Administration

3rd edition

NVQ LEVEL 3

Carol Carysforth
Maureen Rawlinson

D0263969

Student Handbook

Heinemann Educational Publishers,
Halley Court, Jordan Hill, Oxford OX2 8EJ
A division of Reed Educational & Professional Publishing Ltd

Heinemann is a registered trademark of Reed Educational & Professional Publishing Limited

OXFORD MELBOURNE AUCKLAND JOHANNESBURG BLANTYRE GABORONE
IBADAN PORTSMOUTH NH (USA) CHICAGO

© Carol Carysforth, Maureen Rawlinson 2001

First published 2001
2005 2004 2003 2002 2001
10 9 8 7 6 5 4 3 2 1

A catalogue record for this book is available from the British Library on request.

ISBN 0 435 45166 9

Typeset by Wyvern 21 Ltd., Bristol

Printed and bound in Great Britain by Biddles Ltd, Guildford

Please note that the examples of websites suggested in this book were up to date at the time
of writing. It is essential for tutors to preview each site before using it to ensure that the URL
is still accurate and the content is appropriate. We suggest that tutors bookmark useful sites
and consider enabling students to access them through the school or college intranet.

Tel: 01865 888058 www.heinemann.co.uk

To all our friends and colleagues
who were part of the team.

RIP FMT – 1989–2001

Council for Administration

This NVQ/SVQ publication is based on the national occupational standards developed by the Council for Administration (CfA), which is the Government-approved body representing the sector of Administration. Copyright of the national occupational standards is the property of the CfA and, as such, the standards may not be reproduced or transmitted in any form or by any means without written permission from the CfA.

For further information on the work of the CfA, including the Administration Standards, please contact:

The CfA
18/20 Bromell's Road
London SW4 0BG
Telephone: 020 7627 9876
Fax: 020 7627 9877
Email: nto@cfa.uk.com
Website: www.cfa.uk.com

Contents

SPECIAL NOTE

Guidance on the following skills and finance option units is freely available on the Heinemann website at

www.heinemann.co.uk/vocational/NVQ:

Unit 311 – Contribute to organising events
Unit 313 – Support and record business meetings
Unit 314 – Organise repairs to premises and equipment
Unit 315 – Contribute to the development of teams and individuals
Unit 316 – Lead the work of teams and individuals to achieve their
         objectives
Unit 317 – Contribute to the selection of personnel for activities
Unit 322 – Prepare documents from shorthand notes
Unit 323 – Produce documents from complex recorded speech
Unit 324 – Recording income and receipts
Unit 325 – Making and recording payments
Unit 326 – Investigate arrears and recover debt

Please see page 428 for further details of how to access these units.

Acknowledgements

The authors would like to express their gratitude and appreciation to all the friends and colleagues who gave so generously of their time to advise on many of the specialist units in the scheme. Particular thanks are due to Christine Blackham, Alison Chadwick, Sue Willetts, Antony Carysforth and Vince Higham for their IT expertise and advice; David Walsh for his specialist help with the finance units; Carolyn Lee for her input on customer care; Gillian Lee for her advice on recruitment and interviewing techniques and Karl Faulkner for his knowledgeable contributions in relation to premises repairs and maintenance. Their assistance was invaluable in ensuring that these units were totally up-to-date and focused on the needs of today's administrators in the workplace.

Thanks must also go to Roger Parker and Helen Kemp for their expert editing and proofreading, and to Anna Fabrizio who battled feverishly, yet cheerfully, against very tight deadlines in an effort to ensure target publication dates were met.

As ever, Margaret Berriman, our publisher, has played a key part in this project from its inception to completion and her advice and encouragement has been invaluable throughout.

Carol Neild
Maureen Rawlinson

July 2001

Introduction to NVQ awards, the structure of this book, Key Skills signposts and choosing your option units

This section gives you information on NVQ awards, which is particularly valuable if this is the first time you have taken an NVQ. It also explains how this book is organised and how it has been designed to help you. In particular, you will find explanations about the Key Skills signposts useful if you are also taking Key Skills units.

This section also summarises the option units available and explains how these have been covered in this book and on the Heinemann website. You will find advice and guidance on choosing the best options to link with your own job role.

Understanding NVQ awards

If you have already taken an NVQ award, such as NVQ level 2 Administration, then you can safely skip most of this section – unless you took your award some time ago and need to refresh your memory! However, you are still likely to find the other sections useful and may wish to turn straight to page xv, to see how this book is structured, or direct to the information given on the Group B Option units on page xvii.

If this is the first time you have taken an NVQ award, you are advised to read this section thoroughly. You may have already realised there is a considerable difference between this type of award and other types – such as GCSEs or GNVQs. The main differences are as follows:

- NVQs are designed to be undertaken by people in the workplace or who are able to obtain their evidence for the units through undertaking real workplace activities.
- The aim of an NVQ is to check whether you are **competent** at carrying out certain tasks, linked to the type of job you do. Administration NVQs are designed for people working in administrative jobs.
- NVQ awards are offered at different levels. The level you take depends upon the amount of responsibility you have. Level 1 is the first level for administrators and level 5 the proposed top level.

- An NVQ consists of a number of **units**, each one covering a specific area of work. Each unit is divided into two or more elements.
- To achieve the full NVQ level 3 Administration award, you must do **six** mandatory units and **three** option units. The structure of the scheme is covered on page xv and choosing your option units on page xvii.
- You are assessed on tasks you can do competently. If you are competent it means you can do a task many times to a high standard. You have to demonstrate, or provide evidence, to show that you can do all the tasks specified for each unit. These are called **evidence requirements**.
- You also have to prove that you know and understand what you are doing and why you are doing it. This is called **knowledge and understanding**.
- Many NVQ candidates also undertake Key Skills units at the same time. Ideally you should link your evidence for both awards together where this is possible (see page xv).

Providing evidence

Most NVQ candidates provide evidence in a **portfolio**. This is usually an A4 lever arch file which contains documentary evidence relating to their job. You will start your portfolio almost as soon as you start the scheme. Your portfolio becomes very valuable and should be kept in a safe place. Unless you are certain that your portfolio will be secure you should keep a copy of your evidence in a separate place.

You will be guided through the scheme by your **tutor, trainer, adviser** or **supervisor**. Regardless of their title, this is the person who will help you to understand the scheme and provide the right kind of evidence.

As you complete each unit, an **assessor** will check your evidence to make sure that nothing is missing. Your assessor may be your tutor or trainer or could be someone else. At certain intervals, an internal verifier will check, by sampling, particular units in certain portfolios to see whether they are correct. Your assessors and your internal verifier may want to talk to you about your evidence – they should do this so that they know who you are and where you work, and can check that you fully understand the scheme. An **external verifier**, sent by your awarding body, will also check a number of portfolios as a final quality check. Your awarding body is the organisation which will issue your final certificate, such as OCR or Edexcel.

You will not know which units in your portfolio may be checked by a verifier. However, if your assessor has passed them, this usually means there are no problems.

Organising your portfolio

You will need a set of dividers – to separate each unit. You will also need tracking sheets or other documentation provided by your awarding body. Your tutor or assessor will give you these and tell you how to complete them.

Starting out

It is always best if anyone assessing or verifying your portfolio knows who you are and what you are doing! It is therefore sensible to start with a **title page**, which states your name and the scheme title – NVQ Administration level 3.

Then give **information about yourself**. This should include:

- a CV
- your official job description, if you are employed
- your own version of the job description, expressing in your own words what you do every day
- a short description of your organisation, what it does and the people you work with
- an organisational chart (add this only if you believe it will help people who read your portfolio to understand your specific job role).

The portfolio should also contain a list of all the people who have helped to provide evidence, such as witness testimony (see below), and the names of tutors or advisers or supervisors who have countersigned evidence. List these clearly using the following headings:

- name of person
- job title
- sample signature.

Unit evidence

Each unit will probably start with a **tracking sheet**. This is because you need to link your evidence to specific parts of the scheme. Your tutor or adviser will show you how to do this.

You may then be asked to write a brief **storyboard**. This summarises what you have done in relation to the unit or element, so helping to guide the assessor and verifiers through all the materials. It is often a good opportunity for explaining what you know and understand about the topic – and this can save you time having to answer verbal questions. Again your tutor or adviser will tell you how to write a storyboard. If you are working, it is better if this is on letter-headed paper and signed by you *and* by your line manager at work. This confirms that what you are claiming really happens.

Then include your **evidence**. You do *not* have to fill the portfolio full of paper to gain the NVQ award – there are other ways to prove you can do a task! However, as administrators often deal with paper, it is likely you will include some documentary evidence, as it is called, so we will deal with this first.

Documentary evidence

Documentary (paper) evidence can be described as:

- **primary** (or personal) evidence – which is very valuable
- **secondary** evidence – which is less valuable.

Unfortunately, many candidates like to fill their portfolios with paper, regardless of its value!

Identifying primary evidence

The best evidence comes from **working documents** that *you personally* have produced, or written on, or somehow made your own. They could include:

- a typed list of jobs you were given, on which you made notes about what you were doing and ticked off each job as it was completed
- copies of notes you made over the telephone – then a copy of the message you wrote out or e-mail you sent as a result
- a diary or log you kept over a period of time, listing the jobs you did relating to a particular unit
- a typed document or prepared spreadsheet – with the draft or original manuscript or amended version attached, plus a note clearly showing the instructions you were given.

NEVER think that evidence is better if it is clean and pristine! A beautifully printed document may be the final result, but your evidence will be much more valuable if it shows the vital scribbles and notes you made on drafts beforehand. That is what really proves you had a personal involvement with the work.

Identifying secondary evidence

Secondary evidence comprises documents prepared by other people. These documents may have given you information, but that is all. Examples include:

- formal health and safety policies you have been given
- photocopies from books – such as this one
- photocopies of documents from files and office manuals.

None of these really counts for anything on its own and will not help you to achieve your award. The only time you should use this type of evidence is if you can 'convert it' into primary evidence or if it helps to improve your primary evidence. For instance, if you have to follow a particular procedure and want to include it, you should identify exactly how it relates to a particular unit and element – and how it affects your own job role.

Other types of evidence

It is not realistic to think that there will *always* be a piece of paper to prove you can do something. Sometimes this is not appropriate and there are much better ways of checking what you know and what you competent at doing. This can be called **activity evidence**.

Observation by your assessor

Some people find this a bit unnerving, especially if it takes place on a special occasion. It is better if your assessor can simply watch you working in a normal situation. Normally your assessor will then provide you with an **observation report** to go in your portfolio.

Witness testimony

This is a signed document provided by a colleague, or your supervisor or line manager, confirming that you regularly do a particular job well, or that you have provided help on a certain occasion. Witness testimony must be specific, however! You cannot ask your boss to write five lines to say you are good at everything and just get your award! Again, your tutor or adviser will give you advice. Witness testimony should be written on headed paper and signed by the person who wrote it – not by you! The signature should be included on the list at the front of your portfolio. If you write a statement saying what you have done this must be countersigned to prove it is authentic. Normally, however, you will write your own version in your storyboard.

Oral questioning

Your assessor may find out what you know and understand by talking to you and asking questions. This should be more of a conversation than an oral 'test' and is done to check whether you understand *why* you have done something. You may be given a list of the questions asked, to put in your portfolio, together with a summary of your answers – or you can even include an audio tape on which your conversation has been recorded.

Professional discussion

This is your opportunity to discuss aspects of your work in more detail with your assessor. Use it to describe relevant tasks you have undertaken. Explaining why you did them in a particular way helps to prove your knowledge and understanding. Include, too, other similar situations to prove you can apply your skills in different circumstances.

Final notes on evidence

There are certain other points you should note about evidence.

a   All the evidence must be **recent** and **sufficient**. This means that you can't put in one piece of paper which is five years old to provide all your evidence for one unit!

b   Your evidence must be **relevant** – that is, it must meet the requirements of the unit as specified in the NVQ scheme.

c   All the evidence must be **authentic**. This means the evidence must belong to you and must relate to *your* work.

d   You should not take confidential documents or sensitive information away from the workplace without permission. Often such documents can be used when certain information has been blanked out, or your supervisor may agree to provide witness testimony instead.

e   You can use the same evidence *in more than one unit* if it clearly meets the requirements of both. This is called **cross-referencing**. It will save a lot of effort if you can identify opportunities where evidence can be used more than once. Again your tutor or adviser will give you help until you get used to this.

f   The best type of evidence is that which is **naturally occurring**. This means that you produce it as a natural part of your job. It is a good idea, whilst you are undertaking the NVQ award, to start a box file and put into it copies of documents you produce and evidence of work you have undertaken – so that you can use this to find appropriate evidence when you get to later units in the scheme.

CHECK IT OUT!

You cannot start to identify what type of evidence is required until you have received – and read – a copy of the NVQ scheme. Obtain one now, if you have not already done so. Don't try to understand the whole scheme the moment you receive it. Instead look at unit 301 which is the first mandatory unit covered in this book.

- The first page gives a **summary** which identifies all the things you have to do.

- The next three pages explain the three **elements**. They explain what you must always do and the evidence you must provide in each case.

- Then, on one or two other pages, the **knowledge and understanding** requirements are listed.

All the knowledge and understanding requirements are covered in this book. In addition, the evidence collection sections in the chapters match the evidence listed in the scheme. By the time you have finished the chapters you should feel confident that you could answer questions to prove your understanding and know how to provide the evidence required.

The structure of this book

This structure of this book has been designed to help you in the following ways.

- Each of the mandatory (core) units is covered in detail in Chapters 1–5.
- Both optional group A units are covered, in slightly less detail, in Chapters 6 and 7. *Remember you have to choose one only of these units.*
- Then eight of the option group B units are covered, but in less detail again. It is assumed you have some basic understanding of each area and the opportunities to obtain evidence or you would not be choosing that unit! For that reason, the main guidance is on the knowledge and understanding areas you may need to develop and the evidence you will need to provide.
- The remaining eleven option group B units can be accessed free of charge on the Heinemann website at www.heinemann.co.uk/vocational/NVQ. Full details are given on page 428.

In each unit there are special features to help you. These are summarised below.

Key Skills signposts

There is a Key Skills signpost in each mandatory unit, and in the option group A units. You may find these useful if you are taking a Key Skills award. Discuss with your tutor or trainer which signposts are useful for you – as you may not be taking all six Key Skills units.

The signposts indicate the most logical Key Skills unit to link to that NVQ unit and suggest the tasks you could carry out to obtain most, if not all, of the evidence required for a Key Skills portfolio. In some cases you can refine, extend and map your NVQ evidence to cover a Key Skills unit. In other cases you will have to undertake additional work to obtain evidence.

You can, of course, use evidence from *any* NVQ unit to help achievement of some Key Skills units – such as Communications. Your tutor or trainer will give you further details if you are taking a Key Skills award.

The signposts have been written for candidates taking Key Skills units at level 3. However, in some cases you may be taking a Key Skills unit at level 2, such as Numeracy. In each case the evidence can be simplified relatively easily but you should discuss the changes you would have to make with your tutor or trainer.

Check it out!

These sections give you the opportunity to find information for yourself – often linked to the tasks and facilities you are currently using at work.

Information updates

Here you will find the latest information on a particular subject or area linked to what is currently happening in business organisations.

Test your knowledge and understanding

These sections give you the opportunity to assess how well you have understood information already covered. Sometimes they are in the form of a quiz or self-assessment.

Evidence collection

These are possibly the most important sections of all! Here you will find guidance, hints and tips on obtaining evidence to cover a particular section of a unit.

Key notes (Group B Option units only)

These boxes contain summaries of important facts you should know.

SPECIAL NOTES

1 The knowledge and understanding sections in this book have been written to help you to test that you have a clear understanding of the information which you have just read – and to enable you to check with your tutor or trainer any topics about which you are uncertain. These sections *may* be used to contribute to your knowledge and understanding evidence, but the extent to which you need to provide documentary evidence will be up to your assessor. Sometimes your performance evidence will prove that you understand something or you will have discussed it with your assessor. Therefore, do not automatically expect that you will have nothing else to do to prove you understand something after you have read through a unit and done these exercises! Equally, don't include written answers to prove your knowledge and understanding in your portfolio if you can do this by performance or during a professional discussion.

2 Similarly, the evidence collection sections are intended to *contribute* towards your evidence and help you to identify opportunities for obtaining appropriate evidence *throughout* the unit. However, on many occasions your competency will be assessed in other ways, such as by specific performance or questioning. Therefore, simply collecting a number of relevant documents does not mean that you have necessarily completed a unit. Again you will be guided by your tutor, trainer or assessor on this.

Choosing your option units

- The core of the NVQ scheme at level 2 comprises **five** compulsory units – which you must do.
- You then have to choose **one** unit from option group A. The units in this group relate to selecting *either* paper-based filing *or* using a database package. These units are covered in Chapters 6 and 7 of this book.
- You then need to select **three** units from option group B, which contains a choice of 19 (see below).

For all your option units it is sensible to choose those which link most closely to your job role, so that you can obtain the evidence from your job as it 'naturally occurs'. It is sensible – as well as courteous – to talk about the ones you would most like to do with your line manager or supervisor, who may be able to give you some useful advice and suggestions. If you are not working yet, and will be obtaining evidence largely through placements in a training organisation or on work experience – then it is important to discuss with your trainer or supervisor which options would be best.

More about the group B options

Ten of the group B options are covered in this book and the remainder can easily be accessed on the Heinemann website (see page 428 for details). Read the section below which summarises the content of these units and then study the scheme very carefully and look at some of the option group B units before you make your final choice.

Do note that you can choose *any* three options in group B.

Administrative support options

All the following options are concerned with providing an administrative support service in the following areas.

- Unit 309: **Support users of administrative services**. This unit builds on the work you will do for mandatory unit 304. If you provide support to people who use administrative services in your organisation and are responsible for helping to improve the quality of these services, then this unit would be appropriate for you.
- Unit 310: **Contribute to scheduling activities and resources**. If you enjoy scheduling and coordinating activities and resources to produce a required result then you will find this unit particularly interesting.
- Unit 311: **Contribute to organising events**. If you are regularly involved in helping to organise large events, such as conferences or seminars, then you are likely to find this unit suitable.
- Unit 312: **Order, store and distribute supplies**. This unit is designed for administrators who are regularly responsible for placing orders,

storing items and issuing them appropriately. The supplies may be stationery items, refreshment, cleaning materials or tools or small items of equipment such as spare parts.

- Unit 314: **Organise repairs to premises and equipment**. If you are employed in a buildings or estates department, then this type of work may be a major feature of your job. It involves proving you can assess the need for repairs, order the work to be carried out and monitor its successful completion.

People-based options

All administrators deal with people – their colleagues, customers and clients. Dealing with other members of your team is dealt with in mandatory Unit 301, but some option units also concentrate on other people and may be appropriate if you deal with a variety of people and enjoy this aspect of your job.

- Unit 308: **Develop effective services for customers**. If you regularly deal with customers and assist them with their problems and complaints, then you may find this unit a good choice.
- Unit 315: **Contribute to the development of teams and individuals**. Many people today work as part of a team. This unit builds on mandatory unit 301 and would be appropriate if you are responsible for helping to develop the knowledge and skills of other members of your team.
- Unit 316: **Lead the work of teams and individuals to achieve their objectives**. If you operate as a team leader and are responsible for planning and assessing the work of team members you may find this unit both appropriate and interesting.
- Unit 317: **Contribute to the selection of personnel for activities**. This unit is appropriate if you are involved in selecting people to undertake particular work activities. These may be people recruited internally or on a temporary basis – as well as full-time staff.

Computer-skills options

Most administrators today use a computer. If you enjoy this part of your work then you may find one of the options below particularly appropriate.

- Unit 318: **Support the use of information technology systems**. If you regularly help your team to make the most effective use of information technology by helping to organise and maintain its use and providing them with support, then you will find this unit interesting and appropriate.
- Unit 319: **Produce spreadsheet documents**. If you regularly use your computer to enter, process and manipulate data on a spreadsheet, then this would be a good choice.
- Unit 320: **Design and create complex documents using a computer**. If a major part of your job is designing and creating complex documents, using a computer, then this unit may be a sensible option.

- Unit 321: **Design and create presentations using a computer**. If you regularly design presentations and produce slides using a computer package such as Powerpoint, then this unit may be ideal.

Communication-related options

Communication is an essential skill for all administrators and some useful hints and tips to improve your communication skills are included in the Appendix on page 679. The following option units focus on this area of work.

- Unit 322: **Prepare documents from shorthand notes**. Select this unit if you *regularly* use shorthand as a key part of your job.
- Unit 323: **Produce documents from complex recorded speech**. This unit is appropriate if you regularly use audio as part of your job role.
- Unit 313: **Support and record business meetings**. If you organise, support and record business meetings as an important part of your job, then this unit may be a good choice.

Financial options

If you work in a finance, accounts or credit control office then you might find that these units are best for you.

- Unit 324: **Recording income and receipts**. If you regularly prepare invoices and credit notes and send these to customers, enter this information into relevant books of account and receive and check payments on behalf of your organisation, then this unit may be particularly appropriate.
- Unit 325: **Making and recording payments**. If your job involves processing invoices and credit notes received by your organisation and recording transactions in the appropriate ledgers and then making authorised payments, then you are likely to find this unit would be suitable.
- Unit 326: **Investigate arrears and recover debt**. If you are involved in credit control and a key element of your job is to identify arrears in accounts and arrange for regular repayments to be made, then you may find this unit very useful.

Choosing from different groups

Although in this book the group B option units have been brought together into categories for convenience, *remember that you can choose any you like*, from any category. So, for example, if you regularly use a computer to produce presentations, you organise these events and then analyse the costs of them on a spreadsheet, then you could select units 321, 311 and 319. If you deal with customers, are responsible for all the stationery supplies and regularly type letters from audio, you would choose 308, 312 and 323. The mixture of options is entirely your choice.

When making your choices you might find it useful to start by ignoring all those option units which are *not* related to your job or tasks you regularly do. Then see how many you have left.

a First check whether you have an obvious unit to select for group A. Most people undertake some paper-based filing, so unit 306 will be the most likely choice for many people. If you also operate a database, however, you may prefer to choose this unit to develop your skills.

b Now look through the group B units. If more than three units relate to your job, decide which ones you do the most often. You would also be well advised to read your scheme to see *exactly* what you have to do for each unit. This may help to narrow down your choice.

c If you have fewer than three, you need to see whether there is any other area of work you could request to do, so that you could broaden your skills and your value to the organisation.

Remember that at this stage you don't have to make a definite decision, but it is useful to have a good idea. This is especially valuable if you want to be able to make a note of evidence which you could cross-reference from another area as you progress through the compulsory units.

Linking options to your own self-development – a useful tip!

When you reach the final element of mandatory unit 303 (Manage your work and development), you will have to identify what new responsibilities you could take on – and link these with your on-going learning or development plan. Use this requirement to identify any new areas of work you would like to do that would help with a particular option unit that attracts you. This may give you the opportunity to broaden your skills and your expertise over a wider area of work.

It is also worth remembering that you are likely to have several jobs in your career, and no two jobs will be exactly the same. An individual is more employable – and more worthy of promotion – if he or she *has developed several skills and has a good knowledge of administrative work over a wide area*. For that reason, even if you have not chosen a specific option that is covered in this book, you may find it useful to read the information for interest, or if you want to develop a particular skill. Or you could save it until you decide to change jobs – and read it then! It may help you to sound quite knowledgeable if you are asked a question about that area at an interview.

Carol Neild
Maureen Rawlinson
July 2001

CORE UNITS

Unit 301 Maintain effective working relationships

This unit looks at the way you work with other people.

You may be the most efficient administrator the world has ever known, but you will never be effective if you cannot work productively with other people. Neither are you likely to be very popular! You may relate to other people on a one-to-one basis or as a member of a team. Some people will be your managers, others will work at the same level, and there may be some who are more junior. Some people will be members of your organisation and others will not. Your ability to relate well to all of them is extremely important and is therefore the subject of this first unit.

 KEY SKILLS SIGNPOST

If you are taking your Key Skills award, you can link the evidence you produce for this unit to your evidence for **Working with Others**. You will have to prove you can work with others to meet agreed objectives and contribute to complex work in *both* one-to-one *and* group situations. Remember, the list below equates to level 3. Talk to your tutor or trainer if you are doing a different level.

WO3.1

In your own job, identify how you relate to a colleague or your supervisor over the way work is planned and allocated in your area. Then keep records of discussions you have and copies of documents which show that you have planned your work with other people. Your evidence should show your own contributions, how you have prioritised your work and agreed your responsibilities, and the methods you use to keep your colleague or supervisor informed of progress.

Identify a group event or activity on which you will work with other people. This could be a shared project or assignment or a special event (perhaps organised to raise money for charity). At work this could be a major presentation or event which is being organised by your office or department and with which you are involved. (You will find other examples on page 74 of this unit.)

- Keep records of all planning meetings which are held and identify your own contribution to the group's objectives.
- State the information exchanged which enabled individual responsibilities to be agreed – including your own.
- Summarise the plans that were agreed in terms of the resources that need to be obtained, the deadlines set and the priority of different tasks.
- Identify how the work will proceed – including arrangements for undertaking the work and methods of keeping each other informed.

WO3.2

In relation to *both* your own work *and* the group work or project you are undertaking, give examples of the way in which you obtain and use resources and how you refer to other people for support or assistance.

Explain how you organise yourself to meet deadlines and ensure you are working safely. Identify the steps you take to ensure your work is always produced to the required quality.

Explain how, in both a one-to-one situation and the group situation, you have continually tried to establish and maintain cooperative working relations over a period of about three or four months. Try to include examples of how you have tried to motivate other people, how you have supported others, acted assertively when necessary and taken action to avoid discriminating against anyone. If any difficulties have been encountered, identify your own contribution in helping to resolve any problems.

State the occasions on which you have exchanged information to compare the progress being made, by yourself and others, towards the objectives. Include examples of when you have asked other people for information or progress reports.

Changes are frequently required to ensure plans meet objectives. Identify any changes or adjustments that have been made to the original schedules and explain how these were agreed.

WO3.3

Keep a copy of progress or appraisal interviews you have with your line manager to discuss and review your own work. These should include your own explanation of how successful you think you were in meeting your objectives and the identification of any factors which influenced the outcome. Include information on how you agreed your own development needs or areas for improvement in the future.

When the group project or event is completed, *as a group* identify the extent to which this was successful and any factors which contributed to the eventual outcome. Your review should include how well you think the event was planned and resourced, your views on the contributions of yourself and others, and any unexpected developments or changes which affected the result. Identify what you need to do to improve the way the group works together in the future.

KNOWLEDGE AND UNDERSTANDING REQUIRED FOR THE UNIT

A survey by training company Eden Brown identified that most people consider that having friendly colleagues is the most important element of the job – more important than job security, money or good working conditions. Yet what is it that makes one office happy, sociable and lively and another off-hand, cold or downright unfriendly?

Experts argue that this is caused by four factors:

- the 'mix' of personalities in an office
- the 'culture' or style of the workplace and managers
- the opportunities for getting to know your colleagues better, such as communal rest or relaxation areas
- the individual 'people skills' of those who work there.

You may not be able to do much about the first three factors – although these will be mentioned in more detail in this unit. You are, however, the only person who can improve your own 'people skills' – which is the main focus of this unit.

The importance of effective working relationships

You have already seen that having good working relationships with others is important for your own happiness and well-being. The next thing you need to understand is what, exactly, is meant by the term 'effective working relationships'. This may sound simple, but is actually far from it! Many people are extremely good at the 'task-based' elements of their work but are constantly annoying those they work with, by being patronising or abrupt to customers and dismissive or uncooperative with other members of the team.

They make life difficult for everyone. Your job is not only to be *better* than these people when it comes to relating to other people, but also to manage to cope with them as well! So where do they go wrong – and what can you do to make sure you don't copy them?

Before we look at this, let's start by defining the term 'working relationship'. Again, some people go wrong with this. They think that a working relationship is the same as a friendship. It isn't. If you are lucky, you might make a true friend at work – but this isn't part of the deal! You are actually employed to work cooperatively and harmoniously alongside a number of people who are strangers at the start, some of whom you wouldn't wish to be anywhere near on a night out or to meet on a holiday! You are also employed to keep a number of outside contacts happy. Your customers are one group – and some will be more reasonable, patient and understanding than others. Your suppliers are another – whether they are supplying goods or a service to your organisation. In a 'working relationship' you are expected to:

- liaise with them over work-related tasks, including the supply of goods and services
- cooperate with them as much as you can
- maintain a professional relationship with them at all times.

The last point is often the most difficult, especially if someone is being uncooperative with you!

The basic reason good working relationships are important is that, when they are not good, people are so distracted about their problems they can't concentrate on their work. When everyone is working well together, the focus is on the tasks in hand and how these can be done. Working relationships are said to be *effective* when people cooperate to 'make light work' of difficult jobs because they share them and help each other. Excellent groups often display synergy – which roughly means 2 + 2 = 5. In other words, when those four people get together they operate so effectively they do the work of five people.

For this type of harmony and cooperation to occur the following requirements need to exist.

- Each person and/or group respects the views, needs and opinions of others.
- Each person works for the *good of their team or the organisation as a whole* – not just with their own interests in mind.
- People remember the basic courtesies – such as 'please' and 'thank you' and give consideration to others.
- Each person actively tries to help other people, not impede their progress.
- Everyone accepts that their colleagues and contacts have pressures from outside work which may affect them – and allows for this.
- So far as possible, people are 'self-aware' of their own shortcomings and continually try to improve their people skills.

- No one is so important that he/she cannot apologise for a mistake or for saying something hurtful or demeaning.
- Negative influences such as rival factions, back-biting and political game-playing are strongly discouraged.

Of course, it is rare that you will find any organisation where this idyllic state lasts for ever or between all people. Pressure of work and human nature usually intervene before long. However, in a place where there is mutual respect and consideration, harmony will prevail most of the time. If there is a disagreement it will usually be relatively trivial and short-lived. So the amount of time people spend worrying about what other people are saying or doing behind their back is minimal. They can concentrate on the job they are paid to do!

Your contribution to this process

You may think that the focus of this unit is to try to convert you into a paragon of virtue. You would be wrong! If you were such a person everyone would probably get very fed up with you. There is nothing more annoying than people who think they are perfect or who never make a mistake. The aim of this unit is, rather, to make you more self-aware and more observant and knowledgeable about the ways other people act or respond to people and situations. Simply by doing this you will probably start to lose any 'hard edges' you may possess and your expectations of other people will become more realistic. You should also become rather more tolerant. However, you are not supposed to turn into a doormat either – so you will also learn the skills of assertiveness.

However, there is nothing to stop you looking again through the list of bullet points above and deciding how well you score against each one.

The people who make up your team and their responsibilities

Your team comprises those people you work with on tasks for which you all have *a shared responsibility*. If, therefore, you work in a small office with five other people and you are all responsible for doing the work that arrives in that office, then this is your team – whether or not it is officially termed as that in your organisation. Alternatively, you may belong to different teams – some of which are formed for a particular purpose, such as to manage an important project, and are then disbanded once the work is complete.

Bear in mind that in a team not all members need to have equal status. You may have a team leader, or a supervisor or line manager who has overall responsibility for the work you all carry out. This person is still a member of the team, but has a different job role.

In other teams there is no official leader – but there might be an unofficial one! This may be the person who is the most forthright and outspoken. This does not, however, mean that he or she is the *best* person to lead the team – yet it can be difficult to argue with someone who holds very strong views or who has worked there for much longer than you. Hopefully, some of the skills you will learn about dealing with difficult people in this unit will help you to deal with the difficult unofficial team leader as well!

CHECK IT OUT!

One of the major problems with working relationships is the sheer number of them. Probably you have far more than you ever thought.

- Firstly, the basis for any relationship is two people – you plus someone else.
- As a starting point you can therefore calculate how many possible relationships you have with one other person in your current job role.
- Next, you also relate to groups of people or teams. The smallest number is three, the largest is however many people you are likely to be involved with in a meeting or briefing. The reason for separating all these is because the *nature* of the relationship between people changes depending upon who is there. You notice this with your friends. If you are alone with your closest friend, both the atmosphere and topic of conversation may change if someone else arrives. If that person leaves and a different person arrives, the 'mood' of the group changes again, and so on.
- Therefore you can – if you are so inclined – calculate how many possible relationships you may have at work with all the possible combinations of colleagues there are! If you now 'add in' your external contacts, this number increases still more!

This sort of thinking helps when you come to look at your 'role set' in the next section.

Team job roles

Colleagues at the same level as yourself may have different job roles, but if you work in a team together, then all these job roles (and the job descriptions of the holders) should link together to encompass all the tasks you are expected to carry out as a team. Needless to say, every team should be doing work which contributes to the overall requirements of the organisation. If, therefore, you look at all the teams that operate in your organisation, ideally they will collectively undertake everything that is required at the moment. If the situation changes, then new teams may be formed or old teams disbanded and reformed. This can be quite traumatic for team members, as you will see later in this unit.

Team member responsibilities

Within each team, individual members are expected to contribute to the overall work but will have specific responsibilities. This is important, otherwise no one is accountable for anything and there would be no control over the way in which the work is done. Therefore, in your own job, you have key tasks which are your responsibilities. However, you will be expected to work with other members of your team on tasks which take two or more people and will also be expected to deputise for people who are absent or help out another member of your team if you are quiet and they are very busy.

Team member characteristics

In addition to the work each team member has to do, each of them will also have different personality traits. Some will be lively, others quiet. Some may be workaholics and others may see work as a necessary evil. Some will be confident, others shy.

Such differences are a very important part of a good team ethos – as you will see when you reach element 301.2. However, one expert, Professor Cary Cooper, has argued that three ingredients are absolutely essential.

- The first he calls the Social Emotional Leader. This may or may not be the official leader. However, it is the person who cares about the others, stops potential arguments before they begin, arranges social activities and brings 'balance' into a hard-working team.
- The next is the Task People who are concerned, above all, with completing the job in hand. They are essential if the team is to achieve its objectives and fulfil its responsibilities.
- Finally, there must be one Communicator who makes sure that everyone knows what is going on and who keeps people informed – both within and outside the team.

This is why, when you apply for a job, a good interviewer will assess you not just on your task-based skills but also on whether you will 'fit in' with the existing team. This is more important, if a good ethos is to be maintained, than whether you passed your last exam with distinction!

TEST YOUR KNOWLEDGE AND UNDERSTANDING

1 A role set diagram is one way of showing your relationships with
   other people. The shape of this is shown here for Joanne, who
   works in a team of five. She has drawn some members of the team
   very close to her and others further away – because she has more
   frequent contact with Ben, Lian and Asifa than she does with Lucy,
   who works in a separate office, with Yasmin whose work is more
   specialist. and with Jason the team leader. Study the diagram and
   answer the questions which follow.

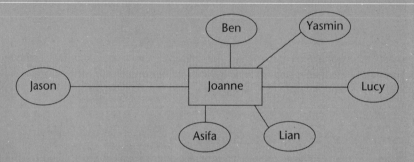

Role set diagram

   a With whom do you think Joanne has the *most* contact, from all
      the members of her team?
   b With whom do you think she has the *least* contact?
   c Which situation do you think would affect Joanne the most –
      and why?
      (i)   Ben, Lian and Asifa have arranged to go out for lunch
            together and not invited her
      (ii) Lucy, Yasmin and Jason have arranged to go out for lunch
            together and not invited her.

2 Each of Joanne's team has various personality traits.

   • Yasmin, Jason and Lian are all very hard workers and apt to bury
     themselves in their work.

   • Asifa is a very caring person. She is the one who takes Jason a
     cup of coffee every morning – otherwise she says he'd forget to
     have one – and who comforted Ben when his girlfriend decided
     to call it a day.

   • Lucy is good fun. She knows her job well but is also lively and
     extrovert. She is the one who puts up the Christmas decorations
     and buys cakes on people's birthdays. ➡

- Ben and Joanne are both new members of the team. Ben was quite shy at the start but, as he finds his feet, is becoming the 'wit' of the group, who can make everyone laugh. Joanne would describe herself as relatively quiet and a very hard worker.

a What do you think would be the effect on the team if Lucy left and was replaced by another 'Joanne'?

b How would the team be affected if Asifa left, and was replaced by another 'Lucy'?

c According to Professor Cary Cooper's categories, what type of person is the team lacking? How may this affect them?

CHECK IT OUT!

There are various ways in which you can analyse your own team to obtain a better insight. The first stage is to identify them and then see how well you know them.

1 Start by copying out the box below and completing as many sections as possible.

2 Now draw a role set diagram to identify your relationships with each person.

3 Analyse your diagram. Which are the people closest to you – and why? Who have you drawn further away – and why?

4 What are the major characteristics of each member – and what are your own?

5 How 'balanced' a team do you think you are? If a new person joined you, what type of attributes would you be looking for – and why?

Note that you may wish to use your analysis as part of your evidence for this unit, but that would be unwise if you have included any characteristics to which one of your colleagues would object, or would find hurtful. Instead, it is better to keep your role set diagram safe until you can expand it to use as evidence (see page 16).

Knowing your team members			
Name	Job title	Main responsibilities	Key characteristics

The business, mission and objectives of your organisation

All organisations are in business for a reason. Your organisation may provide goods or services with the aim of making a profit. This will be the case if you work for a commercial organisation.

Equally, it might provide services for the overall good of others, such as a hospital, college or school. Or you may work for a charity, which produces a surplus (rather than a profit) and uses this for the good of others.

The purpose of your organisation may be summarised in its mission or vision statement – but you are more likely to have easy access to this if you work for a large organisation than a small firm. Your local solicitor may have the mission of 'offering appropriate and expert legal advice to the local community at competitive rates' but may never have actually summarised this in writing. If you are in this situation, you can start by thinking 'what business are we *really* in?' This is the first stage most organisations go through when they are trying to write their first mission statement or revise an old one.

Each year, your senior managers or partners will have to decide on the objectives of the business. However, before they do this they may decide on their major *aims*. For instance, the solicitor may have the following aims (amongst others):

- to offer prompt legal advice to all clients
- to expand the family law section.

The *objectives* will be written as 'stepping stones' to help the achievement of these aims. For instance, in order to offer prompt legal advice it may be decided to:

- open a second office in the town centre
- extend opening hours to 6 pm each weekday
- employ two new administrators for the new office
- move two solicitors to these premises.

You and your team may now be involved in helping to achieve these objectives. You could find yourself moved to the new office, working later or helping with the move itself. Or you may not be involved at all. However, when you read a lengthy list of objectives produced by your own employer, it is unlikely you will find nothing that concerns you – especially if your own team leader or line manager is responsible for ensuring that some of these are achieved before the end of the year!

EVIDENCE COLLECTION

1 Try to obtain a copy of your organisation's mission or vision statement. If there isn't one, try to write one yourself. If there is one, assess it. Do you think it is accurate? How well do you think it describes the overall purpose of your organisation?

2 Find out what the main aims of your organisation are at present and, if you can, what its objectives are. Even if you cannot see the whole list, your line manager should be able to give you those which relate to your own section or department.

3 Look through the objectives and highlight those relating to your own work *or* the work of your team. Then write a brief summary of how you think they might affect you over the coming months.

 INFORMATION UPDATE

Some people argue that the 'culture' or 'politics' of the organisation is more important to working relationships than the objectives. Objectives simply identify the work you need to do to help to achieve stated aims or goals. However, the culture or politics will depend upon the environment and situation the organisation operates in – and the style of management.

Dot.com organisations are a good example of one type of culture. They are often run by relatively young and inexperienced managers, they operate in a highly competitive environment and are often under-funded (i.e. they don't have very much money). To continue to exist profitably their staff may need to work long hours and have to turn their hands to almost anything. Team members are expected to be creative and to work to tight deadlines – often in a large, frenetic open-plan area. There may be terrific angst if a contract isn't won or a job is going wrong. In this type of organisation, expect to be on first-name terms with everyone, to really enjoy the 'highs' but to have a risky job and to be told, straight, if you get anything wrong.

If you then moved to a more traditional organisation, you might experience what is termed a **culture shock**. Let's say you moved to a well-established firm of architects. The senior partner is in his early 60s and likes order, peace and quiet. The company charges quite high rates for its work but has a reputation for producing quality designs. The atmosphere is calm and orderly. Most people have their own offices. The senior administrator has worked there for twenty years and is highly respected. There are standard ways of working to which everyone conforms. Even the decision to open an Internet site took three months and several meetings.

You can decide which one would suit you better – or whether neither of them appeals. But if you suggested a night out at the local pizzeria at the architect's office – or a system for logging all hours worked at the dot.com company – you might find yourself stared at for quite a long time! Therefore, a key factor in your working relationships will be the *expectations* of the people you are with and their style of working – and these will be influenced by the type of organisation and how it operates.

People outside your team

Getting on well with people in your team is crucial – both for your sanity and for office productivity. However, you will find your life runs more smoothly if you can get on well with everyone else as well. This may sound almost impossible – given the number of people involved – but in many ways is easier. Because you don't see as much of these people, you can afford to be charming when you do!

In one organisation, a new administrator discovered to her cost the danger of thinking that only people who were at her own level or above were important. This organisation exported most of its products and was therefore often host to foreign visitors. Given these visitors were considering spending up to half a million pounds, keeping them happy was paramount. However, our administrator was very dismissive of the catering manager, who she considered was somehow inferior because she undertook 'menial' tasks. On one notable occasion, a plane with several Arab visitors arrived four hours late. The buffet lunch that had been ordered was no longer appropriate and a light snack was required for these VIPs on arrival. It had to take account of the cultural requirements of the visitors and their religious beliefs. The administrator desperately needed the help of the catering manager who (guess what?) was nowhere to be found. The moral of this tale is that importance has nothing to do with job titles. It has everything to do with how much you may need the assistance of someone to be able to do *your* job well!

There is an old saying for getting on well with people – 'do as you would be done by'. This is important because often people outside your office do not *have* to assist you in the same way that your team members do. Even if they should help you, some may have some ingenious ways of not doing so if they feel so inclined. The secret is to remember that when you ask people outside your team for something you are asking for a favour. You are more likely to be successful if you observe a few rules.

• Treat everyone with respect for their expertise in *their* own area.

- Do favours for people or help them out when you can. Then you can 'call in' a few when you're desperate. You'll also gain a reputation for being helpful yourself.
- Remember that everyone is under pressure to fulfil their own responsibilities. If someone helps you, be grateful. You now owe them.
- If someone says 'no' they can't help you, try to establish whether the problem is with the procedures (your firm is too rigid in an emergency), because that person is always awkward, or because that person is genuinely too busy. In this case:
  - if the procedures are to blame, have a word with your own boss to see if he/she can help
  - try to find someone else who is more cooperative in that department
  - accept the refusal as graciously as you can, and put on your problem-solving hat or talk through your problem with your team leader.
- Don't fall out with someone over an isolated issue – it isn't worth it. You never know when you may need their help again!

 INFORMATION UPDATE

EQ is one of the latest buzzwords. Whereas IQ (intelligence quotient) signifies your intelligence relative to the average, EQ (emotional intelligence) relates to what you do and – even more importantly – how you do it. According to the experts, even though most people's IQ level is fixed by the time they are adult, EQ can be constantly improved. In addition, if you are skilled at EQ you will do better in your career than if you have a high IQ.

All this is really jargon for putting together a number of skills which have always been needed but are now considered more important than ever. They include self-awareness (knowing and understanding yourself), teamwork, social skills and abilities, self-motivation, empathy with others and communication skills. All this, of course, comes down to having good 'people skills' – and thinking about the needs of other people (colleagues and customers) as well as yourself.

If you feel you need to improve your EQ then there are a range of training courses available – though most are at a price. An easier way may be to adopt some basic but effective measures – such as smiling at people, having a positive attitude, responding well to a challenge, praising and thanking people who do well or do something for you, recognising that even though someone thinks differently from you they have the right to do this – and are not necessarily wrong. In other words – be a 'nice person' to have around!

EVIDENCE COLLECTION

1 Expand your role set diagram to include the other *main* people with whom you have a working relationship outside your immediate team. If you can, try to include some people who are internal to your organisation but not in your team and some who are external to your organisation. Remember that the importance of each person and the frequency of your contacts with them should be denoted by how near or far away from you they are on the chart.

2 Under the chart, write a brief description of the role of each person and your major reasons for contact. This will give your assessor useful information on your most important working relationships.

Element 301.1 **Work effectively with other people**

Know yourself!

If you are going to work effectively with other people you need the type of skills which were described in the information update on page 15. This element looks at helping you develop these skills so that you become better at:

- communicating with other people
- integrating your work with other people
- identifying positive and negative relationships – and what to do about these
- coping with difficult situations.

However, the first stage in dealing with other people is to know yourself. Asking someone else to assess your good and bad points is one way of doing this – but very risky! You will probably enjoy hearing about your strengths and become argumentative, defensive or demoralised when your weaknesses are listed. In addition, everyone you know would probably give you a different list – so you may end up very confused. For that reason, you are better finding out why this can happen and then learning something about the value of self-analysis.

Complex human beings

Why is it you get on well with some people almost immediately but struggle to relate to others? Why do you find some people interesting and others boring? Why is it that some people find you fun to be with and others (awful thought!) do not? After all, very few people go through life *deliberately* trying to be awkward with everyone else, so what is it that often goes right and can also go very wrong with relationships?

Firstly, let's start with a basic. Everyone is different. You know that, but very often people forget it. You expect people to think like you do, like what you like, get annoyed with the same things that irritate you. The *degree* of difference between you and someone else can be important. While opposites may attract for a short time, it is usually people with similar interests and views who form long-term friendships and relationships.

These differences in viewpoint are caused by many things.

- Our innate nature and personality is the first thing. In a family, one child may be lively and extrovert, the other quiet and shy. This difference may stay all their lives.
- The second is the experiences we have in our lives. As an example, if you received constant encouragement as a child and at school you will be

more self-confident than if people have often 'put you down' or demoralised you. If you have always enjoyed excellent health, you may find it hard to identify with someone who is very ill. If you have been taught that 'success is everything' and believed this, then you may be very ambitious – and so on. This results in our belief system by which we make sense of the world. It also affects our perception of events and why we think as we do.

- Finally, we are also influenced by our current mood and situation. Some days we feel good about ourselves, other days less so. This can be caused by a variety of factors in our personal lives – whether we have enough money, feel loved and cared for, have something to look forward to – and so on.

If you put that 'mix' together, is it any wonder that no two people are alike?

TEST YOUR KNOWLEDGE AND UNDERSTANDING

Ryan, Leanne and Perveen have just been introduced to their new team leader, Corrine, who has transferred to their office from another department. She is quite young and has a reputation for being excellent at her job. She has just spent 15 minutes telling them about how she sees their team operating. The three of them have now met for coffee to compare their views.

Leanne is excited about the prospect of working for Corrine. *'I've heard that she's a perfectionist and very hard working – and on her way to the top. Did you see her outfit – it must have cost the earth – and her hair is really great – I wonder where she gets it done? Do you think she'd be annoyed if I asked her?'*

Ryan is less impressed. *'Well, I'm not telling any of my friends I'll be working for a woman. Though I suppose one who drives a souped-up MX5 can't be all bad.'*

Perveen is amazed by this exchange. *'I really don't believe you two. Weren't you listening to anything she said? I think she'll be very fair but she'll want the job doing – and doing well. We'll all have to work very hard to please her, you know. She's keen to get on and she certainly won't let us get in her way.'*

1 What does this conversation tell you about their belief systems? How do you account for their differences in perception?

2 Now listen – really listen – to some of the views expressed by your own team. Especially after you have all been involved in the same experience. What differences are there and how can you account for these?

Getting to know you!

In the exercise above, three colleagues were reacting to meeting someone for the first time. This is an interesting process to analyse – as we all meet new people regularly. When this happens you begin a process which may end very abruptly – or continue for many years. It can be summarised in four stages which are detailed in the table on page 20. Read this carefully and then we will see how it relates to your **working** relationships.

The importance of situation

An important influence on the development of a relationship is *where* you meet someone. If you meet someone at a party, and don't like the look of them, it doesn't really matter whether you walk away or not. It's completely up you. However, there are some situations when this is not an acceptable choice! Meeting someone you will have to work alongside is one of these. Whether you like it or not, this person is going to be part of your life from now on, and – if you work together as members of the same team every day – you have to progress to at least stage 2, whether you like it or not!

You may comfort yourself with the thought that situational friendships are not uncommon. For instance, if you found you were marooned on a desert island with someone, you would be sensible to be rather less choosy than you are now! It is unlikely that you would take yourself off to a lonely cave rather than work at building a relationship of some kind. The same often happens in offices. Because you are with that person every day, you have to make some effort or the situation becomes unbearable. So you learn to 'rub along' even if you don't become fast friends. If you then change jobs, you may never see that person again and not worry about it.

There are some useful strategies you can employ to help to develop a relationship which doesn't seem to be working naturally. These are all related to controlling your reactions to the situation as you cannot control anyone else's!

- Stay open-minded when you meet someone for the first time. Don't be unduly influenced by their looks and appearance, or their manner. For instance, they may be shy and find it difficult to smile or make conversation.
- Don't automatically take it personally if someone doesn't seem pleased to meet you. They may be distracted by work, have serious personal problems or simply be 'running late' at that moment.
- Keep to neutral topics when you first talk to someone. Don't embarrass people by talking about a personal or contentious topic. The good thing is that the tasks you do are neutral, so talk about these and the way the office is organised.
- Remember a conversation should be like a tennis match! Talk yourself,

Getting to know you – and what can go wrong			
Stages in development	Key features	What can go wrong	The outcome
One: Introduction	You are introduced – either formally or informally – depending upon the situation. At this point you assess *what you see*. This includes someone's looks and appearance and their manner towards you (whether they seem pleased to meet you).	You consider them unattractive. They are not unattractive but either ignore you or appear unfriendly.	You will either have a positive reaction ('this person looks nice'), be neutral ('this person looks OK but I'm not really interested') or negative ('I have no interest in this person').
Two: Factual conversation	You talk to this person. The topic will normally be very general – an exchange of views about facts – where you are now, what the weather is like, what type of films you have seen.	You have completely different interests. The other person monopolises the conversation. The other person says very little.	The result of this, however brief, either reinforces your original idea or contradicts it.
Three: Personal conversation	Over time, and in subsequent conversations, you will start to exchange your views on a wider range of 'less-safe' topics.	The other person rebuffs you, doesn't reciprocate, misinterprets you or breaks a confidence.	If the other person is supportive and also shares confidences with you, then the relationship will move to stage four.
Four: Personal disclosure	Intimate and highly personal information is disclosed. There is no limit on the topics discussed. Differences are accepted and acknowledged but in an atmosphere of support.	The other person over-reacts to the situation, wants to influence your views unacceptably or destroys your trust in some way.	Over time, a deep and lasting friendship or relationship can ensue.

then encourage the other person to respond. If someone is shy, this may take some skill. Limit the sessions in the early stages.

- Learn how to listen! It helps if you show an interest in the other person and are talking on 'neutral' territory – such as over a cup of coffee in a rest room or canteen.
- Accept that with some people stage 2 is as far as your relationship will ever get. This is quite satisfactory for many working relationships.
- If you start to build a deeper relationship with someone, *don't* rush it. If the other person backs off, then accept the situation. If they disclose personal details to you, then you will either feel uncomfortable (and back off yourself) or will want to reciprocate.
- If you destroy a confidence or break someone's trust (or vice versa) then this is likely to end the relationship or move it significantly backwards.
- We know people better when we exchange our views and reactions to events (e.g. our feelings) with them, rather than facts about ourselves. However, some people find this very difficult to do and most people are discouraged if they are then criticised or contradicted. Remember that other people have different views and belief systems – for all the reasons you read about on pages 17 and 18 – and it is not your job to try to change these!
- The more open, supportive and uncritical you are with someone the more likely they will be the same with you – but again, take your time!

CHECK IT OUT!

How well do you think you could analyse your belief systems, temperament, attitude and personality? Remember, there are no right and wrong answers as your reaction to situations is very personal and cannot be quickly assessed in a quiz! However, a little self-analysis does help you to spot where you may be rather hasty, be fixed in your views or tend to over-react.

Score yourself on 1 to 5 for each of the following statements, where 1 means you are nearly always like this and 5 means you are never like this. Either extreme is likely to affect your relationships with other people. However, before you aim for a score of 3 every time, remember this would make you pretty boring!

Now look through your very high and low scores and think about how this must affect the other people you meet, socialise and work with. Are there any adjustments that would make life easier for *them*?

Finally, concentrate on one trait about yourself you don't particularly like and make a concerted effort to try to improve this over the next few months.

1 I often agree to things just for the sake of peace, then resent it and get annoyed later.

2 I like to tell people what I think.

3 I often feel inferior to other people.

4 I struggle to control my temper.

5 I often say or do things I regret later.

6 I find it hard to apologise.

7 I enjoy meeting new people.

8 I find it difficult to make friends.

9 I worry a lot about what people think of me.

10 I sometimes tell lies to cover up my mistakes.

11 I think people often take advantage of my good nature.

12 I know I can be greatly influenced by people I admire.

13 People turn to me when they have a problem.

14 I like other people to know me very well.

15 I am good at keeping secrets.

16 I keep all my promises.

17 I hate being proved wrong.

18 I think the only person I can truly rely on is myself.

19 I like telling people what to do.

20 I think carefully before I say or do anything.

21 I know I like to be the best.

22 I think most people are much luckier than me.

23 Criticism really irritates me.

24 I get bored easily.

25 If someone crosses me, they'll regret it sooner or later.

26 The thought of working on my own horrifies me.

27 I enjoy arguing.

28 I am often worried or depressed.

29 Within 5 minutes, I can tell if someone is worth knowing.

30 I am often moody.

The importance of communication

As you have just seen, one of the key aspects of getting to know someone and forming a relationship is being able to communicate with them. Very quickly, after some basic pleasantries, your skills as a conversationalist and a listener start to become important. At work, these skills are important not just to develop or sustain good working relationships but because you have a responsibility to pass on accurate and timely information to other people. This may be verbal or in writing but in every case people are relying upon you for information they need to do their own jobs properly. If you cannot speak or write clearly, or are tactless or careless about details, then you will create upset, annoyance and confusion.

The key aspects of effective communications

All your communications need to fulfil several criteria to be effective. They must be:

- **accurate** in every detail – so they can be relied upon
- **concise and clear** – so people don't have to hunt for the information they need
- **timely** – so they arrive before, not after, they are needed
- **complete** – so people don't have to ask you to fill in the gaps
- **valid** – so they contain objective information and not your own assumptions
- **constructed for the benefit of the recipient** – this means using appropriate vocabulary and being sensitive to the needs and feelings of others
- **be in the most appropriate format** for the message and the circumstances.

To fulfil all these criteria you have to be aware of the following.

- **Accuracy** depends upon having up-to-date facts and no gaps. It means not relying on one person's opinion but researching a complex topic thoroughly. It also means checking that your information is up to date and hasn't been superseded by events.
- **Concise and clear** depends upon your verbal and written communication skills. You need a good vocabulary to be able to express yourself succinctly yet lucidly. (Look up either of these words if you don't know what they mean!) It means having good presentation skills when you create written documents and using headings to separate long text or bullet or numbered points to keep items separate.
- **Timely** means that you do not act as a bottleneck or 'sit on' information which should be passed on. It means you note down information instead of trying to remember it – and then forgetting. It means you use the most appropriate method of communication and then follow this up if you don't receive an acknowledgement or response.

- **Complete** means you have an eye for detail and check your work. You also make the effort to find out things you don't know and never guess or leave things out which should be included.
- **Valid** means you check your facts and don't jump to conclusions. You are aware that you don't know everything – particularly if you are asked to draw conclusions or make recommendations. You are aware of your own personal interests and how these may affect what you say and write.
- **Constructed for the benefit of the recipient** means that you *think* before you communicate – not just about the message and the reason for talking or writing but *about the person*. You think about the 'tone' of your message and choose your words with care.
- **In the most appropriate format** means that you consider the best method of communication, both in terms of the type of message and its urgency. You can correctly decide whether it is best to talk to someone face-to-face or over the telephone, or to write a letter or send an e-mail (and can use all these methods equally well).

Developing your communication skills

From the start of your career you will be expected to communicate with people face-to-face and on the telephone, and to write memos, simple progress reports and send e-mails. As you progress, you will find that you have to initiate a greater range of communications – from speaking to strangers and making them feel at ease, to writing more complex documents including reports, summaries and business letters (see also unit 305).

Very quickly, therefore, your technical skills will be on view. Can you construct (and then say or write) a grammatical sentence? Can you write e-mails quickly with or without your spellcheck? Do you remember to include punctuation in your written documents – and what happens when you have to insert an apostrophe? Remember that the advent of e-mail has meant that people's written communication skills are on view to virtually all their colleagues from day one! If you have any doubts in this area, assess yourself by working through the Appendix on page 679.

Even if you pass all these tests, you need to be able to construct your communications properly. Even the shortest message should have:

- a beginning – where the recipient is told what the topic is (a good place to start is with the facts he or she already knows)
- a middle – when you present new facts or information in a logical order
- an end – when you state clearly the response or the outcome you expect.

This type of construction can be even more important when you are speaking to someone. If you start in the middle, then go off at a tangent with two or three irrelevant comments, and then carry on again, your listener is unlikely to have much of a clue about the point of the discussion.

The next test concerns your **diplomatic skills.** These are not just of concern to government employees! You need to be able to speak and write diplomatically or you may distract your listener or recipient who is more ruffled by your tone than by your actual message. You need to think about both the person and the reason for communicating. For instance, is the recipient someone at your level or senior? How status conscious is this person? What is your relationship to date – do you know him or her well or not? What has been the tone of the person's communications to you – formal or informal?

The **type of message** is also important. It is always more difficult to write (or say) something the recipient doesn't want to hear. (Hence the phrase 'don't shoot the messenger!') Equally, if there is a dispute of some kind, or if your information may be passed to a third person for consideration, you are always better to err on the safe side. Be more formal in such situations. Equally, if you are trying to obtain a favour, your emphasis may be on persuasiveness!

Choosing your method of communication – the facts

Should you choose your method of communication to suit yourself or the recipient? Generally, the latter. Sometimes it is unimportant whether you pass on information when you see someone, phone them or send an e-mail. At other times the difference can be critical. Use the following as a guide.

Choose face-to-face if ...
- the information is personal or highly confidential
- your colleague's reaction could be extreme (e.g. because of bad news)
- you know the recipients well/see them frequently
- you need to discuss the facts of the matter
- you want to persuade someone to do you a favour!

But remember to:
- choose your time
- use appropriate body language (see page 36)
- give people 'thinking time'
- give people 'space' if they are upset or very annoyed by your information.

Choose the telephone if ...
- you are busy and it would take some time to walk to where they are
- the information is urgent
- you need to obtain a rapid response
- the information is fairly basic.

But remember to:
- speak clearly
- repeat yourself if necessary, without sounding irritated

- use your voice to show sympathy or concern
- check that the recipient is clear about what you want before you ring off.

Choose a written memo if ...

- you need to keep a copy on file
- you want a written record
- you are contacting someone who rarely reads incoming e-mails.

But remember to:

- put an appropriate subject at the top
- restrict your memo to that subject (it makes filing easier)
- structure it with a beginning, middle and end
- copy it to other people who need to know, and include the distribution on your top copy
- store it in your pending tray and chase up a response if you haven't received one by the due date.

Choose a progress report if ...

- your boss has specifically asked for this
- you are updating people on an ongoing situation or project
- your organisation routinely uses this method to update staff.

But remember to:

- use an appropriate heading
- set it out clearly, so the key points are easy to read
- stick to the facts, unless you have been told to include your views
- include the date it was produced and your own name/initials.

Choose an e-mail if ...

- the communication is urgent
- the person is often difficult to contact by phone
- you are busy and want to pass on information quickly, at your convenience
- the information is too long or complex to be relayed over the telephone
- you want to send another document as an attachment
- you want a written record that you passed on the information.

But remember to:

- put the subject title as your heading
- keep it relatively brief
- be courteous
- check your spelling and punctuation
- check whether it has been read (or received) if you don't receive an acknowledgement or reply quickly.

TEST YOUR KNOWLEDGE AND UNDERSTANDING

1   Ryan and Perveen both want to take a personal day's leave at short notice, at a time when the office is particularly busy. To this end, Ryan sends Corrine the e-mail shown here. Perveen, on the other hand, goes to see Corrine and explains that she would like to visit her brother next weekend before he goes abroad to work. She says that it would be much easier if she could have the Friday or Monday as a personal day, because of the distance she has to travel. She says she will work late the previous or following week if necessary, to help clear any backlog of work.

From:	Ryan Forbes
To:	Corrine Masters
Sent:	20 November 200-
Subject:	Time off

Hi Corrine

I've just got news that I've got a ticket to the England match a week on Saturday. All the lads are going down the day before and it wouldn't be the same if I wasn't with them. Is this OK? To have the day off on the Friday, I mean.

Cheers

Ryan

a   Corrine is far more impressed with Perveen and more inclined to grant her request. Why do you think this is so?

b   Rewrite Ryan's e-mail to improve his prospects!

2   In each of these situations, which method of communication would you use – and why? Discuss your suggestions with your tutor or supervisor.

a   Three weeks ago your finance department promised you that they would pay an outstanding account. You have just received a telephone call from the supplier to say the money has still not been received.

b   You want your reprographics operator to print you a colour copy of an advertisement urgently.

c   You need to inform all the staff in your office about the new fire risk assessment.

d You need a colleague in marketing to comment quickly on a recent sales report. You are not sure if he has received a copy of the report.

e You need to tell three staff about the changed time of a meeting next week.

f You thought one of your team had posted an urgent document two days ago. She is absent today and you have just found it in her 'out' tray. You have to bring this situation to the attention of your boss, but know he will be very annoyed.

3 Leanne struggles with her written English. She has just produced two documents – a memo about e-mail use and a progress report about the sales conference.

   a Correct the memo, which Leanne has written herself, so that it is suitable for sending to staff.

   b Correct the report which Leanne has typed from Corrine's written notes of the meeting. Expand all abbreviations, expand information written in note form correctly and correct any obvious errors.

M E M O

TO	All staff
FROM	Leanne Ashforth
DATE	25 November 200-

E-MAIL USEAGE

Many staff have asked for gidance on useing e-mails. In addition many of you are also unawear of this companies policy on the use of e-mail. Below are the main points all staff should bare in mind with sending emails.

1 Emails must only be sent on workrelated matters and private e-mails over the Internet should'nt be sent without permission.

2 Staff what have goods for sale should use the electronic bulletin bored, not e-mail.

3 No sallutation is needed for internal e-mails but you may wish to use one on external e-mails (eg Dear . . .) and to end with 'best wishes' or 'regards'.

4 On our package you can mark a message 'high priority'. Only use high priority for important messages not all the time otherwise everyone will take no notice. ➡

---

5   On our package you can also set the system to send an automated reply if you are out. This is a good idea as this means people don't keep phoning to check if you've got it or not.

6   CAPITAL LETTERS are not the thing to do. This is called 'shouting' and is not done.

7   To many e-mails say they have attachments, then don't, so check yours carefully before you press 'send'.

8   Sending nasty e-mails are known as 'flaming'. Staff who do this will be in trouble.

9   Don't send copies to people who don't need them. This clogs up all the male boxes.

10 Dont' 'forward' e-mails you have received all round the building, this has the same affect.

Thanks a lot.

PROGRESS REPORT ON SALES CONFERENCE

A meeting was held on Wednesday, 20 November to discuss arrangements for the sales conference in Feb.

Present: Corrine Masters, John Kelly, Neelam Rani, Stephanie Burns, Dominic McGlynn.

Arrangements made and agreed

- The event wld be held on 20 and 21 February.
- Program for both days decided in outline.
- Seminar rooms had been reserved at Swallow Hotel, Winford, for both days.
- Attendance req'd by all sales team for both days – technical and production staff on day one and marketing staff on day 2.

Arrangements to be made before next meeting	Action by
• All staff to be informed of event	JK
• Accomm to be booked for night of 20 Feb	SB
• Meals and refreshments to be agreed with hotel	SB
• Presenters to state audiovisual aids req'd	NR
• Design of new sales literature to be agreed	DMcG
• Program for conference to be finalised	CM

Next meeting will be held on Friday, 16 Nov in room T45 at 2 am.

Corrine Masters
21 November 200-

EVIDENCE COLLECTION

1 Leanne's e-mail refers to the company policy for sending written communications. Find out the policies or procedures that exist in your organisation relating to your communications. Obtain a copy for your portfolio and personalise these by saying how they affect your choice of method and content.

2 You need to provide evidence that you communicate with other people in *three* of the following ways:

- face-to-face
- by telephone
- in writing
- by e-mail.

Your written communications can include memos, correspondence, progress reports or any other suitable document agreed by your assessor. 'Other people' can include your line manager, supervisor or team leader, other team members, people within your organisation but not in your team, and people external to your organisation – in other words, the main people you identified in your role set on page 16. Your evidence must include communications sent to at least *two* of these groups of people.

The easiest way to do this is to start a file in which you keep copies of written and e-mail communications which are *not* confidential. If you have any doubts about whether to include an item, discuss this with your line manager. Often this is possible if you 'blank out' sensitive information and then take a photocopy.

For your face-to-face or telephone communications you can either produce a written record of what you did, or keep a log of your verbal communications over a short period. In either case you need your line manager to counter sign this for authenticity. Alternatively, you can ask one or two of your colleagues for witness testimony but you should not do this with your external contacts without the agreement of your line manager.

Integrating your work

One of the most common causes of rows and disagreements in a working environment is conflict over resources. This can be as basic as someone repeatedly borrowing your stapler or using your computer, an argument over who has precedence at the photocopier, or whether your boss's need to use the meeting room at 10 o'clock next Monday is so important that the person who booked it first has to go somewhere else!

You get the same sort of arguments in families – 'Who's borrowed my sweater?', 'I told you not to use that without asking', 'How could you take the last one and not tell anybody?' Interestingly, if you come from a large family, where people share everything, then you may find 'integrating your work' easier than if you live a peaceful and ordered life and never need to worry about your possessions vanishing from under your nose! In this case, compromising on ownership may not be one of your strengths.

The reason for all this squabbling is because resources are normally in short supply. This includes one of the most important resources of all – time. So your ability to juggle your priorities is also critical here.

Regardless of the precise reason for a disagreement, if you find yourself in a 'head-to-head' with a colleague about who should do or have what first, there are four possible outcomes:

• you win and they lose
• they win and you lose
• you both lose
• you both win.

The 'win/win' scenario is obviously the one to aim for, but how do you achieve this? Let's start first by looking at the other options.

If you win and they lose because you have been the most argumentative, then you may feel quite triumphant. But your colleague is either annoyed or upset. He or she may decide to get revenge next time, or tell everyone how overbearing you are. So insisting you are right and must have your own way is usually inadvisable.

If they win and you lose, the reverse occurs. You are resentful or upset. Furthermore, you have the added problem of finding an alternative method of doing the job you have been given – and the person who has given you this problem will not be high on your popularity list! You may be prepared to forgive and forget – or you may decide to get even when you get the chance.

If you both lose, however – if you either end up arguing for so long that *neither* of you can finish the job in time, or if you 'split' resources equally but this means neither of you have sufficient – then both of you are at loggerheads for the next few weeks.

So how do you both win? This can be achieved by forgetting 'who is right' and looking at the issue that is involved *jointly*. In other words, if you, on your own, had *both* problems, what would you do? Which issue is the most critical or important? What other ways are there around the problem?

In this case, the person with the most important job or highest priority will 'win' but will also help the other one to solve their difficulty. This may involve an element of compromise — when you can have some of what you want, but not all of it, or have to do what you want in a different way.

TEST YOUR KNOWLEDGE AND UNDERSTANDING

Read each of the following scenarios and decide how the work could be integrated so that both parties 'win' and, where appropriate, how the priorities were agreed.

1 Jenny has just finished the final checks on a 20-page word-processed report. Her boss wants 30 copies by 2 pm. Sofiya has 50 mail-merge documents to get in the post at the same time. Both share the same printer and at 1 pm both are ready to start printing.

2 Ben and Ryan arrive at the stationery cupboard simultaneously. Ben needs 20 presentation folders for sending some sales information to important customers. Ryan needs 10 presentation folders for sending a copy of the new sales literature to all the representatives. Both stare in horror at the box — which contains precisely 21 folders.

3 Leanne needs to book the data projector for the sales conference next month as several presenters are using Powerpoint. When she looks in the book the projector has already been booked by Neil, the personnel administrator, for an hour on the first day as it is used on staff induction programmes.

4 You have been asked to check some figures on a spreadsheet and cannot concentrate because of everyone around you talking, telephones ringing etc. You move into an adjacent, empty office for some peace and quiet. Within five minutes, Lisa, a member of your team, arrives in a panic, pushing a large trolley with numerous boxes. She has been asked to fill 250 envelopes with a mail-shot which must go that evening and wants to use your workspace to spread everything out.

Identifying essential information

Everyone in an office handles a tremendous amount of information every day. You receive information when you talk to people, answer the telephone, open the mail, read your e-mail, attend a meeting or even during your lunch break. Some of this information is trivia, some of it routine, some of it very important or essential — but perhaps to someone else, rather than you.

Identifying essential information – and then doing the right thing with it – isn't always easy. That's why you sometimes hear the plaintive cry, 'But I didn't think it was important!'

Obviously, if someone stands over you and *tells* you something is vitally important, you will react accordingly. The problem occurs with other types of information you may simply come across during your day-to-day work. Often, two of the secrets are having a good memory and being able to make connections. The reasons for this are simple.

- If you have a good memory, then you will remember names and events that have been discussed and be able to retain information quite easily.
- If you 'make connections' then you don't see information in isolation. Instead, you will be able to make links between information you receive in one situation and something you know about from somewhere else. Often, making these links is very important indeed.

As an example, let's say that a few days ago you heard your boss discussing a visit from some customers in Ireland. This morning you hear on the radio that your nearest airport is closed through fog. Even though you don't know whether your customers are flying over that day you should still mention this to your boss. Don't assume he already knows. If your suspicions are correct and several important arrangements have been made, any delay could cause a considerable amount of extra work.

A test of initiative, on occasion, is knowing what to do with information that arrives at the last minute, or when the person who needs to know is elsewhere. Thankfully, mobile phones have partially solved this problem as it is now easier to keep in touch with people who are travelling. Here are some other solutions you might find useful.

- Always consider *who else* could act on the information. If you pass it on to someone senior, then you don't have to worry about it as much as the responsibility is now shared.
- Remember that the way to interrupt a meeting in order to pass on important information is to write the message on a piece of paper, knock on the door, apologise for the interruption and then simply hand your note to the person who needs it.
- Know how to contact your boss in an emergency. Much will depend upon the way in which your organisation operates and the nature of your boss! In some companies, 'out-of-hours' contacts are quite routine; in others they are out of the question.
- Make sure your recipient actually receives the information. If you have to leave a message with someone else, don't give the content, ask for the person concerned to ring you. If you send an e-mail or leave a message on voice-mail, follow up if you don't get a response. And *never* write out critical information and then simply leave it on an empty desk or amongst a pile of papers.

In each of the following situations, identify the critical piece of information and say what action each administrator should take.

1 Leanne has booked a buffet for 35 external visitors next Monday lunchtime and sent out the invitations. By Thursday she has received 15 firm acceptances and 10 refusals and a note that one guest is a vegan.

2 Perveen knows Corrine has arranged to show some very important visitors around later that day. She overhears the fire marshal talking about a fire drill.

3 Ryan is preparing some slides for a presentation Corrine will be making tomorrow morning at a customer's premises. She will be away all day. At 3 pm a warning flashes on his screen that the computer network is about to go down because of a technical problem.

4 At the same time, Leanne is processing the expense claims which have to be with finance tomorrow at 12 noon. She routinely puts queries on one side, where she cannot agree a figure, and this time includes Corrine's claim.

5 Parveen overhears Ryan telling a colleague that he intends to be away during the first week of April, but hasn't got around to booking the time off yet. She remembers that some time around then Corrine had said she didn't want any leave taken because they would be busy with the end-of-year accounts.

EVIDENCE COLLECTION

Try to develop your antennae for identifying important information. Instead of letting information 'wash over you' in future, make a mental note of it, check if there are any associations you can make, and decide whether:

- the information is trivial
- the information is useful, but of no particular importance
- the information could be vital – to someone else, if not you.

Then keep a record of all the times you notify your colleagues or your line manager about important developments so that you can provide your assessor with relevant examples.

The hallmarks of positive working relationships

You have already seen that people work together better when

- they are prepared to compromise and work together to find a solution
- they provide information promptly.

In the first section of this unit you analysed your own behaviour and looked at the ways in which different perceptions are formed. From this it is a relatively small step to identifying the types of behaviour, or the 'hallmarks', of a positive working relationship. Each of the following attributes is normally found in this situation:

- loyalty amongst colleagues
- mutual support and encouragement
- sensitivity to the needs of others
- a strong sense of commitment
- mutual respect and understanding
- professionalism.

The importance of loyalty

When you work with other people you start to form a **psychological contract** with them. That is, they have expectations of you and you have expectations of them. Breaking this contract will damage the relationship, and being disloyal is one of the fastest ways of doing this. These are some examples:

- failing to defend your colleagues if you hear them being criticised (or even worse, joining in)
- betraying their confidences
- reporting a problem to your boss before your colleague has had the chance to explain
- talking about your colleagues behind their backs
- spreading rumours.

Remember, you can only expect loyalty if you are prepared to be loyal yourself.

Mutual support and encouragement

There are times when things go wrong for everyone – and each person you work with will have their own personal concerns and worries. Depending upon their nature, they may find it helpful to talk about this or prefer to keep it to themselves. All you may notice is that their behaviour has changed in some way.

If you suspect someone has a personal problem then the first rule is not to pry. The second is to make it clear you want to give support, and not be judgmental. The third is to be extra helpful if someone is having a difficult time, such as having to cope with illness at home. This may involve you in extra work for the short term, which you should do willingly. You never know when you may need such a favour yourself.

Finally, if you suspect a team member has a serious problem and is becoming seriously depressed, do consider whether you should tell your line manager in confidence. This is particularly the case, too, if you spot serious signs of stress in a colleague. Another useful person to talk to is your **mentor**, if you have one. A mentor is usually someone who is more experienced and to whom you can turn for guidance when necessary. This is one exceptional occasion when total loyalty to a team member may be misplaced if you don't say anything – as, at the very least, arrangements may be made to lighten your colleague's workload on a temporary basis.

Sensitivity

People who are 'sensitive' have a sixth sense in relation to the needs of others. They instinctively know when not to interrupt or how to phrase something tactfully. They 'read' signals without having to have something spelled out. They rarely 'put their foot in it'. You can develop sensitivity only if you learn to watch for signals and read them accurately.

You will be more sensitive if you are relatively skilled at each of the following:

- understanding body language
- listening.

CHECK IT OUT!

1 Body language relates to the way we use our eyes, facial expressions, body position and physical gestures to denote how we feel. For instance:

- you lean forwards when you are interested and away when you are not
- you stand closer to someone you know well than you do to strangers – unless you are in a crowded area such as a lift, when you keep your 'personal space' by not looking at anyone!
- you raise your eyebrows when surprised and frown when you are worried or disagree with someone
- you tap your fingers (or a foot), pace the floor or constantly check your watch when you are impatient ➡

- you use a 'defence' such as crossing your arms or clutching a folder to protect yourself if you feel vulnerable
- you take up a 'mirror' position of someone who is saying something you agree with.

The whole subject of body language is fascinating. Find out more by checking out the books in your local or college library or connecting to www.ask.co.uk and typing in the question 'What's body language' – and investigating some of the sites identified.

2 How good a listener are you? *Excellent* listeners can be identified by their ability to repeat correctly what was said to them. *Moderate* listeners remember the interesting bits, and *poor* listeners hardly remember anything! The danger is that it's always difficult to keep listening if:

- the topic (or person) is boring
- what they are saying triggers a response – so we can't wait to jump into the conversation
- they say something which makes us angry or with which we strongly disagree – because we then want to 'put them straight'
- we are busy, distracted by something else, too hot, too cold, tired, ill or in a hurry.

A key point to remember, therefore, is not to give *someone else* important information when they are distracted, busy, in a hurry etc.

Now test yourself.

a This week, after a conversation, see how much you can recall about the details.

b Identify occasions when you are 'switching off' and deliberately try to 'switch back on' again.

c Guard against interrupting people because you suddenly think of something in reply. Surely you won't forget if you wait five minutes, will you?

d Deliberately try to improve your listening skills over the next few weeks and then test yourself again to see whether you notice a difference. Your colleagues certainly will!

Commitment

Commitment simply means keeping your promises. If you can always be relied upon to do what you have promised then you will be very valued as a colleague. People will not have to wonder if it is possible that you will let them down at the last minute. This doesn't just mean doing jobs you have promised to do, but arriving on time, returning from lunch at the time agreed, repaying favours and helping people when you have said you would.

Mutual respect and understanding

Common sense should tell you that people work better when they show mutual respect for each other and their different needs and beliefs. Today we live and work in a multicultural society which enables us to meet a wide variety of people. You may also work with people who are much older than yourself or who have learned to master a skill even though they have an impairment or disability. Being open-minded and finding different people genuinely interesting is a strength. It encourages tolerance and means you are constantly learning.

Self-awareness is an important feature of tolerance. You may have friends or relatives who hold stereotypical views about particular groups of people. Often this is through fear or basic ignorance, but you can inadvertently accept these opinions as 'fact' simply because you have been exposed to them for so long. They simply perpetuate some of the world's greatest prejudices. Examples include:

- all women are bad drivers
- all Jews (and Scottish people) are tight
- the Irish are charming but dim
- old people are 'out of touch'.

People will cling fast to some of these beliefs, despite meeting an excellent female rally driver, having a generous friend from Edinburgh, knowing a doctor who hails from Dublin, and having an uncle who couldn't live without his mobile and who listens to Eminem!

Remember, everyone is an individual – regardless of age, gender, colour, race or creed. So never judge people as a member of a 'group'; there are far too many exceptions for that to be useful at all.

Professionalism

This is one of the hardest attributes to master – especially when you become close friends with a work colleague. Professionalism actually means that the objectives of the organisation take precedence over your personal relationship. You can jeopardise your professionalism by becoming too close to someone, or by mistaking an excellent working relationship for a personal relationship. Consider these examples.

- One of your friends constantly arrives late, but you daren't say anything because it will cause trouble between you.
- You find a close friend is taking home stationery for her boyfriend, who has just started his own business. She swears you to secrecy.
- Your boss is very friendly and approachable. You think he therefore won't mind if you take long lunch hours and go home early on the odd night.

In each of these situations the professionalism of your working relationship is being challenged. It can be difficult to 'draw the line' between where your loyalty to your colleagues and the organisation should lie – but it is important. People who compromise you aren't your true friends, and this should be pointed out to them, rapidly. So far as your boss is concerned, you are likely to find the boundaries are quickly redrawn if you take advantage of his or her good nature.

The negative side

Just as there are positive behaviours which help to encourage productive working relationships, people indulge sometimes in activities and behaviours which do the opposite. The major types you may encounter are outright aggression, game-playing and operating a hidden agenda.

Outright aggression

Outright aggression is when the slightest possible challenge or comment is met with an immediate – and often upsetting – response. Many people do this – without thinking – as a defence mechanism. They feel vulnerable, so they go on the attack.

Firstly, it is hoped that you never respond in this way; you will soon find people avoiding you. Secondly, if you have to deal with this, learn and practise some assertiveness skills. These are discussed in more detail on page 44.

Game-playing

Everyone plays games to some extent, but you occasionally find someone who makes a career out of it! All games are played for a pay-off of some kind. The game starts when the player adopts a role, to which people respond. At the last minute, the player changes tack, which 'throws' the opposition. The expert on games is a man called Eric Berne and his book *Games People Play* is worth reading if you want to know more.

At work, the most frequently played games are these:

- **Yes, but ...** In this game, no matter what you suggest someone counters it with 'yes, but ...' and then gives a reason why they cannot do something. In this situation you will give up – and the game-player wins. For example:

'Andrea, could you help out in the mail room for half an hour?'

'Yes, but if I do I won't be able to finish this report for Mary and she wants it in half an hour.'

'Well, can you ring her and check if it'll do later. I really want you to go to the mail room.'

'Yes, I would but I saw her leaving her office 20 minutes ago.'

'Well, can someone else do the report, then. I really need you to go.'

'Yes, but it'd take me a while to explain how these figures have to be entered.'

The pay-off for the game-player is not having to do the job but also never having to give an outright refusal.

- **Harried ...** This is the person you never dare ask for help because they are always so busy. They wear a permanently harassed expression, are forever telling you how much work they have on, how they came in early on Monday, stayed late on Tuesday. You'll find one in almost every organisation! The pay-off for the game-player is that everyone will avoid giving him or her extra work because they themselves can't cope with the hassle!

- **Now I've caught you ...** This is a game played by the less than pleasant boss. It is based on the fact that no one is perfect. The poor victim is given ever harder jobs, tighter deadlines and inadequate guidelines. The boss waits until there is a mistake – and then pounces. The pay-off for the game-player is to ensnare the victim.

- **Let him and you fight ...** This is the person who fuels your annoyance against a person or situation and makes all the bullets – with the intention that you will fire them! If ever you hear the words 'I'd tell her straight if I were you' or 'I wouldn't put up with that' – be on your guard. Ask yourself how many times the *speaker* has challenged your boss outright! The pay-off for the game-player is being able to cause trouble, whilst not being actively involved in it.

So, how do you cope with an inveterate game player? The secret is to 'call their game'. So in each of the above cases your counter-ploy is:

- *To the 'yes, but' game-player*: 'I don't think you really want to do this. If you don't want to, why can't you just tell me?'

- *To 'harried'*: 'You are obviously struggling to cope with your job at the moment. You always seem to be under too much pressure and I'm very worried about you. I think you should talk to someone about it. Obviously this situation can't continue.'

- *To the unpleasant boss*: Prepare a list of all the jobs you've been given and ask the boss to help you work out a priority order. Every time a new job is given to you ask for this to be added – at the correct point in the list.

- *To the bullet maker*: 'I quite agree. You won't mind if I say you gave me the idea, will you?'

In fact, if you get good at calling games, you may quite enjoy it!

Hidden agendas

A hidden agenda is an ulterior motive for saying or doing something. If you are totally naive about office politics then you may not realise that everyone is not quite as 'up front' as they seem! You should suspect a hidden agenda when someone acts in a way you find odd or unexpected. Then you need to think about *why* they are acting in this way. However, don't become so paranoid you suspect everyone has ulterior motives all the time!

Typical examples are:

- saying something just to impress the boss
- saying something in public that will deliberately make someone else look foolish – apparently by accident
- someone implying they know more about something than they can actually disclose (to impress everyone)
- someone deliberately going against a new idea because they originally thought of the old one.

Hidden agendas are difficult to tackle head-on, unless you are prepared for a row. The problem is that sometimes people don't even realise how their behaviour is perceived by everyone else, and how unpopular this makes them. Probably the easiest, and kindest, thing is for the team member who is closest to this person to try to explain how their behaviour is being interpreted – again, if you like, 'calling the game'.

CHECK IT OUT!

The difficulty with identifying hidden agendas is that we all say one thing and do another. Even you! According to the sociologist Chris Agyris, this is because people routinely have both an espoused theory (which they declare to the world) and a theory-in-use (which is what they really do!). This explains why:

- the person who preaches most about the environment also manages to throw half a ream of paper away each day

- the person who thinks all criminals should be locked away for years often tries to inflate his mileage claim

- the boss who monitors staff punctuality like a hawk may forget to apply it to himself!

Before you label all these people as hypocrites, think carefully. To what extent do your espoused theories and your theories-in-use differ? And over what issues?

Improving relationships

You may remember, from your study of how relationships are formed (see pages 19–21), that they cannot be rushed. However, there are occasions when an opportunity occurs for you to either improve a relationship or not. Recognising these opportunities is obviously the first step. Here are some examples.

- Someone is struggling to complete a task when you have time to help.
- You can do a favour for someone quite easily. This can be as basic as collecting a cup of coffee or picking up their dry cleaning because you are passing the shop.
- Someone offers to help you. Instead of dismissing them, you can take them up on their offer.
- Someone apologises to you for something. You can accept it graciously and tell them to forget the matter rather than dwell on it and make them feel worse.
- You know someone could help you understand something – but this means swallowing your pride and asking for their advice.
- Someone is on their own, so you suggest having coffee or lunch together.
- There is a problem which affects you and someone else, so you suggest discussing how to solve it together.

In all these situations you are making a step towards improving your working relationship. At this point you are vulnerable to rejection – and it is fear of this that makes many people decide not to bother. Yet, what have you got to lose? The worst that can happen is that the other person rejects your gesture. Therefore, if all you can do is gain, what are you waiting for?

Dealing with difficult people and coping with conflict

In this element, you have already learned about several strategies for trying to improve difficult working relationships. You have also seen that taking the initiative to solve a problem will cost you nothing at all. But what should you do if you are having to cope with a really difficult person – or if there is outright conflict between you and someone else? And what procedures are there in your organisation to protect you if things become really unpleasant?

'Difficult' people

If you have problems dealing with one particular person, there are several questions you should ask yourself before you take action.

Are you alone?

Does this person act in the same way with everyone else, or just with you? If the person acts this way with several, or most, people then the problem is not connected with you personally. A good strategy could be to see how more experienced staff handle this person and/or ask your mentor for advice. It could be you just have a particularly tetchy member of staff to deal with.

How persistent is the problem?

Is this person 'difficult' only occasionally – or regularly – and over one particular issue or over almost everything? If someone is normally fine, then there may be a good reason why they are being 'difficult' on an occasion. For example:

- they have a personal worry
- the issue is something over which they feel strongly
- there is a 'hidden agenda' you don't know about.

There is a lot of difference between, on the one hand, finding out that your finance officer goes mad with everyone who sends in their expenses claims late, but is otherwise great, and on the other hand discovering that it's only when *you* appear he or she starts to become unreasonable.

What are the reasons?

Are there any known reasons why the person acts this way? Experiencing a difficulty which relates to a particular issue is always easier to deal with than a personality clash. This is because it is easier to discuss the matter. You may annoy someone, for instance, because you leave a mess behind when you have been doing a job – yet instead of telling you this person simply becomes off-hand with you.

This is where you need assertiveness skills to raise the matter without causing further problems – as you will see below. If you get the matter out into the open and find out *why* you are being glared at or brushed aside, then you are half way to solving it.

Is there a personality clash?

A serious personality clash can be difficult to deal with. This is when you never really get on with another person. The danger is that you will be apt to store up perceived injustices (real or not) to substantiate your suspicions. If the other person is also doing this, the situation becomes steadily worse. Every single word and gesture start to be misinterpreted and stored up as 'ammunition'. You both enter into a situation known as 'self-fulfilling prophecy' – because you *expect* a sharp retort if you speak to this person, you start off speaking sharply to them (or deliberately withhold information they need). This fulfils their expectations about *you*. And so it goes on ... .

If, eventually, this ends up as open conflict you may need help to solve the problem (see page 45), but there are things you can try first.

- *You* must be the one to break the cycle – because you certainly can't force the other person to do it. Do this by *deliberately* acting in a different manner to confound expectations. Don't go overboard, just be very pleasant and patient. Be sensitive about your body language and tone of voice. Persist with this – the other person now *has* to change their behaviour to you in some way – either to ask you outright why you are doing this or to reciprocate, even if only slightly.
- Decide 'what is the worst you can live with'. Obviously you don't want arguments or nasty comments, but simply having less contact with someone and giving them 'more space' is often quite acceptable.
- Give it time. Very few situations like this go on forever. If you are new to an organisation and the other person has been there many years, it could be some time before you are accepted as an 'insider'.

Is the behaviour really so bad?

Is the person's behaviour simply irritating or seriously upsetting? There is an enormous difference between irritating behaviour and that which seriously upsets you. In all the cases above we have assumed that the situation is more of an irritant than anything else. If that is the case, it is worth taking the initiative to try to solve the problem or to cooperate with anyone else who is trying to improve the situation. In a situation where there is open conflict or someone is making your life a misery, the situation is very different – and that is the subject of the next section.

CHECK IT OUT!

The premise behind 'assertiveness' is that everyone has certain rights. You have the right to:

- consider your own needs
- refuse to do something without feeling guilty or selfish
- make mistakes
- express yourself – providing that you don't upset anyone else when you do.

Bear in mind, everyone else has these rights too! And note that 'refusing to do something' obviously doesn't refer to the work you are paid to carry out.

The aim is that your *verbal* skills allow you to state your point of view calmly, and without upsetting other people. You are neither a doormat, who agrees to everything for the sake of peace, nor someone who rants and raves to get your way! Some people are more naturally assertive than others, but you can check your own abilities.

You are being assertive when:

a   You state your case calmly and unemotionally.

b   You are prepared to give a reason for something but do not hurriedly justify yourself.

c   You start with the word 'I' (to own the statement) and not the word 'You' (which is inflammatory and accusatory).

d   You get to the point without lots of explanations.

e   You consider your own needs are as important as everyone else's.

f   You refer to your own views and feelings – not someone else's.

g   You ask questions for clarification.

h   You act in an adult manner and do not resort to childish tactics or criticism to get your way.

i   You explain clearly why you cannot do something – and don't feel guilty afterwards.

j   You realise you have more control over your own priorities.

Now check out how much work you have to do! If you hate asking people to do things for you, always back down first if there is a disagreement, never say 'no' or speak up for yourself when you get upset, then it's high time you started. Equally, if you give people a hard time by aggressively responding to the merest suggestion, you have even more to do! Practise being assertive in the presence of someone whose feedback you trust. Don't worry if you don't always get the words and the balance right from the start – work at it. It's worth it – and so are you!

Procedures for dealing with conflict and poor working relationships

Firstly, it is important to get the word 'conflict' into perspective. Conflict exists in all normal relationships and in all situations. However, it is the *degree* of conflict and whether this is *constructive* or *destructive* that is important.

There are very few friends who don't disagree from time to time. If they row every day then the situation becomes untenable. If they never disagree then it is more likely that one is agreeing with everything for a quiet life. However, in a well-balanced adult relationship each person can be assertive with the other *without* threatening the overall balance. They can discuss issues on which they disagree and work at finding a way around these.

In many organisations, **constructive conflict** is used very productively. Creative teams are a good example. There may be furious arguments before an idea is developed and 'honed' to everyone's liking. However, if the discussion centres on the issue (rather than people attacking each other) and the aim of the group is to end up with the best possible solution, the conflict has been purposeful. In fact, some people thrive on such situations and feel quite a 'buzz' afterwards.

Destructive conflict denotes a situation which is out of control. It is harmful to those who are in it – and often to the observers as well. It stops productive work and upsets people. This type of conflict needs to be avoided, and most organisations have procedures to control it.

Resolving conflict unofficially

The first priority of any reasonable manager will be to try to resolve conflict informally and quickly, before it can escalate. Only if this fails will official procedures be invoked. There are several strategies which can be tried, but the aim of a good manager will be to:

- establish the reason for the conflict
- get the issue out into the open
- help both parties to save face – in other words, to go for a 'win/win' solution.

The reason for the conflict, as you have already seen, may be a dispute about an issue (such as scarce resources) or a personality clash. Ideally, your manager will want also to know how many people are involved, how long it has been going on, and the events that have taken place so far.

The next stage is to hold a meeting with those involved. If there are two people (or groups of people) a meeting is usually held with each one separately at the outset. A few 'ground rules' help to set the scene. Each side should be expected to:

- focus on the positive – not necessarily the 'best possible' but 'what I can live with'
- express their feelings honestly – and assertively
- back up any allegations or opinions with evidence
- identify areas where a compromise or change is possible
- show a willingness to end the dispute.

The final stage is to negotiate some agreement. A skilled manager will consider solutions which enable *both* parties to claim victory. This means identifying areas where both could benefit from change and issues on which both have indicated a willingness to change (interestingly, these are often different as one person sets greater store by some things than another). The change may be proposed over a trial period and progress monitored. This means neither side feels 'forced' into a situation they may later consider unacceptable.

Resolving conflict officially

In some situations, conflict cannot be resolved by these methods. This may be because:

- the dispute has gone on too long and both sides are too firmly entrenched
- the manager is part of the conflict
- the manager likes a quiet life and refuses to intervene or simply ignores the problem
- the manager orders both sides to conform to his/her instructions – and the conflict continues to simmer under the surface
- the situation is too serious to be resolved unofficially.

For these reasons, all organisations have grievance procedures employees can use if they feel they are being treated unfairly or discriminated against. You should have been notified where you can access these when you received your contract of employment. There are usually three stages:

1 An interview with the line manager at which the facts or allegations are checked. At this interview, the employee can be accompanied by someone else of his/her own choosing, such as a colleague, solicitor or union representative.

2 If the problem is still not resolved, an interview is held with a more senior manager, usually from another department. This may be the personnel or human resources manager. In a serious conflict, there may be a joint committee meeting of union and management representatives.

3 An interview with an outside third party who will make a recommendation, such as the Advisory, Conciliation and Arbitration Service (ACAS).

The reason for these procedures is not only to resolve conflict, but so that the organisation can prove it has taken action if there is a serious situation which violates the legal rights of people at work. These rights are laid down in employment law and are specified in Acts such as:

- the Sex Discrimination Act 1975/1986
- the Race Relations Act 1976
- the Disability Discrimination Act 1995 – which currently applies to organisations with more than fifteen employees.

These Acts focus on the basic principle that all employees should be treated fairly and equally and your organisation may also have an **equal opportunities policy** which reflects these aims.

Discrimination is when you are treated differently because of your gender, race or a disability, and are denied opportunities given to others – in other words, you are treated less favourably than your colleagues. This could be unlawful and action can be taken against organisations which do this – either deliberately or inadvertently – if the outcome constitutes discrimination. Further details are given below, and if you study Option Unit 317 (on the website) you will read more about equal opportunities there.

The Sex Discrimination Act 1975/1986

This Act makes it illegal for anyone to be discriminated against on grounds of gender (or gender reassignment) – either directly or indirectly. In employment this applies to recruitment and selection for jobs and promotion, training, the way you are treated in a job, dismissal and redundancy. **Direct discrimination** is where one gender is excluded, e.g. 'only men need apply'. **Indirect discrimination** is where a *condition* would make it more difficult to one sex to comply, eg 'only those over 6' 6" need apply'. Even if this is done unintentionally, the organisation is still guilty. There are some special exceptions, such as in acting or live-in jobs, if the employer can show a Genuine Occupational Qualification (GOQ) applies. Note, too, that the **Equal Pay Act 1970** means that jobs where the work is of 'equal value' must be paid at the same rate for men and women.

The Race Relations Act 1976

This Act makes it unlawful for anyone to be discriminated against on grounds of colour, race, nationality or ethnic origin. Again both direct and indirect discrimination apply, e.g. 'only white people need apply' or 'only those who speak English as their first language need apply'. Again there are certain special circumstances under which it can be justified, e.g. restaurants for authenticity, but these are relatively rare.

The Disability Discrimination Act 1995 (Currently applies only to businesses with over 15 employees, but from 2004 will apply to all businesses.) This Act is concerned with discrimination against people with disabilities in employment, when obtaining goods and services or buying/renting land or property. The disability may be physical, sensory or mental but must be relatively long-term (i.e. last more than 12 months). Employers must *not* treat a disabled person less favourably than able-bodied persons whether in recruitment, training, promotion or dismissal, unless it can be justified. Employers must also be prepared to make reasonable adjustments to the workplace to enable a disabled person to do the job. Discrimination in this case is not divided into 'direct' and 'indirect' but is 'less favourable treatment that cannot be justified'.

People who suffer discrimination, either on grounds of sex, race or disability, can complain to an employment tribunal.

You are also protected against **harassment** (and stalking) by the Protection from Harassment Act 1997. The definition of harassment is 'unwelcome behaviour' which upsets, offends or frightens you. It is sexual harassment if the behaviour is linked to your gender. It is racial harassment if it is linked to your skin colour or culture.

Your organisation should make it clear to you how to take action if you feel you are the subject of harassment or discrimination.

INFORMATION UPDATE

Most organisations have policies relating to harassment and discrimination but very few have a policy against bullying, despite the fact that a survey carried out by the University of Manchester Institute of Science and Technology of 5000 employees from the public, private and voluntary sectors found that over 50 per cent had experienced or witnessed bullying at work over the last five years.

At work, forget the stereotypical bully. The worst type may be a good-looking charmer or someone who is devious and clever or even your colleague at the next desk who's due to retire next year. They may not be outwardly aggressive but make someone's life a misery by other, more subtle, psychological tactics. Their actions can include obvious intimidation – such as shouting, constant criticism, refusal to grant a personal day's leave – and more insidious behaviour – such as taking away interesting work and replacing it with trivial duties, making you look small in front of your colleagues, setting impossible deadlines, telling jokes at your expense, excluding you from team discussions and social events. This will totally destroy your self-esteem – if you let the situation carry on.

The Andrea Adams Trust is a workplace bullying charity. It gives the following advice in this situation.

a Keep a record of *all* the incidents that occur – the frequency and regularity is important.
b Try to get witnesses to the incidents that occur.
c Avoid being on your own with the bully – keep a low profile while you are collecting evidence. But also find out if anyone else is being subjected to the same treatment and if they will support you.
d Keep copies of all documents you receive which relate to your work and job performance. ➡

e   Find out the grievance procedures which exist in your organisation and inform your manager, union representative or personnel officer.

f   Although the law is on your side, remember that taking the issue to a tribunal may be very traumatic. Think seriously about leaving – better to do this than to feel mentally scarred for life.

Or ring a helpline – such as the Andrea Adams Trust on 01273 704900, the TUC on 020 7636 4030 or Wash (Women against sexual harassment) on 020 7405 0430. Alternatively access Bully OnLine – the website of the UK National Workplace Bullying Advice Line. If you even suspect you *may* be being bullied the information you read will be invaluable.

CHECK IT OUT!

How well do you know your rights at work, and the responsibilities you have to your employer under the law?

The main rights of employees were laid down in the Employment Rights Act 1996, but further rights relating to maternity, parental and family leave were granted to all workers in the Employment Relations Act 1999. The National Minimum Wage Act stipulates the minimum wage rate per hour for all adults and young workers, and your working hours are regulated in the Working Time Regulations. For most employees the working week must be no longer than 48 hours, unless an 'opt-out' agreement is in place, with specified rest breaks and four weeks' annual holiday entitlement. Finally, part-time employees now have the same rights to equal pay, treatment and benefits as full-time workers under the European Directive on Part-time Work.

Further changes are on the way. From 2003, working fathers will have the right to two weeks of paid paternity leave and adoptive parents will have the right to paid adoption leave. From 2004, all employers will have to conform to the requirements of the Disability Discrimination Act – even those with fewer than 15 employees, which are currently exempt.

Knowing your rights – and your responsibilities – and staying up to date with changes is in your own best interests! As a start, consider the following.

1   Check your own rights – and those of your employer – by reading the summary below.

2 Find out whether your employer (and/or your college) has an equal opportunities policy, and see what it says.

3 The minimum wage rates as at November 2001 were as follows:

- £3.70 an hour for all adults
- £3.50 an hour for workers aged between 18 and 21 years
- £3.50 an hour for workers aged 22 and over for the first six months in a new job, if they are receiving accredited training.

Check how your own wage rate compares with this and find out whether there have been any updates (see below).

4 Find out whether there have been any further changes to the aw you should know about. Do this from your library or by accessing the Internet. Useful websites include www.tuc.org.uk, www.open.gov.uk, www.lawrights.co.uk, and www.emplaw.co.uk.

Your rights as an employee

1 To work in safe working conditions and not to be discriminated against on grounds of race, sex or disability.

2 To receive details of your employment terms within two months of starting work. Normally this is in a contract of employment. You have the right to be consulted over changes which will significantly alter your terms and conditions. If your employer makes changes which you consider unacceptable then you *may* be able to claim constructive dismissal and complain to an employment tribunal (but note here employer right number 11!).

3 To be paid a wage or salary which is at or above the national minimum wage and to receive an itemised payslip which shows your gross and net pay and details of any deductions.

4 To be provided with information relating to your rights. For instance, the fact that if you are asked to work on a Sunday you can 'opt-out' by serving notice.

5 To have any grievances properly dealt with.

6 To join a trade union or become a trade union official or health and safety representative.

7 To have time off work for jury service or ante-natal care. All female employees are eligible for maternity leave and have the right to return to work afterwards on the same terms and conditions as before.

Your rights as an employee (cont.)

8 To have paid holidays as long as you have been continuously employed for 13 weeks.

9 To be paid for up to 26 weeks if you are suspended from work on medical grounds.

10 To be treated reasonably and the right to refuse an unlawful request (e.g. to drive a company vehicle if you are not insured).

11 To have a minimum period of notice (between 1 and 12 weeks), depending upon the length of time you have been continuously employed. Your employer would be guilty of wrongful dismissal if you did not receive this.

12 To receive redundancy pay if you are dismissed through redundancy provided you have worked for that employer for more than two years.

13 Not to be unfairly dismissed and, if this occurs, the right to make a complaint to an employment tribunal.

The rights of your employer

1 That you will be 'ready and willing' to work and will do what a 'reasonable' employee would do in any situation.

2 That you will give a personal service (i.e. you will turn up for work yourself!)

3 That you will be reasonably competent and will not have misled your employer at interview by claiming skills and qualifications you do not possess.

4 That you will take reasonable care of your employer's property (this includes equipment and furniture).

5 That you will carry out reasonable and lawful instructions.

6 That you will always act in good faith, i.e. you will be honest, you will not work for a competitor, take bribes or give away trade secrets.

7 That you will comply with the express terms of your contract of employment (e.g. your hours of work, duties etc).

8 That you will comply with all health and safety procedures.

9 That you will work towards the objectives of the organisation.

10 That you will behave responsibly towards other employees.

11 That you will be prepared to change when the job changes, e.g. when new technology is introduced into the workplace.

EVIDENCE COLLECTION

1 Obtain information on your organisation's procedures for solving problems with working relationships – such as informal routes and grievance procedures. Explain in what situation you think you would need to use these, but *first* state what initiatives you would have taken to try to solve the problem on your own.

2 You need to provide evidence that you work effectively with at least two of the following types of people:

- your line manager (or supervisor or team leader)
- other people in your team
- people internal to your organisation, but not in your team
- people external to your organisation.

The easiest way to do this is to keep a diary of your workplace contacts over a short period, say a month. Into this enter *significant* occasions on which you have had to relate to another person, such as:

- when you had to integrate your work to avoid a resource problem
- when you had to pass on essential information
- when you had to adjust your own working style to allow for the needs of others
- when you specifically helped someone
- when you had a problem fulfilling a commitment and had to notify your manager and negotiate with others about your changed priorities
- when you had a difficulty which you needed to resolve through negotiation with another person.

3 Finally, your perception may be that you work effectively with others – but you need to prove that they think so too. The easiest way to do this is to obtain witness testimony – although do obtain your line manager's permission before you ask anyone external to the organisation. This should not be problematic if, say, you regularly liaise with and help a particular customer or supplier. If possible, ask the people who are providing you with witness testimony to be specific. Rather than produce a short paragraph saying how wonderful you are, it is much more valuable if they can give specific examples of when you have worked with them particularly effectively.

Element 301.2 Contribute to improving the work of your team

Your team comprises the group of people with whom you liaise frequently over common goals or targets. A team is distinctive because each member is responsible for achieving the team's goals and objectives and each should put the team's objectives before any personal ambitions. You see this every day if you watch a good sporting team in action. They work together and *complement* each other – so that they achieve a good result consistently.

If you have already taken your NVQ Administration level 2 award, you will have learned much about being a team member and contributing positively towards the work of your team. At this level you have to raise your sights and take a more proactive role towards helping the team to continually improve. You may even be the team leader, in which case you have the official responsibility for their overall performance.

Teams and continuous improvement

Meredith Belbin, an expert on teams, argued that 'although one person can't be perfect, a team can be'. By this he meant that because a team can comprise members with complementary strengths there should be few, if any, weaknesses. However, a perfect team is hard to find. There are three main reasons for this.

1   Members of teams continually have two areas of concern. Firstly they have to think about meeting team goals. Secondly, they have to maintain good team relationships. These areas are likely to be interlinked. If goals are not met then this can threaten working relationships – particularly if it creates stress and some members of the team blame the others. If team relationships are jeopardised in any way, performance usually suffers, which means goals may not be met again. So it can end up as a vicious circle. Yet keeping both areas intact simultaneously isn't easy.

2   Building a successful team takes time. A new team goes through distinct stages of evolution and takes some time to reach the 'performing' stage (see below). If teams in your organisation are rapidly brought together and just as rapidly disbanded, they will never get the opportunity to be highly performing.

3   In some organisations, teams are used for the wrong reasons. Teams comprised of members from different departments (all working in their own department's interests!) is an obvious example. Teams should be used to create a sense of common purpose and a shared goal – or where complex knowledge is required. They shouldn't be formed for no good reason or just because it is the 'in' thing. Similarly, if the organisation only ever rewards *individual* effort, this will mitigate against successful

teamwork (an obvious case of where the espoused belief and the theory-in-use is very different!)

However, a point to note is that highly confident, long-standing teams can become complacent or difficult to change. This phenomena, known as **groupthink**, is discussed further on page 59.

CHECK IT OUT!

Before you can even consider helping to improve your team, you have to be able to identify how well it is performing *now*. There are three ways in which you can do this.

First you can assess how far your team has 'matured'. One expert, Tuckman, identified five stages, each with recognisable patterns of behaviour amongst team members. These stages are summarised in the table on page 56. Work through it and decide how far your team has progressed to date.

Secondly, you can check if high performance is *possible* to attain. This may not be the case if your team is deprived of essential resources or if the circumstances are such that teamwork is not supported by organisational rewards and procedures. To operate effectively the team needs:

- an appropriate number of skilled people for the goals it has to achieve (between five and seven is considered best)
- space in which to work
- appropriate equipment
- achievable goals that, preferably, the team has been involved in agreeing
- either a skilled team leader or procedures whereby any disputes or disagreements can be resolved rapidly
- an appropriate balance of skills and abilities.
- staff development on teamwork, such as team-building activities, to promote compatibility and interaction.

Thirdly, you can check out your team to see how well it would score against the statements in the checklist on pages 56 and 57. Allocate one point for each statement you think is honestly true. Bear in mind that few teams would score 20; but if you score less than 10, you have quite a bit of work to do to improve your team!

Tuckman's stages in team development	
Stage	Identifiable behaviour
Forming	The group is new and members don't know each other. They are anxious or apprehensive and rely on the leader to provide information on the reason for the team being formed, its 'rules' and how it will operate. There is likely to be some informal banter and 'ice-breaking' activities are helpful.
Storming	Differences between members start to emerge. Some may be disillusioned about the team; others feel disappointed. There may be arguments as people voice different opinions and the leader may be challenged. At this stage the leader has to spell out the responsibilities of each member and make certain each person is certain of their own role and place in the team.
Norming	Members of the team have now started to accept their roles and to support each other. Problems are discussed more openly so that solutions can be found which are acceptable to everyone. This leads to a more open exchange of opinions and greater camaraderie. There is more group consensus and harmony and closer relationships develop. Team members start to identify strongly with the team itself.
Performing	Because the human relationship needs of the team are well developed, the team can now focus on task performance. Members feel able to express their opinions and offer solutions. They are flexible about their roles if this will help to achieve team needs or goals. Each member is secure in his/her identity and feels valued. This is the major period of team effectiveness.
Mourning	This is the final stage for groups which disband, when members are about to go their separate ways. Some may feel sad and upset and there are often ritual endings (such as a 'last night out') and promises of reunions in the future.

Checklist for high team performance

How many of the following characteristics can you honestly ascribe to your team?

1   All members know what the team has to achieve.

2   Members have a high level of identification with the team – and use this to describe their role.

3   Members agree with the aims of the team.

4   Members support each other.

5   There is team support for the leader.

6   Members trust each other.

7   Members have confidence in each other's skills and abilities.

8   There is open communication.

9   Information and problems are shared.

10 Members help each other to develop.

11 All members participate in team discussions.

12 All members participate in decision-making.

13 All members feel they can put their case assertively, without causing offence.

14 Members work together to achieve a task.

15 Mistakes are 'owned' by the team, not by individuals.

16 The team learns from its mistakes.

17 Members put the team's aims before personal benefit.

18 Conflict is constructive with the emphasis on the issue, not the people.

19 Personality clashes are dealt with openly and positively.

20 Relationships with other teams are positive and cooperative.

The reason for continuous improvement

Continuous improvement is important because everything is continually changing. Therefore, even a 'perfect' team would fail to be perfect for long if it never changed its methods or style of working. In addition, all teams undergo some change of membership. People leave and are replaced. All team members then have to adjust to the alteration and it will take time for the same level of performance to be reached.

All teams need a mixture of personality types to operate effectively. You have already met this concept on page 9, but in this section a greater range of personalities is identified. The standard five are held to be:

- an **action person** – the risk-taker who is continually pushing ahead, is impatient and reacts quickly

- a **caring person** – who is sensitive to moods and feelings within the group, can mediate in an argument and promote harmony

- a **detail person** – who is concerned with completing tasks, getting the detail right and is prepared to slow down the team to achieve high quality

- a **coordinator** – who can lead discussions and make sure everyone is involved and make sure everyone is performing effectively

- a **creative thinker** – who comes up with good or unusual ideas that give the team new ways of thinking about a problem.

Alternatively, you can classify team roles into those which relate to the *task* and those which relate to *people*. You then need a mixture of these styles and roles. If one or more key roles are missing, team performance will suffer. But if everyone is an Action person, it is likely that the results will be very fast, but pretty chaotic.

1 Check the table opposite and decide whether you are fundamentally someone who prefers to deal with tasks or with people. If you are a mixture, to what degree you prefer each one?

2 Now decide how you would categorise both yourself and your team members. Do bear in mind that people can undertake more than one role (and have to, in a small team). So you may, for instance, be both an information handler and provider.

3 Finally, decide whether there are any key roles missing in your team and whether anyone could try to change their style to make up for this.

 INFORMATION UPDATE

The concept of 'groupthink' was devised by Irving Jarvis. Basically, it relates to a team which thinks it is so good, it can never be criticised or challenged. It regards all other teams as 'weak' or 'stupid' and any member of the team who challenges this view is belittled. You may remember this sort of behaviour from school, when rival groups competed against each other. To be one of the group you had to agree with everything 'it' thought. Regrettably, such tactics are not unknown in the business world too. ➡

According to the experts, this mentality is fostered – even if accidentally – by organisations that hold up certain teams as 'good examples'. This means teams become competitive instead of cooperative.

The most drastic solution is to move people around regularly, so that teams don't become too set in their ways. A more moderate measure is to break up the team into subgroups to solve the same problem, so that different ideas are encouraged.

Task roles	People roles
Initiator/energiser Creative, imaginative, suggests new ideas and ways of solving problems. Often dynamic and enjoys a challenge.	**Information provider/communicator** Ensures all members of the team and external contacts are kept informed and encourages participation by everyone.
Information handler Collects appropriate information, good at clarifying complex points and obtaining relevant facts and details.	**Team builder** Tactful and a good listener. Helps to strengthen the team by alleviating tension, averting friction and helping to resolve any conflicts.
Co-ordinator Confident. A natural leader. Coordinates activities and combines ideas and suggestions. A positive decision-maker.	**Motivator** Good at encouraging others. Projects warmth towards other team members, praises regularly. Interested in new ideas and proposals.
Evaluator Quietly and objectively weighs up the strengths of weaknesses of any suggestions or ideas and/or evaluates the relevance of information.	**Quality setter** Interested in reputation of team. Likes to achieve but does this by helping to set and raise team goals and standards. Provides useful feedback on group performance.
Implementer/finisher Reliable and efficient. Likes to get on with the job and dislikes too much discussion. Conscientious and delivers on time.	**Follower** Prefers to take a back seat in team discussions and agree with others. Quietly supportive and helpful.

(Adapted from the work of Benne, Sheats and Belbin.)

The importance of feedback

Feedback, as you will see in Unit 303, is an essential element of our self-development. However, you probably already realise that everyone – including yourself – prefers positive to negative feedback.

Positive feedback

Positive feedback is absolutely crucial if the team is to be highly motivated. There is nothing worse than doing a super job for someone in double quick time and never receiving any thanks or acknowledgement. Bear in mind that this is a case where 'little and often' pays dividends. Don't store up compliments and give them to someone once a year at an official appraisal session. Although this is better than nothing, *regular* praise and encouragement is far more valuable as this inspires team members to continue to work hard. And remember, too, to pass on compliments and praise you receive from other people which relate to your team.

'External' negative feedback

Regrettably, on occasion, you will also receive negative feedback from other people – either minor moans or formal complaints. Bear in mind that these may be received from any of the team's customers – either inside or outside the organisation. They are 'external' simply because the complainant is not a member of the team, not because they work somewhere else.

Before you say anything to anyone you need to assess:

- whether a moan or complaint is justified
- what went wrong
- what action is needed to remedy the situation.

Even if a team member made a terrible mistake, always remember that you must show that you are loyal to your team to 'outsiders'. So, right at the outset, start from the position that:

- there are two sides to every story
- few people deliberately make mistakes
- you need to find out what else contributed towards the problem (e.g. lack of information, lack of resources)
- your team (or team member) has the right of reply (to you) to any accusation which has been made.

If your team know that you have inherent faith in their abilities they will be more open about discussing problems because there is less need to defend themselves. This helps you to get to the heart of the matter more easily. You then need to take action as follows:

1 Sort out the problem with your customer, according to your organisational procedures. Don't take the blame. Simply apologise and arrange for things to be put right.

2 When you find out why the problem or mistake occurred, take action to try to prevent any repetition. This may mean obtaining more training for one of your staff or making improvements in communication or information (see also pages 66–71).

Monitoring performance yourself

Team performance should be monitored continually, not just once or twice a year. Remember, you should be concentrating on both team performance and team morale. The areas on which you should focus are given below.

- **Team goals or results.** Do team members know what results are expected? How often do these change? Are team members kept informed? Are expected results still achievable? How often are targets reached or surpassed?
- **Motivation.** Are team members keen to work together? Are they eager to produce the required result? Has any change occurred which may have affected the motivation of any members?
- **Resources.** Are the resources still adequate? Are the equipment and technology still appropriate? If the goals have been changed, have resources been provided to match?
- **Skills.** Have team members the skills and abilities required? Are new skills emerging which the team could usefully use? Can the team consistently identify and achieve the quality of work required? Are they competent to carry out all the operations? Are there any particular abilities which the team lacks?

Don't forget that your team members will have their views on each of these areas – and it is important you listen to these. You cannot possibly obtain an accurate picture on your own. There should therefore be regular team meetings at which any concerns or problems are aired. The focus then should be upon positive methods of dealing with these (see page 66).

Do be aware, however, that team members may have a 'hidden agenda' which will influence what you are told! Equally, just as there are always positive and helpful team members you may also have the odd more difficult person to deal with. The better you know your team, the easier it is to second-guess their reactions and the simpler it is to think of a way to respond to these – as you will see.

CHECK IT OUT!

Just as there are positive team roles, as you saw on page 59, there are also negative roles that impede teamworking and give you a headache if you are trying to identify problems and recommend improvements.

Negative, or dysfunctional, roles are shown in the table on pages 62 and 63. Bear in mind that no one is perfect, so everyone you meet has a tendency here one way or another. However, when the behaviour is so pronounced that it actively affects the team, you need to take action.

Check out your own team against the list in the table and then implement at least one of the suggested strategies to try to cope with your trickiest member!

Problem type	Description	Strategies to try
The ideas blocker	Always negative. Dislikes any change. Pours cold water on new ideas and puts off everyone else.	Ask for solutions, not problems. Make the ideas blocker suggest ideas or ways around identified problems. Or 'call the game' – laugh and say, 'But of course, now we need Tim to tell us why we can't do this!'
The praise seeker	Always trying to please (and flatter) the boss. Boasts to others about own achievements. May act superior.	Try to work out why. Do you (or your boss) respond to this treatment? Do praise seekers get a 'better deal' in your office? If not, counter all boasting by talking about other people's achievements – but make these bigger and better!
The attention seeker	Likes sound of own voice, particularly in team meetings. Prevents progress. Often interrupts – often with irrelevant points. May try to manipulate the group behind the scenes.	Be strict – make everyone keep to the topic in a meeting. Learn to recognise 'red herrings' quickly. On important issues, say you want a contribution from everyone but only for 2/3 mins – and 'guillotine' speakers who overrun. Get a close team member to 'tip you off' if there are problems behind the scenes. Again, call the game. 'Oh, Sarah, I believe you had a problem with that. Do you want to discuss it?'
The work avoider	Will never argue but passively agree to suggestions – but then not do them. If skilled, will always find good reason for this.	Find out if it's 'can't' or 'won't'. If 'can't' then provide support and training. If 'won't' then box them in. Fix a time/date/target when you will be able to see evidence of achievement. Start to list reasons given for non-compliance and produce this when next reason given.
The sympathy seeker	Tries to obtain team sympathy by always having problems. Uses this to avoid work and get attention.	If you *definitely* know the problem is not genuine or is minor but inflated, you could frighten this person by suggesting you may have them transferred to another team where the work is less onerous. Few people actually want this option!
The antagonist	Argumentative and often openly hostile to others in meetings. Wants to win the argument more than to solve the problem.	Step in immediately if there is an open confrontation and say this is distracting everyone (which it is). Focus on the issue. Don't allow insults to be traded. Keep calm and don't become openly hostile yourself or 'fuel' the debate in any way.

Problem type	Description	Strategies to try
The critic	Often bossy. Likes to give orders and opinions. Highly critical of others. May be strongly disliked.	Give this person the role of official quality checker! And say why. This leaves your critic vulnerable if he/she *doesn't* spot an error! And keep them busy – they've then less time to order others around.
The individualist	May only partially listen to ideas, then goes off and does 'own thing'. Uninterested in team suggestions – prefers to do work alone.	Not everyone is a 'team' person. Is this person disillusioned, bored or very ambitious – and feels the team is holding them back? Identify any jobs for which this person can have *sole* responsibility. The situation is tolerable if not affecting team performance or morale.

Giving negative feedback

No matter what strategies you have up your sleeve, there will come a time when you have to give direct negative feedback to a team member. For instance:

- when, despite all your loyalty and investigations, a problem reported by a customer is valid and was caused by one of your team
- when you have identified a problem yourself, such as a team member not doing his or her work or not completing it to the required standard
- when unacceptable behaviour is affecting the working relationships within your team.

On page 60 and in Unit 303, you will see how to cope with *receiving* negative feedback. Never forget your own dislike of this when you are giving negative feedback yourself. The first rule is: 'do as you would be done by'!

First, remember that your approach should vary depending upon whether this issue and/or this person has been a problem before. A first-time incident should be treated differently from a recurring problem.

Second, never forget that negative feedback should be given in private. *Never*, ever, criticise someone in front of his or her colleagues – they will 'lose face' and are unlikely to forgive you.

Third, remember the key points on the list below.

1 Prepare in advance and make sure you have your facts right. If there is any evidence, have it available.

2 If your team member knows there is a problem, don't delay the meeting. Call it as soon as possible and make sure you have uninterrupted privacy.

3   Allow an appropriate length of time. The more important the problem, the longer you are likely to need.

4   Get to the point quickly. Don't make it into a guessing game.

5   Make it clear immediately that you want to be supportive and help to find a solution, your aim is not to be highly critical.

6   Focus on the issue – don't bring personal characteristics into it. This is the case even if you have a 'problem person'. The *issue* in this case is how the team or team performance is being affected.

7   Give specific examples, and back this up with evidence if necessary. For instance: 'Yesterday you sent through this document which contained twelve errors;' or 'Yesterday you were highly critical of three suggestions made by the team and nearly reduced Maggie to tears. This meant the meeting had to end without us getting any nearer to a solution.'

8   As soon as you have made your point, focus on the positive. Don't enter into a long debate. Say what you want to be the case – or the action that must be taken: 'Obviously we must send through mailable documents;' or 'It is very important we all work together to find a solution at the next meeting.'

9   Remember the other person has the right of reply. But if you have double-checked all your facts and have not personally attacked your team member, this will reduce the need for defensive explanations.

10   Make sure that you both agree the problem, its effects and what action should be taken to put things right: 'I will speak to Ben about his handwriting but *you* must agree to check words you cannot read and to proofread your documents carefully;' or 'I'm glad you agree that it is off-putting for people when everything they suggest is criticised. I really need you to support me next week. If you can think of any good ideas yourself, please let me know.'

11   Don't hesitate to offer support and help yourself, if this will help. This may include talking to problematic colleagues such as Ben and, in the above case, even offering to double-check difficult documents yourself for a while.

12   Don't hesitate to suggest a follow-up meeting at which the other person can consult you if there are ongoing problems – such as Ben continuing to hand in unreadable documents, disappearing all day and then wanting a perfect version immediately he returns!

TEST YOUR KNOWLEDGE AND UNDERSTANDING

There are two ways in which you can do this exercise. The first is to read the questions and then make suggestions as to what you would do. The second, and better, way is to do this and *then* select one and, with a partner, 'role play' the part of team leader giving critical feedback. Then ask your partner to assess you. It is important your partner takes on the role of the person concerned – and expands this in any acceptable way. Bear in mind that their assessment of your performance will test your own ability to receive some critical feedback!

1 Suzie's attitude to visitors is casual, to say the least. She notifies the person they have come to see and then forgets all about them. Yesterday, a row broke out when a visitor had to wait over half an hour in reception.

Suzie's defence is that she gets engrossed in her other work. Yesterday she was monitoring the waiting area and trying to type up a long report at the same time. If she could just concentrate on reception she'd be OK.

2 Jack is responsible for checking and processing your section's invoices and logging these on a spreadsheet, before they are passed for payment by finance. He is normally very competent. Recently you have had two complaints – firstly from a supplier who wasn't paid for weeks (it turned out that Jack had put the invoice in the wrong file) and secondly – and more worryingly – from finance. They say there is a backlog and invoices are being sent in huge batches and in every batch recently there have been mistakes which haven't been spotted.

Jack's defence is that the first error could have happened to anyone – it was a simple mistake. He says the reason for the delay and problems lately is that his workload has increased dramatically over the past few months and he is struggling to cope.

3 Juliette is a new trainee. She often makes mistakes and you are beginning to doubt her abilities. You have had complaints about the mail being delivered wrongly, faxes not being sent on time and photocopies being crooked, crumpled and on one notable occasion, collated back to front. Yesterday your boss asked her to send some papers to three people and to arrange for them to attend a meeting in his office to discuss these at 2 pm. When the the people arrived they had no idea why the meeting had been called and hadn't received the papers. He tells you to 'sort her out'.

Juliette's defence is that your boss scribbled some instructions on a Post-it note on top of the papers. He never said clearly what she had to do, just wrote 'ask these people to attend a meeting' and listed their names. She didn't realise the papers needed to be sent. When you check the note you see she is right. She also claims that, although she was promised help and training, nothing has been provided and she's just supposed to get on with the job. Then she bursts into tears.

Suggesting improvements

You can suggest improvements at a one-to-one meeting at which you are giving feedback, or you can make general suggestions during a team meeting. This is often the best forum for continual improvements. One-to-one meetings are apt to be more focused on specific improvements which must be implemented in response to an identified problem.

However, do remember that you must be tactful if the improvement has emerged because of some problems experienced by a particular member of your team. Talk about the issue in general terms – on the basis that it may affect any one of the team.

Remember, too, that improvements which bring an obvious benefit to the whole team (such as a new, faster photocopier) will always be received more joyfully than those which bring benefits just to one or two people, or those which will require more work and effort!

For any improvements you want to suggest you are wise if you:

- have the basis of the idea before you start, but are prepared to accept recommendations from your team that will improve it
- don't suggest improvements that you can't deliver (like a new photocopier) – always first consult your own boss about resource issues
- move the discussion away from problems and negative ideas and on to constructive proposals as quickly as possible
- welcome suggestions from your team, however bizarre, so that you encourage even more!

Some common issues

You can often second-guess reactions by looking at the type of issues and suggestions which tend to emanate from each area you are continually monitoring.

Team goals or results

Expect your team to be defensive if goals or results are not being met. Try to separate valid reasons from excuses (which isn't easy). Ask for evidence to support accusations and assumptions (such as 'my workload has doubled recently' or 'John never tells us anything').

Then focus on a key result area to improve and ask how performance can be improved in this one area, as a start. Make the goal achievable.

Finally, identify what additional support the team needs – from you or anyone else.

Motivation

If this is a problem then you should have noticed! If your team was previously keen and hard-working and is now dispirited and fed-up there must be a reason. It may be work overload, staff shortages or a particular stressful event.

Separate the solution into the short term and the longer term. In the short term, identify a 'treat' with them (extra half day off, lunch out, evening out) that would give everyone a boost. Then look at team-building opportunities they would enjoy.

At the same time, unless it was a one-off event, discuss with your line manager how more serious and ongoing threats to team motivation can be solved.

Resources

A word of warning! There will never be enough resources in the organisation – ever – to keep everyone happy. If you encourage too many requests in this arena then you will have to disappoint people on a regular basis, and that isn't a good idea.

Separate 'wish lists' from reality. Check the validity of moans and groans about equipment or supplies. Check claims that more staff are needed because of increased work or that current equipment is inappropriate or defunct.

Cost out suggestions. Bear in mind your line manager will have an eagle eye on the budget! Don't make any promises to your team – except that you will pursue valid suggestions with vigour on their behalf. And do so!

Skills

Encourage your team to be positive about any 'skill gaps' which exist. Identifying these accurately is a strength, not a weakness. Encourage staff to be proactive in improving their skills and abilities and support them – this is to the overall benefit of team performance and will enable you to meet your organisation's objectives more effectively.

Find out – if you don't know already – what types of staff development activities, training and support for attendance on outside courses exist in your organisation, so that you can make appropriate suggestions. Then ask for your line manager's support in relation to any financial or work-release requirements.

Always ask for a team member's assessment of the value of a course of study or training they have undergone. Then you can decide whether it is worth sending anyone else. And don't forget to use their new-found skills or no one will benefit!

Finally, encourage your team to be constructively critical of themselves as a team. This doesn't mean constantly focusing on their weaknesses. It means being able to stand back from personal agendas and assessing *themselves as a team* objectively. If they can do this, and use any negative feedback as a source of good ideas for change, your team will continue to go from strength to strength. And that is the true meaning of continuous improvement!

 INFORMATION UPDATE

Brainstorming is used by many teams who want to find a solution to a tricky problem and by many creative teams who have to come up with new or novel ideas – from the design of a car to the name of a new after-shave. It works because no criticism is allowed – even of the most 'off-the-wall' ideas – in the early stages.

Start by asking for ideas, no matter how bizarre. Scribble these down on a whiteboard or flip chart. After a fixed period, say 15 minutes, identify each idea as Possible, Probable or Wacky. Then try combining some ideas to see what you come up with. The results are normally far more inventive than otherwise – and the technique effectively stops the critical member of the group spoiling everything!

Coping with responses to your suggestions

With the best will in the world, you can think about a problem, identify an improvement and put it to your team constructively and in an appropriate time and place. They can then all disagree with you and with each other! In this situation, you may feel somewhat desperate.

You can take heart by the fact that this happens to all team leaders from time to time – and often quite unexpectedly. Improvements you *think* they may be against are accepted quite happily and then, all of a sudden, something you think wasn't a problem goes out of control. Why does this happen and what do you do?

First of all, this happens because you cannot know everything about the background to a situation and the reason for your team's current state of mind.

It could be as basic as a customer who has always seemed very reasonable to you but has been a nightmare for them. You then mention that this person gave a criticism and whoosh – it's like setting light to touchpaper!

So, accept as fact that this will happen occasionally and focus on how to handle it. The following list may provide some useful ideas.

- It helps if you aren't totally committed to the improvement you are suggesting. Otherwise you will defend it to the hilt and not be willing to hear alternative views.

- Teams often perform best if you let *them* suggest improvements – rather than handing them a ready-made solution. However, you may have to rein in the most fanciful suggestions.

- Be prepared to listen to team members who have strong views on a subject because of a personal experience. Listen – you may learn something. Note that this doesn't apply to those who have strong views on everything!

- After the first few minutes, focus everyone back on the key issue of finding a positive, constructive solution.

- Try to involve everyone in the discussion.

- During this time, soak up information and ideas. Mentally check each one against how your line manager would react. Which are feasible? Which are not – and why not?

- If views are very polarised don't push for a solution at that time. Summarise the main suggestions and try to check the strength of feeling for/against each one.

- If one of your suggestions is rejected, don't take it personally!

- Make people give *reasons* for rejecting ideas and suggestions – not just rejecting them out of hand. Two to watch for are 'it's never been done before' (or 'we've always done it like that') and 'we tried that a few years ago, and it didn't work'. These are negative. Times change. New ideas need trying from time to time (or old ones revisiting).

- Explain that you will take the best of their ideas, think about them and – where appropriate – may wish to discuss them with your own line manager to see what is feasible.

- Fix another meeting to discuss the outcome.

Finally, another phenomenon which frequently occurs – as well as a team reacting strongly to the unexpected – is that of 'time putting things into perspective'. Often, by the time you hold the next meeting, there are other problems and possible improvements on the horizon and this one has less impact. A skilful team leader will use this to advantage and sometimes just allow five minutes to settle the first debate. Because everyone is now focused on something else, agreement takes hardly any time at all!

Providing support

The word 'support' has been mentioned throughout this element. One of your key roles in relation to your team is to provide ongoing and unwavering support. However, this can take many forms and some are more exhausting than others! You will need to provide support when:

- a member of your team is experiencing personal or professional problems and needs someone to talk to in confidence
- there has been a complaint about the team that is worrying or distressing them
- they are having problems undertaking tasks they have been given – because of resource problems, lack of information or lack of skills
- they are being given conflicting instructions
- they are being given unreasonable requests or instructions
- they are being treated unfairly or unreasonably by a member of staff outside the team
- there are personality problems and difficulties within the team.

First, always remember that 'people' problems are more difficult – and more time consuming – than 'task' problems. Someone's inability to input data on a spreadsheet is easier to solve than two people constantly at loggerheads. It also takes less time to listen to someone's problem with filling in a new form – and make sensible suggestions – than it does to listen to how they are having problems with their partner or teamworker.

Support should be provided in two ways:

- **moral support** for their personal problems means you are always ready to listen, loyal, discreet and emotionally supportive
- **practical support** for their task problems means that you will do your utmost to help to find a solution by making practical suggestions, providing information and advice, showing them how to do something or even having a word with more senior colleagues when necessary.

Remember, however, that imposed support is never welcome. Only offer support – don't insist on providing it (unless there have been repeated failings). In personal matters, a team member may just want to talk. Don't expect to come up with solutions and move into his or her personal life to implement them! On practical matters, sometimes people would prefer to try something on their own first. Be sensitive to the other person's self-image and pride. Simply knowing you are there may be enough. If, however, your offer of support is welcomed, make sure you do what you promised. Otherwise, you will do more damage than if you had never offered it at all.

Eleanor has just become a team leader. You are her closest friend. How would you advise her to cope in each of the following situations?

1 She is having a problem managing the team rota for holidays. The organisation is open 50 weeks a year and each section must be covered properly throughout the summer. Four members of her team of six want the same weeks in July and are arguing bitterly about this. One is saying her partner can only have these two weeks, another is saying she is going with her parents at this time. A third claims to have already booked and the fourth says she always has these two weeks as it covers both her and her partner's birthdays.

2 The demand for skills to prepare presentation materials has been increasing considerably over the last three months. One member of the team is an experienced Powerpoint user but the others are not. One person, Tim, has tried to learn it recently, using a manual, but his work has been criticised by Eleanor's line manager. Tim now says he's not doing it any more. Eleanor now has two urgent requests on her desk. One requires sophisticated Powerpoint skills but the other does not. Both must be finished by next Wednesday.

3 Every member of Eleanor's team uses a computer and each has an old inkjet printer attached. These are now giving problems, not helped by lower quality paper which constantly misfeeds (or won't feed at all). The speed, too, is creating problems – especially when her line manager asks for long documents to be downloaded from the Internet and printed.

Eleanor's team are asking for new printers or a laser printer. Until they get one of these, they argue, they cannot be responsible for the quality or speed of printouts. Eleanor's line manager is reasonably supportive but says there is no chance of any replacements until at least next April, when he has more money in the budget.

INFORMATION UPDATE

If your idea of team building activities is a night out clubbing or lunch in the local pizza place, think again! The type of activities you can now take part in ranges from paint-balling and abseiling to landing on the moon, working on a farm, crossing a field criss-crossed with pyrotechnic tripwires (with only your team to talk you through) and assembling a robot. Or you could collectively make a film or television programme! In a day! Which certainly requires team cooperation.

The general focus of all these activities is that the team is given a challenge. Unless the team *works together* they will be unlikely to succeed. Afterwards, feedback is given on how you all performed. So if you abandoned one member because she couldn't get through the 12-foot fake spider's web and left another marooned on a desert island surrounded by crocodiles, expect to be criticised!

CHECK IT OUT!

Find out what team building activities you could undertake with your team which would help you to function more effectively as a unit.

Do this by investigating:

- what type of activities have been offered by your workplace to other teams (ask your Training Manager or supervisor)
- other alternatives that may be a possibility (scour your Yellow Pages, visit a library and read through some Training journals or surf the Internet)
- the type of activities your line manager can suggest/would support (both morally and financially!).

Then discuss your draft ideas with your team. Remember to respond positively to *their* ideas (look back to page 69). Remember the eventual choice must be a team decision, so that you have their commitment from the start!

If the end result is a really useful team building event, keep a record (you could even take photographs) and describe what happened and the outcome to your assessor.

EVIDENCE COLLECTION

For your evidence for this element you must show that you can provide *both* positive *and* negative feedback to one of the following types of team members:

- one with similar levels of responsibility to yourself
- someone with fewer responsibilities
- someone with more responsibilities.

You must also show that you can provide *both* the following types of support:

- the giving of information and advice
- showing someone how to do something.

1 It will be relatively easy to prove that you have provided positive feedback. It is unlikely that any of your team members will object if you ask whether you can produce a brief summary of the feedback session and ask for a counter-signature. Alternatively you can ask your team member for witness testimony.

2 Providing evidence about giving negative feedback can be more difficult. If you have to tell your line manager something he or she did not really want to hear, then this is an obvious example. Choose a different time to ask if you can include this in your portfolio! *Don't* include confidential information about a team member unless you remove his or her name – so that you just give *examples* of what you did, without naming individuals. It is better to discuss your negative feedback sessions with your assessor and say how you handled them. You will do even better if you can assess your own performance and identify what you would improve on next time.

3 Providing support is easier to document. The best way is to make a list of all the improvements which were identified by you and your team. State how the improvement was identified, what suggestions were rejected and when the final improvement was implemented. Finally, identify the support that was required and provided by you and ask for this to be counter-signed – either by your line manager or by your team.

Element 301.3 Jointly plan and carry out work with other people

The previous element looked at the way in which you can help to improve the work of your team. Yet on a day-to-day basis you are more likely to be involved with your team in undertaking a wide range of tasks, some of which people can do alone and some of which they cannot. You will then have to plan how this work can be undertaken to use their skills and abilities (and time and resources) most effectively. Additionally, there will be occasions when you have to plan how to carry out work with your line manager – or your own team leader or supervisor – and, probably less frequently, other people in your organisation and people external to it.

The reason for joint planning and working

The phrase 'joint planning' is used to cover a wide range of activities, from moon launches to emergency rescues. It is often essential when a task is complex or needs several skills. Imagine, for a moment, the chaos that would ensue if the police, fire brigade and ambulance services all arrived at a major crash scene and just 'did their own thing'. The fact that each unit has specialist skills and employs these in a coordinated way with the other units means that everyone benefits – including the wounded, for whom a rapid response is essential.

Although offices operate in far less dramatic circumstances, the same principles apply. Joint planning is the most effective way of undertaking many tasks quickly and effectively. Examples include:

- a major new initiative, such as the creation and launch of a company website
- the production of a document, such as a newsletter or brochure, which needs an input from several sources
- arrangements for a special event, such as the arrival of VIPs, the AGM or a sales conference
- a visit by an external body, such as health and safety inspectors, auditors or VAT inspectors – when a variety of documents and files will need to be available for checking and staff on hand to answer queries quickly
- a particularly stressful period when an urgent deadline has to be met, such as the end of the tax year.

Agreeing realistic targets with other people

Depending upon the task, you may have to reach agreement about various aspects of the work with one person or several people. Usually, unless you are dealing with someone who is particularly difficult or unreasonable, it may be easier to reach agreement with one person than several, especially if each person has differing problems and concerns to take into account. However, if several people *are* involved, it is sensible to get everyone together for a discussion, rather than see each person separately. At the end of the session agreement should have been reached on all the main areas. These are likely to be:

- the **objectives** to be achieved (if you have forgotten what objectives are, look back to page 12)
- the **resources** that are required
- the **working methods** which would be best
- the **schedule(s)** for undertaking the work.

Ideally, you need some sort of brief or outline before you enter into any discussions. Otherwise you are wise to say you must think about the proposals and will respond later. The brief should state what the job entails and any relevant completion dates. At least you then have some idea what you, or your team, will be involved in.

Your initial response may be largely determined by your natural tendencies. If you are normally very confident, you may be apt to *overestimate* your own – or your team's – abilities to deliver. If you are normally lacking in confidence, even the proposal itself may sound horrific. In this case, you may be prone to *underestimate* what can be done. Remember, if everyone works together, this enables results to be achieved that would be impossible for one person. Despite your natural inclinations, it would be sensible to consider the following:

- what other work you (or your team) are involved with at present that *must* still be done
- what you know you can offer to contribute without any problems
- what you know you can commit your team to doing without any problems

- what you could consider – but would have to gain further agreement
- what might be possible – given sufficient resources
- what is absolutely impossible (but be careful here – you will probably need to have some good reasons ready).

In other words, you should have a relatively good idea how much and what you can do – and what you can't. You won't be asked to do the impossible, but you never know!

In any discussions, however, it is important that you remain positive. There is nothing worse than someone whose immediate response is 'It can't be done.' Turn this around. Consider that there is no such thing as a problem, only an opportunity – and try to think of ways around a difficulty. You will be valued for it.

Finally, in any organisation you will find a clutch of 'gung-ho' colleagues. These are people who are prepared to cut corners and perhaps be even slightly unethical if it will get a result. If someone is suggesting that the work would be done quicker if you ignored a particular procedure and didn't follow the normal methods of working in your organisation, say that you cannot possibly agree to this without permission. Otherwise, if anything goes wrong, you could find yourself in a very difficult situation.

TEST YOUR KNOWLEDGE AND UNDERSTANDING

Read the following scenario and then answer the questions that follow. Check your answers with your tutor or supervisor.

Crista works for a firm of architects. They have been approached by a Spanish company who are buying plots of land in Southern Spain on which to build villas and apartments. The partners are eager to win the contract to produce the designs for these, and have been asked to submit a lengthy proposal and quotation. Most of the firm is involved in helping to produce these.

Crista and her team have been asked to produce a portfolio which shows similar buildings the firm has designed. Her brief is to:

- *arrange for a photographer to visit six similar sites (these are specified on a list) and take photographs of the exterior and interior in each case*
- *arrange for the architect who did each design to write a brief summary and then word process this*
- *obtain the drawings for each site and copy these to an appropriately reduced size*
- *have everything translated into Spanish*
- *have everything bound and ready for dispatch to Spain.*

Crista has three administrators who work with her, and is aware that the day-to-day work must still be undertaken. At the initial planning meeting, the date for despatch is proposed for two weeks' time. The partner in charge of the project thinks that any later bid would not be successful.

1 What do you consider to be the overall objectives of this job?
2 Which tasks do you think your administrative team could carry out without any problem?
3 What resources would you ask for?
4 How flexible do you consider the deadline to be?
5 Draw up a schedule for completing the work assuming the deadline is not negotiable.
6 State what you would do if one drawing was missing and a colleague suggested you substitute a different one on the basis that 'no-one would notice'.

INFORMATION UPDATE

A very modern example of 'joint planning' relates to the actions you must take if your purse or wallet goes missing containing all your credit and debit cards. If you report your cards missing within 48 hours, you may have few problems. Beyond this, the card companies will probably hold you liable for any bills which are run up on your behalf.

Firstly, you may be tempted to phone everyone you know and everywhere you have visited to check whether your cards have been found. This is a luxury you cannot afford. The first priority is to tell the bank(s). Then you need to phone the police. Then you need to arrange to get new cards and cancel all your other cards. Oh, and if your keys have also been stolen you may want to change your locks. Then you may need to find out how to obtain cash until your new cards arrive – especially if you are away from home.

Bearing in mind all these problems, a number of services exist which will do all this for you. In a sense they are 'joint planners' and coordinators. You can register with Card Protect Plan or Sentinel, for instance. These organisations will do everything for you. You can register all your cards, keys, driving licence and passport details. They will not only cancel everything for you, but arrange for emergency cash to be available and air ticket replacements and hotel cover when needed. All you do is make one phone call.

Now *that's* the value of joint planning and coordination!

Agreeing individual responsibilities

It is fairly obvious that if Crista had one member of her team who was a qualified photographer and another who spoke fluent Spanish she would give the first the job of taking the photographs and the second the task of doing the translations – and not vice versa! However, whilst this may sound common sense, it is amazing how many jobs are divided amongst team members without any consideration of individual strengths and weaknesses.

Remember that strengths and weaknesses don't just encompass 'special' skills, such as speaking a foreign language. They also relate to individual personalities and attributes. For instance:

- one person may enjoy meeting VIPs and be good at thinking 'on her feet' whilst another would rather curl up and die than do this
- another may be good at writing difficult communications – whether letters, e-mails or even a newsletter
- one person may have excellent IT skills
- another person may be good at researching and checking details
- another may be excellent at working accurately and speedily to achieve a deadline – without getting stressed.

If you assign tasks to people who enjoy that type of work you will not only get a better result, but will please your team as well. The biggest mistake you can make is to try to 'test' people by giving something to do they will find very difficult – especially if someone else could do it more easily. This is game-playing, which you learned about in element 301.1 (see page 39).

Of course, on occasion, you will have a job to delegate that no one could do easily. The questions to ask now are:

- What *additional* resources do you need?
- Could the job be divided amongst several people?
- Is there someone particularly talented, who would enjoy the challenge?
- What *additional* support or training would you have to provide?

Negotiation skills

Negotiation implies you are trying to achieve a 'win/win' situation which was first described on page 31. The need to negotiate means that you haven't reached an agreement easily. You are trying to avoid a deadlock. So how do you cope if you are arguing one thing and someone else is arguing the opposite?

First, it is obviously rather different if the other person has a higher status than you. Some people would argue that if your boss says 'Jump!', you should simply respond 'How high?' Hopefully, if your line manager's aim is that the job will be done effectively and by the required deadline, you will be allowed rather more input than this, but the point is still valid. You are likely to have more negotiating space with colleagues at your own level, your own team members and *some* other people internal to your organisation than you are with your line manager (or a very senior manager) or an important customer. If you want to win an important contract, you may have no choice in the quantity of information that has to be provided and the date by which it must be available. So there are times when even the most senior member of the organisation has little room for manoeuvre.

In a situation, however, where there is some scope, you need two skills: the ability to see the situation from the other person's point of view, and the ability to recognise when a *mutual advantage* can be achieved. With regard to the latter, you have to consider what you have that you can 'trade' to the other person.

Consider again Crista who works for a firm of architects (see page 76). Let's assume that Crista has found that finance just happened to employ Maria Gonzales last year – a native of Madrid. She is fluent in English and Spanish. Crista thinks it would be better to ask Maria to translate the documents than to give the work to an outside company because it would be cheaper and easier to control. If Maria did not understand any of the architectural terms used she could check these directly with the architect. Crista's line manager tells her to negotiate with the head of the finance team, Matt, to see whether Maria can be released for a few days. Matt's response is that they are far too busy at present but he agrees to meet to discuss the problem.

Crista has several choices. She can:

- give in (he wins, she loses)
- have a row (both of them lose)
- go to the senior partner and insist he backs her (she wins, Matt loses)
- negotiate (in the hope that both of them will win).

Key aspects to negotiating

Before the meeting, Crista needs to think carefully about each of the following points.

- What is Matt's 'mindset'? In other words, why has he responded like this? He may be genuinely busy and worried that his own area will suffer if Maria has to work elsewhere. *Or* he could be protecting Maria if she doesn't want to do the work.
- What do Crista and Matt have in common? Presumably, they both want the firm to be successful, and gaining the contract will help to ensure this. There is another common area – Matt is in finance and should appreciate Crista's attempts to keep costs down by getting the work done internally.

- Where could they compromise? Does Maria have to do all the work? Do the summaries have to be very long? Could her involvement be reduced in any way?
- How could Crista help Matt? Could she offer one of her own team to replace Maria for a day or two? Matt might reject this but appreciate the offer. Could she do anything herself that will help?

At the meeting, Crista should do the following.

a She should start by outlining the problem for the firm – not for herself. Because Matt is equally interested in its future prospects she is defining some common ground.

b She should give Matt information about the work – and the lack of flexibility with the deadline. He can now more readily appreciate Crista's dilemma.

c She should state that she appreciates his problem – and sympathises.

d She should ask whether there are any problems she doesn't know about – such as Maria not wanting to do the work.

e She should suggest some ideas which would help them both – such as reducing the work for Maria or 'exchanging' staff.

f She should listen to any suggestions that Matt might have. He may have brought along a solution himself if he, too, is skilled at negotiating.

g She should try to reach an agreement which will suit them both. This isn't possible on every occasion, but the better you are at negotiating, the greater the likelihood of success!

TEST YOUR KNOWLEDGE AND UNDERSTANDING

Try to find a partner with whom you can carry out this exercise verbally. Otherwise, prepare a written response and ask your tutor or supervisor to give you their comments.

At the last minute, you have been asked to arrange a social event for a member of your team who is leaving to join her sister who emigrated to Australia several years ago. You approach your canteen manager, Joanne, herself an Australian, and ask for a finger buffet to be provided on Friday lunchtime for 20 people. She says this is impossible as she has three other important business events that day and hasn't the staff to cope. She says you will have to go to a local restaurant. You know that all your colleagues have different lunch breaks and it would be impossible to organise this. Your one ray of hope is that you have agreed to meet Joanne tomorrow to discuss the problem.

1 Prepare for the discussion with the strategies on pages 79–80.

2 If possible, have a discussion with a colleague 'role-playing' the part of Joanne – and see whether you can both 'win'.

Monitoring progress and evaluating results

No matter how well a job is done, there is very little in life that couldn't be improved upon. Therefore, at the end of any major job, it is important to see what lessons can be learned for the future. It is vital that this be done promptly, otherwise it is too late – key points will be quickly forgotten. That is especially true if everyone is exhausted and simply wants to crawl into a hole to recover!

Monitoring progress

If you are monitoring something then you are *continually* checking what is happening. You can monitor progress in various ways; for example:

- by *listening* to what is being said
- by *observing* work being undertaken
- by *asking* people for progress reports
- by *holding* regular update meetings at which you check progress against an action plan.

Always remember that it is perfectly possible to plan a job properly, ascertain and obtain the resources and be extremely well organised, but for something still to go wrong. Sometimes you will have no control over these events – especially if they are external. For instance, if on the day Crista's photographer is due to take the photographs every property is blanketed in thick fog, she has a problem. And no one could blame her planning or organisational skills for that!

The key point is that regular monitoring enables you to identify a problem quickly and to take action. If Crista's photographer phones her immediately to alert her to the problem she can try to do something about it – such as booking him for the next day or arranging for him to do it on the next fine day – and checking the weather forecast. This is impossible if she has no idea. So monitoring and continually collecting information is vital.

Dealing with problems

It is impossible to give guidance on dealing with specific problems as so many things can go wrong. If your planning has been good then these will only be unforeseen issues. If a situation is critical it is always best to have a

contingency plan. This is another way of doing things if the very worst happens. Sometimes, at important planning sessions, a contingency plan is devised on a 'just-in-case' basis at the same time as the plans are being made. As an example, if you were sending three people into outer space, you would plan what to do if there was a serious problem before it occurred.

Sometimes, in this situation, brainstorming can help (see page 68). If you are really desperate, you can expect everyone to offer to help. However, on a more mundane level, the main points to consider are:

- what has gone wrong (or could go wrong)
- what should be done
- what resources are needed (additional time, materials, skills)
- who must be informed
- whose help or expertise you need
- what is the 'best' you can achieve
- what is the 'worst' you can live with.

If, upon analysis, the issue relates to poor planning or organisational skills, you need to take these lessons on board. If you are responding to a foreseeable emergency, you should ask yourself *why* no contingency plan was considered. If it is a relatively unforeseeable emergency the situation is different. Keep a cool head. Assess the alternatives. Negotiate with everyone to find an acceptable solution. And then learn from it!

INFORMATION UPDATE

In May 1999 NATO forces bombed Belgrade during the Kosovo conflict. The mission was planned and the target chosen carefully. It was an arms agency, in a large building next to a warehouse structure.

The information and precise coordinates of the target were passed to a bomber squadron at Whiteman Air Force Base in Missouri and programmed into the guidance system. The bombs would be released with precision accuracy, using the latest technology including global-positioning satellites.

Nothing could go wrong. Except that the map on which the target was identified was several years out of date. It never identified the fact that the old Federal Directorate of Supply and Procurement had been converted into an embassy – the Chinese Embassy – which received the full force of the three 2000-pound bombs.

This was the worst blunder of the whole conflict. Simply because everyone had thought there was so little to go wrong, they hadn't even bothered checking the date on the map.

The moral of this story? No detail is too small to be checked – and technology only does what it is told. It cannot think for itself.

For each of the following problems linked to earlier scenarios in this element state:

- whether the situation was foreseeable
- whether there was any lack of planning or organisational skills
- what you would do *at the time* to solve the problem
- what you would do next time to prevent a recurrence.

a   At the leaving buffet for your colleague who is going to Australia, many of your colleagues are vegetarians. Yet the canteen manager, unknowingly, has prepared a variety of meat sandwiches.

b   Maria is absent with 'flu on the day she is supposed to start work on the translations.

c   The photographer phones you on the day the photographs are due to say his camera developed a fault, he has three days where he is booked solidly and is then away on a week's holiday.

d   Your boss is flying to Spain to negotiate the finer points of the contract – which they look like obtaining. Two hours before leaving for the airport he asks you for his ticket. You can't remember receiving it.

e   You ordered six special presentation folders for the information for Spain. When these arrived you put them in the stationery cupboard, clearly labelled. Now when you want them you find only four are left.

f   Your boss told you to organise a quick meeting before he leaves for Spain. Only six out of the nine people invited arrive. You check but find the other three didn't know about it.

g   Your boss asks you, at the last minute, to give him a copy of the presentation materials to take to Spain. You ask your team member for a copy and she responds that she never realised she had to *keep* a copy – she sent everything off to Spain.

Evaluating results

Truthful evaluation is always slightly painful. This is because it involves focusing on what when wrong, not on what went right. If the team sit around afterwards in a self-congratulatory frame of mind, this may be appropriate if there was a successful outcome. But even then it is doubtful that there is *absolutely nothing* that couldn't be improved upon next time.

Allow five minutes for self-congratulation and then refocus the discussion. The aim is to identify:

- what problems occurred
- how these were dealt with
- whether they could have been prevented
- whether they could have been foreseen
- whether they could have been dealt with better
- whether the work could have been divided more effectively
- whether *anything else* could be improved upon.

The trick is to note down all suggestions and then keep these in the same file. The next time you are asked to plan a similar event, first read through the notes. This will refresh your memory and enable you to plan better, using the knowledge and experience you acquired the first time around.

EVIDENCE COLLECTION

For your evidence for this unit, you must show that you can jointly plan and carry out work with two of the following types of people:

- your line manager (which includes your team leader or supervisor)
- other people in your team
- other people within your organisation (but not in your team)
- people external to your organisation.

You may find it easier to do this in respect of two large jobs you and/or your team is given, each one relating to *one* of these groups of people.

1 Make notes of all the plans that are discussed.

2 List the objectives, resources, working methods and schedules that are agreed. Attach any relevant documents.

3 Identify any checks you made or discussions in which you were involved whereby you:
   a checked that the plans were in line with your organisation's procedures
   b agreed with others the individual responsibilities for pieces of work
   c considered the strengths and weaknesses of other team members.

4 If there were any serious points of disagreement, state how you negotiated a compromise (or be prepared to discuss this with your assessor).

5 Keep a record of any problems you experienced and state what you did to solve them. ➡

---

6 Make notes at any final session when you evaluated the work and identified how it could be done better next time.

Finally, write a brief summary which links all your evidence and ask your line manager to counter-sign this for authenticity.

Unit 302 Contribute to the maintenance of a healthy, safe and productive working environment

This unit is concerned with your role in the maintenance of a healthy, safe and productive working environment. As an administrator you must not only show an example by following all organisational procedures in this respect, but you should also be expected to take a more proactive role by identifying and remedying possible hazards and encouraging others to do the same.

 KEY SKILLS SIGNPOST

If you are taking your Key Skills award, you can extend your knowledge of health and safety and use this as evidence in your portfolio for **Application of Number**. If you are an AMA, you are likely to be taking this at level 2; but if you have achieved level 2, you will be studying level 3. The list of activities below has been written at level 3, but can easily be adjusted by your tutor if you are taking level 2 by, for instance, issuing you with simpler extracts from the statistics and simplifying the activity you undertake.

N3.1

Your activity is to collate and compare the accident, injury and sickness statistics in your own workplace with the current national picture. This will also involve identifying any trends and comparing these with Health & Safety Executive (HSE) forecasts.

You will also undertake a comparative activity on *two* areas in your workplace in terms of space and safe working.

Your datasets can be accessed on the Internet at www.hse.gov.uk/hsestats.htm. You need to download any *two* relevant sets. These are available in PDF format, so if you don't know how to use Adobe Acrobat™ to read and print these files, then talk to your tutor. Alternatively, your tutor may wish to download the files first or obtain them in hard-copy format from the HSE or from the Operations Unit in Bootle on 0151 951 4842. Recommended statistics include:

- the current *Safety Statistics Bulletin*, which contains a variety of tables and graphics
- the latest edition of the *National Picture*, which gives accident and ill-health statistics – the tables are particularly useful as these break down accidents into different types and categories
- the latest 'HELA report' which is the report on injuries to employees as reported to local authorities – the report on office-based injuries is particularly relevant.

However, do check whether any additional statistics would be more relevant to your study at the time you undertake this. For instance, information on the current costs of accidents would also be useful and is frequently available.

Plan how to undertake this activity and the information you will need to obtain. It is sensible to limit your comparative data to what you can obtain relatively easily, and you may first wish to talk to your line manager or supervisor about this. The same applies to selecting the two areas of comparative study. The aim is to take measurements to compare the degree of safe working in each environment. You may find that your own Health and Safety Officer will be interested in the results of your study!

Write a brief summary which outlines exactly what comparative data you intend to obtain, and how – and justify your choice.

N3.2

Prepare a comparative dataset for your own workplace which also shows trends, percentage and proportional changes, averages and means. You may wish to input this data into a spreadsheet and use formula to obtain your results.

Take measurements of the two areas you have selected and identify the degree to which there is safe working, in terms of traffic areas, clearance distance when drawers are open, and when people are actually using equipment. Identify, too, the range of temperatures normally experienced in both areas. Note that if any part of the room or piece of equipment is inaccessible, you can calculate any missing sides from your other data.

Produce a scale drawing of at least one of these areas.

N3.3

Prepare a report which (a) illustrates your findings and (b) compares the findings and trends from your workplace with national findings and trends. Your report must include at least *one* graph, *one* chart and *one* diagram – which can be your scale drawing(s).

Explain how the results of your calculations relate to the purpose of your activity and identify any way in which you could improve your choice of methods if you undertook such an activity again in the future. You may also wish to mention what national statistics you would have liked to have used to extend your research.

KNOWLEDGE AND UNDERSTANDING REQUIRED FOR THE UNIT

Throughout this unit emphasis is placed on the importance of working in a healthy, safe and secure workplace. In order for you to play your part you must be aware of what employers must do to comply with the law in this area. Both UK and EU law have imposed a large number of obligations on employers which cover virtually all aspects of working life – from the maintenance of equipment right through to the contents of a first-aid box.

You have responsibilities in relation to recognising the types of hazard that may exist in an office environment, and knowing the correct action to take. You also need to be aware of what you should do in the case of an emergency – and in particular, your own personal responsibility in such an event.

The underlying rationale of the whole unit is that health and safety is not an optional extra. It is an integral part of working life and the results of not paying it sufficient attention can be very far-reaching.

Health, safety and security in your workplace

Researchers of the TV soaps *Coronation Street*, *Eastenders* and *Brookside* have discovered that they all depict areas of high risk, with an abnormally high incidence of deaths, serious injuries, illnesses and accidents. Obviously on TV a certain amount of exaggeration is expected, but the researchers made the serious point that most people are unaware that the home can be a very dangerous place. Equally, people who work in offices may think that they are not in any danger. However, the following incidents, each of which took place in an office, might persuade them to change their minds.

- An office worker used some mobile steps in the office in order to reach some folders on the top shelf of a bookcase. The steps were not properly secured and she fell, breaking her leg. She was off work for three months.

- A word-processing operator developed severe eyestrain problems after working at a VDU screen for several hours each day over a period of nine months.

- An administrator was killed when the banister he was leaning against collapsed and he fell down a flight of stairs.

Even if poor working conditions do not cause major injuries, they can still affect employees. If you are working in an area which is too hot, too airless or too cold, or where the workspace is very cramped, then your productivity may suffer because you are too uncomfortable to concentrate on what you are doing. If you work in a smoky atmosphere you may develop breathing problems. If there is constant noise, you may start to feel stressed – and so on.

What can sometimes be overlooked in any health and safety survey is the fact that a workplace is equally unsafe if it is *insecure*. If a door is left unlocked or a window unsecured, this can be an invitation to thieves to enter the premises, ransack desks and filing cabinets and make off with computers, calculators, petty cash, contents of handbags etc. This can obviously also cause a lot of personal distress and can certainly raise levels of anxiety and stress.

TEST YOUR KNOWLEDGE AND UNDERSTANDING

The lack of adequate health, safety and security measures does not simply cause personal discomfort, it can also affect the financial viability of an organisation. The table on page 90 indicates the costs that could be incurred by an organisation that fails to recognise its health and safety responsibilities.

In each of the following scenarios try to determine what types of direct and/or indirect costs could be incurred as a result of these accidents.

a A member of the public walks into your reception area and trips and falls over a vacuum cleaner that has been left in the middle of the floor by the cleaner.

b The production controller hurts his hand on an unguarded piece of machinery and has to have some time off work.

c An administrative assistant throws a lighted cigarette stub into a waste paper basket. It causes a small fire and the carpet and wallpaper are slightly damaged.

d Some goods destined for an important supplier are badly packed and the driver who is loading them on to his lorry is injured when the package breaks open and the contents fall out. The goods themselves are also damaged.

Costs of inadequate health and safety measures	
Direct costs	Indirect costs
Employer's liability and public liability claims	Business interruption
	Product liability
Damage to buildings	Investigation costs
Damage to vehicles	Loss of goodwill
Repairs	Loss of corporate image
Sick pay	Hiring and training of specialist staff

INFORMATION UPDATE

A recent survey showed that approximately two million people suffer from work-related illnesses. Of those two million, around 35 per cent are no longer in work. Of the remainder, a little over half take no time off work; but those who do cause the loss of almost 19.5 million working days. Of the two million, around 1.2 million suffer from musculoskeletal disorders. The next largest category is illness caused through stress, anxiety and depression. Other conditions include asthma and other respiratory diseases, deafness, skin diseases, headaches and eyestrain.

Basic requirements of the health and safety and other legislation in the workplace

Health and safety legislation has changed a lot during the last 100 years. At first the legislation applied only to specific areas or industries. For instance, workers in bakeries were protected by the Biscuit Factories Welfare Order 1927 and workers in factories by the Factories Act 1961. Workers in offices and related areas were protected by the Offices, Shops and Railway Premises Act 1963. However, it gradually became apparent that this legislation was not very effective, firstly because it was too limited, and secondly because there were not enough inspectors to keep a check on whether or not the law was being broken.

For further information on other workplace health and safety regulations, see pages 91–95.

Health and Safety at Work Act 1974

In 1974, the Health and Safety at Work Act (HSW) was introduced. This was known as the 'umbrella statute' because it extended its provision over the existing provision. Rather than applying only to certain specified areas, it set out in general terms what the duties of the employer and the employee were in relation to health and safety at work. This table lists what they are.

Major requirements of the Health and Safety at Work Act 1974
Section 2(1) outlines the general duties of the employer to ensure, 'so far as is reasonably practicable', the health, safety and welfare at work of all his or her employees.
Section 2(2) extends this to cover five specific requirements: <ul><li>the provision and maintenance of a safe plant and systems of work</li><li>arrangements for ensuring safety and absence of risks to health in connection with the use, handling, storage and transport of articles and substances</li><li>the provision of such information, instruction, training and supervision as is necessary to ensure the health and safety at work of the employees</li><li>the provision and maintenance of means of access to and egress from the place of work that are safe and without risk to health</li><li>the provision and maintenance of a working environment for employees that is safe, without risk to health and adequate as regards facilities and arrangements for their welfare at work.</li></ul>
Section 7 states that every person in a business is an employee whatever his or her status, and therefore must: <ul><li>take reasonable care for their own health and safety at work and that of others who may be affected by their acts or omissions</li><li>cooperate with their employer in all things which he or she does in order to discharge his or her health and safety responsibilities.</li></ul>
Section 8 requires all employees not to interfere intentionally or recklessly with, or misuse, anything provided in the interests of health, safety and welfare.

There are three levels of responsibility placed on employers. In various situations under the Health and Safety at Work Act 1974 they must take:

- **'reasonably practicable'** measures – where the health risks are balanced against the time, money and effort required to reduce the risk
- **'practicable'** measures – which must be carried out, if at all feasible, even though costly (such as some of the requirements of the Noises at Work Regulations)
- **'absolute'** measures – which must be carried out no matter what the cost (for instance, the fencing off of moving parts of machinery).

Management of Health and Safety at Work Regulations 1992 (as amended in 1999)

Although the HSW brought about a great change in approach to health and safety in the workplace, there are now a number of additional health and safety regulations which have been introduced as a result of European Union legislation. Although many of their requirements are already met by employers who are satisfactorily fulfilling their duties under the HSW, they nevertheless formalise a lot of good health and safety practice, which is not *explicitly* required by the 1974 Act. One major EU directive is the Management of Health and Safety at Work Regulations 1992 (MHSW) (as amended). The table opposite summarises their contents.

A **Code of Practice** gives advice on how to comply with this law. It has a special legal status in that if employers are prosecuted for a breach of the health and safety law and it is proved that they have not followed the relevant provisions of the Code of Practice, a court can find them at fault unless they can show that they have complied with the law in some other way.

The MHSW Code of Practice recommends that the employer should observe all the following provisions.

• If possible, avoid a risk altogether (e.g. by not using a hazardous substance).

Regulation 3: Risk assessment

A risk assessment should be carried out by every employer and self-employed person if there are more than five people employed in the organisation. See page 115 for further information.

Regulation 5: Health surveillance

The employer must ensure that employees are provided with health surveillance appropriate to the risks to their health and safety as identified by risk assessment.

Regulation 6: Health and safety assistance

The employer must appoint one or more 'competent' persons to assist in the carrying out of his or her statutory health duties. In practice this means the appointment of safety officers or advisers.

Regulation 7: Procedures for serious and imminent danger

Employers must reappraise their existing emergency arrangements to take account of the conclusions of any risk assessment findings.

Regulation 8: Information for employees

Employees (including trainees and those on fixed-term contracts) must be given clear and comprehensible information on all health and safety risks and mitigating measures adopted by the employer.

Regulation 9: Cooperation and coordination

Where two or more employers share a workplace they must cooperate over and coordinate all health and safety matters.

- Combat risks at source (e.g. if steps are slippery they should be cleaned or treated rather than a warning sign being displayed).
- Where possible, adapt the work to the individual, especially with regard to the design of the workplace, the equipment and the working methods.
- Take advantage of technological and technical progress to improve working methods and make them safer.
- Ensure risk-prevention measures form part of a 'coherent policy' and approach with the aim of progressively reducing risks which cannot be prevented or avoided altogether.
- Give priority to those measures which protect the *whole* workplace and those who work there by giving collective protective measures priority over individual measures.
- Provide workers with information, training and supervision so that they understand the importance of role in ensuring health and safety.
- Promote an active health and safety culture through the training of workers and through good communication systems.

As part of her induction a new employee is given a list of the MHSW regulations and a copy of the code of practice. She has difficulty in understanding some of them and asks you the following questions:

a 'What does "health surveillance" mean?'
b 'What sort of things could cause serious and imminent danger in an office? I don't feel in any particular danger.'
c 'What exactly are mitigating measures?'
d 'Why do the regulations specify that two or more employers sharing a workplace must cooperate with each other? Shouldn't they already know what the law expects them to do without any further reminder?
e 'Could you give me some examples of work being adapted to the individual?'
f 'What kind of measures *could* protect the whole workforce?'

Prepare some brief notes to answer her questions.

Workplace (Health, Safety and Welfare) Regulations 1992

Another major piece of legislation affecting the workplace is the Workplace (Health, Safety and Welfare) Regulations 1992 (WHSW). The table opposite summarises its contents.

Try to resolve the following problems by reading the table containing the main requirements of the WHSW. Write short notes of your answers.

a Jamail is extremely tall. He works on a VDU for a large percentage of his time and he frequently complains of leg ache. His supervisor tells him that the workstation and furniture have only recently been purchased, are 'state of the art' and that all that can be done has been done. Do you think that is true?
b Vanessa works virtually full time in the reprographics unit carrying out photocopying duties. The area is quite small and the window is high up and cannot be opened easily. What steps should be taken to prevent a possible breach of the WHSW regulations?
c Terry works in the packing department on a conveyor belt system. He has to stand up all day on an uncarpeted and uneven floor. What are the organisation's obligations under the WHSW regulations?

Major requirements of the Workplace (Health, Safety and Welfare Regulations) 1992

Work environment

- There must be an effective ventilation system.
- A reasonable working temperature must be established during working hours.
- There must be adequate lighting and, in some cases, emergency lighting.
- There must be enough space available for employees so that their health, safety or welfare is not at risk.
- Workstations must be suitable for the people who work at them.
- Workstations outside a building must provide protection from adverse weather.

Safety

- Traffic routes must exist so that people and vehicles can circulate safely.
- Floors must be properly constructed and maintained and have no holes or uneven surfaces. They must be kept free from obstruction and have an effective means of drainage.
- Windows and skylights must be safe to open, close and clean.
- Doors and gates must be constructed so that they are safe to operate.
- Escalators must be safe to use.
- There must be safeguards to prevent people or objects falling from a height or to prevent people from falling into containers of dangerous substances.

Facilities

- There must be sufficient lavatories.
- Sufficient washing facilities should be provided.
- There must be an adequate supply of wholesome water.
- Suitable storage accommodation for clothing should be provided.
- Adequate seating must be available for people at work.
- Rest areas should be provided for reasons of health or safety, including provision for pregnant women or nursing mothers.
- Provision must be made for non-smokers in rest areas.
- Where people eat meals at work, there should be adequate facilities provided for them to do so.

Housekeeping

- All workplaces, equipment and facilities must be properly maintained.
- All workplaces must be kept clean.

The responsibility for health, safety and security in the workplace

Because health and safety in the workplace is such a major issue nowadays, it is unlikely that you will be given the sole responsibility for checking that all the regulations are being followed. In most organisations there are qualified personnel who are employed to do this. This section looks at three such roles.

Safety adviser

Regulation 6 of the MHSW makes it clear that employers should appoint a suitably qualified person to assist them in the maintenance of health and safety at the workplace. Generally a safety adviser will be expected to:

- inform senior management of changes to health and safety legislation
- advise and oversee the implementation of the changes
- carry out safety inspections
- investigate accidents/incidents
- maintain and update the organisation's safety policy
- advise on and organise staff health and safety training.

Safety representative

In many large organisations, you may find that your contact with the safety adviser is limited. You may have far closer contact with your own departmental or workplace safety representative who is appointed to act as your spokesperson on the safety committee and to be on hand to deal with any concerns you may have. He or she is normally expected to:

- investigate potential hazards and dangerous occurrences at the workplace
- examine the causes of any accidents at the workplace
- carry out inspections at the workplace
- investigate complaints by employees about health, safety and welfare issues at work
- talk to the employer about health, safety and welfare issues
- attend meetings of safety committees.

The **Safety Representatives and Safety Committee Regulations** 1977 are binding upon companies having recognised trade unions. They allow trade unions to appoint safety representatives from among the employer's workforce. The **Health and Safety (Consultation with Employees) Regulations 1996** require employers to consult all employees not already represented by trade union safety representatives. So now all workers, not just those represented by a trade union, enjoy the same protection.

Safety inspector

Although your main internal contact will be the safety representative or adviser, your manager may also have to liaise with an externally appointed HSE inspector who has the power to:

- enter premises at reasonable times or at any time where there is danger
- make examinations and inspections
- take possession of samples, articles and substances
- take measurements and photographs
- make recordings
- have something tested, removed or dismantled
- require that certain areas be left undisturbed
- obtain information
- inspect and copy any entry in documents the employer is required to keep.

CHECK IT OUT!

In many organisations, health and safety issues are kept separate from security issues and are carried out by a different set of personnel. In your own workplace, check to see whether the two roles are separate. If they are, what are the functions of those employed to look after security? See page 107 for more information about security issues.

TEST YOUR KNOWLEDGE AND UNDERSTANDING

Most medium to large organisations have a safety committee which is composed of both managers and employees and which regularly meets to:

- investigate and report on accidents/incidents
- review health and safety audit reports
- draw up works rules and instructions on safe systems of work
- oversee health and safety training
- promote and advise on health and safety publicity measures
- consider and advise on impending legislation.

If you look back to the safety adviser's 'job description', you will see that it covers many of the items listed above. The safety representatives' duties are quite similar. Why, therefore, do you think a safety committee, a safety representative *and* a safety adviser are necessary?

EVIDENCE COLLECTION

1 Check that you are aware of the people who have responsibility for health and safety in your workplace. Identify any workplace policies or procedures you must follow in relation to health and safety.

2 Write a brief description of how health and safety is monitored in your own workplace and who you would contact if there was an accident or injury in your area or if you knew procedures were not being followed properly.

Element 302.1 Monitor and maintain a safe, healthy and secure working environment

In a recent survey of administrators, several quite senior staff claimed that health and safety was not relevant to or part of their job. What they meant, presumably, was that they did not have an 'official' health and safety role in their job description. Nor were any specific tasks listed for them in that area. However, it is doubtful whether any administrator on earth can claim that health and safety is not relevant to their job!

Basically, it depends upon your viewpoint. For *any* working environment to be safe, *everyone* has some responsibilities. If you see boxes piled up in a corridor where someone will fall over them, or if you spill coffee all over a tiled floor, you would do something about it, wouldn't you? It is almost certain that the administrators who did the survey would have taken action too – but saw this as 'automatic' rather than as 'part of their job'.

In this element you will learn about the appropriate actions to take in relation to hazards that might affect yourself and others. You will also look at recommending improvements to health and safety. Often this is simply a case of being vigilant and then doing something about what you see. If you are asked to identify your role in relation to any survey *you* then receive – you may find it easier to respond correctly.

Being up to date about information on health, safety and security in the workplace

Health and safety legislation is constantly changing and being updated as revised statutes and regulations are introduced and as different cases are being decided in court. If you don't keep up to date with these changes, you might find that you are unintentionally breaking the law. It is, of course, part of your safety adviser's role, and that of senior management, to keep abreast of health and safety developments and to change working practices as necessary. However, you may be in the position of having to make sure that the people in your own work area not only know about but actually cooperate with any new practices. If, for instance, your health and safety adviser or line manager issues an update on the storage of flammable materials, you should check that the more casual of your colleagues are not ignoring it. It can be a difficult job!

You can speak with more authority if you find out for yourself about any new health and safety developments. It is more difficult for others to argue with you when you show an awareness of the facts. To do this, you can check in regularly published journals such as *Croner's Health and Safety Briefing* or *Health and Safety at Work*. You can also check relevant websites such as www.hse.gov.uk and www.tuc.org.uk.

Being alert to health, safety and security hazards

Ensuring that health and safety procedures are being carried out properly is not just yet another administrative job for you to do. If procedures are not followed and someone is hurt or injured, your employer may find that he or she is in breach of the law and may be faced with certain penalties. For instance, employers are subject to the doctrine of **vicarious liability** which makes them liable for any careless acts carried out by their employees on the premises and during the course of the working day. This could involve the payment of compensation, a fine and even, in some cases, a prison sentence. In one case, for instance, a lorry driver was smoking when he was transferring petrol from his tanker to a store. A fire resulted. It was held that the driver's employer was vicariously liable for the negligence of the driver.

Equally, employees may be held to be negligent if by their actions they cause the injury of another employee. Consequently, where an employee carelessly directed a van driver out of the factory yard and an accident occurred, the employers were held vicariously liable for the injury to the driver. However, they in turn demanded compensation from the employee who had misdirected the driver.

If an accident occurs, the courts will try to establish whether or not the employer owes a duty of care to the injured person and whether or not that duty has been breached. In one famous case a company manufactured ginger beer in opaque bottles. The ginger beer was sold to a retailer who then sold it to someone who gave the bottle to a friend. Upon drinking the ginger beer, the friend discovered a decomposed snail and was made seriously ill. The House of Lords held the manufacturer liable for the illness as he owed **a duty of care** to anyone he could *reasonably foresee* would drink from that bottle.

Of increasing importance to many employers is the recent emphasis which has been placed on the concept of **corporate responsibility** (or 'corporate killing' as it is sometimes now called) if an accident results in death at the workplace and the employer can be shown to have been at fault. Although in theory it has always been possible to prosecute companies and their directors for the manslaughter of their employees, in practice the definition of such a crime has been so vague that it has rarely been possible to bring a successful prosecution. The proposed changes by the government introduce a set of specified offences in this area which are designed to make it easier to get a conviction.

TEST YOUR KNOWLEDGE AND UNDERSTANDING

Establishing a duty of care and deciding what is reasonably foreseeable can be quite difficult. Look at the following cases and try to decide whether or not the plaintiff (i.e. the person making the complaint) was successful by proving (a) that he or she was owed a duty of care and (b) that the damage was reasonably foreseeable. Check your answers with those given on page 148.

a A painter and decorator was working in a house. The houseowner had to go out and he asked the decorator to lock up if he also went out. The decorator failed to do so and the house was burgled. The houseowner claimed damages.

b Two employees of a railway company were assisting a passenger to carry a parcel on to the train when they dropped it. It contained fireworks, which exploded. A passer-by, standing about 25 yards away, was slightly injured by some weighing scales which had become dislodged by the vibration caused by the noise of the explosion. The passer-by claimed damages from the railway company.

c A woman was told that her husband and children had been in a car crash and that one of the children had been killed. She was taken to hospital and saw her husband and the other child still covered in dirt and oil. She suffered from nervous shock and claimed damages from the insurance company of the driver of the other vehicle.

Common health, safety and security hazards and how to identify them

Imagine you have just been appointed as an administrator in a large open-plan office. The office is badly in need of refurbishment. The carpet is threadbare and torn in some places. Cables from various pieces of equipment lie across the floor in all directions. The desks are badly arranged and pushed so closely together that it is difficult to find a way through. The windows will not open and some of the blinds are broken. The central heating is erratic – sometimes it works and sometimes not. Smoking is allowed and there are overflowing ashtrays on many desks. The plastic waste-paper bins are also overflowing with rubbish. The filing cabinets are too full and boxes of papers are stored on the floor and on top of the cupboards. None of the desks have drawers that lock. The telephones are in constant use, as is the photocopier, fax machine and shredder.

After a month, the manager calls you into her office and tells you that the department needs a safety representative and she has nominated you. She asks you first of all to list any possible health, safety and security problems. You hardly know where to start!

List the hazards to health, safety and security you have noticed and keep these for future reference (see page 117).

Tripping and falling

As the above scenario indicates, one of the most common hazards in an office is the danger of tripping and falling. In 1995/96, 5800 injuries caused by slips, trips or falls were reported to the Health & Safety Executive. Since then, the total has risen to around 8500 a year. One of your roles, as an administrator, may therefore be to try and reduce that number.

TEST YOUR KNOWLEDGE AND UNDERSTANDING

1   One method of reducing these accidents is to identify the type of situation which could lead to a fall and then take the necessary action. The table below lists some of the most common situations. In each case decide what action you would recommend. Check your answers with the suggested answer on page 148.

2   One possible reason for accident levels not having dropped is that the risk of falling or slipping is not perceived as being high amongst people working in an office. In fact, many people make light of the risks and a lot of accidents go unrecorded. What do you think could be done to change this view?

Preventing slips at work

- spillage on the floors/stairways etc.
- trailing cables
- rubbish on floors, surfaces etc.
- unsafe mats
- slippery surfaces
- change from wet to dry surfaces
- poor lighting
- changes of level
- steps

 INFORMATION UPDATE

An anti-slip floor and stair covering has been designed to reduce the risks of employees suffering slips, trips and falls in the workplace. ➡

The covering consists of a series of flat sheets which can be fitted to existing walkways and staircases to provide an anti-slip surface.

The incidence of slipping and falling is highest in the food and drink industries. The Health & Safety Executive has therefore launched a campaign to attempt to improve matters in this area. Its *Recipe for Safety* lists the elementary precautions, which should be observed.

Injuries caused through lifting

For some reason bad backs are often associated with either old people or lazy people. Young energetic people are not expected to suffer from that disability. However, statistics show that absence from work through back pain accounts for 80 million lost working days a year. A lot of it is work-related and could be avoided if, for instance, employees:

- remembered to use any appropriate equipment
- learned how to lift packages and other objects properly.

The **Provision and Use of Work Equipment Regulations (PUWER)** 1998 cover virtually every type of machine, appliance, plant or tool used at work. Although many of the items covered by these regulations may have little relevance to people working in an office, some of them do. For instance, included in the list are an overhead and slide projector and even a stapler.

The regulations oblige employers to:

- ensure that equipment is suitable for the task for which it will be used
- take into account the working conditions when selecting the equipment
- ensure that appropriate information and training is given to employees.

The **Manual Handling Operations Regulations** 1993, which cover a wide range of manual handling activities, require employers:

- to arrange work to avoid manual handling wherever possible
- if manual handling cannot be avoided, to undertake a risk assessment to identify the risks to workers' health and safety (for more information on risk assessment see page 116)
- on the basis of that risk assessment, to implement preventative and protective measures to reduce the risk of injury to employees.

CHECK IT OUT!

Either in your workplace or at college, identify objects that are regularly lifted and moved about by staff. Check also whether there are any instructions available on how these objects have to be carried. If there are, compare them with the set of instructions outlined opposite. State which you prefer and why.

MAGELLAN MANUFACTURING LTD

Safety notice to staff

Instructions for lifting

1   Remember that it is not the *weight* of the object that is to be lifted that causes the risk. Any object picked up awkwardly can cause damage to your back – if, for example, you are moving a file from the top shelf of a cupboard.

2   Where possible, avoid lifting the object yourself if there is a machine available to assist you.

3   If you have to lift the object, remember to take into account:
   - your own physical capabilities
   - the area in which you are working – is it well lit, is the floor surface secure etc.?
   - the weight and size of the load.

4   Remember:
   - Do not carry more than you can manage. Get some assistance or make two trips.
   - Do not carry the load on one arm.
   - Keep a firm grip on the object.
   - Distribute the load evenly.
   - Bend with your knees, **not** your back.

Office furniture

Lifting is not the only office hazard that can cause back pain. Chairs are often another cause. You may be unaware that you are sitting all day at work on a chair that is the wrong height and at the wrong angle. Workers who use a VDU are protected by the **Health and Safety (Display Screen Equipment) Regulations** 1992. (See page 107 for further information.) However, even if you rarely touch the computer keyboard, you should still:

- if possible, test out any new chair for a couple of days
- ensure that your chair enables you to put both feet flat on the floor (or can be adjusted to allow you to do so)
- consider the use of a foot rest
- be able to adjust the backrest, if relevant, to support the small of your back
- check that the seat has a curved 'waterfall' edge deep enough to support the full length of your thighs but not so deep that there is pressure behind your knees when using the backrest
- be able to change position comfortably.

Remember that a chair, however suited to your physique, should not be allowed to do all your work for you. Remember also not to remain stationary for long periods unless absolutely unavoidable. Stand up and stretch at least every 20 minutes.

 INFORMATION UPDATE

The Health & Safety Executive (HSE) and Health and Safety Commission (HSC) campaign 'Good Health is Good Business' has now linked forces with the government's 'Our Healthier Nation' to form the Healthy Workplace Initiative. Its aims include:

- identifying and promoting examples of good practice for the management of key workplace health issues such as back pain
- making appropriate and up-to-date information available
- encouraging improved access to services and helping to bridge the gap between prevention, treatment and rehabilitation
- helping to encourage compliance with relevant workplace legislation.

Noise

You have probably become very used to noise. Even areas such as libraries, where traditionally almost complete silence was expected, have now partially transformed themselves into learning centres when a certain amount of noise is not only tolerated but welcomed.

At work, you may take for granted that you will be carrying out your duties to a general background of noise from the telephone, the photocopier, the fax, the printer, individual conversations etc. You may also work in an area where you can hear the noise of machinery or traffic. In order to survive you are likely to exercise a 'switch off' mechanism in your brain to allow you to shut out noise and to allow you to concentrate on what you are doing. However, there can come a time when the level of noise is so high that you just cannot ignore it. Not only is this a nuisance, it may eventually become a hazard.

One writer maintains that noise is probably the most widespread and underestimated of workplace hazards and that three million employees are exposed to noise levels which could result in their suffering permanent noise-induced hearing loss at some point in the future. Employers are therefore required to ensure that a noise assessment is carried out by a competent person to comply with the **Noise at Work Regulations 1989** and to introduce measures to control the auditory risks at source or to enclose the source of the noise. For instance, it may be that a piece of office equipment could be less noisy if a protective hood or cover is used. A well-used telephone could be situated in a less busy area in a soundproof booth, and so on.

However, if such measures are not possible, then the employer must provide effective hearing protection such as ear protectors – although this is normally regarded as the last resort. In fact the **Personal Protective Equipment at Work Regulations** 1992 (PPE) require employers to provide suitable equipment and clothing which protects the employee from risks to his or her safety – only if all other safeguards have first been put into place.

CHECK IT OUT!

Sit down for five minutes in your own immediate work area or in a selected area of your college or training institution, and during that time make a note of every different type of noise you can hear. Try to classify which noises you think are acceptable and which too loud. If you think any of them are too loud, make a note of what measures you think could be put into place to improve the situation.

Use of VDUs

Nothing could seem more harmless than the sight of a group of office employees working on their computers. Note, however, the following – probably a fairly typical conversation.

LINDA: How's everyone this morning? OK?

KAREN: My hands and wrists are aching like mad. Do you think I've got rheumatism?

TYE: You always seem to have something wrong with you and it never seems to amount to anything. I happen to have a splitting headache at the moment but you never catch me complaining. It must be my contact lenses. I knew the moment I saw that optician that he had as much idea about fitting contact lenses as I have about deep-sea diving.

RONNIE: Do you know what I think is wrong with all of us? It's stress. I can't sleep and I've taken up smoking again. My wife says that if I mention work just one more time, she's going to strangle me. I work such long hours the kids can hardly remember who I am. Even the dog tries to bite me on the rare occasions he sees me.

LINDA: I wish I'd never started this conversation. Roll on the next six weeks when my maternity leave starts. Coping with a baby can't be worse than listening to your moans.

Linda may be quite right – the others may just enjoy having a moan. However, they may have a genuine cause for complaint. Working on a VDU for long periods can cause some health problems. It may, for instance, cause repetitive strain injury (RSI) or upper-limb disorders to your hands, wrists, arms neck, shoulders or back. Although the Health & Safety Executive says that research has shown that there is no evidence that VDUs can cause permanent damage to the eyes, it admits that long spells of VDU work can lead to tired eyes and discomfort. There is also a possibility that people who wear contact lenses or bifocal spectacles experience particular difficulties. Headaches can result from screen glare, poor image quality, reading the screen for long periods without a break, or poor posture. Stress levels may also rise. Although recent research has shown that there is little if any link between miscarriages or birth defects and working with VDUs, there have been anxieties in the past that there is such a link.

CHECK IT OUT!

There is quite a lot you can do to assist in preventing any damage to your health if you use a VDU frequently. Use the accompanying checklist to assess whether or not you are doing as much as you can.

VDU Checklist

1. Do you adjust your chair and VDU to find the most comfortable position for your work?

2. Do you have enough workspace for your documents or other equipment?

3. Have you tried different arrangements of keyboard, screen, mouse and documents to find the best arrangement for you?

4. Have you arranged your desk and VDU to avoid glare or bright reflections on the screen?

5. Have you made sure there is sufficient space under your desk to move your legs freely?

6. Have you thought about using a footrest? Have you adjusted your keyboard to get a good keying position?

7. Do you always remember to keep your wrists straight when keying and to keep a soft touch on the keys?

8. Do you make sure that you have positioned the mouse within easy reach and that you do not grip it too tightly?

9. Do you adjust the brightness and contrast controls on the screen to suit the lighting conditions?

10. Is your screen surface clean?

11. Is the text setting large enough?

12. Do you make sure you take regular short breaks?

Many of these concerns have been recognised by the **Health and Safety (Display Screen Equipment) Regulations** 1992 which require employers to minimise the risks in VDU work by:

- analysing workstations to reduce risks by examining the workstation and equipment and also the work being carried out
- noting the special needs of individual staff
- ensuring that workstations meet minimum requirements (details of which are set out in a schedule to the regulations)
- planning work so that there are breaks or changes of activity, bearing in mind that short frequent breaks are better than longer, less frequent ones and that, ideally, the operator should have some discretion over when to take the breaks.
- on request, arranging eye tests and providing spectacles if special ones are needed
- providing health and safety training and information.

Security hazards

If you have ever had some money stolen from you or gone out to the car park and found that your car has been broken into and your radio taken, you will realise what an unpleasant experience it is. Modern offices can be quite inviting to thieves who regard them as a potential source of supply for all types of office equipment and for petty cash. Consequently most managers are now aware of the need for increased security measures and expect their employees to be equally aware of their role in preventing theft and vandalism.

Security of equipment

Most organisations have in place a series of measures designed to prevent theft of equipment – or at least to assist in its return if stolen. These include making sure of the following points.

- When not in use, equipment should be stored in conditions that reflect the level of risk attached. The greater the risk, the more secure the storage. A member of staff should be responsible for making regular inspections of equipment and for recording the results on an inventory list. This should include the make, serial number and model number.
- All valuable equipment is security-marked with details of name, address and postcode by, for instance, the use of an ultraviolet pen, etching, chemicals, paints or stamping.
- The *true* value of the piece of equipment is assessed. Quite often that value becomes apparent only after the theft (e.g. in loss of working hours, hold up in production etc.). For instance, computer disks may not in themselves be high-value, but their loss, theft or damage could carry a high financial penalty. Security consultants often advise employers to

leave a safe door unlocked when it has nothing valuable in it or is empty. This avoids forced entry and consequent damage to the safe and its contents.

CHECK IT OUT!

At your workplace, college or training organisation.

1   Check on the procedures for marking, recording and checking equipment.
2   Check also on the methods used to keep the following documents safe: chequebooks; bank statements; blank invoices; letterheads; order forms.
3   Write a short note of your findings, where relevant suggesting any improvements.

Security of keys

If a key is lost or taken, the problems this can cause are often tremendous. Even though no one actually knows whether the key has been misplaced or stolen, for all practical purposes security has been compromised – which normally means that locks have to be changed and security systems altered. It is worth while, therefore, putting some thought into key security. Many organisations operate a system of key control, for example:

- **Access keys** afford access to a building from outside and are issued only to members of staff who are permitted to enter buildings at times when they are officially closed.
- **General keys** give access to all areas within the building but not to external doors. They are issued to staff who need access throughout the building.
- **Departmental keys** give access to specific sections of the building and are issued only to heads of departments or their authorised nominees.
- **Individual keys** give access to a particular area and should be issued to the prime users of that area.

Cash carrying

Today a lot of money transactions are carried out without any money actually changing hands. Most employees are willing to receive their wages as a cheque rather than actual cash. Most suppliers are willing to do the same. However, there may be circumstances in which the movement of cash from one place to another is unavoidable. You may work in a small organisation and be expected to take money to the bank. You may have to walk around the organisation to empty drinks machines. You may simply be in charge of the office kitty for presents, leaving parties etc. If so, there are certain precautions you should take.

- If you are not expected to collect and transport the cash yourself, make sure that the person who does so is not a new or young employee.
- Even if you do collect and transport the cash yourself, never do so alone. Always have a second person with you.
- Don't collect or transport the money at the same time of the day or week. Vary it. Vary the route as well.
- Use a car where possible – never a bus or taxi.
- Use special cash-carrying equipment, such as devices that can raise an alarm or spoil the cash contents with a chemical marking agent should the carrier be destroyed.

 INFORMATION UPDATE

Even if you work in a small organisation, which is not able to afford to employ a security company to carry cash, it is possible nowadays to become a member of a cooperative with other businesses in the area to make use of such services.

Personal safety

One personal safety consultant maintains that workplace violence is much more frequent than employers realise. Retail staff, nurses, teachers, taxi drivers, traffic wardens, ambulance drivers, bar staff and social workers are all prime targets. He estimates, for instance, that there is an assault on a retail employee during every minute of every day. Obviously employers of those most likely to be at risk have a duty to try to minimise that risk (the law recognises that accidents at work include 'non-consensual' acts of violence and requires employers to take all reasonable measures to prevent such acts). In such cases the Health & Safety Executive has suggested that employers should:

- find out if there is a problem
- decide what action to take.

One major petrol company was simply not aware of the extent of the problem faced daily by forecourt employees until it consulted them. If your organisation is in that position, what it should do first of all is to consult staff both formally and informally to find out whether they have ever felt threatened. It can then make a record of any reported incidents, including an account of what happened, the people involved, the location and the outcome (including working time lost). If the incidents are numerous, they should then be classified into levels of seriousness and the results used to determine not only who is most likely to be at risk but also where and at what time violence is most likely to happen.

One course of action may be to train staff most at risk to spot early signs of aggression, and to avoid it or cope with it. Another would be to look at the actual workplace itself and decide whether or not action should be taken to improve security. This could include:

- the provision of video cameras or alarm systems
- coded security locks on doors to keep the public out of staff areas
- the presence of a security guard
- the provision of external lighting
- the provision of personal staff alarms
- an open plan office layout staffed by a number of people
- where relevant, wider counters and raised floors on the staff side of the counter to give staff more protection
- the provision of better seating, decor and lighting in public waiting rooms, with more regular information given about delays – in order to try to pacify the potentially aggressive members of the public.

TEST YOUR KNOWLEDGE AND UNDERSTANDING

Imagine you work for a small organisation, which employs fewer than a dozen people. The receptionist arrives at work by car half an hour earlier than anyone else in the morning and leaves half an hour later, during which times she has to answer the telephone and deal with any early or late visitors. During those periods she is on her own, the only other person being the caretaker who is occupied in either unlocking or locking the other exits and entrances to the building and the internal doors to offices. She has her own key to let herself in and out of the office. When she first arrives she opens the safe and takes out the petty cash box. She also starts dealing with the mail. At the end of the day she puts the cash box back in the safe, puts out the lights and locks up. She then walks to her car, which is parked in a nearby side street.

List the precautions you would suggest should be put in place to protect her from any potential threats to her personal safety (bearing in mind that cost will be a consideration). You may want to look at the specimen risk assessment form on page 117 for some ideas.

Workplace stress

If you carry out a small experiment with the people you work with and ask each one in turn how they feel you will get a variety of responses. Some will say they are fine; others may say they have a headache or that they are feeling tired. What you may also find, however, is that at least one or two say that they feel under pressure or 'stressed out'. Workplace stress is fast becoming one of the most worrying areas of health and safety management. According to the Health & Safety Executive, around 279,000 UK employees believe that they have suffered from work-related stress and a further

254,000 claim that they may have developed an illness caused by increased stress at work. The Department of Health estimates that stress-related disorders costs UK industry at least £5 billion a year in absenteeism and staff turnover.

In addition, in recent years, there have been a number of court cases involving claims by employees that overwork and unsympathetic employers have brought about work-based stress. In one case an employee was off work twice with nervous stress but was still not given any assistance on his return. He won his case.

It is obviously worthwhile, therefore, for employers to try to identify the major causes of work-based stress and to try to remove them where possible.

Modern management theorists maintain that people vary widely in their ability to cope with stress and that a major predictor of who does and who does not cope is the amount of *resiliency* they have developed. This resiliency is associated with balancing the various aspects of life.

Assume that the circle below represents resiliency development. Each wedge in the figure identifies an important aspect of life that must be developed in order to achieve resiliency. The most resilient individuals are those who achieve life balance. For example, if the centre of the circle represents the zero point of resiliency development and the outer edge of the circle represents maximum development, shading in a portion of each wedge represents the amount of development achieved in each area. Individuals who can best cope with stress can shade in most of each wedge, indicating that they have not only spent time developing variety in their lives but also that the overall pattern is relatively balanced.

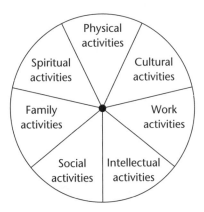

Resiliency circle

If you do find that certain aspects of your working life are causing you stress, any or all of the following suggestions can help.

1   Refreshed and relaxed minds think better. Even if you are totally

overwhelmed at work, try not to take work home or work all over the weekend. Give yourself a break.

2 Remember that work makes work. Set yourself a time limit for the completion of a set number of jobs and then stop or have a break.

3 If you can, share your workload. Delegate if possible.

4 Try not to panic when faced with what seems to be an enormous task or an impossible deadline. Slow down and remember the **wasp** sequence – wait, appraise, slowly proceed.

5 If you feel tense, ease the tension in your shoulders and neck by gentle massage or try closing your eyes and picturing a pleasant setting.

6 Do not neglect mealtimes. Skipping an occasional meal doesn't matter. Skipping a huge number of them does.

7 Do not try to go it alone. Talk over your concerns with either your boss or a colleague. If you have a partner, use one another to bolster self-confidence. If, for instance, you are having difficulty with your job and feel your job security threatened, the fact that your partner has a secure job should make you feel less financially insecure at least.

TEST YOUR KNOWLEDGE AND UNDERSTANDING

Read the checklist below. Select the *five* issues that you feel are likely to cause you the most pressure. In each case, decide how you would try to reduce the pressure. Make brief notes of your answers.

I become stressed when:

a   too many people are telling me what to do

b   there is too strict supervision and control

c   I have too much responsibility

d   the work is boring and repetitive and there is no room for creativity or personal input

e   I have too many jobs to cope with at any one time

f   the deadlines are unreasonable

g   I don't get on with my boss

h   I don't get on with the rest of the staff

i   I am being bullied

j   I am discriminated against because I am female/black/disabled etc

k   I have no contact with other people

l   the workplace is uncomfortable and depressing

m   there is no job security.

Fire precautions

The danger of fire exists no matter in which type of workplace you work. Nowadays, most organisations pay attention not only to the action which should be taken if a fire breaks out but also to the action which should be taken to prevent one from starting. Most of these are put in place as a result of a fire risk assessment (see page 116 for further information).

Smoking

There can hardly be anyone living in the UK who is not aware of the health risks attached to smoking. It is estimated that it is responsible for around 120,000 deaths a year, and far outweighs any other single occupational cause of death. What is becoming of increasing importance, however, is the impact of 'passive smoking' on the health of non-smokers exposed to tobacco smoke, particularly in the workplace. If they do become ill, the employer could be in breach of the Health and Safety at Work Act 1974.

He or she could also be in breach of the **Control of Substances Hazardous to Health Regulations 1994 (COSHH)**, the purposes of which are:

- to keep to a minimum situations where workers are exposed to hazardous substances
- to warn employees of the dangers and the measures taken to minimise their exposure to them
- to provide suitable protective clothing and equipment where exposure to hazardous substances is unavoidable
- to ensure medical review and feedback on the results for those employees exposed to hazardous substances.

Many employers have taken note of the potential risk of passive smoking and have therefore introduced a number of measures to reduce it. Examples are:

- a total ban on smoking throughout the workplace
- designated areas for smokers
- the provision of ventilation systems.

 INFORMATION UPDATE

- A Social Security Commissioner decided that an asthma sufferer's exposure to smoke at her workplace could be classified as an industrial accident, entitling her to specific social security benefits.

- After a smoking ban had been introduced at the factory where he worked, another employee resigned and claimed constructive dismissal – i.e. that he had been forced out of his job. Employees had been given four months' notice of the ban in order to give smokers time to adjust to the new ruling, but no facilities were provided for smokers. The employee claimed a 'right to smoke'. The industrial tribunal, however, decided that there was an equal right for employees who did not smoke, not to be placed in an environment with those who did.

Although it is obviously in everyone's best interests to allow a total ban on smoking to be imposed in a workplace, this can lead to certain problems. Look at the following situations and write brief notes on how you would try to resolve the issues raised.

a   No smoking is allowed anywhere at all in your workplace. However, you entertain a number of visitors, many of whom are very good customers – and some of whom are smokers.

b   The sales team works well together and is very successful. All smoke and maintain that smoking helps them to concentrate, to brainstorm new ideas and to achieve their targets. They are incensed when they hear of a proposed smoking ban throughout the organisation.

c   Because of the smoking ban in the organisation, all the smokers congregate on the front steps of the building when they wish to have a cigarette. They block the entrance and the area is constantly dirty with trodden in ash and cigarette ends. It creates a very bad impression for visitors.

How to identify risks

The old saying that prevention is better than cure is very relevant to current thinking about health and safety in the workplace. Emphasis is now placed on trying to identify what could cause a problem rather than deciding what to do when the problem arises. The process is normally referred to as **risk assessment**.

Note that a **hazard** means anything that can cause harm (e.g. electricity, working from ladders). A **risk** is the chance, whether great or small, that someone will be harmed by the hazard.

Under Regulation 3 of the Management of Health and Safety at Work Regulations, employers are required to carry out risk assessments on all types of work activities that may potentially cause harm or ill health. In practice, this means that they must look carefully at what is going on in their workplace to see whether or not they have sufficient precautions in place. The diagram on page 116 outlines the five steps which should be taken.

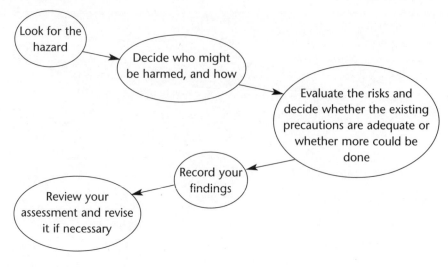

Stages in risk assessment

Specific risk assessments

Although the risk assessment checks should be applied throughout the workplace, there are certain areas in which they are particularly important. One such area is fire risk. Under the **Fire Precautions (Workplace) Regulations** (in force from December 1999) all employers are legally obliged to assess fire risks in their workplaces. In order to do this, they must:

- identify any potential sources of ignition which could start a fire (e.g. hot processes such as welding work, faulty or misused electrical equipment, potentially flammable materials)
- identify who is at risk from fire hazards
- identify where people work (e.g. at permanent workstations or in a number of different areas)
- evaluate the risks and decide whether existing fire precautions are sufficient or whether further action is necessary to reduce these risks (e.g. by storing highly flammable substances in fire-resisting stores).
- examine the existing fire precautions in the workplace, including firefighting and fire escape routes, and decide whether they are sufficient to deal with the remaining risks.

If more than five people are employed at the workplace, the employer must record the findings of the assessment – including the significant fire hazards and any suggestions for further action aimed at reducing the risks. The assessment must be reviewed and updated at regular intervals or when new fire hazards are introduced at the workplace.

Another specific risk area is security. See page 126 for further information about security risk assessment.

1 Refer back to page 110 and the office scenario in which you were asked to list potential hazards. Look at your manager's handwritten draft risk assessment form below.

a Prepare a word-processed version of the form.

b Complete columns 1 and 2.

c Assess against each of the identified hazards those which you think are high risk, medium risk and low risk, and complete column 3. The following are questions you could ask yourself:

(i) Is the law being broken?

(ii) Can the hazard be completely removed?

(iii) If not, can something else be done?

- Is there a less risky option?
- Can access to the hazard be prevented, such as by a guard or other safety device?
- Can the work be reorganised to reduce the risk?
- Can personal protective equipment reduce the risk?
- Can better welfare facilities be provided?

d List suggested action under column 4.

2 Certain groups of workers may be more vulnerable and therefore require more attention. List who you think they are. Check your answers on page 149.

3 'A risk assessment is only as good as the person doing it.' What personal characteristics do you think you should possess in order to carry out an effective assessment?

N W Frankland Ltd
Sales Department

Risk assessment report form

①	②	③			④
Identified hazard	Person(s) at risk	Risk			Proposed action
		High	Medium	Low	

Signature:

Date:

Hazards you can put right yourself

General considerations

Health and safety is such an important issue that responsibility for it is placed firmly on the shoulders of the head of an organisation. However, in fulfilling that responsibility, he or she must have the cooperation and support of *all* members of the organisation. Obviously much depends on your role in the organisation. If you are a safety adviser, a director or a member of the senior management team, your responsibility will be greater than that of an office cleaner. If you are a senior administrator your responsibility will be greater than that of your staff, and so on.

Normally you will be made aware of your health and safety responsibilities either during your induction period or through a staff development activity. These could include one or more of the following:

- making regular checks of your immediate workplace for obvious hazards, such as trailing cables, broken furniture, torn carpets or flooring, missing or faulty lightbulbs, doors and windows that won't open, filing cabinet drawers left open, fire doors wedged open, heavy files on tops of cupboards
- taking action where appropriate, such as checking at the end of each day that filing cabinets are locked, windows closed and computers turned off, closing filing cabinet drawers, removing obstructions in the path of the fire doors, keeping coffee areas clean
- participating in or holding regular meetings with staff to maintain awareness of the need for a safe and secure workplace.

Cleaning

One major cause of accidents in an office is lack of cleanliness. Good cleaners are worth their weight in gold and you should try to give them as much support as possible. You can do this either by organising an effective cleaning programme covering all aspects of the workplace or by ensuring that someone else does so. You should, for instance, check the following points.

- The regularity with which cleaning takes place. Floors and traffic routes should be cleaned at least once a week, while interior walls, ceilings and work surfaces should be cleaned at suitable intervals.
- The timing of the cleaning. Ideally it should be outside working hours. If that is not possible, there should be sufficient warning signs available to make sure that staff are aware of potential hazards.
- How staff are trained in the use of cleaning equipment and safety precautions. They should also be made aware of manufacturers' instructions for the various cleaning agents and/or equipment.

You should keep records of the cleaning schedules, any problems encountered and any training programmes organised.

1 Check what the procedures are for cleaning the floors and walkways at either your workplace, college or training institution. Summarise them.

2 When choosing a floor surface, you should consider who will be using the area and how often, whether the surface will be suitable for the type and amount of traffic likely to use it, how the surface will be cleaned and how frequently, and whether or not it is suitable for the work activity in that area. Select one area, either at your workplace, college or training establishment, research to what extent the above issues have been taken into account, and write a brief report of your findings.

3 There are many different types of office equipment cleaning products on the market. Look at the table, which is an extract from a sales leaflet from a firm of suppliers of cleaning products. Examine the equipment in your immediate work area or in a section of your college or training establishment and (a) find out what cleaning products are used, and (b) compare them with the list in the table below. Try to determine whether there are any gaps in the provision.

Cleaning products	
Product	Uses
Screen cleaner	Ideal for cleaning glass and silk/anti-glare filters. Helps to reduce eyestrain, nausea and headaches – complaints associated with dirty screens
Multi-surface cleaner/foam cleaner	For plastic casings and keyboards
Solvent activator	Specially formulated for dissolving inks and correction fluid on printers, typewriters and fax machines
Screen wipes	For VDUs
Telephone wipes	For telephones
Hand wipes	For general purposes

Hazards you must report

In some cases, the type of hazard you identify may be one that you are personally unable to do anything about. If, for instance, you note that the electric kettle has a frayed cord it is not good policy to try a spot of DIY work with a roll of tape. Nor is it a good idea to try to open the back of a jammed shredder with a screwdriver 'just to have a look'. In those cases you must follow the appropriate reporting procedures.

Up to 750 people are seriously injured each year as a result of coming into contact with electricity, and office workers form part of that number. It is therefore important to make sure that office electrical equipment is checked regularly. A system of portable appliance testing (PAT) sets out the steps that employers can take to maintain portable electrical equipment. That includes office equipment which has a plug or a lead and can be easily moved around – such as kettles, lamps and vacuum cleaners.

CHECK IT OUT!

1 Below is an example of an accommodation check form. Investigate in your own workplace, college or training institution to see whether a similar form exists and how it is used. Write brief notes of your findings.

2 Obtain a copy of the HSE leaflet *Maintaining Portable Electric Equipment in Offices and Other Low Risk Environments,* and check whether your organisation is conforming to the requirements of the Electricity at Work Regulations 1989.

HAWORTH & FREEMANTLE

Accommodation inspection of: . . . .

Date: . . . .

Inspection by: . . . .

Distribution to: . . . .

Room number	Action to be taken	By whom	Date action completed
B1			
B2			

Accommodation checklist

Warning others about hazards

Shouting 'look out' to your colleagues each time you see them about to trip over something or collide with somebody isn't the end of your obligations in this respect. If someone is injured it is important for you to show that you took sufficient precautions to warn that person of the risk. Otherwise your organisation could incur both legal and financial penalties (look back to page 99 for more information).

It is unlikely that you will always be on the spot to point out the existence of a hazard or potential hazard. You therefore have to take steps to ensure that any hazard which cannot be put right immediately is made known to all staff. Much, of course, depends on the nature of the hazard. One that is high-risk (such as a suspected gas leak) would justify you reporting it immediately to your line manager who would probably consider evacuating the area. (See page 122 for information on emergency procedures.) Other lower-risk hazards you may be expected to deal with yourself.

One method of doing so is to have a supply of warning signs readily available such as a 'cleaning in progress' sign outside a lavatory or refreshment area. Other methods include the use of e-mail, which enables you to relay a message to a number of people within a matter of seconds. Failing that you may have to use surface internal mail, although if your organisation has a loudspeaker system or CCTV network in operation you may be able to use those means of communication to ensure that the information is disseminated as quickly as possible.

TEST YOUR KNOWLEDGE AND UNDERSTANDING

Look at the following list of potential hazards. In each case state what you would do.

1 You note that the cleaner is using a vacuum cleaner with a frayed flex.

2 There is a broken window in the storeroom which overlooks the back yard of the premises.

3 The younger members of staff propel themselves along on their castorised chairs from desk to desk. There are frequent collisions or near collisions.

4 You are about to go out for lunch and the workplace is half empty. As you come out of the office you see someone you don't know and who is not wearing a visitor's badge. When he sees you he turns abruptly and starts to go down the stairs again. (If necessary, check on page 126 for information about security measures.)

INFORMATION UPDATE

Employers have a legal duty to display an up-to-date 'Health and Safety Law' poster in a prominent position in the workplace, or alternatively to provide a copy of the leaflet to each of their employees, outlining health and safety legislation.

EVIDENCE COLLECTION

Undertake a weekly routine hazard review of your own working area and other areas in the workplace for which you have some responsibility. List any hazards you identify and what you think should be done. Note that this shouldn't prevent you from noting down hazards you spot between these reviews – but a weekly formal check will help you to remember. For your assessor, explain:

a which hazards you spotted and could correct yourself – and what you did

b those hazards which you had to report to someone else and the action you took in the meantime to warn other people of the risk.

Finally, state the outcome of your report – how the hazard was finally dealt with.

Your organisation's emergency procedures: how to follow them, and your responsibilities

---

Illness and accidents

People at work can become ill and need immediate attention. They can also have accidents. In a large organisation, if the illness or accident were serious you would normally call in the organisation's doctor or occupational nurse.

In smaller organisations, 'an appointed person' is responsible for taking charge when there is an accident or when someone is ill. He or she can perform such tasks as calling an ambulance and looking after the first-aid box but cannot carry out the first aid. In larger organisations 'first-aiders' are required who have to undergo an HSE-approved training course

Your organisation will probably have procedures in place to deal with minor illnesses or injuries. The **Health and Safety (First Aid) Regulations 1981** require employers to provide 'adequate and appropriate' equipment, facilities and personnel to enable first aid to be given to employees. Minimum requirements include a suitably stocked first-aid box and an appointed person to take charge of first-aid arrangements.

Adequate and appropriate measures

What is adequate and appropriate depends on the circumstances in the workplace and on a number of factors, such as:

- any specific risks (e.g. working with hazardous substances or dangerous tools or machinery)
- the differing risks in different parts of the workplace
- the past history of ill health and injuries
- the number of people employed
- the extent of their experience
- the pattern of working hours
- the distance from any available medical services
- the use of works experience trainees
- the number of visitors to the premises.

See the table below for suggested numbers of first-aid personnel.

Number of first-aiders		
Category of risk	Numbers employed at any location	Suggested number of first-aid personnel
Lower risk eg shops, offices, libraries	Fewer than 50	At least one appointed person
	50–100	At least one first-aider
	More than 100	One additional first-aider for every 100 employed
Medium risk (e.g. light engineering and assembly work, food-processing, warehousing)	Fewer than 20	At least one appointed person
	20–100	At least one first-aider for every 50 employed
	More than 100	One additional first-aider for every 100 employed
Higher risk (e.g. construction, chemical manufacturers, work with dangerous machinery)	Fewer than 5	At least one appointed person
	5–50	At least one first-aider
	More than 50	At least one first-aider for every 50 employed
	Where there are additional hazards for which additional first-aid skills are necessary	In addition at least one first-aider trained in the specific emergency action

In your workplace, college or training institution, check out the following list and prepare a brief report of your findings. Also, obtain copies of the free leaflets *Basic Advice on First Aid at Work and First Aid at Work – Your Questions Answered* published by HSE Books, PO Box 1999, Sudbury, Suffolk CO10 6FS. Check to see how far their requirements are being met by your organisation.

a Where is the first-aid box, and what does it contain? Ideally it should include:
  - a leaflet giving guidance on first aid
  - 20 individually wrapped sterile adhesive dressings (assorted sizes)
  - two sterile eye pads
  - four individually wrapped triangular bandages (preferably sterile)
  - six safety pins
  - six medium-sized individually wrapped sterile unmedicated wound dressings
  - two large sterile individually wrapped unmedicated wound dressings
  - one pair of disposable gloves.

b How often are the contents inspected?

c How many first aiders are there, what are their names, and what is the extent of the area each covers?

d What are the arrangements if one of them is absent?

e How have they been trained?

f How are staff kept informed about the first-aid facilities (including those who may have reading or sight problems)?

g What arrangements are there for visitors who become ill?

h What arrangements are there for people who work off-site?

i What is the extent of the liaison with local medical services?

j What is the extent of your responsibility?

Fire

Preventing a fire from happening is obviously less fraught with danger than trying to put one out. However, if despite all precautions a fire does occur, you must be in a position to deal with the situation immediately and comprehensively. All organisations are responsible for ensuring that their premises can be vacated easily and swiftly, and for providing appropriate fire-fighting equipment.

CHECK IT OUT!

1 In your own workplace, college or training establishment obtain details of:

   a the fire drill procedures in operation and how often these take place

   b any follow up action identified after the last fire drill and whether or not it has been carried out

   c how staff are trained in fire-drill procedures.

2 Check also on the extent of your own responsibilities.

   a Are you responsible for making regular inspections of fire hazards and reporting back to your line manager?

   b Are you a marshal who is responsible for clearing a specific area of a building if the fire alarm sounds?

   c Have you taken part in a fire drill? If so, how successful did you think it was?

   d Have you been trained in the use of fire-fighting equipment?

3 Write a brief report of your findings.

Bomb alerts

In many ways the precautions to be taken in the event of a bomb alert are the same as those for fire. However, because of the urgency of evacuating a building if a bomb threat is received, most organisations have in place additional precautions. In this case, for instance, people might be asked to take their bags with them to assist the fire brigade in any search made of the premises and to avoid them having to include a search of unattended baggage. There may also be a different alarm system to indicate that the alert is a bomb and not a fire alert.

Regulation 7 of the MHSW now requires employers to plan for a possible evacuation of a building by:

• establishing emergency procedures with adequate staff to implement those procedures

- naming and/or appointing competent staff to carry out the evacuation procedures
- allowing people to stop work immediately and go to a place of safety if there is a threat of imminent danger
- preventing them from entering any area where there are health and safety risks until they have been properly trained.

Breaches of security

Protecting your premises against thieves and vandals can take many different forms. These can include a wander around the premises by the caretaker or office manager. On the other hand, your organisation may have employed a firm of security consultants to carry out a much more sophisticated survey of the building and premises.

CHECK IT OUT!

Check out the list of questions contained in the specimen risk assessment form on page 127 in relation to your working environment.

EVIDENCE COLLECTION

For your evidence for this unit, you must prove that you can follow emergency procedures in all the following situations:

- illness
- accidents
- fires
- other reasons to evacuate the premises (such as a bomb threat or gas leak)
- breaches of security.

You obviously cannot 'arrange' an emergency to prove you know what to do! However, if there is an emergency in which you are involved whilst you are undertaking your award, write a description of what happened and how you coped. Ask your line manager or supervisor to countersign this for authenticity.

Otherwise, be prepared to discuss with your assessor what you would do – or write a brief account covering all these areas. You will be expected to know the organisational procedures you would have to follow in this situation and how you would respond quickly if you hadn't time to read these in advance! It is therefore sensible to give some thought to how you would cope if there were a *real* emergency and everyone was depending upon you to take the appropriate urgent action.

Alarm systems

- Is there a burglar alarm?
- Is the alarm installer a member of an approved security association?

Keys and locking up

- Is there a proper system to control the issue of keys?
- Is there an established procedure for locking up?
- Are rooms checked to see there is no one in the building when it is locked up?
- Is there a procedure for periodically checking security fittings such as locks, catches and bolts?

Security during working hours

- Are visitors encouraged to use the main door and is this signposted?
- Is it possible to monitor the arrival and departure of visitors?
- Are visitors asked for identification?
- Are visitors asked to sign in and out?
- Are visitors escorted to their destination?
- Do staff challenge strangers they see in the building?
- Have adequate arrangements been made for staff working in isolated areas?

Security outside working hours

- Are the premises regularly checked by the police or by a security firm?
- Are the premises well lit when not in use?
- Is external security lighting provided?
- Is the caretaker on-site?
- Is he/she easily accessible?
- Can he/she quickly contact the police and fire service?
- Is the timing of cleaning arrangements designed to facilitate supervision?
- Have adequate arrangements been made for staff working overtime or late?

Theft

- Are there secure areas for storing valuable equipment?
- Are staff advised on the need to safeguard personal property?
- Are cash holdings kept to a minimum?
- Is cash counted out of sight?
- Is money removed from premises overnight?
- Is equipment marked so as to identify the owner, and are signs displayed to this effect to deter thieves?

Security risk-assessment form

How to recommend improvements in health and safety

Consider the following scenario.

HAMID: I'm sorry I'm late. It's so dark that I've practically had to crawl on my hands and knees across the hall today. Is there any coffee going?

LUKE: That's brave of you.

HAMID: Caffeine doesn't worry me.

LUKE: I don't mean that. There's a very odd smell in the kitchen. It must be the drains again. Every time we get a hot day, it smells as if there's a dead body hidden in there.

HAMID: On second thoughts perhaps I won't bother. Where's Minnie?

LUKE: You don't know what you've missed. She went down to get the post and tripped on the loose stair carpet. What a performance! She's not exactly silent at the best of times but you should have heard her. She's upstairs in the staff room having a cigarette to calm her nerves.

HAMID: I thought the staff room was a no-smoking area.

LUKE: It is. Do you want to mention that fact to her – in the mood she's in at the moment?

HAMID: Best not.

One of the most difficult problems a safety representative has to face is employee apathy. Even though staff may notice that a light is not working, that there is a horrible smell in the kitchen and that the stair carpet is loose, quite often they will do nothing about it other than to complain to each other. As an administrator you may be expected to keep a check on health and safety issues and to make recommendations for improvements. You may also be expected to encourage others to do the same. There are various ways of doing so, depending on your level of responsibility. They include:

- raising specific issues at staff meetings and during staff development sessions
- sending e-mails/memos to staff asking them to report any hazards and to recommend improvements
- sending details of any obvious risks to your immediate line manager with recommendations for improving the situation
- feeding back to staff the results of any risk assessment surveys and asking for their comments
- ensuring that safety notices are visible and updated
- ensuring that safety information is current and sent to staff at regular intervals.

Although staff may be encouraged to report health and safety hazards and to offer suggestions for improvement to either the safety representative or line manager, most of them are very reluctant to report a colleague for causing a hazard or disobeying a health and safety rule. In the above scenario Hamid and Luke did not want to have an argument with the highly strung Minnie. Write a brief note on how you would have handled the situation.

Health and safety records you may have to complete, and how to do so

The possible consequences of a failure to have a safe workplace are so serious that most organisations make sure they keep very extensive documentation relating to all health and safety issues. This includes minutes of the safety committee meetings, reports from the safety adviser and the individual safety representatives, risk-assessment surveys and the follow-up action taken, summaries of fire drills undertaken etc. Much depends on your job description, but it is probable that at some stage in your career you will be called upon to take notes of safety meetings and to prepare risk-assessment reports for certain areas, either independently or in liaison with your line manager or safety adviser. You may also be expected to keep a record of any accidents or illnesses in the workplace.

The **Reporting of Injuries, Diseases and Dangerous Occurrences Regulations 1995** (RIDDOR) requires the reporting of:

- work-related accidents – i.e. where there is death or major injury or where there is an absence of over three days because of an accident
- diseases – i.e. where a doctor notifies the employer that an employee suffers from a reportable work related disease
- dangerous occurrences – i.e. where something happens which did not result in a reportable injury but which clearly could have done.

If you work in an office, a retail or wholesale outlet, a warehouse, a hotel or catering facility, a sports or leisure facility, or residential accommodation other than a nursing home or a place of worship, you should normally report to the environmental health department of your local authority. For all other types of business you would be expected to report to the area office of the Health & Safety Executive.

The information to be provided should include:

- the date, time and place of the event
- personal details of those involved
- a brief description of the nature of the event or disease.

Accident reports

Even where an accident is not sufficiently serious to warrant immediate reporting, most organisations have a system whereby accidents or injuries, however minor, are recorded and a summary of them presented to the safety committee, safety adviser or a member of the senior management team for consideration. See the sample form printed here.

ACCIDENTS IN .... BETWEEN .... AND			
Reference Number	Person	Accident/injury	Action taken

Safety representative reports

At some stage in your career you may agree – or be 'persuaded' – to become the departmental safety representative. As already mentioned (see page 121) one of your duties will be to investigate staff concerns and to report back to the safety committee or to your line manager. In addition you may be required to investigate and report back on specific incidents. In the case of an accident, for instance, you might consider the use of a checklist covering such items as:

- the working environment
- the injured person's job experience, the extent of the training he or she has undergone and the amount of supervision he or she was given

- information available to the injured person on health and safety issues
- the adequacy of maintenance of any equipment involved
- the provision of personal protective clothing
- any possible breaches of the law
- management action already taken.

Element 302.2 Monitor and maintain an effective and efficient working environment

The conditions under which you work and their effect on effectiveness and efficiency

A responsibility which administrators sometimes accept without thinking is their role in keeping a working area clean, tidy and well organised. They also have responsibilities for machine maintenance and performance. If the photocopier or fax machine suddenly makes an odd noise, or starts to smell of burning, it is likely someone would tell you quite quickly!

However, taking positive action to maintain a pleasant and well-organised working area is also beneficial in terms of improving health and safety. A pile of dusty box files scattered over a rickety shelf, a stack of dirty coffee cups or discarded drink cans and a mass of wires across a room not only looks unsightly but is hazardous to you and everyone else.

In this element you will see the relevance of keeping your working area tidy and should gain some useful ideas for a 'review' of your own area. If you have never thought about a grand style 'tidy up' before now – perhaps now is your chance!

You might be the sort of person who says that you are oblivious of your surroundings at work. You just concentrate on what you are doing and don't let external conditions bother you. If you are, you are in a minority. Most workers *are* affected by the conditions in which they work. That is why the **Health and Safety at Work Act 1974** covers not only health and safety at work but also welfare at work and the various sets of regulations specify which sorts of working conditions are acceptable and which are not.

Your effectiveness will be increased if you are working in well-lit surroundings that are maintained at the correct temperature, where the desks and chairs are suited to your physical needs, and where the noise is at an acceptable level. Your efficiency will be increased if the office layout helps you and your colleagues to communicate, if the equipment you use is well maintained and suited to your requirements, and if the systems and procedures are designed to assist rather than impede you.

Organising your own work area so that you and others can work efficiently

Your desk or workspace

Brendan is constantly getting into a mess because he can never find anything. When the telephone rings he never has a pen to hand to take a message or, even if he borrows one, he has then lost the telephone message pad. When he wants to reply to a customer he has to spend hours looking through all his desk drawers and filing cabinets to try and find the original letter. Every time he reaches to answer the telephone he knocks over his desk lamp. He has no room to spread out any papers. In fact his desk is so crowded that he has to balance his portable keyboard on top of the printer unless it is actually in use. He has lost his mouse mat weeks ago. He can hardly open any of his desk drawers because there is so much in them. He tends to like a snack during the day and frequently has opened bags of crisps, cans of coke and packets of sweets littered about on his desk or pushed into one of the drawers.

Phil's desk on the other hand is immaculate. In response to his manager's wishes he operates a clear-desk policy and has on it only the essentials – his diary and address book, a telephone, a VDU and printer, a container for his computer disks, three wire baskets containing incoming mail, outgoing mail and pending correspondence and a desk organiser containing paper, envelopes and manila files. His desk drawers are equally well organised. There are baskets and containers for pens, pencils, computer labels, staplers, staples and paperclips. He stores spare computer disks in the drawer that has a lock on it. He never keeps food in any of the drawers and limits personal items to a minimum.

> **CHECK IT OUT!**
>
> Check your own desk area. Write down what you have on it at present. Check each drawer if relevant and carry out the same exercise. Decide whether (a) you want to remove any of the items or (b) rearrange any of them to improve your personal effectiveness.

Your immediate work area

Even if you are totally satisfied with the way in which your desk is organised, you have also to be equally satisfied with the way in which the furniture and equipment in your immediate vicinity are arranged. If you have to squeeze past two desks each time you want to use a photocopier, or have to walk 50 metres to the filing cabinet, you are preventing yourself from being as effective as you could be.

INFORMATION UPDATE

One writer maintains that the muddled desk with papers stacked high is a remarkably efficient working environment until mass clean-ups disrupt 'people's self-constructed information retrieval systems'. He maintains that the old joke that people cannot find things after they have been forced to tidy up is true because they have lost visual prompts that jogged their memory. According to him, many desks resemble 'volcanoes' of paper with papers originating at the centre crawling to the end of the desk and, like lava, flowing slowly to the edge and eventually dropping off, where the cleaner eventually throws them away and no more is said about them. The very fact that they do drift towards the edge of the desk, he says, indicates their uselessness!

The traditional rectangle desk does not easily accommodate the personal computer with its three components of VDU, keyboard and printer. Many modern desks comprise worksurfaces which allow the user three-quarters of a square worktop to allow the easy positioning of the computer equipment. An alternative is to keep the desk free from computer equipment and to make use instead of a computer workstation on a portable trolley situated immediately adjacent to the desk

On page 103 you were given some information about the correct type of chair to use to prevent backache. Similar considerations can apply to desking. Height adjustability of desks is now considered so important that in the Netherlands, for instance, it is compulsory, and in the UK the new standard ISO/EN9241 has recommended adjustability for all desks at which computer users sit.

CHECK IT OUT!

Ask your line manager whether you can carry out this exercise.

1 Sketch a diagram of your immediate work area, including your own desk or work unit, those of staff working in the immediate vicinity, the type of and positioning of any office equipment, filing cabinets etc.

2 On paper, try out one or two variations which you think may improve workflow. You may, for instance, want to rearrange the positioning of the desks or filing cabinets.

3 Ask for the opinion of your manager and, where relevant, consult your colleagues and health and safety adviser or representative.

4 Prepare a second sketch and brief report to your manager outlining any improvements you would like to make.

Following your organisation's requirements for how you organise your working area

Your organisation's policy towards the work environment will obviously affect the way in which you organise your own working area. Are you working in an organisation which favours the more traditional style of office layout, where managers tend to have rooms of their own and the rest of the staff work together in small areas? Is your work area completely open-plan so that no one other than perhaps the very senior managers has their own room? Are you part of a very modern organisation where 'hot desking' or 'hotelling' is used – that is, no one even has his or her own desk but instead makes use of whatever workspace is available?

Open-plan offices – particularly those which try to incorporate some of the advantages of the traditional office – are growing in popularity. Many of them have quiet areas in which staff can work on tasks requiring concentration or talk to colleagues on a one-to-one basis. Some provide social areas furnished with chairs and sofas which staff can use in their breaks. Some make effective use of acoustic screens to cut down the level of noise. Even so, one writer has given some additional tips on how to 'thrive' in open plan surroundings.

- Resist the temptation to have a loud conversation about what you did the previous weekend, just as your colleague has started a telephone conversation with a valued client.
- Recognise that open plan does not mean open house, and that wandering around from desk to desk picking up staplers, pens, computer disks etc. will not make you the most popular member of the workforce.
- Try, however, to avoid regarding your desk as yours and yours alone and becoming belligerent if someone else sits down at it to use your keyboard or telephone.
- Equally, try to assert your individuality in some way, by having something on your desk – photographs, pictures etc. – that reminds you of your own personality, likes and dislikes.
- Capitalise on the advantages of the open-plan system by getting to know as many people as possible.

 INFORMATION UPDATE

The BBC has recently introduced an open-plan style office in one of its areas. All staff sit in sight of a window and of each other. The central space is dedicated to low personal filing cabinets to support a clear-desk policy. Armchairs are arranged ready for informal meetings at any moment. As well as conventional meeting rooms, there are individual study booths and private spaces for people ➡

who are busy or want privacy. At the centre there is the 'hub' –
the kitchen and the printing facilities in one space with plenty of
floorspace and chairs to encourage social interaction.

TEST YOUR KNOWLEDGE AND UNDERSTANDING

Whatever the layout used, you will already probably have discovered
that it has both advantages and disadvantages. The table below lists
the advantages of three major types of office layout. Try to decide
what disadvantages each may have. Then turn to page 150 for a
suggested answer.

Types of office layout	
Office layout	Advantages
Traditional	• There is less noise. • Confidentiality is easier to maintain. • Groups of staff can meet without disturbing others. • It is easier to maintain concentration without interruption from others. • An individual office is sometimes regarded as a 'reward' and as part of a promotion package. • Customers and clients feel more comfortable if they are talking to someone away from the rest of the staff.
Open plan	• It allows for standardisation of systems (e.g. communal filing systems can be established). • Standardised working conditions can be maintained more easily – heating, air conditioning, lighting etc. • Communication can be quicker and easier. • Staff feel less isolated and a good rapport can be established. • It is more difficult for staff to be idle when their colleagues can see what they are doing. • Better use can be made of limited office space.
Hot-desking or hotelling	• The best possible use can be made of limited office space. • As with open plan, there can be a complete standardisation of conditions and systems. • It discourages staff who should be out of the office from loitering in the building (e.g. salespeople).

Organising your working area for a positive impression on other people

Your manager has asked you to meet a very important client and to keep him happy until she finishes off an important meeting. You agree to do so. Ten minutes after the client is supposed to have arrived you decide to check in the reception area to see whether he is there. Apparently he is and he is none too pleased at having been kept waiting. The morning receptionist has gone off duty and the afternoon receptionist has not yet arrived, so no one has asked him what he wants and who he wants to see. He is sitting in the corridor next to the cupboard containing cleaning materials and the only person he has met so far is the cleaner who has complained to him about the state of the cleaning materials and the fact that no one in the organisation cares whether the place is clean or not.

You apologise and ask the visitor to come with you. The lift is not working and the stairs are uncarpeted and badly lit. At the top of the stairs, the visitor trips over a packing case and you have to help him up. His temper is not improved by this incident. When he reaches your office you can see that he is not impressed by the brown paint, the ancient, mismatched furniture and the wilting spider plant in the plastic margarine tub. When he sits down the chair creaks and he is obviously anxious that it won't bear his weight. The air conditioning has stopped and after a few minutes he is perspiring heavily and demanding a glass of water. All you can offer him is a plastic cup of hot chocolate from the drinks machine. He refuses this and looks pointedly at the clock. When your manager arrives the scene is set for a very uncomfortable interview. Unsurprisingly, your manager is unable to persuade the client to give her an order.

As that scenario indicates, *first impressions do count*. When visitors come into your office or working area, they should feel quite comfortable at spending some time there, rather than making plans for an early escape. As previously mentioned (see page 133), your desk or working space should look well-organised. Other steps you can take are given below.

- Office equipment such as your VDU or photocopier should look clean and not be heaped with discarded pieces of paper.
- Filing cabinets should be labelled, and the drawers should be easy to open. Visitors are generally surprised if you have to ask them to give you a hand to open a drawer which is so full of papers that it jams when you try to retrieve something!
- Any visual aids you have on display should look attractive. Noticeboards full of out-of-date material which is crumpling round the edges and faded by the sun are not impressive. Neither are notices which have been scribbled on by the office wit and are stuck to the wall with sellotape or drawing pins. Wall planners hanging half off the wall which have obviously been bought in a fit of enthusiasm and never used after the first week are equally unpleasing to the outside eye.

- Drink-making facilities that are in view must be clean and tidy.
- Plants or flowers should look healthy, not brown withered skeletons of their former selves.

Finally, 'jokey' personal belongings should ideally be out of sight. This includes any holiday postcards, cute cuddly toys or mascots and photographs of you in relaxed mood at the office party. You might find them funny, but visitors may not share your sense of humour!

 INFORMATION UPDATE

Apparently one of the most difficult things to overcome in modern offices, whether traditional or open-plan, is draughts. Even if all the windows are double-glazed there still remains the problem of open doors, particularly if the area is one that has frequent visitors. Devices to overcome this include the construction of lobbies with inner and outer doors so that both doors are not open at the same time when visitors are passing through, and the use of wood or glass screens placed round doorways. In the majority of cases, however, most writers admit that reduction of draughts has to be left to the 'ingenuity' of the staff!

CHECK IT OUT!

There are some aspects of the office environment for which you are not likely to be directly responsible. These include the actual decor, the type and age of the furniture and equipment, the heating and lighting facilities and the method of ventilation. Nor are you likely to have control over the acoustics. However, one of your managers is likely to have such a responsibility. In your own organisation, check:

- who is responsible for choosing or deciding upon the office decor
- whether there is an organisational style (e.g. whether all areas have the same type of decorations and furnishings) and, if so, what it is
- what, if any, specific arrangements are made for reception or waiting areas.

Write a short report of your findings.

EVIDENCE COLLECTION

You need to prove to your assessor that you can:

- organise the work area for which you are responsible so that you and other people can work safely
- organise your work area so it meets your organisation's requirements (for instance, in terms of what you can put on the wall or store on top of cabinets) and presents a positive image of you and your team
- identify any conditions which interfere with effective working – this could be poor layout, lack of blinds, temperatures which are too hot or cold – or any other issues which you have read about so far
- put right the conditions which you can and report the others.

1 Start your evidence by carrying out a survey of the work area for which you are responsible. Identify the organisational requirements with which you must comply. Suggest any changes which will help to give a more positive image.

2 Assess the conditions and note down any factors which you think prevent or impede effective working. Identify those you can remedy yourself, immediately. Report others to the relevant person together with your suggestions for improvements.

3 Note that 'good housekeeping' means that you need to be alert thereafter – so decide how frequently you will monitor the area.

Now write a summary of all the activities you have undertaken and attach any relevant documentation which relates to these, such as your report to your line manager and his/her response.

Working in a way that shows respect for other people

Not many people work in isolation. Most work in a group or a team where personal characteristics have at least the same importance as technical expertise or administrative skills. You may be a very efficient administrator in the way in which you carry out your work. However, you will not be an effective administrator if no one wants to work with you and your line manager keeps trying to have you transferred elsewhere because he or she is fed up with having to deal with the grumbles of the rest of the staff. Equally you will not be able to do your job properly if your colleagues behave in a way that hinders rather than helps.

The following are things to avoid:

- interrupting someone who is in the middle of a conversation with another person
- making personal telephone calls during working hours
- using the Internet during working hours to check on holiday flights, football scores etc.
- refusing to keep quiet when someone is taking a telephone call from a client
- refusing to take a message for someone else or doing it so carelessly that you omit important details such as a correct telephone number
- coming in a little late each morning and leaving a few minutes early
- having an extended lunch break if the boss is out
- going through other people's desks and removing calculators, scissors, rulers, staplers etc. to replace anything you have mislaid
- having so much on your desk that papers overflow on to the floor, window sills etc and get in other people's way
- insisting on having all the windows closed – or open – regardless of other colleagues' wishes
- when the heating goes off unexpectedly, taking possession of the one portable heater and huddling over it all day
- never washing up your coffee cup
- always trying to avoid making the coffee
- filing documents so carelessly that no one can find them – or not even bothering to return them to the filing cabinet
- noting that the photocopier is out of paper when you have used it and doing nothing about it
- not bothering to note the number of photocopies you have taken or to record details of any photocopies for copyright purposes
- jamming paper in the photocopier and walking away.

The following are things to actively encourage:

- cooperation in establishing and following organisational procedures and systems
- an understanding of and compliance with the organisation's rules, ethos and etiquette
- a professional approach towards the maintenance of well-organised and attractive surroundings
- consideration for others not only in relation to the way you carry out your work but also in the way you assist others to carry out theirs.

Manufacturers' instructions and organisational procedures for your use of equipment

Manufacturers' instructions

VDUs, printers, fax machines, photocopiers, calculators, overhead projectors, CCTV, dictating machines, telephone and voice answering machines are a normal part of office life nowadays. So too, for some workers, are electric kettles, coffee percolators, vacuum cleaners and floor polishers. All are designed to improve your working life and in most instances they do so. However, problems can arise in two different ways.

The first occurs when a new piece of equipment arrives in the office and you are so eager to begin to use it that, instead of listening carefully to the salesperson's advice or bothering to read the manufacturer's instruction booklet, you make a dive for the machine and start pressing buttons at random. The second problem arises when a machine, upon which you have become almost totally dependent, suddenly goes wrong just when you are in the middle of preparing documentation for a major conference the following day. Bursting into tears and/or trying to coax it into life by kicking it is no substitute for knowing what may have happened and what can be done about it.

Reading and absorbing the information in manufacturers' instructions can be a fairly long task and it is sometimes difficult to understand some of the language used. A good way to start is to check the contents page to see which of the items are likely to be of most use to you. At this stage, also, it is an equally good idea to determine the extent of your responsibility for the safety, security, maintenance and upkeep of the machine. In many cases other people will share that responsibility.

TEST YOUR KNOWLEDGE AND UNDERSTANDING

Look at the example of a contents page of a manufacturers' instruction leaflet for the use of a mobile telephone opposite. At first sight, which of the items do you feel may be of most use to you? Are there any you feel may be of particular use to other people in your organisation and, if so, who?

Safety instructions

Whatever else you may try to skim read, safety instructions should not be one of them. You have already read about the importance of health and safety in the workplace and the need for your cooperation. Making sure you are aware of what you should and should not do when using office equipment is part of that obligation. In most cases, the safety instructions are merely common sense. For instance, they will advise that you do not:

- turn off the main switch when a machine is in operation
- put anything heavy on top of a machine
- open a machine and touch any of the moving parts inside it
- use the wrong type of cleaner or solution
- try to 'mend' a fault without referring to the manufacturers' instructions
- spill coffee on it!

Service agreements

The manufacturer's instructions may advise that regular maintenance is essential – which normally involves entering into a service agreement with the manufacturer or supplier. However, though it is generally good practice to enter a service agreement, there can be drawbacks in doing so without making sure that you fully understand exactly what the agreement covers.

Your phone	**Function menus**
Handset features	Menus and the compass key
Display features	Navigating through menus
	Extras
Getting ready	clock and alarm
Battery installation	stopwatch
Battery charging	biocalendar
Activating your account	calculator
Buying calltime	Phone book
Getting confirmation	Quick dial
Monitoring calltime credit	Messages: text and voice
	Callback service
Basics	Calls
Turning on/off	Settings
Making calls	Security
Receiving calls	
Who's called?	**Special features**
Calling emergency services	Automatic redial
International calls	Scratchpad
Locking/unlocking the keypad	Touchtones
Entering text	Hide your identity
Useful phone adjustments	
	Troubleshooting
	Do remember
	Safety
	Did you know?
	Accessories
	Contact numbers

Contents page for a mobile telephone manual

CHECK IT OUT!

At your workplace, college or training establishment, find out whether the equipment you use has service agreements. Make notes of what these agreements say.

Exclusion clauses

Some manufacturers' instructions or service agreements might have exclusion clauses which attempt to limit their liability if the equipment goes wrong. Within reason they are allowed to do this, and if you sign a document containing an exclusion clause it might be difficult to say at a later date that you did not agree to it. In such circumstances, you would obviously consult your immediate line manager before entering into such an agreement.

The courts are reluctant to allow manufacturers to rely too much on exclusion clauses and to disclaim responsibility for all faults. In one case, for instance, a customer hired a cycle from a shop. Under the contract, the shop was exempted from liability for any personal injuries to him. The cycle was faulty and he was injured. However, although he could not claim under the contract, the court held that he could still claim under another legal heading – that of negligence. The hirer won his case. See also page 145 for information on the **Unfair Contract Terms Act 1977** and its effect on exclusion clauses.

Guarantees

Many manufacturers' instructions include a guarantee. Although this can be useful, particularly if a piece of equipment develops a fault at an early stage, again you should take care that you or someone in a position of responsibility reads it carefully.

TEST YOUR KNOWLEDGE AND UNDERSTANDING

Read the following extracts from a manufacturer's mobile telephone manual which outlines the terms and conditions under which the guarantee will operate.

a 'This guarantee applies, provided the product is handled properly for its intended use, in accordance with its operating and care instructions. Proof of purchase will be needed. ...'

b 'The guarantee may not apply if:

- the proof of purchase has been altered or is illegible in any way
- the product has reception or operation problems caused by signal conditions or network reliability
- the model or production numbers on the product have been altered, deleted, removed or are illegible
- damage has been caused by leakage from batteries other than those originally delivered with the product
- unauthorised repairs have been carried out
- the product has not been bought brand new
- the damage is caused by accidents including but not limited to falling, shock, lightning, liquid, fire, misuse or neglect. ...'

One of your colleagues is not very good at reading or following instructions. Nor is he particularly careful with his own or the organisation's possessions. Write short notes on (i) how you would try to ensure that he is made fully aware of the importance of looking after his telephone, and (ii) how you would try to monitor that he continues to do so.

INFORMATION UPDATE

Although you may not have the sole responsibility for negotiating contracts with suppliers, you may be the first point of contact if a problem arises. In such circumstances an outline knowledge of consumer protection legislation is useful, particularly if the sales representative with whom you are dealing tries to rely upon any statements made in the relevant instruction manual. The major legislation includes the following:

- The **Unfair Contract Terms Act 1977** makes exclusion clauses or disclaimers invalid unless an organisation can prove these terms are fair and reasonable. If, for example, in one of the service agreements there is a clause which states that the manufacturer will not be responsible for any faults in the equipment whether or not caused by its negligence, it is unlikely that the company would be able to rely upon it.

- The **Consumer Credit Act 1974** places strict controls upon organisations providing credit facilities in the course of their business.

- The **Sale of Goods Act 1979** and the **Sale and Supply of Goods Act 1994** provide that any goods for sale have to be *as described* (i.e. match any description given of them), *of satisfactory quality* and *fit for the purpose for which they are intended.*

- The **Supply of Goods and Services Act 1982** extends the protection of the 1979 Sale of Goods Act to services as well as goods. If, therefore, you find that a piece of equipment has been installed incorrectly or a vastly inflated price has been charged for the work, you may be able to claim that the Act has been breached.

- The **Consumer Protection Act 1987** makes it an offence to mislead consumers about the price at which goods are available. If, for instance, a sales representative has told you that the price charged is far below the recommended price, or you find out that the price quoted does not include a number of 'hidden extras', again you may be able to claim that the law has been broken in this area.

Organisational procedures

Because manufacturers' instruction manuals can be complicated, many organisations choose not to rely upon them completely and prepare instead a summarised version based on the manual but in a much more 'user friendly' format. For instance, see the table below for a list of instructions on how to store photocopying paper. In addition most organisations take matters a stage further by instituting a set of procedures for use each time a new item of equipment is purchased.

Paper storage

Paper should always be stored properly because poor paper condition will result in poor image reproduction, creased copies and paper jams.

Do

1 Store paper on a flat surface.
2 Store open reams of paper in the package.
3 Use older stock first.

Don't

1 Store paper in humid areas.
2 Store paper where it will be exposed to heat.
3 Place any heavy objects on the paper.

Extract from an organisational manual on the correct way to store photocopier paper

If your line manager asks you to prepare some procedures for the staff to follow, you will probably need to have your own procedure for doing so! Points to bear in mind include:

• deciding first of all what the procedure is designed to achieve
• who will be expected to follow it
• who will be responsible for ensuring that it is followed
• who should be consulted
• when it is going to be implemented.

The next stage is to decide on the format. The normal method is to use a step-by-step approach or list of actions to be followed. In most cases this is sufficient but occasionally the use of graphics or diagrams can help. If, for instance, you have been asked to prepare a procedure for the use of a new fax machine, you might find it helpful to include in the list some illustrations from the manufacturers' instruction booklet.

Your manager leaves the following note on your desk. Prepare a suitable response for him.

FAIRCLOUGH AND DERRY

MEMORANDUM

To: (You)

From: Leslie Bernstein

Date: (Today)

Photocopying

The new photocopier has just arrived. I know everyone will be wanting to use it as soon as possible particularly since the training session yesterday. What I'm worried about, however, is that they will go mad and start photocopying everything in sight. I don't want an astronomical bill for paper at the end of the month. I'm also a bit bothered that one or two of our 'handy andies' might try to take matters into their own hands if anything goes wrong. Another point – Yuhana from Computer Services has told me that she has never dealt with more arguments since the installation of their new photocopier. This is in a room that is meant to be locked but, according to Yuhana, the number of people who have walked off with (or even 'hidden' the key!) has been unbelievable. Again, although we agreed we would copy the Computer Services first come first served system, Yuhana tells me that some people are always trying to beat the queue by claiming that their photocopying is urgent.

Can you have a think about it and draft out a list of procedures that I can discuss with the staff at the next meeting?

PS: I've just walked past the photocopier in Computer Services. There is paper thrown about all over the place, the machine is still switched on even though it's long after the time most people have left, and one of the doors is open! I don't want us to be in the same situation.

At your workplace, make a note of all the equipment you use on a regular basis. In each case, check to see whether or not there are any organisational procedures in existence. Where there are not, ask your line manager to discuss the advantages and disadvantages of introducing them. Make a note of his or her answers.

EVIDENCE COLLECTION

You need to prove that you can use and maintain equipment in accordance with the manufacturer's instructions and your organisation's procedures. Write a summary of all the equipment you routinely use and identify any specific instructions or procedures you or your team have to follow. Then note down how you have dealt with faults, problems or an emergency in relation to equipment and its use – or how you *would* deal with these, if they occurred.

KEYS

Suggested answer to 'Test your knowledge and understanding' on page 100.

a   The houseowner succeeded. The court decided that the decorator had a duty of care towards his employer to ensure that the premises were secure. He could have reasonably foreseen that leaving the house unlocked could have resulted in burglary.

b   The court decided that the railway company owed a duty of care to the passenger but not to the passer-by. It could not have been reasonably foreseen that the vibration from the explosion would have dislodged the scales.

c   The insurance company was held not to be liable for the nervous shock. It could not have been reasonably foreseen that the woman would meet her husband and child at the hospital in that condition.

Don't worry if you guessed wrong. High Court judges frequently disagree with each other about this type of case!

Suggested answer to 'Test your knowledge and understanding' on page 101.

See the table opposite for the suggested action to be taken.

Suggested answer to preventing slips at work	
Situation	Action to be taken
Spillage on floors/stairways etc.	Arrange for spills to be cleaned immediately. Use suitable cleaning agents. Use appropriate warning signs to indicate that the floor is wet/slippy etc.
Trailing cables	Position equipment to avoid cables crossing pedestrian routes. Use cable covers to fix to surfaces.
Rubbish	Arrange for regular clearing. Do not allow it to accumulate.
Mats	Ensure that mats are securely fixed and do not have curling edges.
Slippery surfaces	Assess the cause. Carry out any relevant cleaning treatment.
Change from wet to dry surfaces	Warn of the possible risks. If relevant, advise on suitable footwear. Place mats between the two surfaces.
Poor lighting	Improve the lighting. Check in particular that the light placement is correct to ensure even lighting in the workplace.
Changes of level	Use suitable lighting.
Steps	Provide handrails. Use floor markings. Check on any worn treads. Use anti-slip coating.

Suggested answer to 'Test your knowledge and understanding' on page 117.

These could include staff with physical disabilities, visitors/members of the public, subcontractors, new or inexperienced staff, young workers and pregnant women.

Suggested answer to 'Test your knowledge and understanding' on page 125.

Ways of avoiding an arson attack:

a Ensure that a senior manager takes responsibility for preventing arson from occurring.

b Check security in the workplace. For example, if possible have entrances staffed all the time; erect outer fences, walls and gates which are strong enough and high enough to deter possible intruders; avoid storing material of any kind adjacent to fences or walls where it could be set alight from the outside; ensure doors and windows are in good repair and locked when not in use; use good-quality locks and padlocks; fit letterboxes with metal containers on the inside; avoid having large gaps under doors; invest in external lighting.

c Ensure that staff are aware of the possibility of arson attacks and ask them to challenge visitors not wearing badges.

d Check the credentials of outside contractors.

e Ensure the fire-fighting equipment is in good order.

Suggested answer to 'Test your knowledge and understanding' on page 136.

Disadvantages of various office layouts:

Traditional

- It is wasteful on space.
- Staff can sometimes feel isolated.
- It is more difficult to standardise systems and to ensure that everyone is following standardised procedures.
- Supervision of staff may be more difficult.

Open-plan

- It can be difficult to concentrate on a complicated task because of the noise of other staff or activities.
- It is sometimes difficult to hold confidential discussions.
- Meetings can be difficult to arrange because of the possible disruption to the work of the other staff.

Hot desking or hotelling

- It is suitable for only certain types of organisations, such as those whose staff spend only a small amount of time in the office.
- Surveys have shown that not many staff like the arrangement.

Unit 303 Manage your work and development

This unit is concerned with how you plan and organise your work. It also focuses on your personal development to enable you to evaluate your own performance, recognise where improvements are needed, and develop the skills to take on new responsibilities. The aim is to give you the abilities and confidence to meet future goals.

 KEY SKILLS SIGNPOST

If you are taking your Key Skills award then you can extend your knowledge and abilities from this unit and use this as evidence in your portfolio for **Improving your own Learning and Performance**. Your progress file, learning plan or any other action plans you complete can also contribute towards your portfolio evidence. You need to provide at least *one* substantial example of meeting the following standards to achieve level 3. Remember, if you are working at a different level, talk to your tutor or trainer about any changes you need to make.

LP3.1

Access various sources of information which will help you to identify what you want to achieve in the future, not just in your learning or your career, but also in your personal life.

Identify any factors you think may affect your plans – either positively or negatively. These may include financial considerations, your own health and safety, your personal commitments or situation, what opportunities are available to you, and how motivated you feel.

Hold discussions with your tutor, trainer, supervisor or other appropriate person to discuss and agree targets you could achieve over the next 3–6 months. Make sure all the targets you identify and agree are SMART ones (see pages 165 and 211).

Create a clear action plan to show how you will achieve these. This means identifying action points, working out realistic timescales, assessing where you may need additional support, and making arrangements to review your progress regularly. At this point, identify any difficulties you think you may experience, and suggest how you could overcome these or how your plans could be changed to allow for them. Make sure your action plan includes all these points.

LP3.2

Keep clear records or a weekly log of your achievements which clearly shows how you took responsibility for your own learning over a period of 3–6 months. This should show:

- how you prioritised your actions to achieve targets
- how you handled any difficulties
- the deadlines you achieved, those you didn't and why
- the revisions you had to make to your plans, and why
- details about the feedback, help and support you received from other people and its value
- the way in which you assessed your own learning style (see page 217) and identified the ways in which you prefer to learn.

In addition, you must show that you tried different methods of learning over this period:

- how you studied a complex subject (this could be a topic in this book you found difficult, for instance)
- how you learned through a practical activity (e.g. by watching and copying a demonstration on how to use an item of equipment or by being coached by someone how to do a particular task)
- how you undertook independent learning (e.g. by researching on the Internet, using distance learning materials or an IT package/manual, or improved your abilities on your own such as by working through the Appendix in this book).

LP3.3

Review your own progress and achievements by producing various documents.

- Produce records which show the quality of your learning and performance. This should include a summary of what you have learned and how you learned it. If you were able to use information from one area or task to help to undertake something new, make certain you include this.

- Collect examples of what you have achieved and what you learned when you studied a complex subject, a practical activity or undertook independent learning.

- Generate any other evidence of your achievements, such as actual examples of the work you have produced and statements by your supervisor, tutor or colleagues (you can cross-reference appropriate evidence from your portfolio here).

- Complete your updated action plan which clearly shows the targets you have met and the targets you are thinking about for the future. Include information on the ongoing discussions you have had with other people to agree how you could continue to improve.

KNOWLEDGE AND UNDERSTANDING REQUIRED FOR THE UNIT

Throughout this unit, you need to understand why it is essential to be able to plan, prioritise, organise and develop your own work. This is important not just for your own personal success but also for your current organisation and any future employer.

All the information you need is contained within this chapter, but fundamentally you should appreciate that this unit is concerned with the key aspects of administrative work.

- **Planning** means being able to look ahead, to forecast what is likely to happen so that you can take routine events in your stride and meet unexpected challenges or changes. In an administrative role it means that you have foreseen and made arrangements in advance, thought about the consequences of your actions, anticipated possible changes and complications. You are therefore much less likely to be fazed by sudden developments or changes to deadlines.

- **Prioritising** means that, no matter how much work needs to be done, you are able to identify what should be done *first* and meet deadlines reliably. It means working 'smarter' not 'harder' – by doing the right job, not just doing the job right!

- **Organising** means that you can bring order to situations where there could otherwise be chaos. You make arrangements that run smoothly, you know exactly what you are doing and why, you can find things quickly, you can remember key facts, you can respond calmly and efficiently even in a crisis.

- **Developing yourself** means that you are never satisfied with what you did, or could do, yesterday but constantly want to improve your performance so that you can take on and meet new challenges. It also means that you are prepared to take responsibility for your own self-development and don't expect other people to coax you along.

These requirements are not an easy remit for anyone – and if you are only young and in your first job then you may find them rather overwhelming. However, it is unlikely you would have been attracted to administration as a career if you were not relatively good at planning and organising – and if you did not enjoy seeing a job through to successful completion. You should remember that even the longest trek can be completed if you take it a step at a time. It is therefore wise not to think of how you would like to be (or how much you would like to earn!) in five years' time but to think about what you would like to know and do in the next three or six months. If you think about self-development in manageable chunks, even your wildest dreams may be achievable.

Finally, before you start to study the first element of this unit, it is important to realise why planning, prioritising, organising and developing skills are so important to your employer.

All organisations are involved in:

- developing new areas of work and generating new business
- consolidating existing operations
- making arrangements for various events or different people
- handling huge amounts of paperwork
- constantly communicating with external contacts
- producing and storing countless documents.

Good administrators are vital to all these processes. *Excellent* administrators – who think ahead, make useful suggestions or provide helpful advice, are superbly well organised and can be depended upon even in the worst crisis – are worth their weight in gold. They can recognise and even create business opportunities. They keep customers happy. They support their managers and colleagues. They can anticipate problems and help to avoid serious repercussions. Organisations which possess such administrators benefit through increased business, satisfied customers, effective managers and a focused workforce. So now you know just how important your role is – if you really take it seriously!

INFORMATION UPDATE

Several surveys have indicated the importance of planning and organisational skills for administrators. One report, by employment agency Gordon Yates, produced in association with *The Guardian*, identified that more than half the human resources managers surveyed believed that being proactive and self-prioritising had become increasingly important for secretarial and administrative staff. The top abilities identified were word-processing skills, but immediately behind this were organising, project management, prioritising, problem-solving and planning – as well as IT skills and Internet knowledge. Typing, audio and shorthand skills were relegated to the bottom of the list.

This trend is due to the increased number of people for whom administrators and secretaries have to work. There is a greater emphasis on being a member of a team. In a separate survey, teamwork was again emphasised – with 'a good attitude' being identified as the top skill of all. But you learned this in Unit 301, didn't you?

Element 303.1 Plan your work to meet requirements

Everyone makes plans. We plan where to go on holiday, which film to see, when to go shopping and what to buy. We make lists of essential items we mustn't forget to buy and of important jobs we mustn't forget to do. We discuss our plans with friends and relatives and may – or may not – take their advice. So why do we plan?

The aim of planning is to enable us to:

- clearly identify what we want to achieve – the overall **aim** or **goal**
- work out the steps we need to take to achieve the aim or goal – sometimes called **objectives**
- take the actions which will mean we achieve each objective – and therefore our aim – within the time limit or **deadline** (this usually means devising a **schedule** for each stage of the work).

Good planning also incorporates constantly comparing progress and adjusting our actions if a problem occurs. (See diagram opposite.)

Some plans are relatively easy to make and achieve. This is because:

- the task is a routine one we have done before – so experience helps us
- the task is simple and straightforward
- the task is easy to achieve in the time allowed
- we are in total control of every stage of the plan
- it is a job we enjoy doing.

Plans are far more difficult to achieve when:

- we are tackling something new and unknown
- the task is complex
- there is a tight deadline
- we are reliant on other people as part of the plan
- it is a tedious job or one we dislike
- things keep going wrong.

However, it is almost impossible to achieve anything if we just 'trust to luck' and don't plan at all! Think of a good plan as being like a journey. You may meet a few hold-ups on the way, and have to change your route and speed up once or twice, but at least with a plan you know where you are going, when you should be there and know when you've arrived.

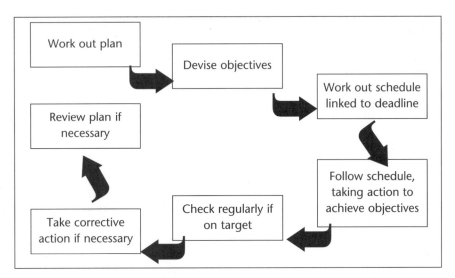

The stages of planning

Lucy has made the following personal plans. In each case identify:

- two or three objectives she could set in order to check regularly whether she is on target
- the actions she needs to take to achieve her goal in each case
- what sort of problems she could encounter
- what corrective action she could take if she met these problems
- which of her plans is likely to be the easiest to achieve, which the hardest – and why.

1 Lucy wants to go shopping in her lunch hour for two presents, two birthday cards and a new outfit.

2 Lucy's knowledge of the Internet is meagre and she wants to learn more as soon as possible. She has recently seen a short course advertised at her local college one evening a week.

3 She is going on holiday with three friends this summer. They have already made the booking and paid a deposit. She has agreed to act as 'treasurer' and to collect the money for the balance at monthly intervals from each person.

4 Lucy herself needs to save £100 a month to pay her share – but normally she finds saving very difficult.

5 Finally, Lucy wants to lose weight before she goes – she is hoping to lose about ten pounds.

Establishing requirements

If a plan is like a journey, then establishing requirements is the equivalent to studying a map and deciding the best route. The requirements should give you clear information on what you have to achieve and the best way of doing it.

For most administrative jobs this means identifying, for any particular task:

- the standard of work that is required
- the quantity of work that is involved
- the deadline for completion
- what working methods must be used.

You need all this information before you formulate a plan – as the details of the task will affect the time frame and the overall resources you need. It obviously takes longer – and requires different resources – to produce a high-quality fifty-page report for an important customer than it does to create a two-page information sheet for your colleagues. Key points to note are given below.

- The **standard** of work can affect not only *how* the task must be done but also *who* does it. You may have the ability to delegate some routine jobs to other people – or to ask for assistance from other members of your team. However, you are unwise to ask someone who is inexperienced to help if the task is particularly important, complex or must be produced to the highest possible standard – unless you are prepared to check their work every step of the way. Producing work to a very high standard can also affect the time required and the resources and specialist skills needed.
- The **quantity** of work involved can affect resource planning too. You may have to select and order in advance additional materials for a special or large-scale job – and schedule the proposed delivery date into your plans. Equally, if the task will take a long time to complete, this too must be scheduled into your plans.
- The final date for completion – the **deadline** – is critical. However, if the deadline is internal or if the job is less important, then the deadline may be negotiable in a crisis or if you have other priority jobs to complete. If the deadline is non-negotiable then you need to give the work top priority for completion.
- You also need to know the **working methods**. This means knowing, firstly, what action you can and cannot take in a particular situation. These should be defined in your organisational procedures – but beware, some may be 'custom and practice' or just unwritten rules in your firm! Secondly, you need to be able to identify the methods that will be most effective in helping you achieve your goals.

Do make certain that the requirements for the job are *clearly* agreed with the person who has given you the task. You are well advised, particularly for important jobs, to note the requirements in writing and send a copy to the originator. This prevents any disagreements or misunderstandings. This is extremely valuable if some of the people who give you jobs are notorious for giving instructions quickly, changing their minds at regular intervals, or two days later completely forgetting what they originally asked.

The consequences of failing to agree requirements in advance are fairly obvious. You are likely to waste a considerable amount of time, and materials, doing the wrong thing. You may also miss the target deadline if the work has to be redone. Quite apart from the inconvenience, everyone is likely to be annoyed and despondent if they have to start a job all over again or are blamed for something they think wasn't their fault because they were given imprecise information or ambiguous instructions. Whilst you may never totally solve this problem with someone who is particularly disorganised, at least you can minimise its likelihood and can prove, if necessary, that you did all you could to check what was needed at the start.

Finally, it is always better if you can develop a relationship with your colleagues where you are *consulted* about important jobs and where key requirements are *negotiated* rather than 'demanded'. You will be able to achieve this more easily if you have a reputation for knowing what you are doing and the expertise to think through the different aspects of an important job in order to make helpful suggestions. You will then find your comments are valued and you will have a greater input into the planning process than simply being the recipient of instructions. Some expert administrators recommend always trying to negotiate a longer deadline than you need and then always completing the job ahead of time. This way you will not only gain a reputation for reliability and efficiency, you will also find people who give you jobs won't keep asking you for regular progress checks. The downside is that you may be considered a wonder-person who can do anything with five minutes' notice!

Organisational procedures and policies

The longer you work in an organisation the more familiar you will be with its ways of operating – and to know what you can, and cannot do. For instance:

- You need 200 special covers printed for an important document. Can you just arrange this through the local print shop, have you an 'in-house' reprographics section which must do them, or do you have to organise this through a separate department after a budget transfer has been agreed?

- You want to order some additional stationery for a special job. Can you do this yourself, or do you have to refer it to a purchasing section? Do you have to use a specific supplier?

- Last night three burglars were apprehended trying to break into your office building. This morning the press are on the telephone asking for a statement. Can you talk to them – if not, who should?

- The travel agency telephones you to say that the cost of a one-day return rail ticket for your boss is higher than they thought as no cheap seats are available. Your boss is out of the office. Can you accept the higher priced ticket? If not, what must you do?

There are no 'model' answers to any of these questions. It all depends upon where you work and their policies and procedures. If you change employers, you are likely to find yourself operating to a whole new set of rules! As a new recruit in an organisation you might find yourself constantly checking with colleagues before you do anything new, just to make sure you don't overstep the boundaries and limits on the ways in which you can operate.

The golden rule is to *ask*, if ever you are in doubt. You should do this at the outset, when you are establishing the requirements for a particular job. If the person giving you the work cannot confirm your parameters, then check with another colleague. In a large organisation you should be able to refer to the office copies of any official policies and procedures to see what they say. Ask for help interpreting these if necessary, until you understand them.

Beware the unwritten rules!

As you saw in Unit 301, every organisation consists of individuals who have their own personal preferences and habits. In addition, the type of work carried out, the history of the organisation, the way the departments are structured and its size will all influence the 'culture' in operation. To take two extremes, one firm may be relatively relaxed about time-keeping, provided that people 'put in the hours', allow staff to work from home when they can and encourage informal dress and team socialising out of hours. You are likely to find this type of culture in a small firm comprising young, creative individuals. At the opposite end of the scale, a more 'traditional' organisation may check punctuality regularly, have a more formal dress code, more rules and regulations and a raft of procedures to be followed.

To add to the confusion, individual line managers will also affect the way particular offices or departments run. One manager may be an excellent delegator and encourage staff to take on new and interesting tasks. Another may be a little disorganised but very supportive and helpful in a crisis. A third may be more autocratic and like to retain control and check what is happening very closely.

For these reasons, when you change employer, department or even if you suddenly inherit a new boss, you may find that some of your methods of operating have to change as well. The best way to learn quickly in a new organisation or department is to find a mentor to advise you (see page 36 for more information). If your boss is new to the job, then there is a settling-in period for everyone – and during that time you will soon find out his or her preferences.

1 Either start a log of work you are asked to do by different people, or devise a simple form you can use to record the requirements of different tasks you are given. Another alternative is to confirm the requirements of each task in writing with a copy to the person who gave you the job, but this might be appropriate only for more involved or important jobs. Your log or form should contain the following information for each task or job:

- who gave you the job
- what you were asked to do
- the standard required
- the quantity required
- the deadline for completion
- any policies or procedures (formal or unwritten) which affected what you could do or how you could do it.

2 Supplement this information by obtaining a copy of policies or procedures which regularly affect the way in which you do your job. Personalise these by attaching a short note identifying exactly how they relate to your own job role and occasions when they have affected your working methods. If you work for a small firm with few formal policies and procedures, write a brief description of the actions you are allowed to take and those you are not. Ask your supervisor to countersign this to confirm you are correct.

Learning to prioritise and integrating new work

Prioritising sounds a simple matter of common sense. Obviously something that is urgent must be done before something that is not, and only the most naive administrator would think that jobs should be done in the order in which they arrive. However, the problem is made more difficult for many administrators because of the following factors:

- some jobs are urgent, some are important, some are both
- if you work for more than one person, each one may have different priorities
- during the day, more urgent or important items can arrive
- you may be constantly interrupted when you are trying to do an urgent or important job
- jobs that are not urgent one day can become urgent if left over to the next

- priorities can change with the next delivery of mail, fax or telephone call – or almost every time you access your e-mail
- computers, apart from helping us, can complicate life by producing even more information and paper to deal with
- every day, there are routine jobs which must be done somehow.

So – how do you take into consideration all these different factors, prioritise effectively and retain your sanity?

Hints and tips

a   Develop a system so you have *one* master list on which you write *every* job you need to do. An alternative is a master folder in which you put every job you need to do. The secret is to make sure there are no 'black holes' (such as pending files or desk drawers) into which you put jobs and then forget them!

b   When each job comes in, identify:

- whether it is both urgent and important (class 1)
- whether it is urgent (class 2)
- whether it is important (class 3)
- whether it is neither (class 4).

c   Always highlight any specific deadline dates or write or type them in red or bold.

d   At the outset, identify any jobs which may create particular problems because you require special resources, or cooperation from another person. 'Star' these jobs because it is likely they will take extra time. The same applies if the job is very complex or must be completed to an especially high standard.

e   At the start of each day, plan to tackle your jobs in 'class order' – i.e. class 1 first, class 2 second. If you have any 'starred' jobs, check resource issues or the availability of the people you need early. You then have a better chance of making progress during the course of the day.

f   Tick off completed jobs on your list as they are done.

g   Don't panic if you have to re-order your jobs because something else crops up. Simply slot the new job in at its obvious place after you've classified it.

h   At the end of the day, reschedule your jobs for the next day. Always make sure that you move forward jobs with specific deadline dates with the aim of completing each one at least a day in advance. This allows some room for manoeuvre if you hit a problem at the last minute. Remember, too, that some job classifications may change if you've put them off for a little while.

INFORMATION UPDATE

A key source of information for many people today is the Internet. If you know what you are doing you can access the information you need quickly and easily – and print it out for reference. The danger is that you amass more information than you know what to do with – some of it irrelevant. E-mail and intranets are other sources of information – and particularly useful if you need a hard copy of internal information in a hurry.

However, rather than simplify the way we work, computers have made things even worse, according to recruitment consultants OfficeTeam. According to a recent poll, 44 per cent of respondents believed that there was either the same amount of paper or more in their offices as a result of computerisation – and this gave them more to do in the course of an average working day, if only to file all the printouts that are made!

TEST YOUR KNOWLEDGE AND UNDERSTANDING

1 You have the following tasks on your 'to do' list. Today is Monday. Re-order these into a priority list.

a   Check my e-mail.

b   Respond to a customer enquiry received on Friday afternoon.

c   Order refreshments for a meeting to be held tomorrow afternoon.

d   Find out information on personal shredders as my supervisor wants to replace hers as soon as possible.

e   Book a flight ticket for my boss to visit a customer in Belfast on Thursday and return the same day.

f   Create a presentation file for my boss to take with him to Belfast, containing one of each of our latest brochures.

g   Log the rep's reports for last week on the computer system.

h   Get my filing up-to-date!

i   Note down messages from the answering machine which is used to log customer calls over the weekend.

j   Photocopy a five-page document needed for 10 people at tomorrow's meeting.

k   Send out an update information sheet that all the people at the meeting need to read in advance.

l   Fax a supplier with an urgent order for a new thermal binder. The old one broke last week and has been deemed irreparable.

m Print out the sales figures for last week which will have been downloaded on to the computer system by 2 pm and are required for a meeting on Wednesday.

n Type up three letters to customers my supervisor has handwritten.

2 For each of the following problems, identify (i) the action that should be taken by the administrator, and (ii) the action you would take in your particular organisation. If you can, compare your responses with other administrators working for other organisations to see how working methods often vary.

a Your boss is writing a job description for a new job and has asked you to obtain an example from your personnel office. Despite asking three times you have received nothing.

b You have delayed doing a job for three days and have planned to have a day off tomorrow. You now realise the deadline for finishing it is tomorrow at noon.

c You have three urgent jobs to finish and it is 3 pm. Despite this your supervisor keeps interrupting you with less urgent work.

d A 10-page document needs photocopying for tomorrow morning and the photocopier suddenly develops a serious fault.

e A member of the sales staff asks you to urgently find out a customer's credit rating but the extension number in accounts is constantly busy.

Planning objectives, working methods and schedules

Talking about planning is all very well, but to be able to plan effectively you need to know the best methods to use to formulate realistic plans and consistently achieve them.

Objectives

Think of objectives as the stepping stones to helping you achieve your overall plan. The main function of objectives is to 'break down' a complex plan into achievable parts. An example is shown below.

Marsha helps the Marketing Manager to prepare the monthly staff newsletter. The newsletter comes out on the first Monday of each month and the central reprographics section needs five days to produce it.

To help her to control this process, Marsha has made out a list of objectives she must achieve each month. Note that this could equally well be described as a **work schedule**.

```
STAFF NEWSLETTER

Objectives/work schedule
1        Identify articles and contributions required and list
         (to cover 4 × A4 pages)                              Day 1–7
2        Arrange artwork/photographs                          Day 10
3        Check received articles against list                 Day 17
4        Chase up outstanding articles/artwork                Day 18–20
5        Complete layout of draft newsletter                  Day 22
6        Send layout master to reprographics                  Day 24
7        Receive printed newsletter                           Day 29
8        Distribute newsletter                                Day 30
```

The benefits from listing each objective are as follows.

- Marsha – and her boss – know on which days she will be heavily involved with the newsletter. This means that she can schedule her other jobs around these days.
- Listing all the objectives means that no important part of the overall job has been omitted.
- The schedule has been devised so that she has some room for manoeuvre if any contributors let her down, or if there are unexpected problems.
- If Marsha is absent then it is easier for someone else to take over the job, as they can see at a glance what needs to be done and when.
- Marsha doesn't have to 'think through' what is required every month. Having done the job properly once, she can rely on this information every time.

Objectives, to be useful, should be 'SMART' (see page 211). This means they should be:

- Specific
- Measurable
- Achievable
- Realistic
- Time-constrained.

It is easy to check whether SMART objectives have been met. If you worked in telesales and had an objective of contacting 20 customers each day then this would be SMART. If you had an objective of telephoning as many people as you could, this would not. Neither would telephoning 500 people a day, as this is obviously not achievable, nor is it realistic.

Marsha's objectives are specific. She can check precisely whether she has achieved each one, so they are measurable. They are both achievable and realistic and in each case she has scheduled a day for completion so they are time-constrained. They will therefore assist her each month. If she achieves her objectives then the task will be done properly.

Working methods

Working methods are likely to be influenced by your own knowledge and skills, the equipment and other resources you have to hand, your previous experiences and whether you are doing a job alone or with help.

As a basic example, if you are asked to send a mailshot to 5000 customers then you have several options of working methods.

- If you have a large automated postroom then they will be able to deal with this easily, using automatic folding and inserting equipment.

- If you decide to use a specific Royal Mail service, you will have to meet their requirements on pre-sorting and despatch to benefit from special discounts.

- If you have no automated equipment then you will have to allow time to 'stuff' each envelope by hand – but it will quicker if you do the job as a team.

- If the postroom is only small, with a limited pre-set amount in the franking machine, they will probably only do the job if the envelopes arrive in batches.

- If you are on your own, then you will have to allow plenty of time for this – and may have to renegotiate the target figure of 5000 if this is not achievable. An alternative could be to subcontract the work to a specialist company.

If you are undertaking a totally new job, with no previous experience, do be prepared to revisit any first ideas you had on working methods if they are obviously *not* working. Never stick hard and fast to your first idea if it is patently obvious to everyone there is going to be a disaster! A useful technique for all large jobs you do infrequently is to review them afterwards, while the experience is still fresh in everyone's minds, and decide what can be improved. If you leave it until the next time you will have forgotten the problems – and will probably experience them all over again!

CHECK IT OUT!

The words 'method' and 'methodical' are not related by accident! A working method which produces results is one that has broken down the overall job into small tasks which, when completed one by one, have a positive result. Good examples of 'working methods' are well-written recipe books and technical manuals which show you how to carry out a new task step by step (preferably with illustrations!).

You will follow these better if you are well-organised, assemble your materials at the outset, read each stage carefully so you understand it and are *methodical* in your approach. For instance, you finish one task (and put away the remnants) before you start another.

Check how methodical you are. The next time you are following any type of step-by-step instruction guide, check your own attitude and approach. Do you read it thoroughly before you start? Do you have what you need to hand? Are you well organised from start to finish? Do you clear up as you go? Do you work out problems you encounter for yourself? And how successful is your normal 'end result'? The answers may be quite enlightening!

Schedules

Whereas a list of objectives or an action plan with dates is invaluable for a basic task, a more complex set of activities, which may use the same resources, requires a schedule. Many organisations routinely use complex schedules as part of their planning operations. Here are some examples:

- production companies which use machinery to produce goods in batches
- airlines which need to maximise use of their planes and minimise turn-round times
- tour companies which plan package holidays
- schools and colleges which devise timetables for students and courses.

Scheduling is often used when several people will be involved in different activities, or when the same people are needed in different places. You may have a format to use (see below) or have to devise your own. Golden rules include the following.

a Make certain you know exactly what *all* the requirements are before you start.

b Make a draft in pencil.

c Be prepared to make several alterations to fill in gaps or to reorganise things.

d Re-read your requirements after you've completed your draft.

e Check and recheck to make sure you can't make any improvements.

f If possible, ask someone to look over your schedule before you distribute it.

TEST YOUR KNOWLEDGE AND UNDERSTANDING

Try your hand at a simple schedule. Imagine you work in the human resources department and are involved with the interviews for a new Marketing and Sales Director. There are six candidates on the shortlist. The interviews and selection will take one day. All the candidates will be met in the morning at 9 am by both the MD and Chairman. They then have to meet the other directors, in teams of two, for a 30-minute talk with each pairing. In between these times they will be taken on a tour of the buildings. All the directors are to meet with the MD and Chairman at 12 noon to give feedback before the individual interviews take place in the afternoon. These start at 1 pm and each is scheduled to last 30 minutes.

Your first job is to schedule the meetings with the directors. The information you have received is as follows.

a The MD wants the meetings with the directors to start at 10 am.

b He is not concerned how the senior managers 'pair up'.

c There are six directors: Human Resources, Production, Finance, IT and Administration, Marketing and Sales (the present director), and the Company Secretary.

d You have been informed of the following, unalterable, commitments by the directors:

- The Finance Director has an important meeting between 11 and 11.30.
- The Production Director cannot become involved until 10.30 at the earliest.
- The IT and Administration Director has asked that you 'leave him out' between 10.30 and 11.
- The existing Marketing and Sales Director is free all morning.
- The Company Secretary has asked to start as late as possible.
- Your own boss, the HR Director, you know would prefer to be 'paired' with the IT and Admin Director.

1 Copy the following blank schedule and complete it to take account of the directors' requirements. You need to decide each pairing and put representative candidate letters (A–F) under the times when interviews will take place

2 Work out an interview schedule for the candidates for the day. Note that the names of the candidates are as follows but they must be interviewed in alphabetical order in the afternoon: Graham Brown, Zahira Choudrey, Marcel Tierney, Adam Appleby, Sarah Wilmot, John McNulty.

	10.00	10.15	10.30	10.45	11.00	11.15	11.30	11.45
Team 1								
Team 2								
Team 3								

Clearly informing relevant people

Any kind of plans you make, or schedules you prepare, will affect other people. It is not only courteous to keep these people informed, it is *essential* if you want their cooperation and if you don't want to have to redo much of your planning because you didn't allow for their own plans and their reactions to yours!

The priority occasions when you need to keep people informed are:

- when you need them to do a specific job you have scheduled
- when you need their attendance at a particular event
- when you need them to supply a resource you require
- when new information will affect the way a job is being done
- if any of the requirements of the job are altered
- if your plans suddenly change for some reason.

The three main aspects of communication to consider are:

- what to communicate
- who to tell
- how to give the information.

What to communicate

The worst possible thing you can do is to keep important information to yourself. If in doubt, communicate! It is better to give someone information they really do not need than to withhold crucial facts from someone who needs them.

Always remember that people need certain key information to be able to interpret a request accurately. This includes details of:

- **what** the job entails
- **why** it is being done
- **when** it must be completed
- **who** else is involved and **who** is coordinating the task
- **how** their contribution must be carried out
- **where** an event is being held or **where** work or resources must be sent.

Who to tell

The people to whom you are most likely to communicate plans, schedules and priorities include:

- your line manager – most likely your supervisor or team leader
- the person who asked you to do the work
- other staff in your team/department
- people from other teams or departments
- suppliers from outside your organisation.

Keeping your line manager informed is normally crucial, as he or she needs an overview of all the work currently being undertaken in the section or by the team. This doesn't mean that you have to involve your line manager at every step of the planning process, but it is courteous to provide information which may affect your line manager and/or any other staff for whom he or she is responsible.

The person who asked you to do the work (who may be your line manager) will often be involved with you regularly to check that there are no unforeseen problems or difficulties. This is the key person to ask if you have a query or concern about the schedule or in relation to acquiring any essential resources.

Other staff in your team/department can be accessed for information and advice, for assistance if you need help or to keep you updated if you are doing a job together. This is particularly important when a job requires the combined efforts of a group of people to be completed successfully. Equally, it is your job to keep your colleagues updated about anything you are doing which will affect them.

You may need to refer to other people in your organisation if you require information or a particular service. There may be specific procedures you have to follow to obtain these and much will depend upon whether the task you are asking them to do is large or small and whether the service can be provided freely or will be charged for. Asking someone for a telephone number and requesting an immediate copy of a 200-page report are slightly different – as is asking a manager to attend a short meeting and requesting a buffet for 60 guests!

Suppliers from outside your organisation can be suppliers of goods, services or information. It may be vital to obtain specific supplies for an urgent job – and you may have to make several enquiries or even 'lobby' a regular supplier to get what you need in time. You may have to obtain quotes and estimated completion dates for services which are contracted out, such as a coloured brochure from a print shop or the hire of a temp from an employment agency. You may contact suppliers for information or advice, such as your firm's solicitor or accountant. Always note down when you made the calls, who you spoke to and what the responses were. Also make a note in your diary to follow up on a specific date if no response has been received.

How to provide information

There are two aspects to this – the method of communication and the wording. Firstly, it is *always* better to put requests in writing whenever you can – either by e-mail or memo to an internal contact, or by fax or letter to an external contact. This is a much safer method of communication because the details are in writing and there is permanent proof that you made the request. Do remember, however, that if you send an internal e-mail you should check that each recipient has read the message – and telephone those who have not. It may be that someone is having problems with the computer system or is even away for a few days. You can't do this with an external e-mail. Instead, send a follow-up (or telephone) after a day or two if there has been no response.

If the situation is urgent or you need to negotiate a new deadline or stress a particular requirement, it may be better to speak to them anyway – either on the telephone or face-to-face. This option is also better if some part of the information is sensitive or confidential.

The style and wording of your communication should obviously be adjusted for different recipients. A letter to a customer or a supplier should be worded differently from an internal memo to another department. An e-mail to a manager should not have identical phraseology to the one to your friend in the next office!

A good tip is to check any communications which may upset other people's plans, or involve them in additional work at the last minute, to make certain that you have:

- apologised for any inconvenience
- asked for a favour and not demanded one as your right
- given sufficient detail for them to understand the request or reason for communicating
- expressed gratitude for their assistance or cooperation.

TEST YOUR KNOWLEDGE AND UNDERSTANDING

Your line manager, Sales Manager Martine Gregson, has informed you that three important overseas clients will be visiting your organisation next Monday afternoon. She wants you to organise the following.

a A chauffeur-driven limousine is required to pick them up from the airport at 12 noon. Their flight number is TK2083 from Qatar. The limousine should return to pick them up from their hotel at 8 am the following morning and return them to the airport.

b A vegetarian lunch will be provided for six people in his office at 1.30 pm.

c There will be a 20-minute presentation of your main products by Joe Marsh, one of your sales coordinators, to be followed by a technical presentation by Ken Havering, from technical services, to last another 20 minutes. The presentation should start at 2 pm and end about 3 pm.

d The presentation will be followed by a tour of the factory – and Martine needs the Production Manager, Bill Stevens, to be informed.

e If the MD is available, Martine would like him to meet the clients at some point during the afternoon, when he is free. The visitors would think it discourteous if they did not meet him, unless there was a very good reason, and Martine is worried that this could jeopardise negotiations.

f Information packs are to be collated by the marketing department and placed in special folders.

g Required from your legal department are four copies of your organisation's terms of business for overseas contracts. This must be the latest edition which was revised last month.

h Hotel accommodation should be reserved at the best hotel in the area for that evening plus a dinner reservation for six people.

Martine wants to hold a preliminary meeting in her office at 9 am on Wednesday to check the details. She would like Bill Stevens, Joe Marsh, Ken Havering and representatives from your marketing and legal departments to be present – as well as yourself. When the meeting starts she will expect you to give an update about how plans are progressing.

1 Write yourself a 'to-do' list which itemises the tasks you have to do *in the order in which you would do them*. Then, briefly, justify the decisions you made when you chose this order.

2 Decide how you would communicate with each person on your list and state why you have chosen this method.

3 Prepare *any two* written communications you would have to send and check your wording with your tutor or supervisor.

4 Which of the following developments would you (i) report to your line manager immediately, (ii) try to solve yourself (in which case state how), (iii) simply raise as queries at Thursday's meeting?

   a The marketing department want you to confirm exactly which 'special folders' you want – there are three types.

   b The Managing Director can only meet the visitors at 2 pm, which was the time scheduled for the presentation.

   c The Production Manager would prefer the tour to take place at 4 pm as he will be off-site until 3.30 pm.

   d The best hotel in the area is fully booked but you can reserve three suites at another hotel which is six miles away.

   e There is an important staff meeting being held in the legal department at 9 am but they can send someone over at 9.30 on Thursday if this would help.

   f The catering department want to know what drinks are required and whether a finger buffet or sandwiches are preferred.

   g Ken Havering tells you that unless someone mends his computer quickly there's no way he can produce slides using Powerpoint.

   h The limousine firm informs you that they often collect people from that flight and last week it was delayed by over two hours.

Organising resources

Resources were covered briefly on page 158, when the importance of deciding resource needs in relation to job requirements was discussed. The resources you need to have available and organised include:

- equipment – e.g. mailing equipment, photocopier, fax, computer
- materials – e.g. stationery items and computer supplies
- information – e.g. details you need to do the job, whether from your own files, internal documents, catalogues or brochures or external reference materials.

Equipment

The type of equipment you have available will affect how you do a particular job – as you saw on page 166. However, you also need to check that all the equipment is in working order, you have access to it when you need it, and you know how it operates.

If you do not have the appropriate equipment in your own department then you may be able to borrow it from another one – or you may have to 'outsource' the job to a specialist. Much depends upon cost. If you regularly need a particular type of equipment you don't possess then you may wish to talk to your boss about purchasing it. However, you are likely to have more success negotiating for a long-arm stapler than for a colour photocopier!

Materials

Ironically it is often specialist materials which are considered and ordered in advance and routine items that are overlooked. You may order 200 transparent wallets for a special presentation and then forget to check there is enough photocopying paper to cope with a large and unexpected print-run. It is useful to have a note of the type of stock levels held by your department, the typical delivery times and how often routine orders are sent. If you know that stocks are always running low towards the end of the month then you can allow for this in your plans.

Information

Some tasks are highly dependent upon information, but to be of any use this must be accurate and up to date. Useful tips include the following.

- Always check that you are using the latest version of documents or books which are produced regularly, such as price lists, reference books and timetables.
- Use the Internet where you can (e.g. for train times or Royal Mail information) – but check on your screen when the page was last updated.
- Make sure, when you access an office file, that no important documents are still waiting to be added to that file.
- Do not rely on verbal information unless you are *certain* that the person who told you is a totally reliable source.

EVIDENCE COLLECTION

For at least three tasks you undertake, prepare and complete a resources list. A suggested model is shown on page 176. Obtain your supervisor's signature to provide evidence that your claims are authentic.

The importance of flexibility

Changing priorities is seen by some administrators as the key facet that makes their work varied and interesting. For others it is just a nuisance. For a manager, there is nothing worse than an administrator who huffs, puffs and sighs in an emergency and who tries to continue doggedly with doing set jobs regardless of how events may change.

However, there is a limit. Even the most flexible administrator is likely to become harassed if priorities *keep* changing. At that point a sense of humour is invaluable. The key point is to respond positively to the situation.

RESOURCES LIST	
Task	
Date work received .... Deadline date	
Resource requirements identified	
Equipment:	
Materials:	
Information:	
Items specially ordered/obtained	**Method of acquisition**
Problems or difficulties encountered and how they were solved	
Candidate's signature	
Supervisor's signature	

Change can be caused by events or by people. Events relate to new information coming to light or new situations which no one can help. It is no use blaming anyone in these circumstances. People can cause change either because *they* notify you of changed events, or because they change their minds. Hopefully you will not work for someone who constantly makes you change your priorities because they never thought the job through properly in the first place. If this happens once it is perfectly excusable. If you are constantly inconvenienced because of someone else's lack of planning, then talk to your line manager in confidence.

You have the following jobs to do this morning in addition to routine tasks such as reading your e-mail and filing.

- Type a six-page report to send to a rep by e-mail by tonight.
- Photocopy three documents your boss needs to take with her to a lunchtime meeting.
- Check 20 urgent expense claim forms for finance.
- Prepare 10 overhead transparencies your boss needs for a presentation tomorrow. She wants to check through these this afternoon.

At 9 am you are told that one of the other administrators is off sick. She normally collects the post from the main office. On her desk are three faxes marked as urgent which haven't yet been sent.

At 10 am your boss informs you that the rep now has to visit the customer this afternoon and asks if you can send the report by lunchtime.

At 11 am she tells you she urgently needs a handwritten table to be keyed and photocopied for the lunchtime meeting.

At 12 am she tells you the meeting has been cancelled and asks if you have finished her overheads.

1 Last night you should have prepared a plan of action for today. In what order would you have scheduled the jobs you knew about – and how long would you have allowed for each one?

2 How would the absence of the other administrator have affected your plan?

3 What adjustments would you have made
   a at 10 am?   b at 11 am?

4 How would you have responded to your boss at 12 am? Bear in mind that the cancellation of the meeting is not her fault!

EVIDENCE COLLECTION

On a particularly hectic day, whilst the details are still fresh in your mind, write your own brief report which identifies the jobs you thought you had to do at the start, and how you had to alter your priorities. Try to identify why and how the urgency and importance of some jobs changed. If possible, include your original plan of action and then state the order in which you finally did the work. Give your reasons for leaving any jobs until the following day.

Again, it is better if your supervisor will sign your report to prove it is authentic – and that you coped with the situation positively.

Element 303.2 Carry out your work to meet requirements

Some people are incredibly well organised. They are very tidy by nature and write everything down. They are also extremely self-disciplined. Regardless of whether they like to do something or not, they do it. They use time effectively, are prepared to change their priorities, and always seem to get through their jobs without getting into a panic or becoming irritated with people around them.

Such paragons of virtue are rare, however. For most of us our organisational abilities are relatively good but can vary – depending upon our mood, the type of jobs we have to do and the pressure we are under on any particular day. However, a fundamental knowledge of the importance of organisational skills and how to acquire these can help anyone to improve. This element concentrates on helping you to make better use of your time and to improve your organisational abilities.

 INFORMATION UPDATE

Even if you have never heard of **displacement activities** it is highly likely you indulge in them every so often. These are jobs you like doing, rather than jobs you must do. The temptation is to fiddle with pleasant little jobs and put off starting another, more unpleasant job. You do this by convincing yourself that the pleasant little jobs must be done!

We all do this to some extent, especially in our private lives. We would probably rather have a shower than iron a shirt. In an office, many people would rather type a non-urgent letter than clear the filing. Try to avoid indulging in displacement activities too often – they can be dangerous as an important job can be put off just too long. The first step is to identify when you are undertaking a displacement activity and to be honest enough to admit why!

Making effective use of your time

Time management is not a new concept. Courses have been run on it and books have been written about it for many years. The aim of all these is to help people to make better use of their time – or, in the work situation, to help them to complete more jobs in an average working day. A good time manager is then left with more 'quality time' to spend with friends and family – because there is less need to work late or to take work home in an emergency.

Time is unique. It is the scarcest resource there is. We cannot make it, we cannot save it, we cannot change it. Each minute that passes has gone forever. It makes sense, therefore, to try to use time wisely. In your private life, this means finding time for the things you really want to do. At work, it means doing the job you are paid to do within the time available, in an organised way, to reduce stress and pressure on yourself and other people.

So – what are you paid to do? You are paid to fulfil a number of tasks in a day. You are not paid to stare out of the window, to chat to a friend on the telephone, to gossip to colleagues, to surf the Internet looking for cheap holidays, to e-mail friends, to arrive late back from lunch or to make such a mess of every job it takes twice as long as it should. This is common sense. However, if you think about the **key activities** which you are paid to carry out, this helps you with your prioritising. Some Americans take this to such an extreme they advocate that anything which doesn't improve your personal standing in the boss's eyes because it relates to the aims of the organisation should be rejected. However, this strategy is likely to do little for your relationships with your immediate colleagues!

However, the basic principle of applying questions such as 'Is this what I am paid to do?', 'Is this a top priority in my boss's eyes?' and 'Is this important to the organisation and the way it operates?' can help you to identify what is really important in your work and to use the time you have to the best advantage.

There are two other aspects to using your time effectively. The first is to reduce time-wasting. The second is related to being well organised – which is the focus of this element. Time-wasting is caused in a number of ways.

- Time-wasting is caused by you – especially on a bad day when you find it difficult to concentrate or have three boring jobs to do and can't stay focused. In this case you are more likely to chat to other people or distract yourself with displacement activities.
- Time-wasting is caused by other people – when they interrupt you (especially with something which isn't important) or distract you with their own problems.
- Time-wasting is caused by lack of planning – so you don't know which job to do when.
- Time-wasting is caused by lack of information – so you know what to do, but not how to do it.

Time-management techniques

There are dozens of different techniques to use – but not all of them will be right for *you*. The quiz at the end of this section may help you to identify how much work you need to do to improve your abilities. In the meantime, the following hints and tips should help you to make a start.

1   If you are often disorganised, think through a job before you start and decide the best order to do it in.
2   Plan collective tasks, such as saving all your photocopying so that you make one journey, and saving up e-mails and sending a batch at once.
3   Learn to do two jobs at once, such as sorting through your in-tray whilst your computer logs on.
4   Never 'play with paper'. If you have a piece of paper in your hand either action it, file it or throw it away. If it must be held back until another day, put it in a specific file, put a note in your diary and make sure you action it then.
5   Do a little job when you have only a few minutes to spare – rather than do nothing. It takes minutes to file a few papers, send an e-mail or fax, make one telephone call.
6   Identify your own productivity cycle. Are you more productive in the morning or do you only fully wake up in the afternoon? (Immediately after lunch is most people's 'low' point.) Force yourself to do the worst jobs when you are at your best in the day (or at the start of the day to get them out of the way) – then treat yourself to a coffee or soft drink as a reward.
7   Get jobs 'right first time' – attention to detail saves time as well as your reputation.
8   Use body language and assertiveness techniques to get rid of time-wasters. Keep your body position where it was – don't turn your body to face the person interrupting you, only your head – and keep your pen in your hand or your hands on your keyboard. Answer briefly (you can still be courteous). If the person is persistent then explain briefly that you are working to a tight schedule and daren't stop. Suggest you talk to them later – when it is more convenient.
9   If you have anyone to whom you can give work then learn to delegate *properly*. This means choosing proper jobs – not all the ones you dislike doing – and showing someone how to do it properly so he or she will learn from the experience.

 INFORMATION UPDATE

Many time-management courses focus on using specific recording systems – Filofax is an obvious example. A diary or shorthand notepad can work just as well. Another alternative is the range of electronic personal organisers on the market – Microsoft, Philips and 3-Com all make these. However, unless you have between £150 and £350 to spend you may decide to set your sights a little lower than that.

At the end of the day, most time-management systems focus on a daily task list. Time-management gurus suggest that tasks should be divided under key activities or your key areas of responsibility.

You can then flick from one to another to check all your 'areas' are up to date. This, of course, is quite possible to record on a sheet of paper or in a loose-leaf binder. The only thing you can't get the binder to do is to 'bleep' a reminder to you – which an electronic organiser can.

This all points to the fact that no matter what technique you use, if you can't list or log tasks or appointments accurately, if you don't check through what you have to do regularly, if you can never remember what day it is, let alone what you should be doing and when, then no amount of expensive gadgetry will help you.

TEST YOUR KNOWLEDGE AND UNDERSTANDING

1 Identify your own key activity areas or key areas of responsibility. Try to keep it to a maximum of seven or eight. Use the test 'What am I paid to do?' to help you to decide. Then try scheduling the tasks you must do each day under each area to see whether this technique works for you.

2 Do the quiz below to find out how good your own time-management is. While this quiz is not meant to be taken too seriously, it should help you to determine your own strengths and weaknesses.

Time management quiz

Identify your strengths and weaknesses by answering the following questions honestly.

1 How good a proofreader are you?
   a) Very good – it's rare you miss an error.
   b) Not so bad – providing the spellchecker is working.
   c) Pretty dire but your boss has got used to it.

2 You are constantly interrupted when you are trying to work. Do you find this
   a) infuriating?
   b) annoying?
   c) a relief?

3 You have three urgent jobs to do. Which would you do first, and *why*?
   a) The shortest?
   b) The hardest?
   c) The nicest?

4 You wonder where the time has gone.

   a) Rarely or never?
   b) Sometimes?
   c) Every day?

5 Your friend is getting married on a Thursday. You have the day off but will be working on Friday, after a very late night! Do you

   a) schedule some *very* routine and easy jobs for Friday morning?
   b) stagger in late, hung-over, and spend the morning telling everyone how it went?
   c) plan to ring in sick?

6 How quickly and accurately could you tell someone what you were doing last Thursday morning?

   a) In two seconds, when you've looked in your diary?
   b) In ten minutes, when you've given it some thought?
   c) Never – unless there was a special reason to remember.

7 On the 'chat and gossip' chart in your office, would people rank you

   a) low?
   b) middling – depends how interesting the gossip is?
   c) definitely top?

8 Hand on heart, how many private telephone calls do you make or receive each week at work?

   a) Very, very few – only if there's a crisis would someone ring you at work.
   b) Two or three.
   c) You've normally lost count by Wednesday.

9 How often do you have to return to your house or desk for something you've forgotten?

   a) Very occasionally – if you have a lot on your mind.
   b) Sometimes – if you're distracted, in a rush or talking to someone.
   c) Regularly – but normally you don't realise you've forgotten it until later.

10 How high is the pile of papers in your filing tray?

   a) It isn't – unless you've had to do a special job and got behind.
   b) It isn't – but only because you'd be in serious trouble if the filing got behind.
   c) You'd be able to tell if you could find the tray under the papers.

Score 2 points for every (a), 1 for every (b) and 0 for every (c).

16–20: You are very good at managing time and very well organised. You constantly focus on completing tasks above everything else. Don't forget to switch off sometimes, will you, and pay some attention to the people around you?

12–16: You are generally a good time manager. Spot one or two areas where you think you can improve. You'll find this useful on particularly busy or chaotic days.

8–12: A considerable amount of improvement is possible! Identify those techniques you could use which would make the most immediate difference.

4–8: You are like a miniature disaster waiting to happen. If your time management in your personal life is as bad as at work you'll miss out on a lot of opportunities. Unless you intend to improve you are advised to never ask your colleagues what you are really like to work with. They may tell you!

0–4: Ever thought of a career change? Preferably to something which needs little self-discipline, such as dog-walking.

Materials and methods!

You will save time without trying if you:

- have materials you need close to hand – and in working condition
- can find what you need quickly.

This seems very basic, but it is amazing how many people waste time because they are so disorganised – such as walking across the office to borrow a stapler, then having to visit the store cupboard because the stapler needs refilling. By this time the papers being stapled have become lost somewhere in a great muddle of papers, files and folders. When the papers are eventually found, there is nowhere to put them down, so they are stapled in mid-air (never a good idea) and consequently either the staple doesn't go in properly or is in the wrong place. Contrast this with the person who simply reaches out an arm for a filled stapler, places the papers on a relatively clear desk and staples them neatly and then starts the next job. If you then multiply the difference in time by about 100, you get some idea of the time you can waste in the average week if you are disorganised – and the standard of work you are likely to produce.

The amount of chaos and disorder in which you can happily exist at home is a personal matter, especially if you live on your own. If you live with your family or a partner then there may be some bickering but ultimately most people negotiate some sort of compromise everyone can live with. At work it is different. Your actions affect other people and if you are constantly borrowing other people's materials, leaving a mess wherever you go and forever mislaying important documents you will irritate – if not infuriate – almost everyone.

Some people, of course, are very neat and tidy – if this applies to you then you can probably safely skip this section. It is worth noting that if you are *fanatically* tidy and have all your possessions in a locked drawer labelled in capital letters with your name you will probably be equally annoying to work with!

Most people are somewhere in between. Generally, we are less tidy when we are rushed or busy than when we have plenty of time. yet once the clutter builds beyond a certain level we get irritable – especially if we can't find what we want.

CHECK IT OUT!

Read each of the following statements and give yourself one point every time you can honestly tick it as correct. Below a score of 7, urgent action is needed!

a   You have one of everything you need to do your job (e.g. notebook, calculator, stapler, stapler remover) and a set of pens and sharp pencils.

b   Everything you need is within arm's reach when you are working at your desk.

c   If you are right-handed your telephone is to your left and your pen to your right (vice versa if you are left-handed).

d   You have basic equipment on your desk for keeping odd items neatly (e.g. a pen holder for pens and pencils, a small tray for paperclips and so on).

e   All the papers you are dealing with are either in your 'in-tray', 'pending tray' 'out-tray' or 'filing tray' and only the ones you are working on are currently on your desk.

f   You are a great believer in 'a place for everything and everything in its place'.

g   You always try to leave a clear desk when you finish each evening. (You might like to note this is considered doubly important on a Friday night as it helps you to start the new week in the right frame of mind!)

h   If you work in another area (such as by the photocopier or near the fax machine) you always tidy up when you have finished the job.

i   Your top drawer is the place where you keep small items. You cleaned it out during the last three months to make sure it wasn't full of dust and paperclips at the bottom.

j   You routinely pre-sort papers due for filing – so you only have to look through a few documents if you need a recent document in a hurry.

k   If you have more than two or three papers on a topic, you start a folder and clearly label this, so you can find what you need quickly.

l   You can find what you put away quickly.

Minimising waste

If you are relatively neat and tidy – and if you *think* before you take action – then you are likely to be a far more environmentally friendly person than if you do not! This is because you are likely to waste fewer materials – especially paper. Many organisations are now committed to recycling paper – and sometimes printer cartridges too – but the amount usually to be found in the waste bins of the average firm is still incredible – especially near printers and photocopiers.

Quite apart from the environment, all materials cost money. Therefore if you are constantly wasting paper, losing things or breaking them you will cost your company far more money to employ you than someone who does not. Hopefully you don't have the type of controls which were in place some years ago – when one resources manager insisted that everyone who wanted a new pen had to bring the old one to her to prove it had run out! However, with a bit of consideration and thought you can *personally* help to reduce your company's stationery budget for the next year.

You will use fewer materials and reduce waste and costs if you routinely:

- check documents carefully before you print or photocopy them
- take a test print or a test photocopy before starting a long print run – as a double-check
- only take the exact number you need – not a 'few more' for spare
- photocopy 'back-to-back' to save paper whenever you can
- store paper so that it is kept flat, in a cool place and away from direct heat, sunlight or damp
- use the correct type and weight of paper for the job you are doing and the equipment you are using
- check if your paper is marked with an arrow or 'this way up' – paper inserted upside down can create paper jams
- 'fan' paper properly before placing it in a paper tray
- convert unavoidable waste paper (such as obsolete letter headings) into scrap pads
- put tops back on to pens when you have used them (especially highlighters and marker pens which 'dry out' if you do not)
- always replace the top tightly on a bottle of correcting fluid
- reuse envelopes to send internal mail
- reuse brown file folders by reversing them
- always separate transparent folders and polypockets from old documents which are being thrown away so that they can be reused
- relabel and reuse A4 ring binders, lever arch and box files whenever they are still in good condition.

The key test is this: If it were *your* business and *you* were paying for everything used, would your working habits be just the same or very different? This simple measure should tell you all you need to know!

Dealing with confidential information

The higher you rise in an organisation, the more likely it is that you will deal with sensitive or confidential information. The types of information which usually need to be treated as confidential are:

- personal details about staff or customers (such as medical or financial history)
- financial information about the company (including proposed pay increases)
- future selling prospects for the organisation and key contacts
- disagreements between staff, between unions and management or between the organisation and a customer
- possible legal actions being taken against the organisation.

However, every organisation is different and wherever you work there will be specific information that relates to your job which you have to treat as confidential.

The first question to ask yourself is whether you are good at keeping a secret. It is said that the second you tell another person something, it is no longer secret. If you have difficulty keeping an interesting item of gossip or news to yourself then you have three choices.

- Write it down in a locked diary at home, where no-one can read it.
- Divulge it *only* to your partner – or lifelong friend – who has nothing to do with your job, your organisation or any of your colleagues.
- Find another job!

Fundamentally, you can destroy someone's trust in you in seconds, by repeating something without thinking. Yet this trust can take years to rebuild. So never, ever, be tempted to risk everything just for the opportunity of impressing someone for five minutes.

Of course, even if you never say a word to anyone about a confidential matter, there are other things you can do which are just as careless – and can enable unauthorised people to see sensitive information. The golden rules, therefore, when you are dealing with confidential information are as follows.

1 Keep such material in a folder and, unless you are referring to it, make sure it is safely stored in a locked cabinet
2 Send any copies of confidential material in sealed envelopes, clearly labelled as 'confidential'.
3 Photocopy such material yourself – and check the glass afterwards to make sure you haven't inadvertently left the original on the machine.

4   Shred spare or spoiled documents – don't just put them in the wastebin.

5   Keep such material well away from public offices and reception areas.

6   Keep another document on your desk which you can use to 'cover' a confidential document if you are unexpectedly interrupted.

If you regularly prepare confidential documents on a computer, then you should have your desk and computer positioned well away from the door and any major traffic routes. Your computer should be sited so that people approaching your desk see the *back* of it first. You can also lobby your boss to buy you a special 'flat' screen which is only visible when the screen is directly facing. In addition it is useful to have a few other strategies up your sleeve, such as:

- setting your screen saver to start very quickly if you fail to press a key (do this by clicking on Start, then Settings, then Control Panel, Display and Screensaver – and shortening the time)

- saving and closing the file if you leave your desk for any reason

- switching off your VDU only *or* turning the brightness down on your screen

- having another document open in another window and switching to this one if someone comes over to talk to you.

Finally, do remember that if you back-up confidential documents on a floppy disk this should also be locked away, together with any hard copies.

CHECK IT OUT!

Identify the type of work which is considered sensitive or confidential in your organisation and make a list of the special measures you already take to prevent its disclosure.

Now assess your own work area in relation to confidentiality. Is it easy or difficult to 'manage' confidential information because of the position of your desk or workstation? How easy is it for someone to read your computer screen? Have you access to a lockable filingcabinet? Where would you store a floppy disk containing sensitive information? If you have difficulties maintaining confidentiality because of the physical siting of your desk and your lack of access to secure storage areas, perhaps now is a good time to discuss this with your supervisor or team leader.

Changing work plans – and still meeting requirements

Work plans may change for two main reasons.

- A situation becomes more urgent, so a deadline moves *forwards.*
- Other urgent tasks intervene, so a deadline has to be moved *backwards.*

You have already learned about the importance of flexibility in the last unit – and why you should *expect* plans to change, rather than resent such changes.

However, it is not unnatural to feel frustration if a change means a major alteration, rather than a minor adjustment. If you have to reschedule the whole job, from start to finish, then this is going to take you longer than if you simply need to make two telephone calls to solve a problem.

The critical points to bear in mind are the following.

- If your boss wants a deadline changed, there is little you can do. This is especially true if the deadline has been changed to fit in with an important customer who does a lot of business with your company or because of a VIP who means a lot to your boss's boss!

- If you cannot meet a deadline, then the sooner you tell people the better (see below).

- If you cannot meet a deadline then you need to assess the reason honestly. To what extent are you to blame? If the reason is unavoidable because of outside factors, then you can explain this quite easily. If it is because you forgot something or failed to plan properly then you are best to own up and be honest. *Never* try to cover it up. Then do your level best not to repeat the mistake.

- *Negotiating* a new agreement is different from 'telling' someone what you can do. Negotiating implies give and take on both sides. You may have to be prepared to alter your own priorities to accommodate someone else if you are responsible for the problem in the first place. However, don't be pushed into negotiating a new deadline which is impossible to meet. Otherwise you'll let the same people down all over again.

From a practical point of view, you now need to make all the relevant alterations in your diary, on planners and schedules to make sure the *new* deadline won't be missed.

Notifying other people

Changes to plans affect everyone, not just you. It is sensible – if not basic courtesy – to keep people informed. Don't expect people to have to keep checking with you that everything is going to plan. Sometimes your boss may appreciate a regular update or 'progress report' – especially if you are doing an important job – if only for reassurance.

Changes and amendments should be notified to everyone who may be even remotely affected. This enables them to amend *their* plans to allow for the alterations and prevents people being unnecessarily inconvenienced.

One of the worst pieces of news you may have to give to anyone is the fact that you can no longer meet the deadline you originally agreed. Even the most reasonable person may suddenly have a rather unpleasant reaction when faced with this piece of information – *especially* if it is an important job and *even more especially* if they have only received this titbit of information at the last minute. There is no book in the world which can tell you how to successfully manoeuvre yourself out of this situation unscathed. So – two golden rules:

1 Give critically important jobs top priority. Defer other deadlines before you try to move these.

2 If something important even *looks* as if it may go 'pear-shaped' then let those who would be most affected know *immediately*. This allows some remedial action to be taken quickly – such as:

- your boss stepping in and giving a few instructions to get things moving again on schedule
- other people being drafted in to help if you are short of manpower
- other jobs being taken off you, so you can concentrate on what is most important.

Conflicting instructions and priorities

Difficulties over prioritising are likely to occur more frequently if you regularly receive jobs either from, or involving, a variety of different people. Problems can occur, for instance:

- if you receive jobs from several different people, all of whom have their own different priorities
- if you regularly have dealings with other departments or sections in your organisation
- if some of your tasks are related to dealing with external contacts, such as customers or suppliers
- if you are often reliant on information from other people – and if this information can often change your priorities.

The problem is that you are the only person with the 'whole' picture of your job. Each other person only knows their own individual link with you. Therefore it is up to you to inform people who are affected if a particular piece of work becomes more urgent or if there are difficulties doing a task to time.

Again there are a variety of people who you may need to contact:

- your line manager (e.g. your supervisor or team leader)
- the person who gave you the work
- other members of your department/team
- specialists internal to your organisation
- specialists external to your organisation.

Your line manager

As a general rule, your own line manager is the obvious person to go to if you feel you have an unsolvable problem or difficulty. For instance, if you are overwhelmed with more urgent jobs than you can cope with in the time available, see your supervisor or team leader *immediately* – whilst there is time to give you extra help. Don't moan and groan – simply explain the problem and make any positive suggestions you can. If no extra help is available, ask your line manager to advise you as to which jobs should be done first.

Another matter to refer to your line manager is a bottleneck somewhere else in the organisation or office, which is affecting your ability to do your work. However, in this case only use your supervisor or team leader as a last resort – *after* you have tried everything you can to solve the problem yourself.

The person who asked for the work to be done

You should see the person who asked you to do the work if there is any problem meeting a deadline or if any updated information you have received has significantly affected the job. If several people give you work and all of them are giving you urgent jobs and expecting you to work miracles, then there are various strategies you can try.

- Explain the problem to each of them and ask them to decide between them which jobs must be done first.
- Send each one a memo or an e-mail with a list of the jobs you have to do, so they see the problem you are facing.
- Discuss the problem with your own supervisor and ask him or her to intervene.
- Erect a whiteboard in your office with ten or twelve numbered slots. Ask each person to write their job in a numbered priority slot. If all the top slots are full and another task comes in, the person giving you that work will have to see one of the other people involved to arrange to 'queue jump'. You simply follow the list on the board each day.

As you have already seen, the golden rule is to keep those people who give you work informed if there are any changes – and consult them in good time – not when it is too late to do anything about a problem!

Other staff members

Other members of your team or department will appreciate being 'kept in the picture' – especially if a crisis is about to occur which will involve them in extra work or in changing their own priorities. However, don't panic everyone needlessly – otherwise you will gain a reputation for simply being a nuisance. *Consulting* them calmly, however, and asking for suggestions can often mean you can find a solution to a possible problem more easily than you thought.

Internal specialists

Specialists internal to your organisation can include anyone across the organisation who you have asked for information, advice or to provide a service – from your health and safety officer to a member of the cleaning staff. Never assume that because someone is 'lower' in the organisation than yourself or does a more menial job than you that they deserve less courtesy or consideration. In more than one organisation, an administrator has learned the hard way that catering staff, cleaners and caretakers who feel they are treated with little respect have some novel ways of ignoring urgent requests from those they dislike!

A useful hint if you are desperate for urgent action from another department is to 'walk the job'. Often your first contact may be by telephone or e-mail, but if you are getting a poor response then turning up in person can often generate action – if only to get rid of you! Be pleasant – but be persistent.

Equally, if they are desperate for information or action from you, which you cannot now provide by the agreed date, turning up in person to apologise and negotiate an extension may take some courage, but will be respected. It is also more difficult to argue with someone face-to-face than on the telephone or by e-mail – so you may find you reach agreement more easily than you first thought.

External specialists

Specialists from outside your organisation will also appreciate being kept informed if deadlines change. In this case you cannot even start to consider how your actions will affect their own work – but early notification, courtesy, an apology and *honesty* will help your cause.

Whatever you do, when you have negotiated a new agreement, do everything in your power to make sure you honour this – particularly if you are dealing with a customer who could easily take his or her business elsewhere.

A final point. It is quite one thing notifying people *occasionally* and for very good reason, that you cannot meet a pre-arranged deadline. It is quite another to have to do it regularly. In that case, something is badly wrong with your planning, isn't it?

TEST YOUR KNOWLEDGE AND UNDERSTANDING

1 You promised a customer that you would send him some literature and a quotation he requested by first-class post tonight. At 3 pm, you find that there are no brochures left in the store cupboard and the sales representative who promised to give you the quotation has left on an urgent call. He is also scheduled to be away from the office for the next two days. What action would you take, and why?

2 Refer back to the exercise on page 166, when you were preparing a folder for an overseas customer. If the customer contacted you today and informed you that he had decided to visit your company to collect it instead – but a week earlier than planned – you would have several people to notify.

   a List all the people or departments you would need to inform.

   b You know that the company photographer will have to complete the work a week earlier than originally planned. You also know he is rather difficult to deal with. Draft a short but persuasive e-mail asking for his assistance.

3 Your boss, the sales manager, suddenly realises that she has three appointments booked next Monday afternoon. She is due to attend a meeting with the sales director, she has two designers coming to see her with some new ideas, and now she has been asked to give

a presentation to an important client. She has already muttered that she could ask the deputy sales manager to go to the meeting and then get him to see the designers afterwards, but can't make up her mind. Her other alternative is to ask the deputy to do the presentation for her instead.

a What are the dangers of being indecisive in this situation?

b List the actions you would have to take if she decided to do the presentation herself.

c For which course of action do you think her deputy will need most warning – and why?

4 Your colleague, Shahida, is normally very efficient and reliable, but has been working under pressure recently preparing for the annual sales conference. Today, when you arrive, there is panic. Shahida has telephoned to say she has a heavy cold and doesn't expect to be in work for the rest of the week. No-one has a clue how far she has progressed with arrangements and whether she has actually booked the venue and sent out the invitations according to schedule.

a What actions could you take to try to rescue the situation?

b What actions should be taken to prevent this type of situation recurring in the future?

5 Your finance office has a deadline of 6 December for expense claims if they are to be paid before Christmas. You have been involved in a considerable amount of additional work and suddenly realise – at 5 pm on 5 December – that you had completely forgotten to check any of the expenses which you locked in your filing cabinet for safety. Normally the task takes you at least two days – and you have several other urgent jobs to do tomorrow. Who would you notify about your predicament, and what would you suggest?

EVIDENCE COLLECTION

You must prove that you can liaise with *three* of the following types of people over changes to work plans:

- your line manager (e.g. your supervisor or team leader)
- the person who gave you the work
- other members of your department/team
- specialists internal to your organisation
- specialists external to your organisation.

To do this, keep a copy of any written documents you send which inform other people about any changes to deadlines (either bringing these forward or renegotiating a new date because of an unforeseen delay). Personalise these by adding your own comments saying why the change had to be made and the other people you informed.

If you negotiate any new agreements verbally, write your own account of what you did. If the agreement was negotiated with someone internal to your organisation, you can ask them to verify this by counter-signing your account.

Finally, you can ask your line manager or other people who give you work to provide witness testimony to prove that you always give them reasonable notice if you cannot meet their deadlines or if plans or priorities change, and are willing to make positive suggestions when negotiating a new deadline.

Element 303.3 Develop your own work

In this part of the unit, the focus is now on *you*, rather than the way you plan and organise your work. How much time do you spend planning what *you* are going to do in future and taking steps to make your ideas reality? When did you last take a long, hard look at what you can do now, what you *could* need to do in the future, what you really *should* do – and linked all these to your personal interests and future ambitions?

The importance of thinking about yourself and your work

In this context, thinking about yourself means taking some time out to consider:

- where you are now
- where you would like to be (or what you would like to do) in the future
- what you have to do to 'bridge the gap'.

If you are young, you may consider that you will bridge the gap almost automatically as you get older and more experienced. However, some people bridge the gap quicker than others (at any age) and some never bridge it at all! Why? What is the difference between these people?

People who bridge the gap quickly normally have a plan. They know what they want to achieve and plan how to do this. That doesn't mean being ruthlessly ambitious or abandoning your social life forever. It means having a good 'work/life balance', moving upwards and onwards – and enjoying yourself at the same time. People who never bridge the gap rarely have a plan. They drift along and let life and circumstances dictate what they do and when. They are never in control of their own lives. This may sound idyllic – for the short term, but over the long term it means you are unlikely to reach your full potential – either in terms of your job, your personal life or your earnings. So, we will assume you want to get somewhere in life and need to plan to achieve this. In this case, your plan relates to your own personal development.

A final point. This is your plan – not your supervisor's, tutor's, parent's or partner's. Plans devised by other people are rarely successful – as you are trying to fulfil someone else's hopes and dreams, not your own. Therefore, if you associate planning for the future with what other people want you to do, now is the time to step into the driving seat and decide for yourself what you want to do in the future, and how you are going to achieve this. If you are successful, then the rewards can be considerable.

Obtaining the benefits

Three criteria have usually to be fulfilled for the maximum benefits to be achieved from any personal development programme.

1   *You* select what you want to do and how you are going to do it. The activities you choose link to your own personal aims and preferences and you are therefore keen and highly motivated at the outset.

2   The 'learning experience' is enjoyable. It doesn't matter whether this is work shadowing someone else, attending a course for one day or six months or experimenting on your home computer. If learning gives you a 'buzz' and makes you feel good, then you will want to carry on.

3   You feel a sense of achievement and a greater sense of purpose than before. This may be because you have acquired a new and valuable skill or because you can now do different jobs or the same job better or because you can now move on to higher things. You get a pay-off for learning.

Of course, in a perfect world, all learning would be like this, but unfortunately we all suffer from negative learning experiences every so often. Try not to let these put you off. If you can try to keep an open-minded approach to learning and take advantage of all the opportunities around you, every day, to learn new things then you are half-way there. Being the owner of an enquiring mind and enjoying trying new things is often the first step to lifelong success!

 INFORMATION UPDATE

In a survey carried out by OfficeTeam looking at the Office of the Future in 2005, a survey of 150 executives of large companies gave the following results:

- 65 per cent thought that admin assistants would become more involved in project management
- 81 per cent thought that admin assistants would be very involved in Internet research
- 71 per cent considered that desktop publishing would be important
- 55 per cent thought that administrators would be very involved with helpdesk or computer training and assistance
- 31 per cent expected their administrators to be involved in Web page development
- 65 per cent expected that the word 'coordinator' would become part of virtually every administrator's title.

For the results of another survey, see page 208.

1 Think back to something you really enjoyed learning.

   a What made you choose this activity?
   b What was there about the 'learning' that you particularly enjoyed?
   c How did you feel afterwards?
   d How useful has this skill or attribute been to you?

2 Identify one thing you would like to learn that you think would really add value to your life now.

   a Why have you selected this?
   b What alternative ways are there in which you could learn this?
   c Are there any barriers stopping you doing this?
   d If so, how could you overcome them?

3 What is your general attitude to learning?

   a Do you associate it with school and think it's a nuisance?
   b Do you learn easily but only if you are enjoying it?
   c Do you welcome the opportunity and think everything you learn has benefit sometime?

4 Apart from winning a fortune, what would you really like to achieve over the next three to five years? What would you like to be doing by then – and what will you need to do to make this dream come true?

Identifying your strengths and weaknesses

If you positively welcome opportunities to learn then you have already identified one of your strengths! We live in a rapidly changing world where technological developments are constantly affecting the way we live and work. If you didn't learn anything new then you would end up being as outdated as the dinosaur.

Identifying your current strengths and weaknesses enables you to establish your position at the moment. You need to do this before you decide in which direction you need to move (and at what speed!) so that you are in a different situation in the future. Note that at this stage this exercise is just for you! You don't have to share it with anyone if you don't want to.

Key areas for analysis

As you are working in Administration, there are several important job skills you need. However, life isn't just about work. You can develop personal attributes as well which will bring benefits in both your work and social life.

The starting point is to undertake a personal self-evaluation of your skills, knowledge and abilities at this moment. To help, read the chart below and decide how you 'rate' for each category. You can, of course, add to these categories if you can think of other areas which are relevant to you or your job.

Key areas for analysis		
(Score yourself from 1 to 5 in each of the following areas, where 1 is excellent and 5 is poor.)		
Skills, knowledge and abilities	Areas to think about	Score
Organisational skills	Ability to plan, find items you have stored easily, meet deadlines, prioritise, juggle several jobs effectively, coordinate a job and keep people informed, keep in control of tasks.	
IT skills	Ability to use PC software including word-processing, spreadsheets, databases and presentation packages effectively. Ability to use Internet, e-mails and on-line services appropriately; undertake Web page design/website maintenance; use hardware such as scanners and Zip drives.	
Information-handling and decision-making	Finding and researching information, checking information, storage and retrieval systems (manual and electronic), extracting and summarising, obtaining and analysing appropriate facts to solve problems and make decisions.	
Communication skills	Good written English and oral skills, telephone manner, face-to-face communications. Assertive, good listener, appropriate use of body language. Negotiating skills.	➡

Skills, knowledge and abilities	Areas to think about	Score
Self-management	Self-disciplined, takes responsibility for own actions and learns from mistakes, committed to giving best in a situation, knows self and reactions to stress/negativity from others, schedules time for personal interests, values own appearance and fitness.	
Money management	Able to plan and *stick* to a budget. Financially self-aware. Good financial knowledge/judgement.	
Numeracy skills	Can carry out basic numeric operations with/without a calculator, can understand basic statistics and trends on a financial document.	
Interpersonal skills	Sociable and approachable. Good conversational and listening skills plus ability to start conversation with strangers. Genuine liking for other people and can identify different needs. Cooperative and helpful.	
Organisational awareness	Understands aims and needs of employer. Can explain products and services accurately. Knows structure and responsibilities of managers. Sensitive to culture and 'office politics'.	
Personal skills	Displays positive attitude, uses initiative. Self-confident with belief in own ability, flexible, open-minded.	
Miscellaneous attributes	Additional skills – such as good recall of facts and names, eye for detail, technical expertise (e.g. with camcorders or audio-visual equipment), knowledge of foreign language, good with graphics, adept at training junior staff, good general knowledge.	

Objectively analysing your strengths and weaknesses

If you are relatively self-confident and a natural optimist with a positive attitude, then you will probably look at your scores in the table above and feel quite good about yourself. Even if you recognise there are several areas for development you may see these as an interesting challenge and real opportunities for the future.

If you lack self-confidence and are naturally pessimistic then you may feel quite overwhelmed by the whole exercise and want to give up now. You may feel that you couldn't possibly improve in all these areas so it's not worth even thinking about it.

Firstly, do bear in mind that no one is expecting you to be perfect in every area or to know all there is to know. No matter how experienced or skilled you become, there's always something new to learn! That's part of the interesting things in life. Secondly, the old maxim that a long journey begins with just a small step holds very true here. What you need are small 'bite-sized chunks' to start with. Setting goals which need a long-term commitment or which amount to a massive challenge may be good for some people, but most ordinary mortals prefer to take things at a steadier pace.

It is therefore important to start by *objectively* analysing your strengths and weaknesses to help you to think about your plans over the short term. Do this by referring back to your results when you analysed your key areas. Then:

1   Separate the different areas in the left-hand column into those which are your strongest and weakest. Put these in a list from one to eleven.

2   Identify which areas are the most important to you *now* in your current job. Put three stars against these areas, two stars against those which are next and one star against those which don't matter at all to you at the moment.

3   Now study the 'three star' areas which are your worst – and select *one* improvement zone in each area.

4   Finally, put this list into a priority order – this time with the improvement you would *most like to do* at the top.

Keep your list safely. You will need to refer to it again later in this unit.

Feedback from other people

At the moment, your analysis of your strengths and weaknesses is purely personal. However, our picture of ourselves doesn't just come from self-evaluation; it is also formed by the feedback we receive from other people. Psychologists argue that our identities have to undergo constant reconstruction if we are to develop and grow and that feedback at work helps us to continually redefine ourselves and move onwards. Comfort yourself with that the next time you are not particularly happy with feedback you have received!

We receive feedback constantly, mainly on an informal basis. If someone says 'Thanks, you've done a great job' then you may feel good about yourself all day. If someone else finds fault with your work and criticises all your ideas – especially in public – then you may feel very low and despondent. If you have a fiery nature you may be tempted to give them a piece of your mind –

though this can be extremely risky if the speaker is your supervisor or employer!

On other occasions the feedback may be formal. This will occur if you have an appraisal interview at work, when your performance since your last appraisal is discussed. Alternatively, if you are an Advanced Modern Apprentice you are likely to be having periodic reviews. In either of these sessions, you should be given the opportunity to do most of the talking – and to focus on what you are trying to achieve and how to do this. At an appraisal, your manager will want to look at how your skills and abilities can be developed to benefit the organisation which currently employs you. You may have grander ideas – but only the most enlightened employers will help you to prepare to move onwards and outwards!

Generally, any formal feedback or review session should be structured. This means that you know what will be discussed, preferably in advance. You should be given time to prepare for the session and to think about what you would like to discuss. You can expect the following items to be on the agenda:

1 A discussion about your performance since the last review or appraisal will include what you have learned since then and how well you have met any targets which were agreed last time.

2 There will be a discussion about your current performance, how well you are coping in your job and your future role. If you have any worries or anxieties, now is the time to mention them. Equally, if you have already decided areas you would like to develop or new responsibilities you would like to take on, you should say so.

3 Once your future role is agreed, you can discuss new targets or areas for development and the time-scale over which these can be achieved

4 The next step is to decide what training you need and when. There are many different ways in which you can learn new skills and attributes as you will see on page 213. A discussion about *how* you can achieve your goals is therefore relevant at this point.

5 Finally, you can expect your supervisor or manager to draw a few conclusions from this session. If you have been interested and positive about your future development then you will have made more of an impact than if you have not. Therefore, not only is your past performance assessed but also your attitude to your own development. If this is consistently negative, don't be surprised if your employer thinks you are completely uninterested in furthering your career.

Good and bad feedback sessions

Good feedback sessions are obviously those when you receive praise! However, a positive feedback session can also take place when you are criticised – if the person giving you feedback is skilled at doing this and finishes on a 'high note' – and if you are prepared to accept the comments as constructive and said to help you. The danger, of course, is that once you are criticised (particularly if this is done tactlessly) you brood about this and ignore everything else! Try to avoid doing this. Keep the information in perspective. This will be easier to do if you like and respect those who are giving you feedback and if you think that they are particularly good at their job. In this case, consider their feedback as valuable information which will help you to form a more accurate picture of yourself and your abilities.

The very worst feedback or appraisal sessions, of course, are those which completely demotivate the staff who attend them. If a manager takes some perverted pleasure in terrifying his or her staff or subjecting them to an inquisition, then this not only defeats the whole object of appraisals and reviews but will actually *lower* overall performance in the organisation. No one can do a good job if they loathe or fear their boss – so if you ever find yourself in this situation you are best advised to find alternative employment as soon as you can.

What is far more likely to happen is that a *well-meaning* or kindly manager or supervisor gives negative feedback rather insensitively. This won't matter too much if you have a thick skin and if criticisms rarely faze you. If will matter very much if you lack self-confidence anyway and such a session completely demoralises you.

Dealing with feedback constructively

It is important to regard all feedback constructively and objectively. This includes praise you receive as well as criticism. Some people will use praise as a method of getting you to do more work or even to impress you. We are all apt to be 'suckers' if someone flatters us. For instance, a representative might 'charm' you into typing up an urgent four-page report because he claims that no-one else is as fast, accurate and reliable in the whole place! Try to take praise from these people with a pinch of salt. Enjoy the moment and then forget it!

Praise from someone you respect and admire should be taken seriously and savoured – especially if you have worked hard to earn it. But again, a word of warning. Don't let it go to your head and tempt you to become complacent from now on. You have been praised for your *current* way of working – don't change this or the feedback may be different next time. And don't brag about it to other people – or your insensitivity to the needs of others may be on the list too!

Negative feedback is different. If one small aspect of your work has been criticised and you know, in your heart of hearts, that the criticism is justified, try to accept it and learn from it. No one is perfect, so consider this a 'learning experience' and try to alter your way of working to take on board the comments.

More difficult to deal with are very negative comments, particularly if you feel these are unjustified. In that case, you are advised to deal with these according to the Dos and Don'ts given in the table below.

The Dos and Don'ts of handling negative feedback
Do
Work out in advance how sensitive you are. Do you over-react to even the *slightest* adverse remark and respond aggressively or defensively? Or do you have the hide of an elephant so your boss thinks issues must be spelt out before you will understand them? In either case, try to 'stand back' from the situation and view it as if you were another person. This will help you get a better perspective.
Remember most people find it very difficult to criticise, even harder to do it tactfully! Allow your boss or supervisor a bit of space for mistakes!
Ask for a specific example if the criticism is vague (e.g. 'you don't meet deadlines') – e.g. 'I'm sorry, I wasn't aware of that. Can you give me an example of a time when I have let you down and not met a deadline?'
Give in gracefully if the criticism is proven (e.g. 'I asked you to prepare the slides for the sales conference and had to ask someone else to help because you hadn't done them').
Point out the facts if the situation was out of your control (e.g. 'If you remember, I could have done the slides but was told the sales report needed completing urgently and I had to drop everything else until this was done'). However, do expect your boss to counter by asking what steps you took to remedy any potential problem yourself! Very few situations are *completely* outside your control.
View the session positively afterwards. If no one ever pointed out our shortcomings, we'd be awful people to know and would never be prepared to improve ourselves!
Don't
Turn the session into a personal argument. Focus completely on the issue that is being discussed and avoid a personality clash. This means never attacking the person giving you feedback (e.g. 'You're always picking on me').
Put the blame onto anyone else. It will simply sound like you're making excuses and aren't a very loyal colleague if you're response is 'Well, Chloe let me down *again* and Mark promised to do it but didn't.' If it genuinely was someone else's fault be generous, (e.g. 'Unfortunately we were all very busy that week and it was overlooked').
Focus on the negative – look for positive solutions and ask for ideas, such as 'This problem is constantly occurring, I'd be grateful for advice on how I can handle it in future.' ➡

Lose your temper or say anything you will later regret. If the situation is going from bad to worse, ask for time to consider the points that have been made and arrange to continue the meeting later.

Brood afterwards or become unduly upset. If your boss is constantly critical ask for a meeting yourself – after you have recovered from the experience – and point out how upset you were. You could point out that you may be able to learn quicker from your mistakes if you didn't feel you were constantly doing wrong.

Shrug it off and ignore everything you have been told! It is very rare that there is no truth, ever, in something someone says to you. In a quiet moment, ask yourself how accurate it is likely to be and what you can do about it.

TEST YOUR KNOWLEDGE AND UNDERSTANDING

In each of the following scenarios a feedback session has taken place and, in some cases, has gone wrong. As office administrator, working directly below the team leader, what would you do in each case to either improve or rescue the situation? Discuss your ideas with your supervisor or tutor.

1   You have noticed that the proofreading skills of one of your colleagues leave much to be desired. At her appraisal interview, your team leader raises this with her, and tells her, quite simply, that she either improves them or looks for another job. She comes to you for help – in tears.

2   The latest recruit in your firm has been labelled as 'idle' by virtually everyone. He puts in the minimum effort and, if anything goes wrong, blames other people for not supporting him. He has recently been chastised for his lack of team commitment but instead of taking this to heart has started 'rubbishing' your team leader in front of your colleagues and several customers and saying what a joke she is.

3   Your friend gets highly indignant over the mildest rebuke. Yesterday she was told by a colleague (rather tactlessly) that there was a much easier way of formatting a spreadsheet she was working on – and took great offence. The result is that neither of them are speaking and the atmosphere in the office is awful.

4   At a feedback session, your office manager – who you normally like and respect – criticises your punctuality. You know this is not your strong point but you are always willing to work late when required – so you think this compensates. On several occasions lately

you have worked until 7 pm for no extra pay or time off. He doesn't agree and argues your presence is just as critical at 9 am as 5 pm. You leave the interview feeling you are undervalued and not appreciated and vowing never to work late again.

5 Your 16-year-old trainee administrator likes her social life even more than her pay packet. On several mornings she has been late after a hectic night out, and has been fit for nothing until after lunch. Last Thursday was her friend's birthday and you weren't a bit surprised when she rang in 'sick' on Friday. You suspect this may be the start of a new trend. The office manager promised to have a word with her during her next review – which she had this morning. It is fairly obvious from her attitude that nothing has been said and you suspect that, as he's fairly soft-hearted with very young staff, he lost his nerve at the last minute.

6 Following a departmental reorganisation you find yourself working for a new boss who asks you to attend an informal feedback session. He has all your records on his desk and accuses you of failing to fulfil your potential. He argues you are bright, capable of developing yourself considerably, but seem to be happy to take it easy and stay in your present job for life. You are simultaneously flattered and annoyed as you feel there is little evidence for this statement. He gives you a week to think about it and then asks you to meet with him again to discuss the matter further.

EVIDENCE COLLECTION

As part of your evidence for this unit, you have to obtain (or ask for) feedback from both the following

- your line manager (which can include your team leader or supervisor)
- other members of your team.

In addition, your feedback should include a discussion about:

- what you are doing well
- areas you could improve
- what new responsibilities you could take on.

Your formal feedback sessions will be easier to document than informal sessions. Your evidence from these is likely to include:

- your formal reviews, if you are an AMA
- any formal appraisal documents.

If you have other, regular discussions with your line manager which are not documented, you can either discuss these with your assessor or ask your line manager for witness testimony or (probably the best option) write a brief account of the discussion, sign it and ask your line manager to counter-sign it for authenticity.

Informal feedback is less easier to document. You are not supposed to be trying to create a confessional document in which you list all the criticisms anyone has ever made about you! The best way is to copy out and complete a self-evaluation form such as the one opposite, which gives space for feedback evidence without detailing any personal criticisms. If you ask your line manager or a member of your team to sign this, and then add your own comments to your assessor, this will suffice as evidence.

New areas for future development

The eventual aim of any self-evaluation or feedback should be to help to move you forwards by identifying areas for future development. This includes identifying possible new responsibilities with a clear focus upon what you hope to do in the future.

Do bear in mind that your own ideas for future development and your line manager's ideas may not be the same. This is particularly the case if you work in a very small firm where opportunities for promotion are extremely limited. In this case, your line manager may actually prefer you to stay exactly as you are! However, this is not in your own best interests in the long term, so whereas we can sympathise with these feelings, you need to learn a strategy to quietly work round them. One trick is to look at new areas of work or methods of working being undertaken in your firm and ask to become involved in one or two which interest you the most.

In a large organisation, with considerable potential for development and promotion, you are likely to be actively encouraged to identify and achieve your future career goals. However, you can reasonably expect your boss to link *your* career goals with prospects in that organisation – rather than counsel you on how you can achieve opportunities elsewhere. Indeed you might find it rather upsetting if you *were* advised that you would do better if you worked somewhere else!

So, in summary, you can realistically expect to have to keep your own counsel on your eventual career goals, unless you work for a very enlightened and magnanimous organisation – or have a mentor who is personally interested in helping you to develop and achieve your career goals.

This does not, however, prevent you from agreeing the best areas you can develop which will help you to achieve both your short-term objectives now and your long-term goals for the future.

SELF-EVALUATION FORM

Name .... Date ....

This form is a summary of my strengths and areas for future development at the date above from my own personal analysis and from feedback received from other people.

STRENGTHS

The following are the areas of work I am doing well:

Evidence:

Personal evaluation (date:)
Feedback evidence (from/date):

AREAS FOR IMPROVEMENT

The following are areas I have currently targeted to improve:

Evidence:

Personal evaluation (date:)
Feedback evidence (from/date):

NEW RESPONSIBILITIES

New responsibilities it has been agreed I may undertake in the future are:

Evidence:

Personal evaluation (date:)
Feedback evidence (from/date):

Name ....

(Title) ....

FEEDBACK EVIDENCE CONFIRMED BY

(Name)...

(Title) ....

INFORMATION UPDATE

One American survey looked at identifying which skills would be the most valuable in the future by investigating how jobs are changing to meet future changes and challenges. According to the experts, the key work areas and skills required by future administrators will include the following:

- total mastery of computer software and a good knowledge of IT – this *includes* total proficiency with the Internet and World Wide Web and learning as much as you can about your company's website

- terrific verbal and written communication skills – to maximise your on-line communications and your customer networks

- the ability to produce professional presentations through software packages such as Powerpoint and to set up and use the accompanying technology, such as data projectors

- excellent organisational and coordination skills so that you can arrange conferences and meetings which never go wrong

- wonderful customer service skills that encourage all your customers (both internal and external) to return to you again and again – this means honing your skills of tact, diplomacy and negotiation to deal with even the trickiest of clients

- the ability to manage quite a complicated project from start to finish without losing concentration at any stage – and delivering to the agreed deadline

- the skill and aptitude to cope with change positively and proactively by suggesting good ideas and taking on board new developments which will help your organisation

- broadening your administrative skills to encompass areas such as accounting and budget management, interviewing, office management and web site management.

CHECK IT OUT!

Study the list of potential development areas above and decide:
- which interest you the most
- which develop skills you already have
- which link most to your current employer's aims and objectives
- which link most to your own career plans.

Then decide which areas you would pursue first, second and third, if you were given free choice.

Developing competencies

As an extension of your English skills consider the following. The word 'competencies' can relate to either a verb or a noun. To be competent means to be able to perform a task to the required standard again and again. A 'competency' is a sub-set of a skill. For instance, if you were learning word-processing there are several sub-skills or competencies involved such as:

- switching on/logging on to the package
- learning how to input and edit text
- keyboarding skills
- proofreading skills
- formatting and displaying text effectively
- saving or printing your work.

You can, of course, break these skills down still further to include many different operations you need to undertake to become totally proficient.

Competencies are easier to achieve than the whole skill. In fact, in many cases you may not need to learn *every* single competency to know enough to do your job well. You may word process documents every day, but you may never be asked to create an index, import graphics or set up macros – even though the package can do all this. What is far more important is that you can undertake the operations you need for your job and know *how* to investigate and master other functions you may need to do in the future.

Breaking down tasks into competencies makes them more achievable. It is easier, for instance, to identify that this week you will master headers and footers than to say that this week you will learn how to use Word 2000 from start to finish!

It is recommended that you concentrate immediately on competencies you need in your current job – but also have a 'weather eye' on competencies you could also develop to help your future prospects.

 INFORMATION UPDATE

All NVQ standards are based upon identifying the major tasks undertaken at work in a particular occupational area and breaking these down into competencies. You can therefore look at the Administration level 3 scheme and see how this works.

- Research has shown that all administrators need to carry out the tasks relating to the mandatory units.
- Administrators may use a paper-based filing system *or* a database – but not all administrators do both of these. Hence these are the Option A units. ➡️

- Administrators may do a range of tasks which are covered by the Option B units – but certainly not all of these. It will depend upon the focus of your job.

Within the elements for each unit you will find the competencies listed under the national standard of work. Therefore, simply by undertaking your Administration level 3 award, you are obtaining evidence that you are competent in these areas.

Identifying other competencies

You can identify these relatively easily. Start by listing all the main tasks you carry out as part of your job at present, such as word-processing, mail handling, photocopying, sending e-mails – particularly if some of the jobs you do are not part of your Administration level 3 scheme. A useful starting point here is to study your job description, and see if this helps. Look back at the chart listing 'Key areas for analysis' on page 198 for other ideas.

Next think about jobs where you know *just about* enough but don't feel totally confident or skilled in that area. An example might be taking notes for a meeting if you are always worried you will miss something important or if your boss always has to improve your final document.

Finally, think about jobs you have been asked to do or know it would be helpful if you could do – if you had the skills.

From your list, select between four and six tasks where you know it would help you *and your employer* if you improved your abilities. Now put these into priority order and use the list as a basis for a discussion with your line manager.

Break down large tasks into separate competencies. For instance, if you were taking notes at a meeting you could split this task into two basic areas:

- accurate note-taking at the meeting itself
- the ability to produce well-written minutes or summaries of the discussion.

If your written English skills are rather dubious, you may have to add this to your list as well!

Learning plans

At the beginning of this element, you looked at assessing where you are now in terms of the skills, knowledge and abilities you possess. Since then you have looked at skills you would like to develop, linked to your career goals. A learning plan brings all this together. In effect, it is a map of the learning journey you are planning to take.

Like all plans and journeys, it may go awry for a variety of reasons, but if you haven't got a plan at all then you would be unlikely to recognise this – let alone make appropriate adjustments.

Rather than seeing developing a learning plan as a chore, try to see it as time when you focus completely upon yourself. Your plan should be a summary of what you want to achieve, broken down into objectives, to help you develop the competencies you have just identified.

Before you start this process, it is important to remember that a good objective is said to be SMART – as you saw on page 165.

Let's look at this in more detail in relation to your own objectives.

- **Specific** means that your objective relates to a stated activity – rather than something general. Therefore: 'learn how to use a presentation package' is specific whereas 'learn more about business software' is not.

- **Measurable** means that you can include 'measures' whereby you can check if you have achieved your objective. Therefore, our objective above could be extended to say 'to learn how to undertake basic operations on a presentation package effectively, including the creation of usable slides with imported graphics'.

- **Achievable** and **realistic** are related in that you are specifying objectives which are a 'natural' next step from your current skills. These also relate to **time-constrained**. You should put a realistic date for achieving your goal. Saying you will learn all about presentation packages in the next 24 hours is neither achievable or realistic, even though it is time-constrained!

Hints and tips on deciding new goals and setting objectives

1 Don't get carried away and list so many things to learn and do that you terrify yourself. Decide on your priorities at the moment.

2 Don't include over-ambitious ideas which you will really struggle to achieve or have no interest in. Equally, do set your sights high enough so that you have to work to achieve them – otherwise you will feel no sense of satisfaction afterwards.

3 Write your objective by starting with a verb (e.g. learn, input, practise, create, sell) – say what you will actually *do*. Then focus on the exact activity.

4 Think about a standard of performance that is acceptable. For instance, in the example above, the words 'effectively' and 'usable' both denote the standard you wish to achieve.

5 Match the time limit to the objective. The more complex the task or skills (or the greater the number of competencies involved) the longer you will need. You might learn to use a presentation package in a month or two but you'd need much longer to learn a foreign language!

6   Think carefully about your time limits. Long-term goals mean that you need persistence and commitment to keep going. However, too short a time may be unachievable and unrealistic, especially if you are busy with your job. Don't forget you need some time for yourself to keep your work/life balance.

7   Remember you will also need more time if you have no skills in a particular area at the moment and are starting from scratch.

8   Pencil in your time limits until you know how much support you will have from your employer or what opportunities there will be to learn in your workplace (see page 213).

TEST YOUR KNOWLEDGE AND UNDERSTANDING

Your new trainee administrator, Nadia, is studying for her level 2 award and is puzzling over writing her objectives. Your team leader has told her to base these on a discussion at a recent review when it was agreed she should:

- improve her keyboarding skills so that she could input text more quickly and accurately
- improve her spelling – which is pretty atrocious
- smarten herself up when she is working on reception
- improve her telephone technique and message-taking skills.

Nadia has been scribbling all morning. Eventually she asks for your help and passes you the following sheet.

1   How would you convert the five objectives she has written into SMART objectives?

2   What competencies do you think are involved with taking accurate telephone messages?

Discuss your ideas with your tutor or supervisor.

Nadia's draft objectives	
Objective	Achievement date
1 Learn to use a keyboard better	Next month
2 Learn to spell some new words every day	On-going
3 Wear my best clothes on reception and comb my hair first	Tomorrow
4 Answer the telephone promptly when it rings and don't say 'Hi'	Tomorrow
5 Write down messages properly	Next week

Learning activities

There are two points you need to note about learning activities.

- These days there are dozens of different ways in which you can learn something new.
- The type of learning which suits you may not suit your colleagues, and vice versa.

Types of learning activity

Traditionally, all learning was designated as 'on-the-job' or 'off-the-job'. The first related to activities learned in the workplace and the second to those undertaken at a different place. Today the division is becoming more blurred. Where, for instance, would you categorise e-learning that you undertook partly at home and partly at work? Where would you place learning more about the Internet if you did this at work and also had access to it at home – but could go on a course at college as well?

A list of some of the options available is given in the table on page 215, but your main task here is to realise:

- the advantages and disadvantages of different locations
- the types of activities which are best learned in certain ways
- where to find out more information relating to your workplace or your area.

Finally, you can link all this to the best ways of learning *for you* that are dealt with later.

Advantages and disadvantages of different locations

The main *advantages* with learning in your own workplace are:

- you learn the operations which are undertaken in your organisation
- you can focus on the specific equipment that is used (e.g. the type of photocopier or telephone system) and/or software
- you learn how to undertake activities in the way your employer prefers
- you can schedule this learning to take place when it is most convenient
- it is cost-effective for your employer – so is often more readily agreed to.

The *disadvantages* with learning in your own workplace are:

- your employer may have little interest in helping you to develop wider skills for use elsewhere
- the person showing you may have few skills at coaching or training you
- you may be distracted if work is still going on all around you
- if you are busy, you may 'keep putting it off' – and never do it.

The *advantages* with learning somewhere else include:

- you can concentrate on what you are learning
- you meet new people – and exchange ideas
- your trainer/tutor is (it is to be hoped) an expert
- you can use specialist equipment not found at work
- you can often achieve nationally recognised qualifications which will help you to obtain promotion or a better job elsewhere in the future.

The *disadvantages* with learning somewhere else include:

- several aspects of the course may not be particularly relevant
- the pace of learning might be too fast or slow for you
- the course may be held over a number of weeks or months – and this needs commitment
- you may be pressurised to 'miss a week' if you are busy at work
- if you take time off during the day, you will have work to catch up on your return, if you attend during a weekend or evening, you may find this very tiring
- you may have no chance to put your new skills into practice – because your boss doesn't really know what you are doing!

Types of activities, and where they are best learned

Just as you are most unlikely to have to stop work one morning while your line manager lectures all the staff on new health and safety legislation, you are just as unlikely to practice customer service training with your company's database at college.

This is because job-related tasks, especially those involving skill acquisition using specific equipment or software, are best undertaken at your workplace. This is why most retail stores, banks and building societies open slightly later one day a week to enable staff training to take place. Equally, if one of the staff wants to work towards a nationally recognised qualification it may be necessary for that person to attend a course of study – though not essential.

The table on page 215 summarises the main choices you have in relation to *where* you learn. It also gives examples of the types of activities often undertaken when you learn in this way. This is useful when you start to consider how best you learn.

The location and type of learning activities

At college

- Nationally accredited qualifications, such as NVQs, AVCEs, GCSE and A levels, skill qualifications in IT, professional and management qualifications in areas such as Personnel, Accounting, Supervisory Management. May be offered part-time (day, day/evening or evening only), on Saturdays or on a flexible basis.
- Activities may include: practical skills training, taught sessions, answering written questions, undertaking case studies, assignments or projects.

Private training organisations

- Short specialist courses held in city centres or hotels linked to specific topics; e.g. Organising meetings and conferences, Assertiveness skills, Time management etc.
- Activities may include: taught sessions, group discussions, workshops, case study analysis.

Outdoor venues

- Many organisations offer team-building events which are sports or activity related.
- Activities may include: orienteering, problem-solving, abseiling, paintball-throwing, sailing.

At own or another workplace

- Secondment (where you work elsewhere for a short time) or work shadowing (where you 'watch and learn' in another environment).
- Activities may include: using different equipment, applying existing knowledge to following different procedures, understanding the work of a different office, department or the job role of someone else.

Training area at own workplace

- Training on job related equipment and software, learning and practising customer service techniques or call handling, understanding basic regulations and requirements (e.g. induction or fire training).
- Activities may include: trainer input, learning from computer-based packages or manuals, simulations and role-plays.

In own job location

- Specific instruction on a job-related operation (e.g. maintenance of new photocopier, use of new software package), observation, coaching by an experienced colleague.
- Activities may include: practising new skill under supervision, undertaking new tasks with support of adviser or mentor.

INFORMATION UPDATE

The government has supported several new initiatives to encourage learning, such as the Campaign for Learning and National Training Awards. You can find out about some of its latest ideas on the website www.campaign-for-learning.org.uk. Amongst the items currently featured is the result of a national survey on e-learning which shows that two-thirds of e-learning takes place at work and a third at home, mainly on the Internet or through the use of CDs. Quite simply, e-learning means using materials distributed over the Internet or a staff intranet so that learning can take place anywhere – sitting at your desk, at home or even when travelling! However, e-learners do value support, such as through an on-line coach, or at least *some* contact with a human being! If you are interested in how e-learning works, try the website www.click2learn.com to see how some organisations have incorporated e-learning into learning and induction programmes for staff.

Another initiative – for those who are not employed or who don't have employer support – is Learn Direct. Their database has information on more than 575,000 courses all over the country. If you are interested in finding out more, you can telephone their free helpline on 0800 100 900 or access their website – www.ufiltd.co.uk. Finally, if accessing a course is not your problem, but paying for it might be, then find out about Career Development Loans by ringing their helpline on 0800 585 505 or check out the website of www.open.gov.uk/dfee/loans.

CHECK IT OUT!

The options available to you will depend upon where you live and where you work. If you live in a remote area – thirty miles from the nearest college – the idea of travelling there one night a week in winter to learn something new may have little appeal. If you live in a large town or city you are unlikely to have this type of dilemma.

Equally, if you work for a large organisation, you may find there is a specialist training section which helps to support employees who want to learn a variety of skills or undertake different activities.

1 Obtain a prospectus or list of courses from your local college and check what is on offer that interests you.
2 If you work for a large organisation, visit your training or staff development office and find out what opportunities are available.

3　Obtain a copy of your local newspaper and see whether any events are advertised. Alternatively, visit your local or college library and look at the training journals you will find there.

4　If you have Internet access, access any of the websites shown above to find out more about e-learning or Learn Direct.

5　Visit the Smart Secretary website at www.smartinformation.com which gives details of how you can progress your admin career and find training courses to suit you. An alternative, if you want to go on a specific course, is to use a search engine which understands plain English, such as www.askjeeves.co.uk, and type in your request.

Learning that suits *YOU*

Many experts have studied how people learn. These studies have resulted in learners being encouraged to recognise their own learning styles or patterns. In this way, they can more easily identify the type of activities which would suit them best when they are learning.

One authority, Kolb, devised a test in which a learner can measure his or her strengths and weaknesses in relation to the four stages of the learning process. This involves:

- learning about the theory
- deciding how best to put it into practice
- doing the activity
- analysing your own performance afterwards – i.e. what did you do well and what do you still need to improve.

Kolb thought that very few people are good at all these stages.

In a study undertaken by Honey and Mumford, another 'test' was devised (which is probably in your college library). This also suggests that learners have preferences and can learn better in some ways than others. Interestingly, if both studies are put together the same type of conclusions emerge. These are shown in the table on the next page.

Kolb styles	Honey and Mumford styles	Common elements
Converger	Pragmatist	Prefer practical activities to theory; undertaking tasks rather than dealing with people.
Accommodator	Activist	Prefer taking action to talking about it, like new challenges and experiences. May take risks and gets bored easily.
Diverger	Reflector	Thoughtful, can see situations from various perspectives. Good listeners. May have many interests and be interested in dealing with people.
Assimilator	Theorist	Enjoy pursuing ideas and theories to acquire new knowledge. Like academic studies and reading.

This may help you realise why some people in an office would love the thought of an outward-bound team-building course and others might faint at the very idea! On *any* course (or in any lesson), however, an experienced tutor or trainer will 'mix' the activities so that everyone can benefit. This is easier with some topics than others. If you are learning word-processing, you will be involved *more* in a practical activity and less with the theory. The opposite would be true if you were studying a theoretical subject, such as law. However, quite apart from their personality, you are apt to favour tutors and trainers who help you to learn in the way you prefer (either accidentally or deliberately). You will also enjoy courses more if they focus on your style of learning.

Even allowing for different learning styles, other differences affect our ability to learn, such as:

- the time of day – are you a morning lark or a night owl?
- how comfortable you are (temperature, ventilation, type of seating and so on) – but do note it is possible to be *too* comfortable!
- the mood you are in
- whether you feel fit, healthy and raring to go or tired, lethargic or even quite ill.

It is also relevant to ask how disciplined you are about learning. Do you actively concentrate and take notes without being prompted? Do you seriously try to put theory into practice? Do you complete tasks you have been given to time? In other words – are you taking responsibility for your own development or do you think this is the tutor or trainer's job?

TEST YOUR KNOWLEDGE AND UNDERSTANDING

1 You have just attended a customer service course with your colleagues. This involved:

- being taught about the importance of customer service and the legal rights of your customers
- role-play, when you had to act out being a customer and/or customer service adviser
- a workshop, when you discussed how the main principles you had learned could be applied in your department
- the production (on your own) of a brief customer service handbook for staff summarising the essentials.

Brad loved the role-play – even though he 'guessed' some of his legal answers – probably because he was bored during the taught session at the beginning. Phillipa enjoyed producing the handbook but hid during the role-play. Kieran was full of ideas during the workshop and was good at looking at problems from the customer's point of view. Tahir was fascinated during the taught session and quite enjoyed producing the handbook, but didn't like either of the practical sessions.

a How would you categorise each of your colleagues, according to their preferred learning style?

b Which activity would you have enjoyed the most and which the least?

c Which learning style do you think this implies you prefer?

2 You have now been asked to learn more about Internet technology. Which type of activity do you think would be best for you, and why?

a A short college course which mixes theory and practice.

b Buying a manual and working through this on your home computer.

c Work-shadowing experts in your computer department, watching them and then using the technology under their supervision.

d A one-day course in a hotel learning about the theory of Internet technology and its potential in the future.

3 As you may realise, not all courses (and not all lessons) can be devised especially to appeal to your own, individual learning style. What strategies could you use, therefore, to retain your interest during the parts of the session which least appealed to you? Discuss your ideas with your tutor or supervisor.

4 You are actively trying to improve your ability to remember names. You have been advised that one way to do this is to keep using someone's name in conversation when you first meet them. Another strategy is to remember a personal characteristic of theirs and link it to the name – or to link them with someone famous. The aim is to form an 'association' in your mind that will help your recall. Try this yourself, not just with names but with anything you are trying to remember, and see how successful you are!

Reviewing your plan

Long-term plans should always operate on a cyclical basis. That is, they virtually go on forever because you are involved in the same monitoring process you saw in the first element of this unit (see the diagram on page 157).

All plans have to be monitored, otherwise they can go so badly adrift they become virtually useless. Remember we likened your self-development to going on a journey. You would hardly set off on a new journey in reality without checking where you were in relation to your final destination every so often, would you?

Plans for developing competencies and achieving objectives can go wrong for a number of reasons.

* You may have been too ambitious and listed too many objectives.
* You may have been under-ambitious, mastered all your objectives but don't really feel as if you've achieved anything at all.
* You may have been unable to achieve an objective through reasons outside your control, such as illness, family problems or new responsibilities at work.
* Your circumstances may have changed so that your objectives have changed, for instance if you change your job. In that case your priorities may have to be adjusted.

It is important that you review your current achievements and revise your plan regularly in consultation with someone who will help to motivate you and make appropriate suggestions to guide you. You need someone who is interested in you and whose suggestions you respect. However, no matter who you talk to, remember that your learning plan belongs to *you* and, as we said at the start of this element, whilst advice is useful the final decision about your future is up to you.

EVIDENCE COLLECTION

You now need to create your own learning plan that you can discuss with your tutor, trainer or assessor. If your employer or college has a model for this then you can obviously use that (you may find that in some organisations this is called a Training Plan). An alternative design you can use is shown below.

You can customise this by creating it on your word-processor, using the suggested headings, and then completing each of the sections. You can obviously adjust any headings or sections you want if this would help you to create a more usable document in your own workplace.

PERSONAL LEARNING PLAN

Name .... Organisation .... Job title ....

Date created .... Review date .... Career goal ....

AREAS IDENTIFIED FOR DEVELOPMENT

Required competency	Objective(s)	Learning method	Target achievement date	Result at review date

Comments (Use this space to record additional or unexpected learning opportunities you have undertaken since your last review; reasons for good or poor progress in achieving an objective; or additional competencies you wish to achieve in the future).

Your signature: .... Reviewer's signature ....

EVIDENCE COLLECTION

When you have completed your learning plan, agree your first review date. You may have an overall review with your line manager, team leader or supervisor, but you may wish to bring to this meeting any other feedback reports you have received on your progress from other relevant specialists. These could include your college tutor, a trainer or staff development specialist at your workplace, someone who has coached or helped you to learn something new, such as an IT expert.

It is always better if you add your comments to any reports you receive. If nothing else, this at least gives you the opportunity to say whether you agree with it or not!

After your first review, update your learning plan and include it in your portfolio, together with any feedback reports you have received on your development.

Unit 304 **Contribute to coordinating administrative services**

This unit is concerned with the administrative services provided by you or your team. This is a key function of all administrators and users of your services will depend upon these being regularly undertaken to a consistently high level of quality, and often to tight deadlines. One of the ways in which consistency can be achieved is through appropriate systems and procedures which everyone understands. The focus of this unit is devising these for new services and identifying improvements that could be made to existing services.

 KEY SKILLS SIGNPOST

If you are taking your Key Skills award, you can use this unit to contribute significantly towards your evidence for **Communications**. This is because you cannot improve or develop administrative services without communicating with other people! If you undertake the activities below you will obtain evidence for level 3. If you are working towards a different Key Skills level, do discuss this with your tutor or trainer.

C3.1a

Assess the current satisfaction levels amongst users with *at least two* of the administrative services for which you are responsible and identify any emerging needs for a new service. Organise *at least one* group discussion:

1 Identify a relevant and appropriate group of users.

2 Prepare for the session by identifying:

  a how you will introduce and develop the topic

  b how you will present explanations to meet the needs of the audience

  c how you will structure the session to take into account the situation and the group to whom you will be talking

d how you will ensure that you obtain contributions from the group.

3 Hold the session and listen carefully to the views of other people. Develop the points and ideas they raise.

Write a summary of the discussion and how this has informed your plans to develop or improve your administrative services.

C3.2

Obtain all the organisational policies and procedures which currently relate to the administrative services you are investigating.

Do research into whether there are any legal or other constraints which apply. For instance, if you are investigating filing or database operation you would need to investigate the Data Protection Act; if you are investigating customer services you will need to investigate consumer legislation. Use your library, the Internet or organisational documentation but note that you must study *at least two documents and at least one of these must include at least one image.* If there are no legal or other constraints then use the same sources to research the type of services offered by other organisations.

Identify the main points from all these documents which relate to the administrative service you are developing or improving, and summarise these so that you can refer to the main points easily.

C3.1b

After you have decided upon the system or procedure to introduce or improve, and have worked out your draft proposals (see page 242), *either* arrange a presentation to your line manager and his/her colleagues at which you will present your ideas, *or* – after obtaining approval and working on your detailed guidelines (see pages 244 and 249) – arrange a presentation to your colleagues to explain the new or revised system or procedure.

Remember that:

- the presentation must be appropriate
- your language and style must suit the topic and the audience
- it must be properly structured (with a beginning, middle and end)
- you must use techniques to interest and engage the audience (such as graphics or images).

Note that your presentation must include at least *one* image.

C3

Prepare all the relevant documentation for users of the new or improved service. This should include *at least two* different types of documents (such as a report in a memo, flow chart or set of procedures). All these types of document are covered in this unit. However, note that *at least one piece of writing must be an extended document and include at least one image.* (If you are also doing option unit 309, which is an extension of this unit, the suggested *Staff Guidelines Handbook* would qualify.) Note that your document must be:

- in an appropriate form for presenting the information
- appropriate in terms of tone, sentence structure and vocabulary for the recipients
- well-organised (with headings, sub-headings, paragraphs, appropriate highlighting etc.) so that it is clear and easy to read)
- proofread properly – so that it is as perfect as you can get it!

Knowledge and understanding required for the unit

Before you can start deciding how to develop, implement and maintain administrative services (the focus of elements 304.1 and 304.2) you need to understand several key aspects relating to these services. One of the problems is that some of the terms used here may sound rather overwhelming – words such as 'policies', 'systems' and 'procedures', for instance. You may not quite realise, either, what the term 'administrative services' really means – even though you provide these every day! Use this first section, therefore, to understand what this unit is all about. You will probably find, as you progress through this introductory part, that you suddenly start to have some quite good ideas about how you could provide examples of evidence from your own workplace.

Administrative services for which you are responsible

What is an 'administrative service' – and which services do you provide?

- First, there are the services you provide yourself.
- Secondly, there are those provided by your team or any staff for whom you have responsibility.

Bear this distinction in mind as you progress through the unit. Whereas controlling the quality of your own work is up to you, this is more difficult to achieve consistently if several other people are involved. That is why 'procedures' are often used – as you will see later.

Administrative services are provided every day by administrators and encompass virtually all the tasks you carry out for other people. The following are some examples:

- photocopying, collating, binding and/or distributing a complex document
- receiving visitors and making sure they are dealt with properly
- taking messages for people out of the building (or office) and ensuring that any information is passed on promptly on their return
- sending communications on behalf of other people – whether by letter, memo, e-mail or fax
- opening and distributing incoming mail
- collecting and despatching outgoing mail
- monitoring stationery stock levels and ordering new stock
- recording payments, processing expense claims or balancing petty cash
- researching and refining information for someone
- storing documents in the correct files and retrieving these on request
- booking accommodation or making travel arrangements
- arranging hospitality for a specific event
- taking minutes or notes at meetings
- producing presentation materials.

The list is virtually endless!

All these are administrative services because you are providing them for other people – whether it be your line manager, supervisor or team leader, other staff in your organisation or external contacts. As you will see in other units, these can all be considered your 'customers'. If they can trust you, and your team, to provide an excellent administrative service at all times, then this has several benefits:

a   They can rely on you to produce high-quality work. For instance, they can trust that:

- your research information will be up to date
- your travel arrangements won't leave them stranded
- a file will always contain the correct documents, in the right order
- notes you produce from a meeting will faithfully represent what happened
- messages will be passed on promptly and accurately
- visitors and customers will be looked after properly
- photocopied complex documents will be good quality, correctly collated, properly bound
- prepared documents will be well-designed and free from errors.

b   The office will run more smoothly. There will be fewer panics and crises and this frees up everyone to concentrate on their own job.

c   you are likely to receive far fewer complaints – either from other departments or from external customers.

The reason for reviewing administrative services

Even if your office always runs smoothly and there are hardly ever any crises or disasters, your administrative services still need to be reviewed continuously. This means that you regularly think about how they operate and whether they could be improved. Nothing stands still! Businesses operate in a fast-moving world where everything is constantly changing – such as the needs of their customers, the actions of competitors and methods of doing business. You only need to think how supermarket and banking services have changed over the past few years and to consider the growth of the Internet and e-commerce to realise how true this is.

So far as your own services are considered, constant review is necessary because:

* the needs of *your* users change over time
* users may give you feedback that indicates improvements are needed
* new technology offers alternative ways of offering many services
* people learn from experience – as you become more expert you can often identify better ways of doing something
* your team may make suggestions which would result in improvement
* people's jobs may change which may result in different types of services being requested or different team members carrying out these requests.

Organisational policies, procedures and constraints that affect your administrative services

It is important to start with some definitions.

An organisational **policy** is a statement of the standards that will be upheld or the minimum acceptable standards. A policy statement tells you *what* will be done. It doesn't tell you *how* it will be done. For instance:

- a college may have a policy of offering all full-time course applicants an interview
- a building society may have a policy of contacting all customers who have a savings account to notify them of a change of interest rates within two weeks of the change being made
- an accountant may have a policy of retaining all client files for at least 10 years
- your organisation may have a policy of undertaking safety checks on all electrical equipment every year.

A **procedure**, on the other hand, states exactly *how* something will be done:

- the college interview procedure will state how applications must be dealt with and how interviews must be scheduled
- the building society procedure will say how customers should be notified
- the accountant's procedure will say how the files should be stored
- your organisation is likely to have safety procedures for various things. In this case, the procedure would state who would check the equipment, how checked equipment is identified and how faults should be reported.

A **constraint** is something which stops you doing something. For instance, if you are constrained for money on a Friday night, you will not be able to go out on the town! At work, constraints are likely to come from:

- organisational policies and procedures which stop you from 'doing your own thing'
- resource constraints – where lack of equipment, time, staff or money means you are limited in your choices
- ethical constraints, which simply mean that some actions in business are frowned upon, such as paying a cheque to a supplier when there is no money in the account or lying to a customer about the capabilities of a product you are selling
- legal constraints – such as having to give a refund to a consumer who has purchased a faulty product (in some cases, the law is used to enforce compliance with certain types of procedures, as you will see below).

All these factors affect the administrative services you offer. Quite simply:

a You have to follow your organisational policies and procedures – which determine what you must do and how you must do it.

b You have to honour your commitments, even though you may be constrained by certain resources.

c You *should* always abide by ethical constraints (because, hopefully, you believe in them); you *must* always abide by legal constraints.

As an example, if a health centre has a policy of offering an appointment to every patient within 48 hours of the request, and the procedure is for appointments to be logged on a computerised system but the patient's normal doctor is on leave that week, the administrator should offer an appointment with another qualified doctor to honour the policy. If the patient accepts, the appointment will be logged under the second doctor's name.

within two days and the unsuccessful candidates are notified within a week. Jenny is struggling a bit today. The member of staff who normally supervises the test is ill, so Jenny is having to do this herself.

EVIDENCE COLLECTION

1 Obtain a copy of any organisational policy documents which relate to the administrative services you offer. The easiest way of doing this is to make a list of the main administrative services you undertake and ask if your line manager or supervisor can spare you a few minutes to give advice on which organisational policies relate to each service – and where you will able to obtain a copy.

2 Now obtain a copy of any routine procedures you have to follow. These may not be headed 'procedures' but may be guidelines or checklists to ensure you do a job in one specific way. Again, you may have to ask your line manager or supervisor for guidance.

3 Try to identify the type of constraints which often limit the type of action you can take. For instance, are you often:

a constrained by people problems, such as not enough staff or not enough skilled staff?

b constrained by time problems, such as too much work given with tight deadlines?

c constrained by equipment problems, such as too little/outdated/malfunctioning?

You might also like to consider the way in which some of your policies and procedures constrain the way in which you have to operate.

Once you have your paperwork together, prepare a brief account for your assessor of the main administrative services you regularly provide, who you provide them for, and which policies and procedures relate to these. If you number the policies and procedures you will be able to refer to them throughout your statement.

INFORMATION UPDATE

Bureaucracies are nothing new – they were first identified over a hundred years ago and originally related mainly to government departments. Today, to call something 'bureaucratic' is often derogatory, because the word implies that it is inflexible and has so much 'red tape' that no-one can do anything. ➡️

Much of this is the 'downside' of too many procedures which are so prescriptive that they remove the ability of anyone to show initiative or move quickly. If you can't deal with basic queries or assist customers without checking which procedure to follow, and if every procedure says you have to have official permission to do anything, then your organisation is going to have problems!

The difficulty is that procedures have their 'upside' as well. A proper procedure related to holiday rotas stops some staff taking advantage and having more days off than others. A proper procedure related to pay means that you don't find that someone younger than you and with less experience is being paid more – and so on. This is why, even the most dynamic 'young' firms – which often comprise a group of staff involved in computer technology or e-commerce – find that, as they increase in size, some procedures are required.

Developing systems and procedures

What is a system?

People use the word 'system' every day, but very few can define what one is! You may want to buy a 'new computer system' whilst your parents are bemoaning the fact that their 'central heating system' isn't working properly. Then you queue to buy a packet of tissues at lunchtime and overhear someone saying that the shop has a 'crazy system for serving customers'.

The word 'system' used to be used mainly for mechanical things – such as central heating, where several parts are connected together for it to operate. Using this type of description, you should understand why the most complex system of all is your own body – lots of parts, all joined together, and all trying to work in harmony. When you are fit and well, your body works more effectively than when you are tired, ill or injured. The same is true of your central heating system – if one part is broken the system will not work efficiently, or at all. It depends which part has failed and how important it is.

The word 'system' has become more popularly used to describe any complex function which operates for a particular reason. Let's look at the shop analogy. The shop exists to sell goods and to do this it has to serve customers. To process sales it needs tills or cash points, trained staff and wrapping materials. The cash point may also contain other devices, such as a barcode reader or swipe facilities for credit and debit cards. The customer might want a receipt, so the cash register has to be capable of producing one.

These are all the 'parts' which make up the sales processing system. If one (or more) goes wrong, then the system doesn't work properly – a shortage of staff, for instance, or a barcode reader doesn't work and the assistant needs help to input the product code. We have all been in situations like this – the system normally breaks down when we are in a hurry to buy something in our lunch break!

Understanding how systems work

Before you can improve a system, you have to understand how it works. To simplify things, there are certain terms used with systems.

- **Inputs** are the items which go 'in' to the system. In your body system, the inputs are food and drink. In your central heating system, the input is cold water and a heat source.
- The **process** is what the system *does*. It works at converting these inputs into something else.
- **Outputs** are the result of the process. Your body converts food and drink to energy. Your central heating processes cold water and makes it hot.
- **Controls** are introduced into every system to regulate the way it works. You *know* when you have eaten or drunk too much – you feel bloated or even ill. You also know when you are hungry or thirsty. So your body regulates the inputs by telling you when it needs more (or less). Similarly, your central heating system will have a thermostat. You can set this for the temperature you want. This will then control the heat of the water and the radiators.
- **Feedback** is information received on the quality of the outputs. For instance, if you feel tired and listless one day, or have stomach ache or feel sick, your body is giving you feedback that all is not well with its 'system'. You will try to take preventative action yourself and if that doesn't work, you will see a specialist – your doctor. If you touch every radiator and it feels cold, despite the fact your system is still operating, you have feedback that there is a problem. You may try to investigate – or call in a specialist – an engineer. As you will realise, feedback doesn't have to be negative – on a day when you feel wonderful, the feedback is positive!

In a system, this is often illustrated graphically. The example shown opposite illustrates the inputs and outputs for a central heating system.

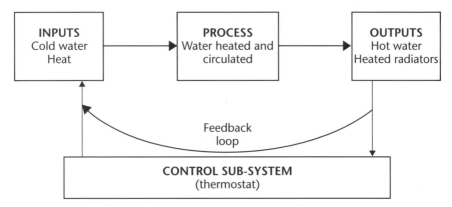

Simple systems diagram for heating

Linking systems and procedures

You may think that systems are all very well, but consider that they have little to do with procedures you must follow or administrative services you must provide.

The link with procedures is quite straightforward. Because systems are complex and comprise various parts, to work properly each part has to be controlled. One of the most problematic parts of systems which involve people is individual behaviour. The shop system may have the latest cash registers and dozens of cash points, but if one of the assistants is clueless, rude or processes a sale wrongly, then the system falls down. Equally, if none of the customers knew where to queue, or how to pay, problems would occur. So procedures exist to control the human parts of a system! These can be written checklists for staff or notices for customers.

Recommended and mandatory procedures

Even though you never think about it, you follow procedures every day of your life – and not just at work. You follow procedures when you ride on a bus or train, light a fire, wash your hair or clean your teeth. You may not think of all these actions as procedures but they are! In some cases, they are important to your safety or the safety of others. If you try to jump off a bus when it is moving, or put a match to a gas appliance after the gas has been on for 10 minutes, you endanger yourself and others. In other cases, following procedures is not as critical. Following the right procedures when you wash your hair is less important than if you were *dyeing* your hair, but cleaning your teeth properly will be stressed by your dentist at every checkup. However, as only you will suffer the consequences if you ignore this advice, no-one is going to force you!

Procedures which are very important are often *mandatory* or 'must do' procedures. In this case, if you don't follow them there are likely to be serious consequences. Mandatory procedures are enforced by the law, in many cases, or by severe punishment. For instance, a candidate in an examination room who doesn't follow procedures is in danger of having his or her paper disqualified.

Procedures which are less critical are normally *recommended*. Most of the administrative service you provide will have recommended procedures – but not all. You are unlikely to face disciplinary action if you fail to log a visitor's name properly in the visitor register. You are certainly likely to do so if you order £5000 of goods without authorisation – so your financial procedures are likely to be mandatory within your organisation.

Administrative services and procedures

Many administrative services – which can comprise complex systems – include a number of procedures. A good example is filing. That may sound very basic, but it is actually quite a complex system. It comprises 'inputs' (documents), the process of storing the documents and, if this is done properly, 'outputs' in the form of neat and orderly files which can be rapidly found. However, the process is undertaken by human beings. Unless they all do the same thing then the system won't work. So procedures are required:

- how to store different types of documents
- where to store different types of documents
- how to use the classification system
- how to cope with requests to borrow a file
- what to do if a document needs to be cross-referenced.

In addition, these will be backed up by organisational policies – such as those which govern the length of time important documents have to be retained – and who can decide what can be archived or destroyed. In an establishment which deals with highly secret documents, some of the procedures may be mandatory for staff dealing with these particular papers.

TEST YOUR KNOWLEDGE AND UNDERSTANDING

1 You use a restaurant where you have to find a table, identify the table number, make your choice from the menu and then order your food at a serving counter. Is this an example of a system or a procedure? Give a reason for your answer.

2 The road traffic system is one of the most complex systems there is and knowledge of the *Highway Code* is essential for all drivers.

   a Why do you think the 'road traffic system' is so called?

   b Using system terms, what is the role of the *Highway Code*?

   c Either as a pedestrian or as a driver, identify two procedures you have to follow.

   d Are these procedures mandatory or recommended? Give a reason for your answer.

   e What controls exist to make sure people follow these procedures?

   f What feedback might you get if you ignored one or two?

3 The health service has a large number of specified procedures for surgeons, anaesthetists, doctors and nurses.

   a What type of procedures would you call these?

   b Why is following them so important?

4 Unless you are very unusual, you will have been part of the UK examinations system at some time in your life.

   a What are the 'inputs' and 'outputs' of this system?

   b How would you describe the 'process'?

   c What procedures do you recall your teachers or invigilators having to follow?

   d What procedures did you have to follow?

   e Why do you think all these procedures are important?

INFORMATION UPDATE

Many organisations have changed their systems because of technological developments, and this has affected the procedures their staff and their customers have to follow. ➡️

A good example is banking. Thirty years ago people queued up to obtain cash and make transactions and received their statements through the post. The advent of cash machines meant that money could be obtained 'out-of-hours' but the procedures had to be clearly visible on screen so that customers could follow the new system for obtaining cash. Today virtually all large banks offer 'on-line banking' which has completely revolutionised the way in which they interact with customers.

Customers who are registered to receive this service can now log-on at any hour of the day or night, access statements, move money between accounts and undertake dozens of other transactions. The design and content of the banks' websites is important as this gives their customers instructions on the procedures to follow. Because of problems with fraud, banks have had to tighten up their security procedures to make sure their sites are secure and that customer confidentiality is not violated. More importantly, customers need to have confidence that their money is safe.

Customer feedback has also resulted in many sites being restructured, so that access is easier and faster. This reduces the amount of time the customer needs to be 'on-line'. Customers are also given a telephone number to ring if there are site problems – to collate any negative feedback and offer an alternative service. Today, virtually the whole range of banking services is available by computer – except the facility to withdraw cash!

EVIDENCE COLLECTION

All organisations have a system for evacuating buildings quickly in the case of fire. Do the following to prove to your assessor that you understand 'systems' and 'procedures'.

1 Describe how this system operates in your own organisation.
2 Describe the procedures people must follow.
3 Explain why these procedures are necessary.
4 Identify which procedures are mandatory and which are recommended.
5 Identify the controls that exist to make sure people follow the system.
6 Explain what feedback is given after a fire drill to evaluate the result.
7 Identify your own role in this process and your own contribution to the effectiveness of the system.

Element 304.1 Help to develop administrative services

The focus in this element is on the development of administrative services. Your knowledge of systems and procedures should give you a good perspective on the services you provide. Unless you can identify the systems and procedures required for your administrative service to function properly, you will develop a good service only by luck – not by planning and good management. That is not the idea. The aim is to be able to identify the components of a service so that you can then develop one properly. It may not be perfect, but it will have a far greater chance of success!

Encouraging feedback

You have already seen that feedback is an important component of any system. It tells you when things are going well or not! Feedback can therefore be usefully employed to:

- identify the need for a new service
- develop an idea for a service
- improve an existing service.

However, the users of your services may give you little formal feedback – apart from the odd moan or two if something goes wrong (which you might be tempted to ignore!).

Basically, there are two types of feedback – positive and negative. We all enjoy positive feedback, but be careful. Praise cannot always be taken at face value. Question its value if:

- you have just done a 'special favour' for someone which isn't generally available
- the person giving you the feedback is trying to flatter or charm you for some reason.

Equally, no-one likes negative feedback. The general tendency is to blame outside influences or to claim that a problem occurred only because of exceptional circumstances. Try not to do this. You will never think productively about developments and improvements if you act defensively every time something goes wrong.

So – first golden rule – remain open-minded about all the feedback you receive. Treat it as the courts treat evidence – find out if it is proven or valid. You can do this only by finding out if the views expressed by, say, one or two people are also held by several others.

To establish this, you need to *encourage* feedback from a wide variety of people. The banks encourage feedback when they offer a telephone number if their on-line service is not accessible. Many lorries today advertise a telephone number to ring if you think the vehicle is being driven badly. These are two ideas for obtaining feedback, but neither of them is particularly appropriate for an administrator. Before you think of ways of encouraging feedback, the first questions to ask yourself are:

a   Who should you ask for feedback?

b   How should you ask for feedback?

c   What 'controls' do you need to place on the feedback you receive?

d   What should you do with the feedback you get?

You can describe this another way. You can say that you need to 'devise a system for obtaining feedback' – and think of it in system terms instead!

Who to ask

Remember that feedback will be your input into the system. You therefore need to think broadly about who is affected by the services you or your team provide. This, therefore, includes both the users of the service and the people who deliver it.

How to ask

Basically, there are two choices. You can decide on a formal method or an informal method.

Formal options include:

- a *short* questionnaire (sending it by e-mail these days is often better than through the internal mail and your response rate will be higher)
- a meeting of your team and users specifically to ask for comments and ideas.

Less formal options include:

- a suggestions box in the office
- a space on all 'job' sheets for your customers to complete when they receive finished work
- chatting to users or team members to ask for their views.

Formal methods normally give you more overall control but are apt to be 'one-off' events, whereas it is often better if people can be encouraged to give regular feedback. However, a more formal method can be used to check whether an opinion is held by several people. For instance, you can log the number of questionnaires you have sent and calculate the percentage response you receive. If only 5 per cent answer you can hardly accept this view as widespread. The situation is different if 80 per cent respond.

However, don't discount the value of informal feedback. A chance remark can often be the basis of an extremely good idea. Much depends upon whether you are (a) listening, (b) interested, (c) able to apply what you have just heard, and (d) just a little bit creative!

What to ask

There are two types of feedback you may want:

- feedback linked to a specific idea or suggestion
- general feedback on the overall quality of the administrative services offered.

Your method of asking should relate to the type of feedback you want. For instance, feedback linked to a specific idea would be usefully obtained through a questionnaire or a short meeting. This 'controls' the type of responses you receive. General feedback is better obtained on an 'on-going' basis, such as comments on job sheets or informal chats – and you would not normally wish to control this to the same extent.

What to do next

You can encourage people to give you feedback by devising methods that are easy for them. You will quickly dishearten them, however, if all their suggestions seem to be consigned to a 'black hole'! In other words, if you ask for feedback, then the best way of encouraging more is to let users know you value it. People will quickly stop putting comments on job sheets, for instance, if they see you glance at them and throw them into your wastebin.

All good systems have a positive output – and this should include your system for 'encouraging feedback'. One obvious output is a new or improved service. If people see their ideas and suggestions being adopted then this is the best reinforcement in the world for even more feedback.

A word of warning, however. You will always receive feedback you could do without – especially if you encourage it. One person, for instance, may think it is now his or her 'duty' to put you right on everything! If this occurs, try to deal with the person tactfully – perhaps by saying that whereas you welcome all ideas, you are concentrating on one or two specific areas at present. Then quickly start a suggestions box (preferably placed in a different office) and ask this person to use it from now on!

Using information to evaluate the effectiveness of administrative services

Feedback from users and staff may be the main way of gaining information, but it's not the only way. Useful information can come from doing the following things.

a   Monitor how successful you – and your team – are at meeting deadlines.

b   Note the number of times work has to be redone because of misunderstandings or errors.

c   Log the number of complaints (and compliments!) you and your team receive.

d   Keep an eye on 'workflow' – i.e. the way in which work is progressed by you or your team (even think of yourselves as miniature processing systems if you want!). Identify what gets held up, where and why, what controls exist, and the extent to which they are operating properly.

e   Identify the number of problems that occur in the course of the average day or week. Which ones *keep* occurring – what could be done about them?

f   Identify the number and type of questions that are routinely asked – both by users and by staff. Could anything be done to reduce these?

The key aspect of all this is *repetitiveness*. 'One-off' complaints, problems, queries and issues are totally different from those that occur constantly. These are giving you important information that a particular service is not as effective as you thought it was.

TEST YOUR KNOWLEDGE AND UNDERSTANDING

Kerry Wright works for a graphics and media production company. She has obtained the following information relating to the administrative services she and her team provide.

1   Identify which ones are significant, indicating that something should be done quickly, and which are less important and can be deferred for now.

2   Then identify the benefits that could arise if there was a proper system.

Check your answers with the key on page 271.

a   An irate e-mail is received from a member of the finance staff – Lucy Merrow – claiming no one has responded to her (repeated) requests for information on sales statistics this month. Your team member says Lucy always leaves it to the last minute to ask, then complains it's not done on time and copies the e-mail to her own boss – putting the blame on your team.

➡

b A visitor has left reception very annoyed. He had an appointment with the Technical Manager who he finds is now not available. Apparently, yesterday a crisis occurred and the Technical Manager has had to go a see a client and will be away all day. No-one thought to tell the visitor – who has just travelled 50 miles. Apparently no one else can help as the visit was about an on-going discussion the two were having.

c For the third time this month an air ticket hasn't been delivered by your travel agent because there was a misunderstanding about whether it would be collected or delivered. Added to that, there are repeated problems as to travel requests being misunderstood over the telephone.

d Your own boss is fuming because he cannot find an important contract he needs for a meeting with the MD this afternoon. It is eventually found beneath several papers in the filing tray.

e There is an argument between two members of staff outside the meeting room as both are booked to use it at the same time. Your team member says room bookings are 'always a problem'.

f A young, ambitious member of staff approaches you in a rage at nearly 5 pm. He is giving an important presentation to a client tomorrow and claims none of his photocopying and binding has been done. He says that office staff always do 'the easy jobs first' and, as a result, his has been waiting for days. When you check with your team, you find he handed in his photocopying half an hour ago and was promised it would be ready for 9.30 am tomorrow – two hours before the presentation.

g Kerry's firm recently started an e-mail service on their website. Anyone with a query or enquiry can e-mail the firm instead of writing or telephoning. Accessing and responding to e-mails is haphazard and this morning Kerry's boss went ballistic. No-one had checked the incoming e-mails for three days and he is convinced a new and important client has been lost for ever.

h A recent questionnaire identified that most users are satisfied with the administrative services provided but the main complaint was 'poor telephone message service' – either messages being put in the normal post system or incomplete information being obtained. It appears most messages are taken by the 'newest recruit' to your team, who left school just three months ago.

i You receive regular complaints from the team member in charge of stock that she can't get her work done because of interruptions for urgent requests and regular complaints from users that they can't get anything unless they order it a month in advance.

Identifying possible improvements and potential benefits

In your own workplace you are unlikely to find as many 'obvious' examples as those in Kerry's workplace – but it will be amazing if you don't find any. This would mean you have perfect systems which always operate wonderfully – which very rarely occurs in real life.

The only way you can identify what improvements are possible in your own area is to spend the next few days (or weeks) gathering as much information as you can, from as many sources as possible. This means 'walking the job' and using your own eyes and ears to see what is going on.

As a first step, it is useful to list *everything* that comes to mind. You can then refine the list into the most and least important – as you did with Kerry's list. Before you finalise this, however, it may be useful to talk to other team members to discover whether they would have a different priority order and, if so, why.

CHECK IT OUT!

Make a list of all the areas where you think there may be a weakness in your administrative services. This may be because there is no proper system or because a system doesn't work very well. Don't think of this as personal criticism – try to stay objective. That means concentrating upon the issue or problem and not the people (or yourself!).

Now prioritise your list so you have one or two definite areas on which to concentrate. Think of all the benefits that would be gained (and by whom) if you could improve things.

Discussing possibilities with your line manager

Depending upon the structure of your organisation, your line manager may be your supervisor, team leader or someone else. However, involving your boss at this stage is crucial. First, your boss may be able to make some excellent suggestions and help to improve your ideas. Secondly, unless you have support for your plans you are unlikely to get very far. If you are wise, therefore, one of the first things you will identify is the benefits *for your boss* (and the organisation as a whole) of the changes you would like to make – rather than focusing just on the benefits for yourself or your team.

Your boss's reaction to your proposal is likely to depend upon three factors:

- his or her overall personality and preferences
- what you are suggesting (and how much it will cost)
- how and when you suggest it.

There are various types of boss. If you are very lucky, you will have an open-minded, approachable and reasonable boss who welcomes positive suggestions no matter how and when they are made. However, this is rather unrealistic! In reality you can expect to be employed by a normal human being. For instance, you may have:

- a boss who dislikes all change or ideas unless he or she first thought of it
- a boss who couldn't care less what you do
- a boss who takes an interest at first, but quickly forgets what was agreed
- a boss who is good on some days and awful on others.

There isn't space in this book to provide guidance on how to deal with all the different types of boss you may encounter during your career. However, a good 'rule of thumb' is to remember that you should vary your approach to take account of your boss's main likes, dislikes and personality traits. You can then adapt this technique no matter who you work for.

- If you have a boss who dislikes ideas which weren't his/hers, only give an outline of the idea and stress how much you need additional input. Listen avidly to every word. Then thank your boss for having such a good idea.
- If you have a boss who is 'laissez faire' (in other words, lets you do what you want) then it is still courtesy to keep him/her informed. The downside is that you are unlikely to get much praise (or support if things go wrong). The upside is that if you make a few alterations to your original plan, it won't matter.
- If you have a boss who quickly loses interest, arrange a meeting so you get his/her full attention and can get some good suggestions whilst interest is high. E-mail or memo a summary afterwards – then you have proof about what was discussed if you need it.
- If you have a 'good' and 'bad' day boss then pick your day and time carefully. If necessary, book a short appointment in advance. Be prepared to postpone this if the day turns out badly and your appointment is for 4.30 pm!

The points that follow usually apply to *all* bosses.

a Think through your idea before you start the discussion, so you know what you're talking about. In other words, do your homework! If you are going to quote issues or problems, have the facts at your fingertips, be accurate and don't exaggerate.

b   Play 'devil's advocate' with yourself before the meeting. This means trying to identify snags yourself first – and think about how these could be overcome.

c   Don't take forever to get to the point. State your case politely and in a straightforward manner.

d   Start by saying you are *thinking* of improving (or introducing) a particular administrative service, *not* that you are going to. Otherwise it sounds as if you are running the office, not your boss!

e   Have the benefits at your fingertips.

f   Be aware that a suggestion that costs money will always be less welcome than one that saves it. Your boss will expect you to have thought about the resource implications of any new idea. Be realistic. Anyone can improve their photocopying service with a machine costing £10,000 and three new staff – but the costs of this will normally outweigh the benefits.

g   Leave scope in your plan for your boss's feedback and suggestions, and welcome these! Hopefully they will all be useful (some may be invaluable). If any of them horrify you, try not to let this show. The default here, if you are absolutely stuck, is to implement them and see how you go. Don't assume it won't work because you didn't think of it. If an idea of your boss's *doesn't* work in reality, then you may be able to quietly discard it later.

h   Promise your boss you will keep him/her informed (the importance of this will depend upon the type of boss you have) and thank him/her for helping you.

Working out detailed proposals

Once you have your boss's agreement to move your idea forward, your next task is to work out detailed proposals for your improved service. You may find it helpful to consult with other people, such as:

- other users
- your team members
- anyone else who has expertise in this area.

This is important. If people know what you are planning, and have some input, they are more likely to cooperate with you when you try to implement it. However, do be wary of contacting *suppliers* for advice – as each will have a very vested interest in helping you to solve your problems by purchasing their products! Therefore, the first stage is to consult as widely as you can (and have time for). The second stage is to narrow down your group to 'hone' your idea and decide the detail. You should note that it is also courtesy to make sure you involve anyone else who will be directly affected by your plans.

There are several advantages to consulting other people:

- Some will have more experience than you, others will be more expert and knowledgeable on particular issues or areas.
- Other people will have different opinions and ideas – which is useful – although too many completely diverse views may create problems (see below).
- You need the cooperation of the key people who will help you to make the new system work. You are unlikely to get this if they haven't had any involvement.
- A team may have one person who they see as their unofficial leader. If this person agrees the proposals with you, the whole team suddenly comes on your side!

Problems with consultation

Consultation doesn't always go smoothly – particularly if you have certain individuals in your workplace who hold very strong views. You may wish to bear this in mind when you decide who to talk to. If you have a choice of three people and one is amenable and positive, another talks for the sake of it and a third is always negative and obstructive, then you don't have to be a genius to work out who to select!

You can also have problems if you consult so many people that you end up with a vast number of different views and don't know where to start. For that reason, deciding who to consult can be very important. If you need guidance on this, draft a proposed list and show it to your line manager. This is a double check to make sure no one important is missing and no one who would cause real problems is included!

Omitting the consultation process altogether

The only time you can – and should – circumvent the consultation process is when a mandatory procedure must be introduced quickly. This may happen if:

- everyone has to comply with a new legal requirement
- everyone has to comply with a new organisational policy or procedure
- there is a sudden, important emergency
- there is a very minor alteration to a basic procedure (such as a change in the date to submit travel expense claims) which staff would accept without question.

In this case you would just need to agree what has to be done with your own line manager, and then inform other people.

Kerry has been asked by her boss, the Administration Director, to solve the e-mail problem. He has asked her to devise a system so that all e-mails sent to the website will be dealt with quickly. She agreed with her boss that she would consult:

- her own team
- the technical and sales staff who have to answer the e-mails
- the IT manager.

She has now obtained the following feedback.

a Her own team of four have mixed views. Rubia is concerned it will take up a lot of time and thinks the firm should employ someone else specifically to do this job. Jason, however, welcomes it as he loves IT work. Sarah suggests that it should be incorporated into the normal mail system for receipt, distribution and despatch. Ben argues this is impossible, because e-mails are more urgent.

b Sam, the IT specialist, has advised her that he can help in several ways.

- The e-mails received on the website can be set up to be accessed by any named administrators.
- The system can be set up to send an automatic acknowledgement to the sender.
- A simple database can be used to log e-mails received. This would provide the added benefit of a list of e-mail addresses of enquirers.
- The existing e-mail system enables automatic 'out-of-office' replies to be sent. These can be used to identify quickly which members of the technical or sales staff are away as any messages forwarded to them will then receive that response.

c The sales and technical staff, who will have to answer the queries, have suggested that time will be saved if each incoming e-mail is forwarded to them electronically. They suggest that if they are off the premises, the e-mail should be forwarded to the manager. They think it would be easier if they replied direct themselves, but Kerry is worried that there will then be no check on which e-mails have been answered, so would prefer replies routed through the office. She is also a bit dubious about the spelling and grammar of some of the technical staff, but doesn't like to say this.

1 What reasons can you give for Kerry's choice of people to consult?

2 Why do you think she thought it was better to talk to each group rather than just e-mail them or send a memo?

3 Kerry decides to think about the problem in 'system' terms, to see if this helps. If she does this, what will be:

- the inputs
- the outputs
- the process which must be undertaken to convert her inputs into outputs?

4 Kerry is concerned about controlling the system.

- How important do you think these controls are?
- Can you suggest any controls which would 'monitor' the system?

5 After considering the problem for some time, Kerry draws up four possibilities:

(i) Employ a new member of staff who is responsible for receiving and logging all incoming e-mails, acknowledging these and forwarding them to the right technical or sales person. This person would then be responsible for sending all responses and monitoring any outstanding e-mails. This person would need his or her own computer on which to do the work.

(ii) Identify an existing member of staff to check the incoming e-mails twice a day and forward these to the sales or technical staff. The sales or technical staff then respond direct to the enquirer or customer and are asked to copy the named admin person with their response.

(iii) As for (ii), but the sales/technical staff send their responses to the named administrator who then checks each one quickly and forwards it to the customer or enquirer. This person keeps track of any outstanding responses and reminds the person concerned.

(iv) The e-mails are printed out twice a day and distributed with the morning and afternoon mail. Attached is a form which the staff complete and return to the office. The forms are numbered, to help to keep track of the e-mails. As the numbered replies are received they are crossed off and the message typed and sent by an administrator.

a Identify the benefits and the drawbacks with *each* of Kerry's ideas.

b Do you think the number of e-mails received daily should be considered? If so, in what way?

c From the information you have so far, what would be your own preference – and why? Can you suggest a better idea yourself?

INFORMATION UPDATE

The Regulation of Investigatory Powers Act, which came into effect in October 2000, has changed the e-mail and Internet procedures which operate in many organisations. This Act gives organisations the ability to monitor e-mail and Internet use by staff. You may also find that you have a 'waiver clause' in your contract which states that your employer can do this. Using your employer's computers and Internet link to e-mail your friends, passing on jokes to your colleagues, surfing holiday sites, job vacancies or (even worse) adult sites can result in disciplinary action – as several employees have found to their cost.

Good employers make certain that staff are aware that monitoring is taking place. They do this by having an IT Use Policy, which states clearly what is and is not allowed. They set up a monitoring system electronically by using software such as Minesweeper which trawls for certain words or phrases, such as CV, job, holiday and sex. They then make sure that all staff are aware of the procedures which would be followed if monitoring identified misuse on their computer.

Some employees have tried to use the excuse that someone else was logged on to their computer. This is not acceptable. Everyone on a network has their own log-on ID and password, so giving this to someone else is likely to be yet *another* breach of the IT policy!

CHECK IT OUT!

Find out if such a policy exists in your organisation and whether your computer use is monitored. If you are studying your award at a college, you should check out what would happen there.

Then identify whether your team is aware of the situation and if new staff are informed properly. If not, you may want to think of a procedure to do this.

Devising detailed proposals

At this stage we will assume you have

- your original idea (for a new or improved service)
- your boss's feedback
- suggestions and information from other people and other sources.

You now have to refine these into a workable proposal. Where do you start? Hopefully, by now, you are not just sitting looking at a pile of paper, but have given the matter some thought. You may have various options in your mind – or drafted on paper like Kerry – but are not sure if these will work.

Step one

Start by concentrating on converting your inputs into outputs. What process is required to do this? In Kerry's case she can list these as follows:

- receive the e-mails
- log the e-mails
- send (by whatever means) the e-mails to the technical/sales staff
- obtain responses
- check responses are suitable for sending
- log response and date
- send reply.

This is the 'process' which will be undertaken by the system. Basically it is a list of all the actions that must take place, in sequence. It is important to check at this point that nothing is missing in the sequence.

Step two

Think about what could go wrong and how you could control these problems. Kerry's list might be as follows:

a The administrator who operates the system is absent.
b The technical or sales staff don't reply because they
   (i) are absent
   (ii) need to find more information before they can answer, or
   (iii) are forgetful and/or disorganised!
c The reply doesn't make sense.
d The punctuation, grammar or spelling needs correcting.

She might also add bigger problems, such as the computer system failing, but that is out of her control so is not part of *this* system.

Step three

Kerry now has to think about what could be introduced into the system to 'solve' each of the problems automatically. She could suggest these options.

a   Share the job between two people.

b   (i) Send the e-mail to someone else to deal with – *if* the absence is
        known – which relies upon the absent person setting up their 'auto
        reply' system.

    (ii) 'Buy' more time by notifying the customer of the reason for the
         delay and giving an estimated date of response.

    (iii) Send a reminder and then notify the manager.

c   Ask the author for clarification.

d   Make sure the e-mails are dealt with by administrators capable of
    correcting this themselves.

Step four

As a final check, Kerry assesses her proposed service and the system she has
devised against the checklist shown below.

Checklist for proposals

- The benefits are greater than the costs.
- The idea is simple, straightforward and easy for people to follow.
- The 'process' will convert the inputs into the right type of outputs.
- The idea meets the aim of the improved system.
- There are no (or very few) negative side-effects.
- The proposal is in accordance with all current organisational policies and
  existing systems and procedures.
- The needs of all major users have been considered.
- The needs of all operational staff have been considered.
- Input from relevant experts has been heeded.
- There is some 'control' over the system to enable it to be monitored.
- There are no serious constraints which could stop the new system or
  service from operating effectively.
- Consideration has been given as to who will take overall responsibility for
  the service and what will happen if that person is absent.

Step five

At the stage when you think you have made as much progress as possible, it
is sensible to go back to your line manager and talk through your detailed
proposals. You may also want to talk to the key group of relevant people
who have helped you. Then if you have forgotten something very important
someone may spot this.

Don't expect everyone to be madly enthusiastic about your plan from the
word 'go'! You would be very fortunate if everyone was 100 per cent positive.

Settle for being satisfied if everyone thinks it has a good chance of working. If you have to convince someone to try it, the best way is to suggest doing a 'pilot scheme' first. Everyone can then suggest improvements after an initial period of, say, two months. This is a useful safeguard anyway, as many new systems need a little adjustment to refine them; not all snags can be foreseen at the beginning. This strategy also gives people the feeling that they will have a say in possible changes they feel should be made.

TEST YOUR KNOWLEDGE AND UNDERSTANDING

Kerry knows she will have to obtain her boss's approval before she implements her plans. She decides to prepare a memo which states her final proposals for the new e-mail system. She will then arrange a time to talk to her line manager about it.

Read Kerry's memo below and then answer the questions that follow.

1 Why do you think Kerry decided to give her proposals to her boss in writing *before* seeing him to talk about them?

2 What additional benefits has Kerry identified in the memo?

3 Kerry has decided that two members of staff should be responsible for this service. Can you identify:
   • *three* benefits of involving two people
   • at least *two* drawbacks?

4 Can you suggest any ways of minimising the drawbacks you identified?

5 Do you think Kerry has forgotten anything, or do you consider her proposals are complete? Give a reason for your answer.

M E M O

TO   John Wade

FROM   Kerry Wright

DATE   15 January 200-

Proposals for dealing with e-mails to website

I have spoken with the office staff, the sales and technical staff and received advice and help from our IT staff and from these discussions I should like to propose the following new system:

1   The named administrators who will do this work are Jason Young and Rubia Khan. Both enjoy working with IT, and having two staff means there is cover if one person is absent.   ➡️

2　The incoming e-mails will be logged on to a database by Jason and then forwarded to the correct member of sales or technical staff to answer the query. The database will give us the added benefit of keeping a record of enquirers' e-mail addresses.

3　The member of staff responds to Jason and Rubia and the response is logged on the database.

4　The response is checked to make sure it is clear and that the spelling and punctuation are correct. If there are any queries about content these will be referred back to the author.

5　The message is then sent to the customer or enquirer.

6　'Out-of-office' responses – which means that when a member of the technical or sales staff is absent the e-mail is redirected to the Sales or Technical Manager.

7　Staff will be reminded of any unanswered e-mails after 48 hours. If the delay is for a good reason (such as technical information), Jason or Rubia will e-mail the enquirer to state when a final response can be expected.

8　Unacceptable delays will be referred, as appropriate, to the Sales or Technical Manager.

If you agree with these proposals, I will work on preparing the documentation required for users.

Documenting detailed proposals

The first question Kerry's boss asks, when he sees her, is how many e-mails are currently being received each day. He also wants to know whether her staff can cope with the additional work. He suggests looking at the other jobs they carry out to see whether these can be reduced a little or re-allocated. Kerry knows only 10 or 15 e-mails are being received every day, but agrees that if these increase dramatically, she will keep her boss informed.

Kerry's boss also questions whether it would be useful to have a paper (hard) copy of the e-mail at any stage. Kerry is unsure but says she will think about this.

Kerry's boss then advises her that she needs to write clear procedures for everyone to follow. There are various possibilities.

- She could prepare a sequence of activities to be followed and type this out as a list. However, the activities might vary for different types of user.
- She could prepare a flow chart to illustrate the procedure.
- She could use graphics if these were applicable.
- She could write the procedures in a specification which would give full details of who will do what and when.

If you open a packet of tablets, a bottle of hair dye, your fax or photocopier manual or a book on car maintenance you will see documented procedures. These may, or may not, have illustrations to guide you. It will depend upon the topic – illustrations are obviously more useful showing you how to change a printer cartridge than how to swallow a tablet!

The quality of user manuals and instructions is very variable. That is why there have been so many jokes about assembling flat-pack furniture and other items of equipment! The secret to producing clear procedures is to draft them out and then ask someone to try them out before issuing them to everyone.

Flow charts are more often used with technical instructions and in computer manuals. They are useful for identifying any 'control loops' that exist (or should exist!) as well as the steps through a process. A flow chart for Kerry's proposals is shown on page 254. Check that you can follow it and see how it works. The actions which must be carried out are shown in rectangular boxes. Every time the administrator must make a decision, this is shown by a diamond. The arrowed lines show the direction of the whole process, and you should be able to see what actions must be taken each time a problem occurs.

Note that some people prefer to draw a flow chart, other people prefer to prepare a list. It doesn't matter which you use, so long as it works.

Procedure specification

Kerry has decided to start by drawing up a specification. This is useful when there are several people involved in operating the system because the role of each person is shown. She starts by dividing up her proposal into small steps – listing one by one all the separate actions which must take place, one by one. She then decides who will carry out each action and by when. In some cases, this type of specification also includes a 'where' column – when different people have to do things in different places. This isn't particularly necessary for Kerry's plan, so she omits it.

Kerry's specification is shown on page 255. In each case she has tried to include every step – starting at the beginning and methodically working through to the end.

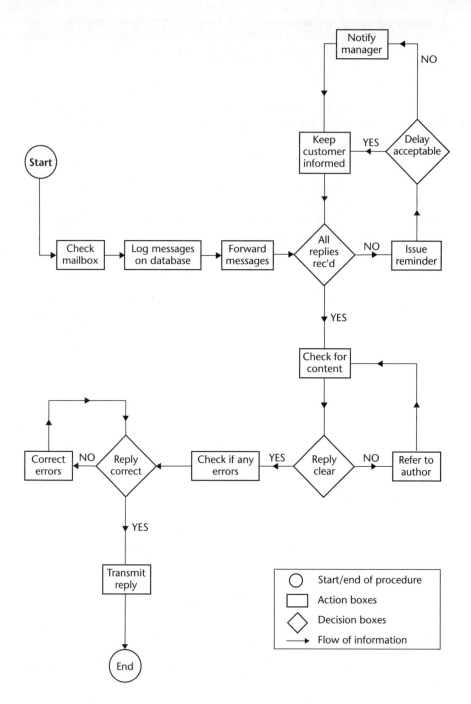

Flowchart for the system to deal with e-mails on the website

Procedure specification		
Action	By whom	When
Incoming e-mails checked	Admin staff	Daily – am and pm
E-mails logged on database	Admin staff	Daily – am and pm
E-mails forwarded to sales/technical staff	Admin staff	Daily – am and pm
E-mails response sent to Jason	Sales/technical staff	Daily
Responses logged on database	Admin staff	Daily
Responses checked for content, style etc.	Admin staff	Daily
Queries on technical content referred to authors	Admin staff	Daily
Queries on technical content answered	Sales/technical staff	Daily
Delayed responses notified to staff	Admin staff	Daily
Reason for delay identified	Sales/technical staff	As required
Customer notified of expected response time	Admin staff	As required
Unacceptable delays notified to managers	Admin staff	As required
E-mail responses forwarded to sender	Admin staff	Daily

Procedures as a list of actions to take

Kerry then works on a set of procedures for Jason and Rubia. This lists all the actions they must undertake. The procedures are useful because both of them will do the same thing and, even more importantly, both will know what the other one must do.

Kerry bears a few key principles in mind when she writes them. These are to:

- keep them simple and easy to follow
- refer to additional information which may be attached or found elsewhere, rather than including it
- deal with the main procedure first
- then deal with exceptions under clear headings
- put her name at the bottom and the date.

The last point is important. If the procedures are revised in the future, people need to be able to compare dates to see which is the latest version.

1   Study the set of procedures for the administrative staff, illustrated below. Then use this to produce a set for the sales and technical staff. These will be shorter than the administrative procedures, but you have to include a reminder to these staff to set their e-mail to send an automatic 'out-of-office' reply if they are going to be away. You should also state that they should notify the administrative staff if there is likely to be a delay answering a particular e-mail.

2   Now think of a job you or your team do every day and write out a set of procedures to cover it. To start, think of a simple task, such as:

   • logging on to your computer system
   • making a photocopy
   • answering the telephone
   • greeting a visitor.

Prepare this step-by-step. Afterwards, state what action to take if a problem occurs. Then, if you are feeling ambitious, draw a flow chart to illustrate it. Again cover the main process first and then draw in the actions to take if there is a problem.

PROCEDURES FOR DEALING WITH E-MAILS TO WEB SITE

1   Check mailbox twice daily (am and pm).
2   Log all messages received on database.
3   Forward message to correct member of sales or technical staff (see list).
4   Check responses for readability, content and style. Refer technical queries to author and correct grammatical or spelling errors.
5   Log response on database.
6   Forward response to sender of e-mail.

Delayed responses

If no response has been received within 48 hours of forwarding message:

1   Check reason for delay with member of sales or technical staff concerned.
2   Ascertain likely time when response will be received.
3   Keep customer informed when reply is expected.
4   If delay is unacceptable or no response is received to reminders, notify Technical or Sales Manager.

Staff absences

All technical/sales staff emails will respond with an automated reply if the member of staff is out of the office. In this case, redirect the enquiry to the relevant manager.

Kerry Wright   1 February 2002

EVIDENCE COLLECTION

On page 242 you were asked to identify one or two administrative services you could either develop or improve. You can stay with your original ideas or you might have thought of other systems or procedures you could usefully introduce. It is sensible not to be too ambitious. Trying to introduce something involving half the workforce is too difficult at this stage – focus on something more controllable for your first attempt.

For your evidence for this element you need to prove you can help to develop administrative services. If you carry out all the tasks below, you will have provided the evidence required.

1 Decide which service you would like to develop or improve from feedback you have received or information you have obtained. Write a brief description of what you would like to do and give details of the feedback or information you have received that has enabled you to make this decision.

2 Arrange a time and date to talk to your line manager about your idea. Before you attend this meeting, list the benefits you think would be gained. Discuss with your line manager who may be the best people to work with to agree the detailed proposals.

3 After the meeting, confirm what was discussed in writing – put a copy in your portfolio. Make a note of the feedback and information you received from your line manager that you need to consider.

4 Discuss your proposals with each group of relevant people you have identified and record what was suggested. Then draft your proposals bearing these in mind. Check these with the checklist on page 250. Attach a summary for your assessor which identifies the amendments you made because other people had different views and ideas.

5 You need to agree your detailed proposals with *at least two* of the following types of people:
   • your line manager
   • the users of your service
   • other people in your organisation with relevant expertise.
   Identify who you should best consult in this situation (normally your line manager should be asked for agreement out of courtesy) and then write an account of the discussions for your assessor (or ask these people to respond to you in writing).

6 Draw up a set of draft procedures for users. This could be a specification, a flow chart or a list of actions to take.

Keep your evidence safely. You will be adding to it in the next element.

Element 304.2 Implement and maintain administrative services

There is obviously little point devising a new service or thinking of improvements to an existing service if your ideas remain on paper in the bottom drawer of your desk! The next stage, having got this far, is to decide how and when you will implement them. In other words, you need to decide from what date will they take effect. The date you decide will depend upon:

- the number of people who must be informed
- the information users will need
- the training people may need
- the on-going support users may require
- the availability of any specialist equipment or resources you need.

These factors can vary tremendously. If your organisation decided to upgrade its computer system and change its software, then this obviously couldn't be done overnight. Chaos would ensue unless people had been told about the change in advance and had been trained how to use the new system.

Alternatively, if you designed (or redesigned) a simple form people had to complete when submitting photocopying requests, you could just send this around with a memo (or attach it to an e-mail) and tell people where stocks could be found and from what date they must use it.

Involving relevant people in planning the implementation

The people you consult in relation to planning the implementation will often be the same group you chose to agree your detailed proposals. Sometimes, however, you may have to involve additional people. In Kerry's case, her original group was:

- her own team
- the technical and sales staff
- the IT expert – Sam.

All of these people now need to be involved for the following reasons:

a She needs her team's advice on the best date to start using the system. It is no use, for instance, choosing a week when Jason or Rubia is on holiday.
b She needs the cooperation of the technical and sales staff. They, too, need prior warning of the date – and time to study the procedure.
c She needs Sam to set up some of the IT systems first. This is a constraint – as if Sam is very busy she may have to wait a week or two until it can be done. Only when they have been installed and tested would Sam be happy to 'go live'.

In addition, Kerry's line manager needs to be kept informed and consulted on the best date. He wants this to be as soon as possible and will expect Kerry to have a good reason if it is delayed. However, he also advises her that she may need to involve additional key people:

- the technical and sales managers – for courtesy reasons and because they will be dealing with some e-mails themselves
- the training officer, if Jason and Rubia first need a day or two of specialist training in using the system and the database.

Kerry had originally hoped to operate the system from next Monday. However, Jason and Rubia are pleased about the idea of specialist training and the training officer cannot arrange this for two weeks. An added complication is that the sales manager is at an overseas exhibition in two weeks' time and doesn't want the system starting whilst she is away. Kerry now has to amend her plans to take into account this feedback and eventually settles for a date three weeks on Monday. Until then, it is agreed that one of Sam's staff will print off the e-mails and send them direct to Kerry's boss who will deal with them himself.

TEST YOUR KNOWLEDGE AND UNDERSTANDING

1 Why did Kerry's boss want the system to start immediately?

2 Why was this not possible?

3 If the start of a system is delayed, why is it important to agree a temporary way of coping until then?

4 Why did Kerry have to consult with a greater number of people this time than she did originally?

5 Write a list of all the tasks which must be carried out before the system 'goes live'.

6 Given the time schedule, at what point do you think Kerry should notify everyone about the new system?

7 What method(s) of communication do you think she should use – and why?

Communicating the plans

The method of communicating plans will vary, depending upon the number and type of people involved and the complexity of the new system.

New users normally want four criteria to be met:

- clear information (in writing) on what they have to do – so they can refer to it when they need to

- details of what training they will require, if necessary, and when this will be held
- information on the support and help they will receive if they encounter problems
- answers to any questions they have when they read the details for the first time.

It is therefore sensible to have worked through this list yourself, before you start to communicate anything. Then you need to select your communication options. You can choose:

- verbal or written
- formal or informal.

There are advantages and disadvantages to each of these, but the best choice must be tailored to the type of procedure which is being introduced.

Verbal communication has several advantages:

- many people can be informed simultaneously (e.g. at a meeting)
- questions can be answered as they arise;

but:

- big groups can become difficult to handle if they have dozens of questions
- it is time-consuming to have to see lots of small groups.

A *formal* verbal method is a structured meeting of staff. This is more appropriate for a system which is complex, instigated by senior management or vitally important for legal or official reasons.

An *informal* one is a discussion with different groups. This is normally better for administrative systems which affect only certain groups of users. It is not usually appropriate for 'external' users.

Written methods are useful because:

- there is a document to refer to
- it is quick and easy – for sender and recipient;

but:

- you may need to build in a system whereby questions can be asked
- it is quite 'impersonal' and some people may resent just receiving a list of 'instructions'
- it is inappropriate if the procedure is very complex and would take pages of text to explain.

A *formal* written method is a letter or a formally phrased memo to staff with new procedures attached. Organisations normally notify customers in writing about new procedures.

Informal written methods include less formal memos and e-mails. Be careful, however, not so be so informal that staff think it doesn't matter whether or not they read it!

A combination of methods may be used in certain circumstances – such as a meeting of staff at which user documentation is issued and discussed.

Kerry decides to send everyone involved a memo and attach to it the procedures that they will use. Below is the memo she prepared and which she asks her line manager to approve. He agrees it but suggests she may be wise to send a reminder e-mail to everyone on the Thursday before the system is due to start!

M E M O

TO   All administrative, sales and technical staff

cc   Administration Director, Technical Manager, Sales Manager, IT
            Manager

FROM   Kerry Wright

DATE   8 February 200-

WEBSITE E-MAILS

The new administrative service to process e-mails sent to the website will come into effect on Monday, 1 March 200-. The system which will be used has been devised after consultation with all relevant staff and will enable us to offer a faster and more efficient response to enquirers and customers.

The administrative staff will receive and log all e-mails and forward them to the relevant experts. Responses *must* be sent direct to the administrators so that these, too, can be logged before the reply is forwarded to the enquirer.

Attached are the procedures which relate to your part in the process. I should be grateful if you would read these carefully and contact me direct, either by memo or e-mail, if you have any queries.

After two months we intend to review the system with all staff to check whether everyone is satisfied it is operating effectively, or whether any changes need to be made.   *KW*

Communicating with other relevant people

Kerry has copied her memo to Sam, the IT manager who has been helping her, her own boss and the sales and technical managers. She now needs to communicate with the IT trainer – which she may do by memo or e-mail.

You should note that it is often advisable to vary your method of communication or style with different groups of people – especially if they are at different 'levels' in the organisation. You may, for instance, prefer to talk to your manager before you send a copy of an e-mail or memo. Kerry may prefer to attach *another* memo to Sam's copy, which is more personal and thanks him for all his help. She may decide she would rather go and talk to the training department, rather than write to them, so that she can agree dates whilst she is there.

The only thing to watch, when you do this, is that you don't give the impression you are 'favouring' one group of people rather than another. Therefore, if you have to inform several groups of people at the same level, it is sensible to use the same method each time.

You won't go far wrong on this if you always consider which method would be best for *the particular user or group of people* – rather than which would be easier for you!

Training, information and support

Kerry simply has to arrange a short training session for Jason and Rubia. In some cases, training may need to be more widespread (such as when a new computer package is purchased or new safety regulations come into effect). Usually it will be undertaken 'in-house', but occasionally, if specialist skills are not available within the organisation, it may be necessary to send someone on a short training course. This may be the case if the system is complex or someone is taking on an entirely new role.

The amount of information provided can range from a one-page document (such as Kerry's) to a whole computer manual. High-level users of new complex database systems may find that they are presented with a 100-page manual at the end of their training! This is acceptable *provided* the key points in the manual have been highlighted during the training session and there is a clear index. People tend to refer to paperwork only when they are stuck, or need to check something they believe to be correct but are unsure about.

The support people receive may be on-going and continual or offered just for a short time – until everything settles down. On-going support is offered by facilities such as computer helpdesks, which can be contacted by either telephone or on-line. Specialist staff are trained to deal with a range of problems users may encounter and are supported themselves by experts who will give advice and assistance when required.

For most administrative services, it is likely that people would be very surprised if you ran a two-day training course, produced a 50-page manual and started up a helpdesk! However, all these principles apply to all systems, on a smaller scale. Kerry's method of arranging training for Jason and Rubia, producing clear procedures and offering herself as a contact if there are queries, means that she has considered all the relevant factors and the needs of potential users at this stage.

EVIDENCE COLLECTION

You are now going to develop your evidence for the administrative service(s) you identified and prepared plans for on page 257. Do this in the following way.

1 Identify all the people you need to consult about a possible implementation date, and agree this list with your line manager.

2 Consult your relevant people and note down any feedback (especially constraints) you receive which you need to consider when setting your implementation date.

3 Identify any training, information or support your proposed users will need. Consider how long this will take to arrange and prepare.

4 Identify an appropriate date for implementation which takes into account all these factors and agree this with your line manager.

5 Make a list of all the tasks you have to do to ensure you meet your scheduled date.

6 Decide how you will communicate your plans to at least two of the following people:

- your line manager

- users of the service

- other people in the organisation with relevant expertise

and how you would communicate if the third group was involved.

Consider at what stage you will provide training or documentation.

7 If you decide to communicate in writing, take a copy of any memos or e-mails you send. If you decide to communicate verbally, prepare a plan to show the key points you intend to cover and make notes afterwards. Remember that you may need to vary your communication method, depending upon the needs of the other people involved.

Finally, prepare a short summary for your assessor which describes what you have done and how you have done it and which covers all the points above. Attach any documents you have produced or received as further evidence.

Coping with problems

After all your preparations, it may seem incredible to have to think that anything might go wrong – but unfortunately it often does. Some problems are minor, others major. Some might mean you just have to change your implementation plans. Others may affect the whole proposed system and/or the documentation you have prepared.

Kerry thinks she has covered everything and, to be fair, it is unlikely that anything will go wrong on a major scale. But what if she is really out of luck? What should she do if each, any or several of the following problems occurred in the next two weeks?

- There is a major computer failure which Sam has to solve. This keeps him busy for at least two weeks and means he has to put Kerry's system on 'hold' for the moment.
- Jason gives in his notice.
- The procedures that were prepared and photocopied for distribution have been discarded in error and the photocopier has now broken down and can't be repaired until next Tuesday.
- The training officer is off sick and sends in a doctor's note for a month.
- A member of the technical staff, who was absent during the consultation, takes offence at the fact he will get 'reminders' from a member of the office staff if he doesn't respond promptly. He argues that his workload is such he cannot always guarantee this. He stirs up the rest of the technical staff who all refuse to cooperate.
- Rubia is trained by someone else and comes back saying she doesn't understand the database or the e-mail system, and doesn't want to do the job. The other two staff say they don't fancy it either.

Whereas problems of this magnitude – all at once – are unlikely, this should give you an idea that they *can* occur. It is wise never to be complacent and think that nothing can go wrong!

Coping skills – first identify a strategy

The strategy to use will depend upon the type of problem you get. Firstly identify the type, scale and scope of the possible problem.

Identify the *type* by remembering that problems are related to either:

- resources (e.g. equipment, people operating the system, documentation, time-scale) *or*
- 'people' issues (e.g. people changing their mind, arguing, becoming uncooperative).

Usually (but not always) resource problems are easier to solve than difficulties with people.

Identify the *scale* by working out its importance. This means looking at the possible impact on the plans which have been made.

- Those which deal with resources usually have 'delaying' effects – some of which are more serious than others. The photocopier problem is relatively minor. The IT staff being tied up for two weeks is a nuisance. The trainer leaving is a nuisance, too, but there should be a substitute somewhere. Most of these problems can be solved by moving the implementation date.

- Those which deal with people could result in the plans being abandoned altogether. Therefore the most serious issues are problems with the administrative staff and the non-cooperation from the technical staff.

Finally, identify problems you can solve and those you can't. Don't try to solve those where the *scope* is so large it involves other people over whom you have no influence. Look at Kerry's case.

a   She can talk to her administrative staff and try to persuade them to cooperate. The best strategy is to find out why they are so against the new system. Are they worried their skills will let them down? Was the trainer really bad so that Rubia may change her mind if she sees someone else? Are the staff worried they are overworked? If Kerry can find the reason behind their feelings she may be able to suggest some solutions – like a temporary member of staff to cover Jason's job until a replacement is found or suggesting a part-time member of staff works additional hours until then – and agreeing these with her own boss.

b   She cannot hope to influence the technical staff – who may be senior to her anyway. This issue needs to be discussed, and solved, by her boss and the Technical Manager. Whether they decide to enforce compliance or agree to make some adjustments to the procedure to appease the staff will depend very much upon the style of the managers and the culture of the organisation.

Consulting your line manager

If you have a problem, it is sensible to talk it through with your line manager. He or she may be able to suggest some solutions you hadn't thought about – and also has the power to enforce or change things that you don't.

However, you will be admired if, rather than bursting through the door in a rage or in despair, you sit and think of a few solutions yourself. Then approach your line manager to say that there has been an unexpected problem which could delay implementation. You have thought about it and have a few ideas but would be grateful if you could talk about these first. Even if your boss has better ideas than you, the fact you took a positive approach will be noted. And don't take it to heart if some of your solutions are rejected – there could be reasons you don't know about which mean they were not feasible.

Finally, if there is likely to be a delay in implementation or changes to the procedures, you must notify all the people concerned. If the reason is straightforward then you can state this; for example: 'Because of serious problems with our computer system, it has unfortunately been necessary to delay the start of the new e-mail service. This will now start on 15 March.' If the reason is a 'sensitive' one, then be more diplomatic; for example: 'Unfortunately, through unexpected events, there will be a delay in starting the new e-mail service. I will, of course, keep you informed if a new implementation date is agreed.' This doesn't commit anyone to anything!

EVIDENCE COLLECTION

Possibly, absolutely nothing will go wrong with your plans. If it does, then you should record what went wrong, at what point you consulted your line manager, what was discussed and what solutions were agreed, and then how you informed other people involved of the changes.

However, you still need to provide evidence that you *would* cope appropriately if problems occurred. So if nothing goes wrong, the best action to take is as follows.

1 Think of all the things that *could* go wrong – until you have a list of about five or six problems (like Kerry's)!

2 Identify the type, scale and scope of each problem and then state which you think:
   • you could solve yourself
   • you would discuss with your line manager (and note down any practical suggestions you would make)
   • would be beyond your control and *must* be discussed with your line manager urgently.

3 Select one of these problems, assume it has occurred, and state how you would communicate the agreed change to the following people, assuming they were all involved:
   a your line manager
   b users of the service
   c other people in the organisation with relevant expertise.

On-going monitoring

At the beginning of this unit, you learned that a major reason for reviewing administrative services is because:

- times, people and requirements change
- there may be flaws or problems in systems which annoy or inconvenience people.

This, therefore, means that even those administrative services you have improved or instigated need checking. In fact the whole process should be circular, as you can see in the diagram.

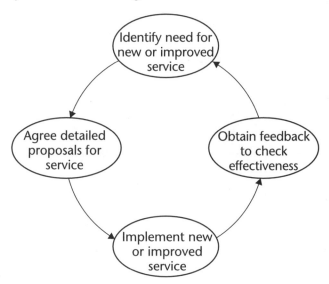

The review process

In some cases, with a new system, it is sensible to schedule a review a short time after it has been in operation. Two to three months is often a good timescale. You need to allow people to get used to operating the system before deciding whether it needs to be altered in any way. Only after a period of time will any snags show up. After the stated time, the simplest thing is to devise a short questionnaire to ask users whether they are satisfied or whether they can suggest any improvements. Or you may meet with them instead. Both of these methods were discussed under 'formal feedback' on page 238.

On page 242 you also read about how to 'walk the job' yourself to obtain information on whether a service is working correctly – and other monitoring strategies you can try. You need constant confirmation that users are satisfied and are using the service and following the procedures correctly. This should be objective and broad-based, so you know it is valid.

Read the developments with Kerry's system and then answer the questions that follow.

After two months, few problems had emerged with Kerry's system so no alterations were made. Six months later, however, she has the following feedback and information on her desk.

- The number of e-mails is growing daily. Jason, who decided to stay with the organisation, thinks this is great but Rubia is unhappy and struggling to cope.
- There are queries coming in which can't always be dealt with by sales and technical staff. For instance, last week a past employee e-mailed asking for details of his national insurance payments, and they have received several enquiries, about where video films or DVDs can be purchased, which are not relevant to their business.
- The sales manager is excellent at making sure her staff answer e-mails promptly but the technical manager is more 'hands off'. Rubia has told Kelly that when staff are absent he often takes several days to respond to a request, but she daren't send *him* a reminder!
- The database now has over 400 names and e-mail addresses on it but no-one has time to look at it.
- Sam has warned Kerry that in two months' they are upgrading their e-mail system and says she will need to consider how this will affect her e-mail service. He has suggested they meet very soon to discuss it.

1 If Kerry had consulted *only* Jason, would she have received an accurate version of the situation? Give a reason for your answer.

2 Which changes signify:
   a a minor problem, when a small readjustment to the service may be possible
   b a major problem, when the complete service may have to be reviewed?

3 Which information is useful, but not strictly relevant to Kerry's investigation of the service?

The answers are discussed in the section which follows, but try not to glance at this until you've thought about the issues yourself.

Making changes and adjustments

Changes can be small, incremental adjustments where you 'tweak' your system to take account of new factors. Or they may result in a complete overhaul of the service and the devising of a different system. Again, you need to consider the type of change or problem and its scale and scope.

- Rubia is struggling. She may need retraining or her job reviewing. A quick way of ascertaining this is to check how many e-mails she is 'processing' a day and how many problems she is struggling to solve. It may be necessary to train (or recruit) another member of staff to help her.

  These would all be adjustments to the system.

- The number of e-mails is increasing. This is significant and can impact on the whole service and system.

  This could result in a complete review of the service.

- Unusual queries can be handled by:

  a the service being extended so that other departments are involved (including customer service)

  b having a designated e-mail administrator answer 'one-off' queries.

  Both these could be an adjustment to the existing system.

- The technical manager may have to be tolerated unless Kerry's line manager can do anything about it. An adjustment could be for e-mails only to be referred to managers if the staff absence is going to be for a week or more. This would reduce the number of e-mails he handles.

  This is an adjustment to the system.

- Strictly speaking, the database is irrelevant to the service, but Kerry should mention this to her boss as their marketing department may wish to utilise it.

  This has no effect on the system unless it is deliberately integrated as part of Jason and Rubia's role.

- Kerry cannot tell what impact the new e-mail system will have on her own service until she has more details.

  However, this could result in a major review of the service.

A word of warning, however. A system which is regularly 'adjusted' in little bits can become unmanageable. If there are number of adjustments to make, it can often be easier to go back to the drawing board!

Again, you should talk through your findings and recommendations with your line manager. Again, too, you will be valued if you recommend the appropriate action to take. This proves you have thought through the issues and are taking a positive attitude to changing the service – rather than burying your head in the sand!

INFORMATION UPDATE

Organisations whose services are seen or used by members of the public often obtain feedback they would rather not receive. In one town in England, the council had a policy of trimming grass verges at regular intervals, so that the grass looked neat and never impeded the view of drivers. The system was straightforward with set procedures for the council workers. Each week, specific verges were identified for clipping in the spring and summer months so that, systematically, all the verges could be maintained.

The problem arose in spring, when hundreds of daffodils were due to bloom. In accordance with their procedures, the council workers set about clipping the grass. Unfortunately, because of the way their equipment operated, the daffodils were included – only the stalks remained. The townspeople went mad. Drivers stopped and accused the workers of vandalism. Gardeners alleged this would kill the bulbs forever more. The local paper took up the crusade. The council defended its actions by claiming it was simply following its 'policy and procedures' – but agreed a review may be necessary!

With an administrative service you are unlikely to find a problem you encounter as headlines in the evening paper, but do consider what parts of this system *you* would change before next spring!

EVIDENCE COLLECTION

1 Over a six-month period, review the service you have implemented. Note down the feedback and information you receive and the views of users, experts and your line manager.

2 Identify any improvements or changes which you think need to be made. State whether these can be accommodated by an adjustment to the service or whether more radical action is called for.

3 Produce a draft plan of action and discuss your ideas with your line manager. Then implement those which were agreed.

Note that if you don't receive any information which tells you that adjustments or changes are required, you will still have to prove this to your assessor! For instance, what evidence do you have to support your view that everything is working and being used correctly?

You will also need to show your assessor that you *could* suggest and implement changes if these were required. One way of doing this is to forecast the future! Think about one or two changes that *may* be required over the next few months and then suggest appropriate actions to take.

KEYS

Suggested answers to 'Test your knowledge and understanding' on page 229

a   Jenny is responsible for scheduling interviews and greeting candidates on arrival and showing them to the waiting room. (Procedure)

b   Many of them are nervous, especially if they have to take a word processing test which Jenny organises in the small room next door. (Procedure)

c   Her employer insists that all applicants for administrator jobs take a short word processing test which also tests their spelling and grammar. (Policy)

d   Today Jenny had a problem as the waiting room was being redecorated. (Constraint)

e   All applicants are interviewed by two people – usually the Human Resources Assistant and the line manager or team leader from the specific area advertising the vacancy. (Policy)

f   Jenny must prepare a list of all applicants in alphabetical order. (Procedure)

g   The test takes 10 minutes and then Jenny has to allow 20 minutes for each interview. (Procedure)

h   After the interviews, an offer is made to the successful candidate within two days and all the unsuccessful candidates are notified within a week. (Policy)

i   Jenny is struggling a bit today. The member of staff who normally supervises the test is ill, so Jenny is having to do this herself. (Constraint)

Suggested answers to 'Test your knowledge and understanding' on page 240

a   Lucy Merrow may be a nuisance but if finance want sales statistics each month, why haven't you set up a system to provide this automatically? Not urgent, but should be done.

b   Upsetting visitors is not a good idea – particularly potential or existing customers. It's probably one of the fastest ways of going out of business! You need a system for logging staff movements and cancelling diary appointments properly. Treat this as very important.

c   If there are repeated problems about travel you need to do something quickly – before a real crisis occurs. This one is important.

d   There needs to be a separate tray for important papers – or someone specifically designated to deal with them. This is just an adjustment to your existing system so could be put in place very quickly. It's important only if it keeps happening and/or you often handle 'special' papers.

e   People squabble about resource issues more than anything else. Set up a system for this which allocates rooms as fairly as possible – and do it quickly.

f   In this case there is nothing wrong with your photocopying system – but you need to adjust it to protect your staff from unfair accusations from people who leave complex photocopying requests to the last minute. Consider it important for everyone's sake.

g   This is very urgent. The potential benefits of having a website and e-mail service are completely destroyed if the service is poor.

h   It is unfair for a new recruit to be asked to do an important job with no guidelines. This is an obvious example where a set procedure would help as it will specify exactly what must be done. Messages are important as wrong or delayed information can cause real problems for staff and customers.

i   A situation where you are getting 'regular complaints' from both sides means something is sadly wrong – and must be put right as a matter of urgency.

Note that it is normally sensible to prioritise all those areas where a poor system is affecting the service you provide to customers. *Then* focus on the internal systems.

The benefits – in all cases – are a better service to all 'users' and more protection from unfair accusations for your staff.

SPECIAL NOTE

If you have enjoyed this unit and if, as part of your job, you regularly provide support to users of administrative services, you should consider doing Unit 309 as one of your options. That extends the knowledge you have learned here, and a simple strategy for obtaining relevant evidence is suggested. The unit is covered on page 461.

Unit 305 Research, prepare and present information from a variety of sources

This unit is concerned with the way in which you make use of a variety of sources to find information. It is important for you to know where you can locate relevant information and how to record it properly once you have done so. It is equally important for you to be able to present the information in the most appropriate format – one which the reader finds understandable, easy to read and well organised.

 KEY SKILLS SIGNPOST

If you are undertaking your Key Skills award you can use or adapt a research task you undertake linked to this unit to contribute to achieving your **Information Technology** Key Skills unit. Alternatively, an appropriate research task is suggested here. If you undertake the activities below you will obtain evidence for level 3. If you are working towards a different Key Skills level, do discuss this with your tutor or trainer.

IT3.1

1   Your brother is a landscape gardener and is considering leaving his employer to set up in business himself. He wants to set up an office at home and to use IT equipment to contact suppliers, advertise on the Internet, produce advertising material, prepare his garden designs, do his accounts and write to clients. His knowledge of gardens is considerable but his knowledge of IT is not. He has therefore asked for your help in identifying the equipment and software he is likely to need, the likely price, and what he will have to do to start up his website. He also has some concerns about security of information and issues such as viruses and would like you to take this into account. He wants you to accompany him to give a presentation when he meets his bank manager and another potential financial backer with the costs of this and the rationale behind the purchase.

2 Your employer is giving a talk on relevant trends that relate to your industry. He has asked you to investigate government and other statistical sources and obtain relevant information. He tells you that you can access these on www.statistics.gov.uk, then StatBase, then StatStore and download relevant statistics on the labour market or relating to your particular industry. As a first stage, he would like you to scan through the statistics available, find what you consider will be useful and then supplement these from other sources. (If you work in a particularly obscure industry, talk to your tutor about an alternative area you can investigate.)

Although you have been given initial guidance by your employer, you have received none from your brother. You have to plan which sources you will use to obtain the information you need in each case, and how you will use your judgement to make selections based on relevance and quality.

If you obtain information via an IT source, such as the Internet, make sure you take a printout and note on the top the searches you made and why you selected this particular item of information.

IT3.2

1 Draft a report for your brother which uses the information you have obtained.

    a Identify the type of equipment and software he will need and what he would use it for – preferably including at least two downloaded images as illustrations.

    b Analyse the range of prices available and give him a competitive price for each item you have selected.

    c Identify the difference in cost if he deferred some purchases, or bought some items at the cheaper end of the range – but state how this might affect his business operations at the outset.

    d Make recommendations as to the most appropriate purchases for his purpose.

    e Identify the benefits to his business of making the suggested purchases.

Send a draft of your outline report to your tutor for comments, using an IT method of communication. Take into account the response you receive when you start IT3.3.

2 Obtain relevant statistical data which relates to your own industry or that identified for you by your tutor. Sort this information so that you can use it to predict future changes on the assumption that current trends are maintained. Then investigate if there are

any factors which are likely to substantially change this hypothesis and adjust your forecast accordingly.

IT3.3

1 Prepare the presentation you will make with your brother, bearing in mind your audience. You will be expected to illustrate the talk with at least one image, and have detailed projections of likely expenditure. Your presentation should be well structured and incorporate any suggestions you received from your tutor. The image and figures should be easy to read, and clearly related to the aims of the presentation.

2 Prepare a written report for your employer about the current and forecast trends in your industry. Illustrate this with a graph or chart, substantiated by relevant, clearly structured data. Ensure that your report, too, is well structured and clear and meets the needs of your employer. Proofread your report and all your data carefully before submitting it.

KNOWLEDGE AND UNDERSTANDING REQUIRED FOR THE UNIT

Throughout this unit, emphasis is placed on the importance of agreeing what is expected of you and your ability to select the information most appropriate to your specific requirements. Many people, faced with research tasks, do not know where to begin or, conversely, collect so much information they feel as if they are drowning in a sea of paper! Access to the Internet and other electronic sources of information has made this all too easy. The skills of researching, therefore, are not confined to knowing how and where to find the information but understanding what to do with it afterwards.

It helps, therefore, if you are relatively selective from the outset. If you know where the most appropriate, up-to-date and relevant information is to be found, then this not only reduces the 'search' time but means you are less likely to have to sort through a mass of irrelevant information at the end. This unit covers all these skills – including the best way to present the information afterwards.

Researching information can be a very fulfilling part of your job as an administrator. You acquire a number of different and transferable skills – such as persistence and the ability to make a judgement about what is and is not relevant. The more experienced you become, the more valuable you are to your organisation and the more likely it is that your responsibilities in this area will increase. In addition, you will find good research skills are not just useful at work but are often invaluable in your personal life. You can adopt the techniques you learn here to finding the best holiday for your money or the best insurance quote for your car.

Agreeing and recording requirements and making sure they have been met

Agreeing and recording requirements

Imagine you work in the human resources section of a large engineering organisation. Your line manager has a specific responsibility for representing the organisation at industrial tribunal hearings should there be any claim for redundancy, unfair dismissal or discrimination. She is also expected to liaise with the safety adviser over the legal implications of any health and safety issues. Your job is to provide her with administrative support.

At the beginning of what promises to be a very busy week, she leaves the following note on your desk:

> I'm out all day but shall be back first thing tomorrow. Can you please make sure that you have all the following information ready for me.
>
> 1 The personnel file for James White – can you extract any relevant items and summarise them?
>
> 2 The latest thinking about stress in the workplace.
>
> 3 The general opinion on Rosie Threlfall.
>
> 4 An update on the accident on the shopfloor.

You don't find this a particularly difficult task. You extract all the favourable comments about James White from his file and summarise them. You spend a long time researching stress in the workplace and prepare a very detailed report covering the increase of stress-related illness in the workplace and the latest thinking on how it can be alleviated. You use your own initiative and make recommendations about the action that could be taken in the organisation to relieve the stress many staff are currently experiencing. You ask Rosie's boss for his comments about her – which aren't very good and which he makes in front of a number of the staff. You ask the shopfloor manager about the accident and he tells you that the worker concerned had suffered no real injury, was back at work and didn't intend to pursue the matter.

When your line manager returns, however, you can tell immediately that she is not too pleased with your efforts. Apparently the information you have provided is not what she wanted, for a variety of reasons.

a   James White is an ex-member of staff who left the organisation recently but who now alleges that he was forced to leave because he was suffering from nervous stress. He wants to take his claim to the industrial tribunal.

b   Rosie Threlfall has complained that her supervisor is constantly treating her less favourably than the men who work with her.

c   There have been two accidents on the shop floor. One of them was minor but the other was far more serious and the worker had to be taken to hospital with an eye injury. The safety adviser is certain that he will make a claim for negligence.

The fault was not entirely yours, because your manager should have been far more explicit in stating her requirements, and since she was away you had no opportunity of checking with her what she actually wanted. Wherever possible, however, it is important that you agree *exactly* what you have been asked to do before you begin your research. In most cases, verbal explanations are sufficient. However, where a large amount of information is required, where the research is likely to take a long time or if the information may be of considerable significance, it is sometimes a good idea to ask for your terms of reference to be in writing. Alternatively, you can always put in writing what *you* think is required and ask for confirmation. Here are some of the points you may want to raise.

- What is the specific purpose of gathering the information, and in what format should it be displayed – a summary, a list of relevant documents, a list of references etc.?
- What should be the limits of the research? The amount of information about stress in the workplace, for instance, is now quite vast. In that case, you could ask whether your research should be limited to the more recent publications or whether more detailed information is required.
- If your line manager asks you to find out some information, he or she may well have some ideas of where you should start or to whom you should speak.
- How much time is there? If the information is required for the next day, it is probably going to be less detailed than if you are given more time to research.
- How confidential is the information (i.e. to what extent can you let people know why it is wanted)? For instance, you might have talked differently to Rosie's supervisor if you had known how confidential that information could be.
- Is cost a factor? You may want to make a library search for which a fee will be payable. You may want to spend some time on the Internet. You may have to contact outside sources and incur costs of time, travelling expenses and possibly a consultant's fee.

Making sure that requirements have been met

In most cases, it is obvious to you and to the person asking you for the information that you have provided what is required. In some cases, however, you may have to keep a check that you are not digressing from the point or researching the wrong area. You may find it helpful to write down your initial terms of reference on a Post-it note and stick it on to the edge of your word processor so that when you are summarising your findings the note acts as a constant reminder of exactly what you are supposed to do.

Alternatively you may want to keep a checklist of what you have done and what you have still to do, so that each time you tick off an item you are again reminding yourself of your objectives.

Where the information required is important or complex, you will need to liaise with the person who has requested it. It is rather disheartening to complete what you think is a very well-researched and comprehensive piece of information, only for your line manager to say that that wasn't *quite* what was wanted and could you start again please! Quite often you will find that the discussions you have will lead to amendments to the initial terms of reference and ultimately to a better final result.

TEST YOUR KNOWLEDGE AND UNDERSTANDING

Your line manager is very busy. He travels a great deal and is sometimes away for several days at a time. He relies on you to provide him with information on a number of different issues – products, clients, competitors, costs etc. Much of the information he requires is complicated and some of it is highly confidential. You are quite confident about undertaking any initial research but on many occasions would like to be able to consult him before presenting him with the final document.

Write a memo to him explaining your concern, pointing out the advantages of consultation and setting out a suggested procedure for doing so.

Legislation covering information searches and the use of information

One problem you may have to face when asked to carry out research is how to distinguish between fact and opinion. Many writers like to be controversial and to deliberately blur the distinction between the two. Journalists realise that they need to sell newspapers and again may 'stretch' the truth slightly or exaggerate the significance of their findings. The same thing can happen when you are having a chat with someone and he or she gives you information which may be coloured by a personal opinion. In most cases, this is merely an inconvenience even if you do report back exactly what was written or said without attempting to refine the information in any way.

On occasions, however, the repercussions of doing that might be more serious. Suppose, for instance, that you have arranged to talk to the safety officer about the safety committee and, in particular, his opinion of how effective it is. This is his reply:

'If you only knew the half of it. I daren't tell you what really goes on in this place or we'd all be up in court. Did you hear about the accident in the car park last month? It was blatant negligence on the part of the lorry driver and he was very lucky to get away with it. He'd been drinking you know – I don't know how he managed to climb into the cab never mind drive the lorry. No wonder it crashed into the wall. You must know who I mean – it's Bill Fox – he's been here for years. He's one of the union representatives so he's allowed to do what he likes of course. I put all the details into a report to the MD but he didn't want to do anything about it and completely refused to let me contact the HSE inspector. He doctored the report so much that when it went before the safety committee it was unrecognisable – and that's by no means an isolated incident.'

You are shocked and you write a memo to your line manager describing in detail what the safety adviser has told you. In doing so, you've probably caused yourself and the safety adviser considerable problems in that you may be in breach of the law of defamation. What the safety adviser has said about the lorry driver and the MD could be held to be slanderous. What you have written about both of them could be held to be libellous. The only real defence would be to prove that what was said was true and without malice – but that may be very difficult to do.

No matter how indignant you feel about something you have researched, it is always wise to sit back and think about it before putting anything in writing or indeed of bursting into your manager's office and saying exactly what you think. If you are in any doubt, have a quiet word with him or her and ask for advice.

 INFORMATION UPDATE

Most people are aware that if they say or write something untrue about someone they may be breaking the law. However, some people seem less aware that if they publish something on the Internet, or print off from it, the same rules apply. The Internet service provider (ISP) can rely upon the same defence as anyone else (i.e. section 1 of the Defamation Act 1996) which allows them to claim innocent dissemination if they are unaware that the material is defamatory and have taken reasonable care to prevent such material being published. However, the amount of material being put on to the Internet is so vast and ever-changing that potentially defamatory material can be published without the ISP being immediately aware of the fact. This has led to claims that this 'diverse and dynamic' source of reference may be unduly restricted as ISPs withdraw or refuse admission of material, however potentially interesting, to avoid taking the chance that it may be defamatory.

See pages 289 and 292 for further information on the Internet as a source of reference.

Confidentiality, data protection and copyright

Confidentiality

The Data Protection Acts are designed to preserve the confidentiality of much of the information relating to people within an organisation. (See pages 281–284 for further information on this point.) However, other documents are equally confidential not because they make reference to the staff but because they contain information about sales figures, legal issues, pricing policies, costs, strategic plans, new developments, capital expenditure etc. It is therefore important that you know what you can and what you cannot access without having first obtained permission.

Many organisations establish levels of responsibility. Some documents are available to all members of staff, some to a limited number of managers and some only to senior management. If the information is stored electronically, limiting access is quite easy. The approved users are given an authorised password which, to preserve confidentiality, is changed at regular intervals. It is less easy to prevent access to paper documents. The obvious devices of locked filing cabinets with keys issued only to approved users will preserve a certain level of confidentiality, but it can be very easy to forget to lock a filing cabinet or to leave it open during the working day because you need constant access to it. In such circumstances you can almost guarantee that the person in the office who takes it upon himself or herself to be the unofficial information gatherer – and distributor – will take advantage of the unlocked drawer the moment your back is turned.

If you are aware that this is happening, it might be worth while dropping into the general conversation that having someone access your files without your permission is not simply an annoyance, it can also have legal repercussions. If the offender discloses information to someone else who makes use of it to the detriment of the organisation, both may be regarded as having broken a term in their contract of employment (known as the 'good faith' term) because they have not acted in the best interests of the organisation. They could be dismissed.

Much depends on your working environment and what is regarded by your organisation as being very confidential. Generally speaking, however, the law recognises that to be confidential:

- the information must be of use to business rivals if it is made public
- the owner of that information must reasonably believe that it is not already known to other people.

In addition, a distinction is made between confidential information and the 'know-how' of employees. If, for instance, you are responsible for the pricing strategies in your organisation and decide to disclose that information to a business rival or write a journal article about it, the courts might decide that you are merely talking about your own personal expertise and not revealing information confidential to the company. Much depends on:

- the nature of the information itself
- whether you are aware of the sensitivity of the information.
- the emphasis your manager has placed on its being confidential and whether it is capable of being easily detached from other information which is not regarded as confidential.

INFORMATION UPDATE

Many organisations are so concerned about confidential 'leaks' by their employees that they insert an express confidentiality clause into their contracts of employment. It is then much more difficult for employees to claim that they were unaware they were doing something wrong in giving certain information to other people.

Data protection

When you have worked for an organisation for a number of years your personnel file may be bursting at the seams with all sorts of information about you – your initial application form, various job descriptions, training and staff development courses you have attended, details of your pension rights, your performance appraisal etc. There might also be less pleasant information such as details of any disciplinary proceedings taken against you, copies of memoranda from your line manager criticising your work etc. In normal circumstances you would not be aware of this – which could come as a shock to you should you ever want to request a reference, apply for promotion or be involved in a grievance etc.

If your organisation is efficient it will have protected this information in some way – locked filing cabinets with limited access to keys, access to the files restricted to specified users etc. If it is not, then virtually anyone can spend an interesting few moments poring over details about you which you would rather not have been made public.

Prior to 1984 there was very little you could do about this, but the government realised that a lot of confidential information was being transferred on to computer databases, allowing access to it by a large number of people. As a result, it introduced the Data Protection Act, which required employers using a computerised database to register as data users. One major drawback to the **Data Protection Act 1984** was that it applied only to *databases*. Information stored in a filing cabinet was not covered by it – although the **Access to Health Records Act 1990** allowed employees to access any health records held by their employer whether in manual or computerised format. If, therefore, your personnel records had not been transferred to a database, your legal rights would be very limited.

The Data Protection Act 1998

Because of growing concern about an apparent loophole in the 1984 law, the Data Protection Act 1998 was introduced which replaced the original Act. This extended several of the original requirements and, in particular, covered data held in manual filing systems as well.

Organisations were given until 23 October 2001 to check that all their new data and files comply with the Act, although manual data held in filing systems prior to 24 October 1998 will not be completely covered by the Act until October 2007. This extension period is to allow data controllers – businesses and organisations which hold personal data – time to check which files must comply with the law and take the required action.

If an organisation fails to comply or contravenes the Act, the Information Commissioner has the power to issue an *enforcement notice* or an *information notice* against that data controller. An enforcement notice instructs the data controller what action it must take (or what activities it must cease). An information notice is a request for details. The Commissioner also has the power to apply for a warrant to enter and search premises if there is evidence of contravention. Failure to comply with a notice or to obstruct a search are criminal offences.

The table below gives more details of the Act and the information it covers.

The Data Protection Act 1998
The Act requires all organisations and businesses which process personal data on individuals (a **data subject**) to give notification that they should be included in a register of **data controllers**, unless they have already registered under the 1984 Act. They must state
* their name and address and the name of their representative, if any
* a description of the personal data being processed and the types of data subject which it covers (e.g. customers, employees, students etc.)
* a description about why the data is being processed
* a description about any recipients to whom it may be disclosed
* a description of any countries outside the EU to which it may be sent
The term 'data' which is covered by the Act relates to:
* information recorded or processed by computer
* information which is part of a relevant filing system or forms part of an accessible record, eg health records, social services records etc. ➡

All data controllers must comply with the eight Principles of the Act in relation to the handling of personal data.

* Data must be obtained and processed fairly and lawfully. Normally this means the individual has given his/her consent. Explicit consent is required for 'sensitive' data relating to religious or political beliefs; racial origin; trade union membership; physical or mental health or sexual life; criminal convictions.
* Personal data must be held only for one or more specified and lawful purposes and should not be processed for another reason.
* The data should be adequate, relevant and not excessive.
* Personal data must be accurate and kept up to date.
* Personal data must be kept no longer than is necessary.
* It must be processed in accordance with the rights of data subjects (see below).
* It must be stored to prevent unauthorised or unlawful access, loss, destruction or damage.
* It must not be transferred outside the EU unless the country to which it is being sent also protects the rights of data subjects.

The rights of individuals (data subjects) include:

* the right to access data held about them
* the right to prevent processing which would cause damage or distress
* the right to prevent processing for direct marketing purposes
* rights in relation to automated decision-taking (e.g. evaluating job performance or credit-worthiness on the basis of personal information)
* the right to take action to correct, block, erase or destroy inaccurate data
* the right to compensation if damage is suffered through contravention of the Act.

Exemptions

The Act allows for certain exemptions, although in many cases specific conditions are attached. Broadly, the categories of exempt data include that held for:

* purposes of national security
* crime detection and taxation purposes
* health, education and social work
* research, history and statistics
* domestic use only.

The key point to note is the central principle of the Act. All personal information a business has about an individual is the property of that individual. He or she should have full rights over the data, can see it at any time, and can seek compensation should the records be incorrect or damaging – even if they have not been shown to anyone else!

INFORMATION UPDATE

Although the 1998 act is now in force, recent research by an information solutions provider has shown that over 60 per cent of businesses are not aware that there is a new Data Protection Act and nearly 90 per cent are unsure how it affects them. Even worse is the situation with new Internet start-ups. Many of these are young people who simply set up in business with a computer and a good idea but very scant knowledge of their legal obligations.

Those who are fully aware of the Act tend to be people who are particularly affected by it – the banks, those organisations which rely heavily on obtaining personal data from third parties, such as direct marketing and credit referencing, pharmaceutical companies which conduct clinical trials, and airlines because they tend to transfer data outside the UK. However, financial services organisations have also had a bad press – mainly because staff who work there do not realise the new rights of individuals in this respect. So if you are turned down when you ask for details on your personal data from such an organisation, you now know how to argue your case!

CHECK IT OUT!

As an administrator, the data protection legislation can work both for you and against you. It protects you personally but it can also hamper you if, for instance, you are asked to research some material which involves access to the personnel files.

At your workplace, college or training institution, check to see whether there is a code of conduct or set of procedures in place informing staff what access rights they and other people have to certain information. Make a brief note of what they are.

Copyright

Not all information is free! Information you obtain from internal sources is likely to be provided without charge – although some modern organisations are so firmly committed to internal trading between departments or sections that your department might be billed for the time it takes to produce the information required, the cost of photocopying etc. Charges from external sources vary. Some government or local government departments regard the provision of information as a public service. Others ask for a nominal charge to cover expenses.

One external source of reference you might expect to be free of charge is the public library – and to a certain extent that is true, apart from a fee being charged for an information search. However, indirectly, much of the information you obtain from a library will incur a cost as a result of copyright legislation.

When you visit a library and find the information you require, you can make notes of what you have found. You may also want to photocopy relevant sections of a book or journal to save time and to ensure accuracy. The law allows you to do this but stipulates certain restrictions – otherwise the writers and publishers of the books and journals would suffer financially if everyone chose to copy their works rather than buying them. If someone writes a book, composes a song, makes a film or creates any other type of artistic work, he or she is allowed to claim property or copyright in it. Anyone else who wishes to use it must get permission to do so and, in some cases, must pay a fee.

The major piece of legislation in this area is the **Copyright, Designs and Patents Act 1988**. See the table for an outline of some of its contents.

Extracts from the Copyright, Designs and Patents Act 1988

Works protected by copyright

* literary, dramatic, musical and artistic works
* sound recordings, films, broadcasts and cable programmes
* the typographical arrangements of published editors (i.e. the whole layout of the printed pages of a published edition of a work)

Length of copyright period

* *Literary, dramatic, musical and artistic works:* Copyright expires at the end of the 70th year after the year in which the author died.

* *Sound recordings and films:* Copyright expires at the end of 70 years from the end of the year in which the work was made or released.

* *Typographical arrangements:* Copyright expires at the end of the 25th year after the year in which the edition incorporating the arrangement was first published.

Rights of the copyright owner

* to copy the work
* to issue copies of it to the public
* to perform, show or play the work in public
* to broadcast it or include it in a cable programme service
* to adapt it.

Collection agencies

In the past, one difficulty for authors and composers was how to collect the fees owing to them. It was impossible, for instance, for them to keep a check on every photocopier in every library. It was equally difficult for them to check on every entertainment venue to see whether their music was being played. Nowadays, however, they are assisted by a number of collection agencies whose role is to ensure that the payments are made. See the tables below for a list of the more important agencies, and other organisations concerned with copyright protection guidance and assistance.

The more important collecting agencies

Copyright Licensing Agency (CLA)
CLA licenses schools, colleges, universities, government departments, public bodies and commercial organisations to copy extracts from books, journals and periodicals.

Design and Artists Copyright Society (DACS)
DACS is the copyright and collecting society for the visual arts in the UK.

Educational Recording Agency (ERA)
ERA issues blanket licences to educational establishments covering recording off-air from broadcast and cable programmes for the purpose of educational instruction.

International Federation of the Phonographic Industries (IFPI)
IFPI licenses public performance, broadcasting and cable distribution rights in certain sound recordings, mainly foreign recordings not commercially available in the UK market.

Mechanical Copyright Protection Society (MCPS)
MCPS represents composers and publishers of music and acts as a centralised collection and distribution agency for mechanical royalties, which accrue whenever musical works are recorded.

Newspaper Licensing Agency (NLA)
NLA was created by national newspaper publishers to enable organisations and companies to legally copy extracts from newspapers.

Performing Right Society (PRS)
PRS administers the performing rights in copyright music on behalf of composers and music publishers both in this country and abroad. The performing rights are the right to perform music in public either 'live' or by mechanical means (e.g. by playing a tape or turning on a television set), the right to broadcast music and the right to diffuse music (e.g. by cable television). ➡

Phonographic Performance Ltd (PPL)
PPL administers the public performance, broadcasting and distribution rights in the main repertoire of sound recordings protected in the UK.

Video Performance Ltd (VPL)
VPL licenses the public performances, broadcasting and cable distribution rights in music video recordings in the UK.

Copyright protection organisations

Anti Copying in Design (ACID)

Association of Authors' Agents

Association of Illustrators

Association of Learned and Professional Society Publishers (ALPSP)

Association of Photographers

Association of Professional Composers

Author's Licensing and Collecting Society (ALCS)

British Academy of Songwriters, Composers and Authors (BASCA)

British Actors' Equity Association

British Computer Society (BCS)

British Institute of Professional Photography (BIPP)

British Phonographic Industry Ltd (BPI)

Broadcasting, Entertainment, Cinematograph and Theatre Union (BECTU)

Business Software Alliance (BSA)

Chartered Institute of Journalists (CIOJ)

Chartered Society of Designers (CSD)

Composers' Guild of Great Britain

Federation against Copyright Theft (FACT)

Federation against Software Theft (FAST)

Musicians' Union (MU)

Music Publishers' Association (MPA)

National Union of Journalists (NUJ)

Patent Office

Periodical Publishers' Association (PPA)

Publishers' Association (PA)

Publishers' Licensing Society (PLS)

Royal Photographic Society (RPS)

Society of Authors

Training Media Copyright Association

Writers' Guild of Great Britain

Exceptions

In certain circumstances you will not infringe the Copyright, Designs and Patents Act 1988. Exemptions apply if you are:

- using the work for private research or study
- criticising or reviewing the work – provided the identity of the author and the title of the work are acknowledged
- reporting current events – provided the identity of the author is acknowledged
- incidentally including any work in an artistic work, sound recording, broadcast or cable programme (e.g. a shot in a film showing a book lying on a table with its title visible)
- using it for educational purposes (except where a licence has been negotiated)
- reporting parliamentary or judicial proceedings, the proceedings of a Royal Commission or astatutory enquiry
- copying an abstract of an article on a scientific or technical subject published in a periodical containing both the abstract and the article.

 INFORMATION UPDATE

Specific regulations for libraries and archives are contained in the **Copyright (Libraries and Archivists) (Copying of Copyright Material) Regulations 1989**. The main privileges they enjoy are to make copies for readers requiring them for the purposes of research or private study. The person requiring the copy must:

- use it only for research or private study
- pay a sum to the library sufficient to cover the cost of making the copy and a contribution to the general expenses of the library

- sign a declaration form.

No more than one copy of one article from any issue of a periodical publication may be made and no one else with similar or related requirements may have received a copy of the same material.

Copyright and software

Copyright legislation also affects computer users. All software has its own **licence agreement** which gives the purchaser the right to use it in an agreed manner (you are, in effect, purchasing the licence, not the software itself – which remains the property of the company or person who wrote it). You cannot, for instance, copy software held on another machine and use it on your own without permission. Nowadays many organisations purchase special licences in order for them to be able to put a piece of software on to the file server and allow access to it by several users.

Copyright and the Internet

A source of reference which is growing in importance is the Internet. Nowadays you can access the Internet for an almost limitless amount of information. Again, however, it is important to remember that the material is subject to copyright and Web pages are themselves regarded as literary works. Provided you are authorised to access a particular page (e.g. on the staff intranet or a page that is password protected and you have used your proper username and password), you are not likely – at least up until now – to be in breach of copyright if you print some material from it. However, copying from other Web pages may be subject to copyright legislation. If the copying is not specifically covered in the page's own copyright notice, you should check on the copyright restrictions – many websites contain a copyright notice detailing how the material they contain may be used.

Many organisations are so concerned about possible breach of Internet copyright that they have appointed copyright advisers to check on the ways in which staff use the Internet and in particular how frequently they copy material from it. The advisers are also responsible for what their own organisations place on their website and whether or not their copyright has been or is likely to be breached.

Element 305.1 **Research, locate and select information from a variety of sources**

The type of sources you can use to access information will vary, depending upon the type of organisation which employs you. When you first start in a new job, it often takes some time to understand all the technical terms or 'jargon' used by the business or industry, let alone get to know all the people who have specialist knowledge in the organisation. Therefore, even if you have been an excellent researcher in one area, you may have to adjust your techniques – and your sources – if you change your employment.

People who work for organisations where information needs to be obtained quickly, such as journalists and television researchers, have recourse to a variety of on-line specialist sources. The organisation considers paying for these is a worthwhile investment, because they are used regularly. Your organisation, too, may have specialist on-line sources you can access.

Throughout this element you will find a range of suggestions you can use, no matter where you work, to obtain relevant and up-to-date information on a variety of topics.

The range of information sources commonly used by your team

Paper-based sources

The longer you work in an organisation, the more likely it is that you will have gathered together a considerable amount of information for your personal use. In all probability you will have lists of internal telephone users, as well as names, addresses, e-mail addresses and fax numbers of clients/customers and suppliers – office/computer suppliers, travel agencies, employment agencies, the Job Centre, solicitors, accountants, banks, the local tax office, relevant local authority departments, car hire firms, garages, restaurants and hotels, electrical/plumbing, heating specialists, the local library etc. If not, you may be able to access the BT On-line service which allows you to check telephone numbers of both businesses and private addresses.

An important point to remember here is that the information is not going to be of much use if it is hopelessly out of date. That is one problem of taking over someone else's personal file. They will have some idea of how current the information is. They may know some of it is no longer correct but have not got round to amending it. You will not. In such cases it is useful to spend a few minutes each day checking and updating the information until you feel in a position to be able to rely on it.

Your **filing system** is – or should be – an invaluable source of reference for you. Again, it is particularly useful because normally you will have organised it yourself and know what information it holds. You may, however, find it helpful to regard your system as one that needs regular review.

- How is the information stored? Even in a relatively low-tech area such as that of storage and retrieval systems, things change. A glance through a business or office equipment journal can give you some good ideas as to how to improve yours.
- Is the classification and index system the most appropriate for your needs? If, for example, you have always classified your files by subject and have made little or no use of an index system, it is sometimes useful to consider whether or not to make a change.
- How quickly can you access information? If your filing cabinets are in another room, down a badly lit corridor or simply too far from your desk, you are causing yourself possibly needless problems.

In Group A Options, Unit 306 provides further information on effective storage and retrieval systems – see page 345.

Computer-based resources

Databanks

An increasing amount of information is now held in computer databanks. You may be able to access your own organisation's management information system, which could comprise any of the following.

- **Office support systems** such as electronic mail, word-processing and computer networks provide assistance with many office tasks.
- **Data processing systems** such as accounts, payroll, production and stock control records keep account of everyday office activities.
- **Decision support systems** such as spreadsheets and forecasting techniques provide management with assistance in planning and decision-making.

In Group A Options, Unit 307 provides information on company databases – see page 380.

Most libraries now allow access to the Internet and to a wide variety of CD-ROMS (sometimes known as an Electronic Reference Library). There, for instance, you can look at back copies of newspapers and journals or research the major encyclopaedias and dictionaries in addition to specific subject-based material. Some libraries also offer access to on-line databases stored on a mainframe computer and linked to the library computer. The 'help' facility on the computer database normally guides you in the right direction. If not, there are usually instructions displayed near each system.

There are also public computer databanks such as *Teletext* and *Viewdata*, although the Internet has gained so much in popularity recently that these are becoming less well used.

Private viewdata (for which a subscription is normally necessary) is normally a private database created for a particular organisation or organisations. The travel industry, for instance, makes considerable use of these to enable them to gain access to a wide range of travel information.

The Internet

Within the Internet is the World Wide Web which is the multimedia computer network offering text, sound and pictures. In the early 1990s, Web pages were seldom more than words and pictures with links to other pages of words and pictures. Increasingly, the technology allows the audiovisual medium to be integrated almost seamlessly into the Web as a whole.

The basic requirement for viewing a Web page is the graphical interface called a **browser**, which turns Web documents written in HTML (hypertext markup language) format into understandable information. Currently the two most popular browsers are Netscape's *Navigator* and Microsoft's *Internet Explorer*. These are available for both Apple Macintosh and Microsoft Windows formats. In their most recent versions they have integrated multimedia features.

If you have a new computer you will probably find that it has been preloaded with one or other of these browsers. If you are using an older computer, the institution or commercial organisation that provides your access to the Internet should be able to supply you with browsing software. New versions of Navigator and Internet Explorer appear quite frequently and can be downloaded from the Internet free of charge.

 INFORMATION UPDATE

The *Sunday Times* recently published a list of the 'top 100' Internet ventures. They included:

- www.sportal.com, which covers sport in eight countries and provides forums, chat rooms and live celebrity chat shows
- www.boxman.com, which is an online retailer of home entertainment
- www.mondus.com, which enables small and medium-sized businesses to find the best deals for goods and to obtain feedback about suppliers used by other companies
- www.peoplesound.com, which provides free music (but a recent court ruling may limit the growth of such websites as being in breach of copyright)

- www.moreover.com, which aims to be the automatic distributor of news to other Internet sites

- www.epo.com, by which the investment process from publication of a prospectus to registration and distribution of shares is carried out over the Internet

- www.silicon.com, which aims to be the leading news site for all matters relating to the business of information technology

- www.e.exchange.com, which puts buyers and sellers into 'neutral' contact – i.e. it has no ties to manufacturers or preferred suppliers.

Many critics claim that current Internet search engines only access about 15% of the estimated 60 million businesses worldwide. Needless to say, plans are afoot to improve this. The first step is to increase the number of available domain names by allowing new suffixes, such as .biz, .info, .pro, .aero – and many more. The second is to create a global directory of businesses on the Internet. IBM is backing a venture whereby a list of companies will be prepared, regardless of size, and allocated to country and region. The aim is to place this information in a giant, searchable, database.

An intranet

An additional source of information, which also appears to be growing in importance, is a staff intranet or in-house information network upon which (in theory at least) all previously paper-based information related to an organisation can be placed, and to which all staff have access. There are many benefits in doing this. Think, for instance, of your internal telephone directory. Even the most efficient administrator can forget to insert the regular updates or can lend it to someone who forgets to return it.

If such information is on the company intranet, these problems will not arise. In addition, very important information such as health and safety or disciplinary and grievance procedures, if put on the intranet, makes it more difficult for employees to say that they were not aware of what they were expected to do or that they have never had a copy of the relevant information. It is hardly surprising, therefore, that intranet usage is increasing in popularity. At the end of 1998 it was estimated that 38 per cent of European companies and 59 per cent of US companies had an intranet, and those figures are predicted to increase dramatically.

However, there are some problems with an intranet. According to a recent survey of 300 of the UK's top 1000 companies, although many organisations have been eager to introduce one, a number of them have done so with no real idea of what they want to put on it. In some cases an intranet has not done much more than replace the office noticeboard. In others the organisational structure itself has hindered developments by trying to duplicate departmental and managerial hierarchies, so that users do not have direct access to the information they want.

Such mistakes have resulted in an unwieldy mass of 'infojunk' – data that is not useful, is out of date or totally inaccurate. Many organisations are now giving their information management staff the task of improving the service. Microsoft, hardly surprisingly, is one of the leaders in this field. The computer software giant has encouraged its customers to consider integrating their intranets with existing computer applications, so that eventually it could be the way in which users access databases and communicate with customers and suppliers.

CHECK IT OUT!

Organisations setting up an intranet for the first time are advised to consider the following key points.

a Allow *all* staff access. Restricting access means it can never be the primary means for communication in a company.

b Remember security. Access to confidential or highly sensitive information should still be limited to a number of authorised users.

c Avoid too much junk information. Don't clear out the contents of the filing cabinets on to your intranet without thinking exactly what is and what is not relevant.

d Keep it up to date. If users don't trust the system, they won't use it.

e Don't try to do too much at once.

f Make sure that the information looks good. Avoid inputting organisational documents of 20 pages in length. Try instead to use small amounts of text with clear headings.

g Make use of the Web by introducing external information sources.

h Consider what use could be made of it by suppliers and customers.

In your workplace, college or training institution check to see whether you or other staff have access to an intranet. If you have, try to assess it against the key points listed above, and write a brief report on how far you think the system meets those criteria.

If you have not, ask for an interview with your line manager and obtain his or her views on the advantages and disadvantages of an organisational intranet as a source of information.

INFORMATION UPDATE

- The point has already been made that to be effective, information must be up to date. It is therefore interesting to note that recent research has indicated that many people are over-trusting about the information they read on an intranet. Apparently, information that they would not take for granted as being up to date if it were in written form, tends to be accepted without question if it is on an intranet. That is not always the right thing to do!

- It might be quite hard to believe but the Internet is now officially 'old fashioned'. Scientists are in the process of developing the Grid that will deliver computing power in the same way the National Grid provides electricity. It will be able to handle petabytes of information – ten million billion bits of data per year – a thousand times faster than today's fastest computer networks.

Telephone information sources

Accessing information via the telephone is quick, simple and direct and is a very useful starting point for many researchers. A telephone directory not only provides you with names, addresses and telephone numbers but also with a wide variety of other information. The contents page of one local directory, for instance, provides you with a summary of information about:

- the community – local libraries and community centres; emergency numbers such as casualty, electricity, gas and water services and charity helplines
- employment – starting your own business, business advice from enterprise trusts, Job Centres
- health – health authorities, health information, community health councils, doctors
- travel – airports, bus/train enquiries, car rental, minicabs, taxis and private hire firms
- street maps
- sports and fitness centres
- restaurants and hotels
- financial and business services – accountants, insurance companies, financial advisers, financial services
- trade associations.

People-based sources

A major source of information is your own team. You will all have different skills, knowledge, experience and backgrounds, so the amount of information you will be able to exchange with each other is probably quite extensive. It is another cheap, easy and convenient way to start a search.

TEST YOUR KNOWLEDGE AND UNDERSTANDING

Imagine that you are part of a group working together for a firm of management consultants.

After leaving school, Des spent a couple of years backpacking abroad. He then came back to the UK and worked for a firm of printers. He loves music and is lead singer with a local band which performs at weddings, special birthday parties etc. He is now the office manager.

Farmin looks after the accounts. He has a business studies degree and a professional accounts qualification. He used to work for an airline company and enjoyed the travel perks. He then had a period in the local branch of a large multinational company.

Mel is the expert on computers. She has worked in schools and colleges and has also spent some time in a Job Centre working with the unemployed. She is also a local councillor.

You assist Des with all administrative matters, but report to Sally Lane, your line manager. She specialises in advising clients on how to obtain European funding to assist in the employment, training and retraining of their staff. She wants to hold a seminar next month and asks you to do some preliminary research on whether or not the local area is one which will attract European funding and how many people in the area are unemployed.

She also asks you to select a suitable hotel for the seminar and to draft out a preliminary invitation to the existing clients. She would like to widen the invitation to other potential clients. She is keen that the seminar be given a 'European' flavour and asks you for some suggestions as to how to do this.

She is willing to invest in high-quality course literature which is 'high tech', eye-catching but not too lightweight, and would like some suggestions before she calls in graphic design consultants.

Before you start to investigate other sources, how could you best use your colleagues' knowledge to assist you with this research?

Accessing specialist information support services

If no one in your own organisation can give you the information you want, you have to start looking for external sources. Obviously much depends on the type of research you are carrying out, but some of the more common sources are listed in the table below.

Outside sources of reference
General
Local/regional libraries
Local government/central government departments
Local councillors and MPs
Citizens' Advice Bureaux
Newspaper information services – *The Times, Daily Telegraph* etc.
Consumers' associations and watchdogs – OFTEL, OFWAT etc.
Individual advisers – solicitors, accountants, Inland Revenue, VAT, Health & Safety Executive etc.
Police/fire brigade
Security firms
Medical centre/doctor's surgery
Maintenance firms – plumbers, electricians, carpet cleaners etc.
Office/computer services suppliers
Travel/hospitality
Travel agencies
Tourist information centres
AA/RAC/National Breakdown
Airline offices
Local car hire firms
Passport offices
Hotels/restaurants
Rail companies
Business
Public relations departments/named contacts of large organisations/clients/suppliers
Local and London Chambers of Commerce and Industry
Professional bodies
Trade Associations
Banks

TUC/local and regional branches

Fundholders – local government departments concerned with urban/rural
    regeneration: local enterprise trusts: business centres etc.

Customs and Excise

The Stationery Office (tSO)

British Standards Institute

Department of Trade and Industry

Commission of the European Union

Personnel

Job Centres

Department of Social Security

Local employment agencies

Local colleges

Private firms of management/other training consultants

Advisory, Conciliation and Arbitration Service (ACAS)

CHECK IT OUT!

Bearing in mind your own organisation and its needs, research the
addresses and, where possible, any relevant points of contact for the
sources in the table, and include them in a personal file. However,
don't despise the humble telephone directory, local directory or
Yellow Pages – they can sometimes be of great help, particularly
initially.

Libraries

Because information is ever-changing and the expense of keeping a private
library is so great, most organisations rely upon public libraries (and the
Internet) for book- or journal-based information. If the local library is not
equipped to offer the appropriate service, other libraries are likely to be able
to do so. If in doubt, you could access a search engine such as Yahoo!, Ask
Jeeves or Google for a list of appropriate libraries, or you could consult:

* *Libraries in the UK and Republic of Ireland*
* *The Guide to Government Departments and other Libraries*
* *Guide to Libraries in Western Europe.*

Journals can be a particularly useful source of reference as by their very
nature they tend to be up to date. See the table below for examples of the
more important business-related journals.

Major business-related journals

Accountancy

Accounting Review

Administrator

Bulletin of Comparative Labour Relations

British Economy Survey

British Journal of Industrial Relations

Business Equipment Digest

Business Law Handbook

Buying Business Equipment and Services

Computer Bulletin/Weekly

Consumer Law Journal

Croner's Briefings on Business, Health and Safety, Exporting, Importing, Europe,
   for Employers

Employment Law

Equal Opportunities

European Law Review

Export Digest

Health and Safety at Work

Human Resource Management Journal

Incomes Data Service – Briefs/Reports/Studies

Industrial Relations Journal

Journal of General Management

Journal of the Market Research Society

Labour Market Trends

Management Today

Marketing

New Law Review

Occupational Pensions

Purchasing and Supply Management

What to Buy for Business

Reference books, too, can be a useful source of information provided you remember to follow two basic rules.

- Always look at the date on the book. Old editions can sometimes give a very misleading picture.
- Check whether it is a UK or US publication. It is obviously of little use, for instance, looking up a legal point in a country which operates a different legal system.

Given the huge number of reference books now available (not all of which are likely to be displayed in every library), a useful first step is to consult those reference books that inform you about *other* reference books! See the table for some examples. You can also make use of the library catalogue, and ask the staff for assistance. (See page 302 for further information.)

Where to start: major sources
How to find out about books
British National Bibliography
Whitaker's Cumulative Book List
The Bookseller (published weekly and brought together quarterly in *Whitaker's Cumulative Book Lists*)
Management Bibliographies and Reviews
Current British Directories
Directory of Information Sources in the UK
How to find out about periodicals and newspapers
British Humanities Index
Guide to Reference Material (Library Association)
British Sources of Information (Jackson)
Facts in focus (Central Statistical Office)
ANBAR Abstracts (various)
Books about newspapers
Willing's Press Guide
UK Press Gazette (trade press, mainly for journalists)
Ulrich's International Periodical Directory

A useful initial source of information is *Croner's A–Z of Business Information Sources*. That offers:

- a list of sources of business information alphabetically by subject area and then alphabetically by source
- a telephone number for each entry
- a loose-leaf format so that sources can be kept permanently up to date through a regular quarterly amendment service.

Your evidence for this unit must show that you have used three of the following information sources (you will also need to explain how you would use the fourth):

- paper-based
- computer-based
- telephone information services
- people internal or external to your organisation.

From now on, make a note of all the information you are asked to find. Some of this may be routine, other types may take much longer to find. In each case, keep a record which states:

a how you checked the clear requirements of the person who wanted the information (including whether you could use chargeable sources, for instance)

b the information sources you identified which met these requirements

c any specific permission you had to obtain or any conditions which applied to either searching for, or using, this information

d any specialist sources you identified.

Carrying out effective and efficient information searches

Planning and organising the search

If you are the type of person who wants things to happen yesterday, or preferably sooner, you may find searching for information hard work – a good researcher is painstaking and patient. What you should always try to do without too much hesitation, however, is make a start! Very often the most difficult part of research is at the beginning. Once you have found out some information, however trivial, it will inspire you to further efforts.

Try to follow these guidelines:

1 Allocate a sufficient amount of lead time. If your findings are needed urgently, you have to move fast. If you have more time at your disposal, make certain that you use it wisely. It is far better to put aside a set amount of time for your research than to try to fit it in alongside your other tasks.

2 Decide on the various sources of information you will use. For example, do you need to telephone someone inside the organisation? Should you contact your local Job Centre? Is a visit to the public library necessary?

Remember also to prioritise if you feel that you have more chance of success with one particular source than another.

3   Get some help, particularly if the research is likely to be time-consuming. For instance, you might want to ask someone to check all the paper-based information whilst you undertake to telephone or speak direct to various individuals.

Recording the information

Remember the basic rules for recording information.

1   Prepare your 'tools', such as a notebook, a pen or pencil, and change for the photocopier. Make full use of the photocopier and/or a laptop computer if you have one.
2   Use a separate page for each topic and number each page.
3   Use cross-referencing as appropriate.
4   Use note form and easy-to-remember abbreviations.
5   Make sure your handwriting is legible, even if you are in a hurry and the caretaker is standing over you waiting to lock up!

Paper-based searches

You should be able to access your own files without too much difficulty. If you cannot, you need to take a serious look at your filing system (look back to page 291 for information on this point) and to check that you are using the most appropriate methods of classification and indexing.

Accessing information from a library may be slightly more complex. Nowadays, however, most libraries are user-friendly. The best way to start is to make yourself familiar with the way in which the library is laid out and how the information is catalogued. Many libraries have leaflets for first-time users, so it may be useful to obtain copies of these before you make your first search. See the table opposite for an example of the introduction to one such leaflet.

By far the most usual method of accessing a library catalogue nowadays is via a computer. In its simplest format, all you have to do is to make a subject search by keying in the appropriate word or phrase and pressing the Enter key to see the results. In most library computers systems, the information displayed indicates:

* the name of the author, the title and the class number (see below for further information)
* whether the book is available now or out on loan to somebody
* whether it can be borrowed on a short loan, or is for reference only
* whether it is not available because it has been lost or stolen.

> **Remember:**
>
> Information comes in many different formats – printed, audio visual and computerised. Some of these sources have to be filed separately, but in most cases the same system is used for arranging the items.
>
> For every subject there is a corresponding *subject number.* In order to find the information you want, therefore, you will need to know:
>
> * the location of the different types of materials
> * the number for your subject.
>
> The best way of finding the numbers for your subject is to use the library catalogue (either by looking in the appropriate filing cabinet or by accessing the information on computer) ...

Extract from a 'Help' page of a library guide

Each book and journal in a library is given a class number to tell you where on the shelves it can be found. The first three numbers indicate the general subject area. You may, for instance, want to check the psychology section of the library. The catalogue will tell you that those books are classified under 155. You can then look for the shelves containing books with that number on their spine. If you wish, you can then narrow your search still further by looking at the numbering sub-divisions. Child psychology books, for instance, are classified under 155.4 – and so on.

Searching for articles in a journal can also be made easier if you check to see whether or not there is an edition which lists all the articles published in that journal over the past year. The articles are normally listed in a number of ways – by date, by subject, by author etc. – and that can speed up your search considerably.

One problem which may arise is if the topic you want to research is rather general. If, for instance, you have been asked to find out about funding available to small businesses, it may be difficult for you to locate the information in the library catalogue or database without first thinking of the 'search' words you should use. You may decide to look under 'start your own business', 'small to medium enterprises', 'government funding', 'local government funding' etc. The more references you can check, the easier it is likely to be for you to locate the information you want.

Remember, however, that the best initial approach is often to ask someone. Librarians expect to have to advise you and can either guide you in the right direction or at least give you a good start. The more specific you can be the better. Unless the information you require is very confidential, it is far better to say to the librarian that you are trying to find out the latest sales forecasts of Microsoft rather than muttering that you want to know something about the major US computer firms!

If you want to access some information not contained in the library databank, you can possibly ask the library staff to search other online databases for you – usually for a fee. You will be required to complete a search form, so obviously it is to your advantage if you think carefully of what you want and what search words or phrases may assist the searcher. See below for an example of a search form.

Online Search Form
Name: **Date:**
Address:
Company:
Telephone no:
Search topic:
Key words and phrases (please indicate as many as possible):
Restrictions on search (where appropriate):   *By date:*   *By language:*   *Other:*   **When required:**   **Signature:**

Search form example

TEST YOUR KNOWLEDGE AND UNDERSTANDING
You have been asked to find some information on the comparative
advantages and disadvantages of travelling by rail, road and air in the
EU countries. Using the foregoing table as a guide, decide on what
your search topic will be, as well as the key words and phrases you will
include to assist the search.

Computer-based searches

Using the Internet has already been discussed on page 292. The biggest
problem you may have with it, however, is finding the information you want
in the midst of the thousands and thousands of other items on the Internet.
Fortunately the computer experts have realised this and have developed ways
of indexing the Web though means of **search engines**. If you have already
used the Web you will know that there is normally a search button that will
present you with a list of links to search engines.

Originally these search engines were based on student projects. Nowadays,
however, they have developed into areas run by commercial organisations
that finance themselves by incorporating advertising into their pages.

These search engines will trawl through the pages of the Web for you and
present you with an index that, hopefully, will compare with your request
for information. The indexing and retrieval methods used by the various
search engines vary, but generally speaking each site gives on-screen help
with search strategies. Yahoo!, for instance, asks you whether you want a
world-wide search or whether you want to confine it to the UK.

An easier method, if you struggle with searches, is to use a site that
understands plain English and will search other sites for you. The best-
known is probably Ask Jeeves at www.ask.co.uk. However, if you have a
query that is better answered by their American site (such as details of the
next spaceshuttle launch!), access www.ask.com instead.

Even so, recent research by the NEC Research Institute has found that even
the most comprehensive Internet search engines typically index fewer than
half of the documents on the Web. Large Web crawlers like Hotbot and Alta
Vista indexed only 34 per cent and 28 per cent of an estimated 320 million
pages – and they were the best! Excite found only 14 per cent and Lycos
3 per cent.

If you use the Internet regularly, and frequently access search engines or use the 'search' facility on large sites, it is worth spending some time refining your search technique. You will find guidance on how to do this on most sites you use. They will also instruct you how to carry an 'advanced' search. The better you are at searching, the less you will be faced with heaps of irrelevant sites or information. Next time you search, remember the following:

- Search engines need correct spelling. Asking for information on William Haig will not get you far if you are looking for the former Conservative leader (William Hague).
- Multiple words or a phrase in inverted commas mean the search engine will look for these words together – e.g. 'Tony Blair' or 'Blair Witch Project'.
- You can insert the word AND if you want both facts related – e.g. Blair Tony AND Cherie.
- You can insert the word NOT if you don't want a particular aspect – e.g. Blair Tony NOT Cherie.
- You can also use both words together – e.g. Hague AND Blair Tony NOT Cherie.

Practise these skills and then develop them by finding out a few more. Perhaps some of your colleagues can advise you, too.

Possible shortcuts

If time is a problem and you must make the most of it on the Internet, you might want to consider the following 'free' shortcuts when you are browsing the Web.

1   View multiple pages at once by loading one page while reading another. Simply press Ctrl and N and open another window.
2   Eliminate all time-consuming pictures, sounds or movie clips by clicking on Tools, Internet Options and the Advanced tab to deselect the relevant multimedia elements.
3   Instead of typing the full address, visit some sites (such as Yahoo!) by entering their name on the address panel.
4   Alternatively, in Internet Explorer, type a company's name into the address panel and press Ctrl and Enter to insert the 'www.' and '.com' either side of the name and you will automatically be allowed access to the site.
5   Remember to access the Internet as early in the day as possible. The Web tends to slow down in the afternoon as the USA wakes up and demand increases.

6   Do not wait for a page to load before clicking on to a link. If you see what you want on screen, click immediately.

7   Make sure you have the latest version of your browser. Check this on www.microsoft.com/ie or www.netscape.com/download.

8   Keep as many pages as possible as temporary internet files. Set limits for these files in Internet Explorer by clicking on Tools and Internet Options. This stops them consuming too much space.

Push services

Even with the help of a search engine it can be time consuming to find the information you want. In some cases you may wish to arrange for 'push' technology Web pages to be sent direct to your computer. With PointCast, for instance, you can customise the service to deliver only the type of news that interests you – politics, world events, health, weather, stocks and shares etc. The appropriate pages will then be sent through the Internet to your computer for viewing off-line. If you have direct connection to the Internet via a local area network (LAN), the pages may update every few minutes. If your connection is via a modem the pages may update just once a day.

Microsoft and Netscape have push services called 'channels' built into their latest browsers. These cover an ever-increasing range of subjects. Once you have chosen to take a particular channel, you need simply click a desktop icon for the most recent update.

Some services include an interactive element. Compuserve, for instance, promises that with their forums the customer is instantly in touch with a 'global community of like minded people' who face the same problems and can help with possible solutions. Examples it quotes include the opportunity for the customer to discuss share dealings in the UK Money Forum with people who own the same shares.

Once you have found an area on the Net that you will want to revisit on a regular basis, you can make use of the bookmark (or favourites) system which allows you to store that area and go direct to it any time you wish.

If you are really having problems with accessing the Web page you want, ask someone. If no one in your organisation can help you – possibly because you are the most computer-literate member of staff – you can get assistance from other sources. Your supplier may be able to help you. So too, may the information services operated by many major newspapers. For instance, *The Times* publishes a regular supplement in which there is a queries page aimed at assisting with computer or Internet problems. You can also access many daily newspapers on-line, such as the *Electronic Telegraph* (www.telegraph.co.uk) the *Guardian* (www.newsunlimited.co.uk) and the *Financial Times* (www.ft.com). It is quick and easy to search archived material if you need facts relating to something reported some time ago, as well as specialist articles on anything from travel to IT.

INFORMATION UPDATE

Even with all the help now available, it can sometimes be a frustrating experience trying to find information from the Net. Some psychologists have identified what they call 'cyberstress', which they say is caused by frustration at not being able to make effective use of the Net. To counteract this, they advise Internet users to:

- maintain realistic expectations – you are not going to have complete success every time
- set specific goals for each Internet session, to avoid ending up with too much irrelevant information
- seek help – there are many people on the Internet who will enjoy giving you some advice (e.g. www.deja.com may help you to resolve a technical problem)
- bookmark high-quality sources of information
- take frequent breaks away from the computer screen
- treat other people with respect rather than using the anonymity of the screen to be rude – otherwise you will find that you are spending a lot of time in needless squabbling
- make a commitment to continuous learning.

CHECK IT OUT!

If you already make use of the Internet you may have a list of useful websites. If not, think about what types of information you need to access frequently – for example, rail and/or airline information, stocks and share prices, hotels and restaurants, business information updates, addresses and telephone numbers of central government/local government departments, the Inland Revenue, the Office of Fair Trading, the Health & Safety Executive.

Then go to the appropriate search engines and compile a list of what you think may be relevant websites. Keep a note of them either via the bookmark system or on file.

To give you a start, look at the table here for some examples of potentially useful areas. Remember that national or international websites may be of less use to you than local websites. If you look in your local paper, you will discover websites that relate to local suppliers, local employment agencies etc.

General

How to have your own website

Advice and registration and domain names

Travel

Bookable flights online

Late deals

UK Hotels and Accommodation

Travel insurance

Route finding

Maps – Ordnance Survey, Mapblast – worldwide maps, Easy Map – free street and motorway maps of UK; UK Street Map – particularly London

AA

RAC

London Transport

Transport

Railway/airline timetables

Insurance

Premises/equipment/personal

Weather

BBC

International weather

Meteorological Office

Recruitment/training

Training and staff development

Job opportunities

Employment agencies

Business information

Share-dealing

Information on other businesses/companies

Foreign-exchange trading

Finance arrangers

Consumer advice

Independent consumer advice

Suppliers

Stationery suppliers

Office furniture/equipment

Electrical goods

Computer services

Examples of potentially useful web site areas

Telephone-based information searches

Finding out information by means of the telephone is effective provided you are thoroughly prepared. It is not a good idea to ring someone and start speaking without *first* having decided exactly what questions you want to ask. Get into the habit of jotting down what you want to ask so that you can refer to this during the course of the conversation.

Unless the query is simple, it is probably better to put your request in writing or in an e-mail so that the recipient has time to consider a response. He or she is then also able to prioritise your request alongside others and doesn't feel pressurised into making an immediate reply – which could be 'no' if you have chosen just the wrong time to ask! A written request also allows you to clarify *to yourself* exactly what it is you are asking. If you receive a reply to your request and decide it isn't really what you wanted, it is far more difficult to ask for information a second time round.

It is also important to listen carefully to what is being said. If you skim-read a journal article and then realise you haven't fully understood what it says, you can return to it. It is more difficult to keep telephoning someone – even the most amiable of people will eventually crack under that sort of pressure!

Make certain, too, that you write down what is being said to you, either as it is being said or very shortly afterwards. If, for instance, you are checking train or plane times, you need to be sure that the information you have is totally accurate – not just a wild guess at what you think you have heard.

One of the more difficult things you may have to do is find information from a particular organisation (particularly a large organisation) when you have absolutely no idea whom you should contact. If you are lucky, the person who answers the phone may be able to give you some advice and to direct you to the right person immediately. If not, you have to be prepared to give some more specific information. Try to be patient – even if you feel you are being passed from one person to another. Generally speaking, someone will eventually give you the information you want – if you go about it the right way!

People-based information searches

Much the same rules apply to personal conversations as to telephone conversations. In addition, however, you will probably get a better result if you

- ring up beforehand to ask for an interview time
- turn up on time
- do not outstay your welcome.

1 How would you deal with each of the following situations?

   a The Health & Safety Adviser who is senior to you refuses to give you any information about the organisation's safety policy.

   b Your own line manager gives you some information which you are pretty sure is out of date but you feel hesitant about going back to see him about it.

   c The HR manager is a talkative soul and spends a couple of hours with you telling you about the impact on employment of the new EU legislation – when all you wanted was a brief paragraph about the organisation's disciplinary procedures to be included in a standard job description.

   d You can't understand a word the Computer Services Manager is saying when you ask him for some information about the company's intranet. He is far too technical.

   e Each time you make contact with the secretary of the local chamber of industry and commerce, he says that he cannot let you have any information because it is too confidential.

2 You have just been employed as an administrator to a young entrepreneur who is in the process of setting up her own Web page design agency. She is the 'artistic genius' behind the venture but leaves you to do all the practical things. The month before the agency is scheduled to officially open, she has a meeting with you and you find to your concern there are a number of issues to be resolved.

   a She doesn't know the difference between a sole trader and a limited company. She asks you which would be the most suitable business entity for her and how she should start to set it up.

   b Although she has offered you a job and you have accepted it, she has no idea of how to go about sorting out a contract of employment for you.

   c The same is the case for the new advanced modern apprentice (AMA) who is about to start next month as a trainee administrator. She doesn't know whether he should have a contract of employment and doesn't know what her rights and obligations are – particularly as regards the training he should be given. She wants to know what training courses are possible.

   d It's the first time she has been self-employed and she has a feeling she should be sorting out her tax position with someone.

e As she is starting up in business for the first time, she wants to know whether there is any funding available to her – and what advice, if any, she can access.

f She needs some business cards printing, the name and address of the business putting in *Yellow Pages*, and a series of small advertisements placed in the local press and any relevant business journals.

g She wants to know something about her possible business rivals.

h She needs someone reliable to clean the premises each week.

i She is a bit worried about security, given all the expensive equipment she has leased, and wants to know what burglar alarm system she should be installing.

She looks hopefully at you! Make brief notes of the sources of reference you will access to obtain the information she requires.

Maintaining the goodwill of sources of information

Even if you are convinced that you will never use a particular source of information again, it is still good practice to make sure that you *could* do so if you wished! Follow the recommendations already made and you should create a good impression of both you and your organisation. Otherwise, you risk losing that source altogether.

TEST YOUR KNOWLEDGE AND UNDERSTANDING

You frequently ask your assistant, Trevor, to find some information but he is very rarely able to do so. You cannot understand this until one day you overhear him speaking on the telephone:

'Hello, who am I speaking to? Who? Right – I'm trying to find someone who'll give me some information about – now hang on a minute – some information about the new working hours directive. Can you help? Well why not? OK – put me though to her. [Silence – Trevor starts accessing his e-mails and reading through his messages.] Who does he think he is – I'm not a miracle worker – Oh sorry, I didn't realise you were back on. I want to know about the new working hours directive. Well, everything there is I suppose. Is it a long document? I didn't know that. Still, if you read it out to me quickly I'll be able to get the gist of it. Yes I will – I'm very quick on the uptake you know. Well if that's impossible can you chuck a copy of it in the post to me? Why not? How much? You must

➡️

be making a fortune. I don't know if my boss will pay that. Incidentally are you the person I should speak to about the new licensing laws? OK, no need to get nasty – if you don't ask you don't get. [Sarcastically] *Thanks awfully for all your help.'*

He puts the phone down. Still unaware that you are there he then says 'Drat it – I haven't given her my name and address. I'd better give her a ring back some time.'

Prepare some notes of what you are – tactfully – going to say to him to make him aware of what he should have said during the telephone conversation, and why it is important.

EVIDENCE COLLECTION

You need to prove to your assessor that you have correctly used efficient research methods when locating information. Note that this requirement applies to all the information sources listed in the Evidence Collection point on page 301.

For at least two substantial research tasks you undertake, note the methods and the techniques you used to make sure that the information met the agreed requirements.

Attach to your explanation a copy of some of your draft documents (preferably with key sections highlighted) together with the final document you prepared, so that your assessor can see how you undertook this task.

Element 305.2 Integrate, prepare and supply information from a variety of sources

Obtaining information is one thing; putting this into the most appropriate type of document – and in the most appropriate order – is quite another.

It is sometimes easier when you given explicit instructions about the type of document to create and how to order the information. This is necessary if you have to abide by criteria set externally – as is often necessary for public sector organisations who must submit returns to a government body or inspectorate. The only difficulty you may then have is including all the required information appropriately, if the number of words or pages is restricted.

If you are given a 'free hand', that can make life easier or more difficult. As you progress in your career you may reach the point where your line manager expects you to advise on the most appropriate type of document and its format.

The key, of course, is always to think about the *reason* for the document and the needs of the *user(s)*. A school administrator faces a completely different task when she is preparing a leaflet for parents from when she is producing a report for the school governors.

This element will alert you to all the many aspects you need to consider when creating your document – as well as the problems that can occur if you ignore them!

Selecting an appropriate document style from the standard ones used by your team

Document types

Imagine you have just returned to your office after a week's leave. In the in-tray there are:

- several memos from your line manager asking for information on a variety of topics
- a draft staff handbook for you to read and amend
- a number of letters from clients requiring a response from you
- minutes of the weekly staff meeting
- a copy of the annual report to the board of directors
- a report from the Health & Safety Committee
- some completed telephone message forms
- notes from various colleagues.

That is only a small sample of the types of document that appear on your desk each day!

This table outlines some of the more common types of document used in organisations. Check them against the documents you are expected to prepare in your workplace.

Standard documentation

General documents

*   Letters
*   Memoranda
*   Reports
*   Notices
*   Agendas
*   Minutes of meetings
*   Summaries of information
*   Schedules
*   Invitations
*   Itineraries
*   Programmes
*   Work rotas
*   Forms
*   Information leaflets
*   Questionnaires

Finance

*   Balance sheets
*   Profit and loss accounts
*   Financial statements
*   Statistical/financial tables
*   Invoices
*   Expense forms

Sales/purchasing

*   Sales brochures
*   Information packs
*   Order forms
*   Estimates/quotations
*   Export documentation

Marketing

*   Press releases
*   Publicity material
*   Promotional material
*   Market research information
*   Presentation material
*   Conference material/delegates' briefing packs
*   Corporate brochures
*   Staff/customer newsletters

Human resources

*   Job advertisements
*   Job descriptions
*   Contracts of employment
*   Personnel record cards
*   Application forms
*   Curricula vitae
*   Standard letters to referees/invitation to interview/post interview letters
*   Letters of acceptance/refusal/ resignation
*   Staff handbooks

Administration/secretariat

*   Policy documents
*   Annual reports
*   Legal documents
*   Information/instruction manuals

Purposes of documents

On one day, Terri was kept busy emptying her in-tray. At the end of the day she was pleased that she had sent all the following and in doing so had achieved her purpose of:

- informing
- requesting
- persuading
- congratulating
- confirming and acknowledging
- criticising and reproving
- complaining
- selling.

a   An e-mail to all staff telling them about the success of a number of the team who had just obtained their NVQ 2 or 3 levels in Administration.

b   A memo to the MD inviting him to hand over the certificates to the successful candidates at a presentation ceremony next month.

c   A letter to the rather shy editor of the local newspaper, asking her to say a few words at the ceremony – and to cover the event in her newspaper.

d   An individual letter to each of the successful candidates congratulating them on their successes.

e   A memo to the catering staff confirming receipt of the estimated cost of the function, and a letter to a firm of outside printers acknowledging receipt of costs of printing invitations, programmes etc.

f   A crisp note to one of the staff telling him that her line manager did not find comments about the successful candidates amusing (he had been overheard saying to them that it was sad that they had nothing better to do with their time) – he, of course, hadn't been successful!

g   A letter to a firm of booksellers expressing some concern that the books used by the candidates had taken so long to arrive.

h   A memo to all new staff outlining the advantages of undertaking the course.

TEST YOUR KNOWLEDGE AND UNDERSTANDING

One of your customers is always late paying her bills. Even though she always pays eventually, her late payments make it difficult for the accounts department to produce accurate financial statements. You ask your assistant to send a letter to her. He does so, but the customer is so enraged that she takes her business elsewhere. This is an extract from the offending letter:

'We note that you have not yet paid your bill amounting to £243.10. Please do so within the next 7 days or we shall be forced to take action against you. ...'

1   What was the purpose of sending that letter?

2 Suggest possible reasons for the customer's annoyance at receiving it.

3 Draft a letter which you think will achieve its purpose without causing the customer to remove her business from you.

Intended readers

Most forms of communication are written for the attention of a specified reader or group of readers. Even notices that are ostensibly directed towards the public at large tend to have a certain audience in mind – the young, the retired, the active, women etc. When preparing a document, therefore, you should make sure that what you write is suitable for the intended reader. The table below lists some of the people, both internal and external to the organisation, who may be expected to read what you have written.

Possible readers of business documentation	
Internal	External
Individual members of staff	Customers/clients
All members of staff	Shareholders
Senior members of staff	Subcontractors
Senior management team/board of directors	General public
Members of staff in one department/section	Sections of the general public – the old, women, ethnic minorities, unemployed, disabled, non-English speaking
Cross-organisation members of staff (e.g. members of the Safety Committee or Management Information Systems)	Other organisations offering the same product/service
Permanent staff	Other organisations offering different products/services
Temporary staff	Local government departments/ Central government departments (e.g. Inland Revenue, Department of Employment, Customs & Excise, Trading Standards, Office of Fair Trading etc.)
	Health & Safety Executive/Commission
	Medical Health Officers
	Local councillors/MPs
	Newspapers
	Funding bodies (e.g. borough funding, European funding)
	Consumer bodies
	Solicitors/accountants

A document's style

You may find that you have spent so much time researching and then preparing a document that you forget to be objective about it. Even if your document is written in the appropriate **house style**, contains all the relevant information and is free from grammatical, spelling and punctuation errors, it may still fail to have the impact you wanted because, for instance, it is ambiguous or too vague – or simply doesn't give the right impression.

If someone sends you a letter complaining that the wrong goods have been sent for the third time, replying in a light-hearted jokey manner will add to, not lessen, your problem. If you are trying to encourage staff to attend the Christmas party, requesting 'the pleasure of their attendance, suitably attired' is not likely to serve the purpose!

> 'Dear Sir
>
> I note with interest your letter of 15 August. The response the organisation gave to the local paper is contained in the edition published on 3 August and I suggest you refer to that. The HSE is adamant that its rules must not be broken.
>
> Yours faithfully'

a Draft a more suitable reply.

b Prepare some notes of what you are going to say to your assistant to indicate that he has not responded as effectively as he might have done.

2 Your organisation wants to encourage all staff to become members of its pension scheme. Rewrite the following paragraph which your line manager wishes to be put into the staff newsletter so that it is informative, encouraging but not threatening.

> 'The company pension scheme is an excellent scheme and everyone should join as people without occupational pensions are going to find it difficult to exist on the old age pension alone. Full details are available from the Personnel Office on request and those of you who are not in the scheme are advised to obtain them immediately. Requests must be in writing not via the telephone. Please note that the present terms and conditions of the scheme may not be available indefinitely.'

Formal versus informal styles

The more formal the occasion, the more formal the language should be. If you are preparing a set of minutes for the Senior Executive you should try to avoid contractions – don't, can't, won't etc. You should also try to cut down on the use of cliches or stereotypes. If your boss insists on using phrases such as 'If it ain't broke, don't mend it' and is resistant to your changing it, soften the overall impact by putting quotation marks round the phrase.

In general, formal documents are written using whole sentences, not notes: 'The team agreed that a request for an additional member of staff would be made to the Human Resources Director' *not* 'Request for new member of staff to be made to HR Director'. Formal documents may also be written in the past, not present, tense. This is particularly the case for formal minutes: 'The members were concerned about the lack of progress made' *not* 'The members are concerned about the lack of progress made.'

Other points to note about formal documents are:

- avoid the use of slang – e.g. 'The fire drill did not work as smoothly as it should have done' rather than 'There was mass panic. People were dashing about all over the place.'

- use titles of people rather than names – e.g. 'the Human Resources Director' rather than 'Damil Shah'
- avoid the first person – e.g. 'the team agreed' *not* 'we agreed'.

TEST YOUR KNOWLEDGE AND UNDERSTANDING

Your assistant is trying to help. He has volunteered to draft a letter to major clients inviting them to attend a lunch to celebrate the opening of the new call centre section in your organisation. You read what he has written but think the style may not be appreciated by some of the more important clients! Rewrite it in a more formal style. (See page 335 for information on the writing of invitations.)

'*Dear* ____

Want a good time? You'll get one if you come to our bash on Friday 12th June at 1 pm. Free nosh, free drinks and even the chance to look round the new call centre. Dress how you like. If you're up for it, give Stephanie a ring on extension 2333.
You won't get a better offer this week!

Cheers'

Presenting documents using the standard styles

Having gathered together a large amount of material in response to a request for some information, you have to decide what to do with it. You may simply have to hand over your notes and photocopies to someone else for them to use. It is more likely, however, that you will be expected to put your research material into some sort of order – either as a summary, a list of key points, a report, an insert into a letter or as part of a presentation.

If your organisation has specific rules about how you should prepare such documents, obviously you would follow them. If not, you have to rely upon your own experience and common sense. The following guidelines may help you.

Standard document conventions

Short internal memoranda are often handwritten, to save time and expense. Generally speaking, all other documents should be either typed or word-processed. Only in the most informal circumstances (such as a scribbled note from a colleague or a social invitation) will a handwritten communication be acceptable.

Formal documents should also be:

- laid out in a structured way – with numbered pages, in paragraphs, with suitable headings and sub-headings
- in sentence form, not as notes
- grammatically correct, properly spelled and punctuated, and free from jargon
- written in an appropriate style (look back to page 318 for further information)
- dated and, where relevant, signed.

Standard numbering systems

The reader's life is made very difficult if a business document is written as a continuous narrative. In most cases a numbering system has to be used. The two most popular systems are:

- a combination of figures and letters
- the decimal system of numbering.

The following are examples:

1 ...	A ...	1.0 ...
a ...	1 ...	1.1 ...
i ...	a ...	1.2 ...
		2.0 ...
		2.1 ...
		2.2 ...
		2.2.1 ...
		2.2.2 ...

CHECK IT OUT!

House styles vary a lot. However, most organisations today expect their paperwork to have a logo. Documents to be seen by people external to the organisation will be pre-printed with details such as the name and legal status of the organisation, its address and e-mail address, its telephone and fax number and, if relevant, the name of a training award such as IIP (Investor in People) or a quality kitemark.

In your own organisation check to see whether there is a house style for documents. If there is, describe it.

Presentation of a summary

On occasions you may be asked to summarise your research findings for inclusion in a report or other document. Like a number of other people, you may find this to be the part of the exercise you like least – and try to put it off as long as possible! The secret lies in breaking the task down into a number of simple steps.

1 Skim read all the information you have collected.
2 List the main points in note form.
3 Check your list against the original information to see that you haven't omitted anything important.
4 If you have noted that information on the same topic occurs in several parts of your research, now is a good time to link them together.
5 Draft your summary from your notes – *not* from the original research material.
6 Add a suitable heading (and sources of reference if required).

The next stage is to check what you have written!

1 Ensure that it is accurate – that you have not misread or misunderstood anything.
2 Delete any irrelevancies.
3 Check grammar, punctuation and spelling.
4 Ensure that you have written in the past not the present tense: 'the information was contained in' *not* 'the information is contained in'.
5 Check that the summary is in sentence form: 'the advantages are considerable and outweigh any possible disadvantages' *not* 'advantages outweigh disadvantages'.

TEST YOUR KNOWLEDGE AND UNDERSTANDING

Your manager has recently had a discussion with a part-time member of staff who has no interest in working full time and says that her views are similar to a large number of other part-timers. You are asked to do some research into the reasons for this, and you find a journal article which lists some of them. Your manager glances at it and asks you to reduce it to about half its length so that he can include it in a short report to the HR director.

'Many workers have a personal preference for part-time work. These include not only those already working part-time but also those working full-time because they cannot find suitable part-time work. One UK survey, for instance, found that more than half of the people currently working as word-processing operators would like to change to part-time ➡

employment if the opportunity arose. Similarly a German research project indicated that the most common reason for part-timers leaving their former employment was that they were asked to work too many hours.

'However there are other reasons for the increase in the number of people seeking part time employment. One is the lack of full-time employment available. For instance, the trend towards the "deskilling" of jobs has resulted in previously full-time jobs being converted into part-time ones. One major example is the retailing industry where jobs such as stock-taking and price marking have become less time-consuming.

'The main reasons, however, for the large number of people looking for part-time work are their personal and domestic responsibilities. One survey, for instance, found that whereas only 3 per cent of those interviewed stated that they worked part-time because full-time work was not available, 69 per cent gave as their reason the need to look after family and home.

'Other reasons for undertaking part-time work included age and infirmity. Older people and those with physical disabilities tended to feel that they could cope only with a part-time rather than a full-time commitment. Similarly, people in receipt of a pension were looking for part-time work because they wanted to preserve their pension rights.'

Presentation of a report

There are many different types of report. Some examples are:
- the **work report** where an account is given of the work accomplished over a certain period
- the **eye-witness report** where an account of an accident or other incident is required
- the **research report** where you have obtained some information and are presenting your findings (in some cases you will also include your conclusions and recommendations).

Standard report layout

All reports tend to follow a similar format. They first outline the purpose or terms of reference. Then they give details of any research carried out, state the findings, give a conclusion and, where requested, make recommendations. For a detailed example see pages 324–326.

Example of a report	
TERMS OF REFERENCE This may simply be a heading.	**Report on the proposal that reception and central office staff should wear a uniform**
It could, however, be more detailed. It could also make reference to the person instigating the report so that everyone reading it would immediately be aware of its importance. If, for instance, the chair of the company has asked for the report, it is likely to carry more weight – or be responded to more quickly – than if a junior in the computer section has decided to raise an issue of particular significance to that section. Remember, however, that in an effective organisation, all reports are taken seriously even though some may take priority over others.	At the Human Resource Director's request, I give below details of an investigation I have undertaken into the advantages and disadvantages of introducing a uniform policy for staff working in the reception and central office area of the organisation.
PROCEDURE In some reports you may be expected to state your sources. For example:	
Direct – e.g. 'going and looking': checking personally on a situation	I checked on the number of staff (including the supervisory staff, their approximate ages and their gender) working in the reception area.
	I visited the public reception areas of several local organisations to see their policy on the wearing of uniforms.
Personal – e.g. what you know already or the information you have obtained from talking to someone else	With the permission of the supervisor, I interviewed all the staff to obtain their views. I also talked to several visitors to find out what they thought of the proposal.
Written – e.g. what you have obtained from various outside sources	I contacted a number of clothing suppliers specialising in the provision of office style uniforms and obtained their catalogues. I also contacted several high-street stores to see whether any of their clothing ranges would be suitable as uniforms.

FINDINGS	
A summary of the information you have obtained.	3.1 Of the staff I interviewed, four were fully in favour of wearing a uniform, two were uncertain but willing to consider the possibility, and two were totally against the idea. The supervisor was in favour of it. Age and gender did not appear to have any bearing on the views given.
	3.2 All the visitors seemed in favour of the idea.
	3.3 Four out of the six local firms I visited required their reception staff to wear uniform. The uniforms were quite basic – normally a skirt, jacket and coloured blouse for the women and a jacket, trousers, shirt and company tie for the men. All staff were wearing name badges. The supervisors' uniforms were similar but distinguished slightly to show their status.
	3.4 The catalogues of the four main suppliers I contacted all contained a selection of different types of uniforms in varying price ranges. I attach photocopied extracts.
	3.5 The high-street retailers all had suitable ranges and were interested in discussing further the possibility of supplying them to us at reduced prices for bulk purchase. I attach details of their individual responses.
CONCLUSION	
This is normally a very short section. Otherwise you run the risk of repeating yourself in the recommendations.	4.1 The proposal does appear to have some merit and could be worth considering further.

RECOMMENDATIONS

The recommendations should be more detailed and, where possible, should follow the same order as the findings. This makes it easy for those readers who want to concentrate on one particular point throughout the document.

I therefore recommend that:

5.1 The proposal should be discussed further by the senior management team, a decision taken on whether it should be adopted and, if so, what budget is available and who is to be responsible for it.

5.2 A further meeting should take place with the reception staff to look in more detail at the proposal and the catalogues containing details of the uniforms.

5.3 Individual interviews should be held with those staff who expressed an unwillingness to wear uniform to see to what extent their objections may be overcome.

5.4 The managers of the high-street stores should be invited to discuss their proposals with a member of the senior management team.

Signature and date

It is normal to sign and date a report.

Jan Stocks

25 July 2002

Circulation list

Much depends on the level of confidentiality of the document. If it is highly confidential, circulation will be limited to only a few people. If not, it is usual to list the people authorised to read it at the end of the report. In most cases the title is sufficient, although some organisations prefer to list the name of the person, his or her title and the department or section in which he or she works.

Circulation list:

The HR Director
Members of the Senior Management
  Team
Reception supervisor
Reception staff

Final review

Even if you are following a set format, reports can be very time-consuming to prepare, so it is very tempting – after you have signed one and dated it with a flourish – to throw it into your out-tray and heave a sigh of relief. However, just before that stage you should try to make one final effort and read it through again, asking yourself whether:

a you have achieved the objective of the report

b you have made your terms of reference clear

c you have made it completely understandable *for those people likely to read it* rather than aiming it at no one in particular

d the report is arranged logically (e.g. in the way outlined above)

e nothing important has been omitted.

f the style is acceptable – neither too informal in a formal report or vice versa

g all the footnotes, references, appendices, bibliographies etc. have been included (see page 339 for further information on this point).

CHECK IT OUT!

If your organisation has a report-writing house style, compare it with the standard format laid out above and see how similar – or dissimilar – it is.

TEST YOUR KNOWLEDGE AND UNDERSTANDING

Imagine you work for the Human Resources Director of an organisation in which staff turnover recently has been much higher than usual. She thinks that one of the reasons for this is that many organisations offer staff an attractive package of employee benefits – such as private medical insurance, share options, a company car, free membership to a leisure centre etc. She intends to make a presentation to the board of directors but asks you first of all to (a) find out in more detail about the types of employee benefits that are currently being offered by many organisations and (b) to talk to a cross-section of the staff to find out their views.

Research the area of employee benefits and write a report to your manager outlining your findings and making some recommendations. Remember to include your sources of reference.

Preparation of a presentation

Giving presentations forms an important part of the work of many people nowadays. Sales people in particular have to show a great deal of expertise in this area. So too do staff involved in training. Increasingly, however, staff in all areas are expected to acquire presentation skills. Middle managers may be required to make presentations to senior management. Computer service personnel may be asked to give presentations to all staff each time there is a new computer update – and so on.

Information required for presentations tends to be quite specific. It normally includes statistical data – as, for instance, in a presentation by a manager on his or her departmental budget. It tends also to be required in chart, graph or pictorial form, particularly where the presenter merely wants to illustrate a point such as his or her organisation's increased share of the market of a particular product.

Charts and graphs can be a very effective method of presenting information to a group of people. The most widely used are the pie chart, the line graph, the bar chart and the pictogram.

Statistical information

Statistics are usually presented in tabular form. There are some important points to note.

- All tables should be clearly headed and, where appropriate, should have equally clear footnotes.
- The figures must be correct! It is easier to make mistakes when keying in figures than with text. A spell-checker will pick up spelling errors, but it can't perform the same function for figures. In a presentation it is particularly important that the figures are accurate. The presenter normally has enough to do, without having to handle awkward questions from the floor about why sales for last year had increased by 0 per cent!
- The less complicated the information is the better. In some cases – where, for instance, the financial director is presenting budgetary information to the board of directors – complexity is unavoidable. In others, a simpler version is preferable with, possibly, reference being made to a more detailed version for those who wish to read it.

Pictorial information: the pie chart

The pie chart is one of the more eye-catching features for use in a presentation. It is in circular format and can be divided into proportional segments (usually indicating percentages). The information it contains has to be very simple but this is normally what is required by a presenter.

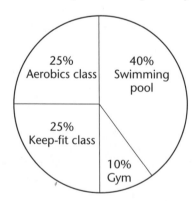

Pie chart: Analysis of participation of members in activities at Halcombe Leisure and Recreational Centre

The steps you should take to draft out a pie chart are as follows.

a Draw the circle as accurately as you can.

b Calculate the percentage that each subdivision will represent – remembering, of course, that the finished result must add up to 100 per cent.

c Calculate the angle needed for each subdivision by multiplying its percentage by 360 (e.g. a subdivision representing 30 per cent will need an angle of (30/100) × 360 = 108 degrees).

d Subdivide the circle as necessary into segments.

e Decide on what colours or shadings you will use for the segments.

f Add colour if required.

g Add a key (unless the information can be included clearly in the chart itself).

h Add an explanatory heading.

Pictorial information: the line graph

Line graphs can be useful in a presentation as they can give an immediate impression of growth or decline. They also make comparisons easy.

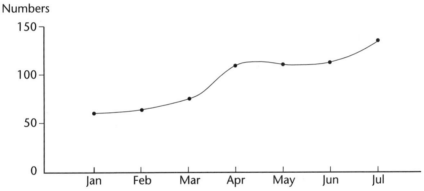

Line graph: Participation in aerobics classes from January to July

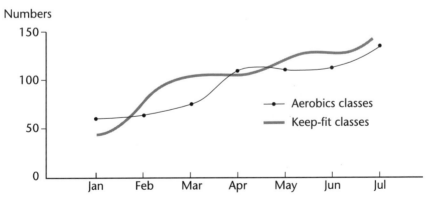

Multi-line graph: Comparison in participation in aerobics classes and keep-fit classes from January to July

If you want to draft out a line graph you should do the following.

a   Look at the statistics you have to include on the graph and select a suitable measurement. Are you going to use 10s, 100s, 1000s etc.?

b   Draw and label the axes – the horizontal and vertical lines. Time is normally shown on the horizontal axis, reading from left to right. Numbers are normally shown on the vertical axis, with the lowest number being placed at the foot (although this convention varies).

c   For a multi-line graph, decide on what colours or different types of line you are going to use.

d   Put in each dot in pencil and *then* join the lines.

e   Add the key.

f   Add the title.

Pictorial information: the bar chart

Horizontal and vertical bar charts can be used in much the same way as line graphs. They are particularly effective in a presentation because of the way in which they lend themselves to colour.

When drawing a bar chart, you can follow much the same rules as for a line graph. The bars (all the same width) to represent individual items of information. The bars may be close together or separated by small (even) spaces. Shading or colour can be used and it is normal to include a heading and a key.

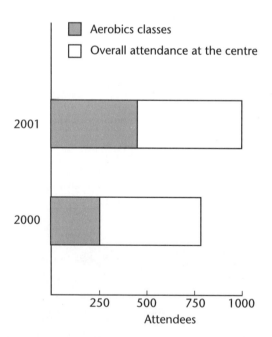

Horizontal bar chart: Comparison of attendance at aerobics classes with overall attendance during 2000 and 2001

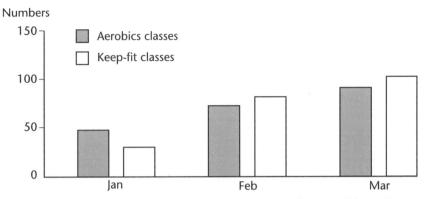

Vertical bar chart: Comparison in attendance at aerobics classes and keep-fit classes from January to March

Pictorial information: the pictogram

Pictures are always popular with an audience. If a presenter wants to indicate that the number of customers has increased over the past five years, this can be done simply by showing a picture of a small person five years ago and a second picture of a much larger person at the present day. An alternative would be to show the first picture of one or two people and the second picture of dozens of them. It makes the point!

Nowadays pictograms (and the majority of other graphs and charts) are nearly always produced through a computer package.

Presentation of correspondence

The letter

As an administrator you will probably have composed many letters, and will have used either the official house style or one you felt best suited the situation. It would usually have been printed on letterheaded paper bearing the name, address, telephone and fax numbers of the organisation, and pre-printed with the logo and any awards or kitemarks that had been achieved.

As a rule of thumb, a standard letter should comprise:

- an introduction or opening paragraph stating the reason for the letter
- the body of the correspondence, bearing in mind the usual conventions – using paragraphs which follow on logically, giving the most important information first, using chronological order where relevant, and moving from the 'known' (what both parties already know) to the 'unknown'
- the closing paragraph stating what is expected and preferably by what date.

The format should follow the rules of the organisation with regard to positioning of the recipient's name and address, the reference number if any, the date and the subject heading. There should be appropriate initial information, such as 'Personal' or 'Confidential'.

You should use the appropriate salutation and complementary closure.

- 'Dear Sir/Madam' requires 'Yours faithfully'.
- 'Dear Mr/Mrs/Ms' requires 'Yours sincerely'.

Finally, there should be correct positioning of the name and title of the sender of the letter, correct positioning of annotations ('Encs', list of attached documents etc.), and a reference to the appropriate number of copies – on the top copy or only on the file copy.

TEST YOUR KNOWLEDGE AND UNDERSTANDING

You have been asked to draft the following letters for the signature of your line manager. Select one and prepare the draft:

a a letter to a customer acknowledging an order for some goods but informing him that they will not be despatched for another three weeks because of production difficulties

b a letter to a customer who has complained about the apparent rudeness of your receptionist when he called in earlier in the week

c a letter to an employment agency giving details of a temporary maternity leave vacancy in the accounts department and asking, if possible, to have someone available within the next two weeks.

Make sure you have an opening paragraph, two or three points to go into the body of the letter, and a suitable closing paragraph. Where possible, use your own organisation's house style and headed paper.

The memorandum

The standard layout for a memorandum (memo) tends to vary only slightly no matter what the organisation. It is usually printed with the name of the organisation, the title 'Memorandum', 'To:', 'From:' and 'Subject:'. In most cases a memo needs no salutation or complimentary closure, nor is a full signature always required – initials are sufficient.

A memo can be relatively short and written in one paragraph. However, some memos may be almost as long as a report – in which case the standard letter format of introduction, explanation and conclusion is used.

A memo is circulated to one or more people. Where multiple circulation is required there are a number of methods. Depending on the system in operation in your own organisation, you can send a separate copy to each individual (with all names being typed on the top copy and ticked off individually). You can list all the names at the top or bottom of the memo and send a blanket copy to all. You can route one copy with an attached circulation slip. Memos are normally sent without an envelope unless the information is confidential.

INFORMATION UPDATE

The traditional methods of circulating multiple copies are: in alphabetical order, by location, according to rank, or according to job priority.

However, recent research has indicated that circulating copies according to rank can cause problems. If a document is sent to a number of people from the managing director downwards, there is a danger that the MD will assume that someone else is dealing with the matter, so too will his or her deputy, and so on down the line. Consequently no action may be taken at all. The most junior recipients of the memo will assume that, because they are at the end of the list, there is no point in reading the document in detail. ➡

One organisation ran into difficulties when – perhaps out of old-fashioned politeness – its circulation list placed the names of all the female members of staff first followed by those of their male colleagues. Some of the male members of staff were upset by the apparent discrimination!

The e-mail

One of the quickest methods of sending written communications is by e-mail. These tend to be relatively informal and written in note form. The e-mail addresses of both the writer and recipient may be in code form and, in this case, can be checked through an address book linked to the system if necessary. So too are the e-mail addresses of those designated to receive copies.

Many e-mail facilities enable the sender to also send a 'blind copy' of the message to someone else. 'Blind', in this instance, means that the recipient is unaware that this other person also has a copy. According to recent reports, this facility is over-used and can seriously upset people if it is used maliciously or to undermine the original recipient.

The accepted rules for presentation of information in an e-mail are still developing. However, the following commonsense rules apply.

1 Where possible restrict the information to a small number of short paragraphs or a list of numbered points. If you want to send someone a 20-page document, it may be better to think of a paper-based method (unless, of course, you are making use of the attachment facility whereby you can attach a word-processed document to an e-mail and send both at the same time).

2 Care must be taken to make sure that the information is correct, is written in the appropriate style, is presented properly – and is not libellous. If an e-mail is printed off and distributed to others, the sender sometimes gets a shock at how badly expressed it really is. Again occasionally information is transmitted by e-mail which the sender would not dream of sending in any other format. The law still applies!

3 Be aware of certain e-mail conventions – such as NOT USING CAPITALS (called 'shouting').

4 Apparently, 'Dear ...' and 'Hi' are the two most popular salutations, and 'Best wishes' and 'Regards' the most common closes. Leave the 'smiley faces' off your business e-mails!

5 *Always do a final check before you press the send button*. Because e-mails are so easy to create, they can be sent far too hastily – before you have checked that what you have said makes sense, that your spelling is OK, and that you have remembered to attach the promised attachment!

6 Never send an e-mail in haste to express your annoyance. Wait a day and then find a better method of showing your disapproval.

Some people consider that e-mails are over-used because they are so easy to compile and send. There are obvious advantages over trying to reach a busy person by telephone or by writing a letter, but sometimes e-mails are used when an alternative method would be a more appropriate. Apparently the same thing happened when the telephone was first invented – people stopped visiting each other – even socially, for a while. Think of e-mails as just one method of communicating – with advantages and disadvantages.

 INFORMATION UPDATE

As with everything new, e-mail is spawning its own jargon.

- **Flaming** is sending an e-mail which publicly reprimands the recipient in some way. This is not a practice to be recommended and can obviously be very upsetting to the recipient (who may not have the ability to respond if the 'flame' came from above).

- **Spam** is the term used for junk e-mails – so be careful who receives your e-mail address or you could return from a short break to find your mailbox clogged with rubbish.

Other written forms of communication

Invitations

If an invitation is sent in a letter, then the reply should ideally be in the same format. On more formal occasions, however, invitations are usually displayed on plain A5 cards (see the example).

Computers Galore
34 Versailles Avenue
Leeds
25 November 200–

The Directors of Computers Galore have pleasure in inviting

....

to the opening of their new showrooms on Friday 14th December between 1 pm and 5 pm. Light refreshments will be provided.

RSVP

Example of formal invitation

Durand & Partners
12 Lyons Promenade
Leeds
2 December 200–

Mr L. Stroeve thanks the Directors of Computers Galore for their kind invitation to the opening of their new showrooms on Friday 14th December, and has much pleasure in accepting (*or* but regrets that he is unable to attend).

Example of formal response

- If the name of the recipient is to be included it is customary to handwrite it rather than type it (although nowadays that custom is sometimes ignored if the invitation is to a large number of people).
- The information should include the date, day and time of the function, the place and the purpose.
- In most cases, the third person (e.g. 'the Directors') should be used in preference to 'We'.

Notices

Unlike many documents that are designed for the attention of either one or a specific number of readers, a notice should be written so that *everyone* can understand it. The language should be clear and simple and the style should be informal. It should be as *short* as possible. It is difficult getting people to read any sort of notice – virtually impossible to get them to read long notices.

Points of presentation include the use of headings and subheadings and, where possible, numbered points rather than continuous prose. Clip-art can make the notice more eye-catching.

There should be a date and signee so that the person whose job it is to check the noticeboards and remove out-of-date material can judge how long the notice has been displayed and refer, if necessary, to the person who issued it.

Staff bulletins and newsletters

Very formal bulletins and newsletters tend to be produced in the publicity department or by a firm of outside contractors – in which case your job as an administrator would probably be limited to providing any information required and in supervising the circulation of the documents. However, many organisations use informal bulletins and newsletters to encourage staff to become more aware of what is happening in the workplace. If you want to make sure that staff read a particular item of information, you have more chance of success if you include it in such a document than if you send round yet another e-mail or memo. You can also use it for 'fun' items – who's won the inter-departmental golf match, who's just become engaged etc.

Formats differ depending on the organisation. Some merely collate the information in a series of numbered points under a main heading. Others imitate the newspaper style and display the items in two or three columns with different fonts and subheadings.

 INFORMATION UPDATE

If the bulletin or newsletter is written in an informal way, and the majority of the information is light-hearted, it would be wrong to include items of great importance. One organisation, for instance, included, in an otherwise jokey newsletter, a list of offences which carried the penalty of instant dismissal. When it did dismiss someone for one of those offences, the industrial tribunal held that it was an unfair dismissal because an employee could not be expected to have recognised the significance of the information given the nature of the communication in which it was included.

Press releases

If you are asked to prepare a press release for either your local or a national newspaper, there are certain rules to follow, designed to assist the paper's sub-editor:

1 Use A4 paper and make sure there is a explanatory heading.
2 State the facts clearly and concisely – the sub-editor will put his or her own 'spin' on it. Double-check your facts. A misspelled name or an incorrect age can cause you problems with the people concerned! If you are not clear about something, check it with someone.
3 If you include a photograph, make sure that the caption or information is written on a label attached to the back of the photograph – not on the photograph itself because the pressure shows through. Make equally sure, of course, that the label does not come adrift and that you find that under your photograph of a retirement presentation there is a caption congratulating the winner of a bonny baby contest!
4 Include a name, telephone number, extension number and e-mail address of someone the press can contact for further information.

Advertisements

If you are asked to draft an advertisement, the newspaper or journal in which you want to place it may give you some guidance on what to do. Bear in mind that you will be charged for the number of lines or words you use, so try to keep it as brief and as concise as possible. Advertisements should be:

• factual
• informative
• complete.

It is a waste of time and money if you forget to include the relevant telephone number, or give the wrong time or date for an advertised event.

Acknowledging your information sources

It is worth repeating that a good researcher is one who pays attention to detail. If you have spent an afternoon in the library or on the telephone obtaining useful information, you can congratulate yourself on a job well done. But it is a job only half done if, when you come to use that information in a report or other document, you cannot remember where you obtained it. In such circumstances you may face several problems.

One problem is that it is difficult to use it as evidence. If, for instance, you present a report to a committee and one of its members disagrees with some of the information, it is helpful if you can refer directly to the source you used – particularly if you have included it as a footnote or in a bibliography within the report itself. A named information source also allows a reader of a report to investigate a particular point if he or she so wishes.

In addition, making a note of a specific source at the time you are carrying out your research should help you if you want to go back there for further details. Ploughing through the library databases again, or nerving yourself to telephone someone for a second time, is frustrating.

Again, house rules normally dictate how you should make the appropriate acknowledgements. In general, however, they can be categorised.

Footnotes

You may want to make a general reference to some more detailed information in another source. If, for instance, you have used a quote from the Data Protection Act or from a book on business management, you could acknowledge that source in a footnote.

DUTIES AND RESPONSIBILITIES

You will be responsible to the Departmental Administrator for:

- word-processing a wide range of business documents
- collecting and distributing the internal and external mail
- photocopying duties
- inputting daily, weekly and monthly sales figures on to the computerised system
- providing general clerical and administrative support.

You should note that the above is not intended as a specific job description and that the duties of the post will be subject to review.

Essential requirements

You must possess:

- good keyboarding/word-processing skills
- a systematic approach to tasks
- the ability to work in a team
- the ability to work under pressure and to tight deadlines
- good oral and written communication skills.

Desirable requirements

You should preferably possess:

- relevant experience
- spreadsheet/database skills

HOURS OF DUTY

You will be required to work from 9 am to 5 pm from Monday to Friday, although there may be occasions when the hours will be subject to change to allow for busy times of the year.

HOLIDAYS

You will be entitled to 25 days per year plus Bank Holidays. The timing of all holidays will be subject to the agreement of your line manager.

SALARY SCALE

From £10,500 to £12,802, depending on age and experience.

Extract from Job Description for Clerical Assistant

Nowadays there are two basic ways of displaying footnotes.

- The traditional footnote starts by including a small superscript numbers, e.g. [1] at the end of the sentence or word in which a quotation or other reference point is included. The full reference is then displayed either at the bottom of the page or in a list at the end of the section or chapter.
- An alternative is to use the so-called Harvard method where, instead of entering a footnote number in the text, you put instead some basic reference material in brackets, e.g. (Roberts, 2000, pp. 22–25) and then display the full details in a bibliography.

Appendices

If the information to which you make reference is very extensive, and yet you feel you need to include it in the document rather than merely refer to it in a footnote, you should include it as an appendix. If, for instance, you felt that the Data Protection Act itself – or at large sections of it – should be included, you would use this method. Try, however, not to over-use this device. It is very appropriate if you have been asked to read through and summarise a long document and you attach the document to your summary. It is less appropriate if you have taken the easy way out and included a series of off-the-shelf manuals as appendices rather than taking the time to extract the relevant material from each.

Bibliography

In some documents you might want to include details of the books, magazines, journal articles etc. you have used. Again, much depends on house rules, but it is normal to put the information in list form displayed alphabetically by surname, and in a consistent format; for example:

Roberts, T.C. *The Business Manager* (Heinemann 2000)

CHECK IT OUT!

In your organisation, try to find a document containing footnotes, appendices and a bibliography. See how they are displayed and keep a note for future use.

---

[1] Roberts, T.C. *The Business Manager* (Heinemann 2000), pp. 22–25

INFORMATION UPDATE

You may sometimes want to cite a reference you have found on the Internet or in an e-mail. If so, the following guidelines will help you.

If you use a database, either on-line or on CD-ROM, to access an article from a journal you then want to quote in your work, you must state:

- name of author
- source (e.g. journal or newspaper name)
- article title and year of publication
- journal volume or part (the full date of a newspaper)
- page numbers
- the medium (e.g. CD-ROM or Internet)
- database/CD-ROM name
- publisher/producer.

If you are quoting from an Internet source then you need to add the URL and the date on which you accessed the reference; for example:

> Sparrow, A. (2000) 'Shareholders are to get veto on directors' pay' Online *Electronic Telegraph* issue 1798, 27 April 2000. Available: www.telegraph.co.uk [15 May 2000]

In the case of an e-mail, state the sender's e-mail address, the date of the mail, the heading and the recipient's name. If the e-mail was forwarded to you, you should state this and also add the date you received it. If you are quoting from an attachment, provide as much information as possible on the attachment itself. For example:

> E-mail forwarded to the writer by Mark Scott (markscott@hotmail.com) on 26 May 2001. The original e-mail was sent to Mark by Liam Brown on 24 May (liambrown@hightown.ac.uk) and was headed Copyright Issues. It included an attachment from Brown and Nuttall, Legal Advisers, dated 20 May 2001, which specifies copyright considerations when using Internet sources.

EVIDENCE COLLECTION

For this element you need to show how your research results in a particular document. You need to produce at least two of the following types of document:

- reports
- presentation materials
- correspondence.

You must also be prepared to discuss how you would produce the third type.

Obviously you can use the document itself as evidence. However, attach a brief summary for your assessor which puts it into context. In particular, you need to include the following information:

- with whom and how you agreed the information that should be integrated
- with whom and how you agreed how the information should be presented
- why the particular document style was selected
- the sources of information you used and where these have been acknowledged
- whether there were any particular conditions or restrictions placed on your use of this information
- whether any amendments had to be made after the person who requested it had checked it.

The last point does not indicate a fault, because people often change their minds! It indicates that you were sensible to check whether the final document met with that person's approval.

Finally, it would also be sensible to ask the person for whom you undertook the research and produced the document to counter-sign your account for authenticity.

GROUP A OPTION UNITS

Unit 306 Maintain and develop a paper-based information system

> This unit is one of two in Option Group A.
> Select *either* this unit *or* Unit 307 – but not both!

This unit is concerned with the way in which you maintain and improve paper-based information systems such as filing systems and small libraries. Although nowadays an increasing amount of information is contained on computer databases, it is still unlikely that you will find yourself working in a completely 'paperless' office. As an administrator you will almost certainly be expected to establish and develop systems which allow paperwork to be stored and retrieved with the minimum amount of difficulty. The more pressurised the workplace, the more essential it is that you, your line manager and your colleagues are able to find a document at a moment's notice. A lost document can cause not only loss of time but also loss of income if an important client is offended, a bid does not go in on time, an order is not placed and production is halted – the list goes on.

 KEY SKILLS SIGNPOST

If you are taking your Key Skills award, you will find there are opportunities in this unit to obtain evidence towards the **Problem Solving** Key Skills unit at level 3. If you are working at a different level, then you should discuss the matter with your tutor or trainer.

Element 306.2 is concerned with continually improving an information system and liaising with other people over issues being experienced with the current system. As you will see, various types of problems can occur with maintaining and using an information system.

- The system is shared by many people, not all of whom understand exactly how it operates. Mistakes can mean considerable inconvenience for other people and serious difficulties if an important document is mislaid. If the number of problems with 'lost' documents becomes excessive, steps must be taken to reduce these.

- A small system, which meets the needs of an organisation or an office originally, may become inappropriate or insufficient if business is increasing. A more appropriate system needs to be identified, in addition to the best method of implementing this and training staff.

- Access to confidential papers needs to be limited and the requirements of the Data Protection Act in relation to structured paper files has also increased legal obligations for companies. A review of whether these requirements are being consistently met by everyone may be essential.
- The number of documents routinely printed out or photocopied in your office has become excessive with many items being duplicated amongst files. This is leading to severe congestion. Not only do the files need pruning, but a better system of coping with multiple copies needs to be sought.
- Your organisation is moving to new premises in the city centre where the rental costs are much higher. One of the problems will be the cost of storage, so your boss wants to know how the amount of information stored can be reduced. However, he is concerned that all legal requirements regarding document retention still be met.

For *any one* of these situations (or for an alternative complex problem you have agreed with your tutor or supervisor) undertake the following tasks.

PS3.1

a   Explore the problem and analyse its features. Talk to other people involved and agree how it could be solved successfully.

b   Select and use a variety of methods to suggest ways of tackling the problem.

c   Compare the main features of each of your options, including the risk factors involved, and then justify the option to decide which would be the best.

PS3.2

a   Plan how you would carry out the option you have chosen and obtain agreement from the appropriate person.

b   Implement your plan, demonstrating that you can effectively use support and feedback from other people.

c   Review your progress towards solving the problem, and revise your approach as necessary.

PS3.3

a   Decide on the methods you can use to check whether the problem has been solved, and check these with the appropriate person.

b Apply these methods accurately, and then draw conclusions and describe the results in detail.

c Review how you approached solving the problem, and say whether you think alternative methods and options might have been more effective.

KNOWLEDGE AND UNDERSTANDING REQUIRED FOR THIS UNIT

Throughout this unit emphasis is placed on your ability to choose the most suitable form of filing system for the documents in your workplace, to keep your line manager and colleagues informed, to seek their advice and support where necessary, and to make sure that once a system has been established, it is effectively maintained.

Any filing system must match the requirements of your line manager, colleagues and other file users – and it is for this reason that regular reviews are essential. Any changes you make must be consistent with the overall system and, if an organisational policy exists, it is not sensible to introduce a system which varies from this.

In Unit 305 you learned that consultation with users means that changes are then – usually – more acceptable. In Element 306.2 you will see how this relates to information systems and the storage of documents in your area.

Establishing and running an effective filing system is not a boring and routine task. If you neglect the task, the overall efficiency of the workplace will suffer. If you prove to be particularly capable in this area, your talents are sure to be recognised!

Information stored and used by your team, and its importance

In Unit 305, a table listed all the types of documents normally used – and stored – in an organisation. Look back to page 315 now and check its relevance to the documents used in your own workplace, or look back at the list you prepared for that unit.

No matter what documents you have listed, it is unlikely that when you walk through the work area you will see all of them on desks or shelves. If you do, then your job as an administrator is likely to be exceedingly difficult! Look at your list again and, at the side of each item, make a note of exactly where each document is (or should be) filed – in a filing cabinet, cupboard, on a computer database etc. It is also helpful to prioritise them. You may, for instance, decide that the documents that are used most frequently are the most important in your workplace. You may think that legal documents such as leases, deeds or contracts of employment should take priority. You may be convinced that financial documents such as orders, invoices, bills etc. are of exceeding importance given the nature of your work. Once you have done this, keep your findings for future reference as you read through the rest of this unit.

Storing information securely and for ease of access

You work in an office with a group of talented but not too well organised people. You are all expected to use the departmentalised filing system and to cooperate with the procedures laid down for its use. You follow the procedures, but unfortunately very few others do. Matters come to a head when your line manager receives an urgent phone call from the PA to the managing director asking for last month's budget figures which are required immediately.

You cannot find them in the filing cabinet – which is hardly surprising since a number of the folder headings have fallen off and it is obvious that most of the files have been crammed into the drawer without any attempt at putting them back in the right places. You therefore decide to ask the departmental financial assistant for his suggestions. The resulting conversation doesn't help!

'The departmental budget figures do you say? Yes, I've seen them quite recently but I haven't a clue where they are now. You say you've tried the filing cabinet – I could have told you that wouldn't be much use. Once in there, lost for ever – that's my opinion. No, I'll have put them somewhere safe – but where, that's the question. Yes, I know it's urgent but there's no point hassling me. It'll come to me soon. I know what to do – let me have a look on my desk. Yes, I know it's a bit of a tip but I always believe that a tidy desk shows a sick mind. No, I know you don't agree with me – you're making it only too obvious. [Coldly] I'm fed up with all this. If it's not one thing it's another. Every time I turn round someone is badgering me for something. I've got a headache. I think I'll have to go home.'

Eventually you track the papers down, but it has taken you at least three times as long as it should have done.

Such incidents should not occur in a well-regulated office. Otherwise you will always find yourself at a disadvantage.

- You will never be able to respond properly in a crisis.
- You will have difficulty making an adequate response to any enquiry.
- You may never have a complete set of information upon which you can rely to assist you in preparing an important document.
- You will create an impression in the minds of other people both inside and outside the organisation that you don't know what you are doing. This is bad enough if it truly is your fault. It is even worse if it is other people who are letting you down. However, it is very difficult sometimes trying to persuade others to follow procedures, however essential.

Procedures that are relevant for using and maintaining your information system

General procedures

One way to try to overcome difficulties is to ensure that procedures are clear and simple, and known to everyone. Much depends on the type of storage system you have established, but there are certain general rules which apply in all situations.

It is helpful, for instance, if everyone in the office knows *how* to file (although see page 356 for details of the advantages and disadvantages of centralised filing). Because filing is often regarded as a boring task, it is often left to the newest or youngest member of staff! However, filing is *not* unimportant, so it is worth taking some time to persuade colleagues on a few issues.

1 They should know how to file alphabetically (see page 350 for more information). Most people know how that B follows A. Fewer people can deal consistently with names such as Macdonald and McDonald. You can either arrange for some explanatory notes to be produced and circulated or, if you feel that staff will do so, ask them to follow the alphabetical system as used in the telephone directory. See the accompanying table for simple guidelines on placing names in alphabetical order (indexing).

2 They should be aware that documents are filed in date order within each folder. The most recent document should be placed in the front or on the top of the papers in the folder. They should also be filed neatly and squarely – which is best done by first removing the folder from the drawer or cabinet.

3 Filing should be done regularly – preferably every day. The more documents are allowed to pile up on desks or filing trays, the more reluctant people become to file them. They are simply overwhelmed by the task.

4 If there are a number of documents to be filed, they should be pre-sorted into the appropriate areas so that they can be filed in batches. It assists the process if the names under which the papers are to be filed are underlined or circled in red. It is also good practice to avoid the use of too many paper-clips, which tend to fall out, so documents become separated.

5 Folders should not be overcrowded. Ramming another paper into an already bulging folder simply means that it gets crumpled, torn and unreadable. (See page 363 for information on possible weeding-out procedures.)

6 Papers relating to two or more files should be cross-referenced. (See page 367 for further information).

7 People should not borrow and fail to return files! (See page 368 for information on absent file procedures).

Rules for indexing	
Rules	**Examples**
1 Place the surname before the first name. If the surnames are the same, the first name determines the position.	Atkinson, Anne Atkinson, Bryan
2 If both names are contained in the name of an organisation, the surname is written first, followed by the first name and finally by the remainder of the name.	Robinson, John & Co. Mugaran, Hanif plc
3 If an organisation has several names, the first is taken as the surname.	Seedat, Williams & Lyons
4 When 'The' is the first word of the name, it is either omitted or put in at the end.	Counting House, The
5 In hyphenated names the first name is used.	Harrington-Smith, Colin
6 Names beginning with Mac or Mc may be treated as if they were spelt Mac.	McArthur, Ian Macdonald, James
7 Names which begin with St may be treated as if they are spelt Saint.	St Claire's Hospital
8 For impersonal names such as government departments, the name that distinguishes it from others is used.	Social Security, Department of
9 Names which begin with a number should either be listed before the alphabetical names in numerical order or converted to words and placed in the appropriate alphabetical position.	6 Times Table restaurant or 'Six'
10 Names which consist of initials are placed before full names.	ABC Co. Ltd Accrington Brick Co.
11 Nothing comes before something, i.e. a name without an initial comes before a name with one.	Tharman Tharman, H.

Cataloguing and classification systems

Common systems

There is no point in trying to persuade your colleagues to file documents properly if they are unaware of the order in which they should be doing it. They need to know, for instance, whether the classification system used is alphabetical, numerical, alphanumerical, chronological, geographical, or by subject.

- **Alphabetical**: There is a separate file for each correspondent and organisation, and the files are then arranged in alphabetical order, from front to back, in a suitable storage container. There is normally a miscellaneous file for each letter of the alphabet in which individual documents can be stored until they become sufficient in quantity to warrant a separate file.

Allinson, P.	
Agwar, H.	
Adamson, J.	
A	

Alphabetical

- **Numerical**: Files are arranged numerically with each correspondent being allocated a number. At the same time an index card is prepared with the name of the correspondent and arranged in alphabetical order in an index card drawer or box. Files are retrieved by first consulting the appropriate index card.

103
102
101

Numerical + Card Index

Alphabetical index

R. Fazal	103
L. George	102
S. Jackson	101

- **Alphanumerical**: This system is a combination of the above two. The guide cards are in alphabetical order, but within each alphabetical division the files are numbered as they are entered on to each index card.

Banerian, Z.	B4
Brown, D.	B3
Bagshot, L.	B2
Baker, T.	B1

Alphanumeric

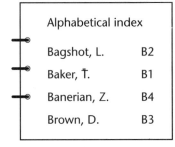

Alphabetical index

Bagshot, L.	B2
Baker, T.	B1
Banerian, Z.	B4
Brown, D.	B3

- **Chronological**: The files are organised in date order, the most recent being at the front.

9/1	Press cutting, Evening Telegraph
12/1	Article, Business Management
15/1	Information from TUC
27/1	Trading standards information

Research File

Chronological

- **Geographical**: Documents are classified according to location – country, county, town, street, number.

Farnworth

Darwen

Blackpool

Altham

Lancashire retail outlets

Geographical

- **By subject**: Instead of being filed under the name of the correspondents, documents are filed under subject headings. The subjects are then filed in alphabetical order.

Staff handbook

Recruitment guidelines

Interview procedures

Grievance procedures

Personnel file

Subject

INFORMATION UPDATE

Although the numerical system of classification has a number of advantages, one of its chief disadvantages has always been considered to be that if numbers are transposed (e.g. 1321 being written as 1231), it is extremely difficult to find the appropriate document. Some organisations have tried to introduce numerical systems that do have some meaning. It might, however, be easier for you to try this out in your personal filing system first. You could, for instance, put all the documentation relating to your car under the numerical part of your car registration number. You might want to file all documents useful to your CV under the year of your birth, and so on.

Terminal digit filing

This is a variation of the numerical method of classification. Files are arranged according to the last pair of digits of a number, instead of the first as in the traditional numerical method. File numbers are broken down into groups of digits (e.g. 489 63 21) and all files ending with the same two numbers are grouped together behind a primary guide. The section allocated for 21 would, for example, contain file numbers 21, 6321, 721 etc. Within the 21 section of the filing cabinet the files are further subdivided into a secondary section according to the two digits immediately preceding the final pair. The file number in the above example would therefore be 63. The files are then arranged numerically according to the digits at the beginning of the number. For example document 489 63 21 would be placed before document 490 63 21. To find that document you would look first in the filing cabinet drawer/shelf under 21, then in the folder 63 to finally locate document 489.

Because this is so complicated, it is a system little used in business organisations. However, its level of accuracy makes it ideal for certain documents such as medical records.

TEST YOUR KNOWLEDGE AND UNDERSTANDING

In an attempt to encourage your colleagues to appreciate the importance of an effective filing system, your line manager asks you to give a series of briefing sessions at the weekly staff meeting. In order to stimulate discussion, you decide to outline all the systems of classification that could be used and to highlight the advantages and disadvantages of each. You make some brief preliminary notes and ask your assistant to word process them for you. Unfortunately she muddles up your notes and fails to include the classification headings. Rewrite the information so that the relevant advantages and disadvantages are placed under the appropriate system of classification.

Advantages and disadvantages of various methods of classification	
Advantages	Disadvantages
• Simple	• New headings can be introduced without disturbing the system
• Useful for miscellaneous papers	
• Accurate	• Considerable cross-reference needed
• File number used as a reference on correspondence	• Index required
	• Difficult to incorporate miscellaneous files
• Useful where location is important (e.g. sales departments)	
	• Difficulties in forecasting space requirements
• Useful for keeping all documents on one topic together	• Time-consuming to prepare
	• Difficulties caused by transposed figures
• Direct filing (no index required)	• Too specialised for general use
• Unlimited expansion	• Geographical knowledge required
• Useful in specialist areas such as research	• Congestion under common names
	• Difficulty in deciding on subject title – and possibility that more than one file might be opened for the same subject
• Index can be used for other purposes	

Check on the system of classification used in your own organisation. Write brief notes on how effective you think it is as part of your overall filing system. Consider the other systems of classification to which reference has already been made, and decide whether any of them would be just as effective.

Legislation covering the collection and storage of information, including health and safety issues

Handling documents has certain legal implications. For example, confidentiality has to be maintained (see page 364). You must take care that you do not breach the requirements of the Data Protection Acts. You must be equally careful that you are not storing any defamatory information. For further information on all these issues, see pages 281–284.

Paper-based information systems are not normally health hazards. However, you still have to remember that health and safety legislation covers such areas as lifting heavy packages (such as bulky files). The law also requires certain fire precautions to be taken, one of which would be to ensure that documents are stored in non-flammable containers and are free from other potential fire hazards. For further information see page 124.

EVIDENCE COLLECTION

Make sure that you know, and possess a copy of, all the organisational policies and procedures which relate to the storage of information. Check that your information covers:

- how materials are stored
- how they are indexed, classified or catalogued
- retention policies
- how materials are disposed of or archived
- the type of records which must be completed.

Now personalise these by stating which ones relate directly to your own area and how you make sure they are followed.

Element 306.1 Maintain an information system

The importance of following agreed procedures

It is relatively easy to formulate a set of procedures – as you saw in Unit 304. From your studies of that unit, you should also know why procedures are vital in this area – given that there are usually multiple users. You should also have no difficulty in understanding the terms 'system' and 'procedures' that are regularly used. However, if you have forgotten what they mean, refresh your memory by looking back at pages 231–234.

One of the main problems with procedures is ensuring that they are followed!

TEST YOUR KNOWLEDGE AND UNDERSTANDING
State how you would reply to the following comments.

a Can't Sue do it? She doesn't seem to have anything else to do at the moment and it's better having one person doing the filing rather than having everyone getting in on the act. That's a recipe for disaster if you ask me.

b It beats me why we're still in the dark ages. Why can't we have a computerised filing system and do away with filing cabinets altogether?

c I can find everything I want to at a moment's notice. Why bother me with a lot of meaningless procedures?

Checking storage conditions and reporting deficiences

Storage conditions

In Unit 302, importance was placed on organising your working area so that it improved your efficiency and effectiveness, as well as making a positive impression on other people. Your filing system and the way in which it operates can assist or hinder you. If your line manager is in discussion with a client and asks you for a file which turns out to be torn and scribbled over with half the documents missing, no one is impressed. If files are left out on a desk and a cup of coffee is spilled on them they become almost unusable, and so on. It is your responsibility as an administrator to try to ensure this does not happen. If you are able to encourage or persuade your colleagues to use the system properly the problem should not arise. However, it is unlikely that you will achieve complete success, particularly when the pressure of work builds up and people suddenly find they have other 'better' things to do. Apart from persisting, you may have to find additional methods of keeping the system in the best possible state of repair.

You may, for instance institute a daily or weekly 'sample' check of some of the files, noting whether or not they are still in an acceptable condition. If they are not you should then try to identify the possible causes. Can the fault be traced back to one particular individual? Is the filing cabinet not easily accessible or are the drawers or shelves difficult to open? Are the drawers so full of material that documents become crumpled and torn when someone tries to remove or return them? Are the folders of poor quality so that they last for only a short time? Are the tabs on the folders constantly falling off and getting lost? Despite your best efforts is there a general lack of interest or cooperation?

The importance of maintaining good storage conditions, however, is not simply limited to making a good impression. Many business documents are so important that their loss or destruction would cause huge problems. In such circumstances you would need to check that they were stored in such a way that they were protected not only from careless handling but also from damp and dirt. You would also have to make sure that they were stored securely to prevent them from being stolen and to prevent unauthorised access. (See page 364 for information about confidentiality.) Obviously they would need to be in storage containers which prevented them from being damaged by fire or water.

Some of these problems you can solve yourself. Others, of course, you may have to refer to your line manager for decision.

In order to be able to check on the effectiveness of storage conditions, you must be aware of the types of storage available to you – not only in your current workplace but also in others in which you may subsequently be employed. If you start work in a new area, one of your responsibilities may be the maintenance of an effective filing system. Then one of your first tasks should be to check on:

- whether the system is centralised or departmental
- what type of storage equipment is used
- the indexing systems, if any.

Centralised storage systems

Read the following transcript of a conversation between two administrators with differing views about filing.

LUCIEN   Am I glad we took the plunge and set up a centralised filing system. You've no idea what we found when we started collecting together files from all the filing cabinets scattered across the department – not to mention those we found on desks, shelves and pushed into the back of cupboards.

GARY: How did the staff take it? Were they cooperative?

LUCIEN: The vast majority were. You'll always get one or two who'll resist any change to the bitter end. Jon was particularly difficult and I know for a fact that he has been very awkward with the new filing staff when he wants anything finding. He keeps saying that the papers he uses – mainly drawings and plans – don't fit easily into a centralised system.

GARY: Isn't a centralised system a bit inconvenient at times? I must admit that I like to have my files in a filing cabinet near to my desk – and my phone! – so that I can access them at a moment's notice.

LUCIEN: It can be but I still think the advantages outweigh the disadvantages. At least we have one set of procedures rather than half a dozen. It's far more difficult for a file to get lost – and, of course, we have managed to buy some state-of-the-art storage equipment which we would never have done if we had to buy one for everyone in the department.

GARY: So you only allow certain staff to file?

LUCIEN: Yes, of course – and they do nothing else.

GARY: They must be bored to death. Surely there is a high staff turnover. I expect I'm old fashioned but I always think it a good idea to let all junior staff take a turn at filing. They learn the system and they also find out a lot about the organisation at the same time. I know I did when I first started.

LUCIEN: No system is perfect of course. At least with the centralised system the filing isn't piling up on someone's desk because he or she is away sick or on holiday.

GARY: What do you do about confidential information? I don't think I'd be too keen if I thought all the filing staff were reading details about my last performance appraisal interview.

LUCIEN: They're warned not to do things like that – but it depends on what guilty secrets there are in your file.

GARY: Nothing much unfortunately. I think the most exciting thing in it is my date of birth.

TEST YOUR KNOWLEDGE AND UNDERSTANDING

Make brief notes of the advantages and disadvantages of a centralised filing system. State also how you think some of the disadvantages might be overcome.

Individual storage systems

The type of storage system used in an organisation normally depends on the types of document to be filed and the quantity of information. If only a handful of documents are filed each day, a less elaborate filing system need be used than if there are hundreds of documents to be filed.

The type of system also depends on how quickly the information is required at any one time. Receptionists in health centres require files immediately, while administrative assistants helping university professors with their research can perhaps afford to take more time.

It also depends on the space available within the organisation to house filing equipment, and the expense involved. In many city organisations, for instance, the amount of 'non-productive' space to be used for storage systems will be very limited.

Also relevant are:

- the number of people using the system – if there are several, the more robust the equipment the better!
- the length of time the documents are likely to be stored
- the degree of confidentiality required
- the location – filing cabinets in a reception area are normally very different from those in the basement!

Storage containers

Vertical filing

In this system the documents are placed upright one behind the other in filing cabinets. If the cabinets are fitted with pockets suspended vertically from metal runners fitted inside cabinet drawers, the folders are held clear from the bottom of the drawer and therefore protected from wear and tear. The titles of each file can be displayed on both the pocket and the inner folder in a variety of ways, the most common being upright tabs supplied in perforated lengths which can be covered with shields of cellulose acetate.

Very large documents can be stored vertically in a chest plan file where the documents are suspended, one behind the other, or in stand-alone dividers.

Another variation on the vertical filing system is the mobile file container in which suspended file holders are incorporated into trolleys so that they can be easily moved from place to place.

The *advantages* of vertical filing are:

- it is in widespread use and therefore most people know how to use it
- the files are easy to label
- the folders are not exposed to public view
- the mobile system is particularly useful for open-plan areas.

The *disadvantages* are:

- a large amount of floor space may have to be used
- only one person at a time can use it.

Lateral filing

This system allows documents to be placed side by side in a cabinet, cupboard or open shelving, again usually in suspended pockets. Some systems incorporate both lateral and vertical filing in one multipurpose cabinet. In rotary suspended filing systems, files are suspended and linked on rotating platforms to enable quicker and easier access.

The *advantages* of lateral filing are:

* it makes the best possible use of floor space, because it is possible to store records virtually from floor to ceiling
* more than one person can access the files at the same time
* every file within the cupboard can be seen at once.

The *disadvantages* are:

* it is not as easily accessible as a vertical filing cabinet, since sometimes steps or other access devices are required
* it is more difficult reading file titles which are also displayed laterally.

Also, the files may become dusty because of their almost constant exposure – many lateral filing systems are only concealed from public view at the end of the day when the dust covers are lowered. This is particularly important in an office to which the general public or a large number of visitors have access.

Horizontal filing

This system is normally used to store plans and drawings horizontally one above the other.

The *advantage* of horizontal filing is:

* it is useful for 'awkward' documents or documents of varying sizes which cannot easily be contained in a vertical or lateral system

The *disadvantages* are:

* it is too specialised for general use
* it is difficult to extract and return documents from the system.

Electronic/automated filing

The electronic filing system allows files to be accommodated in automated units and retrieved at the touch of a button. When a file is required, the operator keys in its index code on a pushbutton panel at the front of the filing unit and presses a retrieve button. This activates the system to locate the required file container and deliver it automatically to the operator. Once the file has been retrieved the restore button is pressed and the file container is returned to its storage location.

The *advantages* of automated filing are:

- it is useful for speed of access
- it can be space-saving
- documents are less easy to lose
- it meets the requirements of disability legislation.

The *disadvantage* is:

- the cost.

Microfilm

This system is suitable for an organisation with a large number of documents to accommodate in a limited space. Documents are reduced in size on film so that they can be stored in much smaller units than would otherwise be possible. The major types of storage media are roll film, microfiche and jacket film.

- Roll film (like a normal camera film) gives maximum storage capacity and is relatively inexpensive to prepare. Its continuous roll format ensures minimal misfiling. However, it is difficult to update, and sequential access (rather than random access) makes it hard to locate information quickly.
- Microfiche (a rectangular sheet of film containing several images) is quick and inexpensive to prepare and convenient to post. It is difficult to update and sometimes is of lesser quality.
- Jacket microfilm is a combination of the film strip and microfiche. Short lengths of film are slotted into holders for quicker reference and ease of handling.

The *advantages* of microfilm are:

- it is space-saving
- it almost eliminates the costs of filing and indexing equipment
- it removes the need for weeding out old files
- it is more durable than paper
- very important documents can be microfilmed and then stored in a high-security area.

The *disadvantages* are:

- the cost
- the time taken to film and index the documents
- the inconvenience of having to use a viewer or terminal every time reference is made to a document.

 INFORMATION UPDATE

Increasing use is being made of computer databases to store a wide variety of organisational information. See page 291 for further information.

Other types of document folder

In many workplaces, although the filing cabinet may be the major storage area for documents, there are other, smaller types of container which are used almost as frequently. They may be used independently or as part of the overall system. See the table below for a brief description of some of them.

Types of document containers	
Box file	A cardboard, metal or plastic box usually provided with a spring clip or other retaining device.
Lever arch file	A heavy duty file in which papers are retained by means of loops which pass through holes punched in the margin. The loop is opened by means of a lever to permit documents to be entered into or removed from any position in the file.
Concertina file	A series of light cardboard pockets attached together, normally used for alphabetically classified material.
Ring binder	A folder fitted with metal rings, cut and hinged to enable it to be opened for the insertion or removal of papers.

In addition there are a number of container systems prepared specifically for use within the filing cabinets themselves:

- The plain folder consists of a sheet of manila cardboard folded to form a cover. The fold is usually off-centre to that the back of the folder projects behind the front, providing an area on which to write a reference title.
- The suspension folder or pocket is fitted with an attachment to enable it to be suspended from the rails of a vertical or lateral filing cabinet into which either the manila folders or individual documents can be placed. They are thus protected from wear and tear from contact with the sides or bottom of the filing equipment.

Indexing systems

If you look back to the section on systems of classification and the advantages and disadvantages of each, you will find that in several instances the need for an indexing system is highlighted as an advantage in that it can be used for other purposes. It can, for instance, be used for recording information such as postal addresses, e-mail addresses, fax numbers and telephone numbers. It can also include information such as the name of the person in the organisation who is responsible for that particular file or customer, the credit limit on the account etc.

There are a number of different indexing systems available.

Vertical card index

This consists of a number of cards each relating to one item of information. The reference heading is written along the top edge of the card and the remainder of the space can be used for other information. The cards are normally arranged vertically in a drawer or small container and tabbed guide cards added for easy reference. An automatic card index can also be used where trays of cards are suspended from revolving mechanisms to allow the user to obtain quick access to a large number of cards.

Strip index

The strip index consists of a frame into which strips of card containing one line, or at the most two lines, of information can be fitted in any required order. The frames can be fixed to the wall, made up into book or folder form or arranged on a rotary stand. Strips of various colours can be used to differentiate different types of information.

Visible-edge card index

In this system a series of index cards are arranged so as to overlap, leaving a strip of each card exposed. The exposed edge is used for the reference heading and the remainder of the card for the other information. Again the cards can be housed in a cabinet or kept in book or folder form.

CHECK IT OUT!

Make an inventory of the filing equipment in your immediate working area. Specify the type of equipment (vertical, lateral etc.) and its storage capacity (two-drawer, three-drawer, height etc.).

Look at the table on page 315 of Unit 305 – or your own prepared list of documents most commonly used in your workplace – and prepare a grid similar to the one outlined below. Highlight what you think are the most suitable storage containers for each one of them. Assume you are in a 'green field' situation and are not limited by a set budget!

To assist you, look at any office suppliers' catalogues you already have at your workplace or can obtain locally.

Document grid									
Document	Equipment				Cataloguing method				
	V	L	H	O	A	N	A/N	S	M	O
Letters										
Catalogues										
Minutes										
Insurance policies etc										

Code: V Vertical filing   A   Alphabetical   M Microfilm
       L Lateral filing   N   Numerical   O Other
       H Horizontal filing   A/N Alphanumerical
       O Other   S   Subject

The disposal and archiving of materials

One of the problems in maintaining an effective filing system is over-full storage containers. The more documents are put in, the more overwhelming the problem becomes to sort out. What you must avoid doing is seizing a bin bag and tipping half the contents of a filing cabinet into it. That may solve your short-term problem but it will surely cause you bigger problems later! As always, what is needed is a systematic approach. Many organisations now have a set of procedures relating to how long documents should be kept, and what is to be done with them when it is decided that they should be removed.

There are normally three options:

- to *transfer* all old records to reserve filing areas
- to *destroy* all unwanted documents
- to *microfilm* all documents.

The choice of a records retention policy depends on several factors:

a   How much low-cost space is available? If, for instance, you have large premises with ample space in the basement, you might decide to keep all documents for 25 years. If you are working in smaller premises in the heart of a city, where even the space for a desk comes into the overall cost calculations, you have to be much more ruthless.

b   How many documents are in the filing system? If there are not many, you have few problems. If there are masses, again you may have to dispose of some of them more quickly.

c   How often are documents referred to? If you work in an area where constant reference is being made to back files, then you have to make provision for easily accessible storage.

d   There may be legal requirements. Certain documents *must* be kept for a specific period. Contracts and VAT documents, for instance, must be kept for six years. Contracts under seal must be kept for 12 years.

Although you may not have been involved in drawing up the retention policy and procedures, as an administrator it is likely that you will be involved in seeing that they are implemented. What you will probably be expected to do is decide which papers need to be retained, which destroyed and which placed in reserve storage. You may also have to decide how often someone should check the system and perform the weeding out process.

Make sure that both you and other staff are aware of the different lengths of time each document must be kept. You may find it useful to draw up a programme for everyone, listing the various documents and their 'shelf life' (1 year, 2 years etc.).

You need to make provision for those documents which must *never* be destroyed – by, for instance, storing them in different coloured folders or in separate filing cabinets.

CHECK IT OUT!

In your own workplace, find out whether there is a record retention policy. If there is, compare it with the suggestions given above, and write brief notes on how they compare. If there is no policy, decide what you think it ought to be, and write a brief memorandum to your line manager outlining your suggestions and giving reasons for them.

Maintaining confidentiality and security

Confidentiality

You come into the office one morning and find two of your colleagues engrossed in a conversation about the row that had erupted at the staff meeting the day before. You have just settled down to do some work when a friend of yours puts his head round the door to tell you about a conversation he overheard in the lift. During the coffee break you all settle down for a gossip about the boss.

Most people are curious by nature. They like to know things – and they like to tell other people what they know. In most cases this is just good fun. In some cases, however, particularly in the office, it can cause problems. Normally, the more senior a position you hold, the more likely it is that you are in possession of information that is not for broadcasting throughout the organisation. You must be discreet. Obviously you don't come dashing out of a meeting to find your best friend and tell him or her what you've just heard about the latest sales figures or how much the managing director was paid last year. Nor do you allow yourself to be tricked into giving information to someone who is very persistent and persuasive or who gives you the impression that he or she already knows what you know and merely wants to discuss it with you.

It is more difficult, however, to keep a secret if it is written down. It is awkward for you if, for instance, you work with someone who likes to wander around the workplace when it is quiet and to look on desks and in filing cabinets for interesting information. It is equally awkward if he or she comes into speak to you when you are working and tries to read upside down what you are writing or to look over your shoulder at what you are inputting on to the screen of your word-processor.

The contents of your filing cabinets are an obvious target for the office gossip, so you may be in a position of having to adopt some strategies to prevent any really confidential information falling into his or her hands. Obviously your first step would be to impress upon all the staff the need for confidentiality and the consequences if it is breached. (See page 280 for further information.) What you should also do, however, is to take certain practical precautions.

- With extremely confidential documents, allow no-one but yourself and senior managers access, and make sure you file them yourself.
- Draw up a procedure for the locking and unlocking of filing cabinets, and nominate the people with access to the keys.
- Keep the filing cabinets in lockable rooms so that the rooms themselves can be locked at the end of the day.
- Limit access to keyholders (see page 108 for information about key security).
- Make certain that when you are preparing confidential documents no-one is within reading distance.
- Decide on a policy for destroying the documents at the appropriate time. Shredding is normally advisable.

Confidential documents tend to be at their safest when they are actually in a filing cabinet. They are at their most vulnerable when they have been borrowed for use. What you need to impress on your staff is that when using confidential documents they should be careful to keep them out of reach and sight of the casual caller. They should:

- lock them away if they have to leave the room for any purpose
- take care when photocopying not to leave the original on the glass of the machine – or spoiled copies in the wastepaper basket
- send confidential documents in sealed envelopes marked 'confidential'.

INFORMATION UPDATE

Files stored on computer databases can be protected by a password system to which only authorised users have access. In some cases there are several levels of user, with some being allowed access to only part of the information and others to all of it. Normally, as an extra precaution, these passwords are changed at regular intervals.

Physical security

No matter how careful you are to keep documents confidential, even greater problems can occur if you fail to keep them physically secure. Documents destroyed by fire or a burst water pipe are gone forever, unless there is a back-up somewhere. You may lose a whole batch of correspondence with an important client. You may have been in the middle of arranging an event and find that you have to start from the beginning again. You may have prepared a series of guidelines and checklists for your own use and these have disappeared.

Furthermore, inconvenience may be the least of your worries. Lost documents normally equate to a loss of money. The time you spend trying to re-sort the filing system and begin certain tasks again will incur expenditure. It will cost even more if you have lost documents on a tender for some work or a bid for funding and you have to start again or, in a worst-case scenario, cannot submit it by the date required.

It is important to store vital documents in containers that are fireproof, waterproof and – as far as possible – burglar-proof. (See page 107 for information on the maintenance of security in an organisation.)

CHECK IT OUT!

Use some office suppliers' catalogues to identify the types of storage equipment designed specifically to protect documents from fire, water and theft. Compare these with the equipment you use in your workplace. Make brief notes of any improvements you would recommend, budget permitting.

Dealing with problems that users are likely to encounter

The system works quite well because you keep a close eye on it. However, when you are away it works less well. You decide to raise this matter at a staff meeting and, to your surprise, find that some of the staff are not satisfied with the way the system is operating. Here are some of their comments:

a 'I can never find the file I want. The system is too complicated.'

b 'Why do we have a filing system that stores information on the same topic in three different files. It's hopeless.'

c 'I know we have a system for borrowing files but I seem to be the only one who uses it. Everyone else seems to borrow files when they want and no-one seems to bother.'

d 'The cabinets are too high. I can't reach to the top shelf.'

e 'I took out the file on the Bahamas project this morning. Half the documents seem to be missing and the rest are virtually unreadable – I daren't show them to the client.'

f 'Have we a records retention policy? If so, it doesn't seem to work. Some of the documents in those filing cabinets are so old, they should be in the British Museum.'

g 'There's only so much time in the world. I just simply can't file every day.'

h 'I hate having to get up from my desk and go all the way across the room every time I want a file. It takes a lot of time and it breaks my concentration.'

i 'I thought our papers were meant to be confidential. The lock on one of the filing cabinets has been broken for at least six weeks.'

TEST YOUR KNOWLEDGE AND UNDERSTANDING

From what you have already read, draw up a list of possible solutions to the problems outlined above, ready for discussion at the next staff meeting.

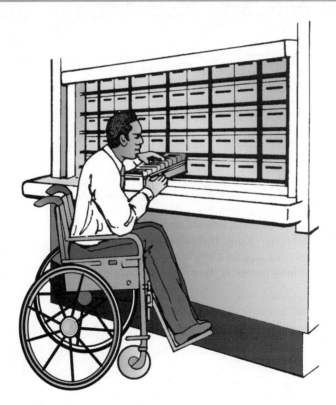

A filing system at a height to suit all users

Records relating to the system

A paper-based filing system is a record in itself. However, in order to make sure that it runs as effectively as possible, other records may need to be kept. A good administrator, for instance, would institute at least two back-up systems, consisting of some form of cross-referencing, and a record of what files are borrowed and when they should be returned.

Cross-referencing records

Look back to pages 350–353 to remind yourself of the various systems of cataloguing and classification. Some of them are quite self-sufficient, particularly those which are numerically based. Others require a system of cross-referencing. If, for instance, you operate a subject classification you may find that in one filing basket alone you have:

- a letter from a local government department referring to two different enquiries
- a letter from the Inland Revenue referring to a number of staff
- a health and safety information update covering a number of departments.

In some cases, of course, you can take a photocopy of the document and place one in each relevant file. In other cases it may be easier to use a cross-referencing system so that the original document is placed in the 'master' file and there is a brief note of its existence made on an index card and placed in the secondary file or files. See the example of a cross-reference slip overleaf.

CROSS REFERENCE SLIP	
For information on:	Staff contracts
Refer to file(s)	ACAS Staff welfare Staff terms and conditions of employment Staff committee Health & Safety committee

Example of a cross-reference slip

Follow-up systems

A standard follow-up system consists of a series of 'absent' folders which are inserted in the place of a borrowed file. Ideally they should be in a different colour to make them easily noticeable to anyone who wants to make a quick check on the number of absent files. A slip of paper is then placed in the folder giving the file title, who has borrowed it, on what date and when it should be returned.

To be completely effective the system should be linked to a **bring-forward system** (sometimes known as a 'tickler' file). It can be housed in a concertina file, a wallet system or a card index box which contains:

- 12 divider cards for each month of the year
- 31 index cards for each day of the month.

It is then a simple exercise for you to look at the appropriate guide card each day and to check on any reminders you have placed behind them. One reminder, of course, is that of files that have been borrowed and are due back by that day.

CHECK IT OUT!

Check on the follow-up systems, if any, in operation in your work area. Make notes of what they are and how effective you think them.

EVIDENCE COLLECTION

Your evidence for this element must show that you can maintain two of the following systems:

- alphabetic
- numeric
- alphanumeric
- chronological
- geographical
- by subject.

You must also be prepared to explain how you would maintain the other types.

1 Keep a log of the tasks you undertake in relation to maintaining your particular systems over a period of 6–8 weeks.
2 Identify the degree to which you think confidentiality is important and the extent to which you think it is maintained.
3 Give examples of occasions on which you have had to provide support to users who have had problems locating or storing information.
4 Obtain examples of records you have completed over this periods, and identify in each case why they were used.

Element 306.2 Continuously improve an information system

The importance of reviewing the requirements

You are responsible for a filing system which consists of a series of vertical filing cabinets with a set of open shelves for ring binders and box files. The documents are stored alphabetically. No form of indexing is used. You have instituted a follow-up system but there is no organisational policy on how long documents should be kept.

The system works reasonably well and, because you work in a busy area, you never seem to find the time to review it. You work on the principle 'if it ain't broke don't fix it'. There are risks in doing nothing, however.

- You may be missing an opportunity to improve the system so that everyone benefits from it.
- You may not be aware of what the staff actually do think about the system because you don't give them the opportunity to state their views. They may want to criticise but they may also want to offer some helpful suggestions.
- You may not be fulfilling your obligations as an administrator. Your line manager may rely on you not only to run a system but also to ensure that it is the best possible system by constantly reviewing it and making changes for the better.

If you feel that changes are necessary, you can, of course, go ahead and make them if your terms of reference allow you to do so, and if you are the only person involved in operating or using the system. However, it is normally much better if you consult other people and take their views into account. You may feel that the alphabetical system of classification is fine; your colleagues may disagree and might be able to give you very good reasons why they would prefer another system. Your line manager may have noticed that the filing systems in other parts of the organisation are more extensive and more up to date than yours, and may be able to give you advice. It is also always a good idea to consult your manager if you want to spend money on making certain changes!

Comparing the existing system with user requirements

Sometimes users outgrow a filing system. You may, for instance, set up a system in your workplace which is staffed by two or three people and which covers a fairly small area of work. You find later, however, that although the work has grown and become more diverse and the number of staff has increased, you are still operating the same system which no longer fully meets the requirements. You may have inherited a filing system which seems to be adequate for your needs and you have other priorities to attend to before actually beginning to check on whether or not it is the best possible system. In both instances, you should try to make a regular commitment to checking the system and comparing it with user requirements. You can do so by:

- raising the issue at one of your regular staff meetings
- asking for suggestions
- talking to the most regular users to see what they think about the system
- checking in other areas of the workplace on other systems in use
- making a regular check of business and office equipment journals (or the information available on the Internet) to discover the latest developments in this area.

If you have taken over a filing system or are aware that it is no longer as effective as it was, it is sometimes a good idea to devise a small questionnaire to be distributed to the users asking them for their opinions. You can then analyse the findings and discuss them with the group as a whole and with your line manager before you start effecting any changes.

EVIDENCE COLLECTION

Either adapt the questionnaire on page 372 to your own requirements and prepare a copy of it for distribution – leaving a suitable space for the replies; or prepare one more suitable for your own particular work area. Ask as many users as possible to complete it. Analyse the findings and write a brief report on what changes you think could be made as a result of staff feedback.

As part of your evidence you also have to consult with your line manager, team leader or supervisor. This is not only sensible but courteous. If your line manager has no strong opinions, then you can consult him or her when you reach the next stage of checking your suggested improvements (see page 374).

Making changes that are consistent with the overall system

Nowadays many organisations are concerned with their corporate image. They have logos on all their paperwork. They ask everyone to conform to a house style when preparing documentation. They organise the environment so that the same colour scheme is used throughout the building. They buy in bulk from purchasers to ensure that all furniture and fittings are standard. In such circumstances, the same principles will apply to the filing systems in operation. If you are unhappy with your filing system or you feel that certain

Filing system questionnaire	
Organisation:	Department/Section:
Name:	Job title:

1 Do you think that our storage systems (*include here what they are*) are suitable for our requirements?

2 If not, state whether you would prefer any of the storage systems set out below:

   ....

   .... *etc.*

3 Do you think that the (*state what it is*) system of classification is suitable for our requirements?

4 If not, state whether you would prefer any of the systems of classification set out below:

   ....

   .... *etc.*

5 Should we have an indexing system (*OR* Do you think our indexing system works? If not, what changes should we make?)

6 Do you think our system to check on absent files is effective? If not, how can it be improved? (*OR* Should we have a system for checking on absent files? If so, what should it be?)

7 *Repeat the same questions for records retention system.*

8 Are there any other changes you would recommend? If so, what are they?

Signature: **Date:**

amendments will improve it, you should check first of all that your recommendations are consistent with the overall ethos. If the general rule is that all filing cabinets should be of a certain style and colour and should be grouped in a certain way in each area, you can suggest that you would like a change. It would be unwise of you, however, to simply go ahead and make the change without first seeking permission.

Even when the changes you want to make are within your remit, you should still be careful that in altering one part of the system you are not making the rest of it *less* effective.

If you feel that all the filing cabinets in your immediate work area should be grouped centrally rather than positioned by individual desks, you should make sure that you are not making it harder for your sales people to access customer files when answering telephone calls.

If you think it is old-fashioned to have a card index file of names and addresses and want it all put on to a computer database, by all means do so, but make certain that:

- everyone knows about it
- they have easy access to a computer
- they know how to use it!

If you decide that you want to alter the system so that it is a combination of centralised and individual filing, you must make certain that staff know what document is filed where. Otherwise confusion will reign!

TEST YOUR KNOWLEDGE AND UNDERSTANDING

1 In each of the following cases, make brief notes of the difficulties you could face if you tried to implement the changes.

   a You want to change the system of classification from alphabetical to subject.

   b You don't like the present system of cross-referencing and want everything to be photocopied with copies being placed in each folder.

   c You want to replace the old cupboards with open shelving.

2 You want to make some improvements to the present filing system. You have had a staff meeting and there is general agreement that changes need to be made. However, some members of staff begin to cause you concern. In each case, state how you would deal with the issue.

   a Yim is the only one of the group who feels that no changes at all need be made. However, he is one of the major users and also senior to most of the other staff, so his views have to be taken seriously.

   b Dietrich is very keen on changing to a numerical system of classification. Most of the others support him but you know that he and two of his colleagues are rather slapdash. You feel he will have great difficulty in mastering the system and think it will be chaos if the filing clerk is away.

   c Lisbeth likes the idea of everyone having access to all files. So do most other people. However, although nothing can be proved, you suspect her of leaking confidential information to people outside the department. You cannot, of course, accuse her of that and use it as a reason for not allowing open access.

   d Hilda is in tears. Up until now her main role has been to act as the department's filing clerk. She feels that any changes will put her job at risk.

Consulting the users and your line manager

Unilateral action is sometimes unavoidable. However, it can be quite dangerous, particularly when you rely upon the goodwill of your colleagues to assist you in your job. You may think you are more knowledgeable than either your line manager or the rest of the staff when it comes to filing systems. You probably are, but that does not alter the fact that implementation of any changes is far easier if you have the cooperation of the users. As already discussed, you may also find that they have some very good ideas! However, there can be problems with this approach.

EVIDENCE COLLECTION

As a result of the feedback you have received from users, identify how your current systems could be improved in a way which is consistent with the overall design of the system. Note that for this element you need to demonstrate that you can improve *two* of the following areas of your information storage system:

- cataloguing
- storage
- security
- disposal and archiving
- guidance and support
- record-keeping.

You should also be prepared to discuss with your assessor how you would improve the other areas.

Now find out what relevant people think of your ideas. Note that as your evidence for this element you need to consult with *both*:

- system users
- your line manager, team leader or supervisor.

Even if your line manager did not provide feedback for the evidence identified on page 371, you should certainly consult with him or her at this stage.

How to implement and test changes

A common fault when trying to make changes to a system is to do so piecemeal. You may feel that the system is overloaded, so you order a new filing cabinet. You think the records retention system is a bit woolly, so you institute a new one. Although individually the changes made may be good, quite often they have an adverse impact on the rest of the system. If you want to change your system it is a good idea to do so in a methodical, step-by-step way.

You take over an existing filing system which you want to change. What you might decide to do, first of all, is to list how the present system operates under the following headings:

- cataloguing or classification
- storage
- security
- disposal and archiving
- guidance and support
- record-keeping.

Your next step should be to examine each of these issues in turn and decide:

- whether or not they exist eg record-keeping systems
- if so, whether or not they are effective
- if not, how they should be changed.

Cataloguing or classification

When looking at the cataloguing or classification system, you should, of course, check:

- what system is being used
- the types of document being filed
- whether or not the present system is the most suitable.

If the present system is not working well, it is normally up to you to suggest an alternative and to present this to your colleagues and line manager with your reasons. If the system is quite good but you think it needs certain improvements, you should carry out the same exercise – although in those circumstances you may be able to implement the changes more quickly. You may, for instance, like the numerical system of cataloguing but be rather concerned that the indexing system is not being fully implemented. You can talk to the staff concerned and encourage them to make the necessary entries on the index cards.

Storage

The same principles apply when you examine the storage system in which the information is filed. However, in this instance, if you are unhappy about what you see, any changes you make may incur some expense. It is of little use in a small office suggesting that the present storage system is inefficient and that you want a state-of-the-art automated filing system. It may be equally useless in a large organisation if the policy is to have a standard type of storage no matter what is being stored in it. You can, however, suggest that the present system of, say, lateral filing cabinets be augmented by the addition of a couple of cupboards to house bulky files or by a series of mobile lateral filing cabinets for use by each desk. Whatever your suggestion, you should accompany it with projected costs. Otherwise your line manager might prolong the process by sending the suggestions back to you with a note asking you how much all this lot will cost!

Security

In checking on whether or not security is adequate, you have first to be aware of the level of importance of the documents in the system. If 99 per cent consist of general office correspondence with only one or two documents being confidential, the need for you to pursue the question of security will be less pressing than if the reverse is the case. It is a good idea for you to check with your line manager how confidential he or she regards the documentation, and then to determine whether or not the system is the best possible to prevent breaches of confidentiality. If it is not, you might regard it as a matter of urgency and suggest that changes be made to the way in which the documents are stored and the number of people who are allowed access to them.

If you are concerned about physical security – risk of fire, theft, water etc. – again you should check with your line manager – and with any security personnel who may be employed in the organisation. If you feel that additional storage containers should be purchased for this purpose, you are justified in putting your point quite strongly to your line manager.

Disposal and archiving

Getting rid of unwanted documents is probably at the bottom of everyone's list! So no matter how effective the system, disposal tends to be the least effective part.

The problem is easy enough to identify – overflowing filing cabinets, difficulty in opening desk drawers, papers spilling out on to tops of cabinets, window sills etc. It is equally easy to find out where the unwanted documents (if any) are stored. They are normally put in the most inaccessible place possible in bulging folders with indecipherable titles. You can, of course, keep your fingers crossed that no one is going to ask you to find a copy of a letter dated five years ago.

The alternative is to make an attempt to improve the situation. Again a step-by-step approach is best. Your most urgent task is to improve the state of the filing cabinets themselves and to make sure that all papers are at least kept away from public view. What you need in this instance is time, not money (although you may have to aquire small items of equipment such as a shredder to encourage staff to get rid of unwanted material). You may be able to persuade the filing clerk to cooperate with you in tidying up the system. If that is possible, draw up a plan covering a period of a few weeks in which a certain time is put aside each day to sorting out at least one part of the system (e.g. one filing cabinet drawer per day). If all else fails you can lead by example – by making sure that everyone sees you filing correctly and tidying up as you go along.

If there is a records retention procedure which has fallen into disuse, you can again ask your line manager to remind staff of it.

With regard to the archiving of documents, you may want to suggest to your manager that a new approach be taken. For instance, if the policy states that all materials are to be kept for five years but it is normal practice to put everything into the archives and forget about it altogether, it could be suggested that all material over five years old should be examined and disposed of if possible. (Look back to page 363 for further information.) Alternatively you might want to have the material rehoused and relabelled so that it is more accessible should it ever be required.

Guidance and support

In this unit, emphasis has been placed on the need for cooperation in operating a successful filing system. What is also required, of course, is a general understanding of how the filing system works. There are a number of ways you can assist with this.

a Make certain that there are written procedures available – although you should realise that no matter how often these are circulated there will always be some people who will insist they have never seen them!

b Prepare summarised versions of the procedures for display on or near the filing cabinets.

c Raise the issue of filing regularly at weekly staff meetings and highlight any concerns then.

d Request that the operation of the filing system be part of the induction course for all new staff.

e Make it clear that you do have time to explain to individual members of staff how the system works, at a time that is mutually convenient.

EVIDENCE COLLECTION

Identify the changes you agreed with users and your line manager, and then write a brief summary which explains how you implemented and tested these. State the actions you took to ensure that both the system and the users were subject to the minimum of disruption.

The importance of giving clear information and guidance on changes

You want to make some changes to the filing system. You go the line manager who seems to be engrossed in reading a set of documents. You ignore this and start talking to her.

'I know you're busy but I want to talk to you about changing the filing system. It's a complete mess — at least it's not such a mess as it was, but it still won't win any prizes. Only the other day Mr Melling said that it took him longer to get a document out of the cabinet than it did to write it in the first place. Of course, I know he is always a bit sarcastic but I have to say he's hit the nail on the head there. And another thing I want to talk to you about is getting staff to cooperate over the way files are borrowed. Jordan is the worst culprit — he leaves papers all over the place and then loses his temper when anyone starts asking him to return them. We had to keep a client waiting in reception yesterday while we hunted for his file. We found it in the refectory of all places on top of the drinks machine. I don't know why it was there because that machine hasn't worked for ages. I'll have to have a word with the refectory manager about it. Anyway … What's the matter? You're looking a bit upset. Have I said anything wrong?'

Management of time is one of the major issues in a busy workplace. If you want to give some information to your line manager or a colleague, or to ask for their assistance, support or advice, you should be very clear about what you are going to say before you actually begin the conversation.

1 Decide *exactly* what you want to say. Do you want to inform your line manager or colleagues? Do you want to ask for their support and advice? Do you want a decision?

2 Decide on the most appropriate form of communication. Do you want to talk to people individually? Do you want to see them as a group? Do you think the information is better in written form? If so, what?

3 Prepare beforehand what you want to say. Have you all the facts at your fingertips? Have you anticipated what arguments there may be so that you are ready with an answer? Are you at this stage prepared to make further changes?

4 Treat the communication process as on-going. Do you think the information needs to be communicated once only? Should it be communicated regularly? Should you give regular updates? If so, when?

TEST YOUR KNOWLEDGE AND UNDERSTANDING

You have spent some time with the filing clerk changing several individual filing systems into a standardised departmental system. Your line manager has agreed to the changes and asks you to outline them briefly to the rest of the staff at the next staff meeting. Prepare brief notes on what you are going to say and in what order.

Evaluating changes

Setting up or changing an existing filing system is hard work. When you have finished, it is very tempting to sit back with a sigh of relief before starting the next job. If you do this you are making the assumption that the system or the changes are, without question, the right ones. They probably are, but as a good administrator you should be prepared to revisit them at regular intervals to evaluate exactly how effective they are. If, for instance, you have changed the procedures for borrowing files or have reallocated the job of filing to a different member of staff, you need to check whether or not these changes have brought about an overall improvement. You can evaluate in a number of ways.

a **Going and looking:** If you have introduced a change to the system of borrowing files, a look in the filing cabinets should give you an indication of how many absent file folders there are and how they are being used. If you have persuaded staff not to leave folders on desks or to remove the full file from the cabinet rather than individual papers, again a walk round the area should show whether or not the procedures are being followed.

b **Asking:** You might want to ascertain the effectiveness of a particular change by asking your line manager or the file users their opinions – either by means of a questionnaire or through discussions with various individuals or at a group meeting.

c **By independent audit:** Sometimes you can get too close to a situation and find it difficult to take an objective view. If you have spent a lot of time altering a filing system, you may find it better to ask someone else – another administrator for instance – to look at what you have done and to give an honest opinion.

d **By results:** If generally there are fewer complaints about the system, fewer files are lost, some compliments are recorded etc., you may feel satisfied that the changes have worked.

EVIDENCE COLLECTION

Retain copies of all the documents you have provided to your line manager and users which provide information or guidance on the changes that have been made and how the system now operates.

Record their responses and the results of on-going evaluations that you have undertaken to assess the success of your system. Do not be overly concerned if you have identified flaws or snags that need addressing. As you learned in Unit 305, this is natural with a new system or procedure, and reviewing it after a few weeks is sensible. If you have plans to further improve it, however, do include these.

Unit 307 Maintain and use databases

This unit is concerned with the operation and use of a computerised database. This may be a database that contains a limited amount of information and is used to help a small firm to operate more efficiently, or one that is shared by a small number of users in a workgroup or department. It may have been purposely designed using a software package such as Microsoft® Access. Alternatively, your database may be very large and complex and may have been professionally designed for your specific industry, customised by specialist staff in your organisation and be simultaneously available to several users on a computer network as well as – partially – to external customers over the Internet.

SPECIAL NOTE

To obtain this unit you need to use a database to retrieve and enter data, to extract required information and to output this information to a specified destination. One of the requirements for the first element is that you create fields with specified characteristics and modify these as required. In the second element, you need to be able to format certain database documents. If you are a database operator on a large, complex, networked system then you may find that these tasks can be carried out only by specialist staff in your organisation. In that case you should talk to your assessor about how you can obtain evidence for this part of the element. Options may include the following.

- Obtain permission to work with your specialist team and carrying out these operations under supervision.
- Create fields and define their characteristics on a PC, using a package such as Access (you could also count this towards your IT Key Skills evidence).
- Undertake a query and/or create a report on the same package and format the resulting document(s). However, you will need to have a basic knowledge about how to set up a database to do this. ➡

• Use evidence from an IT award you possess (such as IBT 3 or ECDL) – where a requirement is that you have to know how to undertake these operations. However, you are likely to have to provide evidence that you actually did so as part of your preparatory work or assessment.

Important note on terminology

If you use Microsoft® Access, you will be aware that your database consists of tables. You will not normally refer to 'files' in your database and do not have this option on your Desktop. The situation may be different if you are operating a large, corporate database.

The unit 307 NVQ scheme frequently refers to 'database files', particularly in element 307.1. Microsoft® Access users may find it easier to substitute 'tables' for this term throughout, although both terms have been used in this book and the actual difference is defined on page 389 and in the diagram on page 391.

If you have any queries, ask your tutor or supervisor for clarification.

 KEY SKILLS SIGNPOST

If you are taking your Key Skills award, you will find there are opportunities in this unit to obtain evidence towards the **Problem Solving** Key Skills unit at level 3. If you are working at a different level, then you should discuss this with your tutor or trainer.

The following types of problem can occur with maintaining and using a database.

• A database is shared by a number of users, not all of whom are very knowledgeable about how it operates. This means that mistakes are made which cause problems and additional work for other staff.

• A small 'flat' database which worked well for customer records is insufficient for current company needs. Frequently sales staff are asked about delivery dates for supplies and financial staff would like the database to include customer account status.

• You and your colleagues need regular access to your company database to answer customer enquiries, but the database is only available on two linked PCs. To make matters worse, the printer you use creates problems because it is quite old and constantly breaking down. Your boss is apprehensive about additional expenditure on IT equipment just to improve database access.

- New users of the database are constantly taking unnecessary printouts or failing to check their work before making a printout. The result has been a huge surge in the amount of paper required and excessive wastage.
- The number of reports available on your database system is limited and no one has overall responsibility for designing and developing these. You feel that this means the database isn't used to its full potential in your organisation.
- Your company has recently purchased a new database from a specialist company. This is a complex, powerful, relational database and your boss seems to think that so long as your IT specialists know about it, this will suffice. You know you can make a strong case for arguing that staff training for all your colleagues is absolutely essential or the potential benefits will never be obtained.

For any one of these problems (or for an alternative complex problem you have agreed with your tutor or supervisor) undertake the following tasks.

PS3.1

a   Explore the problem and analyse its features. Talk to other people involved and agree how it could be solved successfully.

b   Select and use a variety of methods to suggest ways of tackling the problem.

c   Compare the main features of each of your options, including the risk factors involved and then justify the option to decide which would be the best.

PS3.2

a   Plan how you would carry out the option you have chosen and obtain agreement from an appropriate person.

b   Implement your plan, demonstrating that you can effectively use support and feedback from other people.

c   Review your progress towards solving the problem and revise your approach as necessary.

PS3.3

a   Decide the methods you can use to check whether the problem has been solved and check these with an appropriate person.

b   Apply these methods accurately and then draw conclusions and describe the results in detail.

c Review how you approached solving the problem, and say whether you think alternative methods and options might have been more effective.

KNOWLEDGE AND UNDERSTANDING REQUIRED FOR THIS UNIT

In this part of the scheme you need to know the person(s) from whom you need to gain authority to access your database facilities. However, there are various degrees of access rights for database users and these relate closely to security controls to protect the structure of the database and data integrity. This issue is therefore also closely related to staff training – given that untrained staff are likely to find their access is strictly controlled to prevent any loss or damage to critical data.

For that reason, this section covers three main areas:

- access rights and security
- staff training
- basic facts about database operations that all users should know.

The last section is included in case you feel you would personally benefit from a review about databases and how they operate.

Access rights and security

Before you can use a database, you obviously need the authority to access the facilities available. To obtain this unit, you must therefore have access to a PC and/or networked computer and permission to access the database package itself to undertake a range of operations. These include accessing files (or tables), inputting and updating data, creating fields, saving files, interrogating the database and producing documents to a required layout.

Whilst staff who can access general information may need little training, it is not usual for anyone to be allowed to enter or modify data unless they have received specific training. Fundamentally, this is to prevent users making errors that could result in the storage of inaccurate information or the deletion of important data. However, on a smaller database where some users may have more extensive access rights, errors could be more serious and create significant problems if the design or structure of the database is altered in any way. Finally, all users must be aware of the confidential nature of certain types of information – and their responsibilities in this area (see pages 280 and 423).

The freedom you have to undertake certain operations will be determined by your access rights. For any database, there will be a designer or administrator who has the ability to allocate access rights or give permission to undertake operations to specific users. The broad categories are shown below.

Broad categories of access to database operations		
Level	Allowable operations	Typical job role
5	Administration of the database, design and structure of database, on-going developments, assigning access rights to other users, authorising the design and development of new reports	Database Administrator in large organisation Database creator in small firm
4	Modification of structure to meet on-going needs, deletion of historic data, design and creation of new forms and reports	Specialist database operator
3	Access to view most areas of the database and to view, modify and delete data from specific records, ability to run reports for own purposes and suggest new reports	Administrator with responsibility for database maintenance
2	Access to view job specific areas of the database and create new records/update specific records, ability to run pre-determined reports.	Administrator with responsibility for keeping database up to date
1	View access only on restricted areas, ability to view but not run reports.	All staff requiring access to database information

In virtually all systems, there will also be logging-on and/or password controls. If you use a networked computer system you will be aware that you have to 'log on' with your user ID and password to gain access to the network. You may then have to enter a *second* password to access the database system. This control can be in place even on a small database operated on a PC – regardless of whether it is used by one person or a workgroup. Note that if you forget your password then you need to contact the database administrator or creator, who can 'clear' your old password electronically and allocate you a new one.

When you log on, your user ID and/or password will define the areas you can access on the database. Some parts will be completely restricted – don't expect to be able to find out about your boss's salary, for instance! Only at the highest level would you have access to every type of data stored on the system.

Staff training

The amount of staff training needed will depend upon the access level assigned. Level 1 users – who simply use the system to find information – may receive little training and learn their skills by searching the system, using a manual or help sheet or asking a colleague for advice. They simply need to have a good appreciation of the type of information on the system and what they can find that will be useful in their job. Needless to say, if the system is complex, it is sensible even for this level of user to receive some basic training to prevent them wasting time searching for data ineffectively.

At the other end of the scale, database administrators in charge of a large networked system will be specialist computer or systems staff. In a small firm, however, someone with high-level computer skills who has experience in setting up a small database could do the job.

Between these levels, staff training will depend upon the complexity of the system. However, any staff who have the ability to modify and amend important data or whose errors could cause significant problems should receive special training. This should include a basic appreciation of how databases operate:

- types of database
- their basic functions
- their structure
- their components
- their benefits and drawbacks.

INFORMATION UPDATE

Even if you are new to using a database, it is possible that your details are included in several databases held by different organisations.

- You are likely to be in a staff database held by your employer.
- If you attend college to study for your NVQ, then you will be in their student database.
- You are probably in a database held by any large organisation where you are a regular customer – your bank or building society, insurance company or supermarket – and by the health centre or doctor's practice where you are registered as a patient.
- You will be in several national databases, such as those held by the Inland Revenue (all taxpayers) and the DVLA (all holders of driving licences/car owners).
- If you pay bills, own a credit card or bank account or have ever bought goods on credit, then you are likely to be in a Credit Reference Agency database, which will give your credit rating to certain types of enquirers.

You should be comforted to know that you do have some protection in law to prevent people storing *incorrect* information about you or passing this on to other people without your permission. For more details, look back at the information on the Data Protection Act on page 282.

Basic facts on databases

Databases are growing in popularity because of the growing importance of up-to-date information about people, objects or events in an organisation. They enable transactions to be undertaken more quickly, staff to work more efficiently and customer needs to be satisfied. With a database, the required information is literally at the fingertips of staff and can be accessed by pressing a few keys. Other database functions enable staff to update information quickly and find exactly what they need in a particular situation. This type of response is considered essential in today's highly competitive business world.

The basic functions of a database

A computerised database is a collection of structured data held electronically. The word 'structured' means that the data is 'organised' in a particular way to enable rapid input and retrieval. Think of the difference between a filing cabinet with folders containing papers on specific subjects, all neatly filed in date order, and a cabinet where all the papers have been thrown into it in a heap. The first is structured, the second is not. Once data has been entered into a database it can be manipulated and sorted in a variety of ways to provide information of value to the organisation.

At this point it is worth noting the fundamental difference between 'data' and 'information'. Data are facts which, on their own, have no meaning. For instance, 21.10.81 is meaningless on its own, so is 'Chloe' and so is 'Smith'. However, if you know that Chloe Smith was born on 21.10.81 then the data becomes meaningful. It is now information and of some use – particularly, for instance, to a nightclub which wants to invite Chloe to celebrate her 21st birthday with them in October 2002!

Benefits and drawbacks of databases

There are several *advantages* for an organisation which stores and updates its information electronically.

- The database can be designed for the benefit of the organisation as a whole.
- On a networked system (where the computers are linked together) multiple users can access the information simultaneously.
- Because each set of data is held only once, it is easier to update and check. One update is sufficient to change the entry throughout the system. Users then have access to accurate data which is the same throughout the organisation.
- The system can be designed to help to prevent users from making fundamental errors or omitting key information.
- Because access to data can be limited, there is greater security since access to confidential data can be restricted.
- The whole organisation can operate more efficiently as orders can be processed and queries can be handled more quickly.

However, the system is not without its *drawbacks*.

- The system can be expensive to set up, especially if there are multiple users who all need access to a terminal or PC.
- Input errors mean that all staff are accessing incorrect information.
- Specialist staff are required to design and modify a large database to continually meet the needs of the organisation over time.
- Computer failure means that data is not available until the system is operational again.

Types of database

Your organisation may utilise any of the following types of database, depending on its size and the type of data to be handled.

Individual databases

In this case a specific database has one or two users. It is located on one computer and provides the user(s) with information relevant to their job. For instance, if you keep an address book on your personal computer, this is an example of an individual database.

Departmental or workgroup databases

These are databases shared by a small number of users. The database helps them to link their work and prevent duplication. An example would be a health centre where patient appointments are recorded on a database and can be accessed by reception staff, and patient records and appointment information can be accessed by medical staff and doctors.

Organisational databases

These are large, complex databases that store and process data used by a large number of staff for different reasons. Senior management may use reports for decision-making, middle managers to keep track of operations, administrative staff to obtain information on request, and sales staff to process customer enquiries quickly.

Flat and relational databases

A **flat** database consists of only one table. An example might be one you create to keep a simple record of all the CDs you own. A **relational** database, on the other hand, is one containing several tables which have links (or relationships) between them. This is the type you are more likely to use in business and it requires DBMS (database management system) software. However, don't be misled by this term – it is perfectly possible to create a relational database on a package such as Microsoft® Access.

A relational database is required if you would be adding so much information under one file or in one table – some of which may be duplicated or inappropriate – that the database would be unmanageable.

This is the case, for example, if you start a customer database to list names and addresses but then want to set up a database of the products you stock. It would obviously be useful to link these, because your customers buy these products – so you want not only to check what you have sold, but who you have sold to. You therefore set up two tables, one for customers, one for products, and *link* the two. Then if you update a customer record (because a customer had bought something), the product item record is automatically updated too.

The components of a database

There are some basic terms you need to know. These are explained below.

A **file** is a collection of records which can be grouped under one heading and stored as one unit electronically. It often comprises a number of **tables**.

A **form** is designed to enable data on one entity to be entered. An entity can be a person, object or event, such as a customer, spare part or visit by a mechanic to service an appliance. Once the form is completed, it becomes a record. Forms are used by people who input information into a database but don't need to have any knowledge of how the database works or how to add information in a table format (such as shoppers on-line at Tesco).

A **field** is a section on a form where a specific piece of information must be entered. There are various types of fields and these can be specified by the database designer (see pages 396 and 399) to help to control data entry.

A **table** stores data in rows and columns. Each row relates to a record; each column relates to a field. Whether you need to access tables as a user of your system will depend upon how your database is structured. If you operate a relational database and wanted to store information on your customers and on your suppliers, this would require two tables. If you decided to add staff details as well, this would require a third table.

A **query** is a method of interrogating the data to extract what you want.

A **report** is a summary of specific data, usually printed out for reference. It is designed to present relevant data in an easy-to-understand format.

A **wildcard** is a key which can be used to find text if you are not sure of the exact term. The most common wildcard characters are * and %.

INFORMATION UPDATE

You may not think of schools, colleges and universities as business organisations needing powerful databases, but they do! These are highly complex relational databases that hold tables not only on the students, but also on all other related features. The illustration below shows you some of the range of tables you may find. The reason for all the different types becomes more obvious if you consider that:

- not all applicants attend for interview
- not all interviewees become students
- not all students take examinations
- students are sometimes absent from class
- fees may apply to some courses but not all
- courses need rooms, but so do examinations.

These are only a few of the considerations that database planners have to bear in mind! By having separate tables, but linking them, the system is both more flexible and more powerful and duplication of stored information is minimised.

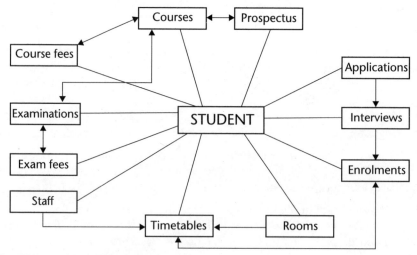

A complex relational database

The structure of databases

The structure of a database relates to the way in which the data is organised. You have already seen there are several components to any database, but they have to be organised in a systematic way. For *each* file in the database, you are likely to find the data organised in a hierarchical system – from files at the highest level down to data at the lowest level. The illustration below shows this graphically.

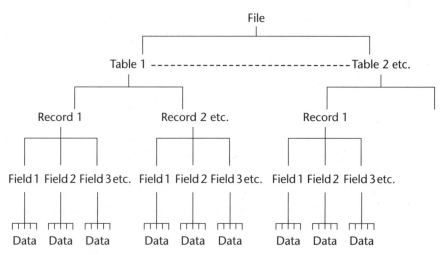

The structure of a relational database

In a relational system, the tables will be linked together by means of relationships between specified fields. In this case, as you have alreadyseen, updating one table updates the others. The links between data and tables and between different types of table determines the *structure* of the database. In element 307.1 you will find that you have certain responsibilities to *maintain* existing data structures and conform to current systems if you make any developments. There is more information about this on page 394.

Some of your tables may be described as 'master' files – which contain semi-permanent data – whilst others are simply reference files which provide you with information on the screen (such as a price list). A third type are sometimes known as transaction files – which are updated regularly. For instance, a college database may have student records as master files, the description and size of its classrooms as a reference file, and register data as a transaction file.

Your system will also be structured so that you enter data on a form in a particular way, depending upon the design of the form and each type of field on the form. The type of queries you can carry out and the reports you can access will also be structured in a particular way and, depending upon the complexity of the system, you may be able to amend these significantly only by submitting a formal request to your database administrator.

Find out how your database is structured by identifying:

a what type of tables exist in the database

b what subjects or topics are covered

c how the tables relate to each other

d what guidelines or 'rules' you must conform to when you enter data into a form

e what type of reports are available on your system at the moment.

Write a brief account which makes it clear to your assessor the database structure in place and the procedures with which you must comply.

Element 307.1 Retrieve and enter data to update databases

Databases are useful only if they are kept up to date. This means entering new data and updating existing data *very* regularly – preferably daily. Before you can enter or update anything, however, you have to be able to find the correct record in the correct file. You also need to know your access level, to know what you are allowed to update. This element is concerned with the critical operations required to maintain an existing database and the operations sometimes required to meet new needs specified by a user.

Meeting customer requirements

In this context your 'customers' are all those people who contact you and need information provided by your database. These may be 'internal' or 'external' customers. For instance, your line manager may want to know the value of all goods sold last month by each sales representative. A customer, on the other hand, may telephone to find out if a spare part is available and, if it is in stock, to place an order. In all these cases you would use your database to find the required information. To deal with the first query you would need to know how to obtain the specific information required. In the second, you may simply have to access your spare parts database to find the answer and then know how to process the order, which is likely to entail accessing a *different* part of your database, such as your customer or order files.

It is worth noting that your customers will not know what your database can do! Neither may they know exactly what they want. Added to this is the fact that you may not be allowed to divulge particular items of information to certain types of customer – particularly 'external' customers. For instance, you should never pass on personal information on other members of staff, such as their address or home telephone number.

Interpreting a customer request can therefore be problematic. It might be necessary to make suggestions as to the best way to meet the requirements. The following points should give you some ideas.

On an **individual database** it is usually possible to input a query to meet the needs of an internal request. You may also be able to design forms and reports to meet the needs of your customer. However, check that the request isn't simply a 'one-off' which can be satisfied in another way – before you promise something which will take a considerable amount of work.

On a **workgroup database** you may have to consult with your line manager if you receive a particularly unusual request. Also, it may be necessary to liaise with your boss or a specialist if you are asked to design a new form or report.

On a **complex organisational database**, the queries you can undertake will be pre-set – but there may be a comprehensive list. Check your manual to find out.

When using a complex database you would have to submit a formal request for a new type of form or report to be created, as this would be done by a specialist department. However, they would require full details of *your* requirements, which means giving careful thought to what is required in relation to what is possible! They would then also need to be convinced that the new addition would be of value, in terms of the time spent implementing your request.

Locating and retrieving database files or tables

The first operational sequence you will learn is how to access the files you need. On a computer network, as you have seen, you will have to log in as a user and enter your user ID. Then you need to know where your database package is located. Often this will be identified by a special icon on your Microsoft® Windows Desktop screen. In this case, pointing to the icon and clicking will give you access to the system.

You are then likely to have to enter your password to gain access to the files. Each user on the system will have access rights (see page 383), so once the system recognises who you are, this will determine the files or tables you can see and the data you can enter or update.

In a complex system, you then need to know how to find the appropriate table. Some complex systems are designed in a similar way to Microsoft® Windows Explorer. In this case, you will see a list of folders. Those folders having a '+' sign at the side have files or tables within them – click on the '+' to list them.

In other cases your folders and files may be displayed graphically as icons, or simply as a list in a dialogue box. With any of these options, if you are using a Windows-based package, double-clicking on a folder or file will open it.

If you use a package such as Microsoft® Access, you should be aware that a file contains different database objects, such as tables, forms, queries and reports. These will be identified on your screen, but their position will be determined by the version of Access you are using.

How to maintain data structures

For this element you have to prove you can maintain existing data structures and retain these in any new developments. Data structures were discussed on page 391 but, fundamentally, this requirement means that you must understand:

- how your database is organised
- how the reports, forms and queries have been set up
- how data must be entered and in which format
- the limits of your authority – i.e. what you are allowed to do and what you are not allowed to do.

A golden rule is *never* to make a modification or adjustment which you do not understand. If your database has been structured correctly, with appropriate security devices, then the system should stop you from doing anything disastrous. However, a colleague who has designed a small, simple database for use by a few people may not have installed such rigorous protection systems as a large organisation – and herein lies the danger. A few key depressions at the wrong time – or a bright idea gone wrong – can quickly cause havoc and undo hours of work.

 INFORMATION UPDATE

A very large database with multiple users is likely to be backed up every night. This is a security precaution because the following day, if a significant problem is found, the database administrator can 'step back' one day and compare the data. If necessary, the existing data will be overwritten with the back-up data – which should put the system right again.

This is a useful technique to use yourself if you use a small database. If you back up your database each evening, and then make a critical mistake the following day, you can replace your existing version with your back-up at any point.

TEST YOUR KNOWLEDGE AND UNDERSTANDING

To understand the concept of database design more fully, check through the sequence of operations carried out by Cathryn Payne, when she designs a database for her boss. This will help you to see how a small database is constructed as well as to appreciate its potential. Later in the chapter you will see how Cathryn develops her database. Start by reading the following and then answer the questions that follow.

Cathryn works for a small garage, Valley Motors, which specialises in car services and MOT tests. Recently she overheard a customer complaining that he had forgotten his MOT test was due and he had been using his car for a month without a valid test certificate. The customer is annoyed that there is no formal system for reminding drivers when their test is due.

Cathryn suggests to Paul, who owns the business, that it might be valuable to set up a database with tables that record customer information, the make and model of their car and the last date the car was tested. She would then print out reports each month showing the cars due for testing, and write to these customers to remind them to book their car in.

1 Identify at least two benefits *to the garage* of setting up this database.

2 Can you think of any drawbacks?

3 How will the garage's customers benefit?

4 What type of database is Cathryn suggesting – individual, workgroup or organisational? Give a reason for your answer.

5 Will the database be flat or relational at this stage? Again, give a reason for your answer.

6 To what extent is Cathryn 'interpreting and applying her customers' requirements' by making this suggestion?

7 How will Cathryn's database be structured? Use the diagram shown on page 391 to help you to explain this.

Creating fields and field characteristics

One of the most critical stages in the development of a database is its design. This means deciding what needs to be included and how the database should be structured. Expert designers spend a long time over this process, otherwise much work is wasted when the database is actually set up. In most cases they start by considering the 'end' product – what they want their database *to do*. Cathryn knows what she wants her database to do – she wants it to provide her with information on MOT tests that are due, by date, by customer. The next stage is for her to consider what information she needs to collect which will provide this result. She knows that she cannot expect the database to analyse information it hasn't been given!

Cathryn is sensible. As someone 'new' to databases she is keeping her database simple. This means having only a few fields to contain important information. She also knows she must abide by some 'golden' rules in relation to fields:

a Each field must relate to the subject of the table – in this case her customers.

b It is helpful if the fields are listed in a logical order – though Cathryn knows she can alter the order if necessary at a later stage.

c Each separate piece of information should have its own field (e.g. first name and surname = two fields, not one).

d Each field needs a different name.

e The length of the fields should be varied to allow for the expected (or maximum) number of characters.

f The type of data to be entered into each field should be specified (e.g. numbers or text).

g The format of certain types of entries should also be specified.

Field lengths, data types and the format of certain fields are all measures which help to prevent errors in data entry.

Cathryn is using Microsoft® Access 2000. She starts by using the Table Wizard to help her to design a table quickly. The wizard suggests field names to her but allows Cathryn to alter these to suit herself. Cathryn's list is shown in the table below.

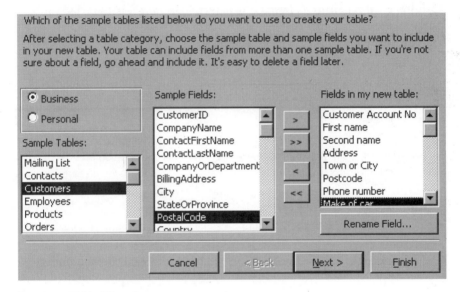

Database Table Wizard

 INFORMATION UPDATE

Wizards are a feature of many software packages. They enable you to undertake quite complex operations more easily by giving you assistance. In other words, they do much of the work for you. If you use a wizard, you may find your overall options are more limited but you are also less likely to make a mistake! You will also do the job quicker. Never underestimate the value of wizards when you are learning how to do something new.

Deciding field characteristics

Cathryn now has to consider each field in turn, in relation to its size, its type and its format.

The size or length of field is determined by the amount of data which will need to be entered. In the illustration on page 401, you will see that Cathryn has chosen a field size of 20 for the field named 'second name'. This is because she thinks this is a sensible number of letters – few people have surnames longer than this.

There are different types of field. Cathryn can choose between:

- **text fields** – which contain either just text (e.g. surname) or a mixture of text and numbers (e.g. address line) or numbers not required in calculations (e.g. telephone numbers)
- **numerical or number fields** – which contain numbers to be used in calculations (e.g. quantities)
- **date and time fields** – where exact dates and times must be entered
- **currency fields** – which contain monetary values
- **yes/no fields** – which provide options (e.g. true/false, yes/no, on/off)
- **memo fields** – which contain long text entries, such as notes and comments.

Finally, Cathryn can specify the format of the data to be entered into a particular field. This helps to validate the data and control the type of entry that can be made. Examples include:

- setting the maximum number of characters which can be entered into a text field
- identifying whether any numbers must be whole numbers (integers) or decimals
- controlling the range of numbers which can be entered into a number field (e.g. between 10 and 20)
- identifying that data *must* be entered into selected fields before the record can be accepted (e.g. the customer's name).

The format must also specify whether duplicate entries are allowed on different records, as when more than one person lives in any one town, more than one person owns a Ford car etc. However, only one person would have a car with a specific registration number.

It is also necessary to set the specific format for an entry (called an 'input mask' in Microsoft® Access). For instance, a date could be required as DD/MM/YY and a postcode as requiring a minimum of six and a maximum of seven characters, with the mix of letters and numbers specified.

Finally, if Cathryn is very experienced, she can link certain fields and set a **validation check**. Then the record will be saved only if these fields *together* meet set criteria. For instance, if the garage guaranteed customers that all

MOT tests would be scheduled within 10 days of being requested, then a 'date requested' and 'scheduled MOT date' field could be linked. In this case, the record wouldn't be accepted unless the date entered into the last field was within 10 days of the first field.

If a user tries to complete a record without complying with the validation rules set, it will not be accepted and the offending entry must be changed.

Identifying a primary key

Cathryn works hard deciding on the characteristics for each of her fields. She has also had to respond to a prompt from her Wizard about setting a primary key.

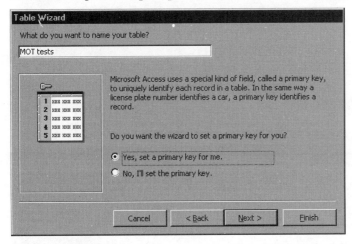

Cathryn's prompt

Primary keys

When she investigates, she finds that primary keys are valuable because they identify one unique field that can always be used to identify that particular record. Although with a 'flat' database, a primary key isn't essential, Cathryn decides to set one anyway. Access promptly inserts a 'key' icon next to the field she has selected to denote this is the primary key field. The database package will now automatically give each new record its own unique number.

 INFORMATION UPDATE

An obvious application of databases is in a library. All the members of the library can be held in one file and all the books in another file. The books can be logged in terms of subject classification, title, author(s), publisher and ISBN. The term 'ISBN' means international standard book number and is unique to every book. This can therefore be used as the primary key.

In a library, as in a supermarket, technology can be enhanced by scanning equipment. A scanner is placed against the barcode on the product or book and this immediately 'reads' which item is being sold or which book is being logged out or in. This saves the operator from having to key in the code and is usually a more efficient and more accurate method of checking items in and out of a computerised system.

In a library there will be several benefits to installing a database. Reminders for overdue books can be sent out automatically, current book stock can be checked immediately, book reservations can be logged on the system. The library will operate more efficiently for the benefit of both customers and staff.

TEST YOUR KNOWLEDGE AND UNDERSTANDING

1 Cathryn's field names and data types are shown in the illustration opposite. Use this to answer the following questions:

   a Which is the primary key field?
   b Why do you think Cathryn chose this field as the primary key?
   c Why has Cathryn selected 'text' as the data type for phone numbers?
   d Why is 'account status' a currency field and not a number field?
   e For which field has Cathryn decided there are only two possible options?
   f The field properties for 'second name' are shown – how do you explain the entries showing?
   g What would happen if Cathryn accidentally set 'no duplicates' in her field properties for 'model of car'?

2 A video shop already has a database of all its members. It now decides to list on a separate file all the films it has for rent – it can then link the two so that members can check which films they have seen already if they can't remember the titles. The fields the manager is considering are listed below. Use this list to decide:

   a which should be the primary key field
   c which fields should be required before the record can be saved
   d which fields can be duplicates
   e the type of field in each case
   f an appropriate field size in each case.

Fields: title, principal actors/actresses, type of film, date of issue, video reference number, category (PG, 15, 18 etc), rental fee, no. of copies held, comments.

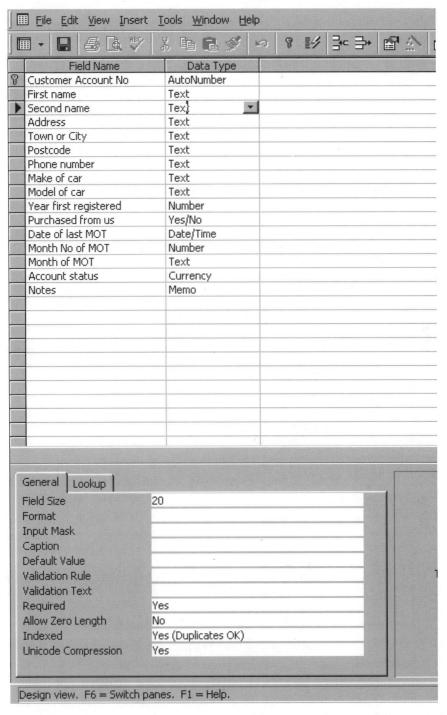

	Field Name	Data Type
🔑	Customer Account No	AutoNumber
	First name	Text
▶	Second name	Text
	Address	Text
	Town or City	Text
	Postcode	Text
	Phone number	Text
	Make of car	Text
	Model of car	Text
	Year first registered	Number
	Purchased from us	Yes/No
	Date of last MOT	Date/Time
	Month No of MOT	Number
	Month of MOT	Text
	Account status	Currency
	Notes	Memo

General | **Lookup**

Field Size	20
Format	
Input Mask	
Caption	
Default Value	
Validation Rule	
Validation Text	
Required	Yes
Allow Zero Length	No
Indexed	Yes (Duplicates OK)
Unicode Compression	Yes

Design view. F6 = Switch panes. F1 = Help.

Database field types

Modifying fields, obtaining guidance and using program Help files

Cathryn encounters a problem when she tries to enter her data in one field. She discovers that she cannot enter the 'year of purchase' as a date/time field because her software requires a specific date (DD/MM/YY) and won't accept a four-figure number. She therefore has to modify her date field and decides to change it to a text field. As she becomes more experienced, she will learn about other options available, such as **input masks** which define the exact type of input (e.g. 00/00/0000).

Cathryn may not have known why she was having a problem, but she could either seek guidance from her program Help facilities or from another person whose knowledge of databases is greater than her own.

In addition to changing field characteristics, Cathryn may wish to make other modifications, such as:

- add a new field
- delete a field
- move a field
- rename a field.

All these operations can be done quite easily in Microsoft® Access from her customers' table. However, it is important that such refinements are done as soon as possible during database construction. Later, when Cathryn has designed a form on which the data can be entered, or has created a query or report which uses certain fields, such alterations are more difficult. This is particularly true if she tries to delete a field which is used in a form, query or report.

CHECK IT OUT!

1 On page 403 are two tables constructed to hold information on members of a fitness club.

   a How many changes have been made between the first table being constructed (Table A) and the final one (Table B)?

   b Can you suggest why these changes have been made?

   c Which field do you think is the primary key field?

   d What characteristics do you think each field will have?

2 Find out how to add, delete, rename and move fields on your own database package. If you wish you can start by creating Table A and then change this to Table B by making the modifications. Print out a copy of both tables to use as evidence. Use your program Help to guide you, but check with your tutor or supervisor if you are still unsure what to do.

Table A

First name	Last name	Membership no.	Date first registered	Renewal date	Membership category	Phone no.
Jack	Parker	204	21.05.1998	21.05.2002	Gold	01323-457583
Catriona	Weiss	312	09.11.1999	09.11.2002	Silver	01736-878274
Julie	Stroud	368	05.01.2000	05.01.2002	Bronze	01829-487383
Liam	Kent	430	29.02.2000	29.06.2002	Gold	01323-394828

Table B

Membership no.	First name	Surname	Phone no.	Membership renewal date	Membership category	Membership fee
204	Jack	Parker	01323-457583	21.05.2002	Gold	£78
312	Catriona	Weiss	01736-878274	09.11.2002	Silver	£52
368	Julie	Stroud	01829-487383	05.01.2002	Bronze	£35
430	Liam	Kent	01323-394828	29.06.2002	Gold	£78

Entering and checking data

On most databases, data entry is made on **forms**, not directly into tables. Form design can be quite complex. The aim is to create an electronic form on which the data for each record can be entered quickly and easily by users.

In Microsoft® Access, data can be entered directly into a table to create records and it is a simple matter to amend and delete records in a table. However, most people refer to work with forms – especially in a large database where the number of records in a table could be enormous. A form represents one particular record and all the data for that record is viewed at once. Users can either move through records, or select a blank form for a new record, or select a specific record if they want to view or amend specific data.

Cathryn designs the form shown below. She then checks that the layout is acceptable to her boss and that all the data they both need will be clear and appropriate to the overall purpose of the database. Then – as well as testing it herself – she asks a colleague to do so. This is a double-check that all the fields are easy to understand and that simple errors have been minimised as much as possible through the design of the fields and the specific characteristics she has assigned to them.

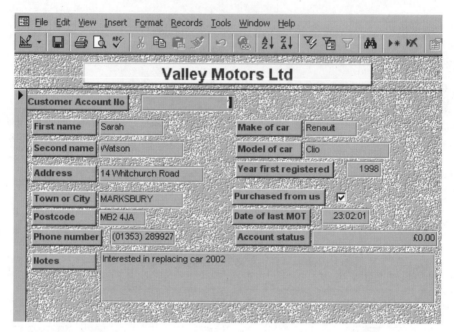

Cathryn's customer record

EVIDENCE COLLECTION

As part of your evidence for this element, you have to prove that you can create fields with *all* of the following characteristics: name, type, size and format.

In addition, you must meet your customer's requirements in relation to: layout, purpose and time.

The easiest way to produce evidence is to create a table (or form) showing fields you have designed. In Microsoft® Access, you can print out your field types from 'design' view. Then state why you have chosen each type and selected other relevant characteristics.

Finally, state any requirements on layout, purpose and time you had to meet, and how you achieved these.

Entering data accurately

You have already seen that the design of a database can help to minimise some errors. However, no database designer can possibly incorporate safeguards to eradicate *all* possible errors. Typical mistakes include:

- accurate data entry but into the wrong record
- inaccurate data entry through keying-in errors
- inaccurate data entry through spelling errors
- inaccurate data entry because of other errors, such as a failure to check data or to 'think' about data entry.

Remember that many people may make decisions and take action on the data you have entered. It *must* be accurate. Therefore, careful proof-reading of every record you create, before you save it, is essential.

Selecting the correct record

If you are locating a record by means of the primary key, then you will have only one record to choose from. However, you may not know the primary key and may be entering other data to find the record. For instance, on a staff database, you may know the name and department but not the staff ID number. If you then find three records displayed – all for 'Smith' in 'Sales' – then you will have to search further to find which one is the right one. (See page 409.)

> **CHECK IT OUT!**
>
> As a first stage you should know the keys to use which will enable you to move through a record easily (usually the Tab key) and from one record to another in a sequence (usually the arrow keys and page up/down keys). Check that you are familiar with all the methods you can use to move from one record to another easily and through a record swiftly on your own database system.

Keying-in errors

Everyone can make keying-in errors – and no database designer can prevent you from typing Jack instead of John or Wilkins instead of Wilkinson! Errors in names are likely to offend or irritate your customers, and errors in addresses can mean that any mailings sent from your database never arrive. Errors in amounts owing or account status can be very serious – and mean good payers are reminded about a debt and people who owe money are left in peace! In fact, you can create chaos quite easily if you fail to check your work when inputting data into a customer record.

Spelling errors

These are likely to be most noticeable in any lengthy entries, such as in a comments or notes section. In Microsoft® Access and many other database packages you can take advantage of the automatic spell-checkers (through the ABC button on your toolbar), which can be used to check your spelling. This is invaluable if you are sharing a multi-user database, where your lack of skills will be on view to everyone who uses the system!

Other errors

One of the most common mistakes on forms is to enter the current year instead of the correct year for 'date of birth'. It may not be possible for your designer to prevent this by means of a verification check. For instance, if you work in a doctor's surgery the current year *will* be correct for a newborn baby! The key point is to *think* about what you are doing and use a simple rationality check to see whether the data seems reasonable. If it does not then make the effort to check what the data should really be – don't guess it!

INFORMATION UPDATE

The largest database in the world is known as the Schengen information system. Data entry began five years ago and it already holds more the nine million files, accessible from 50,000 terminals around Europe. Most of the files relate to stolen cars, passports and identity papers, but 1.3 million relate to individuals – mainly immigrants rather than criminals. The database is the first experiment in the sharing of sensitive data to reduce crime, and to find people who are missing or wanted for extradition.

However, whilst the idea of inputting all this data is mind-blowing, you may be interested to know there are also several problems being experienced. These include poor quality of data, no formal systems for correcting or updating data, and no clear criteria on the reasons why entries should be made in the first place. The result has been valid citizens being refused entry into their own country because they had been listed incorrectly or because names have been confused.

The UK plans to join the database and, in time, it could be available to all police forces both here and in the rest of Europe. The effects of inaccurate data entry are almost too worrying to contemplate.

Saving database records

When you are absolutely certain that your data is both accurate and complete, then it must be saved. As you have already seen, most database systems will not allow you to save a new record (or resave an updated record) if you have made a fundamental error or not complied with all the field and record characteristics specified by the designer.

You may find that your database has been structured so that:

- updated or newly created database records are *automatically* saved when you exit the screen – provided all the required fields have been completed
- updated or newly created database records are saved automatically to a specified location
- the way in which you must name new records is also specified and is automatic.

This is unlikely to be the case if you are working on a small database or one where you have constructed the table and/or designed the form yourself. Then you should note the following tips.

- Save your work frequently (or set this as an automatic function on your computer) so that you never lose very much work if you encounter a system problem.
- Back up your database each evening (see page 395).
- When prompted to save at regular intervals by Microsoft® Access and most other packages – particularly if you are trying to exit a screen *without* saving – always read the prompt carefully and *think* before you respond.
- Name your database with a distinctive title. This is especially true if you are working with several databases.
- Use distinctive names for each set of files you create (customers, suppliers, cars etc.). You should know the extension under which your system saves database files if you are working with any operating system earlier than Microsoft® Windows 2000. This means you can quickly and easily recognise database files and folders.

Remember, however, that database components are linked. Therefore, if you update a customer record and there is a linked table, this will also be updated automatically. There is no need to access the table separately to try to update it. Equally – as you will see – in a relational database, updating one table or record will update any *linked* file records.

Finally, do be aware of your organisation's procedures for database security. This means not divulging any passwords you have or any information you have obtained as part of your job to those with a lower level of access than yourself.

Updating records

If you are given the task of updating database files you have to be able to:

- find the correct record
- move to the data which is now incorrect
- know how to delete this data and replace it with the correct data
- resave the record with the updated information.

You should also know how to delete an entire record that is no longer required, and how to create a new record.

Do check if there are any specific requirements you must follow before you delete a record. This will be very important in some databases if the data contained in the record has a relationship with another part of the database. For this reason, you may have to obtain special permission before you can carry out this type of operation.

EVIDENCE COLLECTION

You must prove that you can accurately retrieve and input both numbers and text into database records and save database files. Retrieving specific information is covered in the next element, but you should start to obtain evidence which proves that you can:

a accurately retrieve the correct record

b enter numbers and text accurately – either into a new record or to update an existing record

c save database files using your organisation's procedures for frequency, location, naming conventions and security.

One method of proving that you can do this is to print out a copy of customer records before and after you have made amendments. You can then write a brief description of any procedures you must follow when saving files. Ask your supervisor or line manager for witness testimony that you regularly carry out all these operations effectively

---

Element 307.2 Extract the required information

There are various ways to find a particular item on a database. One way, of course, is to trawl through every record you have in a table (or every record). Quite obviously this is both slow and tedious and, in a large database, would be completely impractical. Therefore, it is important that you understand how to interrogate your database to find what you need quickly.

Data interrogation facilities

There are usually four methods you can use to extract information from a database for a specific purpose:

- **search** for specific data
- **filter** records
- **sort** records
- **query** records.

The method you use will depend upon the question you have been asked and whether your query is a 'one-off' or whether you want to save it to use again and again.

Searching for specific data

Cathryn's boss, Paul, wants to contact a customer quickly. He knows her first name is Susan and that she drives a VW Golf. He asks Cathryn to find out the customer's full name and telephone number as quickly as possible.

In doing a search it is sensible initially to select the field in which there are likely to be the least number of records. Cathryn has a choice of three fields to search – the customer's first name, the make of car, and the model of car. She decides to try to find her customer under 'first name' as she doesn't think they have many customers called 'Susan', whereas she knows several own VW cars many of which are Golfs.

In Microsoft® Access, Cathryn highlights the field for 'first name' in datasheet view and then clicks on the 'binoculars' icon on the toolbar. This is her Find button and brings up a 'Search and Replace' dialogue box. Cathryn now has three options:

- If she knows the name and enters 'Susan' then she will be looking for an exact match – and will select the option 'whole field'.
- If she cannot remember whether the customer is called Sue or Susan then she can enter the letters 'Su' (or 'Su*') and search under 'start of field'. This would bring up all the records which start with the letters Su – including Sue, Susan and Suzanne.

- If Cathryn is worried that the customer may have two first names, she can enter Susan and search under 'any part of field'.

If this is the only method Cathryn knows for finding a record, then she will have to read through all the records which Microsoft® Access now finds with the customer name Susan in them, to see which also include VW Golf cars. However, this can also be done automatically by filtering records.

Filtering records

If you apply filters when searching the data, you can instruct the database to do this over and over again so that you methodically refine the number of records you can see. You do this by stating the criteria, or conditions, which apply to the records you want to find.

In Cathryn's case she could start by filtering her records first under VW, then under Golf and finally under Susan. Each time the number of records would decrease because those which didn't match the criteria are rejected.

Filters are ideal when you are asked to find certain records which relate to particular types of information – such as a list of all the customers who live in Marksbury who own a Ford car which is over three years old. If this type of filter is used regularly it can be saved, so that it can be quickly applied again when it is needed.

Sorting procedures

If you sort through your records, you specify the order in which the records are displayed. As an example, if Cathryn wanted to find out which customers owe the garage the most money she could sort the records so these records are displayed first. In this case, Cathryn would sort on the Account status field. In Access she can go to her table, highlight this field and click either the Sort ascending button (which sorts from A to Z, 1 to 9 or, with dates, earlier to later) or on the Sort descending button (which sorts from Z to A, 9 to 1 or from later to earlier). Therefore sorting under 'descending' would put the customers who owe the most money at the top.

Equally, Cathryn could list her customers in alphabetical order of surname, simply by applying 'sort ascending' to the 'second name' field.

If Cathryn wanted to sort on two fields she could do this by putting these next to each other (by clicking on the field title and dragging it next to the other one), in the order she wants them to be sorted. When she highlights both fields and clicks the Sort button she wants, the records will be sorted according to both fields.

Querying records

A more sophisticated way of finding what you need is by entering a **query** into the database. Entering a query simply means asking the database a question. Queries can be 'AND' questions, 'OR' questions or both.

• If Cathryn asked her database to list all customers who live in Marksbury and own a Ford car, this is an 'AND' question (Marksbury AND Ford).

• If, however, she wanted the database to list all the customers who live in Marksbury or Helsby, that is an 'OR' question.

• If she wanted the database to list all the customers who live in Marksbury or Helsby and own a Ford car, she would enter an 'OR' and an 'AND' question.

Entering a complex query properly can be quite difficult and, in a large database, a specialist will have entered these for you. However, for this element you should be able to enter a simple query and obtain the correct result.

Knowing the principles on which queries are based will help you to understand what you can and can't do, and why you have to be careful what you enter.

If you try to query something on which your database has no information you will receive an error message. For instance, if Cathryn wanted to know how many customers owned an estate car she wouldn't be able to find out because this isn't part of her database.

Other points to note

A few databases are **case-sensitive**. This means that if you have data entered in capitals then you must enter your query in capitals; equally, lower-case entries are required for lower-case text. Today, most databases can understand either type of entry and apply them. You are more likely to find case-sensitive conditions when you are entering a password or a word critical to your security operations.

Databases cannot cope with spelling mistakes – they look for an exact match!

Even adding an 's' in the wrong place will mean your query won't work. Also, query terms must be exact in relation to the type of entry, any punctuation marks and any spaces. So entering 1.8 XL would *not* find 1.8XL.

There is more flexibility over numeric criteria because you can use mathematical signs to help. For instance, if you wanted to find the customers who owe you exactly £500 then you would enter that figure. If you wanted to find those who owe you more than £500 you enter >£500, and if you want to list those who owe you less than £500 you enter <£500.

TEST YOUR KNOWLEDGE AND UNDERSTANDING

Cathryn is set a problem one morning. Paul tells her that they have to inform all their customers who own either a 1998 Ford Ka or a 1998 Ford Escort that their vehicle has to undergo a special safety check. Cathryn needs to find the records for the customers which match these criteria.

She starts by selecting the fields to include in the query. In this case she must include the make of car, the model and the year first registered. In Access™, a design grid enables Cathryn to select these fields – and any others relating to her query. Fields she 'ticks' will show on her printout.

Cathryn's query is shown in the illustration opposite. Study this carefully and answer the questions that follow. Check your answers with your tutor or supervisor.

1 Which fields, from the ones shown, will appear on Cathryn's printout?
2 What would happen if Cathryn thought that the Ford 'Ka' was spelled 'Car' and entered this spelling?
3 If Cathryn wanted to list all the owners of cars registered after 2001, what would she enter on this line?
4 The final column gives 'Date of last MOT' (not shown in the illustration). Cathryn has asked for this to be in ascending order. What does that mean?
5 Assuming Cathryn's dates are entered DD/MM/YY and she wants to list everyone who had their last MOT test before 20 August 2001, how should she input this query?

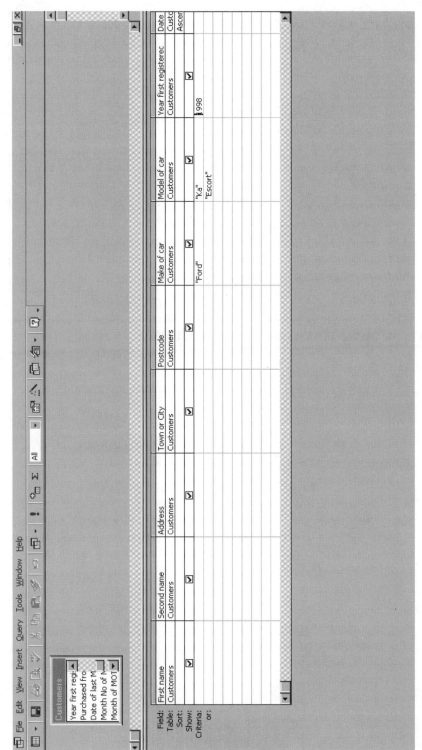

Database query

Producing database documents

After you have found a particular record you may wish to print it. Equally, you may wish to print the results after you have sorted records in a table or entered a query. In this case you will be printing a refined table which just lists the required records.

Another option, and the one most commonly used for answers to queries, is to print a report. Reports are created for printing the results of queries to a specific design.

You may remember that the reason why Cathryn suggested the database in the first place was to print out MOT dates so that she could remind customers when their cars were due for testing. For this unit you do not need to be able to design a report – that is quite a difficult task – but you do need to know how to print available reports and how to format any documents you print to meet the needs of your customer(s).

Printing a record

Printing a record is usually quite simple and you will have the option to print when a record is showing on screen. The record will usually have been designed to fit on one sheet of A4 portrait paper.

Printing a table

Tables are larger than a single record, particularly if you want to show several fields and several records. Basically, the more fields you try to include, the more likely you are to run out of space across the page! In this situation you have the following choices:

- On some database packages you can reduce the width of the fields – though you may lose sight of some of your data (or parts of the headings) by doing this.
- It is not necessary to show all the fields in a table. You already know that you can select the fields to show when running a query. You can also select the fields to include when you are using filters or sorting records. It is sensible to show only those fields that are needed for the reader to understand the printout.

Alternatively, you can change the page layout of your table. This is dealt with below.

Printing a report

Your reports should be designed to fit properly on to A4 paper. The layout of the data within a report is specified at the design stage. In this case, the layout relates to the way the data is organised on the page, such as in columns, in a table or justified. The designer can also select which headings to include, the font and size of the headings and any other design features.

CHECK IT OUT!

Cathryn started by setting up a query which listed the dates of MOT tests in ascending order. This meant that the dates start with the earliest and end with the latest. She then used the Report Wizard in Microsoft® Access to design and structure her report so that it will summarise the data she wants.

Her finished report is shown overleaf. Note the design features Cathryn has included and the way she grouped the data so it is easy to read.

Page layout requirements

The page layout requirements you specify for your design will depend upon several factors:

- your customer's requirements
- the size of the document
- the type of printer you use or other destination you choose (see page 419)
- the options available on your particular database.

If you use a large, specialist database the options may have been pre-determined by the designer, in which case you may be limited in what you can decide yourself. On most Windows-based packages, however, you will be able to select the **page size** for the document. Under normal circumstances this will be A4 – and you may be limited to this size if you intend to print it on a standard printer unless you can use other sizes by manual feed.

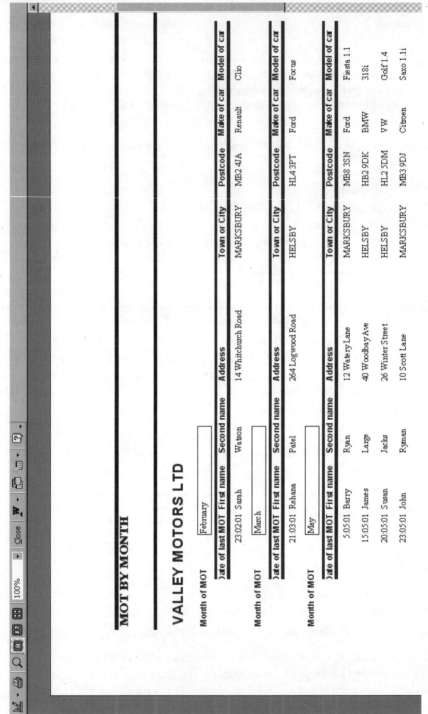

Database report

You will be able to choose the **page orientation** – portrait or landscape. Select portrait if your document is longer than it is wide and landscape if you have a wide table or report and want to include all the headings.

Page numbering is a sensible choice if you are preparing a long report, in case someone drops a printout on the floor! Numbering also makes it easier to find your way around a document and to identify selected pages to print.

Headers can be inserted at the top of the document and **footers** at the bottom. In some organisations, for instance, it is standard for the date the document is produced to be included as a header and the page number to be included as a footer.

Specifying the width of the **margins** gives you additional flexibility if your document is very narrow or very wide, to ensure it is positioned sensibly on the page.

CHECK IT OUT!

Investigate the options you have available to vary page layouts. You can use your program Help files to do this, or you can look at the options under File/Page Setup if you are using Access or a similar package. Find out, too, if you have Print Preview available. This enables you to see the final version on the screen before it is printed. Using this option is environmentally friendly as it saves producing several unusable versions on paper!

 INFORMATION UPDATE

Data capture needn't just be on a keyboard. Data can also be captured by scanning. A third method is through a camera. This is the method the DVLA wants to use to find and stop drivers who have not paid their road fund tax.

Cameras already exist to photograph motorists who break the speed limit. The new cameras will not only read the registration plates but will also compare these with the database records held on the DVLA computer at Swansea. If no tax disc has been purchased for the vehicle then the owner will be sent a court summons.

Eventually, government ministers would like to develop the system to link it with insurance company databases, so that drivers without insurance cover would also be identified immediately. ➡

Finally, there is the obvious benefit for the police that a database of car movements would help to show which cars were in an area when a crime was committed.

The Government has given assurances that all vehicle records would be covered by the Data Protection Act, but civil liberties organisations are concerned that this type of surveillance seems very 'Big Brother-ish' – someone, somewhere will be watching over drivers all the time in the future, it seems.

EVIDENCE COLLECTION

For this element you must prove that you can make all the following adjustments to a page layout when preparing a database document: page size, page orientation, page numbering, headers and footers, and margins.

The types of document (record printout, table printout, report etc.) to which you have to make these adjustments are *not* specified, so you should choose either a document you regularly produce or the one on which you can most easily make adjustments on your package.

The simplest way to obtain your evidence is to select one document and then make various changes, each time taking a separate printout for your portfolio.

If you have any particular restrictions because of the design of your database or because of the printer you use, discuss how you can overcome these difficulties with your assessor. One method may be to select a different output destination (see page 419). Alternatively, if your printer accepts only A4 paper, you could demonstrate on screen how you *could* change the paper size if this option were available to you.

Element 307.3 Output specified information to the required destination

To achieve the last element of this unit you have to prove that you can extract selected information and then use your software facilities to prepare a final document which contains all the required information in an appropriate layout.

The obvious next step would be to print the document you have prepared. However, other options are available if you use a database, and selecting a particular destination is one part of this element.

Selecting the required destination

Modern database packages are designed to be compatible with many other software packages, such as word-processing and spreadsheets. Another common use of database information is a website. If you access a bookshop such as Waterstones on the Internet, you can scroll through all the books they stock and select the ones you want. When you do this you are simply accessing their product database on the Web – though this is usually specially designed so that it is user-friendly to external customers.

Finally, database files and documents may be saved to disk or sent to other people – either on an internal network or attached to e-mail documents. The choice these days is almost endless!

Selecting output devices that meet your customer's requirements

It is useless selecting an output device that your customer – or recipient – cannot access. Equally, it is futile sending your database document or file in a format that your recipient cannot read. To understand this concept, you need to know something about files and file extensions.

Saving a file

When you save a document you can choose various options.

Where the document will be saved

You can choose between your hard disk (normally drive c:), a floppy disk (normally a:) and – if you operate on a network – your 'home' area (often h:). You can also choose which folder to save it in on that particular drive. On your hard drive, for example, you should organise all your files into separate folders so that they are easy to find.

The name to use

This should be a name that is easy to recognise and which is unique to that file or document. A useful tip is to insert your document name as a footer so you can always access the file quickly from the footer reference.

The format in which to save the document

The format can be identified from the **file extension** suffix which follows the full point after the document name – although this doesn't show in Office 2000. Some useful formats which are still useful to know are:

- .mdb – the format used automatically for Microsoft® Access database documents unless you specify a wish to save in a different format
- .rtf – rich text format is useful as it can be read by many packages and most of the formatting commands are retained in this format
- .xls – the format used by Microsoft® Excel, a spreadsheet package that is compatible with Microsoft® Access
- .html (or .htm) – the extension used when a database file will be used on an Internet browser.

Remember you need to select a format that your recipient can read. As an example, imagine you are in charge of maintaining a database of customer records. You receive a request for a list of names and addresses from your database to be used by the marketing department which wants to send a mailshot to all customers in a particular area. You can obtain a listing by sorting your records with a filter to denote the area you want. Then you send the list to the marketing department. They need to receive it as an 'rtf' document which they can use with their word-processing package to create a mail-merge. It saves them having to retype the names and addresses of the customers all over again.

Finally, if you want to attach your database document to an e-mail, remember to pick a format that your e-mail recipient can open and read!

Network users

A multi-user database on a company network is accessible by all authorised users simultaneously. You may therefore think there is no need to send a document to anyone because they can always access it. However, that is not always the case. Examples of when documents may be transmitted include:

- 'new' or 'developmental' documents which are not yet available to all users
- documents which have restricted access because they are confidential.

As an example, if you operated on a complex database but asked the database administrator for a new report, this would be developed 'off-line'. The database administrator may design the draft report and attach it to an internal e-mail, asking for your views.

Only when the final design is agreed will the report be downloaded on to the network for access by all database users.

Equally, as you saw on page 383, certain areas of the database – and therefore certain types of queries and reports – are restricted for security reasons. However, there may be a particular reason why someone is granted permission to see the results of a certain query or a report containing confidential data. Again, rather than print out the report it may be transmitted across the network to a named user.

TEST YOUR KNOWLEDGE AND UNDERSTANDING

Cathryn has plans to develop the database at Valley Motors still further. She has recently been on an IT course at her local college and now thinks she has the skills and expertise to create various files and link these together.

As a first step, she discusses this with Paul. They decide to have three files, one for customers, one for cars (which is a type of 'product' database) and one for accounts. Cathryn uses her database wizard to set up the files and then attempts to link these. She then saves this under a new database title – so that she can continue to develop it when she has some spare time.

A summary of Cathryn's development work is shown below.

1 What *type* of database is Cathryn now developing?

2 Why will this be more useful than her original database?

3 Why is Cathryn developing this database under a different title, rather than simply overwriting her original database?

4 Cathryn is worried that her suggested fields and her links may not be correct. Her tutor has agreed to look at what she has done so far and give her advice.

   a State three ways in which Cathryn could send this information to her IT tutor.

   b Identify the checks Cathryn should make before she decides which method to use.

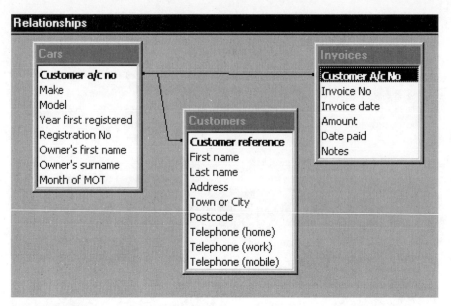

Relationships

Cars
Customer a/c no
Make
Model
Year first registered
Registration No
Owner's first name
Owner's surname
Month of MOT

Customers
Customer reference
First name
Last name
Address
Town or City
Postcode
Telephone (home)
Telephone (work)
Telephone (mobile)

Invoices
Customer A/c No
Invoice No
Invoice date
Amount
Date paid
Notes

Cathryn's draft expanded database

EVIDENCE COLLECTION

For this element you have to show that you can output a database document to a printer and *also* to an electronic store for use by other people. This may be on a floppy disk, on your hard disk (if you share a workstation), across a network, attached as a file to an e-mail or even to your Internet browser for use by your website developers.

It is suggested that you select *one* of these options, in addition to printing the document. You will need to prove that:

- you produced the document
- you saved and/or transmitted the document
- the document was readable by the recipient.

The easiest way to do this is to take a hard copy of your document, then make a note of the electronic storage medium you selected and ask your recipient to provide witness testimony to prove you saved the file correctly so it was easily accessible.

Setting output parameters

If you are printing a document then you must be able to set the output parameters to produce:

- the required number of copies
- the page range (either a single, specified page, or selected pages or the whole document)
- the required page size.

Page sizes were discussed on page 415. The options may be limited if you are using a standard printer, in which case you may have to explain to your assessor what you *would* do if you had a greater choice in this area.

You will normally select all your output parameters from your computer screen and *not* by touching the printer. It is worth investigating all your Print options – and using your program Help facilities if you don't understand anything you see. Normally, when you select File and Print you will see a dialogue screen which enables you to select the pages you want and the number of copies you require. In addition, you may also be able to specify the quality (draft, normal or best) and even whether to print in reverse order (saving you having to re-organise pages in a long document).

Final checks

Do remember that before you save, print or transmit any final document it is sensible to make some final checks. This is especially true if the document is very long or complex and/or is being sent to an important individual. The best test is to do this in three stages:

1 Check it yourself first, making sure that nothing obvious is missing or misspelled.
2 Check it using your Print Preview screen.
3 Print out *just one page* and check this with your recipient or customer – or with your supervisor.

Only when you are certain it is complete and totally accurate should you make the final printout or save it for posterity.

Preserving confidentiality

Remember that you need to preserve confidentiality if your document contains sensitive or personal data. You can do this sensibly by:

- transmitting the document only to authorised recipients
- taking only the exact number of copies you need
- sending hard copies in a sealed envelope, marked as confidential
- filing your own copy promptly, not leaving it lying around on your desk
- keeping your password and user ID to yourself – but then, you would do that anyway, wouldn't you?

INFORMATION UPDATE

Most people think of the CIA as the American law enforcement agency – the Central Intelligence Agency. However, to database designers who put their system on the Web, it stands for the three magic words of Confidentiality, Integrity and Accessibility. The aim is to produce a computer database system where private information is kept private, the data can be trusted to be accurate and staff can always gain information when they need it.

To guard systems from hackers, software bugs and viruses isn't easy. One of the most critical pieces of software is a **firewall**, which checks all data travelling between the computer system and the Internet in both directions. It is designed to stop hackers getting into the system and only allows appropriate information to come on to the system from the Net. **Anti-virus software** is also invaluable. This detects and disables viruses on a system. Because new viruses are being developed all the time, antivirus updates are often available on-line. Some firms offer a 24-hour support service.

In addition, every organisation needs an **IT security policy** so that staff know what they are allowed to access and what they are not, when accessing the Internet on office computers. Finally, **encryption software** can be bought, particularly for laptops. This scrambles the information on the hard disk so that, even if the laptop is stolen, critical information remains secure.

However, all the protection in the world won't help if employees don't follow security procedures or pass sensitive information to others. All staff should be trained to recognise the importance of security and confidentiality and to be vigilant at all times.

EVIDENCE COLLECTION

You need to prove that you can print a database document and specify the required number of copies, the page range and page size.

The simplest way to provide evidence is to take an additional copy of non-confidential database printouts you produce which have required different output parameters. Alternatively, ask your supervisor to provide witness testimony that you can reliably produce database printouts as requested, using the output parameters required.

Finally, write a brief commentary about the security and confidentiality procedures in force in your organisation. Give examples of the precautions you take when you are handling sensitive data or are asked to transmit this to another person.

GROUP B OPTION UNITS

Introduction to Group B Option Units

There are 19 Group B Option Units in the NVQ level 3 Administration scheme. You have only to do **three** of these. Eight of these units are covered in the following pages and the remainder are freely available on the Heinemann website (for details, see below). You can therefore obtain information on all of these quite easily.

MAKING YOUR CHOICE

Although the units in this book are in numerical order, this should not influence your choice. You should choose those which are the most appropriate to your job, so that you have no difficulties obtaining evidence. It is sensible to discuss your preferences with your line manager or supervisor to identify which would be the most suitable. This is certainly the case if you will need support or assistance to access certain facilities or want to use a unit to help to develop and extend your existing skills.

THINKING IN GROUPS

Important guidance on choosing your options was given in the Introduction, pages xvii–xx. You may wish to turn back to these pages now, to refresh your memory. This section mentioned that the options can be thought of in groups – and this, too, may help your choice. For instance, there are:

- 5 admin support options – Support users of administrative services; Contribute to scheduling activities and resources; Contribute to organising events; Order, store and distribute supplies; Organise repairs to premises and equipment
- 4 'people' options – Develop effective services for customers; Contribute to the development of teams and individuals; Lead the work of teams and individuals; Contribute to the selection of personnel for activities
- 4 computer skills options – Support the use of information technology systems; Design and layout complex documents on a computer; Produce spreadsheet documents; Design and create presentations using a computer
- 3 communications skills options – Prepare documents from shorthand notes; Produce documents from complex recorded speech; Support and record business meetings
- 3 financial units – Recording income and receipts; Making and recording payments; Investigate arrears and recover debt.

IMPORTANT NOTE – COMPUTER SKILLS OPTION UNITS

It is assumed that you will not be undertaking any of the computer skills option units unless you *already* possess a good working knowledge of your organisation's computer systems and software. Although the information for these units reviews the key points you need to know, it mainly focuses on the additional points relevant to the knowledge and understanding requirements for your award as well as specific guidance on evidence collection.

If you are concerned that your skills in any area may be insufficient there are a variety of ways in which you can improve. You can:

- purchase a simply 'user-friendly' guide to the software you are using
- obtain a relatively inexpensive book at a good bookseller
- attend an in-company skills training course on your software package
- develop your skills methodically by the use of a software manual, the use of your 'help' screens and assistance from experts in your workplace
- take a short course (flexible options are often available) at a nearby college to improve your skills in a particular package.

UNITS AVAILABLE ON THE HEINEMANN WEBSITE

Guidance on the following option units is freely available on the Heinemann website at www.heinemann.co.uk/vocational/NVQ (password GROUPBOPTIONS):

Unit 311   Contribute to organising events
Unit 313   Support and record business meetings
Unit 314   Organise repairs to premises and equipment
Unit 315   Contribute to the development of teams and individuals
Unit 316   Lead the work of teams and individuals to achieve their objectives
Unit 317   Contribute to the selection of personnel for activities
Unit 322   Prepare documents from shorthand notes
Unit 323   Produce documents from complex recorded speech
Unit 324   Recording income and receipts
Unit 325   Making and recording payments
Unit 326   Investigate arrears and recover debt

THE LAST LAP

If you have worked through the scheme methodically, you may have already completed six of the required nine units. You are now on the last lap to achieving your award. You are also used to finding evidence and building your portfolio. For that reason, the notes given for the Group B Option Units are shorter than for the other units. The focus is on the knowledge and understanding you must have and the evidence you need to collect. Hopefully they will answer all your queries and enable you to obtain your remaining units without any difficulty. Good luck!

Option Unit 308 Develop effective services for customers

FOCUS OF THE UNIT

To obtain this unit you must be able to:

- build effective **working relationships** with customers
- **maintain reliable services** to customers
- **assist customers** with problems and complaints
- **improve services** to customers.

EVIDENCE COLLECTION

It will make evidence collection easier if you can obtain the following information:

a   a description of your own job role in relation to your contribution in developing effective services for customers

b   a copy of all your organisation's procedures for dealing with customers, recording customer information and dealing with problems and complaints (personalise this by highlighting those which specifically relate to your own job)

c   a description of how your organisation's customer database operates (without breaching confidentiality) and the way in which you use this to obtain or store information

d   examples of formal and informal methods of seeking customer feedback – and of how you have analysed and acted upon the information received.

Developing effective services for customers

The customer

The most traditional definition of a customer is the person who buys a product or a service from an organisation. A more modern approach, however, is to treat 'the customer' – particularly business customers – not as a single entity but as a number of people, all of whom have had an input into the decision on whether or not to place the order. See the diagram overleaf for an illustration of this approach.

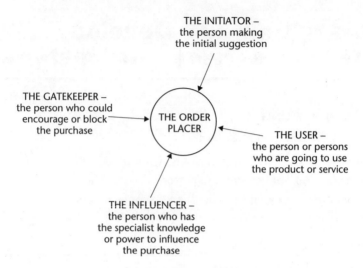

THE INITIATOR –
the person making
the initial suggestion

THE GATEKEEPER –
the person who could
encourage or block
the purchase

THE ORDER
PLACER

THE USER –
the person or persons
who are going to use
the product or service

THE INFLUENCER –
the person who has
the specialist knowledge
or power to influence
the purchase

The different people involved in a decision to purchase

Who are your customers?

No matter where you work you will have to deal with customers – whether internal or external. You may have to deal with members of the general public seeking information, with other members in the organisation for whom you carry out certain tasks such as reprographic, financial, marketing, personnel etc. – as well as with business people wanting to buy products or services. One of your first tasks is to identify exactly who your customers are before you can begin to determine their requirements.

 INFORMATION UPDATE

Many service organisations, particularly in the retail or catering area, spend a lot of time inventing slogans to be displayed in all the work areas – reminding their staff of the importance of knowing their customers. For example:

- 'customers are people who bring us their wants – it is our job to handle them profitably'
- 'customers are not outsiders to our business – they are part of it'
- 'customers are your friends. You don't let friends down'.

EVIDENCE COLLECTION

Prepare a list of the people you think are your customers. Discuss it with your team and ask them for their input. Alongside each group of people you have identified, summarise the type of requests you normally receive from them and your own responsibilities in relation to fulfilling their needs.

Your organisation's procedures for dealing with customers

As a newcomer to an organisation, you should make it a priority to find out the *organisational* procedures for dealing with customers. You may find, for instance, that the organisation has certain structures in place to assist the process. For example:

- there is a discrete customer care unit
- customer care is a sub-section of the marketing department
- one of the senior managers in the sales department has specific responsibilities for customer care
- customer care personnel report directly to a member of the senior management team or a director
- one person from each department or section is part of a cross-organisational team responsible for overseeing the way in which line management deals with customers etc.

What you should also do, of course, is determine your *personal* involvement in customer care. The modern approach is to expect all staff to take some responsibility in this area, no matter where they work or at what level. If, for example, you work in a local council housing department you may have to deal directly with the general public and be responsible for meeting their needs. If you work as an administrator to the finance director, you may have to satisfy the requirements of a number of internal customers, and so on. In such circumstances you need to know what procedures there are in place to assist you in this part of your job.

Although organisations differ in their approach, you will probably find that the majority of them have procedures on the following:

a   dealing personally with the customer:
- telephone enquiries
- people who visit the work area with or without an appointment
- delays in attending to someone
- queues

b   effective methods of communication – including the time in which a response must be made

c   how to prepare all the relevant paperwork, including completing customer records, house styles for letters and so on

d   how and for what reason you should access the customer database and the degree to which you can input or amend data

e   how to find out about and update your information about the products or services offered by your organisation

f   how to deal with complaints

g   how to obtain, analyse and act upon customer feedback

h   how and when to obtain assistance or support.

The importance of effective customer service

There are a number of obvious reasons why you should provide an effective customer service. Armen Kabodian, in his book *The Customer Is Always Right*, outlines some of them.

- Research has shown that customers tell twice as many people about a bad experience as they do about a good one.
- A typical dissatisfied customer will tell 8–10 people about a problem.
- Seven out of 10 customers who complain will continue to do business with you if you resolve their complaint satisfactorily.
- Service organisations depend on existing customers for 85–95 per cent of their business.
- It costs six times more to attract a new customer than it does to keep an old one.

The importance of maintaining and improving customer service

If you lose your customers, you lose your job – and so do others. As the above facts indicate, existing customers form the largest part of an organisation's database and, in theory at least, need less money spending on them to maintain their loyalty. Competition for customers is increasing and the organisations that succeed in winning their support are likely to be those whose service levels exceed those of their competitors.

INFORMATION UPDATE

The Institute of Customer Service was launched in 1998. Its aims are to raise service standards in private and public sector organisations, and it is supported by a number of leading UK organisations. It estimates that three million people in the UK work in customer service activities. That's a lot of jobs to lose!

Key facts on building effective working relationships with customers

The importance of effective relationships

An effective relationship with your customers involves:

- an awareness by customers of your product or service
- initial contact by them to allow you to explore certain possibilities
- the fulfilment of at least one of those possibilities
- an expansion of the relationship on the same basis
- a commitment to further that expansion.

Therefore the first step is to make your product or service sufficiently well known to attract the attention of potential customers. Then, having attracted their attention, you need to ensure that they will become, and continue to be, actual customers.

However, if your potential customers don't know you exist and if even your existing customers find it hard to contact you, you are losing a major opportunity to build an effective relationship with them. Ideally your organisation should be making constant efforts to publicise itself by advertising its existence – in trade directories, journals, newspapers, magazines, fliers, mailshots, on the Internet etc.

It should make certain that its premises are easy to find by having a clear address, providing clear instructions and/or a map, giving details of how to park, giving information about public transport.

It should ensure that customers have relevant details of the staff who will be dealing with them, such as a contact telephone number (together with details of answerphone or voice-mail services), a fax number, a mobile phone number, a pager number and an e-mail address.

CHECK IT OUT!

Being available to deal with customers at all times is a crucial aspect in establishing a relationship with them. However, it is not all that easy. Making certain that someone is available around the clock has all sorts of financial and staffing implications. Organisations that want to make changes are advised to evaluate their current opening hours in relation to their customer needs and in relation to the opening hours of their competitors. They then have to balance the benefits of longer opening hours against the costs involved.

Organisations also have to investigate ways to 'customise' hours to meet customer patterns of working. For example, if the customer database consists almost purely of other businesses, opening on a Saturday and Sunday may not be worthwhile. If the customer database is the general public, it may be.

Check the opening hours in your organisation and try to find out if any recent surveys have been done on how they might be changed to suit customer needs. Make your own judgement on what hours you think may suit your customers. Give a brief summary of your findings.

Accessing information on your customers

Amongst your mail over the past year there would almost certainly have been several requests for you to complete a questionnaire about your lifestyle.

If you wander round a store, bank, hotel or almost any public building you are again likely to find that there will be customer satisfaction feedback forms available. Organisations want to find out about you and they want to use that information to help them to market their product or service more successfully. If, therefore, you work in customer care you have to know what type of information is available to you and how to access it. You may simply have a filing cabinet containing details of your existing customers. You may have all the required information on a computerised database. If your organisation sells on the Internet, you should have a huge database of information available to you through that.

For example, Amazon – which sells books over the Internet – lets customers browse its website and then order books and CDs by completing the Web form pages with personal and credit card details. Amazon's systems capture all this data. It then uses it to:

- send automatic e-mails to customers on the status of their order
- send marketing information to individual customers on books and CDs that may interest them
- mass market its entire customer database in seconds to launch a new initiative.

External customer information facilities

Your organisation may have 'bought in' to certain commercially available customer information facilities, in order to be able to obtain information on **prospective** rather than **actual** customers.

Contact management software packages are often used by telemarketers to hold all customer information on databases which store the address, telephone number and contact information for each organisation. They also enable users to analyse the contact information. Most packages are compatible with laptops so that they can be used, for instance, by sales people.

Another source of potential customers is telemarketing centres. These contact customers not only to sell products or services but also on a more regular basis to obtain certain items of useful information from them.

EVIDENCE COLLECTION

1 Copy out and complete the questionnaire opposite in respect of the customer information you store and are able to access in your own workplace.

2 Give brief details of the way or ways in which the information is stored and who has access to it. If your organisation has a policy for allowing access by only certain members of staff, summarise what it says and state why access is restricted.

3 Give details of any outside sources you use to provide information for you on prospective customers.

Customer information questionnaire		
Item of customer information	Yes	No
Name, address and job title		
Telephone number/mobile number/fax number		
E-mail address		
Details of previous purchases		
Details of previous use of services		
Correspondence		
Details of any promotional literature sent		
Any specialist requirements		
Other information: (give details below)		

Taking the initiative in building relationships with customers

Considerable research has been carried out on how to build a successful relationship with customers. Most of it tends to reach much the same conclusion as to the key principles involved.

- There needs to be **a positive and proactive attitude from staff**. Customers want to deal with a member of staff who is helpful and friendly rather than apathetic and uninterested. They are unhappy if they have to take the initiative in the relationship and have to *persuade* staff to help them
- Customers want **a knowledgeable staff** – who know the product, the nature of the service, how to solve a problem, how to give advice etc.
- There should be **customer-friendly systems** – such as easy-to-complete paperwork, simple payment systems, clear guidance on product availability, helpful signs, easy-to-follow shop/office layouts etc.
- Finally, customers want **a product that works and a service which is efficient** – which means a constant emphasis on quality.

What you should also do, however, is to encourage the customer to *rely* upon you to sort things out. For instance, you should try to make sure you are always there to answer an inquiry. If you say you will look out some information, then do so. If you think of something that is likely to help, then say so. Once the customer realises how useful you are, you are likely to have formed a long-lasting relationship.

EVIDENCE COLLECTION

In your present job role you may be asked to be proactive – to take the initiative in communicating with customers, by contacting them to find out how they feel about a service or product and/or by asking them if you can provide any additional information.

1 In each case below, state whether or not you have used this form of communication to either external customers or internal customers (provided they are not members of your own team):

   a face to face

   b by telephone

   c by fax

   d in writing

   e using e-mail.

2 Select *at least three* of them and give *at least two* examples of when you have contacted a customer using these methods. Explain both the reason and the outcome.

3 State which you find the most successful method, and give your reasons.

Presenting a positive image

Imagine you are in charge of a group of people who work in the customer services area of a large store. You receive a large number of visitors each day. Two members of staff don't see the importance of 'looking the part'. They wear the company uniform reluctantly but try to customise it by removing their ties or scarves and covering their jackets with badges and stickers. Their work areas are untidy and quite often they will leave unwashed coffee cups and the remains of sandwich wrappings in full view of any visitor. They tend to disappear off together at lunchtime and come back a few minutes late when customers are waiting to see them. This means they are talking to them as they take off their coats, switch on their computers etc. Even though they are actually quite efficient at dealing with customer queries, they have created an immediate problem for themselves and the organisation in that they give a bad first impression.

Most organisations involved in customer services have a standard code of practice for their employees who work in that area. The code tends to highlight the necessity for:

• good personal grooming

• suitable dress (unless there is a requirement to wear a uniform)

• adherence to a dress code

- punctuality – to avoid keeping any customers waiting
- a tidy and well-organised working environment – including individual workstations.

EVIDENCE COLLECTION

Check whether such a code or set of procedures exists in your own work area. If it does, compare it with the information just given and comment on any similarities and any differences. If you have no formal code, describe what you think your informal code is in relation to dress, appearance and overall first impressions.

 ## INFORMATION UPDATE

The **Human Rights Act 1998** became law on 2 October 2000. It applies to possible breaches of human rights by public authorities – such as the rights to respect for private and family life, freedom of religion, freedom of assembly and association and freedom from discrimination. However, it also protects freedom of expression, and it has been suggested that a dress code may be unenforceable if it can be shown to infringe on an individual's freedom of expression. If, therefore, one of your staff insists that he or she must be allowed to come to work dressed as a native American as a gesture of support for discriminated-against minorities, you might have to be careful about how you deal with the situation! Remember, however, it is only a suggestion at the moment. There is no case law on the subject.

Judging customer feelings accurately

Your eyes and ears are the best judge of how your customers are feeling. If you listen carefully to what they are saying you are likely to pick up not only any *direct* messages they are communicating but in some cases their *indirect* messages. One customer, for instance, may ask you for details of the price of a certain product. That is a direct communication to you. However, he or she may then tell you that the price of your product is far higher than your competitor's. The message may again be direct. The person is merely informing you of what your competitors are charging. However, he or she may also be trying to ask you indirectly whether you are prepared to lower your prices or reach a compromise deal. If you are sensitive to such indirect messages you are better able to handle the situation – even if you can't give the customer everything.

Remember, too, that body language (see pages 36 and 440) can help you to assess customer feelings. Someone who is tapping their foot or constantly looking at their watch is likely to be running late, impatient and – if delayed in a queue – irritable. A customer who seems very agitated may be extremely upset and on the brink of breaking down unless you deal with him or her tactfully and sympathetically. People who are very shy or nervous may have trouble explaining what they want and will have even greater difficulty if you appear dismissive or impatient.

KEY NOTES ON LISTENING TO CUSTOMERS

Do

- try to identify what the tone of the voice is expressing – annoyance, uncertainty, doubt, irritation, pent-up rage etc.
- decide on the purpose – does the customer want some straightforward information, to make a complaint, to be reassured that something is happening, to confirm what has been agreed etc?
- try to identify any hidden or indirect purpose
- allow a momentary silence to fall before you respond so that the customer feels that he or she has had the opportunity to say everything
- give a prompt if you feel the customer is looking for one
- ask some short relevant questions after the customer has finished speaking to clarify any important points.

Do not

- interrupt – try to keep in your memory the relevant points to which you want to make a response after the customer has finished speaking
- ask the customer to repeat everything immediately after he or she has finished saying it
- show impatience because the customer is talking too much
- try to shut him or her up
- give an immediate negative response – even if you cannot help and have to ask the customer to see someone else, spend at least a few minutes talking to him or her.

Responding appropriately to customer feelings

It is usually quite easy to deal with a customer who is polite, good-tempered and reasonable – and you should be able to determine this within seconds of the conversation starting. The skill here lies in *keeping* the customer in that frame of mind. If you can't answer the queries or give relevant information –

or if you are not in a very good mood yourself and it shows – you may find that the customer responds accordingly.

However, by far the more difficult task is to deal with a dissatisfied customer, particularly one who is angry with the organisation and vents anger on you. The key notes below will help you deal with most angry customers. However, remember that although you are paid to deal with annoyed customers, you should not be put into a position where you have to tolerate verbal or even physical abuse. If this occurs, notify your supervisor immediately.

 KEY NOTES ON DEALING WITH ANGRY CUSTOMERS

- Don't get angry back.
- Use appropriate body language to show that you empathise with the customer – in order to give an overall impression of complete concentration on what the customer is saying.
- Use certain phrases to show that you are taking the matter seriously: 'I'm sorry you're so upset. I'll certainly try to help,' or 'Obviously something has gone badly wrong.'
- Apologise for the fact that there is a problem – although at this stage you should not admit any liability. You need to have all the facts before you or someone else does that.
- Don't interrupt. Eventually the customer will stop talking.
- Make use of effective listening skills (see pages 37 and 438 for information on this point).
- Clarify the exact nature of the problem – write down the details and ask the customer to check them for accuracy. Customers tend to appreciate that.
- Avoid being defensive. Concentrate instead on being positive: 'I think I know exactly what you are concerned about. I'll get on to it right away,' or 'Let me make a start on trying to solve your problem.'
- Tell the customer what you are going to do next so that he or she doesn't feel that it has all been a waste of time. Then do it!

The importance of clear, polite, confident communications

Being rude to customers doesn't help. Being confused and unsure about what you are saying doesn't inspire them with confidence in your ability to help them. Using language or abbreviations the customer may not understand merely confuses them.

The *way* in which you say something is equally as important as *what* you are saying. You obviously have to avoid sounding annoyed, or angry, or sarcastic, or weary, or apathetic and indifferent, or resentful, or incompetent, or patronising.

 ## KEY NOTES ON BODY LANGUAGE

Researchers have found that people receive 7 per cent of any message by listening to the words, 38 per cent by the tone of voice and 55 per cent by watching body language! The message can be either positive or negative.

Negative body language includes:

- giving the customer a blank stare as he or she approaches you
- keeping your head down
- avoiding eye contact
- fidgeting
- drumming your fingers on your desk
- shrugging your shoulders in response to a question.

Positive body language includes:

- smiling
- nodding encouragement where relevant
- making eye contact
- keeping your head up
- sitting still!

TEST YOUR KNOWLEDGE AND UNDERSTANDING

In each of the following cases, state how you would have responded more positively to the customer.

a 'I'm sorry, that's not my job.'

b 'I can't tell help you at the moment. We're in the middle of a restructure and the place is in a shambles.'

c 'I thought I'd made that clear already. Which part do you want me to go over again?'

d 'Can I ring you back? I'm rushed off my feet at the moment, I've never stopped all morning.'

e 'Sorry, not my fault – it's company policy.'

f 'I can't do anything to help you if you can't remember the order number, can I?'

g 'Yes, OK, I'll do something about it when I've got the time.'

Obtaining other useful types of information about the customer

The more you know about a customer the better. If you work in a bank or building society, for instance, and have a number of regular clients you will probably find they appreciate your remembering:

- their name
- what types of account they have
- to ask how they have enjoyed their holiday because the last time you saw them they were asking for travellers' cheques and foreign currency
- how their house removal went because you were involved in sorting out their mortgage.

Not only will most of them be pleased that you are showing an interest, you may find that you can create extra business for your organisation. If, for instance, they start to chat to you about holidays or their children going off to university, you may be able to take the opportunity to remind them of how your bank or building society can help them financially. During the course of a conversation about the cost of a new car, they might ask you about the possibility of a loan or overdraft, and so on.

However, there is a very thin dividing line between showing an interest in a customer and appearing too inquisitive or pushy. If a customer starts talking to you about sorting out his financial affairs it might be a mistake for you to say, for instance, that you thought it about time he started to save for his old age and retirement. A customer might also object if you started talking in a loud voice about the money in her instant access account to the entertainment of the line of people standing behind her.

Your timing is also important too. If, for instance, you are asked to carry out a telephone survey of your customers, you might meet little success if you choose to ring someone with a hungry family at tea time. Avoiding certain times is an important part of your role in being sensitive to customer requirements.

Recording customer information in line with your organisation's procedures

You would probably not dream of sending off a letter without keeping a copy of it on disk or in a filing cabinet, because:

- you need the copy for evidence purposes so that you can prove it has actually been written
- you might want to refer to it again when you receive a reply, enquiry or complaint
- you may want to send some further information to the same person.

This is particularly important if you are dealing with customers. Keeping a file of every communication to them is essential, not only for the reasons just given but also because, as already discussed, the more information you have about the customers the more likely it is you will be able to meet their exact needs. What is also important, of course, is that you follow your organisation's procedures in recording the information. Otherwise no one else but you will be able to find it when needed!

CHECK IT OUT!

Outline your organisation's procedures for recording customer information. Comment on how effective you think they are.

EVIDENCE COLLECTION

Over a period of three or four weeks, keep a log of customers you communicate with and note down key facts about the communication.

a Why did it take place?

b Were you responding to a customer or taking the initiative?

c How did you communicate? (See the list in the Evidence collection box on page 436.)

d How did you judge the customer's feelings?

e How did you respond to the customers feelings?

Then summarise about six or seven of the most interesting contacts you had, making sure that you include at least one customer who was reacting positively to you and one who was reacting negatively.

Key facts on maintaining reliable services to customers

Establishing customer requirements clearly and accurately

Your customers have certain expectations. Some of these are **generic** so, for example, the customers want to deal with an organisation:

- with a good reputation
- with a customer service policy putting the needs of the customer first
- with a helpful and knowledgeable staff
- to which they have ease of access (look back to page 433 for information on this point)

- which is flexible
- which provides them with the product or service they want
- which responds quickly to their enquiries
- which has some value-added features – free service, additional discount, loyalty bonuses etc.
- which checks up on how satisfied they are with the product or service.

Some customers, however, have **specific** requirements. For example, imagine you work in a car showroom. A customer walks in one lunchtime when the two sales staff are busy. Obviously she expects her generic requirements to be met. However, she also expects something more, which might be any or all of the following.

- She knows that the showroom stocks only certain makes of car but she isn't sure which one interests her most.
- She has a certain price range in mind and doesn't want to exceed it.
- She wants to know more about automatic cars.
- She travels a lot on motorways and wants a car to suit that need.
- She is safety conscious and wants to know about the provision of air bags etc.
- She is interested in fuel consumption.
- Ideally she wants a four-door car but much depends on the price.
- She doesn't want to wait too long for delivery.

She hasn't *volunteered* all this information. If you were trying to help this customer until a salesperson became available, you would have to find out a lot of it by listening, asking certain questions, offering her alternatives and giving specific facts and figures. You've still some way to go before making a sale but you are on your way.

After a long discussion she says she will go away and think about it. You are prepared for this and have been noting her requirements as you've gone along. You can provide her with some information she needs – leaflets, brochures, price lists etc. – but you need to check up on other requirements. You agree to send them to her. When she has gone, you complete the appropriate customer requirement form and subsequently take action.

You may not be successful this time. She may go elsewhere and you never see her again. However, you have cut down on the chances of her doing that – and you have all her details which enables you to keep contact with her, to do everything you have promised and hopefully to be the person to whom she returns to agree a sale.

Information needed to plan the service effectively

Almost certainly, if you are unable to answer any of your customer's enquiries or provide any literature, then you will *not* make the sale. In whatever area of customer service you work you need to make sure that you have a very sound information database.

Agreeing and recording customer requirements

Imagine you work in a purchasing and supplies department. One of your department's duties is to supply stationery and computer consumables to the rest of the organisation. You leave a junior colleague in charge one afternoon. When you return the following morning, he mentions to you that someone from finance rang him up in a desperate hurry and asked for an inkjet print cartridge which he left at reception. At this point, the phone rings. It is one of the finance staff who is distinctly cool with you. The cartridge isn't the type she wanted, she actually required six, and she asked for delivery within the hour but it took three hours to arrive. What your assistant failed to do was to agree with her on:

- quality
- quantity
- time and place of delivery.

What you should have done was to make certain that procedures were in place to enable staff to agree and record a customer's requirements as simply as possible. This could be a pre-printed form to be left by each telephone so that your assistant would have a memory jogger to help him determine and agree the customer's requirements.

Support and liaison for staff

If you are responsible for a particular area of work it is sometimes easy to forget that not everyone knows as much about it as you do. You may have set up a number of systems and procedures that you think are capable of meeting all customer requirements. That's all right as long as you are always around to answer the telephone, meet customers or at least advise those members of your team who are doing so. However, there will be times when you are not around. Ideally, therefore, your systems and procedures should be as well known to your team as they are to you. They should also, of course, be designed to support them rather than hinder them!

EVIDENCE COLLECTION

You can use the guidance form below to check on the procedures you have in operation to assist the rest of the staff in dealing with customers.

a   In each case where you answer 'no', state whether or not you think the introduction of that particular system or procedure could benefit your team.

b   In cases where you do not think the staff are aware of the system or procedure, state what steps you could take to solve this problem.

c   Give details of any additional support measures you have in place.

Customer information questionnaire					
System/procedure in place	Yes	No	Are all relevant staff aware of it?	Yes	No
Easily accessible and regularly updated customer database					
Pre-printed forms for • customers' orders • customer complaints • customer queries • customer feedback					
Other pre-printed forms (specify)					
Easily accessible and regularly updated product/service information					
Easily accessible organisation chart and/or details of the main people in the organisation who can assist with relevant information					
A helpline (or emergency contact) to a member or members of staff who can assist with immediate queries or complaints					
Easily accessible copies of the complaints procedure					
Easily accessible information on how to ask for customer feedback over the telephone or in person					
A staff handbook containing details of all these measures					

The importance of checking customer satisfaction

Denzil has a long-standing relationship with a particular customer. As part of an overall check on customer satisfaction, you ask him how he knows the customer is satisfied with his efforts. He is slightly offended and makes the relevant point that if the customer was not satisfied she would have gone elsewhere long ago. He is probably right about that. However, there are times when you need to take a more *formal* approach towards checking on how satisfied customers are with your product or service. This would be so in the following situations:

- when sales are falling and you want to find out what you are doing *wrong*
- when sales are good and you want to find out what you are doing *right*
- when you want to change a product or service and want to check customer reaction to it
- when you have made that change and want to know whether or not you have done the right thing
- when the number of customer complaints has risen over the past month.

Bear in mind that in modern 'management-speak', you must not only *satisfy* your customers, you must *delight* them!

 INFORMATION UPDATE

Each year Kwik-Fit contact over one million customers to ask about levels of service. Every evening its staff telephone 5000 customers within 72 hours of the visit to a Kwik-Fit centre to ensure they have been fully satisfied with the service they received.

EVIDENCE COLLECTION

Keep a record of the contacts you have with customers over a period of four or five weeks, when you have needed to identify their requirements in terms of quantity, quality *and* delivery times.

State how you recorded the customer requirements (or include any forms you completed) and how you then ensured that other people involved in delivering the services or products were informed. If you had to help resolve any problems meeting customer requirements, make sure you record these. State what went wrong, the action you took and the outcome.

Finally, explain the checks you made to ensure the customer was satisfied with the service you gave and how you updated your customer records afterwards.

Key facts on assisting customers with problems and complaints

Your procedures for dealing with problems and complaints

Nowadays virtually every organisation has a well-established complaints procedure. Although formats differ the approach remains similar. You may, for instance, be asked to follow the procedures laid out in the flow chart below or in a similar set of written guidelines.

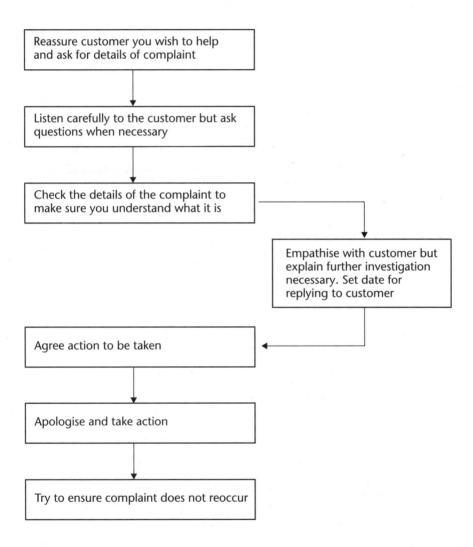

Example of a customer complaints procedure

Most organisations are keen to ensure that their customers know *how* to complain. Large organisations will make sure that complaints procedures are advertised in areas where customers frequently visit and also in any literature it gives to them. See the example here of the way in which one bank tells its customers about its complaints procedures.

A bank's advice to customers on what to do if they need to complain

- Speak first to someone at the appropriate branch or office.

- If the problem cannot be solved straight away, you will be told what is going to be done about it and how long it is likely to take.

- If you are not satisfied, speak to the branch or office manager who will look into the problem free of charge and keep in touch with you.

- If you are still not satisfied, call the Customer Service Line on (Freephone number ....).

- If you prefer to write, please write to the Customer Relations Manager (FREEPOST ....).

- If you are still not satisfied, you can use the free service of the Banking Ombudsman Scheme at the Office of the Banking Ombudsman, South Quay Plaza, 183 Marsh Wall, London E14 (Tel: 0345 660 902).

EVIDENCE COLLECTION

1 Outline your own organisation's procedures for dealing with problems and complaints. Point out, if relevant, where they differ from the procedures illustrated above. Give possible reasons for the differences.

2 Describe the procedures you would follow when dealing with a customer (either internal or external) who:

   a complains about not being given enough information or advice about a product

   b keeps changing his or her mind about requirements

   c complains about a specific service or product.

The importance of collecting sufficient customer information

Hamish takes a telephone call from a customer who says she was treated very rudely by a member of the reception staff. The following conversation takes place.

CUSTOMER:	I wish to complain in the strongest possible terms about the way in which I've been treated by your firm.
HAMISH:	I'm sorry about that. Can you tell me exactly what happened?
CUSTOMER:	I wanted to see my usual contact in the sales department. When I called in, however, I had to wait in a queue for at least 20 minutes. The girl on the desk then kept me waiting until she had a chat with a friend on the phone and then disappeared into the back office – to paint her nails presumably. When I rapped on the counter she came back in and asked me what I wanted in a very offhand manner. She needs the sack if you ask me.
HAMISH:	Did you eventually get to see the person you wanted?
CUSTOMER:	Well, yes – but only after a struggle – and he wasn't too pleasant either. He made me feel I was interrupting something more important. Those two could lose you a lot of business.
HAMISH:	What would you like me to do?
CUSTOMER:	I want them to realise how annoyed I am – and I also want an apology.
HAMISH:	I'll look into the matter for you. Could you give me your name and address please.

Hamish has done some things well. He has been pleasant. He has asked the customer what she wants. He has agreed to look into the matter for her. He hasn't admitted any liability. However, he has made life hard for himself because he hasn't clarified certain points. These are:

- the date and time of the incident
- the name of the receptionist (or a description of her if the customer was too angry to make a note of the name badge)
- the name of the 'usual' contact
- the telephone/fax number and/or e-mail address of the customer.

If he had been given that information he could have begun to make enquiries at once. As it is he has to find out who was on the reception desk yesterday and today and contact them all to see if anyone could give him some details about the incident. He has to search the customer database for details about the customer, and he may have to contact the sales department to find the name of her contact. All relatively trivial points, but time-consuming nevertheless.

The relevant information that should be collected

An important document for you if you are involved in customer service is a customer complaints form. Such a form not only allows you to summarise the nature of the complaint, but also acts as a reminder to you about what information you should obtain. There is then less likelihood of forgetting to ask a relevant question. See the example below.

Customer's name:
Organisation:
Address:
Telephone number:
Fax number:
E-mail number:
Customer reference number:
Nature of complaint
When it occurred:
Where it occurred:
Staff involved:
Action taken so far:
Action to be taken:
By whom:
Any follow up action: (with dates)
No further action required: (Document ready for filing)
Signature: **Date:**

Example of a customer complaints form

Equally, however, you should be careful not to irritate the customer by asking for information that he or she may not have readily available (such as a customer reference number). You can always find out that information at a later date.

CHECK IT OUT!

Compare your method of recording information about a customer complaint with that given earlier on page 447. Highlight the differences, if any, and give possible reasons for them.

Interacting with the customer

The importance of showing empathy

In the example just given, Hamish did his best to soothe the customer. He said he was sorry to hear that she had a complaint. He said he would do something about it. If he had been speaking to her in person he would probably have followed the suggestions for dealing with an angry customer outlined on page 439. If he hadn't done so, he would have made the situation worse. The customer was already annoyed about being treated in an offhand manner by the receptionist and other members of staff. She would have been enraged if Hamish had adopted the same attitude. Quite often, dealing with a customer with a complaint in a pleasant, concerned manner can result in the complaint being taken no further – and, more important – in no loss of future business.

Looking for an agreed solution

Sometimes in trying to be helpful you can cause a problem for your organisation almost by accident. Obviously, you should not agree with the customer to the extent that you are admitting the organisation is at fault. Even if it is, it is likely that a more senior member of staff than you will have to take that decision. What you have also to avoid is promising what you can't deliver – or agreeing a particular solution with a customer when there may be several different solutions. Promising in every case to refund money, replace a product or send a fresh order could cost your organisation a lot of money – and may not be the best solution.

TEST YOUR KNOWLEDGE AND UNDERSTANDING

In each of the following cases, suggest what alternative solutions you would try to offer to the customer (provided you had permission to do so). In some cases you would have to suggest a solution – someone senior to you may have to make the final decision.

a   An important business customer has complained that the order he received was two days late. He wants you to take the goods back.

b One of the sales assistants in the showrooms has sent old price lists to a regular customer, who has ordered some goods and has now been told he has to pay more. He says he will take his business elsewhere.

c A customer wants the car park attendant to be dismissed because he was rude to her about where she should park her car.

d A member of the sales staff shouted at you this morning when he collected a report you had photocopied because you had not done it back-to-back. He accuses you of wasting paper and ruining the environment single-handedly. He is even more annoyed at the fact that he wanted a front and back cover on the report but this information was not recorded on the job request form you received. He wants the whole job to be done again.

Referring problems on to the relevant person

Some problems are just too complicated or potentially too serious for you to handle on your own. You may not be able to pacify a customer no matter what you do. You need, therefore, to ask your line manager for some assistance, particularly since many customers like the thought that their complaint is being dealt with by someone high up the organisational ladder. More importantly, of course, your line manager is the person who must be kept informed if there are likely to be any really serious repercussions as the result of a complaint. If, for instance, you are in the office on your own and a senior manager of another firm storms into the room demanding an explanation for non-delivery of goods, you need back-up – preferably from as senior a manager as possible.

Most organisations include the appropriate chain of command in their complaints procedures so that you should not be left in any doubt as to whom and at what stage you should refer a complaint. If at the moment you are unsure, you should have a word with your line manager and find out who you should contact whenever you feel a situation is beyond you or you need further advice.

The importance of the customer knowing what is happening

Sometimes you are so busy trying to deal with a complaint, particularly if it is rather complicated, that you forget to tell the customer what progress you are making. If at the first stage of any complaint you tell customers that you will look into the matter and get back to them, make sure that you give a date for doing so. If not, the customers are left uncertain about when they are going to be contacted – which can lead to their contacting you again in an even worse mood than at first! If they can see that you are trying to do something, they are likely to be more relaxed about any delays.

Following through agreed solutions and checking that the customer is satisfied

All customers need to be treated well. That goes without saying. However, once a customer has made a complaint he or she tends to need particular attention. Most customers forgive the occasional problem. What they tend not to forgive is a repetition of the same problem or the occurrence of another one.

INFORMATION UPDATE

Some customers put up with a lot! A retired bank clerk moved house 15 months ago and inherited Eastern Energy as his gas supplier. The company used energy consumption figures from the previous occupants to calculate an estimated bill. Although he used far less gas, his efforts to improve the situation got nowhere and he was unable to find out what was going on. Within a four-month period he received five revised estimates.

The bills were finally sorted out in August and the meter was read in September. Unfortunately, however, the new estimated bill was based on the old faulty readings. Whilst he was trying to sort it out, he fell behind with his monthly payments and to add insult to injury he received a 'red bill' demanding £109 but with no details of how that sum had been reached. When he enquired yet again, it was found that the bill was £25 more than it should have been.

At that stage the company admitted that there had been a series of computer and human errors. The customer, however, was not pacified and decided to move back to British Gas.

Dealing politely and calmly with customers who are agitated

Hamish wisely kept his temper with his customer. However, although annoyed, she wasn't abusive or threatening. She was also speaking to him by telephone. If someone had come into the office to complain, in a furious temper and looking very aggressive, he would have had to exercise additional skills. If he followed the suggestions outlined on page 451 he might be able to defuse the situation. If not, he would have to seek assistance from a senior manager. The basic principle in such circumstances is not to leave the customer alone, simmering and getting even angrier. Even if the help offered is not what is wanted, at least the customer knows that *something* is being done.

Research has shown that a large number of incidents of angry customers occur when they have to wait in a queue. Many organisations try to avoid this by:

- having more people available to serve customers, and staggering breaks to maximize staffing at peak periods
- using a master queue feeding to the first available station, rather than independent queues
- having an alerting system to indicate available positions
- having 'roving agents' to deal with problems while people are waiting
- providing seating and using a 'take a number' system
- providing diversions – a reading rack, television, interactive computer terminal etc.
- making sure processes are straightforward, to eliminate the need for multiple queuing
- having fast-track lanes for quick transactions.

 INFORMATION UPDATE

Airline staff are particularly vulnerable to abuse from passengers who have missed planes, whose luggage has disappeared or who have to wait hours because of some delay. As a television series showed, the less they were told the more incensed passengers became. It also showed how the staff were trained to keep their tempers – and how quickly senior staff were on the scene to try to calm everyone down.

Showing determination in solving a problem

Most people can deal with the first stages of a problem. They can reassure the customer and promise to investigate. If there is an obvious solution then everyone is satisfied. If, however, the solution isn't obvious, the problem can sometimes be passed from hand to hand until the customer is frantic! Some organisations try to overcome this by setting out a list of problem-solving procedures for staff involved in customer services. They include:

- initial action to be taken and by whom
- a review within 10 days to see whether the problem is solved
- if not, the follow-up action to be taken and by whom
- a subsequent review within a week – and so on.

This approach prevents the problem from being forgotten by establishing, throughout the process, who is responsible for trying to solve it and creating an inbuilt review mechanism. The customer complaints form quite often acts as the reminder document, particularly if it contains review dates and a 'No further action required' section to be completed before the document is eventually filed (look back to the example on page 450).

Organisational procedures for recording and reporting problems and complaints

Once a customer complaint has been dealt with and filed, that doesn't mean that it should be forgotten about entirely. Many organisations analyse those complaints on a regular basis to see what could have been done to avoid them. Some plot complaints graphically so that they can see the major problem areas at a glance – see the example below.

Complaint	Value
Rude staff	1
Not enough staff	1
Misleading signs	2
Goods not available	1
Poor car parking	8
Too hot	2
Dirty	1

Example of an analysis of weekly complaints received by the customer services section of a retail outlet

INFORMATION UPDATE

It is said that former US President Harry Truman had a slogan on his desk: 'The buck stops here.' Everyone dealing with customer problems or complaints should know when the buck stops with them!

EVIDENCE COLLECTION

Keep a log of problems you deal with over the next few weeks. Your log must include problems relating to:

- the need for information and advice
- changing requirements
- complaints about services or products.

In each case state the customer information you obtained (or attach a copy of the complaints form) and the solutions you suggested. Then state what action you took and how you checked this met the customer's needs.

If you could not reach agreement on a particular occasion, state the procedures you followed in referring the problem to another person, and how you kept the customer informed about what was happening.

Key facts on improving services to customers

Formal and informal methods of seeking feedback

If you don't talk to your customers you will never really be sure that you are meeting all their requirements. Even if a particular product is selling well or there is a lot of use of a particular service, there's no saying that sales or use could not be further improved if adjustments or alterations were made.

The modern approach to customer feedback is to use every available mechanism, both formal and informal. Informal examples include chatting to the customers as they are purchasing a product or making use of a service to find out if there is anything else they might want. Examples of more formal mechanisms include:

- a free-call telephone line – displayed very publicly on correspondence, the product itself, the delivery vans etc.
- comment cards and forms in easily accessible places or sent to customers with a prepaid return slip
- suggestion boxes for use by external and internal customers
- easily accessible customer care desks with staff trained to talk to customers
- customer surveys and questionnaires – sent to both existing and prospective customers
- interviews in person or by telephone, again by specially trained staff.

A modern innovation is a special button on the organisation's website for the user to click. This might be labelled 'Contact us' or 'Let us know what you think'. Clicking the button generates a pre-addressed blank e-mail for the customer to complete and send. The thought that a suggestion will reach the recipient almost immediately is attractive to many customers nowadays – particularly the younger ones.

Other feedback held in your organisation that may be relevant

Imagine you work in a college. You use a number of methods for getting *direct* staff and student feedback. However, you also have a number of other sources within the college that may be able to provide you with additional *indirect* information. They are:

- The library staff: How often is the library used? By whom and for how long?
- The refectory staff: Who are most likely to use the facilities? When and for how long?
- The management information system: Which courses do not recruit, which courses lose and which keep the most students throughout the course of the year?
- The marketing unit: Which leaflets appealed to which type of student?

Which advertisements got the best response?

- The personnel officer: Are a lot of staff leaving? If so, why? Is there a good response to any advertisement for staff? If not, why?

The answers to these questions might give you as clear an idea of the extent of customer satisfaction with your service as do all the more formal mechanisms. The difficulty here, however, is putting procedures into place capable of gathering this information together centrally, analysing it and acting upon the results.

Bear in mind also that customer feedback need not have only one purpose. If a customer is asked to complete a customer feedback card, the questions he or she has to answer might relate not only to the specific product or service but also to a wider range of issues. The extract shown here is from a restaurant's customer feedback card. Not only are there the expected questions about quality of food, staff friendliness etc. but also questions relating to the reasons for visiting the restaurant. The answers could provide useful information – for the library, the shopping precinct, the tourism information centre etc.

---

1   How often do you visit the Singing Kettle? Please tick one box.

    ☐ First visit   ☐ Once a week

    ☐ Once every two weeks   ☐ Once a month

    ☐ Once every three months   ☐ Less often

2   Please rate the following by ticking the appropriate boxes.

	Excellent	Good	Average	Poor
Quality of food	☐	☐	☐	☐
Staff friendliness	☐	☐	☐	☐
Speed of service	☐	☐	☐	☐
Value for money	☐	☐	☐	☐

3   What were your main reasons for visiting us today? Please tick one box.

    ☐ Visiting attractions in the area
    ☐ Visiting friends/relatives
    ☐ Shopping trip
    ☐ Work in the town centre/lunch break
    ☐ Visiting the library

Extract from a customer feedback card

Analysing customer feedback and identifying trends and developments

Gathering together a heap of customer satisfaction feedback forms or cards and piling them hopelessly on top of one another on your desk will achieve nothing other than depress you. However, there's no point in collecting information if you have no intention of (a) reading it and (b) acting on what you have read.

Much depends on the size of your organisation as to the methods it will use to analyse customer feedback. Many organisations, for instance, employ statisticians to process the information obtained from customers. They use specially prepared forms that are capable of computer analysis. This is particularly useful when comparisons have to be made, for instance, between feedback from different departments or stores, or customer's reactions to different products or services, or feedback this time this year as compared with the same time last year. It can help to identify trends over a particular period – increases and decreases of popularity of particular products or services, a rise in a particular type of complaint etc.

It also allows the results to be put into a variety of different formats – tabular, pictorial, graphic – for presentation and analysis by various groups of people.

If you work in a smaller organisation, this process may have to be carried out manually and/or through the use of a computerised customer database which is updated regularly. The use of a form similar to the one in which the number and nature of complaints are identified on a weekly basis is sometimes helpful as you can input the information you receive on an on-going basis. You don't have to wait until the pile grows too high for you to see over your desk!

How to identify and recommend improvements

Any analysis of customer feedback should produce a wide range of issues. It should indicate, for instance:

- which customers are very pleased, reasonably pleased, dissatisfied or very dissatisfied with the product or service
- those areas which are the most highly regarded – the product, the service, after-sales service, delivery etc – and those which are the least highly regarded

- the types of general additional comments made by the customers (e.g. 'It's always cold in the showroom')
- suggestions for improvement (e.g. 'Would it be a good idea to have an additional sign at the entrance to the car park?').

What happens next usually depends on individual organisational procedures. In most cases, however, these would include:

a a meeting of all relevant staff – those who work in the area, those responsible for quality, those responsible for customer care

b the preparation of an action plan recommending what should be done
- to improve areas that have been criticised
- to maintain the level of satisfaction in areas which have been praised.
- to act upon the comments and suggestions

c submission of the recommendations to relevant senior managers for approval

d implementation of the action points by specified personnel

e review dates to check on progress.

EVIDENCE COLLECTION

1 State how, in your own organisation, you collect and analyse at least two of the following types of customer feedback:

- complaints
- praise
- suggestions for improvement.

2 State how you identify and put in place improvements:

- to products or services the customer receives from your team
- to the way in which your team interacts with customers.

Remember that you must clearly specify your own role in this process – not just state, in general terms, what happens in your organisation.

Evaluating improvements and reporting the results

Closing the loop is more difficult than it sounds. It can be quite a satisfying experience to sit down with a group of people and plan improvements. It becomes less satisfying as time goes on, however, if you are constantly reminding other people of what they haven't done or what they have yet to do and you feel you are getting nowhere. That is why regular review dates of the action plan are so important. The more people are reminded of what they agreed to do, the more likely they are to do it – if nothing else but to avoid the irritation of another reminder.

A word of warning, however. The way in which you remind people can be crucial. If you are too abrasive you take the risk that the person concerned will start looking for ways not to cooperate with you. The person might, for instance, always have a perfectly good reason for not having done something he or she promised or may have perfected the art of 'passive resistance' so that you feel you are coming up against a brick wall each time you raise the matter. If you are too gentle and self-effacing, of course, you risk no one taking any notice of you at all. It's a thin dividing line.

The final step in the process is to let customers know what you have done. Everyone likes to think that what they have said has been listened to and acted upon. Actions you could take include:

- in a small organisation, sending a personal response to each customer
- in a large organisation, sending to all customers a summarised version of what action has been taken as a result of customer feedback
- displaying posters or notices in public areas where customers are likely to see them. Some retail organisations have noticeboards set aside specifically to display this information
- putting the information on the organisation's website – for both internal and external customers.

It not only closes the loop – it encourages customers to make any other views known.

EVIDENCE COLLECTION

You can enhance your evidence for this unit by obtaining witness testimony from your line manager and from your internal customers that you regularly meet their needs, assist them when necessary, positively seek to build effective working relationships, obtain feedback and act upon these to make improvements. Do make sure that your witness testimony is specific, however. General praise is pleasant to receive but counts for less than specific examples of, say, improvements you have implemented.

You are advised not to ask external customers for witness testimony unless you have one or two who you deal with very regularly and who would be happy to support you. Even then, do check with your line manager first if this would be acceptable.

Option Unit 309 **Support users of administrative services**

FOCUS OF THE UNIT

To obtain this unit you must be able to:

* **provide support** to users of administrative services
* **contribute to reviewing** support to users.

EVIDENCE COLLECTION

For this unit, you need to produce evidence that you regularly provide support to users of administrative services, and that you review this support on a regular basis. You can do this in one of two ways.

* Choice 1 – You can collect evidence of the support you provide and how this is undertaken and reviewed.
* Choice 2 – You can adopt a different strategy by producing your own *Staff Guidelines Handbook on Administrative Services* as a support document.

Further guidance on both these choices is given throughout the unit to enable you to provide the evidence.

Key facts on supporting users of administrative services

In Unit 304, you learned about systems and procedures. These are crucial to this present unit as you will be providing support to users on your own systems and procedures. The information update below reviews some of the issues, as well as showing how this unit 'fits in' with systems and procedures. If you are still unsure what a system is, or what procedures are, then you are strongly advised to re-read pages 231–235.

 INFORMATION UPDATE

A series of rail disasters led to a great deal of publicity regarding the safety of travelling by train – and considerable havoc for passengers as urgent replacements took place on many rail lines in Britain during late 2000 and early 2001. Now there are plans to install the very expensive European train control system (ECTS) on the first main line by 2005. This system directs drivers from a central control and replaces traditional line signalling. This is a safer system than the cheaper train protection system (TWPS) which is not as effective, but is likely to be fitted on less busy routes. However, fitting any safety systems may cause even more disruption for travellers whilst the work is carried out.

Both the ECTS and TWPS are 'systems' in themselves because they process inputs into outputs. The ECTS monitors data on the train speed and the track (its inputs) and if the data identifies a potential danger it stops the train safely. This reduces the consequences of driver error, because in an emergency the ECTS overrules the driver completely. So the eventual output could be seen as a train which always arrives safely at its destination.

However, rail travel itself can be seen as a system. The main inputs are passengers who want to reach a particular destination. The 'process' transports these passengers. The desirable outputs are passengers who arrive safely at their destination – preferably on time. In the rail travel system, the ECTS and TWPS are control sub-systems which monitor speed and safety. Feedback is obtained by asking passengers for their opinions – which have been rather forceful over the past year or two! (Compare this information with the system diagram on page 233.)

Support is provided for all rail travellers – from information in timetables and on the Internet, to information available at train stations and platform announcements, to station facilities and shops and catering on board. Because travellers know that this 'support' is available, and know the procedures to follow if they want to buy a ticket, reserve a seat or buy a drink whilst travelling, they know how to use the service. However, there are still enquiry desks at stations for people who need particular information and announcements on the train for those unfamiliar with the route or the journey. All these are examples of additional support.

Support becomes even more important if there is a problem. If services are disrupted or delayed then travellers need additional information. At one point, extra staff were hired at London stations to assist delayed or stranded passengers.

All services need to provide support so that users – even if they don't understand completely how the system operates – know what procedures they must follow and why. They may not always agree with these, or be entirely happy with the overall service, but there will be fewer problems if users are kept informed and provided with as much support as possible.

You have probably travelled by train many times, so have used this system. You may have also travelled by air. Air transport can be described in exactly the same way – as a system for taking passengers from one destination to another. You can check if you now understand how systems and procedures operate by seeing if you can answer the questions below.

1 How would you describe the inputs and outputs of the air transport system?

2 What procedures do you have to follow as an air traveller when:

   a you want to book a flight?

   b you check in for a flight?

   c you board a flight?

3 What support is available, both at an airport and on a plane, in relation to:

   a information available for travellers?

   b advice for travellers with a problem?

4 Another type of support can be provided by demonstrating something. When would you see a demonstration on an aircraft? Why do you think printed information is not considered sufficient?

5 What types of additional support are available to travellers at a large airport?

6 To what extent do you think good support improves a service? Give a reason for your answer.

Identifying the services where you are responsible for assisting users

A list of the types of services often provided by administrators was given on pages 225 and 226. If you have completed Unit 304, you may know exactly which services you provide and can identify those where you are responsible for assisting users. If you are not sure about this, then some of the points below may help, simply because, if you think of all the people who ask you for support and why, you may be able to identify the services more easily.

Users to whom you provide support

You have already seen that support means providing assistance and information in the most appropriate way. Sometimes the best way is a brief verbal response to a question – or you may need to take time to give more complicated instructions or advice. On other occasions you may need to demonstrate what to do, or train someone to do something (see page 468).

You are likely to provide support to all users who depend upon you for information and guidance. For example, one of the key groups of people who need support are new staff. When you first start work for a new employer, one of the main problems is the fact that you don't know how things are done. This is why induction courses are held – to give people a quick overview of the main systems and procedures in the organisation.

Your induction programmes may, or may not, include information on your administrative services. If they don't, you are likely to find you and your team are asked a number of questions by any new recruit.

- What must I do to obtain some file folders?
- How can I get a car parking permit?
- How can I book out a camcorder?
- Do I have to tell anyone if I'm off the premises for a day?
- How do I complete this expense claim and how often are they processed?
- Are travel claims paid by cheque or in my salary?
- How does the photocopying system work?
- What do I do if my computer develops a fault?
- How do I book a meeting room and order refreshments?
- What do I do if I need a rail ticket and to book a hotel?

This list could go on and on! Although your questioners will rarely use the terms 'systems' and 'procedures', in all these cases you could substitute these words: 'What's the system for ...?' or 'What are the procedures for ...?'

You can extend this list of 'users' beyond new staff to include:

- existing staff who are not certain (or can't remember) how some of the systems operate because they only use them infrequently
- staff from other departments, if you have your own departmental systems and procedures
- people who frequently work off the premises, such as representatives or technical staff
- potential and existing customers (or suppliers) who are enquiring about your ordering or payment procedures
- all users, if there is a problem with or disruption to a service.

Also included might be visitors who have a particular query: e.g. 'How long will I have to wait?' This is, in effect, a query about your visitor procedures and you may have to provide considerable support if there is an unexpected and lengthy delay.

Agreeing support requirements, discussing problems and performance

The type of support you are expected to provide is normally agreed by your line manager (who may be your supervisor or team leader), or the person in your organisation who has overall responsibility for administrative services, or a specialist. However, you should be capable of contributing positively to any discussion on the type of support that would be most appropriate, particularly in relation to new or revised systems or procedures.

Similarly, if there are problems or if performance is being discussed, then you are likely to be involved with the same person.

Problems may be identified by:

- your line manager or another senior member of staff
- users of administrative systems
- yourself.

For instance, in most organisations, the existence of known systems and specified procedures means there are automatic answers to many of the questions asked routinely. However, if questions are often asked and no-one knows the answer – or likes the one they receive – then this can indicate there is a potential problem in that area. This was clear from the earlier railways example.

If the support is poor or non-existent, then problems will soon surface. Users may be asking the same questions over and over again or not following procedures properly. If no-one attaches a receipt to their petty-cash vouchers, then this is most likely because they weren't told to do this – rather than the whole department having collective amnesia! Therefore information and guidance on this system and the procedure to follow has been poor. If the photocopier is forever breaking because people don't know how to use it properly, or you receive complaints there is never any paper in the photocopying room, then the support you are providing is simply not good enough and must be reviewed.

In this situation you are reviewing the performance of the way in which the systems and procedures are working. For performance to be good, users have to know what is expected of them and additional support needs to be provided to new users and if there are particular problems. This means clear information at the outset and, in some cases, continuing support thereafter.

In Unit 304 you looked at the importance of obtaining feedback and information on systems and procedures. As you will see, this is important for your support services, too.

Record-keeping

In this unit, record-keeping relates to maintaining records on:

- the requests for support you receive
- the support you provide
- feedback from users.

This will provide an objective record to inform your own judgements about whether support is appropriate, sufficient and effective. For instance, if all new staff should attend IT training, but one or two missed the session for a particular reason, a record will identify this and you can arrange a different date for them to attend.

Records will also help you to identify and solve problems and may prove useful in discussions about problems and performance with your boss.

There are many ways in which you can keep support records – much will depend upon the type of support you offer and to whom. One of the easiest methods is to keep a record book (or an electronic record) which logs:

a the support requests you have received, how these were received (e.g. in a meeting, over the telephone, by e-mail) and when

b the name of the person who asked you to provide support – this may not be the user but could be your line manager

c the type of support you provided and the date, together with your own comment on whether additional support is essential, desirable or unnecessary.

You should also ask the person who received support whether they were satisfied with it. This could be a quick check that they now understand the system or procedure and are confident they can now operate it. You could get them to sign or initial your log to that effect – or add a brief comment. At many training sessions this is done slightly differently. Instead you are asked to complete a short evaluation form afterwards, noting down what you liked best and anything about which you still have concerns.

There is further information on feedback on pages 470, 473 and 474.

Key facts on providing support to users of services

Types of support

The type of support provided needs to be considered carefully because what is best in one situation may be inappropriate in another.

'One-off' questions which can be answered quickly are best dealt with verbally, as and when they occur. The importance is that the users know who they can ask to obtain information on the administrative systems and procedures in operation.

EVIDENCE COLLECTION

Select *one* of the following choices as your method of producing evidence for this unit, depending upon the type of support you normally provide.

Choice 1

If you work in an organisation in which you regularly provide support by various different methods, then you will have no problems providing job-related evidence. In this case, at this stage, you should start to prepare and obtain the following:

a a list of the administrative services for which you are responsible for assisting users

b a list of the users to whom you provide support

c a description of the people in your organisation with whom you agree support requirements and with whom you also discuss problems and performance

d a copy of the records you keep requesting support, including details of the support provided and user feedback.

Choice 2

If you work in an organisation where the majority of support needs are met verbally, and there is no official record-keeping system related to providing support, then you may find it more appropriate to undertake the following activity, with the agreement of your line manager.

In consultation with users, you will prepare a *Staff Guidelines Handbook*. This will give information and guidance on the administrative services you provide and how these systems and procedures operate. If a procedure is one staff *must* follow, it may be useful to include the actual procedure as an appendix.

The handbook can be issued to all new staff during induction – and should help to answer many of their questions (such as those listed on page 464). The handbook will state what users should do if they need additional support. It can be revised at routine intervals and this will provide your evidence for element 309.2. If you decide to do this, then first you need to discuss the idea with your line manager or the relevant person in your organisation and obtain outline agreement. Confirm the discussion in writing and keep a copy for your portfolio. This should include an explanation of why such a handbook would be useful to the users of your services.

At this stage, don't start to prepare the handbook. Wait until you have read at least as far as page 471.

Regular, simple, questions may be grouped together and then a fact sheet prepared. On a website, you will often see FAQs pages (this stands for 'frequently asked questions') which is a method of providing support to users of the site. This saves the organisation continually having to answer the same questions. Internally, it is useful for staff to have a document to which they can refer when they need to (such as a user handbook). This is preferable to numerous pieces of paper as everything is in one place.

Complex questions may have to be handled differently – especially if the user is likely to have additional queries. You *can* give advice and assistance in a facts sheet, but often a face-to-face discussion is better. One organisation, which employed a large number of part-time staff, included a one-to-one discussion with an administrator as part of the induction process so that issues relating to pay claims, obtaining a computer ID, obtaining a parking permit and the completion of important forms could be discussed in detail and the administrator could give advice on any points of concern.

Some types of systems and procedures cannot be discussed very effectively. Understanding the procedure to follow to log on to a computer network is much easier if you watch someone do it, and then do it under supervision the first time. Normally, any system or procedure which involves a specific 'skill' process should be demonstrated, preferably with the user then attempting the process under supervision. In the airline example earlier, you should have identified that safety procedures are demonstrated in an aircraft (although many now use video films). In Boots stores, for instance, holders of Reward cards can use a machine as they enter to check the special offers that day. Customers who become new cardholders are always shown how to use the machine by a member of staff who demonstrates what to do.

A complex or very important system or procedure may necessitate special training. This may take 15 minutes or a week or more – depending on what it is. If staff in your organisation have access to a customer database or complex spreadsheets which you maintain, or have to complete forms which are used as part of your quality systems or audit procedures, then they may need specific training so that they know exactly what to do when they are seeking or providing information. You can actually categorise airline safety videos as short training films, under this heading.

Agreeing with users what to do if they need support

Users of your administrative services should be quite clear as to:

- what support is available
- who will provide it
- how or when to ask for it.

Finding out what is available shouldn't be a guessing game! Communicating this to users can be done in a variety of ways – depending upon the situation.

- Forms may have a contact name and number on the bottom in case the user has any queries while completing it.
- Office machinery (such as photocopiers and fax machines) can have a notice nearby which states who to contact if there is a problem.
- Reception areas should have clear notices on what visitors can do if the area is temporarily closed.
- Most organisational intranets have information pages on what support is available to computer users in the event of a hardware or software problem.
- Procedure documents and manuals should have a contact name for users who have a problem or query in complying with or understanding the procedure.
- Unsupervised areas, such as a stationery or equipment store, may have a notice on the door saying who to contact if a user has an urgent request.
- In large areas, where people may be scattered, there may be tannoy announcements to provide urgent information.

For new staff, it should be made clear – as part of the induction programme – who should be contacted for specific types of support or to deal with certain queries.

So far as your own users are concerned, you may have an 'open door' policy (if you don't mind constant interruptions) or you may prefer a more formalised system. All of the above methods will reduce the number of queries you receive personally, but don't make a habit of sticking up notices everywhere rather than communicating with people! It is always helpful if users know that you are available if they have an immediate or important need for support about a particular matter.

Obtaining and evaluating information about users' needs

The information you obtain must be sufficient, valid and reliable. You met these types of requirements in Unit 304 when you learned that the opinions of one person should always be compared with those of other people if you want an accurate and objective view of the situation. One person complaining that a procedure is incomprehensible can be discounted if everyone else has no problems with it – although that person may need *additional* support. If no one can follow it – then you have a problem and the procedure needs revising quickly.

Ideally, you need to know:

- what type of support users need (and prefer)
- what their priorities are.

You can then take the appropriate action. As in Unit 304, you can obtain this information formally (e.g. by a questionnaire or survey of users' needs) or informally (e.g. by talking to people). However, make sure that your sample of people is broad enough to give you a representative and meaningful response. A very quick way of then checking you have valid and reliable information is to quickly memo or e-mail your users with the list of requirements you have collated and see whether they agree with it!

You then need to identify the type of support (see page 468) which is most appropriate for each situation, and put this into a priority order. For instance, if feedback revealed that ten out of twelve people in a department couldn't work out how to complete the latest version of the travel request form, then rather than issue a set of instructions, it may be better to have a quick training session where you demonstrate how to complete it. If many of them are due to travel in the next few weeks, the session should be held as soon as possible.

Keeping users informed

If users give you information and feedback on their requirements, it is only courteous to keep them informed. You need to tell them:

- what type of support has been arranged
- when this will be offered.

If you are organising a training session or demonstration, then try to give people as much notice as possible so that they can arrange to be there. This is particularly important if you are arranging for an outside person to do the session, such as how to operate a new piece of equipment or new type of software. You will feel foolish if you arrange this and only four staff turn up because everyone else is unavailable.

If you are arranging individual sessions with particular staff, negotiate the best time and date – rather than demand they see you at your convenience. If you are issuing documentary support, then simply state the date on which this will be issued and *keep to it*. If you issue it by internal mail, you may wish to 'flag up' on e-mail that it is now available and state where additional copies can be obtained.

Occasionally, of course, you may be unable to meet users' needs for various reasons. For instance, you may not have anyone within the organisation with the necessary skills to do a demonstration or train users, but it may be too expensive to ask for a specialist to do it. In this case you need to discuss the situation with your boss to see whether a mutually agreeable alternative can be found.

Confirming support met user needs and keeping records

After the support has been undertaken, then you need to check that your users are satisfied. The ways to do this – and to keep records relating to providing support – were discussed on pages 465 to 466.

EVIDENCE COLLECTION

Choice 1

1   Obtain information on all the types of support you offer to users of your administrative services. You must provide *at least two* of the following types of support for this element:

    a   information on systems and procedures

    b   advice about using systems and procedures

    c   demonstration of the use of systems and procedures

    d   training in the use of systems and procedures.

    Be prepared to discuss with your assessor how you would provide the other types.

2   Identify all the ways in which you inform users about what they should do if they need your support.

3   Provide evidence that you know what type of support your users require and the level of priority of each of their requirements. State how you obtained this and how you know it is sufficient, valid and reliable information.

4   State the action you carried out to provide the support users required and how you informed them about the availability of this support.

5   Provide evidence that you kept records about the support which was provided and obtained confirmation from users that the support provided met their needs.

Choice 2

1   Inform staff who use your administrative services of your intention to produce a short staff guidelines handbook which will give information and advice on using systems and procedures related to these services. It should also include information on what users should do if they need additional support at any time. You need to find out which information your users consider essential and which less important, so that you can prioritise this if you are short of space. You could do this by issuing a brief questionnaire or by discussing your idea with particular user groups. It is sensible if you work out first what areas need to be covered and ask for people's views on this list – rather than just sending out a blanket request for information.

➡

EVIDENCE COLLECTION (Cont.)

2   At the same time, find out if users have any other issues relating to support which they think should be addressed – either as part of the handbook or as a separate issue.

3   Use this information to draft out a list of systems or procedures which must be included and then work out the best way to provide information and guidance on these. You may want to give brief notes, with the actual procedure at the back of the handbook for reference; or do a facts sheet or even include FAQs for users. This is your handbook and your design, so the style of it is up to you. For some procedures which involve machine operation, for instance, you may want to include illustrations.

4   Prepare two or three draft pages to see whether your ideas are working out in practice. Then ask some of your users, and your line manager, for comments. In particular, find out whether the pages you have prepared meet users' needs for information and advice. Once you are certain that you have the correct format for your handbook, now is the time to produce it!

5   Write a summary of all your consultations for your assessor which shows you have identified user needs, identified the range of support currently offered and obtained user feedback on your proposals and attach any records of your discussions.

6   Note that for this element you have to prove that you provide *two* of the following types of support:

   a   information on systems and procedures
   b   advice about using systems and procedures
   c   demonstration of the use of systems and procedures
   d   training in the use of systems and procedures.

   Your handbook, therefore, should contain both (a) and (b) and you must be prepared to discuss with your assessor how you would provide the other types. However, you can usefully supplement this evidence if you undertake demonstrations or organise training by including information on how you do this, too.

Key facts on contributing to reviewing support to users

In Unit 304 you learned that all systems and procedures need reviewing to take account of change in general and problems or snags which may be identified. The same applies to support as needs may change over time.

Obtaining feedback from users

You will receive informal feedback from users on a regular basis. This may relate to any type of support offered, whether it be information, advice, a demonstration or training. If everyone who talks to a particular administrator about a certain procedure comes away saying how useful it was, then you should make a note of this – if only to praise your colleague for doing such a good job!

If people are always complaining, on the other hand, then you not only need to make a note of it but also need to plan to do something about it – before the situation gets worse.

Over a period of time, you should obtain quite comprehensive records about the quality of support offered. These records can help you to review what is currently available.

Whereas informal feedback can be invaluable as it is often instant and honest, to make sure you have a broader picture before making any changes it is sensible to obtain formal feedback from users as well.

Your contribution to obtaining formal feedback

Formal methods of obtaining feedback may include:

- user questionnaires or surveys
- feedback sheets for completion immediately after a demonstration or training session
- regular performance reviews with users that focus on the degree to which support continued to meet their needs
- discussions with different groups of users.

Your role in this process is to determine which method(s) would be best and to obtain the information. This may mean:

- devising and issuing a questionnaire or survey, distributing it, collating and analysing the responses
- devising and issuing feedback sheets, distributing these and keeping records of the responses over a period of time

- arranging suitable dates for performance reviews to be held (with an appropriate time-period between each), identifying who should be present and the focus of the reviews and taking notes
- arranging dates to talk to different groups of users, leading the discussion and recording others' views.

The topics to cover should include:

- support for existing systems and procedures – including the type of support, the quality of support and the frequency with which it is made available
- support for any new or revised systems and procedures and user preferences on this
- any perceived user needs which are not currently being met.

Identifying trends

The aim of obtaining this information is to enable you to obtain enough data to analyse it and identify:

- where support is good and meets users' needs
- where support is poor and regularly fails to meet users' needs (and why)
- the recurrent needs of users, where you may need to increase the availability of support
- the emerging needs of users, where you may need to offer new or additional support.

Suggesting recommendations

Once you have analysed all the information, you need to consider how you can:

- remedy any problems
- meet recurrent needs
- meet emerging needs.

Remember to match your ideas to the needs of particular groups and the type of support which would be most appropriate (see page 468).

At this point you need to report your findings to your boss, together with your recommendations. This can be done verbally, but is better in writing – not just because it then provides you with useful evidence, but also because your boss can consider the document carefully before giving approval or offering any additional suggestions.

EVIDENCE COLLECTION

Choice 1

1 Make sure that you record all informal feedback you receive from users on the quality of support provided over the next few months.

2 Decide the most appropriate method(s) of obtaining formal feedback and agree this with your line manager. Then devise any written documents or plan any review meetings or discussions.

3 Obtain formal feedback and analyse this to identify users' views and to assess recurrent needs and trends. Then consider how the recurrent and emerging needs of users can be met and how any identified problems can be resolved.

4 Prepare a report for your line manager (or other appropriate person) which summarises your findings and recommendations and then arrange a suitable time to discuss the document. Make a note of the changes agreed as a result of this discussion.

5 Prepare a document for your assessor which summarises the actions you have taken and explains all your documentary evidence in context. Note that you must contribute to reviewing *two* of the following kinds of support:

   a information on systems and procedures
   b advice about using systems and procedures
   c demonstration of the use of systems and procedures
   d training in the use of systems and procedures.

   Be prepared to discuss with your assessor how you would review the other types.

Choice 2

1 Issue your staff guidelines handbook. Keep records of all the informal feedback you receive as a result.

2 After about three months, identify the best method of obtaining formal feedback on the document. You need to find out users' views and whether they would like to see anything added, changed or amended. Either devise a questionnaire or survey or arrange to have discussions with groups of users.

3 Analyse the information you receive and decide how the handbook could best be adapted to meet the recurrent and emerging needs of users and any other appropriate requests you have received.

EVIDENCE COLLECTION (Cont.)

4 Prepare a report for your line manager or other appropriate person which summarises your findings and recommendations and then arrange a suitable time to discuss this document in more detail.

5 Plan to implement the changes when you issue the next version of your handbook.

6 Prepare a document for your assessor which summarises the actions you have taken and explains all your documentary evidence in context. However you should note that you must contribute to reviewing *two* of the following kinds of support:

a information on systems and procedures
b advice about using systems and procedures
c demonstration of the use of systems and procedures
d training in the use of systems and procedures.

In the case of your handbook, you will have reviewed (a) and (b) so you should be prepared to discuss with your assessor how you would review the other methods. However, if you undertake demonstrations or arrange training, you could usefully supplement your handbook with further evidence as to how you review these methods, too.

Option Unit 310 **Contribute to scheduling and coordinating activities and resources**

FOCUS OF THE UNIT

To obtain this unit you must be able to:

- **contribute to scheduling** activities and resources
- **contribute to coordinating** activities and resources
- **organise** travel and accommodation.

EVIDENCE COLLECTION

It will make evidence collection easier if you can obtain the following information:

a a description of your own job role in relation to planning and coordinating activities and resources, together with a list of the types of activities and resources that you are responsible for scheduling and coordinating

b examples of any systems and procedures you operate (including those used in making travel arrangements), including the paperwork or documentation you routinely complete, such as sample pages from diaries and a description of planners you use

c a description of the methods you have used to prioritise the scheduling of various activities and the allocation of resources, particularly when you received conflicting requests

d copies of the documents you prepare when booking rooms, equipment and other resources, with a description of why they are used

e examples of travel request forms you have received, itineraries you have prepared and other relevant documentation, such as letters booking and confirming accommodation (both in the UK and abroad), insurance documentation and written confirmation of car hire arrangements.

Contributing to scheduling and coordinating of activities and resources

Activities and resources you are responsible for scheduling and coordinating

Many administrators have responsibilities for scheduling and coordinating activities and resources for various people. For example, an administrator working in a legal department of a local authority may liaise with a number of solicitors, some legal executives and a back-up support staff. The head of the department is part of the senior management team and is also responsible for attending all relevant council meetings, including sub-committee meetings. His or her team carries out a number of tasks:

- housing issues
- court cases
- negotiation of contracts – both commercial and employment
- consumer law issues
- employment legislation.

The back-up staff are all assigned to a group of solicitors working in a particular area, and they are expected to carry out all the relevant clerical and administrative tasks. The administrator has to coordinate their efforts across the department.

In such circumstances it is important to have certain systems to enable the activities taking place across the department to be monitored, and to ensure that what is supposed to happen is happening.

If you were working in this role, you would need to know, for instance:

- what meetings are taking place – whether regular or one-off
- who is in the office and who is out on business at any particular time
- how long people will be away from the department – when they are expected to leave and when to return
- who is on holiday
- who is away sick
- what visitors have been invited into the department, when and for how long
- what events are taking place – staff training days etc.
- whether anyone is working overtime, when and for how long.

You should also be aware of what resources are available to support these activities. You may be called upon to prioritise tasks. A very important council meeting would take precedence over an internal departmental meeting. A visit from the chief executive would be regarded as more important than a visit from a sales representative trying to sell office supplies. You might also be called upon to:

- allocate various members of staff to support a particular activity
- provide a member of staff with a particular skill (e.g. minute-taking)
- allocate rooms
- make resources available for urgent activities (photocopying facilities, access to a computer database etc.).

As an administrator you have to make sure that the work for which you are responsible is organised in such a way that it meets the requirements of your line manager and your colleagues.

 KEY NOTES ON SCHEDULING AN EVENT

First identify

- who is responsible for its completion (include yourself here if relevant!)
- the other personnel involved
- its level of importance and consequently what priority it may take over other tasks
- when it has to be completed.

Then

- allocate the work to the relevant person, or divide it into a number of discrete tasks and allocate the jobs to different people
- decide approximately how much time is needed to complete each one (counting back from the deadline of the completion date)
- decide the order in which the work has to be completed.

Possible problems

One pitfall you should try to avoid is treating each event separately and making plans for each as it comes along. It is far more effective if you take an **overview** of the work being carried out in your work area and classify it into tasks that:

- are infrequent but which can be anticipated and planned well in advance
- occur more frequently but which can also be anticipated
- occur regularly, but the timing cannot be identified precisely.

Work scheduling table		
Tasks which are infrequent but which can be planned well in advance	Tasks which are frequent and which can be planned in advance	Tasks which are frequent but the timing of which cannot be identified precisely
Annual general meeting	Monthly audit of sales figures	Making appointments for visitors
Review of quality procedures	Weekly departmental meeting	Word processing correspondence
Preparation of new sales catalogue	Monthly check of fire extinguishers	Answering the telephone
Summer holiday rota		
......	......	......

Types of systems and procedures for scheduling activities and resources

You cannot schedule or coordinate activities or resources without a system. You should be fully aware of the benefits of systems and procedures from Unit 304. The most obvious benefit is that there is a standard method, which everyone knows and you and your team can follow. The procedures you follow will rely on paper-based or computer-based planning aids.

Once you have identified the appropriate tasks which need scheduling, and the times at which they are likely to occur, the next stage is to incorporate them into an overall plan and to attach a time element to each. It is no use in such circumstances trying to keep a master plan in your head! You'll never manage it. Make use of all the planning aids that may be available to you. Those you are most likely to use are summarised next.

Lists

The list is the most basic type of planning aid. Even if you do nothing else, you should prepare a chronological list of the events to be organised. Most administrators will make use of a daily list of events. Some like to make weekly, monthly and even yearly lists and pin them up on their noticeboard. They can then see at a glance what they have to do. However, notices get dirty and scribbled upon and are sometimes removed by the office joker! In such circumstances it is sometimes worth investing in one of a number of more sophisticated planning aids.

Planners

Planners can easily be developed from a list. The planning time span for most organisations runs from January to December, although some organisations opt for their financial year – usually April until the following March – and educational establishments often make their planning arrangements from August to the following July to fit in with the academic terms. Whatever the choice, it is the starting point in any systematic work scheduling.

Tasks that can be planned on a yearly basis include:

- the annual general meeting
- the annual sales conference
- dates of sales trips
- dates of quarterly or termly reports
- directors'/senior executive/governors'/councillors' meetings
- financial activities relating to the year end
- cross-section or organisational activities such as the health and safety, quality standards and environmental committee meetings.

Tasks that can be planned on a monthly basis include:

- a regular transfer of events from the yearly planner
- meetings with trade union, equal-opportunities or health and safety representatives
- monthly reports from various managers
- training or staff development courses
- short-listing or interview arrangements
- production scheduling meetings.

If you wish you can devise your own planner, but you may feel that this aspect of your work is so important that you need a commercially prepared planning aid.

A number of office suppliers offer a range of planning aids that claim to ease the work of the office administrator. Read the descriptions given below of some of the planners on offer. Identify those you currently use and decide which others, if any, would be the most suitable for your particular work area and for what purposes. Write brief notes giving reasons for your decision.

a 'The staff and holiday planner is an invaluable supplement for the year planner. There are spaces for 31 names and the planner shows the Monday dates for each week through the year.'

b 'If you prefer a planner on which you can work continuously, this type is ideal. The grid displays months and dates and an individual year is set up with adhesive Saturday/Sunday/Bank Holiday stickers supplied. Half way through the year, the early months can be cleared and weekend stickers set in place for the following year, perhaps leaving a blank month between the current month and next year. If you prefer, the complete chart can be re-set at the year's end.'

c 'This pre-marked planner offers a large clear grid giving a display which is easy to see and use. Divided into weeks commencing Mondays, the actual date can be entered into the small box in the corner of each day.'

d 'This planner has any number of uses since it can be made up to suit your own requirements. Printed in two blocks of six months, each month is printed 1 to 31 across the top. You can commence your year with any month you wish. The left-hand column has spaces for names, machines, rooms, vehicles – indeed anything which needs a control system to keep track of its movements.'

e 'The gridded magnetic board sets out the organisation of various company departments using the accessories in the kit supplied. Magnetic name holders show personnel, adhesive tapes indicate their position in the organisation. By using different colour magnets to mark absences through training or sickness, the staffing level of every department is immediately apparent.'

The diary

The diary is probably the most frequently used planner. Again you will probably use a commercially prepared version, possibly bearing your organisation's name and logo. If you work in a specialist area you may use a diary published by the appropriate professional institute – such as the Chartered Institute of Marketing.

If you schedule the activities of a group of people in a diary you need sufficient space to identify each person easily. So to be useful the diary should be of reasonable size – pocket or handbag-sized diaries have their uses but only in a back-up capacity. The diary should also:

- have at least one page for each day (unless it is particularly large, in which case half pages may be sufficient)
- be subdivided into the time intervals that most suit your purpose – e.g. 15 minutes, half an hour, an hour.

 KEY NOTES ON ADVANTAGES AND DISADVANTAGES OF PLANNERS

Advantages

- They look professional and can be displayed in a public area.
- Most of them are re-usable.

Disadvantages

- Some administrators lose their head when faced with a variety of coloured labels and signals and stick them on at random. They may know what the planner intends to convey. Others may not.
- If the administrator is a perfectionist and insists that all labels must be the exact size etc., the whole exercise can be very time-consuming.
- Some commercial planners have magnetic strips which are permanent. The strips may not be easily adhered to the planner and may fall off.

EVIDENCE COLLECTION

Describe the type of diary you use. State how far you think it assists you to carry out your work responsibilities. Identify why you use it, and the person (or group of people) you use it for.

The electronic organiser

The electronic diary/personal organiser has changed the ways in which diaries and appointments can be managed. The electronic diary usually has some or all of the following features.

- It provides a five-year calendar and diary display.
- It allows you, via fast or slow scroll, to scan diary pages by morning, afternoon or evening: and by week, month or year.

- It enables you to enter commitments, reminders or appointments at any time over the whole period. there is also the facility to block out time periods for uninterrupted work.
- It lets you insert reminders, priority jobs and memory joggers. Some diaries enable you to highlight priority action for the day.
- It gives you access to colleagues' diaries so that you can, for instance, arrange and make the diary entries for a meeting at the first time and date when all members are available.
- It allows you to consult other integrated packages such as a database, spreadsheet or calculator while processing a diary or appointment entry.

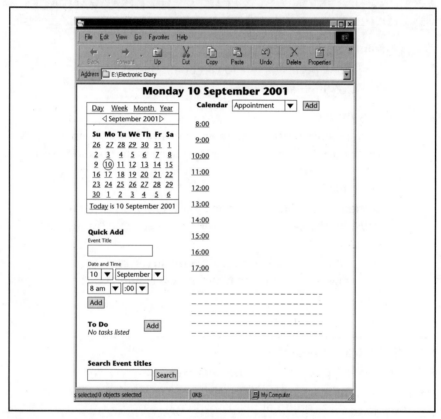

Page from electronic diary

CHECK IT OUT!

If you have access to an electronic diary or personal organiser, write brief notes on the advantages it has over the paper-based diary. If you have not, check the chart opposite which gives information on a range of personal organisers. Make a recommendation on the type of organiser you would find most useful in your own workplace.

Model	Features
Handy Pad 4.0 	Small, stylish and lightweight. One-touch access to 3-month calendar, reminder schedule, expenses, alarm, to-do list. Internet ready.
E-Planner 	Internet information and diary in one compact organiser.
Multi-tasker 	Lightweight personal organiser. 8MB memory. Large widescreen display with diary, addresses, to-do list.
Compact planner 	1MB personal organiser – large widescreen display. Diary, addresses, to-do list. 12 month warranty

Commercial personal organisers

Computer-based aids

Other computerised scheduling aids are a feature in many organisations. For instance, if you work as an administrator in a school or college, you may find that all the timetabling is computer-based. In that case you can not only access but also change all information relating to room, class, staff member and time. If you work in a large organisation and are responsible for coordinating all staff holiday arrangements, you may be able to use your computer to list all staff details, including their holiday entitlement. You can then keep not only an individual check on all holidays booked but also a cross-organisational check to ensure that all vital areas – such as the production departments – are never completely denuded of staff at any one time.

Remember, however, that complete reliance on a computer system can be dangerous. It cannot recognise 'people' problems, and you may be limited in the number of reference notes you can add which are appropriate. Furthermore, it may not always give you the flexibility you would like. For that reason, many administrators also keep a relevant file which relates to an important plan or schedule – which is invaluable, also, if there are any problems with the computer system at a critical moment.

 INFORMATION UPDATE

Growing in importance is the use of calendar connectors – i.e. diary management for mobiles. They present calendar entries on the mobile screen in an easy-to-read format and can show daily, weekly and monthly entries as well as permitting new calendar entries. They also allow the user to search through appointments by use of a keyword.

Scheduling procedures

A planning aid is only a tool! It cannot think for you. No matter how up to date it is, and what features it possesses, it is your use of it that determines whether or not it is going to be valuable. A diary which is illegible and scribbled over and which always goes missing at a vital moment is of little assistance to anyone. If you can, it is worthwhile trying to establish certain basic rules about its use – particularly if you are not the only person with access to it.

1　All the entries should be clearly written and complete. It should be automatic to enter the full name and the telephone or extension number of all visitors to your work area. In cases where the visitor is unknown, his or her name should be printed to ensure that there can be no mistakes of identity.

2　Where relevant, the job title or status of the visitor should be entered.

3　In certain circumstances, an appointment made over the telephone should be confirmed in writing.

4　A brief note should be made of the reason for the appointment – unless it is confidential or unless you work in an area such as an accountant's office when clients may be unwilling to let you know what they wish to discuss.

5　All appointments should be entered into the diary as soon as possible.

6   There is some forward planning. If, for instance, you know that you or your line manager has to attend a meeting each week, those dates and times can be put in the diary well in advance.

7   Provisional appointments are to be written in pencil, to avoid the diary being cluttered with amendments or alterations.

8   Where possible, entries should be ticked off when the appointment has taken place.

CHECK IT OUT!

There are certain danger areas to avoid when making entries in a diary. Look at the diary page reproduced here and compare it with the entries you would have made in your own diary. If you have any queries, the next few pages of this book should clarify some of the issues.

Time	Event	Business	Venue
9.00–10.30	Departmental meeting		D24
10.30–11.00	Councillor Graham		D24
11.00–1.00	Meeting with Chief Executive	Budget issues	Main building
1.15–2.00	Accommodation inspection for health and safety hazards		
3.00–4.00	C. Ingham	Wants to discuss why he wasn't upgraded	D24
4.00–4.45	Meeting at Town Hall		?
5.00	NB CAO to telephone all department heads	Possible industrial action	

Specimen diary page of Chief Administrative Officer

Key facts on contributing to scheduling activities and resources

The importance of clear and relevant information about requests

Scheduling requires slightly more effort than merely writing the appropriate entries in the diary or planner. You have to be completely clear about what is involved. Sometimes this is easy. On other occasions you have to keep your wits about you. The important point is to make sure that you have all the information you need to enable to schedule the event effectively.

Generally, the more important or complex the event and the greater the number of people involved, the more information you need to obtain before you make a decision. For instance, if you manage the holiday rota for the department and staff leave is restricted during busy periods, you would need to know these restrictions before starting to deal with requests to schedule the actual leave.

KEY NOTES ON SCHEDULING APPOINTMENTS AND MEETINGS

Information required includes:

- the names and job titles of those involved
- where the event is to take place
- a brief indication of the nature of the business to be transacted
- an indication, if possible, of how long the event is likely to take
- what travelling time might be involved
- what documentation might be needed.

How to identify the implications of requests for other activities and resources

In some cases, all you need to do is to make the correct entry into your diary or planner. In others, however, you will be expected to carry out other back-up activities.

For example, when entering a meeting into your diary you need also to identify the other arrangements you may be expected to make – booking the room, preparing the relevant paperwork, arranging for refreshments and car parking spaces, notifying reception etc.

If your line manager asks you to book an appointment with one of the staff, you may be expected to have the relevant files ready.

If an outside visitor is booked into the diary, you may have to make sure that he or she knows how to find you, that the receptionist knows of the person's her arrival, that the relevant papers are available etc.

In some cases, the requirement for additional activities or resources may be someone else's responsibility. If, for instance, the scheduled event is a computer training session, it will probably be the responsibility of the trainer to check that he or she has all the training materials and that the machines are in working order. All you may be required to do is check the availability of the room and ensure that the relevant staff are given full details about the event.

On other occasions, you may find that you have received conflicting requests; for example:

- a room – or piece of equipment – is requested for two meetings at the same time and on the same day
- an important meeting is called for a time when your boss already has an appointment.

With resources, it is usually a matter of 'first come, first served' – but not always. If one request has been received from a senior member of staff this will normally take precedence. Dealing with this type of situation is covered more fully below.

EVIDENCE COLLECTION

Either select *at least two* events from the list below in which you have been involved and state (a) what additional activity or resources you had to identify or provide, and (b) what had to be undertaken by others; *or* select *two* other events of particular relevance to your organisation and carry out the same exercise:

a   a staff training event in the office

b   a staff training event in a hotel

c   a health and safety inspection of the work area

d   a visit from a potential buyer

e   a sales conference.

Priorities affecting how you should schedule activities and resources

Prioritising activities and resources is of major importance. Otherwise you may find yourself in the position of making a monthly check on the files to be returned to you instead of making sure that your line manager has all the papers he or she needs for an important conference that very afternoon. The classic approach towards prioritising is that you should classify each job into one of the following categories:

- important *and* very urgent
- important but not urgent
- urgent but not important
- neither very important nor extremely urgent.

An alternative approach is merely to list the activities in what you think is their order of importance. Generally speaking, factors you should bear in mind are:

- the nature of the activity
- its length
- the seniority or status of the people involved
- the location
- the repercussions if nothing is done or the activity is delayed.

CHECK IT OUT!

Look at the example of a chart, opposite, in which certain activities have been prioritised. List the activities in which you or your line manager are likely to be involved in the course of one particular week. Draft another chart indicating what your priorities would be. In each case make a brief note of the possible repercussions, if any, that could occur if you delayed too long in scheduling each activity.

Resolving conflicts

The old saying that if something can go wrong it will go wrong is very appropriate when applied to scheduling activities and appointments – particularly if you are trying to coordinate the activities of a number of people. It is an area where mistakes are readily identifiable and where arguments can erupt at any second. You have to remember that mistakes do happen. You have to be prepared to take steps to resolve the immediate problem and also, at a later date, to review why the conflict arose and how to prevent it from occurring in future.

For example, suppose that your line manager has been double-booked and two visitors arrive at the same time. Your immediate reaction should not be to blame someone else or to make it clear that you think your line manager is an incompetent idiot. With your line manager's assistance, if possible, you should try to identify which of the meetings is the more important or urgent. One of the visitors may be an internal visitor and one external – in which case you would probably try to rearrange the appointment for the internal visitor. One meeting might have been scheduled to last an hour and the other one 10 minutes, so you might therefore want to 'fit in' the shorter meeting first. If all else fails, you have to pacify the visitor who is left waiting by offering coffee, magazines and a comfortable place to wait. Long term, of course, you should identify what went wrong. Did you make a mistake or did your line manager try to 'sneak in' another appointment you knew nothing about? Was the diary entry misleading so that you read 2 pm for 3 pm, and so on? Whatever the reason you should then be well placed not to allow the same situation to occur again.

Prioritising of activities				
Activity	Important and urgent	Important but not urgent	Urgent but not important	Neither very important nor extremely urgent
Attendance at a disciplinary panel	*			
Running downstairs to stop a traffic warden issuing a parking ticket				*?
Daily telephone call to the branches asking for sales figures		*		
Daily telephone call to 3 representatives	*			
Meeting with cleaners who have threatened to down tools because of generally untidy state of offices	*			
Appraisal interview with a member of staff		*		
Meeting with external auditors	*			
Attendance at a staff training session on quality standards		*		
Annual general meeting	*			
Lunch				*?
Brainstorming session about new spring sales campaign		*		
Departmental meeting		*		
Filing today's correspondence				*

In some cases, you will need to study your organisational procedures to resolve a conflict. These may help to clarify areas of doubt such as:

- which of (various) activities normally takes precedence
- the 'rules' relating to the loan and use of equipment
- the regulations relating to staff holiday entitlement
- the number of people who can attend an external event.

If there are no procedures to provide useful guidance, talk to your line manager. Then remember the rationale that was used the next time you have a similar problem!

EVIDENCE COLLECTION

1 *Either* from your own experience indicate which of the problems outlined below you have experienced and in each case state what action you took (a) immediately and (b) in the long term to try to avoid the same mistake being made; *or* state how you would deal with those problems should they arise in the future.

   a The room you want to use for an activity is double-booked.

   b Appointments start to overlap so that people are kept waiting for long periods.

   c An emergency arises but there is not enough slack in the system to allow you to fit in another appointment.

   d A senior member of staff hijacks your schedule by insisting on seeing your manager at that very moment.

   e Someone walks off with your diary.

2 Identify *at least one* type of organisational procedure you would refer to if you were struggling to resolve a difficult conflict over a schedule for which you have responsibility.

Allowing sufficient time between activities

Scheduling activities is not a purely routine activity. A new and young member of staff may think that it is simply a question of entering all events in a diary or on a planner in chronological order. A more experienced administrator realises that other considerations have to be taken into account.

Scheduling too many appointments

If your line manager is constantly moving from one meeting to another with no break in between, not only does this eventually affect his or her energy level, but it allows no thinking time. Nor is it possible to carry out any actions that may have been promised – until a much later time. It is far better for you as the administrator to allow a certain length of time between appointments to allow your manager to write up notes of the meeting, make a few telephone calls, draw up a brief plan of action etc.

Forgetting about location

If your manager has an appointment with someone outside the organisation, you must take this into account when scheduling the person's other activities. What administrators sometimes forget is that, even if the appointment is with someone within the organisation, travelling time might still be required. If, for instance, you have scheduled an appointment from 9 am to 10 am in his or her office and then another appointment at 10 am in another part of the building, you won't be popular. If possible, it is a good idea to try to give both of you some breathing space so that you can hand over papers, check on certain points, pass on reminders etc. in the period between the appointments.

EVIDENCE COLLECTION

You must prove that you can manage *two* of the following types of schedules, using either a paper-based or a computer-based procedure:

- for an individual
- for a group of people
- for a resource.

Check that the evidence you have prepared so far for this unit meets these requirements, and that you have included a clear description of your schedules and how you create and maintain them.

Key facts on contributing to coordinating activities and resources

Bringing activities to the notice of the people concerned

Sometimes being an administrator is a bit like being in the traffic police. You are at the centre of all the activities and are responsible for directing all the events that are occurring throughout the day. On occasions this can be rather trying! An essential part of your survival kit therefore has to be your own organisational skills – particularly when you are asked to coordinate and monitor schedules.

It is not a good idea to assume that just because you have entered an appointment into a diary or planner that everyone will automatically check those entries. As an administrator you may find yourself in the position of having to check for them – and then to remind (or warn!) them of what they are supposed to be doing. It is both sensible and courteous to do this in plenty of time. Always assume that busy managers will not remember their plans in detail but expect (or hope) that you will do this for them. In this respect what you do at the beginning and the end of the day is vital.

At the start of the day

Try to pencil in a few moments each day with your line manager before any activity begins, just to ensure that you are both aware of what is happening during the day and to enable you to make any last minute adjustments. Where this is not possible because, for instance, your line manager has an appointment outside the workplace first thing in the morning, ideally you should have checked this and discussed it at the end of the previous day.

Whenever possible try to arrive before your line manager and colleagues. This allows you some time to check your planners. Where relevant you should move events from your yearly and monthly planner to your weekly planner and/or your diary. Make out a checklist of what actions you and others have to take during the day.

Check your diary and that of others to make sure that the appointments are the same. If they are not, you should make a note of the differences and check with the relevant people as soon as possible on their arrival in the workplace. Make last-minute checks on provisional appointments.

At the end of the day

It is a good idea, particularly when you are a new administrator, to review what has gone on throughout the course of the day. For instance, the day may have gone badly. You may have booked in too many appointments. Your line manager may have been in a bad mood because he or she has not had the time to have a cup of coffee before being faced with another visitor. You may have been so overloaded that you hadn't the time to monitor activities within the office.

In such circumstances, spend a few moments recovering before looking at the diary for the rest of the week to see whether or not you can do anything to avoid the same thing happening. On the other hand, if the day has gone well, you might want to check that you are repeating the success!

CHECK IT OUT!

Complete the questionnaire opposite as honestly as possible. Write brief notes of how you might try to improve your performance in the areas where you put a tick against the 'No' box. Try to encourage your colleagues to carry out the same exercise, and compare notes.

Organisation skills questionnaire		
Question: In each case tick the appropriate box	Yes	No
I am always aware of what my daily appointments are whatever time of day it is.		
I always know where my line manager is supposed to be at any time of the day.		
I always achieve all that I set out to do during the course of a day.		
I arrange my appointments so that I am able to keep a check on my line manager's appointments.		
My diary and/or planners are always up to date, easy to read and easily accessible.		
I constantly check my line manager's diary and that of any other colleagues to ensure that I am aware of any additional appointments they may have made.		
I always allow sufficient time at periods during the day so that I can assess what is going on and to make adjustments if appointments are taking longer than anticipated, an emergency arises etc.		
I never keep any visitor waiting.		

Briefing other people on appointments you helped to make

If you have booked an appointment for someone, obviously you should make sure that you have entered in details of name, title and time. However, your responsibility does not end there. You have to provide as much additional information as possible to ensure that your line manager – or anyone else involved in the appointment – has the fullest possible details of what is going to be discussed at that meeting. In some cases you might also want to provide some information about the people involved!

CHECK IT OUT!

Pick a typical day at your workplace. Look at your line manager's diary for that day and write brief notes on the additional information you had to provide (or make sure that he or she had) for each appointment.

Procedures for booking rooms, equipment and other resources

The first point to note is that, unless you work in a very well-resourced organisation, this is an area where you may frequently receive conflicting requests. Quite simply, there may be insufficient rooms on some days, and not enough equipment or other resources to go around. There may also be special occasions during the year, such as a sales conference, when everyone wants everything – preferably yesterday.

A good system and sensible procedures will help to minimise problems. Part of this should be advance notification for unusual or particularly important requests. For instance, if you are responsible for distributing stationery, this doesn't mean you can suddenly produce 5000 special folders out of thin air if the maximum normally kept in stock is 100!

Stock systems are dealt with in more detail in Unit 312. In the cases of rooms and equipment, there should be a proper booking system which everyone knows how to use. So far as equipment is concerned, you also need a procedure to ensure it is returned, in good condition and to the right place. This is especially important if the equipment is being taken off the premises, when your procedures should also include reference to the insurance requirements.

Other types of support you may need to provide

You can almost guarantee that no matter what the appointment or activity, you will have to provide some additional support to it – as the table opposite indicates. In some cases you can gather together what is required minutes before the activity begins. In other cases, of course, much more time is needed. As always it is a question of planning ahead.

At other times, minor or even major alterations or adjustments to a schedule may have to be made at a late stage. If you need to notify one or several people of changes to arrangements, several communication methods are available – letter, memo, e-mail or telephone, for instance.

If the matter is important and only known at the last minute, ensure that each person receives the information. This can mean ringing everyone yourself or 'walking the job' to find each person. Don't rely on e-mail or people passing on messages in this situation, especially if the information is critical.

Documentation/other material normally required at certain events	
Event	Paperwork/equipment required
Meetings	Agenda: notes of previous meeting: attendance register: supplementary papers: diary: accommodation: refreshments
Presentations/staff development activities	OHTs: PowerPoint® material: own notes: briefing notes for audience: training manuals: attendance register: OHP: accommodation: refreshments
Outside visits	Meeting papers eg sales literature: business cards: laptop computer: diary: map: itinerary: calculator: mobile phone
Internal visits	Meetings papers: diary: accommodation: refreshments
Disciplinary/grievance interviews	Disciplinary/grievance procedures: personnel file: summary sheets for recording discussion/decision: accommodation
Planning the holiday rota	Planner: staff list: staff requests

EVIDENCE COLLECTION

Select an important appointment you organised recently. Write brief notes on what action you took before the meeting to ensure that your boss got all the back-up he or she needed. State how you dealt with any unexpected problems that occurred.

Think, for instance, of occasions where:

- someone misunderstood your requests
- reception was not informed of the visit
- the room was already occupied
- some of the paperwork had disappeared
- the computer database could not be accessed for up-to-date information
- changes had to be made at the last minute.

Other documents to consult when coordinating diaries

Keeping your own diary up to date is relatively easy provided you get into the habit of making any insertions, amendments and alterations *as soon as you know about them* – from, for example, your weekly or monthly planner, any computerised systems for which you are responsible, and paperwork which includes or confirms dates and times of arrangements (such as confirmation letters and minutes or notes of meetings which state the time the location of the next).

If the date and time of a subsequent meeting is agreed at a previous one at which you are present, you should automatically enter it at that time – and carry out the same exercise in respect of any other scheduled activity. If you delay entering any updates – because, for instance, you have scribbled them on a telephone message pad during the course of a conversation – you run the risk of forgetting to transfer the information to you diary. For that very reason, you will rarely see an administrator on the move without his or her diary clasped firmly in one hand.

Keeping a check on a number of diaries poses more problems. Even if you are very well organised and ensure that every amendment is put into all diaries within a short period of time, you may be working for people who are not as efficient as you. Some managers like to keep two diaries – one for the office and one for personal use. Unfortunately entries in one may not totally reflect the entries in the other. Some managers are very good at making appointments over the phone or rearranging meetings at the last minute, but are not as good at letting you know what changes they have made.

Where possible, you should try to train yourself (and your managers) to check and coordinate all diaries either at the beginning or the end of the working day. At least then you will limit the time in which your managers can make unauthorised entries. If you have the overall responsibility for arranging and coordinating a particular activity, it is normally good practice where possible to check with the other administrators who work for the managers involved. They are normally more cooperative!

EVIDENCE COLLECTION

You need to provide evidence that you can review and update either paper-based or computer-based schedules. Do this by preparing a set of schedules for your assessor which cover a range of different dates and which clearly show the updates and changes you made. Then attach an explanation that identifies any unusual occurrences or important factors you had to bear in mind whilst you were undertaking these reviews and updates.

Key facts on organising travel and accommodation

Obtaining clear information on all requirements

Everyone makes mistakes from time to time. Unfortunately, however, some mistakes are more costly than others! If you have misheard your boss who asks you to book a ticket to Dublin and you book one for Dubai instead, that is likely to be a far more expensive mistake than using a first-class stamp rather than a second-class one.

Obviously, wherever money is involved, it is good practice to put in writing what you think you have been asked to do and to check with your manager that what is written down is what has been agreed. In the case of travel and accommodation arrangements you need to know:

- any organisational rules and procedures (if any) which apply to the making of such arrangements – particularly which travel companies or agent you must use, and the costs of the trip
- the date and time the trip is scheduled to take place
- the destination
- the number of people involved
- the purpose of the trip – so that you can begin to gather together all the documentation required
- the type of transport
- the type of accommodation
- how payment is to be made.

EVIDENCE COLLECTION

Some organisations make this part of your work easier by asking all would-be travellers to complete a standard travel request form containing details such as:

- names, job titles and telephone extension numbers of those travelling
- destination(s)
- dates of departure and return
- type(s) of transport required
- insurance
- passport/visa requirements
- vaccination requirements
- method of payment
- other requirements.

You can then be confident that what you are actioning has been agreed. Useful evidence would be completed examples of a similar type of form used in your organisation, together with notes about how you processed each request. Alternatively, you could design such a form yourself or write brief notes of the system you currently use.

Following your organisation's procedures

If you work for a very small organisation, you or your line manager may have complete authority to make what travel and accommodation arrangements you think fit. In larger organisations, however, you will probably have to follow certain procedures when making arrangements.

Many organisations, for instance, have rules and procedures about:

- which travel agent, travel company or hotel booking agencies can be used
- the amount of money that can be spent per night on accommodation (often depending on the status of the person for whom the booking is made)
- what class of travel can be authorised – first or standard class on the rail network, economy or club class if travelling by air etc.
- the mileage allowance permitted if a car is used
- the distance to be travelled before overnight accommodation is allowed
- the subsistence allowance – for meals, snacks, entertainment, other allowable expenses etc.
- how payment is to be made – by prepayment or reimbursement through an expenses claim.

Moreover, if your organisation is one in which a number of employees are engaged in regular trips either in the UK or abroad, you may find that the travel and accommodation arrangements are made through a central unit and that all you need to do is to follow its procedures. Obviously this saves you a lot of time and trouble.

EVIDENCE COLLECTION

If you work in an organisation which does have a standard set of procedures to be followed for making travel and accommodation arrangements, collect together a set of them and identify how they relate to your own role. You can personalise these further by highlighting those which particularly apply to your own job. If you work in a small firm and follow your own procedures, again state what these are and state which type of decisions you would be allowed to take yourself and which you would have to refer to your manager.

How to obtain travel documents

Nearly any trip, however, small, creates a huge amount of paperwork. See the Key Notes opposite.

KEY NOTES ON TRAVEL DOCUMENTATION

Basic documentation

- air, rail, ferry tickets
- rail warrants
- hire car information
- hotel reservations and vouchers
- timetables and map(s)
- passport (and possibly a visa)
- general insurance – medical expenses, personal liability, cancellation or early return, belongings and luggage, money, delayed departure
- additional vehicle insurance if travelling abroad – pre-departure protection, roadside assistance and recovery, vehicle out of use, repatriation of vehicle and passengers, emergency repairs
- current vaccination certificates
- if visiting the EU – Form E111 to prove entitlement to free or low-cost medical treatment.

Documentation you may need to prepare

- a travel folder containing all the relevant information for the trip
- two itineraries – one detailed and one summarised and attached to the front of the folder
- letters and faxes of confirmation for hotels and car hire
- business documentation – contracts, presentation material, sales catalogues and brochures, price lists, reports, journal articles, copies of letters or faxes confirming appointments
- additional notes on the people involved – names, addresses, telephone and fax numbers of organisations, customers, local agents etc.
- names, addresses and telephone numbers of emergency contacts and organisational contacts
- list of travellers' cheques and currency receipts.

Documentation you may need to obtain

- the ATA **carnet** – one document covering all merchandise taken abroad (e.g. samples of commercial products) during the forthcoming year.

Accommodation arrangements to be completed

You may make a hotel reservation direct with the hotel or through your travel agent or a hotel reservations agency. The last two are more reliable methods for hotels abroad, particularly in a non-English speaking country.

Before any booking is made you need to check on:

- the number of people travelling and their names
- the time and date of arrival
- the date of departure
- type of accommodation required
- whether any meals are required (in some countries, such as the US, room only is the most commonly available accommodation)
- how the bill will be settled (e.g. by credit card, cash or through the booking agency).

It is not normal to expect a hotel to send an invoice, unless your organisation uses it frequently and has a credit account.

If your group will arrive late (after about 6 pm), then do make sure the hotel is aware of this so that the accommodation is retained for them. Normally, too, guests in international hotels must check out by 12 noon. If your group will be later than this, ensure there will be somewhere to leave luggage and perhaps a courtesy room available they can use before they leave.

Do remember that if problems occur they may be difficult to deal with – particularly if you are in the office and your line manager is 1000 miles away! Obviously, therefore, you have to be even more particular about the arrangements you make and make sure you have confirmed them in writing by fax, e-mail or letter if you have made the arrangements yourself.

KEY NOTES ON BOOKING ACCOMMODATION

- Make certain you write down all your requirements before speaking to the relevant hotel staff.

- After making your requests clear, ask the reservations clerk to repeat the information to you so that you can be satisfied he or she has understood what you want. Unless you are good linguist yourself, when contacting a hotel abroad ask first of all for someone who can speak and understand English.

- Prepare and send a letter of confirmation (or fax or e-mail) and keep a copy of it to be included in the relevant travel folder. If you receive a travel voucher/confirmation from an agent, check every detail very carefully.

INFORMATION UPDATE

If you have to make independent arrangements for travel and accommodation, you might find the following sources of reference useful:

- *ABC World Airways Guide*
- *International Air Travel Handbook*
- *GB Passenger Railway Timetable*
- timetables from the train operating companies you use regularly. Check websites such as www.rail.co.uk, www.railtrack.co.uk, www.thetrainline.com, www.railtimetable.co.uk
- ferry timetables
- AA guide or www.theAA.com
- *Royal Mail Overseas Business Travel* – tips and guide for the overseas business traveller. Check the website www.royalmail.co.uk
- journals such as *Business Travel World*, *Business Traveller* and *Executive Travel*
- CD-ROMs such as *AA Milemaster*. For the AA Route Planner, travel news and updates check the website www.theAA.com.

Even if you rely upon other internal or external agencies to do this job for you, you might still find it helpful to access the above sources for initial information so that when you discuss arrangements with agency staff you can do so more knowledgeably.

Providing information and documents in good time

Consider the difference between the following two scenarios.

Christina is expected to prepare some paperwork for a number of her line manager's appointments this week. These include a sales staff meeting and interviews for an administrative post. She has to ensure that her manager is provided with:

- briefing notes for the meeting
- a folder containing the interview candidates' application forms, a copy of the job description, an interview schedule and a list of possible questions.

If Christina forgets to prepare one of these documents or to include them in the relevant folder, her line manager will perhaps be irritated but the situation can be remedied almost immediately by a quick phone call to her.

Baz, on the other hand, is responsible for preparing some travel documentation for his manager who is setting off on a sales trip round southern France the next day. At 4 pm Baz's manager comes in to see him in a panic because he hasn't yet been given the travel folder he needs. Baz puts everything together in 10 minutes and his manager is pacified. At 10 am the following day, when the manager is on the plane to Nice, Baz finds the itinerary on his desk – in the rush he has forgotten to include it. The situation is not irreversible – given the existence of modern methods of communications such as fax and e-mail – but it is not one that an efficient administrator should allow to arise.

You need a good system for storing and keeping paperwork relating to one particular trip or visit. Many administrators who make many travel arrangements organise files by date of travel, which is sometimes easier than by a person's name. Make sure everything is complete and neatly stored by checking off all the relevant travel documents against a master checklist, as you receive them. This avoids a last-minute panic because something hasn't been received yet. Then prepare the travel file for your boss in plenty of time. Most managers like to have a quick 'flick' through it to check that everything is there – and this is a useful double-check for you, too.

Problems and how to deal with them

If you are used to dealing with travel arrangements, you are likely to be thinking now: 'What problems *don't* occur?' Problems can arise because of:

- missing, incomplete, incorrect or late travel documentation
- sudden changes to schedules
- accidents, mishaps and loss
- traffic delays and flight delays (often because of poor weather)

to name but a few! Because arranging a trip – particularly one overseas – can be so complicated, you will be very fortunate indeed if you never face any problems. The secret is not to panic if you have to assist in changing plans, notifying other people of changes or obtaining help and advice.

Key sources of advice are:

- your travel agent (for travel rearrangements and problems)
- your travel insurance company (for accidents and loss)
- the British embassy in the country concerned (for loss of passport)
- your nearest passport office (for obtaining a passport quickly)
- the Foreign and Commonwealth office (for serious incidents abroad)
- other embassies and consulates (for direct advice on visas etc.)
- your organisation's bank (for problems/advice on money abroad)
- more experienced colleagues – if you are completely stuck!

The final, critical point is to make sure you know how to contact your boss (and vice versa) at all stages of the trip in an emergency. Mobile phones and laptops which can receive e-mail anywhere have improved communications enormously. If you have a serious problem to solve, the last thing you need is no contact number in a crisis!

INFORMATION UPDATE

Many travel organisers find the Internet invaluable when booking travel. All major airlines, hotel groups and booking agencies have websites, many with on-line timetables. One of the most useful timetables for administrators is the Railtrack site, so it is worth accessing this now to see how it works.

You can also obtain information on any foreign country by accessing the Internet or contacting the appropriate embassy or consultate. The Foreign and Commonwealth Office provides regular updates on travel abroad and is particularly useful if you have staff considering visiting a country where there may be particular problems. The Department of Health, too, provides useful travel advice on its website.

If you identify any particularly useful websites, remember to note them (or add them to Favourites) for future reference. Sites to try at the beginning include:

- www.railtrack.co.uk/travel (then click on *timetable*)
- www.eurostar.com
- www.fco.gov.uk (then click on *travelling overseas*)
- www.doh.gov.uk/traveladvice/information.htm
- www.britishairways.com
- www.easyjet.co.uk
- travel.world.co.uk/index.htm
- city.net/countries.

EVIDENCE COLLECTION

1   You have to provide evidence that you can organise *two* of the following types of travel:

   a   public transport
   b   hired vehicle (e.g. hire car or taxi)
   c   private vehicle

   and organise travel and accommodation *either* within the UK *or* within another country.

   You will find this easier if you collect together information on two trips you have dealt with which cover these requirements. Group together all the relevant paperwork, state which procedures you needed to follow, the travel documents you obtained and the accommodation arrangements required.

2   Look at the list of possible problems given below.

   a   Your manager leaves her travel folder on the plane.
   b   She turns up at the hotel only to find the accommodation unsatisfactory and completely different from what was agreed.
   c   Her car is stolen from the car park.
   d   You get a phone call to say that the departure of the plane has been delayed for three hours, so your boss cannot make her first appointment.
   e   You get a phone call from the host organisation – after your boss has left for the train station – saying that the venue for the meeting in Leeds has been changed.
   f   Your boss wants a technical expert to accompany her on a trip abroad and you find out only at the last minute that this 'expert' hasn't a passport.

   Either select those you have experienced yourself and make brief notes on how you resolved them; *or* give *at least three* examples of other problems you have had to resolve in your workplace and state how you did so.

Option Unit 312 Order, store and distribute supplies

FOCUS OF THE UNIT

To obtain this unit you must be able to:

- **order** the supplies required
- **store** supplies safely and securely
- **distribute** supplies to users.

EVIDENCE COLLECTION

It will make evidence collection easier if you can obtain the following information:

a a description of your own job role in relation to ordering, storing and distributing supplies

b a copy of any organisational procedures with which you must comply – these may include your procedures for adding new suppliers to an approved list, the procedures for placing orders with suppliers, the terms and conditions that are required, procedures relating to the storage of supplies, and procedures relating to the distribution of supplies

c a copy of your approved supplier list – preferably with any updates you have made

d a copy of any documents relating to stock-taking, including procedures you must follow, the results of stock takes and how discrepancies were dealt with

e copies of all the paperwork you use in relating to ordering supplies, recording items in stock and distributing these to authorised users.

Ordering, storing and distributing supplies

Legal and organisational requirements

As a buyer of supplies, your company is protected by consumer legislation. However, it is doubtful that you can expect your supplier to advise on your rights! Although this is a highly specialised area, you need a basic understanding of:

- the law of contract
- the major consumer protection laws.

You will then know better when you have a valid complaint and should take action.

Contractual issues

A **contract of sale** denotes a legal agreement between a supplier and a purchaser. For a contract to be valid, five basic requirements must be met.

- **Capacity** means that each party must be legally capable of making the contract. For instance, they must be of sound mind (e.g. not have a serious mental disorder or be drunk). This is important as your organisation may be able to argue that this requirement has not been met if an unauthorised person or non-employee placed an order and a supplier did not check their authority to do so.
- **Offer** relates to the fact that the buyer must normally make an offer to buy. This can be a verbal or written offer but must be specific and relate to a stated price. The supplier does not have to accept this offer. Furthermore the offer lapses if there is no acceptance within a reasonable time. The buyer can also revoke the offer at any time before it has been accepted.
- **Acceptance** must be communicated to the person who makes the offer. This may be by verbal or written statement or by 'conduct' for example the seller passes the goods to you and takes your money. The acceptance must also be unqualified – it must match the offer. If the supplier argues a changed price then this is a counter offer and you can decide whether or not to accept.
- **Consideration** only applies in England and Wales. Consideration means that the contract must involve some kind of payment or other consideration. Under normal circumstances, the law isn't interested in the price paid. Only if the consideration seems very inappropriate might there be some concern that undue pressure has been exerted on one party to the contract.
- **Intention to create legal relations.** The courts will always assume that if you want to make a purchase you freely intend to create a legal relationship with the seller, unless it can be proved otherwise.

Terms

The terms of the contract may be express or implied.

- **Express terms** are specifically stated, either verbally or in writing. For instance, you may order an item of equipment on the proviso that it is delivered before a specific date, because you need it for a special event. However, the supplier has to comply with this request only if you include it as a condition in the contract. The phrase to use here is 'time is of the essence' and put this in writing, so you have proof later, if needed.

- **Implied terms** are those that the courts accept are the clear, but unexpressed, intentions of both parties. For instance, it is implied that you intend to pay a reasonable price – you can't expect to receive it for nothing.

Note that terms can also be implied by Acts of Parliament, such as the **Sale of Goods Act** 1979 (and its subsequent amendments) – see also page 510.

However, terms can also be categorised in two other ways and this distinction is very important.

- A **condition** is a vital term, so important that the contract is invalid if the term is not met. For instance, you could reasonably expect a computer to contain a processor and memory so that it functions properly. If it does not, you could reject the contract and claim damages.
- A **warranty** is a less important term. For instance, if you had asked for a computer with a sound card, but this was not supplied, this would be classed as a warranty – even though it is part of the contract. You couldn't reject the contract in this situation but could take action to claim damages so that you pay less for the computer unless the sound card is fitted.

In Scottish law this distinction between conditions and warranties does not exist, although a similar distinction is made between 'material' and 'non-material' parts of the contract.

Termination

A contract can be ended in one of three ways:

- by **performance** – you accept the goods and start to use them
- by **agreement** between both parties – you change your mind, the supplier accepts this and arranges a refund
- by **breach** – one party has not carried out his or her part of the contract (it is at this point that the difference between a condition and a warranty becomes very important).

CHECK IT OUT!

The terms of sale for routine supplies you purchase may be stated in a catalogue and on the purchase order. A purchase of expensive equipment or special items may have specific terms agreed which are set out in writing. This is particularly the case if your organisation wants to negotiate certain terms for some reason. A complex contract is normally checked by an organisation's legal department or solicitors before it is agreed.

Find at least three examples of terms for supplies you purchase. In addition, find out if your organisation has had any problems with breach of contract and what action was taken.

KEY NOTES ON CONSUMER LEGISLATION

The main Acts you need to know about are:

- the Sale of Goods Act 1979 and its amendments in 1994 and 1995
- the Consumer Protection Act 1987
- the Trade Descriptions Act 1968
- the Unfair Contract Terms Act 1977.

The Sale of Goods Act is concerned with the condition of the goods. Under this Act, all goods must be:

- as described – they must conform to their description
- of satisfactory quality, in relation to price, description and age
- fit for the purpose for which they are intended – e.g. a pen must write!

In addition, goods must be fit for any specific purpose made clear by the buyer at the time of sale. The buyer of unsatisfactory goods is entitled to a refund from the seller and does not have to accept a credit note. Rights to a refund are not lost if the buyer agrees to a free repair which later proves to be unsatisfactory. Second-hand and sale goods are also covered but a buyer cannot complain about a fault which was specifically pointed out at the time of purchase.

The Consumer Protection Act 1987 relates to price and safety. It is an offence to:

- mislead a buyer as to price (e.g. by not quoting VAT)
- mislead a buyer over sale prices or price reductions
- supply goods which are not reasonably safe.

The Trade Descriptions Act 1968 relates to the descriptions of goods. It is an offence to:

- sell goods which are wrongly described by the manufacturer
- imply misleading descriptions – e.g. pictures in a catalogue which give a false impression
- mislead the buyer over any other aspects of the goods – e.g. method of manufacture, quantity, size, composition etc.

The spoken word of the seller usually overrides the written description of the goods – so a glib salesperson who misleads you would be guilty, though this may be difficult to prove!

The Unfair Contract Terms Act 1977 prevents sellers from limiting or taking away a customers legal rights under the Sale of Goods Act, for example by an unfair term in the contract.

Organisational requirements

If you work for a large organisation, there will be specific procedures you must follow. In a small firm, these may be less precise, but it is sensible if there are some controls over the purchase, storage and usage of supplies. These are needed to ensure that:

- the organisation does not enter into an undesirable or unlawful contract
- there are full records of all contracts and transactions in case a claim needs to be made against a supplier
- competitive prices are paid
- the most economic quanities for need are ordered and stored
- incorrect or damaged stock is not paid for inadvertently
- wastage through depreciation, deterioration or obsolescence is minimised
- the company benefits from suppliers' discounts wherever possible
- critical items are always kept in stock
- pilfering and misuse are prevented.

The requirements are therefore likely to take the form of:

- a specific purchase ordering system, whereby official orders must be signed by an authorised person
- an approved supplier list
- a limit on the amount of stock held and/or capital tied up in stock through budgetary controls
- specific storage arrangements to keep stock in good condition and restrict access.
- specific, controlled distribution arrangements.

See pages 515, 521 and 527 for further information.

EVIDENCE COLLECTION

Investigate the range of organisational requirements that currently exist in your organisation and with which you must comply. Then personalise these by adding your own comments in relation to their comprehensiveness and effectiveness. If there are problems operating these, on occasion, note this and keep your notes safely (see page 515). Do the same if you think the requirements are rather inadequate and should be improved (this may be the case if you work for a small firm).

Supplying to people in your own organisation

If you work in a small firm, you may provide supplies to everyone – but this may mean your own team of six or seven! If you work in a large organisation you may provide supplies to:

- people within your team
- people in your department
- people outside your department.

The system you follow may depend upon:

- the degree to which there are any formal procedures or controls
- the degree to which these are enforced
- whether there is a central purchasing facility for some, or all, of the supplies you manage (or whether you are that facility!)
- whether budget allocations mean that transfer payments must be made for goods sent from one department to another.

CHECK IT OUT!

If you are interested in investigating consumer legislation further then you can contact your local Trading Standards Office for information. Or – without moving from your desk – you could access one of the many consumer sites on the Internet, such as the Office of Fair Trading at www.oft.gov.uk, Trading Standards Central at www.tradingstandards.gov.uk or Tsnet at www.xodesign.co.uk/tsnet. Or you may find your own region has its own site, such as the Oxfordshire Trading Standards on www.oxon-tss.org.uk (from this site you can link to your own area).

It is important that you do this if you work for a small firm which contacts a solicitor only over specific matters, so that you know where to get advice if you think you have a claim against a supplier.

Your level of authority

This relates to the actions you can or cannot take in different circumstances. You are wise if you consider them in the following areas:

- the range of tasks you are expected to do without supervision
- the issues you should query and upon which you need your boss's decision
- the degree to which you are expected or encouraged to use your initiative
- the official authority you have over staff (considerable, little or none!).

Do be aware that exceeding your authority is always dangerous. This is not just because it may annoy your boss and your colleagues but because *you* are responsible if there are any serious consequences.

KEY NOTES ON DEALING WITH DIFFERENT USERS

Team members

- may expect to obtain supplies at any time
- may feel paperwork is pointless
- may resist formal controls.

This might be acceptable in a very small firm, but would compromise you in a large organisation. Be firm and unwavering if you are simply trying to do a professional job and are following procedures. If team members persist, ask them for acceptable suggestions/improvements and ask your team leader to raise the issue at a team meeting. Don't have favourites or bend the rules for anyone, or you make a rod for your own back!

Departmental members

- cannot reasonably expect supplies 'on tap' if it is a large department
- should realise that you need some system to monitor usage (you can't remember everyone!)
- will, however, expect some flexibility in an emergency (this is reasonable – see page 528).

Get people used to the system from the outset (particularly new staff who are not in a position to object). Be flexible, but guard against the abuser of the flexible system whose life is a continual emergency! Refer usage problems to the line manager, don't tackle a colleague direct (see page 525).

Other users, outside your department

- There may be a formal system of requisitioning supplies.
- There may be an accounting system for budget transfers.
- Bear in mind status, if you supply everyone. Senior managers may try to circumvent the systems (and are difficult to refuse).

The larger the number of users you supply, the more formal a system you need. Keep your records up to date, and check new names/requests to ensure authenticity. Have a list of authorised signatories and stick to this to please your finance department/auditors. Keep accounting records up to date to avoid problems if budgets become depleted towards the end of the financial year. Ask for your own manager's support in dealing with unacceptable requests from senior colleagues.

There is a difference between exceeding your authority and using initiative. The latter can be demonstrated by the type of suggestions you make and on which you request approval. There is also often a difference between official authority and 'custom and practice'. If you have always done something, but don't really know if you should be doing it, the key question to ask is: 'Who would be to blame if there was a serious problem?'

Always err on the side of caution, particularly if the limits of your authority are not written down. And if this is the case, why not draft them out yourself? (See below.)

EVIDENCE COLLECTION

To help your assessor, write a brief report on the range of people to whom you provide supplies and identify any differences there are in the ways you deal with the various groups. If you can, provide a rationale to show there is a good reason for this – i.e. it's not just because you are biased towards one group!

If you have a formal job description which clearly specifies your role, add to this with your own comments on your authority. Even better, prepare brief lists of tasks you (a) can do alone, (b) need to refer upwards for approval, and (c) must not do. Ask your line manager to countersign this for authenticity.

 KEY NOTES ON THE IMPORTANCE OF KEEPING ACCURATE RECORDS

Accurate, reliable and up-to-date records are important at each stage of process to ensure that:

- all orders can be tracked by your auditors
- detailed documents are available if there is a dispute or legal claim
- stock-takes can be carried out and the reason for discrepancies identified more easily (see page 524)
- payments are made only for goods that have been delivered in good condition
- payments are made promptly to take advantage of discounts
- goods are ordered only in accordance with organisational procedures
- the quantity and quality of supplies is constantly controlled
- usage is monitored so that action can be taken as appropriate
- only authorised users are allocated supplies.

Recommending improvements

No system is perfect, as you learned when you studied Unit 304. Over time, even the best system becomes out of date and needs changing. There will be various 'signals' to alert you to this. For example:

- users complain of excessive paperwork, lack of flexibility and problems with supplies
- you are asked by finance (or your boss) for paperwork you don't possess or that doesn't exist
- you have forms you never use or which take ages to complete or which don't ask for the right information
- you are still using a manual system even though everything else in the office is computerised
- the system isn't working – records don't correctly reflect stock held, your supplier list is out of date, there are problems during stock-takes, invoices are paid late etc.

In any of these cases it is sensible to review the system – as you will see on pages 529 and 530.

EVIDENCE COLLECTION

Start a file labelled 'suggestions and possible improvements'. Into this put suggestions from staff and ideas you have had to improve the system. This folder will becoming invaluable when you reach element 312.3.

Alternatively, consider devising a questionnaire to obtain the information you need. You might be sensible to complete most of this unit before you issue the questionnaire, in case more ideas come to mind as you progress. However, remember that staff will always be more keen to implement a suggestion they have thought of (even if you've had to modify it a little) rather than one you have imposed upon them.

Key facts on ordering supplies required

Establishing clearly what supplies are required

For routine items the following considerations are critical. It is sensible to determine these at management level to prevent any misunderstandings.

- What routine items must be stocked to fulfil user needs on a day-to-day basis?
- What quantities of each item need to be stocked, considering budget and space restrictions?

- What variances are there in demand during the year (e.g. to meet the needs of organisers of special events)?
- What long-term trends in usage affect the types of item stocked (e.g. changing from deskjet to laser printers will affect the type of cartridges stocked)?

 KEY NOTES ON DETERMINING LEVELS OF SUPPLIES

Three main systems are used.

Periodic review

In this system a set level for each item is determined against current usage. An order point is specified which allows for the keeping of a **buffer stock** to supply users until new goods are received. The identification of appropriate 'periods' is crucial.

If reviews are frequent (e.g. weekly) then there is virtually a continuous stream of orders to suppliers. The main advantage is flexibility. A disadvantage is the need for constant monitoring of stock levels and loss of discounts in some cases.

If reviews are infrequent (e.g. every two months) then larger stocks must be held as reviews and re-ordering occur less frequently. Stock levels must also take into account seasonal trends. An advantage, however, is bulk ordering to maximise discount opportunities. However, the system is inflexible and stock shortages may occur if usage of an item changes before the next review date.

Economic order quantity (EOQ)

The aim here is to find the most financially efficient quantity of goods to stock. This is calculated by comparing the cost of ordering with the costs of storage *for each item*. Goods that are used rarely and which take up little room will therefore be ordered infrequently. Goods used often which take up space are ordered frequently. The advantage is cost-effectiveness. However, it is also complicated to calculate, so rarely used for stationery items.

Just in time (JIT)

Originally formulated for production stock control, this method has been extended to cover other types of stocks, such as stationery. The idea is to find suppliers who will deliver quickly – 'just-in-time' for usage. This reduces storage space and maximises flexibility. The disadvantages are a limited range of suppliers who can offer this service and, possibly, a loss of discounts.

INFORMATION UPDATE

Many large stationery suppliers are taking advantage of the trend towards JIT systems by offering to supply goods in 24 hours or less. Some have websites so prices can be compared and goods ordered over the Internet. Others operate a 24-hour mail-order service to business customers.

In some regions, large companies offer a service whereby *all* stock monitoring and supply can be out-sourced. In this situation *the supplier* is contracted to visit regularly to monitor the stocks and to supply these, as required. This removes much of the work and responsibility from the administrative staff. However, it is important to obtain a supplier who is competitive and who stocks a wide range of goods. If only certain core supplies can be provided, and other items are obtained elsewhere, this defeats the purpose of the exercise.

CHECK IT OUT!

If you want to check websites of stationery supplies you can do this by accessing a search engine, such as www.ask.co.uk, and type in the question 'where can I buy office stationery?' Currently, major suppliers include www.stationerystore.co.uk, www.netstationers.co.uk and fs.officeshopper.com. Alternatively, you can access www.officea-z.co.uk and identify your own nearest supplier.

You can also obtain and compare prices from mail-order suppliers such as Staples (tel: 0800 14 14 14), Neat Ideas (tel: 0800 500 192) and Quill (tel: 0800 496 0644). Alternatively, if you more frequently order specialised computer supplies then Global Direct may be more appropriate (tel: 0870 729 7929 or www.globaldirect.co.uk).

The range of suppliers available

It is doubtful that you will start from scratch with building up a range of suppliers, unless you are employed by a completely new firm. You are more likely to find yourself in one of the following situations.

- You have a central purchasing department which places all orders on behalf of your organisation.
- You have a list of approved suppliers and you can use only these.
- You have a list of approved suppliers for major items but can select your own suppliers for other items. You can also suggest additions or deletions from your own experiences.
- There is no formal list, but there are certain suppliers in your area which your firm normally uses.

It is sensible to review any supplier list from time to time to confirm that their prices and service are still competitive. If this exercise is not undertaken by your organisation then one improvement you could suggest is that this becomes a regular process.

EVIDENCE COLLECTION

Describe how the supplier list in your organisation has been decided. State the degree of flexibility you have in amending or reviewing this. Give examples to support your claims and ask your line manager to countersign your statement.

Attach your current supplier list as additional evidence. If this is reviewed or amended during the time you are studying for this award, attach the updated version, too.

Agreeing terms and conditions

For general goods, the terms and conditions of supply will be specified on the company's website, on the price list or in the catalogue. Remember these form part of the contract. Special terms and conditions would apply when:

- you make it clear, in writing, that the goods must be delivered by a certain date (see page 508)
- you request a particular specification for an item (e.g. paper weight, paper size, colour etc.) and make it clear that substitutes will not be acceptable
- you buy goods subject to a particular offer (e.g. at a special discount).

Remember that your legal rights are still the same, even if the goods you buy are on special offer.

You can also try to negotiate special terms if you are placing a very large order. Your employer may also encourage you to 'shop around' to see which supplier will make you the best offer (see below).

Do make sure that you are well aware of the limits of your authority in negotiating terms and conditions and that you never overstep these. The danger areas to avoid are listed below.

- Never spend more than you are authorised.
- Never contact unauthorised suppliers without permission.
- Never make 'unofficial' arrangements. All your supplies must be ordered following the correct procedures. Otherwise you are likely to be in serious trouble with your finance department and auditors!
- Never accept 'gifts' from a supplier in return for placing an order. You could be accused of accepting a bribe.
- Never agree unusual payment terms without checking first.

Finally, make sure any special terms or conditions are clearly stated on your official order.

KEY NOTES ON NEGOTIATING TERMS AND CONDITIONS

- Don't tell each firm what their competitors have quoted – simply state their *names*. For example: 'We've had an offer from XYZ Co. to supply our new order of photocopying paper. However, as we normally deal with you, I wanted to give you the opportunity to quote as well.'

- Sound surprised (or even horrified) at the first figure, e.g. '£2500, as much as that?' Then wait for a response.

- See what else the sales person will offer. This may be a lower price, other items thrown in 'free' or a better discount if payment is within a certain period.

- If you are talking to a junior member of staff, who hasn't the power to negotiate, suggest the issue is placed before his or her supervisor: 'I'm sorry you can't help us more than that. Given we've been a good customer for many years, could you have a word with your manager about this and get back to me?'

- Never rush to 'close' the deal. There are plenty of other people you could ring. After you've finally asked the key question, 'Is that your final offer?', keep quiet. Let the other person break the silence.

Seeking guidance

There are various occasions when you may need to seek guidance:

- when a supplier contacts you to notify you about a special offer
- when, during negotiations, you are made an unexpected offer or asked to promise specific payment terms
- when a supplier contacts you about a significant problem relating to a delivery or item
- when a supplier cannot agree the terms and conditions you want and tries to renegotiate these.

In some situations you may have to contact your line manager for guidance (or your supervisor or team leader). In others you may need to contact a specialist. This may be someone who is familiar with the needs of the users, the user who needs the item, or a finance person. Alternatively, it could be someone else who knows your organisation's procedures very well and can advise you on how to respond.

Chasing up orders

Finally, it is *your* job to chase up orders with suppliers if they are not received by the agreed date. Make sure you have all your documentation to hand and can quote your order number, date, quantity and any other references. Make sure you obtain the name of the person you speak to. Quote any special terms – particularly if a specific date was agreed. Bear in mind that your response to the situation will depend upon:

- the 'reasonableness' of the excuse for late delivery
- the normal reliability of this supplier
- the effect upon the users (e.g. from marginal to critical).

Do remember to remain professional, calm and polite. You can be assertive without losing your temper. Don't enter into an argument, simply state the facts and ask for an explanation and a *precise* delivery time and date, if the goods are important. If this is not forthcoming then, in drastic circumstances, you may need to be prepared to cancel the order and change your supplier – but check with your line manager before you take that step.

CHECK IT OUT!

You are ordering paper for your office laser printer when you are informed of the following facts.

a Because of a special offer, you would obtain 15 per cent discount if you bought twice as much.

b Because of a special offer, if you bought a minimum of 1000 reams you would receive 15 per cent discount on your laser cartridges.

c Because of distribution problems, your previous order for photocopying paper cannot be met until a week on Monday unless you accept a lower grade of paper than normal.

d The laser printer paper you normally use is no longer stocked and you are asked whether you will accept another brand.

e The supplier has reviewed their policies and is offering 10 per cent discount to all organisations which place a minimum of £20,000 of orders a year. At present you order from three different suppliers and spend about £12,000 with each one.

f You are told that as the last three invoices to your organisation still remain unpaid, no goods can be delivered. This includes the two orders you placed with them last week.

Check, in each case, what you should do to comply with your organisational procedures. If you would need to obtain guidance, identify whom you should ask in each case.

Key facts on storing supplies safely and securely

Suitable storage areas

The main considerations in relation to storage are the following.

1 The area selected should be suitable for the items being stored

Stationery items need to be stored in a clean, dry and well-ventilated area, preferably on slatted shelves. Large items of equipment should be stored safely in a separate area. Whilst all items should be stored in lockable areas, a safe is useful for very small valuables, such as traveller's cheques or foreign currency. A lockable cupboard in a working area is useful for local storage of frequently used items.

2 Health and safety considerations must be borne in mind at all times

- Hazardous items are covered by COSHH (see Unit 302, page 114) and may need to be kept in a separate area. Inflammable items are clearly marked and may also need to be kept separately. It is sensible to draw up your own safety sheet on the action to take if any substance is spilled or inhaled.

- No items should be stored in areas where smoking is permitted.

- Small, sharp items (such as drawing pins or scissors) should be clearly visible and kept in boxes wherever possible.

- Heavy items should be stored on the floor or on low shelves and should be handled properly, in accordance with the Manual Handling Regulations (see Unit 302, page 102). The correct equipment for lifting and moving heavy loads must be available, such as sack trucks. (The origin of this name comes from when sacks were moved around, rather than paper!) If many items are frequently moved around a building it is sensible to have trolleys in different sizes as well.

3 Sensible security precautions should be in force

These include restricted access, a limited number of named key holders and an established procedure for fulfilling orders. It is important to remember that small items, whilst they may be less valuable, are often subject to pilfering more frequently than larger items of equipment which are difficult to remove undetected. Examples of security precautions include:

- tamper-proof labels which clearly denote the owner of the equipment
- security locks and cages which prevent computer tampering or removal.

4 Good housekeeping should prevail

Good housekeeping includes:

- having a place for everything – and everything in its place
- storing new stock below or behind old stock, so the latter is used first – this is known as stock rotation
- keeping working areas (e.g. in front of shelves) clear of boxes and other equipment.

CHECK IT OUT!

Accurate, reliable and up-to-date records are essential. Although the system used by different organisations varies, you can check whether your system is up to scratch by seeing how confidently you can answer each of the following questions.

Within five minutes can you:

a identify exactly which items are currently on order but haven't been received and say when these will be delivered?

b identify any items that are overdue and say why there is a delay?

c list all the items that have been delivered this week?

d list all items which have been received in the last month over which there has been a problem (e.g. incorrect items or quantity delivered) – and state what has been done about this?

e state the quantity in stock of any item?

If you have hesitated over answering any of these questions, perhaps you may have another idea for your improvement file!

Resolving problems with suppliers

Sensible suppliers want to please their customers – for obvious reasons. However, problems can arise because of human error. These may result in you receiving:

- the incorrect goods or an unacceptable substitute
- the incorrect quantity (but check to see if the balance is marked 'to follow')
- damaged or faulty goods
- goods you didn't order at all
- no delivery, when you expected one.

You have already seen how to chase up late deliveries (page 520). In the same way, action must be taken if there is any other problem with a delivery, but in such a way that you maintain good working relations with your supplier. If, later, it is decided that a supplier is regularly unreliable that is a separate issue – and not for discussion when you are querying a particular delivery.

EVIDENCE COLLECTION

You have already seen how goods should be handled safely and what security considerations apply (pages 521 and 522). As evidence for this element you should do the following.

1 Prepare a description of the storage systems for items for which you are responsible. This should include all health and safety and security precautions that are in place. Attach any organisational requirements or procedures you must follow and highlight those which are specifically related to your own area.

2 Prepare a description of the records you keep in relation to the receipt and storage of supplies, together with examples. If you have been involved in any discussions about discrepancies with your suppliers it will help if you can describe these and attach relevant paperwork. Don't forget to state the outcome!

 KEY NOTES ON COPING WITH DELIVERY PROBLEMS

- Count the goods carefully and check against *both* your order, *their* delivery or advice note and *your* goods received note, if your organisation uses this system.
- Check 'unexpected' deliveries against previous deliveries which may have been incomplete.

- Check descriptions against your order, the delivery note *and* the catalogue description.
- Put any unwanted, damaged or faulty items on one side and label these, so they are not used in error and are kept separate for collection.
- Telephone the supplier immediately and explain the discrepancy. Be prepared to quote the order and delivery note numbers.
- Remember your legal rights. You can return goods that are faulty or damaged and substitutes you didn't ask for. You *cannot* as a 'right' return goods you ordered in error. You need the goodwill of the supplier to do this, but if you are a good customer an exchange can probably be agreed.
- If you clearly explain the situation you should have few difficulties arranging for the problem to be rectified. Otherwise, ask to speak to the supervisor. If you are still having problems, say you will investigate further and refer the matter to *your* supervisor or line manager. Don't commit your organisation in any way or accept the blame (e.g. if there is a dispute over who damaged the goods).
- If a return is agreed, mark the documentation so that you (and/or your finance department) know that the returned goods should be credited.

Stock-taking

Stock-taking is the physical process of counting the stock and comparing actual stock with the amounts listed on the stock records. Unless you are very efficient (or lucky!) you may find several discrepancies between both amounts although, of course, the quantities should be identical. Sometimes you may have more stock than is listed, in other cases you may have less.

The first point to note is that scale and value is important. Losing 100 reams of paper is more serious than 100 paperclips! Equally, a missing camcorder is more serious than a missing stapler.

The second point is not to panic! If you find that nearly everything is 'down' by a certain amount there is probably a logical explanation. Perhaps you forgot that the sales staff keep a buffer stock in a locked cabinet in their office, or you counted the delivery that arrived yesterday which you haven't yet entered on the system.

Here are other possible reasons for discrepancies:

- you have miscounted
- an entry was made wrongly on the stock record
- stock has been 'borrowed' (this could be quite legitimate) for a special event but a record wasn't made
- stock has been issued without being 'booked out' properly (or accurately) on the record (such as in an emergency)
- faulty stock has been returned – or put to one side – but no record has been made
- stock was damaged or declared obsolete and has been disposed of
- stock has been pilfered.

However, never make any accusations, jump to conclusions or start to think of hurried explanations. Otherwise you may find yourself having to backtrack or apologise later. Instead, take a more methodical approach to ascertaining the reason for the difference.

1 If you operate a computerised system, you should be able to run an audit report. This will show you every entry on the system both for stock received and issued *and* any adjustments. You can go through this report to find all the entries for the item(s) you are investigating.

2 If you operate a manual system, then you need to ask everyone else who uses the system if they have any explanations. You also need to check all your figures carefully. If necessary, check back against the orders, delivery notes and goods received notes (GRNs). If you use a system whereby items can only be issued against orders or requisitions received from staff, then these need checking against your 'issued' amounts.

3 Finally, if it is the actual stock that is 'down', do a recount and check any other shelves or storage areas where the items may have been placed.

If you still have a discrepancy, inform your line manager. The action taken will depend upon the size of the discrepancy and the value of the stock.

On occasion you may have no discrepancies but notice some goods are damaged or otherwise unusable. In this case adjustments will have to be made to formally 'write off' the stock. It is also important to find out what caused the damage and take steps to prevent any recurrence. Another reason why items may be unusable is because they are now obsolete, such as old letterheaded paper which was printed with a previous telephone code, or old tapes for audio machines which now take digital cards. Such items can either be:

- converted into another use (such as old paper into scrap pads)
- offered to staff for a nominal amount
- 'written off' and disposed of – preferably in an environmentally friendly way!

1 Identify any items in *your* stock cupboard which are obsolete and find out how you should deal with these in your organisation.

2 Check the key notes for minimising stock-taking problems below. Then identify any areas where you could improve your systems and reduce any problems you currently experience.

KEY NOTES ON MINIMISING STOCK-TAKING PROBLEMS

- Restrict stock control duties to a limited number of responsible staff.

- Always enter items received *at the same time* as the delivery is checked and the items put away. This may mean having a separate storage area for goods still to be unpacked and recorded.

- Never issue any items unless you have an authorised requisition or order (see page 528).

- Book out stock on the stock record immediately it is issued.

- Have a system in place to deal with important emergency requests so that items aren't taken without your knowledge (see page 528).

- Write all figures clearly and concentrate whilst you do this – it is easy to transpose figures if you are distracted.

- Have a methodical filing system for your own orders, delivery notes or GRNs and requisitions.

- Never 'lend' stock without the appropriate paperwork being completed. If you have no system for this, attach a Post-it note to the record card and suggest a better system!

- Have a proper system for disposing of obsolete or damaged items so they are 'officially' taken out of the system.

- If you ever need to make any adjustments (such as for damaged items) make a note as to *why* this was done. This is essential on a computerised system but is always valuable so you don't forget.

- If you notice items have suddenly disappeared without your prior knowledge, investigate this immediately. Don't just hope they will be returned.

- Keep the stock cupboard locked to prevent unauthorised access.

When you are doing a stock-take you will normally be issued with a printed form on which the item and the recorded amount are stated. You then enter the real amount alongside, identify whether there is a discrepancy and, if so, give a reason.

If you use such forms in your organisation then retain copies for your portfolio. If you do not, you could easily produce one yourself to the headings above.

You also need to write a brief description of your stock-taking procedures. In particular, make sure you include information on:

a   how often these take place

b   any discrepancies you found and what you did

c   what action you must take if you find goods are faulty

d   what you do to dispose of obsolete items

e   what action would be taken if a sizeable discrepancy could not be explained.

Key facts on distributing supplies to users

Systems for requesting and distributing authorised supplies

If you work in a small firm and the stock cupboard is near your desk, you may be quite happy to issue items as and when they are requested. There may be no formal system, as such – people simply ask for what they need. Your boss may not mind, provided expenditure does not exceed a preset limit.

While this may work at this level, if you work in a large organisation and issue stock to a large number of people, this type of flexibility becomes unmanageable. Firstly, you would be constantly interrupted. Secondly, you would have no way of monitoring usage. While no one is expecting you to count out pencils to your colleagues on a 'two a year' basis, you should be aware if someone is asking for fifteen laser cartridges a week – just in case they are supplying half the neighbourhood as well!

The usual system is for there to be regular days/times on which stock is issued – usually within 24 hours of an order being received. However, there should be an 'emergency' system for providing goods quickly when necessary (see below). Most standard systems require users to complete an internal order or requisition form. This form is to be signed by their line manager or supervisor. Then goods are issued against this request – either daily or two or three times a week.

Your system might vary from that model, but that is not important. The key points to note are that any system should enable users to receive items promptly and orders to be regularly fulfilled accurately. The person distributing the stock must know immediately that each request has been authorised. The usual way to do this is to have a list of authorised signatories and to check the signature on the order against that list. Appropriate entries should then be made on the stock record system, ideally by person, section or department.

The aim is that you have an efficient system which effectively meets users needs. However, this is not always easy. For example, some users:

- regularly need goods urgently to respond themselves to a last-minute request (such as sales staff)
- are disorganised, so often forget to order in advance
- may need to 'borrow' items, such as for a special event like a sales conference
- may regularly underestimate their needs, so you get several orders each week from them
- may regularly overestimate their needs
- may fail to check a delivery and only tell you weeks later that something was wrong or unusable.

If there is a genuine need for an 'emergency' supplies system, it should state the reasons under which goods can be issued. It may also identify additional people who can sign such orders if a line manager or supervisor is absent at the time. On the other hand you may need to get tough with people who are regularly pestering you for items. Practice your assertiveness skills and say 'no' once or twice!

You can consider setting minimum and maximum order limits for items. The minimum is to prevent someone ordering five paperclips a week, the maximum is to prevent someone ordering 50,000 without good reason. Any amounts which would exceed the maximum limit must be agreed and countersigned by the line manager.

The system should have a clear requirement for all users to check the stock they receive and to notify you immediately if any item is damaged or not in accordance with their original order.

In addition, it is helpful if people who know they are going to need an unexpectedly large number of items warn you in advance. Telling you on Monday that 20,000 envelopes are required for a mailshot will probably decimate your envelope stocks unless you have an excellent JIT supplier, and 20,000 letter heads could cause serious problems if your printer takes two weeks to send you any more.

The value of receipts

Whilst you may never think of issuing receipts in relation to stock, they are useful if you need proof that stock has been distributed *in addition to* the authorised order. For example, if items are required urgently and no-one is available to sign the order, you can agree to issue them provided the user signs a receipt for the goods. Other examples are:

- You receive telephone authorisation to issue the items to a member of staff and the manager tells you the paperwork 'will follow'. You then ask the member of staff to sign the receipt.
- Items (or equipment) are loaned for a special event and many, if not all, will be returned afterwards.
- Items are being issued to another department or section that you don't normally deal with – possibly to help them out in an emergency.
- Equipment is being lent to members of staff for personal use. However, this may not be possible unless they can confirm it would be covered by their own insurance.

Some organisations may introduce receipting if they are concerned at current usage levels and want to investigate this in relation to particular sections or individuals. They may also wish to use receipting if there have been disputes about the quantity of items issued or the condition of certain types of equipment. Remember that you issue the top copy to the person who signs the receipt and keep a copy yourself. A small pre-printed receipt book is often all you need for this.

Finally, if ever you have any doubt about whether you should be issuing an item, but are told there is a crisis, asking the person to sign a receipt proves you have tried to be flexible and responsive and yet have 'covered your back' in relation to your own systems.

Encouraging constructive feedback

Throughout this unit you have been introduced to the concept of improving the way in which you order, store and/or distribute supplies. If you took note of the suggestion on page 515, and started an improvements file, then you may have already made several notes on this subject. Now that you are reaching the end of this unit you may want to review the improvements you have thought of and decide which you could make without any further consultation and which you would have to refer to your line manager for approval.

As you also saw on page 515, it is important to ask users for feedback – either by listening to their responses or by issuing a simple questionnaire.

It is a fact that if you ask people for feedback, they will often list their moans and groans rather than make positive suggestions! This can be dispiriting if you are trying to do a good job. You can minimise this by asking people to focus on positive good ideas rather than complaints to help to improve the system you operate.

In the same way, many of the informal comments you hear may be negative: 'I don't know where we get the paper from these days, but it's always jamming in the printer,' or 'These cartridges are running out twice as quickly as the old ones.' Interestingly, when things are running smoothly, your users will often say nothing at all!

You can actively encourage feedback by:

- making it clear that you welcome positive suggestions
- acknowledging complaints and investigating these to see if there is any truth in them
- responding as positively as you can when people complain (even if you have to grit your teeth occasionally!) rather than snapping at them
- *asking* for comments when you change a supplier or even the type of item stocked
- listening to comments relating to storage or distribution and, if there is a genuine problem, doing your best to solve this.

The suggestions you receive are likely to range from the impossible to the extremely useful. Always study even the most off-the-wall idea in case you can convert it into something useful. If you decide to try a user's suggestion, make sure your colleagues know what you are doing. This gives *them* positive feedback that you welcome and will implement their ideas when you can.

Finally, you should note that you gain the psychological advantage if you take on board other people's ideas.

- If users see that you want to use their suggestions to make improvements which will benefit everyone, then they will be more likely to cooperate.
- If you implement an idea which you personally had considerable reservations about, do so for a trial period. You now can't lose. If it works, fine. If it doesn't, then you can 'regretfully' abandon it after the trial period – but at least it can be seen that you were willing to try.

Remember, if you impose only your own ideas your users may doom them to failure through non-cooperation.

1   Identify which of the following comments might be heard in your own organisation – and how you would respond. If none is applicable, then try to think of four of your own which might be.

   a   'When you were off last week, no-one had a clue where the delivery of new Zip disks had been stored.'

   b   'Where I last worked, we could obtain stationery easily any time of the day. I don't see why we can't do that here.'

   c   'The new staplers are useless. More than six pieces of paper and they completely jam. Can't we change our supplier or spend more, next time?'

   d   'We were working late last night and had loads of photocopying to do, but ran out of paper and the stockroom was locked. What are we supposed to do in that situation?'

   e   'I'm sure this paper is damp. Can't we improve our storage facilities?'

   f   'I think it's ludicrous that in this day and age we have to wait nearly a week before we get a delivery of file folders.'

2   Following a recent dispute about stock you issued in good faith, without a requisition, you decided to introduce written receipts for items which are wanted urgently. You bought a receipt book and started this system two weeks ago but have encountered the following problems.

   When you are away from your desk either one of your two colleagues can issue stationery providing the paperwork is in order. One flatly refuses to use the receipting system because she says she doesn't understand it. The other appears to have made users sign a receipt for everything they need.

   You have received nothing but complaints about the system from users, who don't appear to understand it either. One or two are complaining that it shows they can't be trusted.

   a   What action would you take to encourage your colleagues to follow the proper system when they issue stationery in your absence?

   b   What action would you take to ensure that users understand why the system is necessary?

   c   What would you learn from this to ensure that, in future, new systems or procedures meet with more success from the outset? (You may wish to refer back to Unit 304 here for inspiration!)

EVIDENCE COLLECTION

For this unit you have to prove that you can distribute *both* consumables *and* tools or small items of equipment, to members of your team and department *and* to users external to your team or department.

1 Obtain copies of the orders or requisitions completed by users. Attach to these your own explanation of the authorisation system in operation in your own organisation and a description of how frequently you distribute supplies and what you do if an emergency occurs.

2 Prepare a description of any receipting procedure used in your organisation. If this is not used, describe how helpful you think it would be and under what circumstances you may be tempted to introduce this.

3 Prepare a summary of any improvements you think could usefully be implemented. Separate these into:

   • those which you considered yourself
   • those which emanated from user feedback.

   If you issued a questionnaire to obtain feedback, attach a copy, together with the results.

4 If possible, select one improvement and implement this, with your line manager's approval. Then state whether or not it did improve your system and met with the approval of your users.

5 Finally, ask both your line manager and a member of your team to provide witness testimony that you regularly and reliably order, store and distribute supplies to meet user needs.

Option Unit 318 Support the use of information technology systems

Important notes

1 This chapter contains a considerable amount of information which is specifically relevant to Microsoft® Windows. If you use a different system – such as MS-DOS® – or use an Apple® Macintosh® computer – then ask your supervisor or tutor to assist you to 'convert' some of the information provided for your own system.

2 It is assumed that you will not be undertaking this optional unit unless you *already* possess a good working knowledge of your organisation's computer system and software. The information here therefore focuses on additional points relevant to the knowledge and understanding requirements for the optional unit as well as specific guidance on evidence collection.

If you are concerned that your skills in any area may be insufficient, there are a variety of ways in which you can improve. You can:

- purchase a specialised guide to the software you are using (a variety of user-friendly books are available at all good booksellers)
- attend an in-company skills training course on the software package you are using
- develop your skills through the use of manuals and the Help facility, and by asking for assistance from experts in your workplace
- take a short course (flexible options are often available) at a nearby college to improve your skills in a particular package.

FOCUS OF THE UNIT

To obtain this unit you must be able to:

- **help to organise and maintain** the use of information technology
- **help other people** with their use of information technology.

EVIDENCE COLLECTION

It will make evidence collection easier if you can obtain the following information:

a a description of your own job role in relation to information technology support, including details of your IT systems, the names of users who rely upon you and the type of support you regularly provide – countersigned by your line manager ➡

Supporting the use of information technology systems

The limits of your competence and authority

Your ability to assess your own competence and limitations is important – and, in relation to IT systems, it is better to err on the side of caution than over-confidence! Deleting a system program in error, wiping an important floppy disk by mistake or making any problem worse, rather than better, is hardly likely to endear you to anyone. Therefore, unless you are *certain* you know what you are doing, and have the authority (permission) to do that operation, *don't*. No one will think any the less of you for admitting that you are facing a difficult problem and you would welcome another opinion before you do anything.

Organisational systems and procedures

In large organisations there are usually very clearly documented systems and procedures regarding the IT operations. You may have a specialist department which provides computer support, in which case only routine operations would be carried out without their help. This is also likely to be the case if you operate on a large-scale networked system with dozens of users. You may have the competence and authority to deal with minor issues in your own office, but would be expected to comply with the requirements of the computer support section at all times.

If you work in a small office, perhaps where every user has a stand-alone system or where there is a small network, supplied by an outside specialist, then you are likely to carry out a variety of support operations within your own area. You may even be the person who advises your manager on which types of problems should be referred to the specialist and which should not. However, do bear in mind that if your organisation has paid a considerable amount of money for its IT equipment and software, then this should operate effectively. Don't be tempted to do the suppliers' job for them – especially in relation to hardware or software which has recently been purchased and which isn't functioning properly. Otherwise you may breach the terms under which it was installed.

Legislation and regulations that relate to IT

There are several legal aspects which relate to IT work. This is an area that is expanding all the time. It is therefore important you keep up to date with developments as they occur.

- All IT users need to be aware of health and safety regulations – both in relation to the safe installation and maintenance of equipment and its use. There is information on this on page 106.

- In addition, you need to be aware of the current **Data Protection Act** which covers the information stored on computers and in structured manual systems. There is information on this on page 282.

- You should be aware of the main aspects of the **Computer Misuse Act** and the **Regulation of Investigatory Powers Act**, both of which relate to computer users (see the key notes below).

- Software, to be used legally, must be licensed to you or your organisation. Software which is used on a network system is usually configured differently from that for use on a PC and requires either a **site licence** – which covers the whole site – or a **network licence** which is based on a specific number of users. If you buy software for a PC, you are provided with a registration number which must be entered when the package is first installed. This denotes you are the registered user. Pirated software – whether borrowed from a friend or downloaded from the Internet – is illegal and contravenes the **Copyright, Designs and Patents Act** (see page 285).

KEY NOTES ON LEGISLATION

The Computer Misuse Act

This Act is designed to protect organisations against computer hackers or anyone who tampers or alters data or software without permission. Under the Act, it is a criminal offence for anyone to:

- gain unauthorised access to computer material (whether or not there is any intention to cause harm)
- make unauthorised modifications to computer material.

The Regulation of Investigatory Powers Act

This Act allows employers to monitor staff by listening in and recording phone calls, checking the content of e-mails and use of the Internet, and searching the hard drives of PCs and laptops.

Responsible employers issue guidelines which tell employees exactly what is allowed and what is not – but you can take it as read that, wherever you work, sending scurrilous e-mails about your boss, booking your holiday on-line, or accessing 'adult' sites from work is likely to get you into serious trouble. David Pennington and Rupert Beverley found this to their cost. Employees of a Huddersfield engineering company, they forwarded joke e-mails to their colleagues and were sacked – not only for sending the e-mails but for wasting the company's time doing so. In November 2000 their appeal to an industrial tribunal for unfair dismissal was rejected. So now you know!

CHECK IT OUT!

Look back at pages 105–107 and identify all the health and safety regulations that affect your own work with IT. Make sure you are particularly aware of the requirements of the **Display Screen Equipment Regulations** and how they affect computer users.

Then study the information given on the Data Protection Act on page 282 and check how this affects your own work.

INFORMATION UPDATE

The Business Software Alliance (BSA), which investigates leads and tip-offs regarding the use of pirated software, estimated in 1999 that 26 per cent of new business software installed was illegal and that this cost the software industry £7 billion in lost revenue. So don't think that the only pirated or illegal software are games or music downloads! To encourage more people to inform on companies which use illegal software, the BSA has announced a reward of up to £10,000 for information on such users – which is likely to tempt more than a few disillusioned employees (or those who have recently left a firm) to spill the beans.

Software companies are also fighting back. Microsoft has announced an amnesty (not a truce!) on pirated software. Anyone who has bought a Microsoft product which 'looks' authentic and who has proof of purchase can exchange their pirated version for an authentic package. However, to prevent pirated versions of Office 2000 being circulated, Microsoft® has built precautions into the package itself. If, after 50 uses, the software hasn't been properly registered then the program locks out. So if your Office 2000 software suddenly fails, this could be the reason!

Key facts on helping to organise and maintain the use of information technology

IT resources and consumables

Anyone who uses an IT system needs resources – and today a whole industry has developed to support these needs. Specialist suppliers will provide anything from PCs, laptops, monitors, printers and software to hardware components, such as memory upgrades and motherboards; communications equipment, such as cables and adaptors; security systems, cleaning materials and a vast range of general supplies and accessories.

As an administrator, you are less likely to be involved in ordering computers or cables than a computer specialist. Your main responsibility is likely to be for the range of consumable items regularly used by computer users. Your exact needs will depend upon the system installed and why it is used, but broadly you can classify resources into the following headings:

- **input devices**, such as mice and trackballs (companies usually keep a spare supply)
- **printer supplies**, including inkjet and/or laser toner cartridges, paper, film for transparencies, printer labels
- **storage media**, like floppy disks, Zip disks, data cartridges, CDs and DVDs
- **storage equipment**, like disk boxes and CD wallets for transporting media safely
- **health and safety items**, such as wristrests, footrests, glare filters and ergonomic keyboards
- **miscellaneous requirements**, such as cleaning supplies and mousemats and batteries (for laptops).

Quantity, quality and organisational procedures

Your organisation is likely to have rules specifying which supplier(s) you can use, how orders must be placed and who can authorise these. There will be guidelines as to the quantity of each type of item that can be stocked. This should be calculated so that higher levels of essential items are maintained (such as printer cartridges) than inessential ones (such as mousemats).

The procedures might specify the quality of each type of item to be purchased. Cost and overall expenditure needs to be weighed against the pitfalls and damage to equipment of inferior items. Cheap paper in a laser printer can cause serious problems, and a 'bargain' mouse may be a poor buy if it needs replacing very quickly.

The procedures will also cover where and how items must be stored, and the paperwork required before an item can be issued to staff. A very small firm may operate with few controls over the issue of consumables but in a large organisation this would be impractical. The result would be a virtual free-for-all, with key items regularly out of stock plus the temptation for some staff to supplement their home computer supplies at no cost!

CHECK IT OUT!

If you have any doubts about the range of computer supplies currently on the market, either visit a large computer store or, if you have Internet access, go to one of the supplier's websites, such as www.globaldirect.co.uk or www.polka.co.uk and see what's on offer. You may get quite a surprise!

EVIDENCE COLLECTION

Identify the IT resources that you regularly supply to members of your team. List these and, against each item, state what quantities or quality of item you regularly buy. If you can, give a reason for the quantity and/or quality that is specified.

Attach to this list any organisational procedures with which you have to comply when you obtain and store resources. Personalise them by adding your own comments to prove to your assessor how you implement these procedures. For instance, state the suppliers you use regularly, which you find the best – and why – and how you store items. If you can, attach copies of orders and documentation completed by staff when they require an item.

Replacing consumables

While some users may simply collect items they need from the store, others may require a little more help. For instance, you may be asked to replace a mouse, install a new cartridge in a printer or replenish the paper. Installing peripherals is dealt with in the next section.

So far as other items are concerned, you are likely to have few problems if you take the time to read the instructions on the item itself. For instance, paper may be marked 'this way up' and manufacturers may change the design of cartridges and include advice on installation in the package. Similarly, all transparencies contain clear instructions on how they must be put into the printer.

Always check the manual for any output device you use infrequently. Changing the inkjet cartridge on a printer you use every day is a different matter to changing the toner cartridge on a sophisticated laser printer you have never seen before! Never 'assume you know' – always check first.

Installing and checking simple peripherals

Before you can install a peripheral, such as a printer, scanner, keyboard or mouse, you need to understand the connections on the computer system you are using. On some computers – particularly laptops – not only is the **back** of the computer used for connections – but each side as well. If you are really fortunate, you will have an ultra-modern system which has colour-coded sockets and connections – so you are simply looking for 'red to red', 'blue to blue' and so on. If your peripheral is also 'plug and play' (see below) then your life is really easy, as the Microsoft® Windows operating system will automatically recognise the new device the next time it starts. So all you do is turn off the PC, plug in the new device, and restart the computer.

However, life isn't always so easy and you will have fewer problems if you actually understand what you are doing! The first thing to realise is that peripherals are normally added by being connected to an external **port**. A port is simply a socket into which a device is connected. On any computer you will find a variety of ports all of which have different terms and meanings. On other computers – particularly laptops – you will find other options, such as **jacks**. These accept jackplugs to connect such peripherals as a modem, a microphone or other audio device and headphones.

Finally, you can also expect to find a **power socket**. You should always check whether a PC can be plugged into the power supply directly or must be used in conjunction with a universal AC adaptor. In this case, the adaptor is connected to the computer and the power cord goes into the adaptor. Failing to do this, or using the wrong adaptor, can severely damage your computer.

KEY NOTES ON PORTS FOR PERIPHERALS

- A USB (universal serial bus) port is a feature of the latest computers and is used for plug-and-play devices. In this case you don't even have to turn off your computer before you add a peripheral – simply plug it in and Microsoft® Windows should recognise its presence.

- Parallel ports are used mainly for printers and scanners. They allow simultaneous two-way communication (so the cable is slightly thicker than some others).

- Serial ports are used to connect communication devices, such as modems, or your mouse or trackball.

- There is a keyboard port. Note that if you see the term PS/2 this refers to a newer type of port which may be parallel or serial and which has a smaller connection – it can be used for your mouse or keyboard, for example.

- The video port is used to connect your monitor. The most usual standard today is SVGA (super video graphics adaptor).

- An SCSI port is used for rapid communications devices, such as digital cameras or Zip drives. Alternatively, you can install a Zip drive to the same port as your printer by means of a special connection which enables both to operate at once.

- The network port will be in use if your PC is linked to an office network.

- An infra-red port enables a cableless connection to be made with another device having a similar port (such as a mobile phone) – provided they are sited together and nothing is blocking the signal.

INFORMATION UPDATE

Bluetooth is a new set of specifications and protocols for short-range radio communications. It will replace the need for cabling between PCs and printers, between PDAs (personal data assistants) and mobile telephones, and between a host of other devices – which won't even need to be located within the line of sight of each other.

Bluetooth wireless technology was developed by a group of telecoms manufacturers who set up a Bluetooth Special Interest Group in 1998 to create a global standard. If you want to find out more about how this will revolutionise your life, access the official Bluetooth website – www.bluetooth.com.

If you're wondering where the name comes from, Bluetooth was a Viking leader who united much of Scandinavia. The name was chosen because the system will unite your PC and peripherals – so you will be able to say goodbye to sockets and cables.

Protection from unauthorised software

There are various steps that can be taken to prevent unauthorised software being downloaded or introduced into a computer system.

A **firewall** is an electronic 'barrier' which monitors ingoing and outgoing communications between the Internet (or other external users) and the company's intranet (and internal users). The firewall can be designed to 'block' any potentially suspicious items, such as unknown graphics or video files, and prevent these being downloaded.

Most organisations have **virus monitoring software** which not only detects a virus but also eradicates it. This is different from packages such as Scandisk which simply check the system and identify a problem. Proper anti-virus software such as Dr Solomon or Norton Antivirus can be purchased for either a network or PC.

Disks that have been used off-site should be checked for possible viruses

 INFORMATION UPDATE

The problem with viruses is, of course, that as fast as software is developed to identify them, new ones are being developed and distributed. For that reason, most anti-virus software manufacturers regularly send updates to their clients. Others, such as Panda Software, offer a 24-hour, 365-day on-line support service with *daily* updates to users. The system constantly monitors all servers and workstations on a network and provides an immediate alert if a virus is identified.

Solving problems

It is no use offering computer assistance to your colleagues if you don't enjoy problem-solving! This is because, despite your knowledge and best efforts, there will be times when things go wrong with either the hardware or the software. Suggested solutions for some of the more usual problems are given in the Key notes below and on pages 544–545. But first a word of advice. The *best* helper is someone who doesn't give up at the first sign of a problem but – equally – doesn't persist in trying to solve it no matter what! Recognise your own limitations and don't think every problem is a test you *must* win. Otherwise you will spend fruitless hours, on occasion, and may cause considerable damage unless you know what you are doing.

 KEY NOTES ON SOLVING COMMON HARDWARE PROBLEMS

Despite 'plug and play', a new peripheral refuses to work

If this happens you have to add the driver (software) for the hardware.

- Click on the Start button and then select Settings | Control Panel.
- Select Add New Hardware (to start the Wizard).
- Follow the Wizard screens and tell Microsoft® Windows to identify your hardware automatically.
- Microsoft® Windows should search for, identify and install the driver for the peripheral. You can click Details for information.
- If Microsoft® Windows still can't recognise it you must state the device, manufacturer and model. If you have one, load the disk or CD-ROM provided with the device as this contains the driver files required by Microsoft® Windows. Put this into the drive and click the 'Have Disk' button.

An existing peripheral stops working

Check all obvious connections. Note that if you reconnect one, you will have to turn the computer off and on again before it will 'register'.

The computer won't start

First check whether the problem is with the computer or with Microsoft® Windows. If the computer starts but Microsoft® Windows won't load, you have a software problem.

- Start by checking the power supply and power lead.
- Check the monitor settings (the screen may just be switched off).
- Check there isn't a disk in drive A:.
- Find out whether anyone has prepared an emergency start-up disk for Microsoft® Windows. If so you can use that in drive A: (see page 550). Report the fault as you could have a serious hard disk problem.

The system 'hangs' or freezes

Resist the temptation to hit dozens of keys!

- Check obvious connections (e.g. keyboard and mouse).
- Try pressing the Esc key.
- Try pressing Alt + Tab to see whether you can access other open programs.
- Press Ctrl + Alt + Delete (once) to access the Close Program dialogue box. Find the words 'not responding' opposite a program name. Highlight this program and click End Task. The next dialogue box is the Wait/Shutdown box (you might have to give this a few minutes to appear). Then click End Task.
- If the program still doesn't respond, click Shut Down and press Ctrl + Alt + Delete again to reboot your machine.

The system runs very slowly

Learn how to 'defrag' your machine – and clean up your hard disk by removing unwanted data and reorganising existing data.

- Press Start, then access Microsoft® Windows Explorer.
- Use your on-line Help screen to find out what to do next!

A new printer won't work/existing printer won't print

Start by checking the cable isn't damaged – test by substituting another cable. Note that bi-directional cables should be used, especially for new printers. For a printer to work you need the correct printer driver installed. Microsoft® Windows supports many makes and models. Simply select Start I Settings I Control panel and then Install Printers. Choose the one you want from the list on screen. If your model isn't listed, contact the supplier or manufacturer – and note that many drivers can be downloaded from the Internet.

If an existing printer won't work, check all obvious connections. Check that the printer is 'online' and isn't out of paper. Check that you haven't an 'insufficient disk space' error message on screen; if so, delete some old files and try again.

Finally remember that you can access Print Manager to see if Microsoft® Windows has paused the printing operation. Do this by double-clicking the printer icon at the bottom of the screen, if the job is in progress. If the icon isn't showing, click Start I Settings I Printers and click the icon for the printer that is causing problems.

KEY NOTES ON SOLVING COMMON SOFTWARE PROBLEMS

New software won't work

All software must be compatible with the system. You can't use Apple Macintosh software on an IBM-compatible system or vice versa. Neither can you use PC software on a network or vice versa. You also need software which is compatible with your operating system – for instance, whether this is Microsoft® Windows 95, 98, NT, 2000 or XP. So start by checking the label! Next, if you are installing an upgrade of any kind (particularly for the operating system on a PC) *always* back-up all your important data first – just in case. And make sure you have copy system files to hand, too!

- Follow the instructions carefully for installing the new program (usually done from a CD-ROM).

- If you have problems starting the program, try uninstalling the program and going through the installation sequence again. Most new programs include an uninstall utility as well.

- If the program still won't work (or worse, it will but your other programs or devices won't) ask for help. It is likely that some of your system components need to be reconfigured or there is a memory conflict. In either case, you need proper assistance.

Microsoft® Windows won't start

First check there is power to the system unit (otherwise you have a hardware problem). Then check the monitor and all obvious connections. Finally, check your screen to see whether there is an error message showing. If there is, try simple steps to solve the problem yourself (e.g. by removing a disk from drive A:) or report the message to an expert. Do the same if you hear a series of beeps but can't read anything on screen. If there is no message then try starting Microsoft® Windows in 'safe mode', as follows.

- Press Ctrl + Alt + Delete to reboot your computer.
- Press F8 as soon as you see the message 'Starting Windows'.
- From the menu on screen, select Safe Mode. Then tell your technician – from safe mode all your settings can be checked.
- If safe mode won't work, report the problem – you could have a virus.

A program 'freezes'

This is a common problem which causes panic amongst those who fail to back-up their work regularly! Try Alt + Tab to see whether other programs are still OK. Then give your system a few minutes to see whether it is simply running very slowly. If all else fails, go through the Ctrl + Alt + Delete sequence shown under hardware problems and then restart Microsoft® Windows. Bear in mind any data since the last save will now be lost!

Someone accidentally deletes an important file or folder

Teach your colleagues how to 'undelete' items from their Recycle Bin by clicking the bin icon, clicking the right mouse button and selecting Restore!

Providing IT specialists with clear information

In both the tables on problem-solving you should have noted that there are several occasions when you have to report the difficulty to an IT specialist. This may be an external firm or an internal helpdesk. When you make contact, the staff will be grateful if you have carried out fundamental checks yourself first (no one wants to be called out to replace a power lead!), can describe the problem accurately, using the correct terms and without exaggerating – and can also report any error message showing on screen. Having these details to hand means that on an internal network, the matter can sometimes be put right without any need for a personal visit.

If the problem is concerned with a new peripheral you have tried to install, it is worth knowing that the configuration of the different devices on a system can create problems. Sometimes you can solve the problem quickly by simply using a different port. In other cases you may need to report the problem. In that situation you can assist your specialist by printing out a Microsoft System Information utility. This report states exactly what is linked to your computer and where. Do this as follows:

- Click on Start, then select Programs | Accessories | System Tools | System Information.
- Then either print the report or, if it seems to be very long, select File | Export, name the file and save it in a specific location. You could then attach it to an e-mail to your IT specialist if you really want to make an impression!

INFORMATION UPDATE

Many business computer users operate as part of a computer network – so a different range of problems, such as the following, can be experienced.

- A new PC has to be physically linked to the network so must be ordered complete with a network card.
- Laptop users have to insert a network card before they can communicate with the network.
- New users will have to be given a user ID to log-in before they can access the network.
- Problems with the network servers or software can cause the system to go 'down' until the fault has been repaired.

If you operate on a network then the system will be overseen by a network administrator and there is often a helpdesk you can phone if you have a problem.

Finally, a major reason for many calls to helpdesks is because network users have forgotten their password. Try to make sure that isn't you!

EVIDENCE COLLECTION

You need to prove that you have identified and replaced at least one of the following types of resource – storage media (e.g. floppy or Zip disks), printing materials (e.g. paper, toner or transparencies) and software. You must also prove you can deal with both basic hardware problems and basic software problems.

You will find this easier if you keep a log of the jobs you do and the problems you have to solve over a period of time. In each case record the date, what you did and the outcome. Ask the person who you assisted to countersign the entry to prove its authenticity. This will also help you to meet the requirement of keeping clear and accurate records of the work you have done!

Routine cleaning operations

One item in your consumable store should be cleaning materials. A wide range of specialist materials is available to help you to keep your equipment and peripherals in pristine condition. These are infinitely preferable to a damp cloth or a paper tissue!

KEY NOTES ON ROUTINE CLEANING OF HARDWARE

- The biggest enemies of computer equipment are dust and fluff. Eating a biscuit over your keyboard or using a mouse on a dirty mousemat is simply asking for trouble. Using dust covers helps – particularly if the working area is dusty or if building work is going on. Remember that prevention is always better than cure.

- Liquids are fatal. Keep them well away from your equipment. If liquids of any kind are spilled on a processor, monitor or into a keyboard or printer, then obtain expert assistance immediately.

- Use specialist materials made for the job:

  - cleaning cartridges for inkjet printers
  - drive cleaners for CD-ROM and floppy drive heads
  - anti-static spray and/or screen wipes for monitors
  - aerosol sprays which force dirt out of keyboards, or mini-vacuum cleaners
  - specialist scanner cleaning kits to clean the screen and cover.

- Check the handbook or manual for that equipment before you start and note all the 'dos' and 'don'ts'. For instance, check whether the outside cover can be safely cleaned with a damp cloth and proprietary cleaner, and note that alcohol and solvents should never be used near a printer as they cause the rubber rollers to become brittle.

- Turn off the equipment before you start. In some cases you will be advised to disconnect it from the mains.

- Pay special attention to the part of the equipment where performance would be most seriously affected by dirt:

  - the glass on a scanner or monitor
  - the ball in a mouse or trackball
  - the keys on a keyboard
  - the printing head on a printer.

- Never poke around inside equipment or take anything apart – with the single exception of your mouse. The ball can easily be removed for cleaning.

- Having a regular cleaning routine (e.g. once a week or month) is far better than a mad blitz once a year.

Key facts on helping other people with their use of information technology

If you gain a reputation for being an IT expert, you can expect people to ask you for help if they are experiencing a difficulty with the package they are using, or with their equipment. The problem for you is that you may be constantly interrupted with a myriad of different requests when you are trying to do your own work. There are several ways in which you can try to minimise this danger.

Many problems are simply annoying, rather than urgent. For instance, a user's screen display has gone awry – but he or she can still get on with the work – and so can you. Arrange to look at the problem when you have some spare time.

Learn to recognise those problems which are beyond you, so the user (or you) arranges for expert assistance immediately, rather than waiting for you to try to solve the difficulty.

Teach people how to solve a problem so that they understand what to do and can do the job themselves next time. This means *explaining* what you are doing and why (see below) and *not* just tapping a few keys, clicking the mouse a couple of times and then walking away again.

If you are so regularly 'pestered' with basic requests you never have five minutes to call your own, have a word with your supervisor. Either your colleagues need to be trained properly or a short manual or key instruction sheet on basic operations needs to be prepared. Or you need to invest in a few easy-to-understand user guides for the software everyone is using.

Explaining IT problems and solutions clearly

Hopefully, when you looked at the Key notes on pages 542–545 you found these easy to understand. They told you what to do, step by step. You also have a written reference that you can look at when you need it. These are two criteria which should always be met when you are identifying a problem and suggesting a solution. The third, impossible in a book, is to demonstrate – clearly and slowly – what should be done. Then, if possible, ask the learner to repeat the actions while it is still fresh in the mind. If you do this when you are helping people they will learn from the experience and you will benefit in the long run – as they will be less dependent upon you in the future.

Solving specific software and hardware problems

Obviously there are dozens of different problems that people can encounter with their equipment or with their software. Much depends upon the type of equipment and applications software they are using and their experience to date. Within these pages it is impossible to give you solutions to all the problems you may encounter. However, here is some general advice.

1   If you are helping a colleague to set up files and folders, copy or rename them or zip-up files or folders, then you should be a relatively experienced user of Microsoft® Windows Explorer. As a basic you should know the use of the two 'panes' you see, what your right mouse button does and the fact that holding down Shift means you can operate on more than one file or folder simultaneously.

2   You should teach people that all they have to do is to click Start and then Find to find a file which seems to have mysteriously disappeared!

3   If you are asked by colleagues to make any adjustments to their screen display or to reset a modem or install hardware or software, you should know your way around the Control Panel.

4   If you have to solve a printer problem then you should be familiar with that printer, know how to put it on- or off-line, change the cartridge(s) and replenish the paper properly.

5   If you are advising a user of the Internet, then you should know whether you have to dial up your ISP each time or whether your system is constantly on-line. If the latter, then contact your network administrator or IT specialist if there is a problem. If you are on a dial-up system which is causing problems, then you need to know:

- who your ISP is
- how the system works (e.g. you can't dial up from an engaged phone!)
- where all the wires go to – so that you can check the connections (particularly if you have an external modem)
- how to check the dial-up configuration through Microsoft® Windows Explorer
- how to check the modem through the Control Panel.

6 All Internet users may appreciate some basic instruction on how to search for information quickly and how to save it to disk to read or print out off-line (which saves money). Many files are saved in PDF format which means you need to launch Adobe's Acrobat Reader. That can be freely downloaded from most sites as can other useful software (such as RealPlayer to listen to audio transmissions). Knowing how to download (and then launch) packages can be helpful, provided you don't clutter up your system – or anyone else's – with things you don't need!

7 If you are advising an e-mail user, you should note there are two principal types of e-mail operation. The first are the routine operations carried out all the time, such as reading a message, creating a new message, replying to a message, sending or forwarding a message and deleting messages. The next group are those which users may wish to learn to do to enhance their skills, such as attach a file or folder, change the format of an attachment to meet the requirements of the recipient, create folders in which to save messages, mark messages as 'high priority', create their own address book.

8 If you are advising software users then remember that *your* skills in that particular package must be greater than the person you are instructing — or you need to be better than they are at finding the right program Help screen and interpreting it! Never ignore, either, the use of Wizards or even the animated paperclip in Microsoft® Windows if it helps.

9 Before you attempt to solve *any* problems, for anyone else, ever, *always* make sure they have saved what they are doing first. Then, even if you can't help them, at least you haven't lost their work as well!

 INFORMATION UPDATE

If you have a serious hardware fault and your hard disk drive fails, you can take advantage of the fact that your system will automatically default to drive A: to 'boot' the system up if there is a disk installed. Do this by preparing an emergency start-up floppy disk to put in drive A: before you switch on.

- Click the Start button and select Settings | Control panel.
- Select the Add/Remove programs icon.
- Wait until the dialogue box appears and then select the Start-up Disk tab. Then click on Create Disk.
- Insert a blank floppy disk in the A: drive when you are told to do so and click OK.
- When the emergency start-up disk has been created the dialogue box will reappear. Now click OK to return to the desktop. ➡

Some experts advise that you should also access Microsoft® Windows Explorer and copy your system.ini and win.ini files to the same disk.

Although you can now start your system by putting this disk into the drive and switching on, you do need to have your hard disk checked out by an IT specialist as soon as possible. Several useful programs are on the market which analyse hard disk problems and even repair the damage, such as Norton's Disk Doctor, and it is likely that this program, or one similar, will be run on your machine. It is sensible to undertake this operation before you start re-installing your software and data files.

After your hard disk has been checked and repaired, use your original CD-ROM to re-install Microsoft® Windows. Note that you will probably also have to re-enter your registration number. Then re-install all your major software programs, preferably again from the original CD-ROMs. However, you should note that all these precautions will be of little help if you have not regularly backed up your key data *on a daily basis* on a floppy disk, Zip disk or tape streamer.

The importance of sensitivity and helping people to solve their own problems

People who ask for help can be divided into categories:

- type A – those who ask immediately, without even trying to solve the problem
- type B – those who try to solve the problem but, if they have difficulties, will ask for assistance
- type C – those who detest asking anyone anything – and will do almost anything to avoid it.

In an ideal world, everyone would be type B. In the real world, they are not. Type A people can irritate you by constantly pestering, while type C people can be annoying if they create *additional* problems. Then, just to add to the mix, there are those who you helped last week, but have forgotten what you said!

However, you should remember that people very rarely see themselves as others see them (do you?), and no one likes being made to look foolish. Therefore, the way in which you treat people who have problems is as important for office harmony as the way in which you solve the difficulty. Saying 'I don't believe it, can't you remember anything?' *or* 'Not again, am I the only person who can use this system?' is unlikely to endear you to anyone and may actually *deter* most people from asking for help even when they need it. Remember, too, that you can offend people with your attitude and manner – without saying a word. Getting up with a huge sigh and stomping across the office is just as bad as calling someone a nuisance to their face. If you can't do the job with good grace, then don't do it at all.

Perhaps, if someone can't remember what you said, you explained it badly or too hurriedly. This is why patience is essential – and so is the ability to give people the confidence and skills to solve their own problems in the future. Help your colleagues to realise that there is little they can do which will actually *break* their system – and that sometimes investigating a package (such as Windows Explorer) can pay dividends. So, too, can following an excellent well-illustrated textbook on the package.

Recording problems and solutions

If you are constantly encouraging other people to remember what they have done and to learn from solving difficulties, you will look rather silly if you forget what *you* did on a particular occasion to solve a problem! For that reason, it is sensible either to make a note of the problem and how you solved it *or* (at the very least) to note down where you found the answer (e.g. the program's Help file, a manual or software guide).

The best way is to keep a small notebook and divide this into relevant sections, such as hardware problems/solutions and software problems/solutions. Separate your software section into the different applications programs you normally use. If you regularly use the Internet or e-mail, these are also best kept separately.

Finally, you will find it useful to note down useful hints and tips you read about and new operations you learn yourself. IT equipment and software is developing constantly and you have to develop your own skills and abilities to continue to stay abreast of these changes. Otherwise, in a very short time, you will be asking someone else to solve your problems – instead of being able to help yourself!

CHECK IT OUT!

If you have access to the Internet you can help yourself to stay up to date with developments *and* increase your ability to solve computer-based problems through accessing some of the sites which deal with these issues. Check out at least one of these sites yourself and see how it can help you.

*   The retailer PC World is on-line at www.pcworld.com. In addition to information on new products you will also find hints and tips on making the most of your equipment and software.
*   If you need to know more exactly the definition of a computer term – or read about something you've never heard of before – then try www.webopedia.com. ➡

- Virtually all hardware and software suppliers have their own websites. For instance, you can download a printer driver from the Hewlett Packard site (www.hp.com) and find out more about your system from the Microsoft site (www.microsoft.com). Often the best time to visit these websites is in the morning, before US businesses open and Internet traffic increases sharply.

- Many newspapers operate computer help forums which are available on-line. Try www.telegraph.co.uk and click on Technology. This will link you to Connected – which includes Boot Camps and Faqs! Facts! Fax! which answers reader's questions.

- For more specific help, try www.myhelpdesk.com. Here you can read FAQs (frequently asked questions) about various software and hardware, read tips and tricks and even consult a live expert – but you need to become a member for specific help and advice.

- Investigate sources of help listed by a search engine of your own choosing.

EVIDENCE COLLECTION

For this element you have to prove you can deal with application software problems and hardware problems that can be dealt with by a user. To provide full evidence for this element, you are recommended to do the following.

1 Keep a log of the problems you solve. State the date, who you helped, the nature of the problem and the solution.

2 Attach any notes you made to help the person to remember the solution in future.

3 Obtain witness testimony from people you helped that you did so sensitively and helped them to learn from the experience.

4 Obtain witness testimony from your supervisor that you respond promptly but do not endanger your own work priorities and that you solve problems only within the limits of your authority.

5 In addition, either photocopy or lend your problems and solutions log book to your assessor who can then see that you keep a record of solutions to problems you have not met before.

Option Unit 319 **Produce spreadsheet documents**

FOCUS OF THE UNIT

To obtain this unit you must be able to:

* **retrieve and enter data** to create and update files
* **produce** the required spreadsheet by manipulating data
* **output** the spreadsheet to the required destination.

EVIDENCE COLLECTION

It will make evidence collection easier if you can obtain the following information:

a   a description of the type of spreadsheets you routinely create or update, with an explanation of why they are used

b   a copy of any organisational procedures you must follow when you are working with spreadsheets – these may relate to accessing files, entering data, saving files or handling confidential information (see pages 556, 559, 567 and 585)

c   samples of spreadsheets both before and after you have updated or manipulated data

d   samples of spreadsheets showing both numerical data and the formulae you have entered

e   examples of spreadsheet printouts showing a variety of formats, such as complete worksheets, selected cells, portrait and landscape orientation etc.

Producing spreadsheet documents

Spreadsheets are an ideal method of manipulating figures quickly and easily. They enable users to:

- carry out a large number of repetitious calculations speedily, with minimal data entry
- undertake complex calculations accurately
- carry out financial 'modelling' (when exact data isn't yet known or decided, and decisions have to be taken on a 'what if?' basis)
- print out graphical representations of numerical data as charts or graphs.

Gaining authority to access files

Because spreadsheets are widely used for accounting and financial information, often the data held upon them is extremely sensitive. In that case, access to the spreadsheet files may be restricted. In the same way, it is sensible to restrict the ability to input or change data in spreadsheet files, especially when the data is important or is required for particular formulae. Further details of this aspect of spreadsheets are given on page 567.

EVIDENCE COLLECTION

Identify the type of spreadsheets to which you routinely have access as part of your job, and those you need to gain authority to access. Explain the difference between these and the reasons for the access restrictions.

Make sure you know who you would have to contact to gain authority to access specific files, if necessary, and include this information. Your assessor will expect you to know this.

Note that you should know how to protect data yourself. This is covered on page 568.

Key facts on retrieving and entering data to create and update files

Interpreting and meeting customer requirements

Your 'customer', in this situation, is any person (or organisation) upon whose behalf the spreadsheet is being used. This is more likely to be an internal 'customer' – such as your line manager or another department. However, in some working environments you may also keep spreadsheets for 'external' customers. An example would be an accountant who keeps tax records for clients on a spreadsheet or a financial adviser who monitors investment performance.

Your customer may have several specific requirements you must consider.

First, there is likely to be a time constraint on the finished spreadsheet. Secondly, the spreadsheet may be required for a particular purpose. This can influence the format and layout (see pages 570 and 573), the number of copies required, or even the method of output selected (see pages 584–586).

Whatever the pressures, the customer will expect to receive a spreadsheet into which *all* the required data has been input accurately! This means you not only need to run a final spell-check but also need to use your own proofreading skills to check your numerical entries. No spreadsheet package can do that for you!

You should always check whether you have the authority to provide internal or external customers with data they are requesting, unless it is a common request you are used to fulfilling. While you are unlikely to have any difficulty with direct requests from your line manager, if you have concerns because you are being asked to provide sensitive data by someone else, you are always safer to ask your supervisor first. Assuming that you can supply the data, you then need to be able to correctly locate and retrieve it, which is the subject of the next section.

Locating and retrieving numerical files

The basic concepts you need to understand before you can locate and retrieve files are:

- the meaning of worksheets and workbooks
- the basic principles of file management.

If you use a spreadsheet package such as Excel, you should know the following facts.

- **Worksheet** is used to refer to every new spreadsheet you create. The worksheet is the *whole* of the spreadsheet, not just the part you can see on screen.
- **Workbook** is the term used for a collection of worksheets. When you open a new Excel document it automatically comprises three sheets (see the figure on page 558), although you can extend these to a maximum of 256 pages. Think of these as pages in a loose-leaf file folder. This is because you can move them around, just as you can in a file folder.
- **File management** refers to having an organised and structured method of naming and saving files. If you give your worksheets logical names and save your files to specific named directories, then you will be able to find files far more easily than if you don't!

You can, of course, print out a copy of current worksheets and file these in a 'hard copy' workbook. If you have limited access to a computer and are regularly asked for data quickly, then this could be one method of solving the problem. However, you must then remember to take a printout to update your hard-copy file every time you update a worksheet, which can be tedious. You would also have to remember to keep worksheets containing confidential data in a separate file and locked away for security.

The final point to note is that some of your 'customers' will be more precise about their requirements than others. Few will be able to give you the name of the worksheet or directory you should access, for instance! This is where having a *logical system of file names* is absolutely vital, as it prevents misunderstandings from the outset.

CHECK IT OUT!

It is assumed you already know how to switch on (or log on to) your computer system and access the spreadsheet package. If you use Microsoft® Excel, check the screen illustration below and make certain that there are no surprises! This is a Microsoft® Excel 2000 screen, so if you are using an earlier version your screen may look slightly different. You may also find the buttons on your toolbar are different. This is because Excel automatically customises your screen – as you use particular buttons it remembers these, and displays them for you. If ever you need to use a button which isn't displayed, simply click the small button at the extreme right of the toolbar to see what is available to you.

Working with worksheets in Microsoft® Excel

1 Check you know how to **switch between** worksheets. Just click the tab of the worksheet you want and the selected one is shown in white.

2 Remember that if you have many worksheets you may not be able to see all the tabs. On Microsoft® Excel you can **browse through** your worksheets by using the arrow buttons to the left of the worksheet tabs. Click on each one now and see which worksheet appears.

3 You can **add** or **insert** a new worksheet by clicking on Insert, then Worksheet.

4 You can **delete** a worksheet – provided it is not locked or protected – by right clicking on its tab, clicking Edit and then selecting Delete Sheet. If this item does not appear on your menu then you may be able to locate it if you position the mouse pointer over the bottom of the drop-down menu to display all the available options. A warning will appear to remind you that you are about to take a very serious action. Your worksheet will be permanently deleted if you click OK. Remember always to check with your supervisor before you delete a worksheet which contains data.

5 You can **rename** a worksheet by double-clicking on its tab to see the existing name. You then type the new name and press Enter. The limit of the name in Microsoft® Excel is 31 characters and spaces – quite enough to give it a uniquely and easily identifiable title!

6 You can **move** a worksheet by positioning the mouse over the appropriate tab and dragging the worksheet to its new location along the line of tabs. A downwards arrow will show you where the worksheet will appear. Try this now, by changing Sheet 1 to the position of Sheet 3, and then back again.

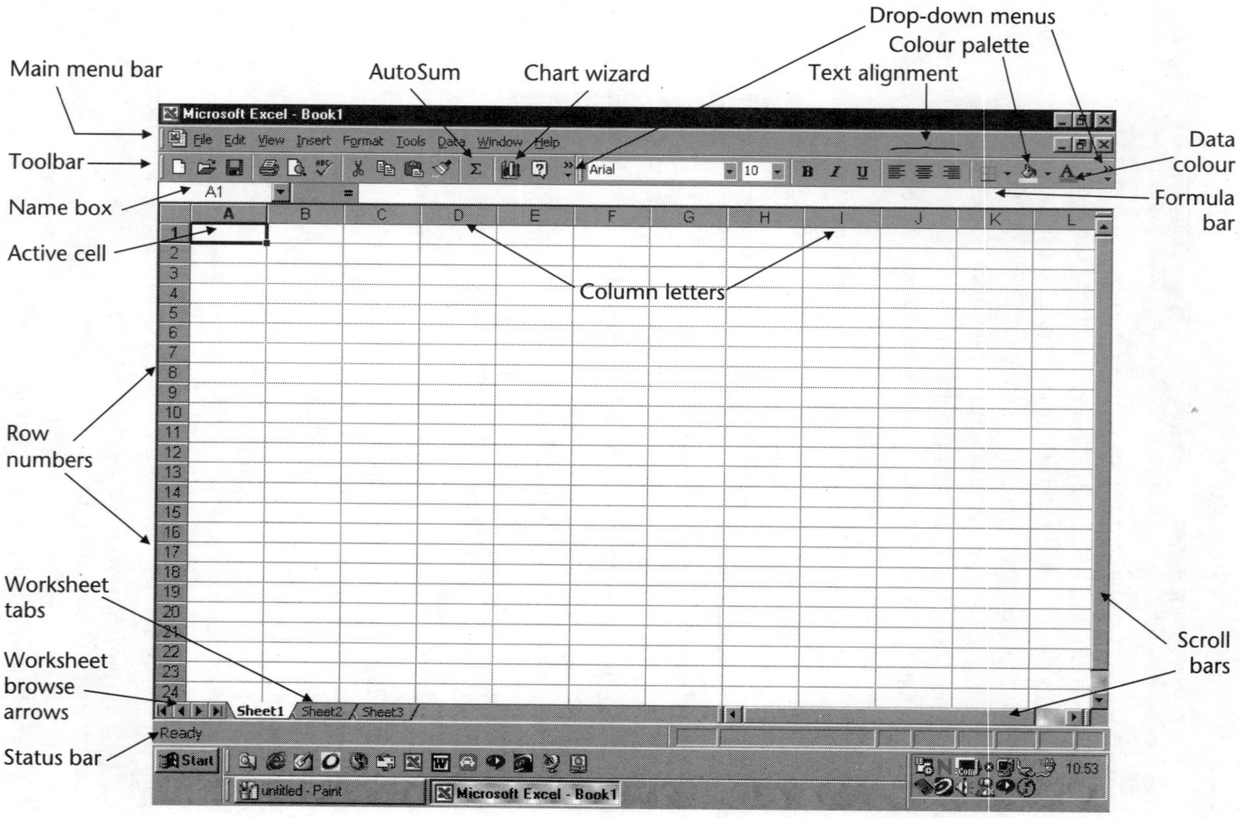
Main menu bar
AutoSum
Chart wizard
Text alignment
Colour palette
Drop-down menus
Data colour
Formula bar
Toolbar
Name box
Active cell
Column letters
Row numbers
Worksheet tabs
Worksheet browse arrows
Status bar
Scroll bars
Microsoft Excel - Book1
File Edit View Insert Format Tools Data Window Help
Arial
10
A1
Sheet1
Sheet2
Sheet3
Ready
Start
untitled - Paint
10:53

The Microsoft® Excel screen

7   **Save** your worksheet by clicking on the floppy disk icon on your toolbar. The Save As dialogue box will appear if you are saving this for the first time. Type a name for the worksheet which you will easily recognise. Now check the 'Save in' box at the top of your screen. This shows you the locations where you can store the file – on a floppy disk (A:), on your hard drive (C:), on any network home area (sometimes H:). Alternatively, if you are using Microsoft® Windows 2000, you can store your spreadsheet in My Documents, on your Desktop, in Favorites (see below) or in Web Folders (see page 586). To select any of these options, simply click the appropriate area to the left of the screen.

However, do make sure that you also follow any of your organisation's specific requirements for saving files – for instance, if there is a specific folder or disk you should use or a particular convention for naming worksheets or files.

8   **Open** a saved workbook by clicking on the open folder icon on your toolbar. When the Open dialogue box appears, click the correct drive or folder to see the contents and then double-click on the name of the workbook you want to open.

 INFORMATION UPDATE

If you use Microsoft® Excel 2000, you can find and organise your worksheet files without interrupting the work you are doing. For instance when you want to find a file and click 'Open' on your 'File' menu, you can access:

- recently opened files – by clicking the History icon

- frequently opened files – by clicking 'Add to Favorites' (American spelling!) on your Tools menus when you save a frequently used file and clicking the 'Favorites' icon when you want to view this list

- files on other disks and in other folders – by clicking the arrow in the 'Look in' box. You then click on a disk to display its contents

- files you have lost – by clicking Find on the Tools menu.

Using **wildcard** characters such as * or ? will broaden your search if you have only the most basic idea of the name. If you eventually track down a difficult worksheet or file it may be worth renaming it, so you find it more easily next time!

Working with workbooks in Microsoft® Excel

1   In Microsoft® Excel, you are not just restricted to one workbook – you can start a new workbook at any time if you need to store data relating to a completely different matter. Simply click on the folded paper icon at the top left of your screen. This new workbook will be titled Book 2, Book 3 or whatever – depending upon the number you have started. A button to identify the workbook will appear on the taskbar.

2   You can switch between your workbooks easily by clicking on Window on the menu bar. You will now see a list of all the workbooks you have open. Simply click on the one you want to see on screen.

3   Excel remembers the names of the last four workbooks you worked on (you can set this number up in Options) and these show at the bottom of the drop-down menu when you click on File. Simply click the name of the one you want to open.

Input devices and the reasons for using them

The most usual input device for entering spreadsheet data is a keyboard. However, on occasion you might receive data in another way or utilise another input device.

For example, digital audio equipment may be linked to a computer to transfer data. For this, the 'host' computer needs voice recognition software installed. One of the most popular versions is IBM's ViaVoice. This will register commands either from audio equipment or from a 'live' voice and is compatible with Microsoft® Excel and Lotus 1-2-3. The latter also has voice-enabled templates which can be downloaded from the Lotus website at www.lotus.com/smartsuiteupdates.

Personal organisers can be used to store data which can then be transferred to a laptop or PC. There are pocket PCs which run Microsoft® Excel, and many palmtop computers will run Quicksheet software, which is rather like a mini Excel. Pocket spreadsheets are useful for those who frequently obtain data whilst travelling – such as sales representatives and repair staff. The data can be logged on site and then easily transferred to a PC in the office.

Data can be scanned into most spreadsheet packages, such as Microsoft® Excel. The data is captured by a scanner and read with an optical character reader (OCR) with a good software package, such as OmniPage Pro 10. The data is 100 per cent readable, but any formulae still have to be entered manually.

A variety of specialist devices exist to help disabled users to input data without a keyboard. These include head tracking systems, trackballs (which can be operated with the feet), and 'touch screen' technology. Most of these options can be viewed at the AbilityNet website at www.abilitynet.co.uk.

Note that, to provide evidence for your award, you only need to *use* one of the devices mentioned above (or the keyboard). However, you do need to be able to *discuss* with your assessor the other available options.

Why use different input devices?

You need to be able to discuss *why* different input devices are used. Some specialist devices will be essential for those users with a disability that makes it impossible for them to use a keyboard. A mouse is not an appropriate alternative, because basic calculations still have to be input on the keyboard. Therefore, either a voice-recognition system, a trackball or a pointer which is used with a touch-sensitive screen may be much better.

Also, it would waste a considerable amount of time to have to input data all over again once it has been captured or recorded. That is why the following methods may be used:

- digital audio – for when data has been pre-recorded
- palmtops and pocket PCs – to download data which has been captured in other locations
- a scanner – to scan in data which has already been input into another (incompatible) document.

EVIDENCE COLLECTION

For your assessor, write a brief account of the input device you normally use. Identify any other devices that are available in your organisation. Then state why each one is used. Remember that even if no audio or specialist devices are available, you will have to prove that you know why they might be required.

If you wish you can supplement the information above with what you have found on sites such as Ability Net (see above), www.microsoft.com and www.pcworld.com. If you don't use Excel, your own software manufacturer's site should prove a fruitful source (e.g. www.lotus.com).

Using available software and automated facilities

There is a wide range of spreadsheet software on the market. Some popular choices are Microsoft®Excel, Lotus 1-2-3 and Quattro. You should have already noted that many of the hints and tips in this section are written for Excel users. If you use a different package, you should be able to convert these either by using your program Help facility or by accessing your supplier on the Internet. Most have FAQs (frequently asked question) sections that you may find invaluable.

As a minimum, you must understand:

- how to open, save and close spreadsheets
- the features you see on your screen
- how to move around the spreadsheet quickly
- how to enter text, numerical entries and formulae (and know the difference between each of these)
- how to make corrections and amendments
- the features and automated facilities which exist on your package to save you work time (see page 565).

CHECK IT OUT!

Check that you can move around your spreadsheet quickly. You should already know the following.

- Clicking on a cell makes it the active cell (when it is also outlined in black).

- The vertical and horizontal scroll bars are used to display different parts of a spreadsheet.

- Arrow keys or Page Up and Page Down can be used to navigate in the spreadsheet.

- You can move quickly to a different part of a spreadsheet by using the Go To command in the Edit menu. Then enter the cell address (e.g. T78) and click on OK.

- You can click on the cell reference or name box, enter the cell address and press Enter.

- Pressing Ctrl + Home will take you to the *start* of the spreadsheet, while Ctrl + End takes you to the *last entry*.

Entering and manipulating data

For Element 319.1 you have to prove that you can enter and manipulate numbers and text (**formulae** are dealt with on pages 576–582), so obviously you should know the difference between these.

- A **text entry** is a word or reference which will not be part of any calculation. This therefore includes all titles and headings, and any reference notes you type *whether or not these contain any figures* (such as a postcode).
- A **numerical entry** consists of figures that will be used in your calculations.

Entering text and data is simple. Just click on the cell to make it the active one, type the data for that cell and press Enter. If you realise at this point that you have made a mistake, either the Delete or backspace key can be used.

If a **text** entry is too long to fit in a cell, the text will try to run on into the next cell. Note, however, that if the next cell already contains data, this will not happen and only part of your entry will be displayed. You can alter your cell in either of two ways to display all the entry.

- **Widen the column** by moving to the column letter at the top of the screen. Position the mouse over the right edge of the heading (on Excel, until you see the thin cross) and then drag the edge of the column until the dotted line shows the necessary width. An even quicker way is to double-click the right edge of the column heading – in that case the column width will increase to fit your longest entry in that column.
- Alternatively, **change the row height** by moving to the row number at the left of the screen. Position the mouse over the bottom edge of the row (until you see the thin cross) and drag the edge downwards until the dotted line shows the depth you want. Again, a quicker way is to double-click the bottom edge of the row – in that case the row will change to fit the largest entry in that row.

If you now want your text to 'wrap' in a cell, click on the cell and select Format, Cell, Alignment and Text Wrap.

If a **numerical entry** is too long you will see the number displayed as ###### (hashes). In this case you will want to widen the column (as it is usually inappropriate to have a numerical entry on two lines), using the technique described above.

Selection facilities

For Element 319.1 you must prove you can select cell(s), a row, a column or a block of cells. Note that when you select any cells they will appear highlighted on the screen. On Microsoft® Excel a flashing dotted line appears around active selected cells. Press Esc (escape) to remove the flashing lines.

You already know that you can **select a cell** by clicking within it. You select a **single row** of cells by clicking on the number of the row. Select **multiple rows** by positioning the mouse over the number of the first row you want to select and then dragging the mouse until all the rows you want are highlighted.

A **single column** is selected by clicking the letter of that column. **Multiple columns** are selected by positioning the mouse over the letter of the first column and then dragging the mouse until all the columns you want are highlighted.

Select **a group of cells** by positioning the mouse over the first cell in your series and dragging the mouse until all the cells you want are highlighted. If you have several groups of cells to highlight, simply press the Ctrl key as you repeat this process. If you include a cell by mistake, click on it to 'deselect' it.

Finally, you can select *all* the cells very quickly indeed by clicking the intersection box at the top left-hand corner of the worksheet, where the row and column headings meet.

Manipulation facilities

For Element 319.1 you must prove that you can carry out all the following manipulations:

- copy
- delete
- insert
- move
- retrieve
- sort.

Remember that in all Microsoft® Windows packages you can use Copy and Paste to copy data. Other manipulations are summarised in the Key Notes below.

KEY NOTES ON MANIPULATING DATA

Copy or move data

You can do this in various ways. 'Drag and drop' data as follows.
- Select the cells to copy or move (see page 563).
- Position your mouse over a border of the selected cells until the 'fat cross' turns into a pointer.
- To **copy** the data hold down Ctrl and drag the mouse to the new position — you will see a grey box to indicate where the data will appear.
- To **move** the data, don't use Ctrl, simply drag the mouse to the new position.

Or use your toolbar buttons.
- First select your cells.
- Then click the 'copy data' button 🖺 or the 'move data' button ✂ .
- Click the cell which you want at the top left of your new location and press Enter.

Insert data
- Click on the cell where you want the data to appear.
- Type the data and press Enter.

Insert a new row
- Select a row (click on the row number).
- Click Insert on your menu bar and then click Rows.
- The new row will appear above the row you selected.

Insert a new column
- Select a column (click on the column letter).
- Click Insert on your menus bar and then click Columns.
- The new column will appear to the left of your selected column.

Retrieve data
- To retrieve data deleted in error (or cancel changes you later regret): click the Undo button.
- To find and retrieve data in another part of the spreadsheet: click Edit then Find. You can also use Find/Replace to change

data quickly this way.

- To retrieve data in another worksheet: copy and move it (see above).
- To retrieve a Word file or other object from a compatible application:
  - click on the Insert menu and select Object
  - scroll down the Object dialogue box to find the type of object you want
  - then click the 'Create from' file tab
  - locate the file by clicking Browse and double-click the file name when it appears
  - click OK.
- To retrieve and insert a graphic:
  - select the Microsoft® Clip Gallery and choose an image you like
  - click on Insert
  - resize the object using the handles. Use the corner handle to retain the same shape
  - move the object, if necessary, by using cut and paste or drag it with the mouse.

Delete data

- *Either* overtype with the new data, *or* use the Delete or Backspace key to remove the entry.

Delete a row or column

- Select the row or column.
- Select Edit from your menu bar and click Delete.

Note: if you delete a row or column containing data for a formula you will see the error message #REF! (see page 577).

Sort data

- To sort data in a row or column: click the Ascending or Descending button on your toolbar. Ascending sorts from A-Z or lowest to highest number ⓐ↓. Descending sorts from Z-A or highest to lowest number ⓩ↓.
- To sort more than one cell range:
  - select the cell range(s) containing the data you want to sort
  - click Data on the menu bar and then Sort to see the Sort dialogue box
  - in the first box select the primary row or column you wish to sort by (eg surname)
  - in the next box select the secondary row or column you wish to sort by (eg first name) – this way your data will be correctly linked together during the sort
  - select a third criterion if you wish
  - finally, click OK.

Automated facilities

The main use of automated facilities is to assist data entry and checking. Once again, the following examples apply to Microsoft® Excel.

AutoComplete recognises the first few letters of an entry. If these match another cell then Excel (and many other packages) will complete the text for you. If you agree, simply press the Enter key. If you do not, just continue keying in.

AutoFill enables you to complete a text series or number series automatically because the package 'recognises' most common series, such as January, February; 2000, 2001 etc. After you have made the first entry, click the cell and then position the mouse at the bottom right-hand corner of the cell until you see a thin cross on the screen. Then drag the mouse over the cells you want to include in the series. If you are entering a number series, you will have to enter the first two numbers of the series. Note that if Microsoft® Excel doesn't recognise the series it will copy the text in the first cell to all the others – then you have to input the correct series yourself!

AutoCorrect is the function which automatically corrects common spelling errors as you input your text – to prevent you spelling words like 'receive' or 'separate' wrongly. You can also run a full spell-check at the end. In Microsoft® Excel, just click the 'ABC' button on the toolbar.

Other useful facilities in Microsoft® Excel include **AutoSum** (see page 577) and **AutoFormat** (see page 573). In addition there is a **Chart Wizard** which is invaluable if you need to do graphics (see illustration on page 558).

EVIDENCE COLLECTION

There are several ways in which to prove to your assessor that (a) you can enter numerical and text data, (b) you can use selection and manipulating facilities, and (c) you know why automated facilities are useful.

- If possible, collect *comparative* spreadsheets which show that you have undertaken all the activities – i.e. spreadsheets before and after data has been sorted, or inserted, moved or deleted.

- If you are not able to collect sufficient examples, try to collect witness testimony from customers for whom you have carried out these operations.

- It may be necessary to undertake all or some of these activities while your assessor observes you, and/or to answer questions on these facilities.

It is sensible to label all documentary evidence and to write a brief summary report linking it all together. Finally, do check that your evidence proves you can undertake *all* the activities required for the scheme.

If any of the automated facilities described above are new to you, then check now how they work. If you are using a different package from Excel, use your program Help screen to see which facilities are available to you.

Preserving integrity

There are various aspects to this. The first relates to your own authority to work with spreadsheets, and the second relates to your organisation's procedures and specific requirements – including those which relate to the safety or security of the spreadsheets you produce.

Your authority and responsibility

You should be aware of the limits of your own responsibility for entering numerical data and updating data files. *Never* change data without permission or 'guess' any entries (particularly numerical ones) – for instance, if you cannot read someone's handwriting. Check with the person concerned if any figures are difficult to read.

Obtaining permission to access certain files was covered on page 556. Some spreadsheets may be protected so that you cannot open, access or change them. Excel provides three levels of protection.

- At the first level, anyone who doesn't know the password cannot open the workbook.
- At the second level, people can open the workbook but cannot save their changes unless they know the password.
- At the third level, designers can choose whether users can open the workbook as a read-only file or as a read/write file.

You can use these strategies yourself to protect your workbooks and prevent unauthorised users either opening or changing your worksheets (see below).

Organisational requirements

Your organisation may have specific requirements when you are working with and saving files. There might be a rule on the frequency with which certain important data must be updated and resaved. This will be particularly important if the data is used by several people or is available over a network. Users will assume it is updated at specific intervals and may be using the data on which to base important decisions.

It is important to be able to find data quickly, so there is likely to be guidance on the naming conventions for files, worksheets and workbooks and on their correct location (e.g. in which set of folders or on which hard drive the files are saved). See also page 559.

Your organisation might also have requirements on the information to be logged in the Summary Information box when you save files. (If you never use this, you can prevent its appearance by clicking on Options on your Tools menu and then clearing the 'Prompt for summary information' check box on the General tab.)

KEY NOTES ON PROTECTING DATA

Locking

You can 'lock' cells or 'protect' key data within a spreadsheet – to prevent other people from altering this even if they can view the spreadsheet. Microsoft® Excel defaults to protecting some cells, so you need to start by unlocking all the cells.

- Select the whole spreadsheet (click the grey intersection box at the junction of the row numbers and column letters).
- Select Format on the main menu bar and click Cells.
- Select the Protection tab and clear the Locked check box.
- Select the cells you want to lock and repeat this procedure, this time selecting the Locked box.

You will see a warning that this procedure will not work unless you protect your spreadsheet, as follows.

- Select Tools on the menu bar.
- Click on Protection and then Protect Sheet. Note that you can protect the whole of your workbook if you wish.

You will have the option to add a password. If you choose this you will then have to retype the password. You will also receive a warning that if you forget it, it cannot be retrieved by your computer system! So if you use this option, either pick a name you will easily remember or keep a note of it in a locked drawer.

Setting a password

- Select the Save As option in the File menu.
- Choose the Options button and select the option you want. For instance, in the 'Write Reservation Password' box you can type a password and press OK.
- In the Re-enter Write Reservation Password box, repeat the password and click on OK.
- In the Save-As dialogue box, click on OK.

Once you close the workbook you activate the level of protection you have selected. If you have selected the 'Read Only Recommended' and someone opens your workbook using the 'read only' button and makes any changes, they would have to save it under a new name – your original cannot be altered.

Note that these passwords are case-sensitive (i.e. to lower or upper case) and that forgetting the password means that you, too, have no means of access!

Check that you can undertake protection procedures by locking and protecting selected cells on a spreadsheet. If you do this properly, you should find that you *cannot* enter or overtype data into your locked cells but you *can* enter or overtype data in the other cells. Remember that you can lock *all* the cells in a spreadsheet if you wish, not just selected cells.

Now create a small spreadsheet and, using Save As and Options, assign a level of protection to it – then test that it works.

Finally, check out how to modify locked cells and remove password protection for a file by accessing your on-line Help facility. Note, however, that if you have protected your spreadsheet with a password, this is when you will need to remember it again!

EVIDENCE COLLECTION

Obtain all the organisational procedures or details of the organisational requirements which apply when you are producing spreadsheet documents. Personalise them by highlighting the ones you use the most and stating how they affect your work. If possible, give specific examples to illustrate the points you are making.

Write an account (or keep a log) which proves that you regularly meet your customer's requirements for layout, time and purpose.

Give examples of occasions when you produced sensitive data and the steps you took to preserve its integrity. You can demonstrate to your assessor how you lock and protect spreadsheets, or write a description of how you do this on your package, and how often.

Finally, write an account or obtain witness testimony to prove that you routinely meet your organisation's requirements for frequency (ie how frequently you must save your work), naming conventions and location for saving files. If you write an account, ask your supervisor to countersign it for authenticity.

Key facts on producing a spreadsheet by manipulating data

You have already seen the importance of identifying and applying customer requirements when retrieving or entering data. This becomes even more critical if you are involved in:

- deciding the final page layout
- deciding how to format your spreadsheet
- carrying out calculations and inputting the correct formulae.

Element 319.2 covers all these areas.

Unless you are very unusual (or lucky!) you will find that some of your customers will have distinct preferences about layout and format. Others may be more laid back – unless the document is required for an important occasion. Everyone, however, will be expect you to be able to enter formulae correctly! See pages 576–582 for information on that topic.

Program Help files are invaluable for providing specific guidance on particular operations you may not know, or have forgotten how to do. A useful tip, if you are not certain that you understand the instructions, is to practise on a small 'test' spreadsheet of your own design. Another safeguard, if you are trying a new technique on an actual spreadsheet, is to save it first. For additional safety you could save a copy with a new name and experiment on that version. Then if anything goes wrong you have not affected the master document.

Many program Help files have a printable option. It is useful to create a small manual of 'help sheets' for operations you often need to access – and this can contribute towards your evidence.

CHECK IT OUT!

Another type of program help is 'wizards'. They help to simplify a new procedure you are trying to learn. For example, creating charts (i.e. graphs, bar charts or pie charts) from data is simplified in microsoft® Excel with the Chart wizard. You start this by clicking on the Chart Wizard button on your toolbar (like a tiny bar chart). Charts are beyond the scope of this scheme, but you might like to investigate this option to *really* prove to your assessor that you can use program help facilities!

Cell formatting facilities

Cell formatting relates to the appearance of the finished spreadsheet. Whereas a worksheet containing black data on a white background with plain headings may be suitable for a standard spreadsheet, often something more interesting and eye-catching is needed if the data is to be included in a booklet or brochure for external customers, or when it is required for a presentation. This is when good formatting skills can really pay dividends and impress your customers!

For this award, you have to prove that you can use *all* the following cell formatting facilities:

- alignments
- borders
- data types
- fonts
- shadings
- widths.

The information you need to undertake these operations is given in the Key Notes below.

 ## KEY NOTES ON FORMATTING

Basic techniques

Alignments

Change the alignment of the text by selecting the cells and then clicking on the appropriate toolbar button. You will find three at the top of your screen – one to align text to the left, one to centre text and one to align to the right.

Borders

Add a border by clicking on the down arrow to the right of the Borders button and selecting the type of border you want.

Data types

- Change the size of the data by selecting the cells and clicking the downward arrow to the right of the number next to the font name. This will show a range of point sizes – the higher the number, the larger the type. This is useful for emphasising a main heading, for instance.
- Embolden data by selecting it and click the bold button on the task bar. Similarly you can italicise or underscore data.
- Change the colour of data by clicking on the downward arrow by the Data Colour button.

Fonts

Change the font (the typeface) by selecting the appropriate cells and then clicking the downward arrow to the right of the existing font name to see the options available. Now choose the one you want.

Shadings

Shade cells by selecting the cells, clicking Format on your

menu bar, then Cells and then the Patterns tab. Choose a pattern from the pattern box. Patterns can also be coloured if you wish. A quick way, if you just want dark or light shading, is to click the appropriate button on your toolbar.

Widths

See pages 563 and 574 for information.

Advanced techniques

If you feel adventurous, try these:

- **Centre a main heading** by selecting the cells you want to centre it across and then clicking the Centre Text button. This is like a tiny chart with two black arrows at the left and right.

- **Format any numbers** you have entered by selecting them and then right-clicking your mouse. Then select the Format Cells option. The Number tab gives you several options, such as currency (£14.32), Integer – which are whole numbers (14), Decimal places (14.3213), Percentage (14.32%).

  Alternatively, use the decimal, currency and percentage buttons on your toolbar. You can choose to put a comma in numbers of four figures or more by using the comma *button* (do not use the comma key on your keyboard for this).

CHECK IT OUT!

It is essential to practise formatting by carrying out *all* the examples above, particularly those you have never used before. It is worth investigating all your format options by clicking Format, then Cells, then clicking all the tabs in turn to see what is available. Use Help if you are uncertain what to do with a new technique – but most are very simple.

If you are experimenting with colour, remember that a professional document should be pleasing to the eye – not overwhelming! It is usually best not to use more than two or three colours, and never use combinations which aren't easy to read – such as blue on red. (Try it!) Remember, too, that using colour is pointless if you haven't a colour printer or will be taking one copy and photocopying the remainder on a single-colour photocopier!

Finally, create a small spreadsheet and experiment with various AutoFormat options to find the ones you like the best.

INFORMATION UPDATE

Microsoft® Excel helps out spreadsheet designers by supplying several 'off-the-peg' versions. These are called **AutoFormats** and consist of a combination of colours, formats, fonts and borders which you can use to create a professional document quickly.

Start by selecting the cells you want to format. Then find AutoFormat under Format on the main menu bar. The dialogue box shows several examples and you can scroll through the remainder. Click on the format you want and then click on OK. Then see the result.

Page layout requirements

Page layout relates to the presentation of the spreadsheet, particularly when it is printed. For this element you must prove that you are competent at:

* inserting gridlines
* headers and footers
* changing margins
* changing the page orientation
* changing the page size.

Again, use the Key Notes below to check your own skills. Remember that you can check the final 'look' of your spreadsheet using the Print Preview window (select the Preview Window on your toolbar for speed). This saves a lot of paper and ink/toner and is far more environmentally friendly than taking several 'test' printouts! And don't forget your Zoom option to magnify areas you cannot read easily. Alternatively position your mouse pointer over an area until it changes to a small magnifying glass and then click to see the magnification. A second click will display the normal page again.

KEY NOTES ON PAGE LAYOUT

Basic techniques

Gridlines

These are the small lines which divide columns and rows and make the spreadsheet easier to read. With Microsoft® Excel, click File on the main menu bar and then Page Setup. The dialogue box will show the option for visible gridlines. Click on this, then click on OK.

Headers and footers

Add a header and/or footer (for instance, to denote your customer's name, your name and/or the date on which you produced the spreadsheet). Click View on the menu bar, then the Header/Footer tab. Now click Custom Header to see the Header dialogue box (or Custom Footer to see the Footer dialogue box). Remember, however, that the middle of the footer is usually used to denote page number. You can automatically add the date by clicking the 'clock' icon which shows on these dialogue boxes – but check first that your 'computer' clock is displaying the correct date and time!

Margins

Margins are set automatically on most spreadsheet packages. With Microsoft® Excel, the top and bottom margins are 2.54 cm and the left and right are 1.90 cm. Change the margins to accommodate special headers and footers, headed paper or more or less data than normal. Do this by accessing Print Preview and clicking the Margins button at the top (or File then Page Setup and click the Margins tab). Next position the mouse over the margin you want to change and drag it to its new location. Repeat these steps for each margin you wish to change.

Page orientation and size

Orientation refers to whether the worksheet is printed in portrait or landscape. The default in most packages, including Excel, is portrait. To change this, select File on the menu bar and then Page Setup. In the dialogue box, click the Page tab and then the orientation you want. Note that this only changes the orientation on the printed page, *not* the way the worksheet appears on your screen.

Page size is another option when you click the Page tab. Remember that any page size you select must be compatible with the printer you are using.

Advanced techniques

If you feel adventurous, try these (all available on the Page Setup dialogue box):

- **Scaling** reduces the size of the print to fit more on a page.
- **Print quality** enables you to print draft versions to save on ink/toner.
- **Row and column headings** includes your row numbers and column letters on the printout, for reference.
- You can **select cells** before accessing File and then Print – so that only the cells you have chosen will be printed.

Design a small spreadsheet and try out all the techniques outlined in the key notes box. You should note that devices such as gridlines and scaling become more important on a large spreadsheet where there is a lot of data to read.

Experiment with headers and footers by putting your customer's name at the top left, then your own name and the date at the bottom left and right respectively. Then check how it looks by clicking Page Preview.

EVIDENCE COLLECTION

A good way of impressing your customers – and proving to your assessor that you can do all the formatting and layout techniques listed on pages 571–572 and 573–574 – is to produce a 'samples' folder of spreadsheets, showing different formats and layouts.

You can even show this to customers who are not certain what would look best for an important spreadsheet. You can discuss with your assessor how you achieved particular effects (or write brief explanations on the specimens).

Using calculation facilities

One of the most critical skills you need to master is the use of calculation facilities. Indeed, without these, spreadsheets would really have no purpose – you could just use tables instead, on a word-processor. It is precisely because complex calculations can be undertaken quickly and easily – and automatic recalculations can take place when data is changed – that gives spreadsheets their value.

Microsoft® Excel has the ability to undertake over 200 types of calculation, some of which are very advanced. You may be pleased that you have to know only the more commonly used functions to obtain this award. However, to use these in different spreadsheets means you must understand them – which is the focus of this section.

If formulae worry you, or if you feel you have never understood them properly, now is your chance to put that right. Simply work through the formula guide below, stage by stage. After each set of instructions you will have the opportunity to practise your skills. Take advantage of this – reading about formulae will never make you competent, whereas using them will!

Formula guide – part 1

1 All spreadsheets require an identifying symbol at the start of a function or calculation. For instance, in Microsoft® Excel this is an equals sign =; in Quattro, it is an 'at' sign @.

2 When you input a cell reference for a calculation, state the column letter *first* and then the row number, like this: =A4+B5. It doesn't matter whether you use upper or lower case for your column letters.

3 Use the following symbols in your formula:

+ for addition =B2+A6 and - for subtraction =F6-E3
* for multiplication =A8*6 and / for division =E10/6.

4 When you create a formula, this appears at the top of your screen in the formula bar. Note that if your formula will give you a total, it is usual to leave a blank cell immediately before it, so the total is clear.

5 Press Enter or click the Tick button on your formula bar to carry out the calculation.

CHECK IT OUT!

Create an expenses spreadsheet using the data shown opposite. Set it out neatly with a heading in bold and your numerical data format as currency. Widen any columns as necessary to fit the text data.

a Now add the total amount of advances by entering a formula to add these three cells.

b Subtract the amount of Kevan Briggs' advance from the amount he spent on travel, by entering a formula to subtract one cell from the other.

c Tom Smith has had the same advance every month. Enter a formula to find out how much he has received in the last 12 months.

d Tahira Patel spent the same on travel in each of the four weeks in September. Enter a formula to find out how much she spent each week.

e Now clear all the cells in which you had entered a formula, but *don't* delete your spreadsheet – you will need it again in this unit.

Formula guide – part 2

1 Large numbers of cells can be added quickly using the SUM function. After the function command, the formula follows in brackets, like this: =SUM(B12:B16). The colon (:) represents all the cells between the two cell references – so your sum would be for B12 *through to* B16.

2 You already know you should leave a blank cell before putting the total. Professional spreadsheet users often include this in their sum. This means that they don't need to change the formula if they add additional figures to the list.

September Representatives' Accounts (£)			
	Tom Smith	Tahira Patel	Kevan Briggs
Expenses:			
Travel	650.00	240.00	820.00
Entertainment	112.00	154.00	158.00
Subsistence	24.00	31.00	42.00
Stationery	8.00	14.00	28.00
Miscellaneous	10.00	12.00	36.00
Expenses totals:			
Less advances	250.00	150.00	300.00
Sub-totals:			
Plus commission			
Amount owing:			
Additional data			
Sales	14,000.00	16,000.00	20,000.00
Commission rate	0.5%	0.5%	0.5%

3 With Microsoft® Excel, you can quickly add up cells by using the AutoSum feature. This is the button on your tool bar that looks like a capital Greek sigma (Σ). Simply click on the cell where you want your total, then click AutoSum. If you are using Microsoft® Excel 97 or 2000, you will see a dotted line around the cells Microsoft® Excel intends to add. Make sure these are the ones you want! If not, you will have to select the correct ones yourself. (Click on the start cell, then drag the dotted line around the correct cells.) Then press Enter.

4 If you mistakenly include the 'answer' cell in your formula you will see an error message – as you have created a 'circular reference'. In that case you will have to correct your formula.

5 You will also see error messages if you:
   • include a deleted cell reference by mistake (#REF)
   • try to divide by zero (#DIV/0!)
   • include a text cell in a formula (#VALUE)
   • mis-key a cell reference, such as BQ instead of B1 (#NAME?).

6 It is easy to copy a formula across cells where you want the same calculation to be carried out. This saves you entering it again and again. For instance, if you have entered a SUM function to add a series of cells in a column, you can point at the bottom right of the cell containing the formula, watch for the thin cross to appear (+), and then drag across the other cells to which you want to copy the formula.

a Can you remember the error message you receive if your number is too long to be displayed – and what you must do about that? If you have completely forgotten, look back to page 563.

b Use the SUM function to add the expenses for Tom Smith. Try to remember to include the next blank cell above your sub-total line.

c Use the AutoSum function to add the expenses for Tahira Patel.

d If you are using Microsoft® Excel 2000 you can use the AutoCalculate function to add the expenses for Kevan Briggs. Select all the cells which relate to his expenses and Microsoft® Excel will automatically add these and put the sum on your status bar, not in the spreadsheet.

e Now clear all your totals except the one for Tom Smith.

f Point the mouse at your total for Tom Smith – check this is the cell containing the formula by looking at your formula bar. Now copy the formula across the other total cells. You can see how your spreadsheet package has automatically changed the cell references for each column by clicking on each total cell with your mouse and referring to the formula bar.

 INFORMATION UPDATE

On the latest spreadsheets, you can quickly add a whole series of rows and columns by selecting all the cells you want to add *including* a blank row for your results, and pressing AutoSum. Use Help to find out whether you have this option.

Formula guide – part 3

1 You have just seen that cell references automatically change when you copy a formula. This is because the cells contain a **relative reference**. It is useful to remember this term.

2 There are occasions when you *don't* want a reference to change. In this case you have to convert the cell containing this data into an **absolute reference**. You do this by typing a dollar sign ($) before *both* the column letter and row number, like this: A6.

3 Spreadsheets carry out calculations using basic mathematical rules. First they <u>m</u>ultiply and <u>d</u>ivide, and only then do they <u>a</u>dd and <u>s</u>ubtract. So $6+2*3=12$ (*not* 24). You can remember this by the sentence '<u>m</u>any <u>d</u>iscounts <u>a</u>ffect <u>s</u>ales'.

4 If you want to change the order in which the calculation is done, put brackets around the part you want to be calculated first. So: $(6+2)*3 = 12$.

Other common functions

These are useful to know:

- AVERAGE – gives the average of a set, like this: =AVERAGE(F6:F9).
- COUNT – counts the number of entries or values in a list, like this: =COUNT(B3:B9).
- MAX – finds the highest value in a list, like this: =MAX(E6:E26).
- MIN – finds the lowest value in a list, like this: =MIN(G10:G54).
- ROUND – rounds a decimal number to a specific number of digits. The number of digits you want is entered after the comma which follows the cell reference, like this: =ROUND(H17,2).

You can view all the functions offered by Microsoft® Excel if you click on the Function button on your toolbar (to the right of the AutoSum button). It looks like a small 'f' with a squiggle at the bottom right. You will now see the Paste function box with the function categories in the left-hand pane and the function name in the right-hand pane. If you ever forget a function name you can select it from this list and read a description about it in the dialogue box. You can now enter up to 30 different numbers, simply by clicking on cells to select them. (If your dialogue box gets in the way, position your mouse pointer over a blank area and drag it to another part of your screen). Note, however, that if you are entering a range of cells (e.g. C5:C18) then you would put this just under the first number box and not split it.

CHECK IT OUT!

It is quite common, on a spreadsheet, to put additional data somewhere else which you will refer to as part of a formula. If this is important data, and the subject of several formulae, then it is sensible to lock and protect these cells (see page 568).

There are two sets of additional data on your representative's spreadsheet – one for sales and the other for the commission rate. This is going to be used to calculate the commission due. However, the rate must not change when you copy the formula – so you are going to refer to it as an absolute reference (see page 578).

a Work out Tom Smith's commission by clicking in his commission cell (where you want your answer). Then enter the formula where the commission *rate* cell is an absolute reference and multiply this by Tom's sales figure cell reference. For instance, if the rate was in cell B9 and the sales figure for Tom in B6, your formula would be =B9*B6.

b Now copy this formula across for the other representatives. Then check your formula bar. You should find that your rate cell reference has remained the same in each one. ➡

c Now practise your formula skills by calculating the sub-total and final amount owing to Tom Smith. Then copy the formulae across so you have a complete spreadsheet for all the representatives.

d Create a formula which will work out how much Tom and Tahira will spend on travel over the next year if they spend the same amounts each month. Enter the cells for their travel figures and then multiply by 12. But add brackets, so that their total travel is added before it is multiplied. Then delete this.

e Practise the other types of common formula given above by moving to a different area on your spreadsheet and entering the figures 10 through to 100 (i.e 10, 20, 30 etc.) down any column. Then leave a blank cell and click on the cell below. Now test the AVERAGE, COUNT, MAX and MIN functions. Then delete your column.

f Practise the ROUND function by entering the following decimal number into a blank cell: 87.40590 and then round it to three digits. Then clear the cell.

Finally, practise displaying and printing a formula on your spreadsheet, as follows.

• Show the formula by clicking on Tools on your menu bar and selecting Options. When you see the Options dialogue box click the View tab and then click the Formulas check box, then OK. (You would have to click this again to revert to numbers.) Note that your cells will automatically widen to show the formula.

• An even faster way of seeing formulae is to press Ctrl and ` (at the top left of your keyboard). If you press it again, you will revert back to numbers.

• Print the formula. Check first how it looks on your Print Preview screen (you may want to add gridlines or change the margins or orientation at this point) and then select print.

• Printing formulae is useful, especially if you think you may need to refer to them again.

Formula guide – part 4

When you reach this point you will already know enough about formulae to achieve your award. However, if you have enjoyed this section and want to know more, there are two more types of formula you may like to try.

Let us look first at **IF** statements, which are used for many reasons. In this section you will see how they can be used as a memory jogger or as a quick reckoner!

A college administrator has been told that only evening classes with more than 16 students can be run. Other classes will have to be closed. Imagine she has 500 courses on her spreadsheet – looking down them all would take some time. Entering an IF statement will do all this work for her. Her spreadsheet for three courses looks like this:

	A	B	C
1			
2	**Course**	**No. of students**	**Close?**
3			
4	Cake decoration	15	
5	Beauty therapy	20	
6	Indian cooking	10	

She enters an IF statement in the last column which is as follows: =IF(B4<16,"Close","Run"), and copies this formula down her 'C' column.

- IF is the function and the formula follows in brackets.
- B4 is the cell she is referring to.
- <16 means 'less than 16' – which is her criterion in this case.
- Close is the word she wants to appear on her spreadsheet if the statement is true (this must be in double quotes and followed by a comma).
- Run is the word she wants to appear if the statement is false.

Bear in mind that she could type any other text into the 'true' and 'false' statements, not just 'Close' and 'Run'!

If she wished, our administrator could make every 'Close' stand out in a distinctive colour, such as red. She would only do this *after* entering her IF statement and copying it down her spreadsheet. Then she would:

- Select (highlight) the cells showing the results.
- Click on Format on the menu bar and then select Conditional Formatting. This shows three boxes which she wants to say
  box 1 – cell value is
  box 2 – equal to
  box 3 ="CLOSE".

- She then clicks on Format and then Cells and then the Patterns tab, and then chooses her cell colour – red.
- Finally, she clicks OK – twice.

The last function we will cover is **LOOKUP**. You already know that you can put useful information somewhere else in a spreadsheet. If you want Microsoft® Excel to 'look up' this information, that is possible.

Claire works for a mail-order company. Its delivery charges depend upon distance and the following table on Claire's spreadsheet shows their rates.

	A	B	C	D	E
1	Zone A	Zone B	Zone C	Zone D	Zone E
2	£2.50	£4.00	£5.00	£6.50	£8.00

Claire decides to call her table 'Delivery'. She tells her spreadsheet this name by selecting *all* the cells in her table, clicking on Insert on her menu bar, then Name, then Define. She then types in the word Delivery and clicks on OK.

When Claire receives orders she enters these in a different part of her spreadsheet as follows:

	A	B	C
15	Name	Amount	Zone
16	John Bates	60.00	C

She can total each order and *also* add in the correct delivery charge by referring to her delivery table. Today, John Bates has ordered a total of £60 of goods and lives in zone C. This total is entered in cell B16. His total order can be calculated by entering the following formula:

B16+HLOOKUP(C16,Delivery,2).

- B16 contains the total for the goods.
- HLOOKUP gives the horizontal look up command – the formula then follows in brackets.
- C16 identifies John Bates' zone.
- Delivery identifies the table.
- 2 identifies the second row on the table where the zone price is.

Finally, you may like to note that it is easier to name a cell by just clicking into the Name box and typing in the name. Check with your tutor (or online Help) if you don't know how to do this.

1 You are responsible for ordering stationery stock. Enter the following items and quantities:

A4 lever arch files	20
A4 paper, white (reams)	14
A4 ring binders	8
DL envelopes, boxes	0

You have the remit to re-order any of these items when they fall below 15. Set up a spreadsheet and include an IF statement to tell you which items need to be re-ordered now – preferably in colour. Imagine how helpful this would be on a stocklist with hundreds of items!

2 You work for a hotel which adds a 'single supplement' to rooms on the following basis:

Class A	£8.00
Class B	£10.00
Class C	£13.00
Class D	£15.00

Enter this into your spreadsheet program and define it as a lookup table using any appropriate title.

Peter Brown wishes to stay with you for four nights in a class B room which costs £75 per night. Enter a formula which will tell you how much he has to pay.

Raising queries

A final word of advice. Never assume you can solve every problem or difficulty on your own. If you are not certain which formula would be best, or if your formula doesn't seem to be working, *always* check with the person who asked you to create the spreadsheet. If you only *think* you are having problems, do a 'rationality check' by working out what type of answer you should be getting and seeing if this matches your result. If you were expecting a five-figure number but the answer is in the hundreds, think again!

If you can't solve the problem, obtain guidance from the person who gave you the task, or someone in your workplace who you know is an expert with spreadsheets. This is much better than spending hours entering formulae only to find they are wrong and your spreadsheet is useless.

Key facts on outputting a spreadsheet to its required destination

Identifying the destination

You have a number of choices in relation to outputting the completed spreadsheet – once you have checked it thoroughly, of course! You can:

- take a hard copy (printout)
- save it on a floppy or hard disk
- attach it to an e-mail (internally on a network or externally over the Internet)
- fax it
- route it to specific people
- publish it on your company intranet
- publish it on the Internet.

In the first case you are using a printer as an output device. In all the other cases you are passing on an electronic version of your spreadsheet. To achieve this part of the award you have to prove to your assessor you can undertake *both* types of operation.

Your choice should be based upon:

- the number of recipients
- where they are
- what facilities they have
- why the spreadsheet is required
- the degree of confidentiality.

For instance, one person standing next to you may want to check a hard copy quickly – or take it to a meeting to show people. Another person may want the spreadsheet saved to floppy disk, to look at it on a laptop or on a computer elsewhere. Twenty representatives working from home – all with e-mail facilities – is a totally different matter. Sending the spreadsheet electronically saves you time, effort and postage!

Output parameters

Another factor that will – or should – influence your choice is the output parameters. These normally refer to hard copies and relate to:

- the number of copies required
- the page range
- the paper size.

Again, if the page range is considerable and several copies are required, you may benefit by sending it electronically. Otherwise you will have to set your printer to match these parameters (see below).

Confidentiality

Do make sure that you are not breaching confidentiality at any point. Check and double-check who is authorised to receive a copy of any sensitive data. *Never* put this type of information on the organisation's intranet or the Internet, and check with your supervisor before sending it over a company network. Probably the safest course of action is to take a hard copy and send this in a sealed envelope, clearly marked 'Confidential'. In extreme circumstances, deliver this yourself – by hand.

Checking output devices

Firstly, you need to know what is available on the computer system you use. Secondly, you need to be on friendly terms with your printer!

You can determine your print options very easily. Click on File then Print and then identify the number of copies and page range you require in the dialogue box. Finally, make sure the page size is correct for the paper you are using and the capability of your printer.

If you want to take an extra copy of your spreadsheet for someone on a floppy disk, then select the Save As option to make the copy and check the device drive is set at A:, and that there is a floppy disk in the drive.

If you operate on a networked system, have internal e-mail or a company intranet, or are expected to publish data on the Web, then it is presumed you already know you have these facilities!

You can attach a spreadsheet file to an e-mail. First save it, then prepare your covering e-mail message if necessary. Then click on Attach, locate the correct drive, directory and file title of the spreadsheet in the dialogue box that appears, and double-click.

You can fax a document (over the Internet) using your Fax Wizard, if you use Microsoft® Excel 2000, and can create a cover sheet in Microsoft® Word 2000. Select File on your menu bar, Sent To and then Fax Recipient. Alternatively, if you have fax software installed on your computer or if your computer is linked to a fax output device, then you can click on File then Print and then select the fax drive in the Name box.

If you work on a company network, you can route the spreadsheet to several customers for comments. On the File menu select Send To then Routing Recipient. Then click Address to see the Address Book dialogue box. Now select the names of the recipients you want and click OK. You can change the recipient order by selecting any name and clicking the up or down arrow next to Move. Now select the routing options you want and click Route to send the file to the first person on your list.

Check with your network administrator or intranet administrator if you want to post your spreadsheet on your company intranet. Normally this means saving your spreadsheet in HTML format. On the File menu, simply click Save As Web Page.

You can also publish data on the Web – even interactive data so that your customers can interact with your spreadsheet. For instance, a building society could create a spreadsheet giving its latest interest rates. When customers key in the amount they intend to save, a final column could calculate their interest per year for each type of account listed. Start by creating your spreadsheet and save it in the Web files folder as an HTML document. Then contact your Internet administrator to find out what to do next – as this varies from one organisation to another.

Your customers' requirements for output

Do bear in mind that your customer may have specific views on the best type of output. However, after reading this section you may be able to make several suggestions! Much depends upon the sensitivity of the data, why it is being distributed and the urgency. At the end of the day, if there is a slight difference of opinion you are always best to accede to your customer's wishes. Otherwise, you may be held to blame if anything goes wrong.

EVIDENCE COLLECTION

It is easy enough to prove that you can use your printer. Simply collect copies of printouts you have produced over a period of time – preferably with different numbers of copies, page ranges and paper sizes. Personalise each one by writing on the top what your instructions were and why this form of output was required.

You can take a copy of any e-mail you send with an electronic attachment, or fax messages you create or routing slips. If you post a spreadsheet on your intranet or the Internet, then you can sit your assessor next to you, show him or her the original spreadsheet and then access the 'live' document on screen as proof.

It will help if you can obtain witness testimony to prove that you can use both electronic output and produce hard copies. There are two ways in which to do this.

- The first is to create a log of all the spreadsheets and related output devices you use over a period of time and ask your customers to initial or confirm each one.
- The second is to ask your customers for specific witness testimony to cover both printers and electronic stores.

Finally, write a brief account of the output devices you use routinely, why you use them and to what degree you discuss this choice with your customers. In particular, state the action you take when you are outputting a spreadsheet which contains highly sensitive data.

Option Unit 320 Design and create complex documents using a computer

---

SPECIAL NOTE

Complex documents can be created on a variety of software packages. For instance, in the Microsoft® Office suite, you can use:

- **Word** to produce complex word-processed documents
- **Excel** for complex spreadsheets
- **PowerPoint**® to produce textual documents to support presentations
- **Publisher** to produce desktop published documents, such as a staff newsletter.

If you produce complex spreadsheets, you will find Option Unit 319 more appropriate. Similarly, Option Unit 321 is suitable if you use Microsoft® PowerPoint® or a similar presentations package.

It is expected that you would want to achieve this unit using a word-processing package. If you more usually use desktop publishing software, you can still undertake this unit but need to check first with your assessor that you can produce evidence to meet all the requirements.

The instructions in this book have been written for Microsoft® Word 2000 users. They also assume a fundamental knowledge of word-processing and the ability to produce and print routine documents.

If you use a different word-processing package (or a desktop publishing package), then please check any specific requirements you need by accessing your online Help facility or by talking to your tutor.

FOCUS OF THE UNIT

To obtain this unit you must be able to:

- **design** complex documents
- **input and edit** text
- **format and lay out** complex documents
- **print** documents.

Designing and creating complex documents using a computer

You should note that information relevant to this section has already been covered in several of the mandatory units, as follows.

Health and safety requirements when using a keyboard and other types of computer equipment

See Unit 302. The major legislation about which you should be aware includes:

- Health and Safety (Display Screen Equipment) Regulations 1992 (pages 103 and 106)
- Provision and Use of Work Equipment Regulations 1992 (page 102)
- Electricity at Work Regulations 1989 (page 120).

Requirements for confidentiality and how to follow these

See page 280 in Unit 305.

The basic legal requirements for data protection

See pages 281–284 in Unit 305.

Key facts on designing complex documents

The types of documents produced by your team

The type and style of documents required by a team depend upon:

- the type of work carried out by the team
- the type of information contained in each document
- the purpose of the different documents
- the overall format or house style of the organisation
- the intended readership.

Information on:

a   the various types of document produced by teams
b   the appropriate designs for such documents, and
c   ways of selecting and adapting designs according to the criteria above

is contained in Unit 305, pages 314–338. You may wish to refer back to those pages now to refresh your memory.

EVIDENCE COLLECTION

List the *types* of document produced by your team. For each, comment on how the original design was agreed, if you know this. Identify all the types of document for which you had a responsibility for the design and creation. If you regularly review different documents, state the time period over which this occurs and your involvement.

If possible, help your assessor by supporting this account with copies of documents with which you are personally involved.

Adapting an existing design, or getting a clear brief for a new design

Imagine these three scenarios. First, one morning just as your manager is going out, she tells you that later on that day she will be interviewing some candidates for the post of computer services manager and she needs an interview assessment form. You spend all morning devising what you hope is an appropriate form, only to find when your manager returns that she meant you to photocopy an existing form, a copy of which is in the filing cabinet.

Second, you are asked to submit a draft design for the front cover of the staff handbook. You obtain copies of staff handbooks from other organisations and talk to a firm of graphic designers about designs, styles and fonts. When you proudly hand over the finished result to your manager, he hands it back to you with the comment that it's far too expensive for him to afford!

Third, you send in a fifth draft of a suggested layout for a client satisfaction questionnaire, and for the fifth time your manager makes some major amendments to it. You try to decide whether it would be worth losing your job simply to have the pleasure of throwing it at him!

These three examples demonstrate that a lot of time – and therefore money – can be wasted if you do not get an absolutely clear brief when you are asked to design a document. Ideally you should consider all the following points.

a Discuss with your manager or colleagues *exactly* what you have been asked to do. You should bear in mind the purpose of the document, the type and style of presentation, the proposed content and the people for whom it is intended. (Refer back to Unit 305 if necessary.)

b You can sometimes save time, energy and money by thinking about whether any existing document can be adapted. It is sometimes easier to recall a complex form or questionnaire you have already designed and alter the headings, rather than start afresh. On other occasions, it is easier to start again. Much depends upon how much of the original formatting was complex and can be retained.

c Determine what your role is. Are you totally responsible for the design or have you only a partial role to play? If so, who else is involved? Are you expected only to carry out the research? Have you to produce a number of different options?

d Determine your budget – if any – and the possible cost options. Is the document high-profile? Is it one that is going to be used across the organisation? Will it be used over and over again? What equipment do you have in-house and what would you have to sub-contract, say, to an outside printer? If you use the latter, will the organisation be prepared to pay for the additional costs involved.

e Make sure you are aware of the time scale. Is the document required immediately or can you spend some time researching and preparing?

f Identify useful sources of reference. You may be asked to design a document from scratch but you have no idea where to start. In such circumstances it is reassuring to feel that you can ask someone else for advice.

Providing colleagues with design options

You are asked to draft out a standardised format for recording the notes of meetings held in your organisation. Once this has been approved it is to be used by everyone for consistency. You provide one version which a group of managers discuss at their weekly meeting. Feedback from this group is that your format is:

- too complicated to use
- not user-friendly.

You make some amendments and the draft is then shown again to the group. Their comments this time are that your design is:

- not detailed enough
- not suitable for use at all meetings.

You decide to invite the comments of individual staff who are frequently involved in meetings. Their response is:

- Why standardise? It is better to have different formats for different purposes.
- The design is too formal.

Obviously, no matter how many different versions you produce of a particular document, you are not likely to get universal agreement for any of them. However, if you produce only one version you give more people the opportunity to reject it – leaving you with no way ahead at all. If, on the other hand, they have to choose from a number of versions, they are less likely to reject *all* of them. Indeed, a frequently used method in such circumstances is to give people the opportunity to prioritise and to select the version or versions they like most.

Like the multiple-choice questionnaire handed out to customers in supermarkets to determine their opinion of customer services, it is essential to make it easy for people to give their opinions. If you ask one of your colleagues in what format he or she would like to see a particular document, you will get little response. If you provide a number of options, the level of response is likely to rise considerably.

Once you have consulted your colleagues, you can feel reassured that the version finally agreed upon is the most effective you can devise – and you should have a document which is far better than any of your original attempts!

CHECK IT OUT!

One of the most difficult documents to design is a simple questionnaire. You need to allow for the size of people's handwriting, that some people may not understand the questions unless they are very straightforward, and the fact that you need a format whereby the answers can be collated quickly and simply. The situation becomes even more difficult if your questionnaire is complex and some questions are dependent on earlier answers.

In this situation, you can usefully look back at an existing questionnaire, rather than start from scratch. You also need to ask people to test any design draft. If they have problems, rethink your design, don't argue with them that they are being dim! Only when you have tested it thoroughly should the final version be issued for general completion.

If you regularly undertake this work, you can improve your skills by being critical of all questionnaires you receive and complete. Also look back at previous ones in your filing cabinet. Assess each for ease of completion and simplicity and note down any key points you notice.

Negotiating and agreeing a final design option

There are normally three stages in negotiations – pre-negotiation, negotiation and post-negotiation.

 KEY NOTES ON PRE-NEGOTIATION

Ideally, when you reach the stage of presenting the final design option to your manager and or colleagues, you should be in the position of being able to do the following.

- Decide what you want and how far you are prepared to compromise. You may, for instance, be prepared to change the font or the graphics, but be very unwilling to change the overall format. You may be quite willing to change anything. You may feel that you should insist that nothing be changed – and that if the design is rejected someone else should take over.

- Make sure that, as far as possible, your colleagues are aware of the limitations of your equipment, software and abilities. You can be expected to do your best, but you are not a miracle worker. Expecting you to fit a complex and lengthy form on one A4 page in a large font is not achievable and you will save yourself a lot of time and worry if you make this clear at the outset. However, do remember to focus on the positive and say what you *can* do. Nothing is worse than someone who keeps arguing that 'it can't be done' for every request and never says what can be achieved!

- Decide what sort of approach you want to take. Do you want to let your colleagues discuss the design in your absence so that they can take a completely independent stance? Do you feel that you should be present to explain the reasons for the design? Do you want to have your say first before anyone else comments or would you welcome general discussion from the start? Do you feel you need your manager's support and that you should therefore discuss the rationale for the design with him or her *before* allowing it to be discussed by anyone else?

- Be prepared to ask yourself the 'what if?' questions: What if no-one likes the design? What if the person who says he or she doesn't like the design is someone whose opinion you distrust or do not value? What if someone says it is too complicated, too plain, too costly, too pretentious? You should then try to provide yourself with answers!

KEY NOTES ON NEGOTIATION

Once you are in the middle of a discussion about your design, you have to be able to think quickly. You may also want to persuade your colleagues that the design should be adopted. If you have prepared thoroughly beforehand, that will help. The following may also help you.

- Try not to monopolise the discussion. If you do, a number of colleagues might simply switch off and you cannot rely upon them for any contribution to the discussion. Others may start arguing with you simply to shut you up!

- Keep your comments simple and to the point. You know the design backward. Your colleagues may not.

- Look confident. If you have faith in your design, let it show.

- Be constantly aware of your colleagues' reactions. If they look sceptical or one or two start muttering to each other, you should be prepared to ask them direct for their opinion – and, if relevant, try to persuade them to change it.

- Avoid going on the defensive. If your colleagues are genuinely concerned about some aspects of your design, be prepared to listen even at this late stage. You may still be able to improve it.

KEY NOTES ON POST-NEGOTIATION

It is important that you agree a design. If you don't, all your work will have been wasted and the original objective not achieved.

- Make a note of the agreement – either at the final meeting or as soon as possible afterwards, write down what has been agreed. Make certain that the notes are distributed to the relevant people – particularly your line manager.

  If you forget this part, you may find that some of your colleagues start arguing with you a few weeks later and denying ever having agreed to what has now been implemented.

- Evaluate the process. If you start off in good spirits, confident that your design is good and then you come up against so many obstacles that your confidence is shaken, ask yourself what has gone wrong. If everything goes smoothly from the start, make a note of what you did and repeat it next time!

Make brief notes of what you would say to your colleagues if they made the following comments about an important document you had prepared for the sales team's annual conference.

a 'I like the overall look but the style is much too informal for such a serious issue.'

b 'It's rather boring isn't it? I couldn't be bothered reading it after the first line – and I'm sure a lot of other people will feel the same.'

c 'The typeface is so small I can hardly read it.'

d 'Could we include some more illustrations?'

e 'I liked the style of last year's better.'

f 'It's wonderful. Well done!'

Capabilities and limitations of the software available to you

Much modern software is very powerful, but the capabilities of your software will depend not only upon the *type* of software you have but the *version* you are using.

You should already be aware of the fundamental difference between different applications packages, such as spreadsheets, databases and word-processing. In addition, of course, there are presentation packages, Web-page design packages, graphics packages and desktop publishing packages – to name just a few!

In the past there was a tremendous difference between word-processing packages and desktop publishing packages, but as these have evolved the boundaries have become more blurred. Today, many of the features you could only carry out on a 'true' DTP package – such as importing and cropping graphics, flowing text around graphics, dividing text into columns and so on – can be done very effectively on a good word-processing package. Only if you need to carry out typographical operations are you now likely to use a specific DTP package.

In addition, software 'suites' have enabled text and graphics to be copied from one document to another using standard 'cut and paste' commands. So it becomes a simple matter to include a logo or graphic at the start of a document, part of a spreadsheet further down, and then import the name and address from your database!

It is useful at this point to know some basic terms.

- **Linking an object** means that updating the object (such as an address) in one application will automatically update it in another application.

- **Embedding an object** means simply copying and pasting from one application to another.

You will only be able to gain the maximum advantage from your package if you understand both its capabilities and limitations. If, of course, you are often asked to include design features which your software cannot cope with, then you may have a case for lobbying for your particular package to be updated!

The second criterion, of course, is your own knowledge and limitations. If you restrict yourself to routine documents and procedures you are unlikely to develop the skills required to get the most out of any package you have. It is quite normal for most people to concentrate on the facilities they use most frequently, but it really is worth exploring possibilities – particularly if you are asked to do something new. Help screens today have improved dramatically from a few years ago. Never say 'no' to a job until you've checked out whether the limitations relate to your software or to yourself!

Obviously, the more you use a particular software package, the more you get to know its functions. Quite often you will learn a new function when you *need* to – where, for instance, you are faced with producing a document requiring a particular format. However, there are certain basics with which you should be familiar right from the outset. You should, for instance, understand the normal screen displays and menus you see. You should know what each of the individual icons represents and how they may help you to produce even the most complex of documents.

In particular, make sure that you can discuss knowledgeably with your assessor everything in the following list, and explain the functions.

- **Menu bar** – lets you choose drop-down menus which hold groups of commands, such as all commands related to Files.
- **Standard toolbar** – contains buttons to help you select common commands such as Save and Print. Move the mouse pointer over a button to view the small box which says what each button does.
- **Formatting toolbar** – contains buttons to help you select common formatting commands such as bold, italic or underline. Again, pointing at the button will show you what it does.
- **Insertion point** – the flashing line on the screen (i.e. the text cursor) that indicates where the text you type will appear.
- **Status bar** – provides information about the area of the document displayed on the screen, the position of the insertion point etc.
- **The ruler** – shows where margins and tabs are currently positioned and can be used to change these positions.
- **The Windows taskbar** – shows what applications are currently active on your system. Clicking on one which is showing will take you to that application.

Toolbars can be displayed or hidden as you require them. On Microsoft® Word 2000 the Standard toolbar has a special icon which allows you to access all icons not currently on display.

When you first start an Microsoft® Office 2000 program, the most commonly used buttons appear on each toolbar. As you work with a program, the toolbars automatically change to remove buttons you rarely use and display those you use most often.

CHECK IT OUT!

Carry out a quick skills test on yourself before reading any further. Answer 'Yes' or 'No' to the following statements. I know:

a how to use the mouse – i.e. how to click, double click and drag objects

b the different options available when I left-click the mouse button and right-click it

c how to access the software I need

d how to exit from the program and close down (or log off) properly

e how to use drop-down menus – and the fact that '...' after a menu option means additional options are available

f the options I can select quickly from the standard toolbar and formatting toolbar

g how to access options not currently showing on either toolbar

h how to move a toolbar or hide my Windows taskbar

i how to use all the Help facilities available (see also pages 602 and 612).

If you answer 'No' to any of these statements, then remedy this gap in your knowledge by accessing Office Assistant or by talking to your supervisor, an experienced colleague or your tutor.

 INFORMATION UPDATE

Times are changing. It is not that long since few executives used their own computer for correspondence. In many traditional organisations this task was carried out by PAs, secretaries or administrators. The advent of the Internet, e-mail and laptops has changed all that. Computer awareness is rising steadily on the agenda of things all executives must know, so information technology training courses for managers are growing in popularity. Such courses tend to concentrate on the information that can be stored and retrieved rather than on hands-on skills – particularly the more complex ones.

However, it is astounding that the vast majority of executives still have to 'hunt and peck' their way around a keyboard – given the time this takes. Some experts consider that keyboarding should be taught in all schools, as a basic skill, like learning to swim or ride a bike – so that everyone can touch-type from an early age.

The benefits of creating document templates and styles

If you count up during the course of a week just how often you prepare a letter, a memorandum or a set of minutes, you will probably find that this occupies a considerable part of your working hours. If that is the case, make good use of the document template features on your word-processor.

A **template** is a pre-formatted file or form which has been designed to a particular layout. In some systems a template is referred to as a **style sheet**. The advantages of templates, or style sheets, are obvious. They save you keyboarding time. They also save you 'thinking' time because you are not required to decide on layout, style, order of content etc. They save reading time as the standard layout allows everyone to find the material they require immediately. They contribute significantly to house style and the organisational image.

There can be disadvantages. Most people like to use some creativity and to alter and adapt their communications to suit the needs of the individual reader. It is more difficult to do this if you are required to use a template. However, most packages also offer you the opportunity of creating your own template and saving it for future use. You can either modify one of the standard versions or produce an original one – as you will see on page 628.

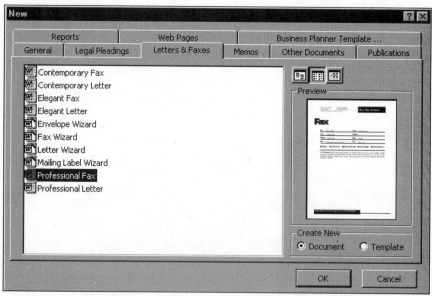

Preview screen of a template

KEY NOTES ON ACCESSING STANDARD TEMPLATES

- Click File on the menu bar.
- Scroll down and click on New.
- Click on the tab of the template you want (see illustration opposite).
- If you wish, click on the icon to preview what the template will look like (in the right-hand pane).
- Double click to select the icon.
- Complete the document with the necessary information.
- When you are satisfied, click File and Save (if you wish to save the information) and follow the Save instruction.
- You can select File and Print to make a hard copy or, if you have completed a fax or e-mail template, you will also have the option to send it.

Note that the information contained in a template is known as **boilerplating**. Templates can be saved either without text (as in the examples on Microsoft® Word) or with information included.

INFORMATION UPDATE

If you have access to the Internet, and are using a Microsoft® Office 2000 product, then you can go direct to the Nicrosoft® Office website by clicking on Office on the Web under your Help options. If you use an older Microsoft product, then you can still get there by entering the website address, which is http:/office.microsoft.com. The site is constantly changing, but it is worth looking around, checking out the clipart possibilities in the Design Gallery and the many options in the Template Gallery. Additionally you can also find out about any updates to the products you are currently using.

Storing the agreed design and any notes safely

If you have spent a long time with your manager debating and agreeing a particular design, you don't want to run the risk of mislaying it. You therefore have two tasks to complete.

1   For any design you have created, make sure it is saved not only on your hard disk (or home area on a network) but also as a back-up on a floppy disk. Use a sensible naming and labelling system so that you can easily identify the correct disk and/or document on screen.

2   Make sure that a hard copy of the design is stored in a 'hard copy manual'. However, do make sure that you include any notes which you have made either relating to the design brief or to the construction of the design. It is therefore sensible, even if you store examples of complex documents in a manual, to have your own back-up file which contains all the notes as well. This material should be placed in a sturdy folder in a filing cabinet. In particular, if your document relates to confidential or sensitive material, make sure that this is stored in a physically secure environment.

EVIDENCE COLLECTION

For *five or six* documents you have been asked to design, produce a brief report which includes a summary of:

a how you agreed and recorded the originator's requirements

b how you checked whether any existing documents could be adapted to meet the requirements

c the number of design options you prepared (where appropriate, attach examples of these), and the degree to which these were influenced by your software capabilities and limitations

d how you negotiated the final option – and the constraints which had to be considered

e how the design evolved (with examples of drafts and final approved version where appropriate)

f the method you used to ensure that the agreed design and any relevant notes were stored safely.

Note that your evidence must include all the following requirements:

- details of the purpose of the document
- information on the style and presentation required
- information on the content
- details of any data to be sourced or imported from other files or applications, such as tables, clipart graphics, logos or text saved in other files.

Finally, you may wish to use this as an opportunity to create a *template* on which you can easily enter the information you need for each of your documents (see page 628) – and then include this as an example of your own design!

Key facts on inputting and editing text

The most basic part of document creation is inputting text. For this element you have to prove you can input both printed text and text handwritten by someone else. This is easy if:

- the text or handwriting is clear and easy to follow
- the instructions are clear
- only basic alphanumeric keys are required
- the person is available so you can check anything you cannot understand
- you know how and where the document should be saved.

The situation is different if you suddenly find six pages of scribble on your desk, containing scientific characters or foreign words with accents, the instructions are vague and the author has just left on a business trip for two days. The only word you can clearly identify is 'urgent'!

In this situation the best you can do is input everything you can read, ask a colleague for help and guidance when you are stuck and put a draft printout on the author's desk for his/her return. To prevent a recurrence, it is sensible to have a few ground rules for when you receive a particularly difficult document – and a mobile number for an emergency contact! Your ground-rules should include checking whether:

- you can read all the text and all the written instructions
- any text is an original document or already exists as a saved file (which can be quickly updated or amended)
- any insertions already exist in a saved file
- the author has any preferences in terms of layout and formatting
- you have to refer a first draft for checking, or whether your first attempt is expected to be mailable – and whether this should be despatched in the author's absence (in which case you are personally responsible for all the checking)
- there are any specific requirements, such as in a legal or financial document
- you have been told the number of copies required.

Keyboard layout

At this stage in your career you will probably be completely conversant with the alphanumeric keys on your keyboard and be able to key in text with little difficulty.

You should also know what additional keys do – such as the function (F) keys, the Microsoft® Windows key and basic keys such as Insert, Delete, End and so forth.

You need to know how to access additional characters. On Microsoft® Word 2000 these are available by clicking on the Insert menu and selecting Symbols. You then have a choice of symbols (in a variety of fonts) or special characters (many of which have been assigned shortcut keys).

You should also check your keyboarding *technique* now and then.

1   Are you using hands and wrists in the way you were first trained, or have you adopted the bad habit of letting your wrists drop on to the keyboard – thus causing yourself possible RSI problems at a later stage?

2   Have you got used to looking at the keyboard even though you knew at one stage how to touch-type?

3   Do you still have difficulty keying in numbers without looking at the keyboard?

4   Do you have such a cluttered desk that you have to type from an original document which is perched on top of a number of files and which falls on to the floor every time the door opens?

5   Do you have a very small work area and therefore prop your originals up against the printer so that you have to crane your neck to read them properly?

6   Do you try to type from an original on your lap so that you have to keep lifting your head up and down to see it?

You may find that even a slight adjustment in any of these areas will improve your overall performance.

CHECK IT OUT!

It is worth finding your way around your symbol and special character options – and printing out a list of the shortcut keys to familiar yourself with those that will be helpful. Access your Help screen for how to do this.

You can assign a shortcut key yourself to any character you use regularly. With the Symbol dialogue box on screen, and the symbol you want to 'shortcut' selected, press Shortcut key, decide the shortcut you want (you will be told if any have already been selected) and then press Assign. The illustration opposite shows a shortcut assigned for a 'tick' – which is a regular feature on many forms and a useful symbol to shortcut.

Finally, investigate how to customise your keyboard through Tools I Customise I Keyboard. You can do this for any particular document or template that you work on or create and which requires special characters or symbols.

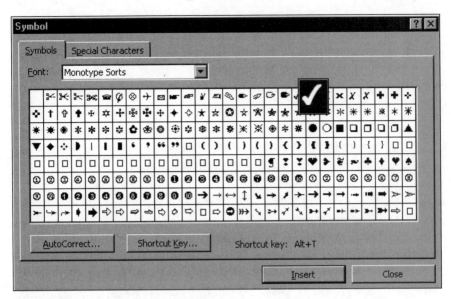

Assigning a shortcut key

Checking a document and computer-based spell-checkers

You have been asked to key a brief extract from a typed document. Before you print it off or before you hand over the printed copy, it should be automatic to you to **proofread** it for errors. The time-honoured method is to read it though, make any necessary corrections and look up any spellings you are not quite sure about in the dictionary.

There are two drawbacks to that method. The first is that you may miss some of the errors, particularly if you are in a hurry or under pressure. The second is that if you do not realise that a word is spelled wrongly you may not realise the need for checking it in a dictionary! If the document is extremely important and the need for accuracy essential – such as a legal or financial document – it is sometimes good practice to ask someone to check it for you as you read it out, or vice versa. If there is a technical term which is not in the dictionary or if there is one about which you have some doubts, you should check back with the person who compiled the original document.

It is likely that on many occasions you will make use of a **spell-checker**. This will identify most misspellings and in most instances will suggest the correct spelling. It may also be able to identify duplicate words (e.g. the the). However, your spell-checker is not a thinking being! Provided the word is an identifiable word it will not be able to decide whether it is the right word in the context of the sentence. It will not, for instance, be able to distinguish between 'stationery' and 'stationary', 'form' and 'from', 'though' and 'through', 'great' and 'grate' etc. The safest approach to take is to use the spell-checker as your first check and then to proofread the document in the traditional way.

KEY NOTES ON YOUR SPELL-CHECKER

Microsoft® Word 2000 can automatically underline misspelled words in red and grammatical errors in green. To correct such errors follow this process.

- Click on the Spelling and Grammar icon on the standard toolbar.
- A dialogue box appears if Microsoft® Word finds an error in the document. It displays the first misspelled word or grammatical error and offers suggestions for correcting the text.
- Click on the relevant suggestion. Alternatively you can correct your spelling manually in the top box of the Spellcheck window.
- Click on Change.
- To skip the error and continue checking your document, click on Ignore.
- To skip all occurrences of the error, click on Ignore All.
- Click OK to close the dialogue box when it tells you the spelling and grammar check is complete.

CHECK IT OUT!

Look at the passage outlined below, which is from the Convention on Human Rights. Decide what errors the spell-checker would be able to identify and what you would have to identify personally.

Everyone has the rite to liberty and security of person. No-one shall be deprived of liberty accept in the following cases:

- *The lawfull detention of a person after conviction by a a competent court.*
- *The lawful arrest or detention of a person affected for the purpose of bringing him before the competent legal authority on reasonable suspishion of having commited an offence.*
- *The detention of a miner by lawful order for the purpose of educational supervision.*

Then, if you have time, input the text and run your spell-checker to discover whether you were right.

INFORMATION UPDATE

Word can automatically correct common spelling errors as you type, such as 'adn' (to 'and'), 'comittee' (to 'committee') and 'nwe' (to 'new'). This is ideal unless you work for an author of an English book who deliberately wanted to include some spelling errors in an exercise!

Using correction methods and the dangers involved in moving blocks of text

The word-processor is a wonderful invention as it provides several ways to correct mistakes very easily:

- by deleting and retyping
- by using the insert function and overtyping
- by using search and replace routines
- by moving blocks of text from one place to another.

You should guard against being over-confident. It is quite easy to select a block of text minus the last sentence and to transpose it elsewhere, to 'cut' a block of text when you really meant to 'copy' it (you won't lose it, but will have to replace it again), or to use the search and replace mechanism and replace a word you did not want replacing.

In particular, trying to cut and paste several items simultaneously is dangerous. You are likely to forget what items are on your clipboard and what items you have replaced! So do them carefully, one by one, to prevent such disasters. And make sure you know how the Undo facility operates before you start.

KEY NOTES ON CORRECTION METHODS

Deleting and retyping

- Make sure the insertion point is at the left of the first character you want to delete.
- Pressing the Delete key deletes characters to the right. Using the Backspace key deletes characters to the left.
- Delete word by word (to the right) by holding down Ctrl and pressing the Delete key.

The Insert key

Your insert function 'toggles' on and off when you press the Insert key.

- When Insert is 'on' (which is the normal default) then typing text at the insertion point will automatically insert it.
- When Insert is 'off' you will overtype text. Beware of doing this and accidentally overtyping text you wanted to retain!

KEY NOTES ON SEARCH AND REPLACE ROUTINES

- Click on Edit on the main menu bar.
- Scroll down and click on Replace.
- Type the word you want to find. Use search options such as Match case (if you want to find Brown, rather than brown) if these will help you.
- Type the text you want to replace it with.
- Click Find to start the search.
- Word will highlight the first matching word it finds.
- Click one of the options – Replace (which replaces the word); Replace All (which replaces the word and all other matching words in the document); or Find Next (which ignores that instance of the word).
- Repeat (using Find Next) until a dialogue box appears telling you the search is complete.
- Click OK to close the dialogue box.

Remember, the search facility is ideal to find any word or phrase in document, even if you don't want to replace it. Check out any search options you are unsure about to find out how they can help you.

KEY NOTES ON MOVING BLOCKS OF TEXT FROM ONE PLACE TO ANOTHER

- Select the text you want to move by highlighting it using your mouse or by holding down the Shift key on your keyboard and then pressing any key which moves the insertion point (e.g. the down arrow). If you want to select all the text in your document, press and hold Ctrl as you press the A key *or* use the Edit menu then Select All.

- If you make a mistake and want to deselect any text, double click outside the selected area.

- Either access the Edit menu and select Cut, or click the Cut icon on the toolbar (the highlighted text is then moved to the clipboard).

- Move to the part of the document where you want to insert the text.

- Click where you want to place the insertion point.

- Click on either Edit then Paste, or the Paste icon on the toolbar.

- Check in both places that all your spacing is still correct.

Always cut and paste one item at a time – regardless of how many your clipboard will hold.

CHECK IT OUT!

Access the 'keys for editing and moving text and graphics' using your Help facility on Microsoft® Word, and print the result. This gives you a list of all the keys you can use to do these operations.

Check through the list to make sure you are familiar with the ones that will be helpful to you. And practise any that are new!

TEST YOUR KNOWLEDGE AND UNDERSTANDING

Input the text shown on page 608, ignoring any correction marks. Then make the required corrections. Make brief notes of which correction methods you used, and why. If you had any problems, practise to improve your technique.

I am becoming ~~increasingly~~ concerned at the amount of money which is being spent on computer repairs / I have checked the repair bills over the (passed) six months and *past* have noticed <u>with some alarm that they have</u> (steadily) increased ~~and that on each occasion the amount has risen~~. As this situation cannot be allowed to continue I have prepared a brief analysis / (a copy of which I enclose for your attention,) of the most common type of repair and also of the computers which most frequently need repairing.

e I shall ensure that the Computer Services Manager is made aware of this so that she can take the necessary measures to ~~a~~ffect improvements but I should also like you to be conversant with my line of thinking.

As you can see, all computer repairs are recorded so that it should be immediately apparent which machines are the most prone to breakdown. A decision is then made ~~as to~~ whether to continue having them repaired or whether to purchase a replacement.
response

end Please consider this matter and let me have a ~~reply~~ by the ~~next~~ of next week.

The record also indicates which makes of computer it would be advisable not to purchase in the future.

Text for inputting and amending

The importance of saving text on a regular basis

Most people who work in an office are hoarders by nature. They hate throwing anything away. The word processor can actually encourage this habit in that all material produced on it can be saved and stored for re-use at a later stage or for evidence purposes. It will therefore be second nature to you by now to use the save function on your machine when you have completed a document.

Unfortunately, familiarity can breed contempt. When you first started to learn how to use a word processor you were probably very careful about how you saved your documents. As you became more experienced, and both your keyboarding speed and the speed with which you carried out the word-processing functions increased, you may have become less cautious. This can have repercussions – if, for instance, at the end of a long document you unthinkingly hit the No button by mistake when the machine asks whether or not the material is to be saved! At this point your work on the document is completely lost. Your only hope is if there is an earlier version on disk – but even then you would have to start making amendments all over again. So no matter what you are doing or how much of a rush you are in, *think* first, exit last!

You can save documents in a variety of files and folders and in a variety of directories. All these are visible in Microsoft® Windows Explorer. This program lists all your directories and folders in the left-hand pane of a split screen. Clicking on a folder will give you a list of files in the right-hand pane.

There is not space in this book to give you information on how to use Microsoft® Windows Explorer, but it is invaluable for file management – including creating files and folders, copying them, renaming them, deleting (and, in an emergency, restoring) them and finding files and folders you thought you had lost.

You can also use Microsoft® Windows Explorer to check the size of your hard drive and the space availability on this and on any floppy disks you have inserted. Do this by clicking on File | Properties.

It is worth spending time identifying the files and folder system you use and seeing if this can be improved to help you find documents more easily.

 KEY NOTES ON SAVING DOCUMENTS

- Click on the Save icon on the toolbar, or click on File on the menu bar and then select Save.
- The Save As dialogue box will appear. If you have previously saved your document, the Save As box will not appear as you have already named it. Instead your original version will be overwritten without any prompting.
- Type in the file name.
- Click on 'Save in' for the area in which you want to store your document.
- Click on 'Save as type' if you want to change the text file formats.
- Click on Save.

Ideally you should have your system set to Autosave your document at maximum five minute intervals and save it yourself before you undertake any special operation such as:

- a tricky cut and paste
- the insertion of an object from a different folder or software package
- a formatting option you have not tried before.

Then you will never have a disaster if your special operation goes completely wrong!

Explore your Save As screen in Microsoft® Word 2000. In particular you should know how to:

- select the drive on to which to save your document
- create a new folder when necessary on that drive
- move from one drive to another
- name your document
- save your document in different format types (see below).

Microsoft® Office 2000 also enables you to save and access documents easily through the icons at the left of the screen, i.e. History, My Documents, Desktop, Favourites and My Network. Check out all of these options and find out how they operate – if you have not done so already.

File formats for saving word-processed documents

Whatever system you are using, it will usually be possible to save your document in a number of different file formats. If you are using Microsoft® Word, for instance, you can do all the following.

- You can save a Word document in a file format that can be read by earlier versions of Word, by Microsoft® Works, by Macintosh users or by Corel® WordPerfect.
- You can open a document created in a different file format by a different program, work on it in Word and then save it in its original format. For example, you can open a WordPerfect document, make changes to it in Word and then save it in either Word format or WordPerfect format.
- You can save a document with a different file extension without changing the file format. For example, you can save a Word document with the file extension '.abc'.
- You can save a document to be used by someone with non-compatible software. The most common options to choose are rich text format (rtf), which saves all common formatting commands, and a text-only option (txt) which saves the text without formatting.

You can see the different options available to you by clicking on the 'Save as type' drop-down menu in the Save As dialogue box. Note that certain file extensions are identifiable as suffixes – '.htm' for instance relates to Web documents, '.doc' to Word documents and '.mcw' to Apple® Mac documents.

The benefit of this is felt mainly when you are sending a document to someone (either as an e-mail attachment or by copying it to a floppy disk) and that person does not have the same version or type of software.

Dealing with problems

Completing the input of a long and complicated document is sometimes not the end of your worries. You may, for instance, face the following problems:

- insufficient storage space
- accidental loss or corruption of data
- duplicated file names.

The table below gives an indication of some possible steps you could take in each case.

Difficulties with access	
Problem	Possible actions
Insufficient storage space	Use a new floppy disk.
	Check the Recycle Bin and empty it.
	Go into Microsoft® Windows Explorer and delete outdated documents to free up space on your hard disk (see pages 609, 632 and 633).
	Consult your computer specialist about compressing the existing data on a disk to make more room or defragmenting your hard disk to create available space.
Accidental loss of data	Click on the undo icon on the standard toolbar or click on Edit and scroll down to Undo if you realise your mistake immediately (NB Control + Z is the keyboard shortcut method).
	Start a major search by clicking on Start, scrolling down to Find, scrolling across to Files or Folders, typing in the relevant information and clicking on Find Now.
	Check Microsoft® Windows Explorer to see whether or not the file has become hidden for some reason (see page 609).
Corruption of data	If the document can be opened, click on File and then Save As, change Save File As type to Rich Text Format, give the file a new name and click OK. Check that the document has been saved.
	Either consult your computer services personnel or your supplier.
Duplicate file names	This should not happen. The system will automatically ask whether a new file name is to replace an existing file name – giving an indication that the new information will override the existing information not add to it.
	If you have been specifically requested to save a file under a particular name, you should change the name of the existing file.

EVIDENCE COLLECTION

1 You need to provide evidence that you correct text by using *all* the following methods:

- typing over text
- using search and replace routines
- moving blocks of text to a new place in the document.

It is logical to extend the evidence you collected on page 600 and to note when you used each of these techniques. The best evidence is provided by printouts of a document both before and after you undertook the particular operation.

2 It will also be helpful for your assessor if you write a brief description of how you normally save documents – and how often – and how you identify the format and location. Attach any organisational procedures you have to follow and highlight relevant parts of these that relate to your work.

3 You will be very unusual if you never meet any problems when you are creating and saving complex documents. You have to prove to your assessor that you have dealt with *two* of the following problems and can discuss what you would do in the third case:

- accidental loss or corruption of data
- duplicate file names
- insufficient storage space.

It is therefore sensible to make a note of any problems you encounter and write a short account of what happened and how you solved it. If no problems occur whilst you are doing this unit, you may have to demonstrate to your assessor what you *would* do in *at least* two.

Key facts on formatting and laying out complex documents

How to achieve various types of text formats

At this stage in your career you will probably be expected to do more than merely key in text and follow instructions. You should be able to make use of all the features on your word-processor, to allow you to format and lay out text in what you feel is the most appropriate way, although if you are in any doubt you can use your online Help or Office Assistant feature for assistance.

Note, however, that although Help features vary from computer to computer, many of the instructions they give can initially be rather confusing. Wherever possible it is better to find a kind colleague who knows the system well and who is prepared to 'talk' you through the function you want to use.

The most frequently used formatting functions include:

- bullet lists and automatic numbering
- different font styles
- different paragraph styles (including justification)
- indentation
- suitable line spacing
- tables
- tabs
- borders and shading
- multiple columns.

It is accepted at this point that you already use routine formatting, such as selecting bold, italics and underscore. The following Key Notes boxes summarise the steps you should take in formatting text in the various ways listed above.

CHECK IT OUT!

Check to see whether on your program there is a **click and type** facility which allows you to insert text, graphics, tables or other items in a blank area of a document. The click and type facility will apply the formatting necessary to position the item where you double-clicked. If, for instance, you wanted to type the book title 'Bleak House' in the centre of the page and the name of its author 'Charles Dickens' to the right of the page, you can double click in the centre of the page and the centre icon will appear. Click again. You can then start typing and the heading will be centred. If you then double click towards the bottom right hand of the page the align right icon will appear and you can then type the author's name which will be aligned to the right-hand margin.

 KEY NOTES ON FORMATTING TEXT (1)

Bullet lists

- Click on the Bullet icon on the Formatting toolbar; *or*
- Click on Format on the main menu bar and scroll down to Bullets and Numbering.

- Select the type of bullet point you want to use and click on OK.
- If you want to create your own version, click on Customize and select the bullet character you want and where you want to position it. You can also change the font if you wish. Click on OK when you have made your selection
- To remove a bullet point at a later date, click on the section of text from which you want it removed and then click on the bullet icon, or click Bullets and Numbering, click on None and then OK.
- If you want to add bullet points at a later date, select the text you want, click Bullets and Numbering, click the style you want to use, and then click OK.

Automatic numbering

- Click on the Numbers icon on the Formatting toolbar and follow the same instructions as for bullet points; *or*
- Click on Format, then Bullets and Numbering and again follow the same instructions as for bullet points but clicking instead on the Numbered tab to see all the options available.

An alternative method for creating a bulleted or numbered list is:

- Type * or 1. followed by a space. Then type the first item on the list.
- Press Enter and Word will (if this option is enabled) automatically start the next item with a bullet or number.
- To end the bulleted or numbered list, press the Enter key twice.

 ## KEY NOTES ON FORMATTING TEXT (2)

Different fonts
For new text:

- Click the arrow next to the box on the Formatting toolbar (which will either be blank or will display a title such as Arial).
- Scroll down and click on the font you require.

Alternatively (particularly if you want to check on what each font looks like before making a choice):

- Click on Format on the menu bar.
- Scroll down and click on Font. The available fonts will be displayed.

- Click on the one you want. Check what it looks like in the Preview section of the window.
- Make your final choice and click on OK.

You can carry out this same procedure to change the size of the text, the font style – regular, italic, bold – whether or not you want the text underlining and other minor adjustments.

For existing text:

- Highlight the area of text you want to change.
- Click on Format I Font, and then on the appropriate font size. Alternatively highlight the text and choose the font type and size from the Formatting toolbar.

Borders and shading

- Click on Format on the menu.
- Scroll down and click on Borders and Shading.
- Select a setting – none, box, shadow, 3-D, custom.
- Select a line style – continuous, broken.
- Select a line width.
- Select a colour from a colour palette.
- Check the preview to see whether you have achieved the effect you want.
- Click on OK.

 KEY NOTES ON FORMATTING TEXT (3)

Indentation
New text:

- Either follow the procedure outlined in Paragraph style (see page 616); or
- Check the horizontal ruler that displays the page width and click on the first line indent pointer. Drag it to the appropriate position. A line will show you where it is.

Existing text:

- For one paragraph only, click anywhere on the paragraph, then click on the Increase Indent icon on the Formatting toolbar. For multiple paragraphs, select those you wish to indent and highlight them. Then click on the Increase Indent icon.
- Alternatively, follow the relevant instructions in paragraphing.

Line spacing
New text:

- If you do not want to use the standard line spacing, click on Format on the menu bar, then on Paragraph.
- Change the line spacing as required, note the Preview and then click on OK.

Existing text:

Highlight the text and then follow the same procedure as above. Word will automatically increase the spacing of lines that contain large characters.

KEY NOTES ON FORMATTING TEXT (4)

Paragraph style (including justification)
New text:

- Click on the icons on the Formatting toolbar for text aligned to the left, centred text, text aligned to the right or justified text. Alternatively, use Ctrl + L for left justification, Ctrl + R for right, Ctrl + E for centred text and Ctrl + J for fully justified text.
- Click the icon a second time when you want to align the text differently. The default is for the text to align to the left if no other alignment has been specifically selected.

Alternatively:

- Click on Format on the menu bar.
- Scroll down to Paragraph and make individual adjustments to alignment, indentation and spacing. You can also choose a hanging paragraph – i.e. where all the text except for the first line is indented.
- Check the Preview to see that you have chosen the style you require.
- Click on OK.

Existing text:

- Select and highlight the paragraph you want to change.
- Click on the appropriate icon or on Format I Paragraph to make individual adjustments.
- Click to remove highlighting.

KEY NOTES ON FORMATTING TEXT (5)

Creating a table

Before you start, make sure you know the difference between:

a cell – one box in a table

a column – a vertical line of cells

a row – a horizontal line of cells.

- Click where you want your table to appear in your document.
- Click on the Table icon on the standard toolbar.
- Drag the insertion point until you highlight the number of columns and rows you want the table to contain. The table will then appear in the document.
- Click the cell where you want to enter text. Then type the text. Use the tab key to move from one cell to another.
- Repeat until you have finished entering all the text.

Alternatively:

- Click where you want your table to appear in the document.
- Click on Table on the menu bar.
- Click on Insert Table.
- Choose the number of rows and columns you require.
- Click OK.

Formatting a table

- Click anywhere in the table you want to change.
- Click Table on the menu bar.
- Click Table Autoformat.
- The Table Autoformat dialogue box appears which displays a list of the available table designs. You can also see a sample of any design you highlight.
- Press the (↓) key or (↑) key until the table design you want to use appears – or use the scroll bar to the right of the Formats section.
- A check mark (✓) beside an option tells you that Word will apply the option to your table.
- Click an option to add or remove a check mark.
- Click OK to apply the design to your table.
- The table displays the design you selected.

Change column width in a table

- Position the insertion point over the vertical line you want to move. The symbol will change to ←‖→.
- Drag the column edge to a new position.
- A line shows the new position.
- The column displays the new width.

Change row height in a table

- Position the insertion point over the bottom edge of the row you want to change. The symbol will change to ⊥.
- Drag the row edge to a new position.
- A line shows the new position.
- The row displays the new height.

Add a row

- To select a row, position the insertion point to the left of the row. The symbol will change to ⤧. Then double click the left mouse button.
- On the Formatting toolbar, click ⊒+⊏ to add a row.
- A new row appears.
- Alternatively, with a row selected, choose Table from the menu bar, and click Insert. You can then decide if you want the new row above or below the selected one. This is useful if you want to add a new first or last row to a table.

Add a column

- To select a column, position the insertion point over the top of the column. The symbol changes to ↓.
- Click ⊔⊔ to add a column.
- A new column appears.
- Again, with the column selected you can choose Table from the menu bar, click Insert and then select either column to the left or column to the right.

Delete a row or column

- To select the row you want to delete, position the insertion point to the left of the row. The symbol changes to ⤧. Then double click the left mouse button.

- To select the column you want to delete, position the insertion point over the top of the column. The symbol changes to (↓). Then click the left mouse button.
- Click ✄ to delete the row or column (or select Delete from the Table menu).
- The row or column disappears.

Combine or merge cells

- Position the insertion point over the first cell you want to merge with other cells.
- Drag the mouse until you highlight all the cells you want to merge.
- Click Table.
- Click Merge Cells. The cells combine to create one large cell.

KEY NOTES ON FORMATTING TEXT (7)

Note that Word automatically places a tab every 1.27 cm across a page.

Change a tab setting

- Highlight the text you want to contain the new tab.
- Click on L at the far left of the horizontal ruler to change it to the type of tab you want: left tab, centre tab, right tab, decimal tab, or bar tab.
- Click the horizontal ruler where you want to set the tab stop. The new tab appears on the ruler.
- To use a tab, click the beginning of the line you want to move across and then press the tab key. The insertion point and the text that follows move to the tab you set.

Move a tab

- Highlight the text containing the tab you want to move.
- Position the mouse over the tab you want to move.
- Drag the tab to a new location on the ruler.

Remove a tab

- Highlight the text containing the tab you want to remove.
- Drag the tab downwards off the ruler. The tab disappears from the ruler.
- To move text back to the left margin, click to the left of the first character. Then press the backspace key.

Setting precise measurements for tabs

- Click Format on the main menu bar.
- Scroll down and click Tabs.
- Type in the required tab stop position.
- Select alignment – left, right, centre, decimal, bar.
- If required select what type of leader dots you want.
- Click on Set.
- Click OK when you have set all the tabs you want.

You can also use this method to clear specific tabs. Click on the relevant tab stop position and then click on Clear.

 ## KEY NOTES ON FORMATTING TEXT (8)

Multiple columns

- Click on Format on the main menu bar.
- Scroll down to Columns.
- Select one/two/three columns either as Presets or by changing the Number of columns box.
- Select a smaller left-hand/right-hand column measurement, or insert your required width and spacing requirements, or choose equal column widths.
- Select the whole document, or from this point forwards.
- Check the preview and then click on OK.

How to achieve layouts and structures

Again, the more experienced you become at producing complex documents using a computer, the more creative you will become at assessing what type of layout to use. What you may have to consider is the use of:

- landscape and portrait orientation
- different paper sizes – normally A4 or A5
- different margin widths and appropriate use of indentations
- different styles and locations of page numbering
- appropriate headers and footers
- automatically generated tables of contents.

KEY NOTES ON TYPES OF LAYOUT (1)

Page orientation and size

- Click on File on the main menu bar.
- Click on Page Setup.
- Click on Paper Size.
- Click for Landscape or Portrait; *or*
- Click to specify exact height and width required; *or*
- Click on Page Setup, then page size and select A4, A5 etc.

Margins

Note that Word automatically sets the top and bottom margins to 2.54 cm and the left and right margins to 3.17 cm.

- Click where you want to change the margin.
- Click on the Print Preview icon on the standard toolbar.
- The document appears in the Print Preview window.
- This area displays the ruler. If the ruler is not displayed, click the View Ruler icon on the toolbar.
- Position the insertion point over a margin you want to change.
- When the pointer changes to a double arrow, drag the margin to a new location. A line shows the new location.
- The margin moves to the new location.
- Repeat for each margin you want to change.
- When you finish changing the margins, click Close to close the Print Preview window.

Alternatively:

- Click on File on the menu bar.
- Click on Page Setup.
- Alter margins individually.
- Decide whether it applies to the whole document or from this point forward.
- Check the Preview and click on OK.

KEY NOTES ON TYPES OF LAYOUT (2)

Inserting page numbers

- Click Insert on the menu bar.
- Click on Page Numbers. The Page Numbers dialogue box appears.
- Click the position where you want the page number to appear.
- Click the alignment you want to use – right, left, centre, inside, outside.
- To hide the page number on the first page of your document, click the relevant option.
- Check the preview and click on OK.

When you add, remove or rearrange text in your document, Word will automatically adjust the page numbers for you.

Inserting headers and/or footers

- Click on View on the menu bar.
- Click on Header and Footer.
- Type information in the Header box; *or*
- Choose from a number of icons – number of pages, format page number, date, time, page setup, show/hide document text.
- Click on Switch between Header and Footer icon to type information in the Footer box.

Automatically generated tables of contents

- Click on Insert on the menu bar.
- Scroll down and click on Index and Tables.
- Select Table of Contents.
- Choose from a number of options – page numbers, alignment of page numbers, leader dots, number of levels required.
- Check Print preview and click on OK.

1 You are assisting the Human Resources Manager to produce a report for the board of directors. So far you have been provided with the following information from colleagues (see the appropriate boxes below):

- details of sick pay and redundancy pay schemes
- some relevant financial information
- a draft induction checklist
- a draft table of contents (with other information to follow).

You are asked to lay out the material you have received in a more suitable way. Prepare the initial draft including at least one example of each of the different types of formats and layouts listed in the Key Notes boxes on pages 613–622.

2 Your junior has problems laying out tables and he asks you for some help. Prepare some notes on how you would advise him to complete the table on page 627 through the use of the arithmetical functions on his word-processor.

Information about sick pay and redundancy

SUMMARY OF STATUTORY SICK PAY RULES

Statutory sick pay (SSP) is paid by an employer to a sick employee for up to 28 weeks and provides him or her with a fixed weekly amount of benefit. If the employer operates an occupational sick pay scheme (OSP), SSP can be deducted from amounts of OSP paid. If the rate of OSP is higher than the rate of SSP, the employers need not adhere to many of the SSP rules although they must still keep basic records. Such employers will still be able to recover an amount equal to the SSP that would have been paid if the rules of recovery are satisfied. Employees who are not entitled to OSP are still entitled to SSP.

Glossary of terms

Period of incapacity for work (PIW)
A period of sickness of at least four calendar days in a row

Waiting days
The first three qualifying days of sickness for which SSP is not payable

Linked PIW

Two PIWs separated by less than eight weeks even if they are for a different sickness. The second or subsequent absence is regarded as a continuation of the first absence. Therefore there are no waiting days for the second absence and it counts towards the same limit of 28 weeks.

Eligibility

An employee is eligible for SSP unless, at the start of the PIW, the employee earns less than the class 1 National Insurance lower earnings limit

- is aged 65 or over
- has a contract of employment for less than three months and works for less than three months
- has already received 28 weeks of SSP in a previous employment and the last day of SSP was not more than eight weeks before the start of the PIV
- is in custody
- claimed incapacity benefit or severe disablement allowance in the 57 days before the incapacity. In some cases the linking period is 52 weeks
- is abroad and the employer is not liable to pay secondary National Insurance contributions
- has done no work under the contract of employment
- is engaged in an industrial dispute, or
- has started her maternity pay period (MPP)

Eligibility for a linked PIW is determined by whether or not the employee was eligible to receive SSP at the start of the first PIW

Notification and evidence

The employee must provide notification and evidence of sickness to the employer. The employer is free to make rules about this within limits. The following rules are commonly used and are acceptable

- Notification must be made on the first day of sickness or as soon as possible. Notification need not be in writing nor made by the sick person himself or herself.
- A self certificate for absences of up to seven days is acceptable. After that a doctor's certificate must be produced.

Statutory sick pay rates

Weekly rates of SSP 1997–2000

Tax year: 1997/1998: – Pay £62: SSP £55.70: 1998/9 – Pay £64: SSP £57.50: 1999/2000 – Pay £66.00: SSP £59.55

REDUNDANCY PAY

An employee is eligible for redundancy pay if he or she

- is under 65 or the company's normal retirement age
- is not on a fixed term contract
- works in the UK
- has two year's continuous service from age 18, regardless of the number of hours worked and
- is not in an excluded employment eg share fishermen, certain Crown employees and relatives in domestic service

Redundancy exists when the employer ceases or intends to cease trading, ceases operations where the employee is based or the requirements for the employee's work have ceased or diminished or are expected to do so.

There is no redundancy if the employee is offered suitable alternative employment.

Amount

The amount of redundancy pay depends on the employee's length of service, subject to a minimum of two years and a maximum of 20 years. For each year's service the employee receives a portion of a week's wages according to his or her age that year. The proportion according to age is as follows:

Age 18–21: half portion of week's wages: 22–40: one week's wages: 41–65: one and half week's wages

The week's wages is subject to a statutory maximum amount, depending on when the employee was made redundant. If the employee is 64, any redundancy pay is reduced by one twelfth for each complete month since the employee's 64th birthday.

Financial information

Ravensbrigg & Nuttall

Expenditure

Staff costs	1999/2000	2000/2001
	£000s	£000s
Production departments	10,860	10,091
Service departments	1,583	1,143
Support staff	400	375
Administration and Central Services	1,549	1,460
Premises	469	433
Other income generating activities	373	164
Catering	204	199
Staff restructure	91	98
Total	15,529	13,963

Induction training

INDUCTION SHEET

Ravensbrigg & Nuttall

Name:

Department/Section:

Job title:

INDUCTION PROGRAMME	YES	NO
I		
• have received a copy of the Staff Handbook		
• have been given individual induction into the job role		
• understand the disciplinary and grievance procedure		
• understand the staff appraisal scheme		
• understand the staff development procedures		
• understand the health and safety procedures and policies		
• have received fire training		
• can send and receive e-mail		
• can access the computer system.		
I know		
• the key areas of the organisation		
• where to go during breaks and at lunchtime		
• where keys are kept		
• where I obtain stationery and other supplies		
• where the car parks are.		

Signature   Date

Signature of mentor   Date

Ravensbrigg & Nuttall

Annual Report to Board of Directors

Table of Contents

Page no.

Table with arithmetical functions

Analysis by age of the number of staff in each department

	Under 18	18–45	45+	Total
HR	5	8	5	
Purchasing	4	7	8	
Computing	11	9	2	
Administration	5	5	6	
Finance	1	7	8	
Total				

How to apply a template

Look back to page 598 for information on the use of templates. Applying a standard template is easy. Preparing an attractive original template takes slightly more artistic flair.

CHECK IT OUT!

Create new letter and memo templates for your manager so that he or she can compare them with those you already use. Write a brief note of how you think you have improved on the originals.

KEY NOTES ON CREATING A TEMPLATE

To base a new template on an existing template follow this procedure:

- Click on File and then scroll down to New.
- Click a template that is similar to the one you want to create.
- Click on Template under Create New and then click on OK.
- On the File menu, click Save As.
- In the 'Save as type' drop-down menu, click Document Template. This file type will already be selected if you are saving a file that you created as a template.
- Templates will appear in the 'Save in' box.
- In the 'File name' box, type a name for the new template and then click Save.
- In the new template. add the text and graphics you want to appear in all new documents that you base on the template and delete any items you don't want to appear.
- Make the changes you want to the margin settings, page size and orientation, styles and other formats.
- Click on Save.

How to apply styles

The computer allows you to be very creative. If you are given a free hand over the layout of a document you have the right to decide on the margins, the pagination, the line spacing, the type of font, the type of paragraph etc.

A word of warning, however – try not to go 'over the top', particularly if you are preparing a business document. Generally speaking the same rules apply as for any other form of communication. The style should be one which most suits the needs of the reader rather than the artistic aspirations of the sender! It is a good idea to experiment with one style at once. You may, for instance, want to check on the different font styles and sizes and to use a different combination on several documents before making your final choice. You might then decide to experiment with different fonts in one document and to highlight certain parts of it in bold or italics. Certainly, if numbers are involved, you have the opportunity to decide whether or not to make use of different tabular forms.

The golden rules include:

- consistency throughout a document – for example, especially between numbered paragraphs and bullet points, and indentation
- simplicity – don't mix styles or fonts within a document unless there is an excellent and specific reason for doing so.

TEST YOUR KNOWLEDGE AND UNDERSTANDING

Retype the following draft advertisement, using a variety of different styles. Justify your use of the styles you choose.

Crickleton College. Committed to Equal Opportunities for All. Director of Curriculum & Quality and Deputy to the Principal. Salary circa £42,000 per annum plus relocation package. Ref. No.113.

Crickleton College is the leading provider of post-16 education and training in the region. It has recently undergone a management restructure which has resulted in the creation of the above post.

As Deputy to the Principal, the successful candidate will have overall responsibility for curriculum management, performance and development. He or she will line manage a team of Heads of Department and will also play a major role in the strategic planning and decision making in the college. For further information and an application pack, please contact the Personnel Manager, Crickleton College, Frensham. FR6 2NM. Closing date for the post: 23 November.

How to access and correctly insert graphics and other files

Using graphics can be fun. Obviously, however, you shouldn't go wild. A member of staff receiving a letter giving him or her four weeks' notice is hardly likely to be impressed if you include as a heading a graphic of someone trudging towards the Job Centre. The board of directors may be equally unimpressed if they receive a set of profit and loss figures festooned with illustrations of garlands of flowers or cartoon characters.

The first step as always should be to find out what your computer can do. Most packages allow you to access Clip Art and incorporate it into relevant documents.

KEY NOTES ON INSERTING CLIP ART

- Click at the point you wish to insert the piece of Clip Art.
- Click on Insert on the main menu bar.
- Click on Picture and scroll across to Clip Art.
- Click on the Clip Art category required.
- Click on Insert Clip, Preview Clip, Add Clip to Favorites or other category or Find Similar Clip.
- Remember that additional Clip Art is also available at www.office.microsoft.com – but note, too, that unless you actually create a graphic you *don't* own the copyright!

In addition, you may want to move some text from one file to another, in which case you may want to make use of the cut, copy and paste functions of your software.

KEY NOTES ON INSERTING TEXT FROM EXISTING REPORTS OR OTHER STORED DOCUMENTS

- Click on File on the main menu bar.
- Click on Open (you can shortcut this process by clicking on the Open icon on the standard toolbar).
- Check the name of source document you want to open and click on that.
- Use the mouse to highlight the text you want to insert.
- Click on the Copy icon on the standard toolbar.
- In your existing document, click where you want the text inserted.
- Click on the Paste icon on the standard toolbar; *or*
- Click on Edit on the menu and scroll down to Paste.

Note that you can have both files open at once and move between them via Winaow on the main menu bar. Or you may choose to close your source document after accessing the text.

Remember you can also insert a whole document in another one by placing your cursor at the insertion point, then choosing Insert File, selecting the file you want and clicking on Insert.

The 'expert' touch is when you can import Clip Art or text or graphics from other applications, and also move them to the best possible position and arrange the text around them attractively.

You can move graphics by selecting them and dragging them to a better position. You can resize graphics by clicking on a corner and dragging the corner sizing handle outwards or inwards (which retains the correct shape). You can crop graphics to remove the bits you don't want. You can wrap text around a picture by selecting the graphic, then – on the Format Picture menu – selecting the wrapping style you want (see the illustration below).

If you don't know how to do any of these operations, or have problems, then you should note that working with text and graphics is quite complex. There isn't space here to give you all the instructions. Your best method is to access 'Working with text and graphics' on your Help facility and then work through the options you need – or just experiment. Try out the different options yourself and/or ask your tutor to show you.

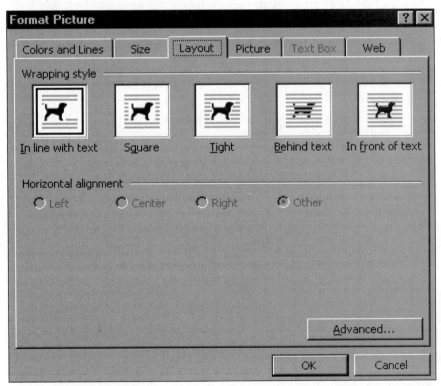

Selecting a wrapping style

Organisational procedures for naming and saving files

Some organisations have established house rules for naming and saving files and require their keyboard operators to name each file in a certain way – rather like a paper-based filing system.

Where individuals are allowed to please themselves, however, problems can arise. Suppose, for instance, you are asked to key in a number of personnel documents. You name them 'jobdesc', 'jobspec', 'jobspecupdate', 'jobinfo' etc. depending on the number of letters at your disposal. You could find it a problem in revisiting the correct file immediately. You might also find that when you input another job description document that you use the same file name and the system asks you whether or not you want to replace the old file. Sometimes you do not. It is worth spending some time, therefore, deciding how you want to reference your files and how you are going to introduce some consistency into your system by, for example:

- using logical file names
- being as descriptive as possible
- avoiding too many abbreviations
- giving a separate suffix to each draft of a document
- including a date code in the file name, e.g. DBA12Apr01.

If you become really discontented with your system you can always access Microsoft® Windows Explorer by clicking on Start and then Programs. Your folders and files will be displayed on screen and you will be able to scroll through the files in each folder. However, do be careful what you delete in Explorer – it is all too easy to delete important systems programs (e.g. those with '.exe', '.dll' or '.bat' extensions).

EVIDENCE COLLECTION

1   You must show that you can format text in all the ways identified on pages 613–620 and lay out and structure your documents in all the ways listed on pages 621 and 622.

The simplest method is to check your existing collection of evidence to see which examples you have obtained already, then make a note to obtain examples of the remainder. If you never undertake certain operations (e.g. tables of contents) then ask your assessor whether you can use a specially created document (such as those specified in this unit) as your evidence for this particular item.

2   Describe the procedures in place in your own organisation for naming and saving files. Explain why you think those particular procedures have been introduced and how effective they are. In particular identify those which especially relate to your own work.

3   Obtain two or three examples of documents into which you have inserted text, tables and graphics from other files. Attach to these a brief account stating how you did this, how you achieved the correct position and size of graphics and how you arranged the flow of text around them.

Key facts on printing documents

Obtaining appropriate permission to access documents

You have been asked to provide some staff salary details for a meeting of the senior executives. You wander into the Personnel Manager's assistant's office. She isn't there and so you talk to a clerk who is inputting some routine data into a computer. You ask him for the information you require. He finds it for you, prints it off and gives you a hard copy. A short time later, the PM's assistant is on the phone to you – and she is not very pleased!

Given the impact of the **Data Protection Act** and **Human Rights Act**, she has every right to be concerned. Handing over information to anyone nowadays carries certain risks. It can fall into the wrong hands and be used for the wrong purpose – staff salary details pinned up on the office notice board for everyone to see or given to a member of the local press as an example of 'fat cat' salaries are not likely to improve industrial relations.

What you should have done, of course, is to talk to the person directly responsible for the information to obtain his or her specific permission. In some organisations procedures are laid down as to who should give permission for various activities, and the printing and circulating of important or confidential documents is often listed amongst those activities. In such circumstances, of course, you should follow the procedures.

See Unit 305, page 280 for further information about confidentiality.

Checking that the document is ready for printing

As an experienced word-processing operator you are unlikely to fall into the traps laid for your less experienced colleagues when preparing to print a document. If a document is required in a hurry and your boss is breathing over your neck when you are completing the last page, it is easy to try to cut corners and to hit the print button the very moment your fingers leave the keyboard. If you do so, you run the risk of spoiling all your efforts by producing a sub-standard document. If you have your own printer your problems tend to be fewer as you have control over it. If you have shared use, you are at the mercy of your clumsiest colleague. If the printer is online and prints out at a distance, whatever the advantages, again you have lost your immediate control.

Achieving the listed specifications

In all cases, before printing a document it is advisable to do the following.

- Use your spelling and grammar checks.
- Proofread to find any errors not picked up by the automatic checks.
- Re-check that you have met the original requirements as to page size, margins, pagination, font size, line spacing, paragraphing etc.
- Make sure that you are aware of the people to whom the document is to be sent and their names and job titles.
- Check that you are using the right printer.
- Check on the printing instructions you have been given, such as the number of copies, whether the complete document needs to be printed out or only specified sections, whether or not a colour printer is required, and any special instructions.
- Where relevant, check on your print preview/printer setup screen that you have matched all the printing instructions (colour, best quality or draft etc.) and that you have entered all the correct option choices for page size or type of document.
- Ensure that the printer is switched on, online and that there is an adequate supply of paper (if you have direct access to a printer).

Remember that if you have a long document to print it is risky to start the printing and then leave the room to carry on with other tasks. Despite the best precautions, printers (particularly those for shared use) run out of paper, get low on toner etc. In addition, some printers, if over-used, have a tendency to jam and, particularly if you know this may happen, you might find it tedious but worthwhile to stay throughout the run.

How to deal with problems

All equipment, particularly well-used equipment, can go wrong. Unfortunately it normally goes wrong when it is most needed, and printers are definitely no exception to this. If you have all the time in the world to print a document, your printer will behave perfectly. If you are under pressure to produce a number of handbooks for a training session to be held that very afternoon, it will almost certainly start to misbehave. You can prepare for this contingency by making sure that you know:

• what can go wrong
• how easy or difficult it is to fix.

A prior knowledge of the instruction manual (or at least of its contents page) can be invaluable if all that is required is a minor adjustment. So, too, is a good relationship with the computer services staff or the office expert! As a last resort, the telephone number of the supplier should also be easily available so that you can make an emergency call if necessary.

 KEY NOTES ON DIFFICULTIES IN PRINTING DOCUMENTS

For general information on how to solve problems, use the Office Assistant facility and/or refer to your troubleshooting page in the printer manual.

Problem	Possible solutions
Printer not selected in software	All printers are delivered with a printer driver (usually on a disk). This is the program which controls the printer and instructs your software what printer you have installed. You can install a new printer by clicking on Start	Settings	Printers. Then choose Add Printer and follow the instructions. If you have a modern computer, 'plug and play' will mean you don't have to close down before your printer will work. Your computer will recognise the printer and be ready for work as soon as you have installed it.
Printer off-line	Depress the on-line button on the printer. If nothing happens, check the cable connections. Check your screen to see whether you are receiving an error message. Shut down Windows (make sure your document is saved!) and restart and try again. If nothing works, report the problem.

Printer out of paper	Restack the feeder tray. Remember to put the paper in the tray the right way – check the packet for instructions. Fan the paper before you load it and make sure you do not put too much in the tray at once.
Printer out of toner/ink	Check on the existing toner/ink cartridge to see if it is empty. Make a careful note of the number and obtain a new one. Remove the old cartridge and insert the new. Save the old cartridge for recycling.
Paper jam	Consult the manual to see what mechanism your printer has for removing jammed paper, if any. Ask for assistance if in doubt. *Never* try to remove the paper by brute force! Carry out a post mortem – was the paper unsuitable for the printer, was the paper damp, were the paper guides set incorrectly, was there too much paper in the paper tray, is there a problem with the actual printer mechanism etc.?

EVIDENCE COLLECTION

1   It is likely that as you have been collecting evidence for this unit, you have already obtained many examples of hard copies. However, you now need to check whether these fulfil *all* the following requirements:

- different numbers of copies
- specified ranges of pages
- printing a document on a requested printer.

It will help your assessor if you also describe the normal checks you make to agree the requirements for printing, how you obtain permission for sensitive or specific documents when required, the routine checks you carry out before printing, and the steps you take to maintain confidentiality when required.

2   You also have to prove to your assessor that you can deal with all the types of problems listed in the Key Notes above. Do this by writing an account of any problems you have experienced and how you solved these *on your particular system.*

If you never have to deal with a printer which isn't selected in your software, you may have to describe this to your assessor or ask for the opportunity to install a printer on a new computer. It is easier to do this on a laptop or stand-alone system than on a networked system, when you would need additional guidance.

Option Unit 321 Design and create presentations using a computer

FOCUS OF THE UNIT

To obtain this unit you must be able to:

- **design** presentations to meet requirements
- **create and demonstrate** presentations
- **print** presentation materials.

EVIDENCE COLLECTION

It will make evidence collection easier if you can obtain the following information:

a a description of your own job role in relation to designing, creating and printing presentation materials

b a log of presentations you have designed and prepared, stating the reason why these were required and who you prepared them for

c printouts of transparencies, handouts and speaker's notes

d a description of the hardware you use to demonstrate the presentation

e witness testimony from people for whom you have successfully designed and created presentation materials.

Health and safety requirements

The major legislation about which you should be aware includes:

- Health and Safety (Display Screen Equipment) Regulations 1992
- Provision and Use of Work Equipment Regulations 1992
- Electricity at Work Regulations 1989.

The major requirements of each Act are outlined in Unit 302 – see pages 102–120.

Key facts on designing presentations to meet requirements

Presentation types and the audience

The simplest form of presentation occurs when a speaker stands up in front of an audience and talks to them on a particular subject. This can be a very effective method of communication if the speaker is a born actor, has an absolutely dazzling personality or is of such importance that everyone else in the room daren't *not* listen. On most occasions, however, speakers find it useful to have other methods of stimulating and maintaining the interest of the audience. These can include the use of:

- an actual physical object to illustrate the main theme – a fire extinguisher in a talk about fire precaution procedures, a mobile phone in a presentation about types of communications etc.
- a whiteboard or flipchart with pre-prepared information on it
- 35mm slides
- video films
- overhead projector transparencies (OHTs)
- presentations on a computer monitor using Microsoft® PowerPoint® – which can be projected on to a larger screen.

Computer-based presentations

This unit is concerned only with the different types of presentation you design and prepare on a computer. However, different 'levels' of presentation are possible using this method.

1 The most basic is a presentation using OHTs that have been produced beforehand on the computer. The presenter is responsible for moving these on and off the projector during the talk.

2 The next level is a presentation using the computer, where the presenter manually clicks the mouse to show the next slide in the series. Some of the slides may include animation effects.

3   A more professional effect is produced when **transitions** and **build-ups** have been added. These are Microsoft® PowerPoint® terms for:

- moving from one slide to another (transitions)
- the way the slide is constructed (build-up).

Slides can appear in different ways – they can fade in and out and other special effects can be included.

4   The final level of sophistication is a fully automated presentation. In this case timings are added which determine how long each slide remains on screen until it fades out and is replaced by the next. In this situation, there is no need for a human presenter at all, so it is ideal for a presentation being shown in a reception or open area which 'loops around' after a certain time.

This unit covers all the skills you need to produce a presentation up to the stage described above as level 2. These are the skills you need to achieve this unit. However, there are obvious benefits to developing your skills, especially if your team has a need for more sophisticated presentations. If you enjoy devising presentations and would like to learn more, talk to your line manager or tutor about more advanced training sessions.

Audiences

Your line manager has been asked to give a series of presentations to mark the launch of some new keep-fit equipment manufactured by your organisation. The first is a general presentation to all the staff. The second is a more specific presentation to the people in the sales department. The third is to existing and potential clients. Although it may be easier for him or her – and you – to prepare one presentation and use it on all three occasions, it would not be good practice to do so. The presentations are being given to three different types of audience with different needs and expectations.

- You need to know who they are. Are they a group of colleagues, a departmental group, a cross-organisational group, a group of managers, a group of customers, a group of volunteers, a social group etc?
- You need to know why they are attending. Do they have to? Is it a form of staff development? Do they need the information? Do you want to tell them something or persuade them to do something? Do you want to update them? Do you want to entertain them?
- You need to be aware of what they already know. Do they know a lot about the presentation topic and merely want updating? Do they know nothing at all? Do they want specific information only – to help them make a strategic or informed decision? At what level should you aim it?

Once you have gathered that information, you are in a much better position to prepare a presentation which fully meets the needs of your particular audience. Not only will they appreciate your attempts, but you will have a better opportunity of hitting home just the message you want to.

KEY NOTES ON THE MAJOR TYPES OF PRESENTATION

Presentation	*Advantages and disadvantages*
Physical objects	Very useful in a training session; e.g. to introduce the staff to the functions of a new photocopier. Less useful in general presentations or where there is more than a small number of people.
Whiteboard or flipchart	Cheap and easy to prepare. No power is required, it is portable and it can both be prepared in advance and used as a notepad during the presentation. It is difficult to see from a distance, and in the case of a flipchart the pages can start to look over-used in a very short time.
35 mm slides	Useful to show a variety of material – text, photographs and diagrams. Creates a professional image. Slides can be expensive to produce.
Videos	Can display moving pictures and sequences of events. Can explain a complex process, which is difficult to describe. Provides a professional image. Specially made video tapes are expensive. 'Off the shelf' tapes may be too general. Normally not suitable for very large groups.
Overhead transparencies	Simple and inexpensive to produce. The speaker can use them while standing in front of the audience and maintaining eye contact. They can be drawn or written on while being displayed as well as being pre-prepared. Their projection is not as large as that of slides and care has to be taken to ensure that the projector head does not obscure the audience's view.
Computer monitor presentations	Combines the advantages of the slide and the overhead transparency. Software can be used to display graphs, charts or three-dimensional images on screen. Moving graphics or animations can be used to show, for instance, how statistics have changed over a period of time. Sound can also be introduced.
	Tables, Clip Art graphics, logos and text from other presentations can also be incorporated into these types of presentations.

Appropriate designs

If you are asked to prepare presentation material for your line manager, much depends not only on your level of experience but also on his or hers. If one of you is more experienced than the other, then that person would be expected to take the lead in deciding on an appropriate design. If both of you are experienced, it can be a mutually agreeable dialogue. If neither of you knows much about it, it is generally up to you to find out – particularly if you are asked to prepare a more sophisticated presentation.

KEY NOTES ON THE BASICS OF DESIGN OF SLIDES OR OHTs

- Favour the top two-thirds of the slide or OHT – i.e. make certain that most of the information is in that area.
- Use the most suitable format – portrait or landscape.
- Use no more than seven lines of text.
- Use no more than six words on a line.
- Use letters no smaller than 8 mm in height on an overhead transparency.
- Use larger letters for titles and sub-titles.
- Centre text and headlines or range them to the left.
- Leave a margin (at least 2 cm on overhead transparencies) from the edge of the frame.
- Leave gaps to make key points stand out.

KEY NOTES ON THE USE OF COLOUR

- Make use of colour where you think it will enhance the presentation – which is nearly always.
- Keep it simple – if you know that colour coordination is not your strong point, use one of the pre-prepared colour schemes your package offers.
- Although it is possible to use a different colour scheme for each slide or OHT, it is not normally wise to do so. You will only succeed in confusing your audience.
- Tailor the scheme to your audience. If they are a senior management group you would probably want to choose more muted colours than if they are a group of your peers or members of the general public who want to be entertained as well as informed.
- Check on your organisation's house style.
- Remember that text slides work best with highly contrasting colour schemes – light text on a dark background or vice versa.

INFORMATION UPDATE

Researchers have found that, although we absorb information through all our five senses, most of it is absorbed through sight:

touch	1 per cent
taste	1 per cent
smell	3 per cent
hearing	12 per cent
sight	83 per cent.

Remember that when preparing a presentation.

CHECK IT OUT!

For your evidence (see page 655) you have to prove you have agreed and recorded certain specific requirements of the person who is requesting the work. Check that you feel confident to do this for each of the following types of requirement:

a   purpose of presentation (see pages 638–639)

b   type of presentation – for instance, whether you have to produce OHTs, presentations on a computer monitor or a projector show

c   style – informal/formal etc. (see page 644)

d   content – the exact information to be included

e   intended user – e.g. the skills of the presenter

f   intended audience (see page 639)

g   notes and handouts required (these relate to speaker's notes and handouts for the audience – see further page 675)

h   data to be sourced from other files – such as tables produced on a spreadsheet package, 'Clip Art' graphics (see pages 657 and 659), logos and text from existing presentations.

Selecting and adapting suitable designs

The structure

Obviously the design of the presentation should reflect its purpose, style, content and intended audience. Your work should therefore follow on from the work your presenter has already carried out in structuring the presentation to achieve the desired objectives.

He or she may, for instance, decide on a structure in which each idea is presented separately and given equal weight. This might be suitable for a formal presentation at which the members of the audience may want to make notes. The structure also lends itself to the speaker making a summary for them at the end of each point.

The structure might alternatively be such that one point is of greater significance than the rest which supplement or augment it. Examples of where this could be used include a talk to already knowledgeable staff about a new product where the product itself is the main topic for discussion.

Or the structure might be such that each idea overlaps so that the first point is further explained by the second, the second by the third – and so on. This is useful in presentations where the subject matter is quite complex and various points need to be emphasised and re-emphasised.

Whatever the structure, the presentation has to be designed to support it to its best effect.

Adapting an existing design

There may be a case for adapting an existing presentation to meet the requirements of the person who wants you to do the work. If there are only minor alterations to be made, that is an easy task and you can then re-save the presentation under a different name for identification. However, don't be tempted to use this alternative as the 'lazy' option if the requirements are so different that the style would really not be appropriate!

The importance of getting a clear brief for the design

Creating a design for a presentation is not the same as following a house style for any other document. It is far more subjective and dependent upon individual taste. If you and your line manager have worked together for some time you may have an idea of the sort of design he or she will like. If you have not, then you may need some detailed discussion prior to the design of any presentation. You need also to be aware that your line manager may prefer different styles for differing presentations. He or she may, for instance, favour a very informal approach with clipart designs and 'jokey' captions in the case of internal presentations. Where the presentation is to be made to an outside (or very senior) audience, he or she may feel happier with a more formal design and style.

It is very important, of course, that you be fully aware of these views right from the start. Otherwise, carried away with artistic fervour, you may waste a lot of time over a design before being told that it isn't what was wanted.

Providing design options to look at and discuss

Sven has started work for a marketing manager, part of whose job it is to make presentations to both internal and external audiences. Sven finds out that, although the manager seems to have a clear idea of what he wants, he cannot seem to put his ideas into words. He sometimes wants something 'dramatic' and 'upbeat'. He occasionally says that he wants the presentation to have the 'feel of a country garden' or to be 'sharp and hard edged'. Initially Sven doesn't have a clue where to begin. As he becomes more experienced, however, he realises that if he shows his manager a number of draft designs in different colours and with different logos or backgrounds, the manager will start to make a number of comments, such as:

> 'Could the background be a little darker?'
> 'No, that's far too gloomy.'
> 'Too young for my audience.'
> 'I can't read the text clearly enough.'
> 'It's too much to take in.'
> 'Should the company logo be on each of the slides?'
> 'I like that colour combination – could it be repeated throughout?'

At the end of each discussion, Sven feels very much more confident that he is getting nearer and nearer to what his manager requires and that the end-result will be one that satisfies them both.

You may, of course, have such a creative line manager that he or she can tell you without hesitation what is wanted. If that is the case, then your work is halved – although there is still nothing to stop you making a few helpful suggestions. Remember that you are probably more technically proficient than your manager and should, for instance, be able to tell him or her just exactly what your computer software package can produce – and give examples of functions that you think may appeal.

Negotiating and agreeing a final design option

One problem that frequently arises when you are engaged in a creative activity is that you don't know when to stop. Once you start discussing various design options it can become so engrossing that making a final decision becomes very difficult. However, a final decision is needed. Hopefully it is a group decision; but if agreement simply cannot be reached, it is normally the task of your line manager to take the lead and decide on one particular option.

When this happens, make sure that you have that decision in writing – either in the minutes of the meeting itself or in a separate memo or e-mail. Not only is this the evidence if someone at a later stage swears that he or she cannot remember 'agreeing' to the decision, it also reminds you of what has been agreed, particularly if the requirements are quite comprehensive. You will, for instance, need to confirm:

- the purpose of the presentation
- whether it is to be presented by means of overhead transparencies or slides
- the style you must follow
- the content
- who is going to use it and what are his or her particular likes and dislikes

- who is going to listen to it (look back to page 639 for a discussion about the intended audience)
- what types of notes and handouts, if any, are required to accompany the presentation
- what data has to be sourced from other files.

Capabilities and limitations of your software

Even Leonardo da Vinci would have difficulty painting the Mona Lisa if he hadn't got a canvas and some paints. You can only be as creative as your resources allow you to be.

You should make yourself as familiar as possible with all the functions of the software you are using – starting with the basics and progressing incrementally to the more sophisticated functions. You should make good and continual use of any manufacturer's instructions and suppliers' handbooks. You should ensure that even if you are not immediately able to carry out a particular function, you at least know where to start looking for instructions on how to do so. Remember that if you have received any training either from the supplier or independently, the course notes you have been given are an invaluable source of reference. Remember also to keep an eye out for other more advanced training courses. It is amazing how much you can gain from them – even if you think you are an expert in this field!

 KEY NOTES ON MAJOR FEATURES OF A MICROSOFT® POWERPOINT® PACKAGE

- Start a new presentation.
- Open an existing presentation.
- Create a master slide.
- Save a presentation.
- E-mail a presentation.
- Create different effects:
  - insert text
  - move text
  - manipulate text
  - change the alignment of text
  - add headers and footers
  - add or change the colour
  - change the font style and size
  - change the line/paragraph spacing
  - use bullet points
  - add tables
  - add autoshapes, charts or clip art
  - animate slides by adding movement and sound effects.
- Re-order slides.
- Change the slide layout.
- View the slide show.
- Create speaker notes.
- Create handouts for the audience.

1 Opposite is an example of a PowerPoint® screen in Microsoft® Office 2000. Check that you:

- are familiar with all the toolbars and terms shown
- know how to select or hide icons on toolbars (View | Toolbars | Customise)
- know how to access additional options on your toolbars (click the downward arrow at the extreme right-hand side)
- know how to find out what each icon represents by positioning the insertion point over it.

2 Check the Key Notes on page 645 and decide which of the functions you feel familiar with. Make a list of the ones you think may cause you concern, and check the rest of this unit for advice and assistance. Remember also to make use of the Help facility.

Selecting appropriate slide designs for effectiveness and consistency

Accessing the system

If neither you nor your line manager has any definite ideas as to the design you want, then use your software package to assist you. If you are relatively new to designing presentations it is important to know that most packages will provide you with a prompt function (a Wizard in PowerPoint) which takes you step by step through the creation of the basic structure of your presentation.

There are also a number of standard layouts or **design templates** which can be used as a basis for any presentation and which save you having to undertake any more complicated functions until you are ready to do so. The only decision to be made is which of the templates to use – and that normally depends on the nature of the presentation and composition of the audience.

If, however, you feel confident about your design skills, most systems will also allow you to take full control over your design by allowing you to access a blank presentation and to experiment with it as much as you wish.

Menu bar – access to lists of commands available

Standard toolbar – to select commands available

Comments boxes – enable comment to slides to be added or viewed quickly

Outline pane – displays all the current text

View button – allows you to change the way your presentation is displayed on screen

Drawing toolbar – for working with objects

Formatting toolbar – to select formatting commands

Common tasks – gives access to New Slide, Slide Layout, Apply Design

Slide pane – displays the current slide

Notes pane – speaker notes for the current slide

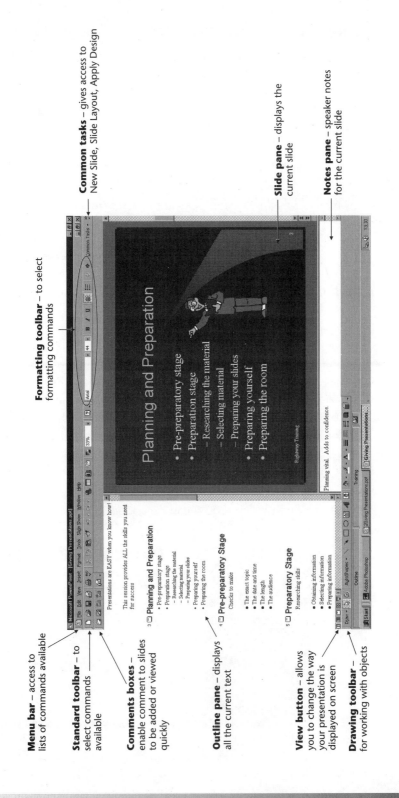

The Microsoft® PowerPoint® screen

- Click on Start I Programs I Microsoft® PowerPoint®.
- The Microsoft® PowerPoint® window appears. The PowerPoint® dialogue box appears each time you start the application, so you can choose to create a new or open an existing presentation. The Office Assistant welcome appears the first time you start PowerPoint.
- Click on AutoContent Wizard to create a new presentation, and OK. The wizard appears (see the illustration below).
- Click on Next to start creating your presentation.
- Click the category that best describes the type of presentation you want to create, and on Next to continue.
- Click the type of output you want to use for your presentation (e.g. on-screen presentation, Web presentation etc.), and on Next to continue. Note that you can click Back at any time to return to a previous step and change your answers.
- Click on Presentation title and type the title you want to appear on the first slide in your presentation.
- To add a footer, click against the Footer heading and type in the required text. Microsoft® PowerPoint® will add the current date and slide number to each slide in your presentation. If you do not want the date or number added, click the appropriate box.
- Click on Next to continue. The wizard indicates that you have provided all the answers needed to create your presentation. Click on Finish to create it.

Note that any items you wish to appear on each slide – such as your company name and logo – can be added to the master slide by clicking on View I Master I Slide Master.

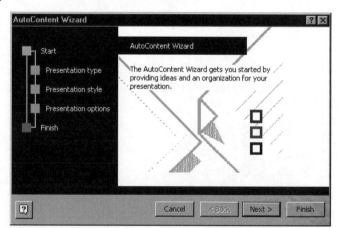

The AutoContent Wizard

KEY NOTES ON USING A DESIGN TEMPLATE

- Click Start | Programs | Microsoft® PowerPoint®. The Microsoft® PowerPoint® window appears.
- Click on Design Template and OK. The New Presentation dialogue box will be displayed.
- Click on the desired template to see it previewed at the right of the dialogue box (see the illustration below).
- Click on OK if you want to select this template.
- Select the slide layout you want from the AutoLayouts shown (see the illustration on page 650), and click on OK.
- PowerPoint will now create a presentation containing one slide which uses the selected design and layout. The slide contains placeholders into which you can enter text and graphics (see the second illustration on page 650).

Note that if you are initially unsure of the look you want for your presentation, you can create a presentation using the Blank Presentation template. This template will create a presentation containing one slide which will have a white background and black text.

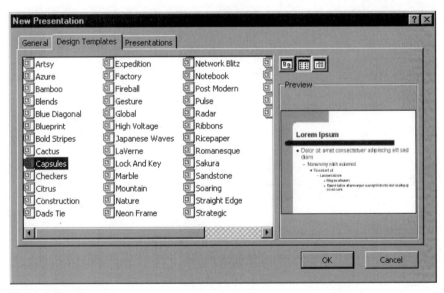

The preview pane

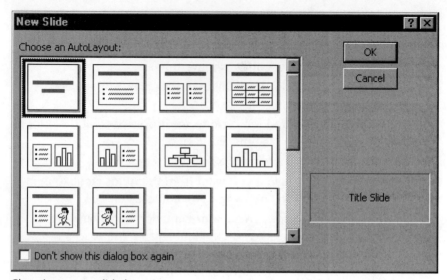

Choosing a new slide layout

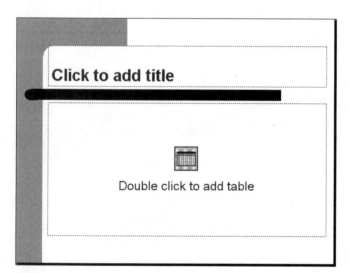

Placeholders

KEY NOTES ON OPENING AN EXISTING PRESENTATION

Note that the Microsoft® PowerPoint® dialogue box appears each time you start the application.

- Click on Open an existing presentation. This area displays the names of the last presentations you worked with. To open one of these presentations, double-click the name of the presentation. If the presentation you want to open is not listed, double-click More Files.

- The Open dialogue box appears. The 'Look in' area shows the location of the displayed presentations. The area to the left allows you to access commonly used folders – such as History, My Documents, Desktop, Favorites, My Network Places/Web Folders.

- Click the name of the presentation you want to open.

- The preview area displays the first slide in the presentation you selected.

- Click Open.

- Microsoft® PowerPoint® opens the presentation.

Slide design formats

Much, of course, depends upon the nature of the presentation. If, for instance, you are asked to prepare a basic presentation to staff about changes to the payroll, you might limit your artistic ability to:

- using a clear font type of an appropriate size
- highlighting in bold certain key points
- inserting bullet points
- including appropriate headers and footers.

If, on the other hand, you are preparing a more lavish presentation for an important conference you might want to use a more elaborate layout and colour scheme and to consider the possibility of adding animation.

What you will probably also want to do, whatever the nature of the presentation, is to ensure that the basic design you have created is repeated throughout the presentation without your having to recreate it each time you begin to prepare a new slide. Most graphics applications packages allow you to create a master design which will automatically be repeated on each subsequent slide. Obviously this not only saves you time but also solves the problem of your having to constantly check back on your preferred design.

KEY NOTES ON SLIDE DESIGN FORMATS (1)

Text colour schemes

- Select the text you want to change to a different colour.
- Click the Font Colour **A** on the Drawing toolbar to select a colour.
- Click the colour you want to use from the pop-up menu ▾. The text appears in the colour you selected.
- To deselect the text, click outside the selected area.

Object colour schemes

- Click the object you want to change to a different colour. Handles appear around the object.
- Click the 'bucket pouring paint' icon on the Drawing toolbar to select a colour. Click the colour you want to use from the pop-up menu ▾. The object appears in the colour you selected.
- To deselect the object, click outside the object.

Colour scheme for the entire presentation

- Click on the icon on the View Buttons toolbar to change to the Slide Sorter view.
- Click Format | Slide Colour Scheme on the main menu bar. The Colour Scheme dialogue box appears.
- Click the Standard Tab. This area displays the available colour schemes.
- Click the colour scheme you want to use.
- Click Apply to All to apply the colour scheme to all the slides in your presentation.

Note that you can change the colour scheme for one slide only to make it stand out from the rest. To do so, click the slide you want to change, then click Format and follow the rest of the steps outlined above including clicking the colour scheme you want to use. Then click Apply (rather than Apply to All).

Fonts

- Select the text you want to change.
- Click the font icon ▾ on the standard toolbar to display a list of the available fonts.
- Click the font you want to use. The text you selected changes to the new font.
- To deselect text, click outside the selected area.

Headers and footers

New presentation using a wizard

- Access the AutoContent wizard (see key notes on creating a presentation on page 648 for some assistance if necessary).
- Follow the designated steps until you reach the point at which the title of the presentation is to be inserted.
- To add footer text to each slide in the presentation, click against footer and then type in the text.

Presentation without using a wizard

- Click on View I Header and Footer I Slide on the main menu bar.
- Complete with date and time, header, page number and footer.
- Click on the Apply to All button.

 KEY NOTES ON SLIDE DESIGN FORMATS (3)

Animations

- Click the object on the slide you want to animate. Handles 🖫 appear around the object.
- Click the icon 🌠 on the standard toolbar. The Animation Effects toolbar appears.
- Click the Animation Effect you want to use.
- Click on the icon 🔯 to preview the animation.
- Click the icon ☒ to close the Animation Preview window.
- Click the icon ☒ to close the Animation Effects toolbar.

Custom animation

- Click on the Custom Animation icon 🎛 shown on the Animation Effects toolbar.

- Select the effect required. If your system is equipped with a sound card, select a sound to be played when the select object is displayed on the screen.

- You can preview the result of each effect you try out before you click on OK.

Note that when viewing your slide show, you must click the slide to display each animated object on the slide. If, for instance, you have animated a list of points, you must click the slide each time you want a point to appear.

CHECK IT OUT!

Describe briefly how your graphics application package allows you to ensure consistency throughout a presentation (such as through the use of a slide master).

Storing the agreed design and any notes safely

Designing a presentation is not often something you can do quickly, and by the time the finished result has been produced it will probably be very dear to your heart! The thought of losing or damaging it is not one you want to contemplate!

Obviously you will make certain that all the presentation material is stored safely before the event takes place, and that someone else knows where it is in case you are unavoidably absent on that day.

There are several reasons why this storage is important.

- You might need to continue working on a design which is unfinished.
- It is useful as a reference if there is any disagreement about the design that was agreed.
- It is a safeguard if you are absent and someone else has to continue.
- Your computer or your hard disk might crash.
- It saves on 'thinking time' for a future similar presentation.

Store *both* the design brief, the design agreed and relevant hard copies of your slides or OHTs in a safe place, in a clearly named file where you can access them easily. An alternative is to have a master folder of designs and presentations in which you store all the relevant papers for a particular presentation or series of presentations.

You should also check on the safety of your material both during and after the event. One problem may be that you are handing over your precious material for someone else to use and you cannot guarantee that he or she will use it with care – or even return it to you after the presentation is over. However, you can cut down on the possibility of this happening in several ways.

- Make certain that all material is saved on disk.
- Keep a hard copy – as above – of all paper-based material, including speaker's notes and handouts.
- Where possible, immediately after the event 'rescue' original OHTs and disks from the room in which the presentation has been given. Even if you are not there you should either try to persuade the presenter of the advantages of collecting together the material and returning it to you – or, if you know he or she may still be too wound up after the presentation to be able to concentrate on doing this – ask someone else attending the presentation to do it for you.

Obviously a lot of presentation material is for a one-off purpose and cannot be re-used very easily. However, it is always useful to have an example of a particularly good design or effective layout on your files next time you need to create another presentation on whatever topic. There is rarely any point in re-inventing the wheel unless you absolutely have to.

EVIDENCE COLLECTION

The evidence you start to collect for this element can be developed and extended for the rest of the unit. In this case, select *at least two* or *three* presentations you have designed and created. For each one, provide a brief report which includes the following information.

1 Write down how you usually agree and record the requirements for a presentation with the person who requests it. Note that you must cover *all* the following aspects:

- purpose of the presentation
- type of presentation
- style
- content
- intended user
- intended audience
- notes and handouts to accompany the presentation
- data to be sourced from other files.

2 If applicable, identify occasions when you have suggested adapting existing presentations to meet these requirements. ➡

Key facts on creating and demonstrating presentations

Selecting and applying slide design formats

As you know already, your package should allow you to select and apply a number of slide design formats. Your final decision should be informed, of course, by the type of information you want to display.

- Do you want to show an organisation chart or display a table?
- Do you want to make use of graphs?
- Is Clip Art to be a feature of the presentation?
- Do you want to make use of animation?

Inputting, checking and placing different types of data

Text

The task of inserting text in your selected slide design is normally quite straightforward. In some packages you will be guided by the use of placeholders on each slide layout into which you can place your text, graphics etc. These enable you to position titles and sub-titles, in addition to the main body of text which can be displayed with or without bullet points.

Remember that checking accuracy and spelling is *vital* if your text will be seen by an audience. Use a spell-checker, proofread word by word, *and* ask someone else to read through printouts on a just-in-case basis!

In PowerPoint you have the ability to work in various views:

- **normal view** – to work on both the text and/or your slides
- **outline view** – to see all the text in the presentation
- **slide view** – to see just your slides
- **slide sorter view** – to see miniature version of all your slides.

Normal view is extremely useful. Your text is given in the left-hand pane of the screen. You may find it easier and quicker to insert, delete and amend text in this pane, rather than in the slide itself in the right-hand pane. If you get it wrong, expect to see a 'lightbulb'. Click on it and you will be told how to make an improvement to your style!

Graphics

A slightly more complicated procedure has to be followed if you are asked to input graphics, although again your software will probably be able to provide you with a user-friendly guide. Most packages, for instance, provide a number of tools that you can use to enhance your presentation slides:

- the Drawing toolbar which allows you to draw simple shapes such as lines, circles and squares and also gives you the facility to access more sophisticated shapes automatically
- a charting facility which allows you to produce charts quickly and easily
- a Clip Art facility which allows you to preview and select one of a wide variety of clips.

See below for an example of a Microsoft® PowerPoint® dialogue box which allows you to access a Clip Art gallery.

Inserting Clip Art

Sounds

Most packages allow you to add sounds. They offer you a variety of sounds – normally designed to last for a short period rather than throughout the presentation – to give you the opportunity of enhancing key points. They might be:

- at the beginning of a presentation – to catch the attention of the audience
- to add humour at certain points
- to highlight any animation
- at certain important stages in the presentation
- to fill in any 'gaps' between certain items of information at the end.

The Key Notes box on pages 653–654 has information on animations, of which sounds are an example.

 ## KEY NOTES ON INPUTTING TEXT DATA

Each slide layout contains placeholders into which you can place text.

- The text in the placeholder tells you what to do to add your own information; e.g. click to add title, click to add sub-title.
- Click on the placeholder. An editing window will appear where you can type your text. The placeholder text is replaced by the insertion point.
- Type the required text. The text will wrap to fit the size of the placeholder. If you want to start a new line, press the Enter key.
- Once you have finished typing, click anywhere outside the editing window.

CHECK IT OUT!

Produce examples of a presentation in which you have input at least two out of the three following materials: text, graphics, sound. State which you use most frequently and why you do so.

If you have never used one of the features, write brief notes on the circumstances in which you might find it useful to do so in the future.

KEY NOTES ON INPUTTING GRAPHICS

Each slide layout contains placeholders into which you can place graphics (see pages 649 and 650).

The Clip Art gallery

- Display the slide to which you want to add a Clip Art image.
- Change the layout of the slide to one that includes space for a Clip Art image; i.e. click Common Tasks and then Slide Layout. The Slide layout dialogue box appears. Click the layout you want. Click on Apply and the slide appears in the new layout.
- Double-click this area to add a clipart image to the slide.
- The Microsoft® Clip Gallery dialogue box appears (see the illustration on page 657).
- Click the category of Clip Art images you want to display.
- Click the Clip Art image you want to add to the slide.
- A menu appears. Click the icon to add the Clip Art image to the slide.
- The handles around the image let you change the size of the image.
- To hide the handles, click outside the Clip Art image.
- To delete an image you do not want, click on it and then press the Delete key.

AutoShapes

- Display the slide to which you want to add an AutoShape.
- Click AutoShapes on the Drawing toolbar.
- Click the category for the type of AutoShape you want to add.
- Click the AutoShape you want to add.
- Position the mouse where you want to begin drawing the AutoShape.
- Drag the mouse until the AutoShape is the size you want.
- The AutoShape appears on the slide. The handles around the AutoShape allow you to change its size. To hide the handles, click outside the AutoShape.
- To delete an AutoShape, click on it and then press the Delete key.

Note that if you want to add text to an AutoShape (such as a banner), click the AutoShape and then type the text you want the AutoShape to display.

Charts

- Display the slide to which you want to add a chart.
- Change the layout of the slide to one that includes a placeholder for a chart; i.e. click Common Tasks | Slide Layout.
- Click the layout containing the type of chart you want to use.
- Double-click the area on the slide where you want to display the chart. A datasheet appears displaying sample data to show you where to enter information.
- To replace the data in a cell, click the cell. A thick border appears around the cell.
- Type your data and then press the Enter key.
- Repeat until you have finished entering the data.
- When you finish, click a blank area on the screen. The datasheet disappears and you can view the chart.
- Note: you can copy and paste an existing chart you have created in another package, such as Excel.

Sound

See Key Notes on pages 653–654.

Achieving different formats

Given that presentations have to be eye-catching, it is up to you to display the material as imaginatively as possible. If you always use the same size of type, never think to display material in a table rather than as text, and cannot bring yourself to experiment with different types of colour schemes, you may produce a sound presentation but it is not likely to be inspiring!

Sometimes the more experienced you are at designing and creating presentations, the less you tend to experiment with new ideas. You become so accustomed to producing what you know is an effective design that you sometimes overlook the fact that there may be ways of improving it if you took the time to check out some alternatives.

KEY NOTES ON FORMATTING TEXT

Fonts

Refer to the Key Notes on slide design formats (2) on page 653.

Note that **serif** fonts have small lines that stem from the upper and lower ends of characters. **Sans serif** fonts do not have such extensions. Generally speaking, larger text in a sans serif font and body text in a smaller serif font usually makes for easy reading.

- Arial is an example of a sans serif font.
- Times New Roman is a serif font.

Lists

Some text placeholders have been set up to format the text you enter as a list of bullet points. When you press the Enter key to begin a new paragraph, a new bullet point is added automatically. Bullet points can be turned on and off by clicking on the Bullets icon on the Formatting toolbar, as can Numbering.

Tables

Note that Microsoft® PowerPoint® comes with a slide layout that includes a placeholder for a table. To use this layout, click Slide Layout on the Common Tasks toolbar. Click through the options, reading the content of each. When you see Table, select this layout by clicking on Apply.

- On the slide, double-click in the specified area to add a table.
- Enter the number of columns and rows required and click on OK.
- Enter the data in the table cells.
- Use the Word tools and menus to format the table. (See option Unit 320, page 588.)
- Click outside the table to return to Microsoft® PowerPoint®.

Note: Don't change the layout *after* you have added an object to a slide. The placeholder will overlap with this and create a very messy look.

Line spacing

- Click anywhere in the paragraph where you want to change the spacing.
- Click Line Spacing on the Format menu.
- Enter the amount of spacing you want and then click Lines or Points.
- Click on OK.

Colours

Refer to the Key Notes on slide design formats (1) on page 652.

Manipulating data

When preparing a presentation, you may want to place a **logo** in a very prominent position on your slide or OHT. You may want to use some graphics or clipart but don't want them to dominate the whole slide. You may want to reposition or rotate some text to highlight a particular point. This is normally quite easy.

Most graphic applications packages allow you to:

- select one or more objects (from, for instance, the Drawing toolbar)
- incorporate pre-prepared graphics or clipart
- align them so that they are in the most attractive position vis-à-vis other information
- place them in the most appropriate position
- resize them – so that they become bigger or smaller
- move them about as often as you like before making your final decision
- stack them one on top of the other to achieve various effects (e.g. a large rectangle containing a smaller rectangle containing an oval)
- change the orientation from landscape to portrait or vice versa.

What is important, of course, is for you to familiarise yourself with what your package can do and to *experiment* with various effects. Remember the golden rule, however, and try not to overdo the effects. If you have so many objects, logos or items of clipart on a slide at the same time, your audience will be far too overwhelmed to take in your intended message.

 ## KEY NOTES ON MANIPULATING DATA

Alignment of text

- Select the text you want to re-align.
- Click on appropriate button on the Formatting toolbar – left align, centre, right align. The text is displayed in the new alignment.
- To deselect text, click outside the selected area.

Achieving the correct orientation

- Click on File | Page Setup on the main menu bar. A dialogue box appears.
- Click under Orientation for Slides or Notes, handouts and outlines.
- Click Portrait or Landscape and OK.

Moving images and text

- Click the object you want to move. Handles ![handles] appear around the object.
- Position the mouse over an edge of the object. (![pointer]) changes to ![move pointer]
- Drag the object to a new location.

Rotating text and drawing objects

- Click the object you want to rotate. Handles ![handles] appear around the object
- Click on the Free Rotate tool ![tool] on the Drawing toolbar. The The pointer will be displayed as a rotation symbol ![symbol] and the selection handles will be replaced by four rotation handles
- To rotate the object, point to one of the rotation handles, hold down the mouse button and drag the object to the required angle. The angle of rotation will be displayed on the status bar.

Sizing images

- Click the object you want to size. Handles ![handles] appear around the object.
- Position the mouse over one of the handles: (![pointer]) changes to a double-headed arrow (↖ ↔ ↕)
- Drag the handle until the object is the size you want. The object appears in the new size.

Note that individual handles can size the object in a different way i.e.

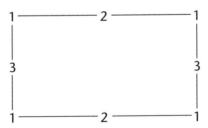

(1) changes the height and width of an object at the same time, but keeps the proportion constant.

(2) changes the height of an object.

(3) changes the width of an object.

Procedures for naming and saving files

Presentations tend to fall into one of two categories. They might be one-offs and prepared for one particular audience on one occasion, such as:

- the introduction of a new computer or management information system
- a general staff reorganisation
- a specific problem – vandalism, petty theft etc.

Alternatively they might be part of a regular programme presentations:

- to those employees about to retire
- to new employees
- to existing and potential clients about the product range
- as part of a rolling programme of staff development
- to the board of directors or senior executives on the overall position of the organisation.

With one-offs, although it is useful to keep the material as evidence or for future reference, it may be unlikely that you will need to re-use it. In the other cases, however, you may be able to use it on several occasions, with either no or only minor amendments. At the very least you will be able to use the layout even if the actual content needs to be changed.

It is therefore a good idea for you to separate the two types of presentation when naming them – particularly if you are dealing with a large number of presentations. The one-offs can be treated individually and separate file names given to them. The presentations that are likely to be accessed more frequently should be dealt with more systematically. If, for instance, you have a number of training presentations which are likely to be re-used, you could create a suitable generic name for that group of presentations and distinguish between each one by the addition of a final set of letters. If your system allows you to do so, it is sometimes helpful to use a combination of letters and numbers – to indicate, for instance, that this relates to last year or the year before, or that it is the third in a series of twelve presentations etc.

Saving important presentations is vitally important, and while preparing them you should, of course, take the precaution of saving the material every few minutes. You might, however, be in a position whereby you design and create the presentations but leave it to one of your colleagues or juniors to produce and save them. If you do so, make absolutely certain that they know how to do it! Make equally certain, if you can, that they are known for their attention to detail!

Refer to the Key Notes on page 672 for information on how to save and print materials.

Selecting and setting up appropriate hardware

Once you have completed a presentation it is sensible to have a 'rehearsal' with the person who is to deliver it. The first stage is for you to give a demonstration. There are both benefits and pitfalls here!

Benefits include:

- checking the equipment that is required and that it is in working order
- checking that the slides (animations and sound in particular) work as you planned
- checking the timing
- checking, if possible, how it works in the actual venue
- having a 'run-through' in time for minor corrections and adjustments to be made.

Pitfalls include the possibility of various suggestions being made about how the presentation could be changed or improved. Many of these suggestions will be made by people who don't understand the work or time involved!

Rather than glare at anyone who dares to make even the mildest suggestion, it is sensible to set the scene at the outset. Simply say this is a 'final' run-through, and minor changes can be considered and any mistakes corrected. However, unless there are months to go before the event 'proper', stress that this is not the occasion for a brainstorming session to rethink the whole idea!

Doing the demonstration and negotiating changes

Don't rush this. Work through the presentation methodically and make sure your audience receives copies of relevant speaker's notes and handouts (see page 675). They may wish to make useful suggestions in relation to these.

Note down any 'glitches' you encounter yourself. If you have software or hardware problems, now is the time to ask for expert help from your computer or AV (audio-visual) technicians.

Do be positive if people make suggestions relating to the viewpoint from the back of the venue – check it out yourself if need be. Remember that the presentation has to be seen and heard by everyone.

It is sensible to organise this session by doing the presentation in silence and then having an 'open forum' to discuss suggestions.

At the end, summarise exactly what you have agreed to change and what should remain the same. (Note that if you are asked to change the order of slides or delete some slides, this is dealt with on page 671.)

CHECK IT OUT!

If you wanted to make the following changes to a presentation, state whether you would make them yourself or consult your presenter.

a You think the presentation looks better in landscape rather than portrait.

b You want to change the Clip Art to give a 'younger' feel to the presentation.

c You think the colour scheme is too vivid.

d You are concerned that one of the graphs gives a misleading picture because the information it gives is too general.

e The presentation is too short/too long.

f You think there should be more bullet points.

Providing support to the presenter

One of your higher risk tasks will almost certainly be the setting up of the equipment 'on the day' as part of your support role. If you are using your own organisation's facilities and are lucky enough to have access to a fully equipped area, then your work is easier. You may find that the equipment is housed permanently in that area and that qualified technical staff check and maintain it on a regular basis. The same might be the case if you are holding your presentation in an external conference venue which is tailor-made to your requirements and which can provide you with any physical or human backup you require.

You have to take extra care when the presentation is to be held in your own work area and the equipment to be used is available to be booked out by one of a number of people. If this is the case you should make sure that you book it in very good time (both for your demonstration and for the actual event). Make an initial check to see that it is in working order and arrange for any repairs or adjustments to be made.

Test the equipment out in the actual room where the presentation is to be held. Moving equipment even a short distance seems to upset it, and a computer which works perfectly in your office often has the annoying habit of refusing to do the same when transported into the presentation area just before the event! Arrange for a spare machine to be available 'just in case' – and don't let that one out of your sight. It is a known fact that if two machines are seen together, one is almost bound to disappear!

Wherever the presentation is to be held, you have to make some last-minute checks. It is not good practice to be seen fiddling with the computer as the audience is coming through the door, but right up to that point your time is your own and you should check and re-check that all is well.

Where relevant, have as many back-up facilities as possible on hand – one of the technical staff either in the room itself or immediately available at the end of a telephone line, a spare machine, a variety of spare parts etc.

You would normally set up the equipment where it best suits the wishes of the presenter. However, you should take into account the size of the room and the audience. See the illustrations below which give you an example of optimum room size and height and the need to consider the sight lines of the audience.

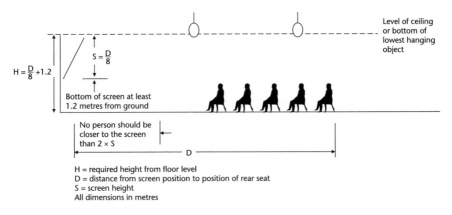

Optimum room size and height when using visual aids

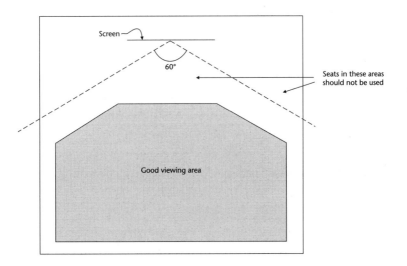

Viewing angles and sight lines

KEY NOTES ON CHECKING THAT EQUIPMENT IS IN WORKING ORDER

- Make sure that you *really* know how the equipment works. Don't content yourself with a knowledge of the basics.

- Check the power supply and take advice as to whether it is sufficient for your purpose.

- Check that there is an appropriate supply of bulbs, fuses, leads etc.

- Have your user manual or manufacturer's instructions to hand so that if a malfunction occurs you can refer to it for initial advice.

- Check all the equipment, but bear in mind the areas where difficulties are most likely to occur – the remote control, the mouse etc.

- Check the entire presentation. It should be perfect at this stage but it is surprising how often items can get out of order or the odd production error can still be spotted. If absolutely necessary you also have the option of changing the design – if, for instance, the background doesn't show up too well or some of the print is not clear enough.

In some cases, in addition to helping with the equipment, you will have a part to play in the overall organisation of the event itself. For further details on these duties, see Option Unit 311 (you will find this unit on the Heinemann website – see page 428 for details of how to access it). You will also have to check in particular that the presenter has everything he or she needs to ensure that the presentation is successful:

- all the 'tools of the trade' – a laser pointer to indicate items on the screen, special marker pens, blank acetate sheets, back up disks etc.

- the speaker's notes, in the right order and of sufficiently large type to be read easily (and have copies of these in case the presenter loses the originals)

- a sufficient number of audience handouts.

You should also remember to check that all the materials your presenter is going to use are laid out in the most appropriate way (first of all checking to see whether he or she is left- or right-handed.) Make sure also that you know where *you* should be standing or sitting. Some presenters are happy that you are just 'there' somewhere in the room. Others prefer you to be nearer at hand and to take a more active part in the presentation – circulating handouts, handing over notes, and so on.

Either write brief notes on what you did when the following problems occurred; *or* state what you would do in such circumstances.

> 'The computer isn't working.'
> 'The power point is too far away.'
> 'There isn't a power point.'
> 'There are no blackout facilities.'
> 'The room's too large.'
> 'The room's too small.'
> 'It's far too noisy here.'

EVIDENCE COLLECTION

For this element, you can extend the evidence you started on page 655. In this element you need to describe how you undertook each of the following operations. You also need to supplement your evidence with relevant hard copies of the presentation materials. Note that your evidence will be far more valuable if you include early drafts of slides and materials in addition to the final 'polished' version, and if you explain the alterations and amendments that were made – and why.

1   How you selected the agreed slide design format.

2   What methods you used to input, check and place data. Note that you must use two types of data from the following list and at least one must be images: (a) text, (b) graphics, (c) sound.

3   How you used software to achieve all the following formats:
    (a) fonts, (b) bulleted lists, (c) numbered lists, (d) tables, (e) line spacing, (f) colours.

4   How you manipulated data in all of the following ways: (a) align text; (b) achieve the correct orientation; (c) rotate images and text; (d) size images?

5   How you saved your presentation. What organisational procedures you had to consider when doing this.

Give details of the demonstration you gave, including the hardware required, the way in which you did the demonstration, changes that were suggested and how these were negotiated.

Finally, outline the support you provided at the actual event.

Key facts on printing presentation materials

Agreeing requirements for printing

Modern computing hardware allows you a large number of printing options. Whatever package you use, you will probably be given the option of choosing to print slides, speaker's notes (with slide plus notes), handouts (with two, three or six slides per page), and an outline view (text content only). You will also be able to choose the number of copies you want to print and the copies you want collating. There is an option to send your output to a file.

You may be asked to print hidden slides – where, for instance, you have prepared a multi-purpose presentation where not all slides will be shown to all audiences and some are therefore 'hidden'.

Obviously what you need to do is to agree the printing requirements before you start the printing process. You need to know the range of slides, notes and handouts that are required and in what quantity.

What you may also have to do in this instance, however, is to advise your manager on what options there are available. He or she may be interested to know, for example, that a number of slides can be produced on a single handout or that a notes page can be produced beneath a copy of each slide for use by the audience during the presentation.

Checking that materials are complete and ready for printing

Preparing a presentation can create a large volume of materials – the OHTs or slides, the hard copies, the speaker's notes etc. An experienced administrator recognises not only this, but also that – particularly in the case of important presentations – changes will be requested continually right up to the last minute.

It is time-consuming (and wasteful of resources) if you arrange for everything to go to print before you are absolutely sure that it is complete and that no further alterations are going to be made. Check the materials yourself, ask a colleague to check as an independent observer, and insist on booking some time with the presenter to take him or her through it in detail before you finally release it for print.

What you should also be able to do is to reorganise the slides that are going to be used to ensure that they are presented in the most logical order.

Viewing the current slide layout

- Click on the Slide Sorter icon [icon] on the View Buttons bar.
- Click the first slide you want to view.
- Click on the Start icon [icon] on the View Buttons bar to start the show.

Changing the slide layout

- Display the slide you want to change to a new layout.
- Click Common Tasks I Slide Layout. The Slide Layout dialogue box appears – which displays the available layouts.
- Click the layout you want to apply to the slide, and click on Apply. The slide appears in the new layout.

Important: Do *not* change the slide layout after you have added an object to the slide.

Reordering slides

- Click on the icon [icon] on the View Buttons bar to change to the Slide Sorter view.
- Click the mouse over the slide you want to move.
- Drag the slide to a new location. A line shows where the slide will appear when you release the mouse button.

Deleting a slide

- Click on the icon [icon] on the View Buttons bar to change to Slide Sorter view
- Click the mouse over the slide you want to delete and press the Delete key.

Selecting the correct printers and media

Having confidence in using your printer is essential. If you approach the machine with dread in your heart because it has a habit of breaking down at the most inopportune moment, or if you know that it is likely to jam after the first few minutes, you should be talking seriously to your line manager about a long-term solution to the problem. Having confidence in the person operating the printer is equally important. It is amazing how much damage an untrained operator can do if left alone with a printer for even a few minutes! It is to your advantage to make sure that he or she is fully trained in its use.

KEY NOTES ON SAVING AND PRINTING A PRESENTATION

Saving

- Click on the Save icon on the standard toolbar. The Save As dialogue box appears.
- Type a name for the presentation and click on Save.

Note that you should do this routinely as you are working and before you make important changes!

Printing

Depending on what you want to print, make sure your paper feedtray is stacked with the appropriate transparencies or copy paper. If you are using transparencies, make sure you have fed them in the right way. If you are not sure, check the box containing the transparencies for the appropriate instructions.

- Click on File | Print on the main menu bar. The Print dialogue box appears.
- Under 'Print what', click the part of the presentation you want to print; i.e. Slides, Handouts, Notes Pages, Outline View.
- Under 'Print range', click an option to specify which slides you want to print; i.e. All, Current Slide, Slides (the ones you specify).
- If you select Slides, type the numbers of the slides you want to print (1,4,5 etc.).
- If you select Handouts, click on the number of slides you want on each page and the order – horizontal or vertical.
- Click on the number of copies you want and how you want them collating.
- Click on Slides and scroll down to Slides, Handouts, Notes pages or Outline view.
- Click to print hidden slides if relevant.
- Click on OK to print your presentation.

Sending via e-mail

- Click the relevant icon on the standard toolbar.
- If the presentation contains more than one slide, a message appears asking you if you want to send the entire presentation or just the current slide. Click the appropriate option.

- A window appears for the e-mail message.
- An icon for the presentation appears in the message box.
- Click the 'To:' area and type the e-mail address of each person you want to receive the message.
- Separate each address with a semicolon.

Dealing with problems

One of the principal reasons for preparing a presentation as far in advance as possible from the event itself is that you are more able to deal with any problems that arise. Finding that the printer is not working two days before the event at least allows you time to do something about it – check the troubleshooting page in the manufacturer's instructions, arrange for the machine to be repaired, find another machine etc. Finding that the printer is not working an hour before the event is a recipe for panic.

It is a good idea to have a regular inspection routine of all the equipment you use – particularly the equipment upon which you rely the most such as the word-processor and printer. It is also good housekeeping to check daily that you have sufficient paper (of all sizes) and OHTs near to hand and that the printer is not on the verge of running out of toner or ink. Thinking ahead is important whether you control your own ordering system or whether you have to requisition for supplies through your organisation's central purchasing and supply system. Otherwise you may be faced with the necessity of having to make a few desperate phone calls either to your local supplier or to a disapproving stock control manager.

Protecting slides and keeping them clean

You spend some time preparing a presentation to be made to a group of senior managers about the latest developments in health and safety legislation. You complete the last one and hand the whole set over to your junior. He has been drinking a can of coke and his fingers are a bit sticky. He picks them up, puts them in a file and sends them through the post to your line manager. Your manager has a look at them and then leaves the OHTs on his desk and they disappear beneath a pile of files and books. When the presentation begins, your manager has a problem. The first OHT he produces has obvious finger marks on it, the second is difficult to read because of the smears on it, and the third is scratched. This creates a bad first impression and your manager has an uphill task to try to persuade his audience that they should listen to what he is saying.

If you are preparing a set of OHTs you should ideally place each one in a cardboard frame. You can then ensure that no one needs to touch the OHT

KEY NOTES ON DIFFICULTIES IN PRINTING DOCUMENTS

For general information on how to deal with printer difficulties, check your Help facility.

Problem	Possible solutions
Selection of correct printer in software	Click on File I Print. Check under Printer name that you have selected the correct printer. Scroll down until you find the one you want. If it's not there you will have to install the printer driver (normally provided on a disk with the printer).
Printer offline	Depress the online button on your printer. If nothing happens, check the cable connections. Check your screen to see whether you are receiving an error message. Shut down Microsoft® Windows and restart and try again. If nothing works, report the problem.
Printer out of paper/OHTs	Restack the feeder tray. Remember to put the paper/OHTs in the tray the right way – check the packet for instructions on this if you are not sure. Fan the paper before you load it and make sure you do not put too much in the tray at once.
Printer out of toner/ink	Check the existing toner/ink cartridge to see if it is empty. Make a careful note of the number and obtain a new one. Remove the old cartridge and insert the new. Save the old cartridge for recycling.
Paper/OHT jam	Check your supplier's manual to see how to remove jammed paper. Ask for assistance if in doubt. *Never* try to remove the paper by brute force! Carry out a post mortem: Was the paper unsuitable for the printer? Was the OHT unsuitable? Was the paper damp? Were the paper guides set incorrectly? Was there too much paper in the paper tray? Is there a problem with the actual printer mechanism?

itself and risk spoiling it. The cardboard frame also allows you to write titles, slide numbers etc. on it – which can help the presenter particularly if during the presentation he or she accidentally gets the OHTs out of order. A cheaper alternative is to use a plastic wallet – but do make sure this is large enough!

Where you want to re-use the OHTs it is important that you store them properly – which doesn't mean shoving them into a desk drawer and dragging them out a few months later in the vague hope that they will still be OK to use. A good idea is to:

- number or name the OHTs (or a hard copy of the slide)
- attach to each a hard copy of the handouts and speaker's notes
- place each set in a folder (preferably a paper or manila folder as the use of plastic folders can result in the OHTs overheating slightly and sticking together)
- place the folder in a filing cabinet – preferably one with a suspension filing system.

Collating and supplying notes and handouts

A presentation normally involves the preparation of not only slides but also notes and backup handouts etc. What an inexperienced presenter can sometimes do is to forget to rehearse when he or she is going to introduce the supplementary documentation. What can happen in such circumstances is that he or she:

- forgets about it altogether and allows the audience to leave without having a copy
- suddenly remembers about it at a later stage and has to hastily back-track
- gives out the wrong handout by mistake
- finds that a multi-page handout has not been stapled together and hands out individual sheets which take 10 minutes for the audience to sort out
- copies an insufficient number for the size of the audience (often people ask if they can have one for a friend who could not attend!).

Obviously you can't do too much to help at that stage – other than trying to take control of the circulation of the documentation. What you can do beforehand, however, is to make sure that all the backup papers are:

- complete – no pages missing, no badly photocopied pages, back-to-back photocopies where required etc.
- clearly labelled – the presenter has no time to read small print
- clearly numbered – in some cases it is a good idea to have a separate folder for each handout so the presenter needs only to open the folder and distribute its contents.

As already discussed, if you are at the presentation you might want to arrange with the presenter that at the appropriate point you distribute the relevant information – or at least hand it to him or her to distribute. An alternative is to put a copy of each handout on the chairs before the audience enters. That normally minimises disruption, but a disadvantage is that people may start reading and flicking through them, rather than listening to the opening!

What you should also do is to make certain that the presenter's own notes are prepared in such a way that they are easily readable – large text, a few lines only on each page, very clear reference to the appropriate slide or OHT etc. Depending on preference, the notes can either be prepared in a set which the presenter works through, or attached individually to each OHT or hard copy of the slide.

See below for a copy of some speaker's notes and printed handouts.

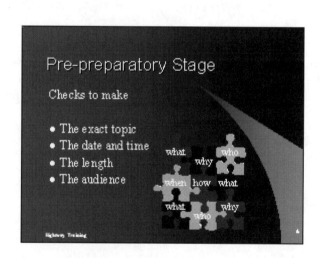

A page of speaker's notes

Slide 2

_____
_____
_____
_____
_____
_____
_____

Slide 3

_____
_____
_____
_____
_____
_____
_____
_____

Slide 4

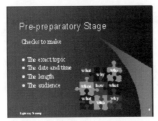

_____
_____
_____
_____
_____
_____
_____
_____

An example of a presentation handout

KEY NOTES ON CREATING SPEAKER NOTES

Either

- Display the slide for which you want to create speaker notes.
- Click the area immediately below the displayed slide (the Notes Pane) and type in the text.

Or

- Click on View I Notes Page on the main menu bar. The notes page for the current slide appears.
- To magnify the notes page so you can clearly view the notes, click the downward arrow next to the percentage setting on your new toolbar 66% ▼ and click the magnification setting you want to use (e.g. 150 per cent). The notes page appears in the new magnification setting.
- You can edit the text on the notes page as for any other text.
- When you finish reviewing the notes, click ▣ under View on the View buttons toolbar to return to Normal view.

EVIDENCE COLLECTION

For this element, you can complete the evidence you created on pages 655 and 669.

1 Add a summary of how you agreed the requirements for printing presentation materials for each example presentation you summarised earlier. Note that your requirements must include both (a) number of copies, and (b) specified range of slides, notes and handouts.

2 State the checking methods you used to ensure the materials were complete and ready for printing.

3 Give examples of occasions when you have used all the following presentation materials:

- transparencies
- handouts
- speaker's notes.

State how you checked that these met the needs of the person, and detail any alterations you had to make. Include copies to support your report.

4 Provide examples of when you have dealt with all the following problems. If you have not experienced one type of problem you will need to discuss it with your assessor:

- printer not selected in software
- printer offline
- printer out of media (e.g. no OHTs or paper)
- printer out of toner/ink
- media jam or misfeed.

5 Finally, state how you keep your slides clean and undamaged and the systems you use to make sure that you always collate and supply handouts and notes as required.

Your final evidence must, of course, be supplemented by examples of slides, speaker's notes and handouts you have printed and issued.

Appendix

Improve your written English

The more skilled you become at producing documents that are grammatically correct, properly punctuated and free from spelling errors, the more valuable you will become to your organisation. First impressions do count and many a contract has been lost because a potential customer has received a letter he or she cannot understand or a draft contract littered with spelling mistakes.

At this stage in your career you will probably be well aware of how proficient you are at producing a high-quality document. However, most people (other than perhaps a Professor of English or the editor of Roget's Thesaurus) feel the need to check on certain points of grammar, spelling, punctuation or vocabulary from time to time.

The following Key Notes are designed as a brief aide memoire for you to check on individual items as you require. The exercises are useful in that they allow you to check both what you do know and what you don't and to concentrate on filling the gaps in your knowledge.

 INFORMATION UPDATE

Some experts blame the rise of text messaging and e-mails for the apparent decline in the quality of written documents, for example the use of:

- RUF2T (are you free to talk?)
- CID (consider it done)
- CMIIW (correct me if I'm wrong)
- I k%d mEt U @ 7 (I could meet you at 7)
- S@RdA (Saturday)
- Prv8 (private).

Spelling

Spelling exercise

Retype the following passage (remembering not to be tempted to use the Word spell-checker) and compare your version with the version given on page 689. There are 23 spelling errors in it. If you get 23 out of 23, move on to the next exercise. If not, check the Key Notes on spelling below.

Thank you for sending the correspondance to me. I have now consulted my colleages, all of whom are members of the Staff Welfare committee. We all feel it is a privilige to be asked to give our assistence in the project you mention. If you send us the full program of events we will certainley consider how we can assist you to fullfil all your objectives.

I should be greatful, however, if you would let us know whether it is permissable for us to act independently ocasionally. We should be dissapointed if we could not.

Is it definate that the event will take place soon? If so we can make sure that all the necessery preparations are made and that we liase with you over all the essential work.

Once I have received the relevent information, I shall call a meeting and find out what is permissable for us to do under our terms of referance. I shall, of course, make sure that the senior management team are kept informed and that I get their permission before proceeding futher with this.

On a final point, I was interrested to note that the letterhead on your stationary has an IIP logo. We are currantly undergoing an IIP inspection. Perhaps we could meet for you to give me any hints on how to make sure we are sucessful.

 KEY NOTES ON COMMONLY MISSPELT WORDS

- Absence ('ce' not 'se')
- Acceptable ('able' not 'ible')
- Accommodation (two 'm's)
- Acknowledge (remember the 'c' before the 'k')
- Advertisement (remember the middle 'e')
- All right (not alright)
- Assessment (two sets of 's's)
- Assistance ('a' not 'e')
- Business ('u' not 'i')
- Certainly (no 'e' between 'l' and 'y')
- Colleague (two 'l's and a 'u' between 'g' and 'e')
- Committee (two 't's, two 'e's)
- Consignment (remember the 'g')
- Consistent ('ent' not 'ant')
- Correspondence (remember 'e' for envelope)

- Currently ('e' not 'a')
- Definite ('i' not 'a')
- Dictionary ('a' not 'e')
- Disappoint (one 's', two 'p's)
- Exceptional ('c' after the 'x')
- Fulfil (only one 'l' in the middle of the word)
- Further (remember the middle 'r')
- Government ('r' before 'n')
- Grateful (not 'greatful')
- Interested (one 'r')
- Liaise ('l' before and after 'a')
- Maintenance ('en' not 'ain')
- Necessary ('a' not 'e')
- Occasionally (two 'c's, one 's', one 'n')
- Occurrence ('ence' not 'ance')
- Permissible ('ible' not 'able')
- Permission (two 's's)
- Privilege (no 'd' and 'e' not 'i')
- Program (if a computer program)
- Programme (if a schedule of events)
- Receive ('i' before 'e' except after 'c')
- Recommend (one 'c', two 'm's)
- Reference ('e' not 'a' between 'r' and 'n')
- Relevant ('a' not 'e')
- Separate ('par' not 'per')
- Sincerely (remember the second 'e')
- Stationery (remember 'e' for 'envelope')
- Successful (two 'c's and two 's's)

Vocabulary

Vocabulary exercise

Correct the following sentences. Check your version with that on page 689.
If, necessary, check the Key Notes on commonly misused words.

1   *I should like to complement you on your contribution to the project. It had a major affect on the final outcome.*
2   *I agree in principal. However, I should like further information before making my final decision.*
3   *He took a personnel interest in the progress of the project.*
4   *Before we precede to the next point, let's check on what action has already been taken.*
5   *What sort of advise can you give me to improve matters?*
6   *Let's practice the exercise again.*

7 *He won't say anything. He's very discrete.*

8 *She is a very good chairperson because she acts in an uninterested way. She never takes sides.*

9 *Can you insure that the report is completed by next week?*

10 *We must look after this customer. We don't want to loose his order.*

 ## KEY NOTES ON COMMONLY MISUSED WORDS

Alternate = rotate, exchange	Alternative = option, choice
Discreet = diplomatic, tactful	Discrete = separate, distinct
Affect = influence, change	Effect = outcome, consequence
Compliment = praise, admire	Complement = balance, match
Personal = individual, private	Personnel = staff, employees
Uninterested = indifferent apathetic	Disinterested = impartial, fair minded
Defer = postpone, put off	Differ = vary, fluctuate
Lose = misplace, mislay	Loose = slack, free
Proceed = progress, move forward	Precede = come before
Principal = main, most important	Principle = belief, standard
Advise = to give counsel (a verb)	Advice = counsel (a noun)
Practise = to rehearse, to carry out (a verb)	Practice = a rehearsal, an exercise, a doctor's surgery, a custom (a noun)
Devise = to find a way, to plan (a verb)	Device = a mechanism, a method, a plan (a noun)
Continual = frequent and repeated	Continuous = without stop
Ensure = make sure	Insure = take out insurance
Practical = concerned with practice not theory	Practicable = able to be put into practice
Dependent = depending or relying on someone	Dependant = someone who is dependent on someone else
Less = quantity (We have less money than we thought.)	Fewer = number (There are fewer people here than I expected.)
Due to = to be used after verbs to be, seem or appear (The delay is due to leaves on the line.)	Owing to = to be used in other circumstances (Owing to a train delay, he was late for work.) When in doubt use 'because of'.

Punctuation

Punctuation exercise

Retype the following paragraph using the correct punctuation and capital letters. Check your answer with the suggested answer on page 690. If it's perfect you need take only a brief glance at the key notes on punctuation. If you've made some mistakes, check the relevant points in the key notes.

at the board meeting held on 25th may the chairperson opened the meeting by welcoming the new members she said that she was pleased to announce that the companys standing had remained high and that profits had risen by 10% given below are some extracts from her speech i am glad to say that our increased sales in the home market have given us the edge over our competitors Its some years since ive been able to say this and i hope ill be able to repeat the same statement next year i also hope that in two years time ill be able to announce an expansion of our export sales i want to congratulate the staff whose hard work enthusiasm dedication and loyalty have made all this possible are there any questions anyone would like to ask

---

 KEY NOTES ON PUNCTUATION (1)

Punctuation mark   Uses

The full stop
- at the end of a sentence (but not a heading)
- traditionally after abbreviations – **i.e., enc.** – although nowadays many abbreviations are written without the full stops – **BA, NHS**

The comma
- to separate words and phrases – **the cup, saucer and spoon** (do not put a comma before an 'and' in such a list)
- after introductory words or phrases – **Having now seen the report, I should like to make the following comments**
- to separate phrases mid sentence – **The Managing Director, Matthew Robinson, will now make the opening address**
- to introduce a quotation – **The actor cried, 'Life is short'**
- if required, in names and addresses and dates in correspondence

Note the use of brackets rather than commas – **Large items (such as filing cabinets) must be moved first**

The apostrophe	• in the place of a missing letter or letters – **You'll regret this** = You will regret this
	• to indicate it is – **It's cold outside tonight** Do not use an apostrophe otherwise – **The building looked at its best in the moonlight**
	• to show possession – **the student's books** (if the books belong to *one* student), but **the students' books** (if the books belong to *a number* of students)

Note:

- A lot of people find the apostrophe difficult. When in doubt consider using the full version. If, for example, you are not sure where to put the apostrophe in 'don't', use 'do not' instead.
- Do not use the apostrophe in ours, yours, theirs, hers. Do use it in one's – **one's own interests** etc.
- Do use it in 'time' phrases eg **one week's time, two years' time**.
- If a word ends in 's' another 's' is not needed – **St. Thomas' Church.**

 KEY NOTES ON PUNCTUATION (2)

Punctuation mark	*Uses*
The hyphen	• in compound words – **up-to-date information**
	• after certain prefixes – post-natal care
The dash	• to indicate a break or to precede a list – **It was a catastrophe – no room, no speaker, no refreshments**
The colon	• to introduce a list of items – **You will need the following: scissors, a stapler, a ruler**
	• to introduce a quotation – **William Wordsworth wrote: 'I wandered lonely as a cloud'**
The semicolon	• to link two parts of a sentence where the pause is intended to be not as long as a full stop but longer than a comma – **We have**

	two different types of machine; one is suitable for domestic purposes and the other for industrial purposes
The question mark	• if there is a direct question – **What are you doing?** Do not use if the question is indirect – **He asked her what she was doing**
The exclamation mark	• in informal communications – **The best money can buy!** Do not over-use
Quotation marks or inverted commas	• to separate direct speech from the rest of the sentence – **The HR Director said 'I am concerned about staff levels'**
	• to enclose direct quotations – **As is often said, 'where there's a will, there's a way'**
	• to indicate a trade name, a book or film or a slang term – **'Apple Mac', 'Lord of the Rings', 'pick n'mix'**
	• for a quotation within a quotation – **He said, 'I always find it difficult to "pick myself up, dust myself down and start all over again".'** Note use of double quotations
The capital letter	• at the beginning of a sentence
	• for titles – **the Duke of York**
	• for proper names – **David Blunkett, Victorian poetry**
	• for headings – **Latest News from London**
	• at the beginning of direct speech in the middle of a line – He observed, **'You have been very patient.'**

Grammar

Grammar exercise (1)

Retype the following passage in complete sentences.

Nice to hear from you again. Many years since we met. Office as busy as ever. Everyone still fine. Need to speak to you about the new contract. 10 am Friday? See you soon hopefully.

For a suggested answer see page 690.

Grammar exercise (2)

Correct the grammatical errors in the following sentences. Read the suggested answers on page 690. If you had difficulty in finding and/or correcting an error, check the Key Notes.

1   We are pleased that we have won the contract. All I need to know now is whose going to be responsible for it.

2   I will be in my office by 10 am tomorrow. Mr. Donaldson will also be there to talk to you and I about the changes in procedures.

3   This is something I don't agree with. I thought it was something I had already spoken to you about.

4   The management team was asked to carefully consider the matter.

5   The Managing Director has agreed that each member of staff, together with their wives, husbands and partners, have the right to make use of the company's sporting facilities.

6   Entering the building, the lifts are directly ahead.

7   The complaint, that had been received by the HR manager, was forwarded to the Head of Computer Services.

8   He was only permitted to sign the contract.

 KEY NOTES ON GRAMMAR (1)

Sentence or note form

- A sentence includes a verb (i.e. a 'doing' word), a note does not.

  You can have your tea now. = sentence

  Tea ready = note

- Avoid an 'unrelated participle':

  Not – 'Coming into the reception area, the desk is to the right of the entrance' – the desk hasn't come into the reception area

  But – 'When you come into the reception area, you will see the desk to the right of the entrance' or 'The desk is to the right of the entrance in the reception area'

  Normally sentence form is required in all but the most informal business documents.

Matching singular and plural

Singular must match singular, plural must match plural:

  Details of the event *are* (not *is*) to be found in the programme.

  The *computer programmer*, who was working with several colleagues, *was* (not *were*) optimistic about success.

If you find this difficult, try to cross out all the words between the two important ones (e.g. between *details* and *are* and between *computer programmer* and *was*). That normally leads you to the right answer.

Matching *I* and *we*	Do not confuse the two:

I am happy that *I* have finished the document.

We feel *we* shall be able to accept the offer.

Difference between *who* and *whom*	*Who* is the subject: *whom* is the object:

Who wants to see me?

This is the new manager whom the committee have chosen.

If you find this difficult think of a way round. If, for instance, you cannot decide in the second sentence whether or not to use who or whom, say instead – The committee have chosen a new manager.

Difference between *who's* and *whose*	*Who's* is an abbreviation for who is: *whose* indicates possession – The car, whose owner had abandoned it, was parked in a side street.

KEY NOTES ON GRAMMAR (2)

Difference between *shall* and *should*, *will* and *would*	I and we are followed by shall or should, unless real intent needs to be shown:

I shall be pleased to see you

We should be interested in hearing from you *but*

We would insist on seeing the document.

He, she and they are normally followed by will or would:

He will be available to see you

They would expect an answer

Do not mix up *shall* and *should*, and *will* and *would* in the same sentence:

> You *will* be pleased to know that you *will* be able to access the network
>
> We *should* be grateful if you *would* come to the meeting

The use of *you and I, you and me*	If you find it difficult to decide whether or not to use *you and I* or *you and me*, translate it into *we* or *us*:

> You and I (i.e. we) must do this as soon as possible
>
> He is coming to see you and me (i.e. us)

The split infinitive	Try not to put another word in between *to* and a connecting verb:

> He promised to deal with the matter urgently – *not* He promised to urgently deal with the matter

The use of prepositions – *to, for, of, with, about* etc.	• Try not to put a preposition at the end of a sentence – She is someone with whom I have always had a good relationship *not* She is someone I have always had a good relationship with

- Be careful to avoid a very awkward construction. If this is likely to happen, find another way round it. Do not say *About what do you want to see me?* Say instead *Why do you want to see me?*

 KEY NOTES ON GRAMMAR (3)

The use of *only*	The meaning of the word *only* changes depending on where it is in the sentence:

- Only we can order these chairs. (No one else but us can do so)
- We can only order these chairs. (We cannot do anything else but order them)
- We can order only these chairs. (We cannot order anything else)

The use of *which* and *that*	In most instances *which* and *that* can be used in the same way. However, *which* is always used if it starts a clause (i.e. a section of a sentence separated by commas, brackets or dashes):

> The letter, which was the cause of the problem, has now been withdrawn

If you are not sure what form to use, rewrite the sentence:

> As the letter was the cause of the problem, it has now been withdrawn.

KEYS

Corrected version of spelling exercise on page 680

Thank you for sending the *correspondence* to me. I have now consulted my *colleagues*, all of whom are members of the Staff Welfare committee. We all feel it is a *privilege* to be asked to give our *assistance* in the project you mention. If you send us the full *programme* of events we will *certainly* consider how we can assist you to *fulfil* all your objectives.

I should be *grateful*, however, if you would let us know whether it is *permissible* for us to act independently *occasionally*. We should be *disappointed* if we could not.

Is it *definite* that the event will take place soon? If so we can make sure that all the *necessary* preparations are made and that we *liaise* with you over all the essential work.

Once I have received the *relevant* information, I shall call a meeting and find out what is *permissible* for us to do under our terms of *reference*. I shall, of course, make sure that the senior management team is kept informed and that I get its *permission* before proceeding *further* with this.

On a final point, I was *interested* to note that the letterhead on your *stationery* has an IIP logo. We are *currently* undergoing an IIP inspection. Perhaps we could meet for you to give me any hints on how to make sure we are *successful*.

Corrected version of vocabulary exercise on page 681

1 I should like to *compliment* you on your contribution to the project. It had a major *effect* on the final outcome.
2 I agree in *principle*. However, I should like further information before making my final decision.
3 He took a *personal* interest in the progress of the project.
4 Before we *proceed* to the next point, let's check on what action has already been taken.

5 What sort of *advice* can you give me to improve matters?
6 Let's *practise* the exercise again.
7 He won't say anything. He's very *discreet*.
8 She is a very good chairperson because she acts in a *disinterested way*. She never takes sides.
9 Can you *ensure* that the report is completed by next week?
10 We must look after this customer. We don't want to *lose* his order.

Corrected version of punctuation exercise on page 683

At the Board Meeting held on 25 May, the Chairperson opened the meeting by welcoming the new members. She said that she was pleased to announce that the company's standing had remained high and that profits had risen by 10%. Given below are some extracts from her speech.

'I am glad to say that our increased sales in the home market have given us the edge over our competitors. It's some years since I've been able to say this and I hope I'll be able to repeat the same statement next year. I also hope that in two years' time I'll be able to announce an expansion of our export sales. I want to congratulate the staff whose hard work, enthusiasm, dedication and loyalty have made all this possible. Are there any questions anyone would like to ask?'

Corrected version of grammar exercise (1) on page 685

It was nice to hear from you again. It is many years since we met. The office is as busy as ever. Everyone is still fine. I need to speak to you about the new contract. Could we meet at 10 am on Friday? I hope to see you soon.

Corrected version of grammar exercise (2) on page 686

1 We are pleased that we have won the contract. All *we* need to know now is *who is* going to be responsible for it.
2 I *shall* be in my office by 10 am tomorrow. Mr. Donaldson will also be there to talk to you and *me* about the changes in procedures.
3 This is something *with which* I don't agree. I thought it was something *about which* I had already spoken to you.
4 The management team was asked to consider the matter *carefully*.
5 The Managing Director has agreed that each member of staff, together with their wives, husbands and partners, *has* the right to make use of the company's sporting facilities.
6 When you enter the building you will see the lifts directly ahead.
7 The complaint, *which* had been received by the HR manager, was forwarded to the Head of Computer Services.
8 *Only* he was permitted to sign the contract.

Index